CACTI OF THE SOUTHWEST

NUMBER FOUR

The Elma Dill Russell Spencer Foundation Series

Echinocereus lloydii.

Cacti of the Southwest

Texas, New Mexico, Oklahoma, Arkansas, and Louisiana

By DEL WENIGER

UNIVERSITY OF TEXAS PRESS AUSTIN & LONDON

Standard Book Number 292–70000–8
Library of Congress Catalog Card No. 78–104326
All rights reserved
Printed by Brüder Hartmann, Berlin, West Germany

To Ellen Schultz Quillin

CONTENTS

ACKNOWLEDGMENTS

Support for this study was graciously provided by a grant-in-aid for research from the Society of the Sigma Xi. Appreciation is expressed to Our Lady of the Lake College which granted me time for the study and made available certain facilities for growing and photographing the plants.

Gratitude is also expressed to many individuals who contributed in various ways to the completion of the present study. First among them is Mrs. Roy W. Quillin (Ellen D. Schulz) who gave constant encouragement and advice and the use of books from her fine library on the Cactaceae. Dr. E. F. Castetter of the Biology Department of the University of New Mexico contributed valuable information and some specimens from New Mexico. He also arranged for the preparation and housing of my collection of important specimens gathered in this study. Numbering over seven hundred specimens of cacti, this collection is, as a result of his interest, permanently deposited in the herbarium of the University of New Mexico.

The cacti of the following herbaria were studied in their entirety, thanks to the help of the staffs and especially of the persons mentioned here: the United States National Museum of the Smithsonian Institution, Dr. Jason R. Swallen and Dr. Velva Rudd being particularly helpful; the New York Botanical Garden; the Missouri Botanical Garden in St. Louis; The University of Texas; Southern Methodist University, with appreciation to Dr. Lloyd Shinners; the University of New Mexico and Dr. Castetter, as already mentioned; and the University of Colorado.

Many others provided valuable information and aid of one kind or another. Appreciation goes to Dr. Barton H. Warnock of Sul Ross College; Drs. Claude W. Gatewood and Bruce Blauch, then of Oklahoma State University; Mr. Charles Polaski of Oklahoma City; Mr. Homer Jones and Mr. P. M. Plimmer of Alpine, Texas; Mr. Clark Champie of Anthony, New Mexico; Mr. Fred Nadolney, Mr. Prince Pierce, and Mr. and Mrs. Earl Newhouse of Albuquerque, New Mexico; Mr. Horst Kuenzler and Mr. Dennis Cowper of Belen, New Mexico; Mr. L. J. Holland, Mr. and Mrs. S. L. Heacock, and Mrs. Ethel B. Karr, all of Colorado; Mr. and Mrs. Walter Heins of Rogers, Arkansas; Miss Lorene Martin of the Arkansas State Plant Board; Dr. T. M. Howard, Mr. Kim Kuebel, and Mr. H. C. Lawson of San Antonio, Texas; Mr. Glenn Spraker of Houston, Texas; Sr. Orton Cerna of Rosita, Coahuila, Mexico; and Sr. Romo Ruiz of Musquiz, Coahuila, Mexico.

Mr. Larry Nichols and Mr. Gibbs Milliken aided the writer in making some of the photographs. The photograph of *Lophophora williamsii* var. *echinata* was made by Mr. David Smith.

The chromatographs mentioned in the text were run by my students, Misses Vicki Perez, Rosemary Drake, and Ethel Matthews in the Biology Department of Our Lady of the Lake College.

INTRODUCTION

Portrayed among the ancient stone carvings of Mexico, woven through the legends of that land, and central in the seal of the nation itself is the strange thick stem or the spiny jointed bush of the cactus. These plants must have been ever present for the people of that land, interesting to them and of some significance to their lives as far back as we can know. How strange to realize then that this fantastic group of plants had never been seen by anyone in the so-called civilized world until after Columbus discovered America. Yet this must be true; for, except for two or three small, inconspicuous, and very uncactus-like species found in places even more unknown to early travelers in the jungles of Madagascar and Ceylon, the cacti grow naturally only in the Western Hemisphere. They are as American as corn, tomatoes, tobacco, or potatoes.

So they must have been seen—and felt—by the conquistadors who drove their horses across America in search of gold. No doubt these men paid little attention to the native flora as they passed, but the cacti they would have noticed for at least two reasons. How could they have failed to see the huge thickets of these devilish plants which blocked their paths to the envisioned gold and which they had to learn to respect? And when, wandering in the arid expanses, they grew hungry and had nothing else to eat, they must quickly have learned from the Indians to spot the cactus species whose fruits were succulent and sweet to the taste. We can imagine the stories they told about these outlandish plants of the New World.

These accounts must have spread very rapidly, for we already have in *The Herball or Generall Historie of Plantes,* by John Gerarde, published in London in 1597, the descriptions and woodcut illustrations of four cacti. Gerarde names them as follows: "The Hedgehogge Thistle," which is clearly seen from the picture to be a Melocactus from the Caribbean area, "The Torch or Thornie Euphorbium," which is easily recognized to be a Cereus, "The Thornie Reede of Peru," another Cereus, and "The Indian Fig Tree," obviously a giant Opuntia. This is already an array of cacti from widely separated parts of Central and South America.

Soon there followed explorers who were more directly interested in the flora of the New World. These early explorers took living specimens of the cacti home to Europe, not only because of their uniqueness, but because they would survive the long sea voyages when other plants, except in the seed stage, would not. They could even be transported all the way without the prohibitive weight of soil on their roots.

Early botanists, beginning to study these plants, faced a problem. Since the plants had been totally unknown in the Old World until this time, there were no words for them at all in classical Greek or Latin. Like John Gerarde, the botanists often thought of these plants, because of their spininess, as new sorts of thistles, and so the Greek word for thistle, *Kaktos,* became somehow applied to them. This has become our *cactus* of today.

There were soon expeditions of botanists just to study the new plants of America. An example was the Ruiz and Paron expedition of 1777 to 1787. This expedition to Peru was commissioned by the King of Spain and encompassed ten years of exploring in most difficult terrain; Spain spent upon the venture twenty million pesetas. Thousands of plant specimens were sent back, with cacti among them.

The interest in these strange plants grew and soon amounted to a "cactus craze." The extent of the "craze" is hard for us to comprehend today. By 1800 businesses were being set up by French, Belgian, and German importers to sell quantities of the plants sent by professional collectors maintained in Central and South America. Societies and wealthy enthusiasts commissioned collectors to travel to America and bring them newer and yet more strange species. Extensive collections were soon formed, grown at great pains in greenhouses. About 1830 the Duke of

Bedford had such a collection of cacti at Woburn Abbey. Other famous collectors in England were the Duke of Devonshire and the Reverend Mr. H. Williams of Hendon.

This cultivation of the cacti must at first have been a very expensive, very genteel hobby, open only to the rich; the plants had to be expensive after having been shipped all the way from the wilds of the Western Hemisphere, and the resources necessary to keep them alive in the climate of most of Europe before the advent of gas and electric heat must have been great. The greenhouse full of cacti may well have been one of the few warmed buildings for miles around on freezing winter nights. Borg has pointed out that the cultivation of cacti has paralleled the cultivation of orchids in many ways, and this is easy to understand, since these are two of the most exotic groups of plants which can be found.

But the cultivation of the cacti became the common man's hobby much more easily than did that of the orchids. With botanical associations and importers putting out long lists of available species, cacti became cheap and available in Europe in large numbers. Soon many a humble home had at least a few of these peculiar plants in a window somewhere. We like to think of this as wonderful and of these cherished cacti as beautiful, but we must admit that even then they were not universally appreciated. Dickens, for instance, must have had an active aversion to them. While attesting to the broadness of the interest in cacti, his description of Paul Dombey's nurse, Mrs. Pipchin, reveals his dislike for them, for he wrote of her, "Among her failings was a fondness for cactus. In the window of her parlor were half a dozen specimens writhing round bits of lath like hairy serpents."

Perhaps Dickens was sensing something cunning and insidious in these cacti, which events proved was there. They were early grown in southern Europe, and it was found that they could be grown without protection in outdoor gardens in southern Italy, Spain, Sicily, and Greece, on the Riviera, and, of course, all along the southern shore of the Mediterranean. In these areas are still today some of the finest cactus gardens in the world, with beautiful, hundred-year-old specimens to be seen.

But once introduced into the Mediterranean area, certain of the Opuntias, the hardiest and most easily spread of cacti, found the hot, arid region too much to their liking and so escaped from cultivation and established themselves as permanent residents of the area. These cacti have now spread through many Mediterranean countries. Though the time required to accomplish this was actually comparatively short, man's memory is even shorter, for so completely are they already accepted as a normal part of the flora that in many areas one finds hardly a resident who realizes that his ancestors could not have known these immigrants. Sometimes one even sees cacti in pictures and movies supposedly reconstructing the time of Christ and the Roman Empire, or in otherwise accurate portrayals of classic Greek times.

In one other place cacti escaped like this and became one of the worst plant scourges ever known. This was in Australia, where several Opuntias, in the absence of their natural enemies and in an arid situation exactly to their liking, took over millions of acres and rendered them useless for anything else. Much money and effort was spent in discovering how to control these cacti in Australia, and the effort has been largely successful. They have been eliminated from huge areas and are being kept in check in others.

But these two instances of cacti escaping and invading new areas are the exceptions. Usually, when taken from their natural haunts, the cacti survive only under very precise conditions and when great care is lavished upon them by their growers. Almost none of them can survive unaided even when only transplanted from one state to another within the United States.

Within the Americas, where they are at home, cacti as a group are very widespread. They range from Alberta and British Columbia in Canada on the north to Patagonia, toward the tip of South America on the south. Their greatest development in both numbers and diversity is in two areas, one along the Tropic of Cancer in Mexico and the other near the Tropic of Capricorn in South America. While flourishing the most in the American deserts, they are far from restricted to these places. Special forms are found in tropical rain forests; others abound along the seashores of the Gulf of Mexico, the Caribbean, and the Pacific Ocean; while some thrive in mountain forests and a few are at home on bleak mountain slopes to as high as fourteen thousand feet. There are also some forms which abound on the Great Plains all the way into Canada, and within the United States it is said that indigenous cacti have been found growing in every state except Maine, Hawaii, and Alaska, although in many states they are so rare and inconspicuous that their presence is unsuspected by most residents.

This picture of far-ranging cacti is misleading if one thinks of any single form as so far-flung. This is the range of the group, which is a huge and diverse aggregation. It is probably fruitless to try to estimate the number of cactus forms that exist, because new publications are constantly adding new-found forms to the list, as well as realigning those already known. But it is said that there are well over three thousand known species in all. Of these, almost none range across from one America to the other. A very few species, considered broadly, may range practically across a continent, and some few cover large expanses of one or the other of the Americas, but the much more usual situation is for each species to inhabit a range measured in a few hundred square miles or less. It is very common for a species to inhabit only a certain valley or mountain range, and there are numerous forms so restricted in habitat that two or three Texas-sized ranches will contain them all.

As we have seen, the cacti which excited the first interest and touched off the first cactus craze were the huge and spectacular Central and South American forms. The cacti of the United States were hardly known until later. Early botanists on the east coast of the United States found only two or three very inconspicuous and uninteresting little prickly pears which they dutifully recorded and no one got excited about. As they pushed west, they found little else until they got beyond the Mississippi River. But once they began to explore the West, the study of U.S. cacti began.

The first great student of U.S. cacti was the famous botanist Dr. George Engelmann. He made his headquarters at the Missouri Botanical Garden, the remarkable early botanical center in St. Louis, and studied the specimens and descriptions sent in by botanists on the early governmental surveys through the West. These botanists—such as Wislizenus, Wright, Bigelow, Parry, and Poselger—were the heroes of early cactus studies in the United States, and some of their names will be met with later, since Engelmann acknowledged his debt to them by sometimes naming cacti after them. They must have been hardy souls, riding on long treks with expeditions such as the Mexican Boundary Survey, the Pacific Railroad Survey, Pike's expedition, and others; and one must admire their stamina, gathering cacti all day on the trail, then, while the others rested, making their records and descriptions and packing up specimens of these unpleasant-to-handle plants to send back to Engelmann. Their routes took them through the heart of the cactus country of the West, and we are amazed at the number of plants found only in places almost inaccessible even a hundred years later, which they located and recorded so long ago.

Beginning in about 1846, Engelmann started publishing the results of these expeditions. He faced the herculean task of listing and describing a huge population of cacti almost unknown before to the world. He coined names for the multitude of forms, worked out something of their relationships, and presented descriptions and some of the finest botanical illustrations ever made for any plants. Although his material was sometimes incomplete and so his descriptions were sometimes deficient, he gave us the first information we have of approximately two-thirds of the U.S. cacti, information so remarkably accurate that in a few cases it has taken us almost a hundred years to verify it. Modern concepts have sometimes revised his ideas of the relationships between the forms, but almost never have we found him in error when he told where a plant grew or what it looked like.

The next effort at studying the cacti of the United States was made by the great botanist John M. Coulter. In 1894 he began publishing a major work on the cacti of North America. Mostly he built on the foundation laid down by Engelmann, with the benefit of much more material collected since Engelmann's time, but he added little really new to what was already known. It is indicative of the difficulty of studying cacti that he is said to have given up the study of this group in disgust and spent the rest of his life with other plant groups after misidentifying a cactus he had earlier named himself.

About the same time as Coulter's study, a large, general work on cacti was being produced in the German language by Karl Schumann. He did firsthand work on the cacti of the then In-

dian Territory and the Canadian River area, but did not travel widely in the United States, and so his work has limited value for us today in the study of U.S. cacti.

A major project on cacti was then undertaken by the Carnegie Institute. Dr. N. L. Britton and Dr. J. N. Rose, with the support of that institution, undertook to list and describe all the cacti of the world. They traveled widely throughout the Americas and visited the European collections, and as a result published a four-volume work, *The Cactaceae*, in 1919 to 1923. Their work had probably the greatest effect of anything ever published on the study of cacti as well as on the growing popularity of these plants. They greatly revised the classification of the group, adding a multitude of new genera and species, and their beautiful volumes, with fine color illustrations, were widely circulated, giving many people, especially in the United States, their first knowledge of the beauty of the cacti. Even today, most people still think of cacti strictly in the terms of the Britton and Rose accounts.

No new attempt to encompass all of the cacti in one large study was made for many years. The task had become just too big. But the great German student of cacti, Curt Backeberg, did not flinch at the challenge, and in 1958 he brought out the first volume of a new world-wide survey, *Die Cactaceae*. It was completed shortly before his death and comprises six large volumes of fine descriptions, with many good pictures of the cacti of the world. It is truly a monumental work.

But the great diversity of the cacti and the fact, already mentioned, that the majority of them are limited to areas which are very small (often single mountain ranges or river valleys), when set against the huge expanse covered by the group as a whole, make it very difficult for any major flora or all-inclusive cactus work to be useful on a local level. Who wants to carry the four volumes of Britton and Rose or the six of Backeberg to the Big Bend of Texas or the mountains of Peru? And if these works were to give really detailed accounts of the cacti found in all of such areas, exactly the information which the local student needs, they would become encyclopedic in size. This fact explains the numerous regional publications on cacti, both articles in journals and separate books. If one is to understand the local cacti, he must refer to these publications, done by people on the scene who have studied the larger picture and then sought out and portrayed the details of the local forms he sees about him. This book is intended to be such a regional guide.

In the United States there has long been a tendency to break down the treatment of cacti into state studies. States are artificial areas and their boundaries have nothing to do with plant distribution, but it has been impossible to ignore them. The present study, however, includes the cacti of five states: Arkansas, Louisiana, Oklahoma, Texas, and New Mexico. These five states make up a unit much more logically considered, cactuswise, than any one of them alone, and a unit for whose cacti there has never been a complete guide. While lists of cactus species and some good descriptions are found in the floras of the respective states (as for instance those of Wooton and Standley for New Mexico) and many articles concerning various cacti in this region are scattered all through the literature, there has been only one complete work on cacti within this area: *Texas Cacti*, by Ellen D. Schulz (Mrs. Roy Quillin) and Robert Runyon. This was published in 1930, covered only the cacti of Texas, and is now out of print.

The need for such a guide for these five states seems, therefore, clear. While the cacti of the far Southwest have been dealt with in numerous publications—Stockwell and Brezzeale's *Arizona Cacti* of 1933, Baxter's *California Cacti* of 1935, Boissevain and Davidson's *Colorado Cacti* of 1940, Benson's *The Cacti of Arizona* of 1950, and Earle's *Cacti of the Southwest* of 1963—none of these covered more than those few forms of cacti which happened to extend their range into our area from the West. And where the cacti of this five-state area have been written about in journals or magazines it has usually been done by students who lived and worked in the far West or even in Europe, and who wrote of our cacti after brief trips through this vast area or from secondhand accounts.

The cacti of this area have not lacked a detailed treatment because they were fewer in number or less diverse than those of the far Southwest. If anything, they may have presented too great a challenge just because of their number. I have found some professional botanists who believed, probably because of the greater size and conspicuousness of the Arizona species plus the greater publicity they have received, that the greatest speciation in the United States occurs in the far Southwest. Actually, this is not true. Texas alone presents more species of cacti than all of the rest of the United States combined. L. Benson lists 60 cactus species in Arizona. California is said to have about 20 natives; and New Mexico, about 50. On the other hand the number of separate species listed here for our five-state area is 119. Earle, the most recent writer on the cacti of the Southwest, lists 121 forms, counting varieties as well as separate species for all of California, Arizona, Colorado, Utah, Nevada, and western New Mexico. Within our area we find 172 different forms. Within Texas alone can be found 106 species and 142 recognizable forms.

The present work, then, lists all of the forms of cacti presently known to be growing within the five states: Arkansas, Louisiana, Oklahoma, Texas, and New Mexico. They are listed by their recognized scientific names, and immediately following (in every case where such exist) are given all of the common names which could be discovered, by which the cactus is known in various localities, including the Spanish and sometimes the Indian names. Spellings of these common names show the local variations found in the literature.

A description of the whole cactus plant, not meant to be tedious but made full enough to be useful for the serious student, is then given. This description is patterned on the original one of the species, but it takes into account other descriptions by more recent students plus our own observations and so may be broader than the original in the case of quantitative characters and may add information not covered in the original.

Following this is outlined the known range of natural distribution for the cactus. This is given in rather general terms, partly because there is still more to be learned about the spread of some of these plants and partly because it is not meant to be a guide telling exactly which mountain slope will provide the collector with the cactus he wants. The publication of such specific information all too often has meant that the slope is bare of any cacti at all the next year. There are no laws protecting cacti in any of the states covered in this study, and the conservation of our cacti is a real problem today. While this work gives no inaccurate or misleading information about where the various cacti are to be found, the exact locations of specific populations are not usually given. Any cactus hunter worthy of the title of "cactophile," once given the general territory where the plant grows, might rather search out the prize himself.

Next follows a discussion of each cactus listed. This is a gathering together of any remarks I might have on anything unusual or especially interesting about the cactus. Included under remarks also, because these are purely my own opinions after studying the plants and the literature upon them, are suggestions concerning its relationship to its fellows, with restatement of the specific characters which distinguish it from its closest relatives.

These relationships are very complex, and the concepts of them have been almost constantly changing throughout the study of the cacti, as can be quickly traced by looking at the synonymy in almost any listing. In an attempt to avoid making this part another series of synonym lists in fine print—or a dry, dead discussion of dead names—this synonymy is presented as a historical account of the vicissitudes through which individual cactus forms, individual plant names, and the ideas of individual students went from their discovery and their first statements until the present. Such a historical approach to this material has not been made before, and it can enable us to understand much about the science of botany and about men, as well as about cacti. Of course, the material is much simplified and rendered as nontechnical as possible. Nevertheless an attempt is made to evaluate fairly, from the vantage point of the present, each important author's arguments and to assign his proposal its proper place in the history of the cactus being discussed.

Lastly, each cactus form is illustrated by a full-color photograph of the plant, in most cases in bloom. A few of these photographs were made in the plant's natural location, but in most cases this proved to be impractical. Most cacti bloom only a few days out of the year, and it was obviously impossible to be in a canyon of the Texas Big Bend, on the Wichita Mountains of Oklahoma, on an Indian reservation in northwest New Mexico, and on an Ozark slope in Arkansas on precisely the days when each cactus chose to bloom. Much effort, therefore, has gone into the work of locating the various forms in the wild, then bringing them in and growing them in such congenial environments that they have bloomed, so that they could be pictured at the right moment. Unless otherwise stated, I made all photographs myself.

The soils and backgrounds visible in the pictures are, therefore, not usually the natural environments of the plants. In fact, the colors of these have often been chosen to contrast with and make as clearly visible as possible the spines and other characters of the cacti. This means that no conclusion about the environments of these plants can be drawn from these pictures. While some readers may consider this a drawback, it should be remembered that most of these cacti use protective coloration and camouflage. Pictures of them in their natural habitats, while of value to the ecologist, usually show little detail of the plants, if they are visible at all. An extreme illustration of this difficulty would be the case of *Mammillaria nellieae* Croiz., where the whole plant is usually totally covered by the moss which grows with it in its rock crevice; a picture of it *in loco* would show only the flower apparently blooming on the moss and would be useless in illustrating what the cactus is really like.

In the verbal description of the flower parts, I was confronted with the choice of employing standardized color names, such as those given in *A Dictionary of Color* by Maerz and Paul, or of using more general terms which would be meaningful to the average reader. I decided on the latter course in the belief that what would be gained in preciseness by the use of terms from *A Dictionary of Color* would be counterbalanced by the incon-

venience of having to consult this reference work in a library in order to determine what was meant by the shade names used.

Although as full as possible a rendering of the beauty of the flowers is an aim of these pictures, this is not their only goal. It is hoped that they may also convey a real concept of the plant body itself and of the spine character; sometimes the flower is shown at less than full angle because of this other aim.

In organizing this presentation, one of the biggest problems was the delineation of the genera. The widest possible range of opinions is held today by the different authorities in the field on the limits of the genera in the Cactaceae. It seems that the present extent of the knowledge of the cacti does not enable anyone to give as definite a list of cactus genera as can be made for many other plant groups. There are several very different systems of genera, each very logical in the light of a certain set of assumptions. I have attempted to re-evaluate these in the light of the latest research available. The work of Dr. Boke at Oklahoma University and results of our own chromatographic studies seem particularly important here. The resulting alignment of the genera is in no case a new one, but in some cases favors one previous proposal and in some another.

Within the genera no attempt has been made to organize the species into tribes or sections, since this sort of thing—as, for instance, various proposals for the genus *Opuntia*—seems still to be based on conjecture, and I find little newer and more solid evidence for any of the various contradictory proposals already made.

PLATES

Measurements given in the photograph captions are the plant body sizes of the specific plants pictured and do not, unless otherwise stated, include flowers. In most cases this size is smaller than the maximum size achieved by the species.

Echinocereus viridiflorus var. *viridiflorus*. Larger plant 2¼ inches tall.

Echinocereus viridiflorus var. *cylindricus*. 4¼ inches tall.

Echinocereus viridiflorus var. *standleyi*. 4 inches tall.

Echinocereus davisii. 1 inch tall.

Echinocereus chloranthus var. *chloranthus.* Young plant (left); mature plant, 4 inches tall (right).

Echinocereus chloranthus var. *neocapillus.* 3½ inches tall.

Echinocereus chloranthus var. *neocapillus.* Immature plant (center), 1¼ inches tall, flanked by mature specimens.

2

Echinocereus russanthus. 4 1/2 inches tall.

(above, right)
Echinocereus caespitosus var. *caespitosus.*
The white-spined "Lace Cactus," 3 inches tall.

Echinocereus caespitosus var. *caespitosus.* The
brown-spined "Brown-Lace Cactus," 5 inches tall.

Echinocereus caespitosus var. *minor*. Largest stem pictured, 2 inches tall.

4   *Echinocereus caespitosus* var. *perbellus*. 2 inches tall.

Echinocereus melanocentrus. 2 inches tall.

(above, left)
Echinocereus caespitosus var. *purpureus.*
3¹/₃ inches tall.

Echinocereus fitchii.
2¹/₄ inches tall.

5

PLATE 6

(above, left) *Echinocereus baileyi*.
White-spined. 4¼ inches tall.

(above, right) *Echinocereus baileyi*. Brown-spined,
clustering. Largest stem pictured, 2¼ inches tall.

(below) *Echinocereus albispinus*. Tallest stem
pictured, 2 inches high.

PLATE 7 (opposite)

(above, left) *Echinocereus pectinatus* var. *wenigeri*.
Stem 4½ inches tall.

(above, right) *Echinocereus pectinatus* var. *rigidissimus*.
6 inches tall.

(below, left) *Echinocereus chisoensis*.
7 inches tall.

(below, right) *Echinocereus pectinatus* var. *ctenoides* (right)
and *Echinocereus caespitosus* var. *caespitosus* (left).
Note typical ovary wall and fruit coverings.

Echinocereus pectinatus var. *ctenoides.* 3 inches tall.

Echinocereus dasyacanthus var. *dasyacanthus.*
Yellow-flowered. 10½-inch stem.

Echinocereus dasyacanthus var. *dasyacanthus.*
Pink-flowered. 12-inch stem.

Echinocereus dasyacanthus var. *hildmanii.* Stems 5 inches tall.

9

Echinocereus roetteri. 4³/₄ inches tall.

Echinocereus lloydii.
12 inches tall.

Echinocereus triglochidiatus var. *triglochidiatus.*
8 inches tall.

11

Echinocereus triglochidiatus var. *octacanthus*.
Stems 4¹/₄ inches tall.

(below, left)
Echinocereus triglochidiatus var. *gonacanthus*.
4 inches tall.

(below, right)
Echinocereus coccineus var. *coccineus*.
6¹/₂ inches tall.

12

Echinocereus coccineus var. *conoides*. 8 inches tall.

Echinocereus polyacanthus var. *rosei*. 8 inches tall.

Echinocereus polyacanthus var. *neo-mexicanus*. 4¹/₂ inches tall.

13

Echinocereus stramineus. Clump, 30 inches in diameter.

Echinocereus enneacanthus var. *enneacanthus.* Clustered stems, 13 inches across.

Echinocereus enneacanthus var. *carnosus.* Tallest stem 8 inches high.

Echinocereus fendleri var. *rectispinus*. Tallest stem pictured, 8 inches high.

(above, left)
Echinocereus fendleri var. *fendleri*. Stem 5³/₄ inches tall.

Echinocereus dubius. Tallest stem 9 inches high. Two specimens of *Lophophora williamsii* in right foreground.

15

Echinocereus papillosus var. *angusticeps.*
Tallest stem pictured, 3 inches high.

(above, right)
Echinocereus papillosus var. *papillosus.*
Sprawling stems, 2 inches high.

Echinocereus pentalophus. Stems approximately
¾ inch in diameter.

Wilcoxia poselgeri. Single,
upright stem, 12 inches long.
Echinocereus papillosus var.
papillosus on ground.

(above, left)
Echinocereus blanckii.
Stem pictured, 10$^1/_2$ inches long.

Echinocereus berlandieri. Tallest
stems pictured, 4 inches high.

Peniocereus greggii. Flowers
2⁷/₈ inches in diameter.

(below, left)
Acanthocereus pentagonus. Flower 6¹/₂ inches
long, including ovary and tube.

(below, right)
Echinocactus horizonthalonius var. *curvispina.*
6 inches in diameter.

Echinocactus texensis.
6 inches in diameter.

(above, left)
Echinocactus horizonthalonius var. *moelleri.*
7 inches in diameter.

Echinocactus asterias.
2¹/₂ inches in diameter.

19

Echinocactus uncinatus var. *wrightii*. 8 inches tall.

(above, left)
Echinocactus wislizeni.
14 inches in diameter.

Echinocactus whipplei.
3 inches in diameter.

Echinocactus mesae-verdae.
1³/₄ inches in diameter.

(below, left)
Echinocactus brevihamatus.
4 inches tall.

(below, right)
Echinocactus scheeri.
2¹/₂ inches tall.

Echinocactus tobuschii.
2⁵/₈ inches in diameter.

(below, left)
Echinocactus setispinus var. *hamatus.*
7 inches tall.

(below, right)
Echinocactus setispinus var. *setaceus.*
10 inches tall.

22

Echinocactus sinuatus. 5 inches in diameter.

Echinocactus hamatacanthus.
12 inches in diameter.

(below, left)
Echinocactus bicolor var. *schottii.* 4 inches in diameter.

(below, right)
Echinocactus flavidispinus. 2 inches in diameter.

Echinocactus intertextus var. *intertextus.*
When collected, 2³/₄ inches in diameter.

Echinocactus intertextus var. *intertextus.* Same plant
after 1 year of cultivation. 2⁷/₈ inches in diameter.

24   *Echinocactus intertextus* var. *dasyacanthus.*
2³/₄ inches in diameter.

Echinocactus erectocentrus var. *pallidus.*
2¹/₂ inches in diameter.

Echinocactus mariposensis. Green-flowered.
1⅝ inches in diameter.

Echinocactus mariposensis. Pink-flowered.
1⅞ inches in diameter.

Echinocactus conoideus. 3 inches tall.

PLATE 26

(above, left) *Ariocarpus fissuratus.* 3⁵/₈ inches in diameter.

(above, right) *Lophophora williamsii* var. *williamsii.*
Largest stem 3 inches in diameter.

(below) *Lophophora williamsii* var. *echinata.*
Largest stem 2¹/₂ inches in diameter.

PLATE 27 (opposite)

(above, left) *Pediocactus simpsonii var. simpsonii.* 3 inches in diameter

(above, right) *Pediocactus knowltonii.* 1 inch in diameter.

(below, left) *Pediocactus papyracanthus.* 2 inches tall.

(below, right) *Epithelantha micromeris.* 1¹/₂ inches in diameter.

Mammillaria scheeri. 6 inches in diameter.

Mammillaria scolymoides. 3¹/₄ inches in diameter.

Mammillaria echinus. Stem 2¹/₄ inches in diameter.

Mammillaria sulcata.
4¹/₈ inches in diameter.

Mammillaria ramillosa. 3¹/₄ inches in diameter.

Mammillaria macromeris. Young plant, not yet clustered. 3 inches tall.

(below, left)
Mammillaria runyonii.
4 inches in diameter.

(below, right)
Mammillaria similis. Typical small plant; diameter 3 inches.

Mammillaria similis. Old plant
in full bloom. Diameter 12 inches.

Mammillaria vivipara var. *vivipara.*
2¹/₄ inches in diameter.

31

Mammillaria vivipara var. *arizonica*. 3 inches in diameter.

Mammillaria fragrans. 2¼ inches in diameter

PLATE 32 (opposite)

(above, left) *Mammillaria vivipara* var. *radiosa*.
2 inches in diameter.

(above, right) *Mammillaria vivipara* var. *neo-mexicana*. Large stem
2¼ inches in diameter.

(below, left) *Mammillaria vivipara* var. *borealis*.
2 inches in diameter.

(below, right) *Mammillaria vivipara* var. *neo-mexicana*.
Young plants, showing juvenile spination on sides of stem and
mature spines at the tips. Larger plant 2 inches in diameter.

33

PLATE 35 (opposite)

(above) *Mammillaria dasyacantha* and *tuberculosa*, growing together.

(below left) *Mammillaria duncanii*. Showing root formation. Spiny portion of the stem 1 inch tall.

(below right) *Mammillaria duncanii*. Same plant, with fruit, after 3 months' cultivation.

Mammillaria tuberculosa.
Main stem 3⅝ inches tall.

34

Mammillaria dasyacantha. Plant pictured, 3 inches in diameter.

Mammillaria albicolumnaria. Plant pictured, 2⁷/₈ inches in diameter.

Mammillaria varicolor. Largest stem 1²/₃ inches in diameter.

(below, left)
Mammillaria hesteri.
4 inches tall.

(below, right)
Mammillaria nellieae. Blooming plant, 1 inch in diameter.

37

Mammillaria roberti. Largest stem 1³/₈ inches in diameter.

Mammillaria sneedii. Blooming stem ³/₄ inch in diameter.

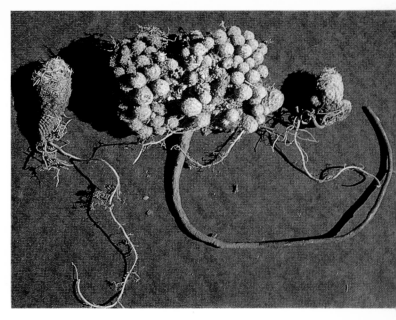

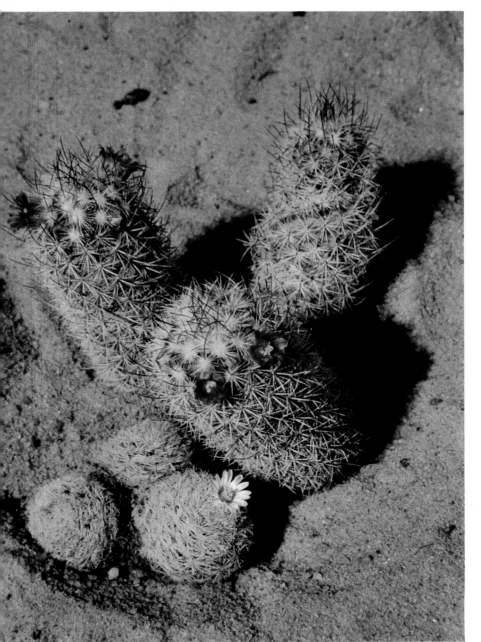

(above, left)
Mammillaria leei. Plants in garden cultivation.
Clusters 4 to 6 inches in diameter.

(above, right)
Mammillaria leei. Typical root formation.
Large clump, 4¼ inches across.

(below, left)
Mammillaria pottsii. Largest stem, 1⅓ inches
across. *M. lasiacantha* var. *denudata* in foreground.

(below, right)
Mammillaria lasiacantha var. *lasiacantha.*
Stem 1 inch in diameter.

Mammillaria lasiacantha var. *denudata*. Stem 2 inches in diameter.

Mammillaria microcarpa. 2 inches tall.

Mammillaria multiceps. Cluster of stems, 4¹/₈ inches across.

Mammillaria wrightii. Stem 1³/₁₆ inches in diameter.

Mammillaria wilcoxii.
Stem 1⁷/₈ inches in diameter.

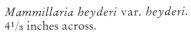
Mammillaria heyderi var. *heyderi.*
4¹/₃ inches across.

Mammillaria heyderi var. *applanata.*
4 inches across.

PLATE 43 (opposite)

(above) *Mammillaria heyderi* var. *hemis phaerica.* 3¹/₂ inches across

(below) *Mammillaria meiacantha*
4 inches across

43

Opuntia stricta. Plant pictured 26 inches tall.

Mammillaria sphaerica. Main plant, with offsets, 4³/4 inches across.

Opuntia engelmannii var. *engelmannii.*
Pad 12 inches long.

Opuntia engelmannii var. *texana*. Largest pads pictured, 8 inches wide.

Opuntia engelmannii var. *alta*. Red-flowered. Blooming pads, 5¹/₂ inches across.

Opuntia engelmannii var. *flexispina*. Main pad 10¹⁄₂ inches wide. White spots are cochineal insects.

Opuntia engelmannii var. *alta*. White-flowered. Flower 3¹⁄₈ inches across.

Opuntia engelmannii var. *cacanapa*. Largest pad shown, 7 inches across.

Opuntia engelmannii var. *aciculata*. Largest pad
6²/₃ inches across.

(above) *Opuntia engelmannii* var. *dulcis*. Largest pad
8 inches in diameter. This plant grew for many years in
an urn by the entrance to the Old Trail Drivers' Museum
in San Antonio.

Opuntia engelmannii var. *subarmata*.
Main pad 12 inches across.

47

Opuntia engelmannii var. *linguiformis.*
Blooming pad 16 inches long. White spots
are cochineal insects.

(below, left)
Opuntia chlorotica. Plant about 22 inches tall.

(below, right)
Opuntia tardospina. 9 inches tall.

48

Opuntia rufida. Largest pad pictured, 7 inches long.

(above, left)
Opuntia spinosibacca. Largest pad pictured, 5³/₄ inches long.

Opuntia macrocentra. Largest pad pictured, 6 inches long.

Opuntia gosseliniana var. *santa-rita*.
15 inches tall.

(below, left)
Opuntia strigil. Largest pad pictured,
7³/₄ inches long.

(below, right)
Opuntia atrispina. Largest pad pictured,
6 inches across.

(above) *Opuntia phaeacantha* var. *major*. Largest pad shown, 8 inches across.

(below) *Opuntia phaeacantha* var. *nigricans*. Old 6-inch pad sprawling; and new, sprouting 4-inch pads.

(above, left) *Opuntia leptocarpa*. Shown in fruit. Plant 15 inches tall.

(below, left) *Opuntia leptocarpa* in foreground and *Opuntia engelmannii* var. *texana* in background.

51

Opuntia phaeacantha var. *brunnea*. Wide-open flowers, 3 inches across.

Opuntia cymochila. Largest pad pictured, 4 inches across.

(above, left)
Opuntia phaeacantha var. *camanchica.* Largest pad
pictured, 4¹/₃ inches long.

Opuntia phaeacantha var. *tenuispina.*
Pads 9 inches long.

Opuntia compressa var. *humifusa*. Largest pad
pictured, 3 inches across.

Opuntia compressa var. *macrorhiza*.
Pad 4 inches long, blooming.

Opuntia compressa var. *microsperma*. Largest pad
pictured, 3 inches long.

Opuntia compressa var. *fusco-atra*. Two specimens from same
locality. Largest pad on stunted plant, 2¼ inches long;
largest pad on vigorous plant, 5 inches long.

Opuntia compressa var. *fusco-atra*. An abnormal form, known as O. *macateei*. Open flower 2 inches across.

Opuntia compressa var. *grandiflora*. Largest pad pictured, 5¹/₄ inches long.

Opuntia compressa var. *allairei*. Largest pad pictured, 6¹/₄ inches long.

Opuntia compressa var. *stenochila*. Largest pad pictured, 4 inches across.

Opuntia ballii. Pad
2¹⁄₃ inches across.

Opuntia pottsii. 6¹⁄₂ inches tall, exclusive of fruits.

Opuntia plumbea. Pad 2¹⁄₄ inches long.

56

Opuntia drummondii. Largest pad pictured, 3 inches long.

Opuntia fragilis. Clump 6½ inches across.

Opuntia sphaerocarpa. In winter condition.
Largest pad pictured, 3¼ inches across.

Opuntia rhodantha var. *rhodantha*. Yellow flowered. 6½ inches tall.

Opuntia rhodantha var. *rhodantha*. Pink flowered. 8 inches tall.

Opuntia rhodantha var. *spinosior*. Larger pad pictured, 4½ inches long.

Opuntia polyacantha. Typical, heavily spined. Largest pad pictured, 4 inches long.

Opuntia polyacantha. With spines few and short. Largest pad pictured, 5⁵/₈ inches long.

Opuntia hystricina. Upright pad, 4 inches long.

Opuntia arenaria. Largest pad pictured, 2³/₄ inches long.

Opuntia grahamii. Pictured clump, 7 inches across.

Opuntia stanlyi. Largest joint pictured, 4 inches long.

(below, left)
Opuntia schottii. Pictured joints, each 2 inches long.

(below, right)
Opuntia clavata. Largest joints pictured, 1¹/₂ inches in diameter.

Opuntia imbricata var. *arborescens*. Branch with ripe fruits. Main branch pictured, 1¹/₄ inches in diameter.

Opuntia imbricata var. *viridiflora*. Pictured plant 15 inches tall.

(above, left)
Opuntia imbricata var. *arborescens*. Section of the main stem pictured, 1¹/₄ inches in diameter.

(below, left)
Opuntia imbricata var. *vexans*. Branch with ripe fruits. Largest fruit pictured, 1⁵/₈ inches in diameter.

61

Opuntia spinosior. Largest stem pictured, 1 inch in diameter.

Opuntia whipplei. In winter condition, 10 inches tall.

62

Opuntia davisii. Largest branch pictured, ⁵/₈ inch in diameter.

Opuntia tunicata. Plant pictured, 13 inches across.

63

Opuntia leptocaulis. Main stem pictured, ¹/₄ inch in diameter.

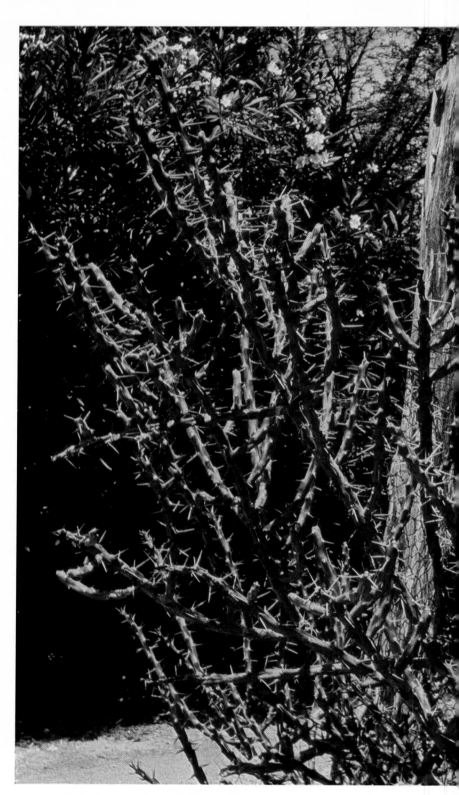

Opuntia kleinei. Plant pictured, 4 feet tall.

CACTI OF THE SOUTHWEST

What Is a Cactus?

Before going directly into the description of the various cacti we might pause to consider, for those who have not concerned themselves about these things before, how a cactus differs from other plants, what is so special about it, and what are some of the problems the uniqueness of its form and physiology bring to it in its natural situation and to us if we desire to raise it.

It is harder to say exactly what a cactus is and how it differs from other plants than one might think. It is obvious that a cactus is a unique plant, with special problems. Imagining how it got that way, learning how to recognize it when we see it, and understanding its adaptations to its special problems—each of these presents us with special difficulties.

The origin of the cactus family remains almost completely a mystery. We are balked here by the fact that there are no fossils of any cacti. So anxious have we been for such evidence that there have been several remains grasped hopefully as being cactus fossils, but all these, such as the famous one optimistically christened *Eopuntia douglassii* Chaney, have since proved not to be connected with the cacti at all. The most primitive and least cactus-like forms that we know are the members of the genus *Pereskia,* still alive, flourishing, and all-cactus, giving us no clear clues as to how they got that way. This leaves us with only theories based on comparative anatomy studies to satisfy us.

Mostly because of certain flower characteristics, it is quite often assumed that cacti are related to the Rose Family. From here one can go as far as his imagination chooses to range, presuming with some that the roses of the West Indies changed in order to adapt to more arid conditions and so gave rise to the Pereskias and through them to all cacti. This is an enchanting story, and I am sure that the cactophiles are pleased with the idea that their favorites might be descendants of the rose, but I am not so certain that the rose enthusiasts are as sympathetic to the idea of appending the cacti to their queen of the flowers. Most agree that the cacti are a young group, maybe 20,000 years old, and an equally big problem is how they could have developed their extreme and fantastic adaptations in such a comparatively short time.

Be that as it may, the cacti are here, and one needs to know how to recognize them. This task is complicated by the fact that most of the obvious characters by which one thinks to recognize them are shared by some plant or other somewhere in the world. This is true of such things as large, fleshy stems, vicious spines, and reduction of leaves, which to an amateur mean cactus every time. There are other plants showing all of these characteristics, some of them to almost the extent the cacti do.

It is a failure to recognize this fact that accounts for the popular articles, nursery ads, and many "cactus plantings," containing mention or actual specimens of completely unrelated plants under the banner of cactus. Although they show some at least of the above characteristics, it must be stated that such things as yuccas, agaves, century plants, sotol, and so on, are not cacti at all, but extremely modified members of the Lily Family. Ocotillo and allthorn are individual residents of the desert community showing some of the same adaptations, but belonging to other plant families. Then there is the whole multitude of African plants paralleling the cacti in almost every feature of stem, rib, spine, and leaf, but all belonging to the huge, world-wide genus *Euphorbia* which also includes such plants as the Poinsettia. We sometimes speak of all these other plants as succulents, setting up the categories of cacti and succulents—although the cacti are also succulent, since the word merely means "fleshy."

How then do you tell a cactus? There is no easy way to do it without close observation of details and something of a botanist's eye. However, a cactus is always a dicot, and its two seed leaves will distinguish it at once from all those members of the Lily Family so often called cacti, since they are monocots and have only one seed leaf.

Then, a feature which all cacti have and share with no other plant is the structure called the areole. All cacti have areoles quite liberally scattered over the surface, and usually arranged in rows or spirals in the most conspicuous places. These are round to elongated spots from $1/16$ to sometimes well over $1/2$ inch in greatest measurement; their surfaces are hard, rough, uneven, and brown or blackish or else covered with white to brown or blackish wool. These areoles are now considered to be the equivalent of complex buds, and it is from these that whatever spines the cactus possesses grow. These spines, since they come from these areoles, are always arranged in clusters, which is another feature not found on other spiny plants, whose spines are produced singly from some source other than an areole.

Beyond this, for the actual features separating cacti from all other plants, one has to look to the flower. Certain rather technical features of the flower are cited, such as its having sepals and petals numerous and intergrading, its having an inferior ovary with one seed chamber and having one single style with several stigma lobes.

The key to understanding why the cactus is such a strange plant is the understanding of its major problem and how it solves it. This is its water problem.

Most plants are great spendthrifts when it comes to water. They stand with their roots in unfailing water supplies from streams or from moisture stored in the soil between rains; and they constantly absorb quantities of water, which they use and then pass on out through their leaves into the atmosphere. This passage of water through the typical plant is so great that we call it the transpiration stream and can best think of such plants as constantly flowing fountains of water. If there is too little water available near them such plants normally solve the problem by developing extra long roots which go where the water is, and if this fails they dry out and die.

But the cactus is typically a resident of the desert or else of habitats where, for one reason or another, the water supply is practically nonexistent at least part of the time. It may be because of inadequate rainfall or because the soil is too coarse or too thin to hold much water. So the cactus has a water problem which it solves in its own way.

The cactus disdains to put out the extreme root systems, often drilling fifty feet deep, used by other desert plants to find the precious water which enables them to stay alive. Instead it sits and waits for the infrequent showers which ultimately do come, even in the desert, or for the rainy season. And when moisture does come the plant is ready. Its finely branching roots absorb water rapidly when it is available, and in a short time it has taken in a large amount. But there will be another drought to come, when it may be able to take in little if any water for weeks or months, so it stores this bonanza of water to the limit

of its capacity, and its adaptations for great water-storing capacity form the basis for the most obvious peculiarity of the cactus.

The commonest and most simple means of storing water found in these plants is by the enlarging of the stem into a thick, fleshy column or even a round ball. A cactus adapted this way becomes literally a water-filled column or ball, actually, in large specimens, a barrel of water—from which comes the common term, "barrel cactus." The interior of such a cactus is not a reservoir of pure water into which you could dip a ladle, as cartoons sometimes show the thirsty prospector doing, but a mass of soft tissue permeated with water. Except for the supporting framework necessary in larger species, that interior is of about the consistency of a melon's watery pulp. When rain comes it fills to the maximum with water, and in times of drought this reserve is gradually reduced. Thus, the cactus stem swells and shrinks according to the water supply, and there is always an arrangement of ribs or tubercles which make this change in bulk possible without the whole stem alternately caving in or splitting open.

In a number of the cacti where adaptations for clambering up trees, camouflage in thickets, or something else limits the thickness or size of the stems, the root may become the water-storage organ instead. In these cacti the root may become a carrot-like taproot weighing up to fifty pounds (in the extreme case of an old *Peniocereus greggii* specimen) or a cluster of tubers (as found on *Wilcoxia poselgeri* and some of the Opuntias).

The cactus, then, is a plant which solves the problem of insufficient water in its habitat by storing large amounts of water within its tissues, and this explains its succulent consistency and bloated stem. Due to this habit it is internally among the softest, most delicate of plants.

But standing there as almost literally a column or barrel of water in the middle of the thirsty desert brings problems requiring still further adaptations, giving us the other remarkable characteristics of a cactus. Since the cactus may have to survive for weeks or months on the moisture it has within it, it cannot afford to be a spendthrift with water like other plants. It has to give up a little at all times to stay alive, but it must sacrifice the smallest possible amount and protect its precious store against the dryness of the desert air which would otherwise evaporate it all in a matter of hours.

For this reason the leaves of a cactus are reduced or eliminated altogether. After all, leaves are for the purpose of increasing the evaporative and light-absorbing surface of the plant, and the cactus needs to reduce the evaporative surface to a minimum, while certainly, in the glaring desert, it need not spread out its surface after light. Therefore, the more strictly a desert dweller it is, the more completely the leaves tend to be reduced or absent and the green stems to take over their functions. Then, its compact form is covered with a thick, waxy epidermis which is impervious to water, and even its stomata are equipped with means to reduce moisture loss. There is great variation in the tenacity with which individual cacti hold water, with the most extreme desert forms said to release up to six thousand times less water in a given moment than an ordinary plant of the same weight.

The thick, dry, protective covering of the cactus is so deceptive to us that we seldom think of the soft, delicate, watery interior which it protects, but we may be sure the thirsty denizens of the desert, where water is life itself, are ever conscious of it. They would eat the plant immediately just for the water, if they could get at it. So the cactus has had to add protection against all the living water-seekers which surround it, and this gives yet another of its peculiarities.

The almost universal solution of the cactus to this problem is to cover itself with an armament of spines. The succulent flesh is entirely covered with a system of spines so sharp and dangerous and so perfectly spreading and interlacing that neither the browsers nor the rodents can get their teeth between them to bite into the plant. The spines are never poisonous, and one can't ascribe maliciousness to a plant for having them. They are there as necessary protection for the otherwise most delicate, most defenseless member of the desert community. It should help one to understand the spiny thing to realize that in the desert, when an injury or a malformation leaves a space wide enough for the jaws of a rabbit or even a mouse to get between the spines and start working, the cactus is soon eaten entirely. If one goes out on the desert and cuts all of the spines off a cactus, it usually disappears overnight. Ranchers have long ago learned to profit by this fact, and in some areas, by merely burning the spines off the huge prickly pears, provide their cattle with tons of free, succulent forage. The water problem, then, is directly responsible for the soft make-up of a cactus and indirectly responsible for its hard, waxy exterior and its often unpleasant but also fascinating array of spines.

The cactus faces another closely related problem. Its habitats are usually extreme in their heat and the intensity of their light. The temperature on a south-facing, rocky desert slope reaches almost unbelievable heights on a summer afternoon. Even the desert reptiles are said to avoid the sun in which the extreme desert forms of cactus have to stand all day. How can they survive this baking heat and searing light?

Of course many cacti could not, and these grow only in the shade of thickets or trees, but the ones which stand and take it are said to depend on their own spines for shade. The spines achieve their shading effect, somewhat after the manner of a lath-house cover, by breaking the radiation up into moving strips of endurable duration. These forms also protect the exposed surface, especially the tender growing area at the top, with a covering of wool or hair, usually white and reflective. One can fairly well judge how extreme a desert situation a species comes from and how much sun it can stand by looking at how extensively this wool is developed or how complete the spine shading is.

With no tender leaves, the compact body of the cactus, with-

in its spiny envelope, is thus remarkably well protected against any of the natural forces or living enemies of its habitat, and it can survive in places where only the hardiest persist. Yet it has one more major problem to surmount. It must reproduce itself. And to do this it must usually produce a flower. Some of the cacti avoid this at all but the most favorable times, and depend instead upon very well-developed vegetative reproduction, but sooner or later all have to bloom.

Now, a flower is an amazingly complex structure of extremely delicate parts. Flowering is a time when the plant must open and expose for the generating touch the most precious centers of its being. It is a time of vulnerability, and not even the cactus has succeeded in armoring the flower. It may swathe the bud in spines and wool, but when the moment comes it must expose the flower to the cruel desert situation as unprotected as any rose or lily. This presents another immense problem for the cactus and its way of solving it gives us both the wonderful beauty for which the flower is famous, and the extreme fleetingness of the flower which exasperates us.

The cactus flower is almost always renowned for its size and beauty, which are said to be for the purpose of attracting insects or other flying forms across the arid distances to pollinate it. At any rate it does not seem to be beautiful for our benefit, because the flower usually lasts so short a period and blooms at such an unfavorable time that we hardly ever catch a glimpse of it and it usually is "born to blush unseen and waste its sweetness on the desert air."

Most cacti have flowers which open in the worst heat of the day, usually for only a few hours, and then are closed and fading before the cool of the evening begins. It is as though the plant waits until the heat of the day drives most of its enemies under the protection of some shade to unfold these tender morsels which it cannot otherwise protect. Thus, in most forms, the flower has its brief life, the reproductive act is completed by the insects which scorn the heat, and the life spark is already down within the spiny ovary before the desert cools, so that its thirsty tribes find only wilted petals for their evening meals.

Many tropical and a few of our U. S. cacti reverse this schedule entirely and open their gigantic, wonderfully fragrant flowers at night to be pollinated by night-flying insects or in a few cases by bats. In most cases these species produce their flowers on tall, spiny stems where no ordinary enemy could reach them anyway, but they fade as quickly as the others, and are usually only sadly wilted remains by dawn. Only the saguaro, whose flowers are inaccessible to almost any enemy, and some other forms protected by especially long, vicious spines seem able to enjoy the luxury of longer lasting flowers.

The cactus fruit, which follows the flower, is usually protected at first by spines or wool, and grows to become a berry with numerous small seeds. In some cases this dries up and the seeds are allowed to scatter, but in many species the ripe berry becomes fleshy and at the same time loses its spines or rises out of its wool covering. Here is probably the only part of a cactus purposely left unprotected. It is never poisonous, and it ranges from sour to very sweet in different species. It is snapped up and carried off by animals and birds who finally get a meal from the cactus, but who pay for it by scattering the seeds far and wide. Some of the sweetest of these fruits are relished by humans. Those of the Opuntias are called "tunas"; and the "strawberry cactus" (of which there are several species) bears this common name because the flavor of the red fruits suggests that of strawberries.

In all of its stages, then, the cactus is admirably adapted for survival in an arid environment, with all of these special features accentuated to the extreme in the forms inhabiting the more severe desert regions and less markedly developed in those of less extreme situations. But these same wonderful features which make the cactus so successful in the desert bring their own problems with them, limiting it in important ways even in its natural environment and making the tough desert thing one of the most vulnerable of plants when brought out of the desert into cultivation.

Its very life, we have seen, depends upon the large amount of water stored within it as watery pulp. But this brings also the greatest danger to the cactus. Everyone knows how easily bruised and how quickly rotting is the watery flesh of melons and other soft fruits. A sharp blow or a gash through the protective covering of such structures causes a breakdown of the soft tissues which often spreads like wildfire throughout, leaving the whole thing a putrid, rotten mass. This is because such soft, nutrient-filled tissues form the perfect media for the growth of bacteria and all sorts of fungi.

The interior of even the toughest cactus is just as vulnerable to fungi. It survives because this tender core is surrounded by the tough, fungus-resistant epidermis. The cactus is only safe when this forms an unbroken barrier covering not only the stem but the roots of the plant. But the slightest injury, any break in this epidermis, may let in a fungus, and if one gets in before the plant can repair the break with scar tissue and starts growing in the interior, the outwardly invincible old cactus will be attacked from within. It will then be quickly permeated by the fungus and will collapse into a foul, oozing thing—often literally overnight. For this reason any injury is a greater danger to a cactus than to most plants, especially if it has been removed from the desert, where fungi are not as numerous, to a more damp climate where they abound.

But the fungi often gain entrance to our cacti in a more subtle way. The epidermis on the roots of these plants is necessarily thinner than that on the stems, and it is in constant contact with the fungus-populated soil. If there is very little rainfall or the soil is open and fast-draining, all will probably be well, but if there are periods of continuous rainfall, or if the soil is close-packed and remains for any time water-saturated, then the normally hard, dry, and impervious epidermis of the roots becomes wet through and softened, and loses its impermeability to the fungi. The defense barrier is dissolved, and almost any

cactus whose roots lie in waterlogged soil for over twenty-four hours or so will be invaded and reduced in about that much longer to stinking carrion. This is the fate of most cacti taken in from the desert and planted in heavy yard soil in a more rainy region or else in a pot which is watered every day along with the geraniums. In general, cacti must have abundant water now and then to replenish their stored supply, but they must not stand in stagnant water at any time.

We have also seen how the cactus survives not only by storing water but by being miserly with it and giving off a transpiration stream of up to several thousand times less volume than other plants. When other plants are wide-open, gushing fountains, the cactus is a dribbling faucet with extra safeguards on all the water exits of its body. This means survival in the desert, but brings problems even there and may mean death in the moisture-laden atmosphere of your garden.

Plant physiologists tell us that the transpiration stream must flow unceasingly in any active plant. If the flow ceases the plant must go dormant—as some plants do in winter or severe drought—or die. They also tell us that the rate of transpiration is directly proportional to the rate of the plant's life processes, including its growth.

Relating this to cacti, we find that, having to restrict their transpiration to a minimum to conserve their stored water, the cacti are limited thereby to very slow life processes and growth as compared with other plants. When looking at a large old cactus one should appreciate the time it took, at this reduced rate, to achieve its bulk. While there is much variation, with the more extreme desert forms, naturally the most slow-growing, the variations exist even in these according to their immediate situation. It is often said that a saguaro cactus one foot tall will be about twenty-five years old, and a barrel cactus one foot in diameter between twenty and forty years old. I have in my own garden a fine specimen of *Echinocactus ingens*, a perfect ball just over twelve inches in diameter, which was planted at the old Shiner Cactus Garden in Laredo, Texas, as a seed, forty-five years ago. It has grown its whole life in a good situation in a plant bed, and while the species might grow somewhat faster in its native haunts in Mexico, its growth has been very nearly typical. Nor is a smaller cactus necessarily younger. I have heard it said that a peyote button two inches in diameter is ten years old. The rates of growth vary from species to species, but almost no cactus is over a fraction of an inch tall at the end of its first year, and they all must have long periods of time to achieve their potential size.

The amount of water vapor in the atmosphere around a plant also affects the amount of water it will transpire. The dry air of arid regions literally drags the water out of the plants, and desert species, including cacti, have to guard their water ardently against this evaporative pull. On the other hand, the water-loaded air of humid regions is reluctant to take up more water, and the plants living in the regions must lay themselves wide open in order to promote the life-giving flow and often live less than the maximum span because of their inability to transpire enough water.

Imagine the problem, then, of that cactus you brought home from the desert and planted in your nice moist yard. Adapted to hoarding its water, with its stomata small and guarded by various means against the pull of the dry desert air, what can it do in the humid air where it is now? It cannot open and lay its moisture out for the humid air. This is not its way. And since this air does not pull water out of its deep recesses, the flow will be less than it would be in the desert, so your cactus, which you thought would respond with prodigious growth to your kindness in bringing it into the moisture, may actually suffer and grow poorly because it cannot transpire and carry on its life processes here.

We have also mentioned the adaptations of the cactus which enable it to live in the extreme heat and light of the desert. These may also bring severe problems to a cactus.

The flesh of most cacti is more or less shaded and protected by the spines and a covering of wool or hair. In the forms which grow in extremely exposed places this covering may be developed to protect against temperatures of well over 100 degrees Fahrenheit and some of the most intense light radiation found on earth. The outer tissues themselves, and even the life processes of some of these species are adapted to such extremes. It seems, for instance, that some of these cacti cannot even begin photosynthesis until the temperature reaches 75 degrees or higher. Everything in them is adjusted for high heat and light intensities.

All this is fine and necessary in the desert, but what about the problems of such a cactus when you bring it home? You want to keep it in your nice cool dark house or your nice shaded garden, and you can't understand why it does not grow, or why,

if it does, it becomes all grotesque and spindly. Don't you see that in such a situation it cannot get light and heat enough through all of its defenses to activate its high-set thermostat and stimulate its growth processes properly? Air-conditioning has marked the end of many a cactus dish-garden because the plants can hardly carry on photosynthesis, in the coolness we maintain, even in a window, and when this is coupled with what is for them little better than darkness, they may not be able to manufacture enough food even to stay alive.

We have seen some of the remarkable adaptations which make cacti so fascinating and have tried to understand the problems these changes are meant to meet, as well as the special problems they can generate for cactus-growers. Successful cactus culture consists of recognizing these problems and helping the cactus meet them naturally. One does not have success with cacti by removing them from all their natural problems. More cacti in cultivation have been killed by too much kindness than by anything else. These are tough plants by nature, and all they ask is that the conditions around them remain within the ranges, rather severe by our standards, for which they are adapted.

It is well to recall that there are cacti adapted for almost every sort of environment, from shady rain forest to extreme desert exposure. All of the problems of growing cacti mentioned above are less critical for those plants adapted to less severe conditions, and these can be grown much more easily than the more restricted ones; some of them can be treated quite a lot like other plants. But these are generally the less spiny, less succulent forms which are, therefore, the ones less fascinating to most of us. It is perhaps unfortunate, but unavoidable, that to grow pitahayas and barrels and other remarkable types one has to simulate to a fair degree the extreme environments of their hot, arid homes.

Key to the Genera of the Cacti

THE KEYS which are given here and before the discussion of each major genus are based as far as possible on the vegetative characters of adult individuals, but it appears to be impossible to construct workable keys for the cacti based on these alone. It was found necessary to refer in some cases to the flowers or fruits and sometimes even to the seeds. This means that the keys will be less than satisfactory in certain seasons and will not identify most juvenile forms at all. Those using the keys will need to have before them very nearly complete adult specimens of the living plants.

The keys are artificial and are my own. They are binomial keys, presenting a series of choices between two alternatives. In use, one reads the first choice (*1 a*) and compares the specimen in question with the description. If the description at *1 a* fits the specimen, he then proceeds to the number given at the end of the description and repeats the process there. If the description at *1 a* does not fit the specimen, then the user abandons *1 a* and moves on to *1 b,* which is the alternate choice. If the specimen matches *1 b,* then he moves to the number given at the end of *1 b,* and so on. When this process is followed carefully with a mature plant from our area, it should lead to a description after which a plant name and page number is given. This is the name of the specimen in hand and the discussion of it will start on that page. If at any point the specimen does not fit either the *a* or *b* choice one has arrived at, there are two possible explanations. Either the user has already made a wrong choice somewhere earlier in the process, or else the cactus he has is not included in this key. Careful reconsideration of all choices should show which is the case. If the user cannot choose between alternatives by studying his specimen, he may have to secure a more mature or more complete example in order to key the form.

1a. Stems of mature plants ribbed—that is, the surfaces of the stems covered with vertical or sometimes spiraling ridges which may be completely uninterrupted, undulate, or sometimes almost completely interrupted by grooves between the areoles, but which are never, on mature stems, rows of completely separate tubercles—2.

2a. Plants possessing spines—3.

3a. Stems of plants upright, prostrate, or clambering, with mature stems more than twice as long as they are thick; the flowers produced on the sides of the stems, with the ovary surfaces spiny; the fruit remaining fleshy and indehiscent or sometimes splitting open laterally—4.

4a. Stems not more than about 6 times as long as they are thick, not over 24 inches long, upright or prostrate, but not clambering, often caespitose; the flowers produced from a rupture of the stem epidermis just above an areole —Genus *Echinocereus* (see key on page 11).

4b. Stems when mature at least 8 to sometimes 100 times as long as they are thick, on old specimens becoming more than 24 inches long, upright or clambering, never caespitose; the flowers produced from within a spine areole—5.

5a. Stems $1/4$ to 1 inch in diameter; spines $1/32$ to $1/4$ of an inch long; roots tuberous—6.

6a. Stems $1/4$ to $5/8$ of an inch thick; ribs 8; spines to $1/4$ or $3/8$ of an inch long; roots clustering tubers; flowers purplish with short tubes and opening during the day —Genus *Wilcoxia* (see page 55).

6b. Stems $1/2$ to 1 inch thick; ribs 3 to 6; spines $1/32$ to $1/8$ of an inch long; root a single extremely large taproot; flowers mostly white with long tubes and opening at night —Genus *Peniocereus* (see page 57).

5b. Stems 2 to 4 inches in diameter; spines $3/8$ to 2 inches long; roots fibrous—Genus *Acanthocereus* (see page 60).

3b. Stems of plants upright, never more than twice as tall as they are thick; the flowers produced at the apex of the stem,

with the ovary surface scaly or sometimes with hair, but never spiny; the fruit opening basally or laterally
                    —Genus *Echinocactus* (see key on page 65).
2b. Plants spineless—7.
      7a. Flowers large and yellow with red centers; ovary scaly   —Genus *Echinocactus* (see key on page 65).
      7b. Flowers small and pinkish; fruit never having spines or scales   —Genus *Lophophora* (see page 95).
1b. Stems of plants smooth or else tubercled—that is, covered with nipple-like projections which may be arranged in spiral rows and which may overlap due to their length, but which are never confluent to form raised ribs—8.
      8a. Plants a fraction of an inch to about 6 inches tall; stems depressed, hemispherical, or columnar, but never jointed; the spines straight or hooked but never barbed glochids; the ovaries and fruits naked or with only a few scales on them—9.
         9a. Plants spineless   —Genus *Ariocarpus* (see page 100).
         9b. Plants spiny—10.
            10a. Fruit becoming dry and splitting open
                    —Genus *Pediocactus* (see page 103).
            10b. Fruit remaining fleshy and not splitting open—11.
               11a. Flowers produced in the axils of the tubercles   —Genus *Mammillaria* (see key on page 112).
               11b. Flowers produced from the tips of the tubercles   —Genus *Epithelantha* (see page 107).
8b. Plants several inches to sometimes 6 or more feet tall; stems jointed; at least some of the spines barbed glochids; the ovary naked or spiny
                    —Genus *Opuntia* (see key on page 162).

Genus *Echinocereus* Engelmann

THE ECHINOCEREI make up one of the largest genera of cacti, both in number of different species and in number of individuals found growing in the area of this study. Many of its members are collected and grown by cactus fanciers all over the world as great favorites because of the beauty of their flowers as well as of the plants themselves.

The name of the genus is composed of two words: *echinos,* meaning spiny, which refers to the very spiny covering of the typical members of this genus, and *cereus,* which means "wax candle," a reference to the stately appearance of the stems of the upright species.

The Echinocerei are oval, conical, or cylindrical cacti, always with ribbed stems. The vertical ribs of some species are more or less divided into swellings which may be called warts or tubercles, but these are never completely separated from one another as in some other genera, so the ribs are always an outstanding character of them all.

These cacti are usually very spiny, as their name implies, and these spines may be straight or curved, but are never hooked, as is common in some other groups.

The stems of Echinocerei are always low as compared with many of their relatives. Most of them are well under twelve inches long when mature, and the few in the Southwest which sometimes surpass that do not usually exceed twenty-four inches long. These stems are erect in most species, but in a few they lie partly or entirely prostrate upon the ground.

The plant body of some species remains a single, unbranched stem throughout life. Others cluster or branch sparingly only when very old; but many regularly form clusters of stems almost from the start. In some these clusters are made up of only a few stems, but in a few of them one plant may with age become a huge, caespitose clump of as many as a hundred or more stems. These stems are never divided into joints however.

The flowers of this genus are borne on the ribs at the spine-bearing areoles, developing just above the uppermost spines of the areoles, where they literally burst through the epidermis of the stem. They may be produced from almost any point on the stem, different species bearing them high or low, but most commonly they appear on the sides of the stems a little below the tips.

The flowers are usually very large and beautiful, so beautiful that many fanciers pick one or another species in this genus as the most beautiful of our native cacti. However, a few of the Echinocerei have small and inconspicuous greenish flowers. The petals of some species remain only partly open, making the flowers funnel-shaped, while those of others open very widely. A perianth tube is always present. The outer surface of the ovary is always spiny and sometimes woolly as well. The stigma lobes are always green on all of our species.

The fruits produced by these cacti are always fleshy, thin-skinned, and often edible. Those of some species are considered delicacies. Something of their character may be imagined from the fact that a number of them are known by the common name of "strawberry cacti." These fruits are also spiny, but the spines become loosened as the fruits mature, and may be easily brushed off.

The members of the genus *Echinocereus* inhabit a wide belt of the North American continent from Utah and Wyoming south throughout most of northern Mexico to a little beyond the latitude of Mexico City, and from central Oklahoma and Texas on the east to the Pacific on the west. Within this huge area more than eighty species have been described by various authorities, but many of these so intergrade that later students have combined various ones. The result is that almost every book or article on this genus has at least a slightly different method of listing them, depending upon the taxonomic philosophy of the writer as well as upon his knowledge of these cacti. This has caused much confusion, and makes it necessary for us to deal with many authors and names in order to know exactly what plant we have before us.

I will attempt to make or follow no formal classification of the species within the genus because it is too large a group and we have in the area of this study only a minority of the forms which would have to be considered in such a classification. Instead, I will group the species in a purely artificial series according to their most obvious characteristics, while concentrating upon describing the various forms properly and calling them, in the light of the most recent knowledge, by their proper names.

The Echinocerei grow mostly in exposed places on dry slopes and hills in the full strength of the southwestern sun. Only a few of them prefer the shade of bushes and trees. With this sunloving characteristic and their inability to tolerate excess moisture remembered, most of them are rather easily cultivated and are, therefore, popular among collectors. They have a wide range of tolerance of cold, those of the north being very resistant, while many of those of Mexico perish by freezing when brought farther north.

KEY TO THE ECHINOCEREI

1a. Stems upright or sprawling, comparatively thick, being two inches or more thick when mature—2.
  2a. Having all three of the following characters: areoles always ¹/₂ inch or less apart; ribs always more than 10; radial spines always more than 12—3.
    3a. Flowers small, 1 to 1¹/₂ inches long and less than that in width, yellow, yellow-brown, or pinkish-red in color—4.
      4a. Areoles elongated; central spines 0 to 3 in number, arranged in a vertical row, and 1 inch or less in length on mature plants—5.
        5a. Plant globose to short-cylindric; radials ¹/₄ of an inch or less long—6.
          6a. Ribs 12 to 18; radials 16 to more than 20; plant 2 inches or more tall when mature—7.
            7a. Spines varicolored red, brownish, or purplish-red and white   —*E. viridiflorus* var. *viridiflorus.*
            7b. Spines yellowish   —*E. viridiflorus* var. *standleyi.*
          6b. Ribs 6 to 9; radials 8 to 12; plant about 1 inch tall when mature   —*E. davisii.*
        5b. Plant cylindrical; radials to ¹/₂ inch long
             —*E. viridiflorus* var. *cylindricus.*
      4b. Areoles broad oval to round; centrals 3 to 12 in number and not standing in a straight vertical row, but instead spreading outward from the center of the areole—8.
        8a. Radials 12 to 23; ribs hardly tuberculate; centrals 3 to 5 in number on mature plants
             —*E. chloranthus* var. *chloranthus.*

        8b. Radials 30 or more; ribs markedly tuberculate; centrals 5 to 12 on mature plants—9.
          9a. Centrals to only ¹/₂ inch long; immature plants having flexible hairs instead of spines; flowers greenish-yellow to bronze and with a glossy surface   —*E. chloranthus* var. *neocapillus.*
          9b. Centrals ³/₄ to 1¹/₄ inches long; immature plants having rigid spines from the first; flowers pale pinkish or brownish-red and with a dull surface   —*E. russanthus.*
    3b. Flowers large and showy, 2 to 5 inches or more in length and width, yellow to purple in color—10.
      10a. Flower tube with long, cobwebby wool and hairlike, bristly spines; spines not recurved against the plant body—11.
        11a. Longest radial spines ³/₈ of an inch or less—12.
          12a. Central spines 0 to 2, porrect and if more than one, then arranged in a strict vertical row—13.
            13a. Centrals usually missing and ¹/₈ inch or less long when present—14.
              14a. Size of mature plant stems 3 to 12 inches tall by 2 to 3¹/₂ inches thick; flower 3 to 5 inches long and nearly as wide, petals 30 to 50, stigma lobes 8 to 22—15.
                15a. Radial spines 15 to 36—16.
                  16a. Spines white to gray or reddish, often with dark tips, but not with the outer parts of the spines conspicuously shiny purplish or black so as to give the plant a shiny blackish aspect   —*E. caespitosus* var. *caespitosus.*
                16b. Outer parts of the spines bright, shiny, purplish or black, giving the plant a conspicuous blackish appearance
                  —*E. caespitosus* var. *purpureus.*
              15b. Radial spines 12 to 15   —*E. caespitosus* var. *perbellus.*
            14b. Size of mature plant stem to only 3 inches tall and 1 inch thick; flowers small, to only 2 inches long and 1³/₄ inches wide, petals to only 20 in number and stigma lobes to only 8   —*E. caespitosus* var. *minor.*
            13b. One black central ³/₁₆ to ¹/₄ of an inch long always present   —*E. melanocentrus.*
          12b. Centrals 3 to 7 and not in a strict vertical row, but spreading   —*E. fitchii.*
        11b. Longest radial spines ³/₈ to 1 inch—17.
          17a. Stems usually caespitose; areoles more than ¹/₈ of an inch long, having no central spines over ³/₈ of an inch long—18.
            18a. Radials ⁵/₈ to 1 inch long; flower rose-red   —*E. baileyi.*
            18b. Radials ³/₁₆ to ¹/₂ inch long; flower pale pinkish   —*E. albispinus.*
          17b. Stems usually simple; areoles ¹/₈ of an inch or less long, having at least the main central spines ³/₈ of an inch or more long on mature areoles
             —*E. chisoensis.*

10b. Flower tube with short wool and rigid spines—19.

 19a. Spines of the plant body strictly pectinate and recurved against the plant body; areoles oval to elongated—20.

  20a. Centrals 2 to 3 in a vertical row; radials slender to medium stout, white to purplish or pinkish and the plant often banded with color, but spines of individual areole not variegated—21.

   21a. Flower purple with white zone and green center
        —*E. pectinatus* var. *wenigeri.*

   21b. Flower orange-yellow with green center
        —*E. pectinatus* var. *ctenoides.*

  20b. Centrals none; radials stout; spines of individual areoles variegated grays or tans and red
        —*E. pectinatus* var. *rigidissimus.*

 19b. Spines of plant body spreading outward instead of being pectinate; areoles oval to round—22.

  22a. Radial spines 15 to 25; areoles 1/8 to 3/8 of an inch apart; flower 3 to 5 1/2 inches long—23.

   23a. Radials 16 to 25 and to 1/2 inch long; plant simple or sparingly branched —*E. dasyacanthus*
        var. *dasyacanthus.*

   23b. Radials 15 or 16 and to only 3/8 of an inch long; plant caespitose   —*E. dasyacanthus*
        var. *hildmanii.*

  22b. Radial spines 10 to 15; flower 2 to 3 inches long; areoles 5/16 to 1/2 inch apart —*E. roetteri* (in part).

2b. Never having all three of the characters listed under *2a* or, in other words, having any one or more of the three following characters: areoles more than 1/2 inch apart; ribs less than 10; radials less than 12—24.

 24a. Flowers scarlet-red and lasting up to 4 or 5 days, with the petals firm and their edges entire—25.

  25a. Ribs 5 to 9; radial spines 2 to 9; centrals 0 or 1—26.

   26a. Spines greatly flattened and usually channeled or furrowed—27.

    27a. Spines extremely heavy—28.

     28a. Central spine absent; radials 2 to 6; areoles 7/8 to 1 1/2 inches apart   —*E. triglochidiatus*
        var. *triglochidiatus.*

     28b. One central present in at least part of the areoles; radials 6 to 8; areoles 1/4 to 3/4 of an inch apart
        —*E. triglochidiatus* var. *gonacanthus.*

    27b. Spines slender to medium thickness; radials 5 to 7; centrals 0 to 1   —*E. triglochidiatus* var. *hexaedrus.*

   26b. Spines round or practically so and slender to medium in thickness   —*E. triglochidiatus* var. *octacanthus.*

  25b. Ribs 7 to 15; radial spines 7 to 16; centrals 1 to 6—29.

   29a. Plant clustering densely into dome-shaped masses of equal, short stems not usually over 6 inches tall—30.

    30a. Centrals 1 to 5; areoles 3/16 to 3/8 of an inch apart; largest central round —*E. coccineus* var. *coccineus.*

    30b. Centrals 3 to 5; areoles 5/16 to 5/8 of an inch apart; largest central flattened   —*E. coccineus* var. *conoideus.*

   29b. Plant clustering sparingly to form flat clumps of unequal stems up to 18 inches tall—31.

    31a. Centrals several—32.

     32a. Ribs 8 to 11; radials 7 to 12; centrals usually 3 or 4 and variable in length from 3/4 to over 2 inches long; all spines round and medium thickness to heavy, whitish to ashy purplish-gray or reddish in color—33.

      33a. Ovary tube with long, flexible hair
        —*E. polyacanthus* var. *polyacanthus.*

      33b. Ovary tube with sparse and short wool
        —*E. polyacanthus* var. *rosei.*

     32b. Ribs 11 to 15; radials 8 to 16; centrals 4 to 6; spines round and white, yellow, or reddish-yellow in color   —*E. polyacanthus* var. *neo-mexicanus.*

    31b. Central 1   —*E. mojaviensis.*

 24b. Flowers purple or yellow with red centers and delicate, lasting only 1 or 2 days, with petals soft and more or less emarginate—34.

  34a. Spines opaque; flesh medium to dark or gray-green—35.

   35a. Mature spines opaque and varicolored or variegated with shades of brown, gray, and white streaking at least some of them; radials 5 to 12; centrals 1 to 3—36.

    36a. Stems more or less flaccid, wrinkled, with broad, somewhat tuberculate ribs; central spine 1, long and curving upward   —*E. fendleri* var. *fendleri.*

    36b. Stems firm and not wrinkled; ribs narrow and not markedly tuberculate; central spines 1 to 3, the main one porrect and straight   —*E. fendleri* var. *rectispinus.*

   35b. Mature spines opaque but not variegated or varicolored; radials 14 to 17; centrals 2 to 8—37.

    37a. Lowest radials as long as the lateral ones in the areole; fruits 1 1/4 to 2 inches long   —*E. lloydii.*

    37b. Lowest radials shorter than the laterals; fruits 1/2 to 7/8 of an inch long   —*E. roetteri* (in part).

  34b. Spines translucent to some degree; flesh light or medium green—38.

   38a. Areoles 1/2 to 1 1/2 inches apart; ribs only slightly tuberculate on mature stems; flowers purple—39.

    39a. Ribs 11 to 13; areoles 1/2 to 3/4 of an inch apart; plant forming a large, regular, hemispherical clump from a single root center; flowers 4 to 5 inches long
        —*E. stramineus.*

    39b. Ribs 7 to 10; areoles 3/4 to 1 1/2 inches apart; plant forming an irregular, sprawling, or prostrate clump, often with adventitious roots; flowers 1 1/2 to 3 inches tall—40.

     40a. Stems extremely flabby; becoming prostrate and to 30 inches long; flower with 20 to 35 inner petals in several series and 10 to 12 stigma lobes
        —*E. enneacanthus* var. *carnosus.*

     40b. Stems sprawling, more or less flabby, and to 15 inches or so in maximum length; flower with 10 to 15 inner petals in one row and 8 to 10 stigma lobes—41.

      41a. Stem to 2 3/4 inches thick, comparatively firm and upright; radials 1/4 to 5/8 of an inch long and straight; areoles 1/4 to 1 inch apart
        —*E. enneacanthus* var. *enneacanthus.*

      41b. Stems 3 to 4 inches in diameter, flabby, and

semiprostrate; radials ³/₄ to 1¹/₂ inches long, often curving; areoles 1 to 1¹/₂ inches apart
—*E. dubius.*

38b. Areoles ³/₈ to ¹/₂ inch apart; ribs extremely tuberculate; flowers yellow with red centers —*E. papillosus* var. *papillosus.*

1b. Stems prostrate and slender, being ¹/₂ to 1¹/₂ inches thick—42.

42a. Central spine present on all or most areoles and ³/₈ to 2 inches long—43.

43a. Stems to only 4 inches long; central spine ³/₈ of an inch long; flower yellow with red center; ribs markedly tuberculate —*E. papillosus* var. *angusticeps.*

43b. Stems 6 to 14 inches long; central spine ¹/₂ to 2 inches long; flower purple—44.

44a. Central spine ¹/₂ to 2 inches long, dark in color, and somewhat aimed and curved downward; flower with a dark reddish-purple throat and narrow, pointed petals —*E. blanckii.*

44b. Central spine ¹/₂ to 1¹/₂ inches long, yellowish-brown, porrect or turning upward; flower with a white throat —*E. berlandieri* (in part).

42b. Central spine usually missing, and if present on occasional areoles only ¹/₄ of an inch or less in length—45.

45a. Radial spines 4 to 6 and some of them ¹/₄ to 1¹/₄ inches long; flower with white throat and narrow, pointed petals —*E. berlandieri* (immature or stunted growth form).

45b. Radial spines 3 to 6 and only ¹/₁₆ to ¹/₄ of an inch long; flower with white throat and broad, blunt-tipped petals —*E. pentalophus.*

Echinocereus viridiflorus Eng.

"Green-Flowered Torch Cactus," "Green-Flowered Pitaya," "Nylon Cactus," "New Mexico Rainbow Cactus"

DESCRIPTION   PLATE 1

STEMS: Single or forming small clusters of up to about half a dozen heads. Each stem is spherical to columnar, varying in the different forms from a sphere or cone only an inch or so across to a column as much as 8 inches tall by as much as 3 inches in diameter. The surface is light green to yellowish-green in color. There are 13 to 15 low ribs with shallow vertical grooves between them. There are definite grooves crossing the ribs between the areoles, giving them a somewhat tuberculate appearance.

AREOLES: Small, narrow oblong to very elongated, up to about ³/₈ of an inch apart on mature parts of the stem. Young areoles are covered with short, white felt, but old areoles lose this and become bare except for a small tuft of wool just above the spines of each areole where a flower has developed.

SPINES: There are 12 to more than 20 radial spines which radiate evenly around the areole. They are straight and rigid, and lie flat upon the surface of the plant or sometimes recurve back toward the grooves between the ribs. The longer

ones sometimes interlock with those of the adjacent areoles. They vary in size from very small, very weak upper ones which are bristle-like and only ¹/₁₆ of an inch long to lateral and lower ones ¹/₄ of an inch long in one variety and ¹/₂ inch long in another. There is great variation in the coloring of these radial spines. They may all be purplish-red or yellow or whitish, but the most typical pattern is for the upper and lower ones in each areole to be white while the lateral ones are reddish—although an occasional specimen displays exactly the reverse pattern. Sometimes individual spines may be white, tipped with red. All of these variations may sometimes occur on the same plant, often in zones, giving the plant a banded appearance.

There is most typically one central spine, much thicker and more rigid than the radials and standing erect in the center of the areole. This spine sometimes is curved upward toward its tip and is usually about ¹/₂ inch long, although in one form it may be up to 1 inch long. This spine may be white with a reddish tip, half and half, or all purplish-red except for a white base. Sometimes one or even two auxiliary central spines, much shorter (only ¹/₁₆ to ³/₁₆ of an inch long) but otherwise identical to the first, may be present, in which case the two or three centrals are arranged in a perfect vertical row. On the other hand, the areoles of many plants lack the central entirely. All the spines have bulbous bases.

FLOWERS: Small, lemon-yellow or straw-color, this often approaching chartreuse or occasionally being suffused with brown and then bronzy. These flowers are about 1 inch long by ³/₄ of an inch in diameter, produced on old areoles on the sides of the stem, usually midway between the base and the top although sometimes even lower. The outer petals are linear, brownish in the midline with lemon-yellow or chartreuse edges. The inner petals are longer and become a little broader toward the tips which are more or less rounded. These inner petals are lemon-yellow to straw, usually with somewhat darker green in the midline. The edges are all entire. The stamens show the same colors. The style is somewhat longer than the stamens and crowned by 6 to 10 dark green, rather fat stigma lobes. Each areole of the ovary has short white wool and 4 to 12 white spines up to ¹/₄ of an inch long.

FRUITS: These are ³/₈ to ¹/₂ of an inch long, egg-shaped, and greenish in color, and have white wool and white spines upon them.

RANGE. From eastern Wyoming and eastern Colorado south through eastern New Mexico to the vicinity of El Paso, Texas, and southeast through the Guadalupe Mountains into the Big Bend of Texas.

REMARKS. *E. viridiflorus* is famed as the most northerly of the Echinocerei. It grows on the bleak prairies and the foothills of eastern Wyoming and Colorado in spite of cold and extreme conditions which would kill most cacti. A few times it has been reported from extreme western Kansas and the Panhandle of Oklahoma, but these reports were mostly fifty or more years ago. If it is not extinct in those areas, it is very rare today. It still may be found occasionally in the Texas Panhandle and in northeastern New Mexico, which is its type locality. The most westerly report of it seems to be just a few miles west of Santa Fe, New Mexico.

Over this whole northern area of its range the cactus is a small, squat, egg-shaped, withdrawing plant, hiding as best it can in the sparse grass and practically invisible during the winter when it is greatly shrunken. The whole plant is seldom over 2 or 3 inches tall in this area. Neither does it produce conspicuous flowers to give away its position in the spring. The flowers are small and greenish-yellow, and even these are borne low on the plant rather than at the top. These northern plants usually have long, up-curving central spines, but their radials tend to be shorter than those of their southern relatives. This northern form seems to be the plant Engelmann had before him which he called *E. viridiflorus* var. *minor*. He stated correctly that this variety from around Santa Fe, New Mexico, northeastward.

South of Santa Fe the species is seen again past Socorro and Roswell, New Mexico, into the Guadalupe Mountains and at El Paso. It then becomes common east and south into the Big Bend area of Texas. But all of the southern plants studied show some differences from their northern relatives. These differences have been considered significant enough from the very beginning to warrant separate variety designations. Much of the confusion in the minds of cactophiles and, therefore, in their accounts of this species and the closely related species *Echinocereus chloranthus* has been due to a failure to distinguish and understand these varieties. The southern forms of *E. viridiflorus* are quite commonly displayed and even sold today under the name of *E. chloranthus*.

Echinocereus viridiflorus var. viridiflorus (Eng.)

DESCRIPTION   PLATE 1

STEMS: As the species except that it is spherical to conical, growing occasionally to about 5 inches high by as much as 3 inches in diameter, but usually much smaller. Usually clustering.

AREOLES: As the species.

SPINES: As the species, except that the centrals are often missing entirely and never observed over 1/2 inch long.

FLOWERS: As the species, except that they are usually lemon-yellow in color and more rarely brownish than in the other forms, with the petals somewhat rounded at the ends.

FRUITS: As the species.

RANGE. From eastern Wyoming and eastern Colorado through

eastern New Mexico to the vicinity of Santa Fe, which seems to be the southern and western limit of its range. It occurs from there east into the Oklahoma and Texas panhandles and is found occasionally in the high plains of extreme northwestern Texas, but this form does not appear to come down into southwest Texas.

REMARKS. This is the more hardy northern form of the species. Small and comparatively insignificant as it is, anyone who has been abroad in its range would be amazed to know how many specimens he has stepped over as it hides in the grass. It takes a real search to locate the plant, but it can easily be grown in northern gardens where most other cacti do not survive. With its clustering habit it soon presents an attractive little clump of heads with varicolored spines.

Echinocereus viridiflorus var. cylindricus (Eng.) Rumpl.

DESCRIPTION   PLATE 1

STEMS: Similar to the species except that it is cylindrical and grows to at least 8 inches tall by 3 inches in diameter. Seldom and sparingly clustering.

AREOLES: As the species.

SPINES: As the species, except that the radials number 14 to 24, their maximum length to 1/2 inch; and the centrals number 0 to 3 in a vertical row, the main central growing to a maximum length of 1 inch on some plants. On many plants, however, the main central may be entirely missing or no longer than the 1/16 to 3/16-inch auxiliary centrals.

FLOWERS: As the species, except that they are more often brownish in color and the petals are more sharply pointed.

FRUITS: As the species.

RANGE. Common from the area of Socorro and Roswell, New Mexico, southeast through the Guadalupe Mountains into Texas. The writer was surprised to find a stand of this variety near Mosquero, in northeastern New Mexico, which marks a great extension of its range northward. In Texas it ranges through the Davis Mountains into the Big Bend.

REMARKS. This is *E. viridiflorus* as it appears in its southern range, a much more robust form, with radial spines about twice as long as and more interlocking than those of the northern form. Its central spines are extremely variable. Almost any collection from the Big Bend will show some plants with only five or six single centrals 3/16 to 3/8 of an inch long scattered over the whole stem, a few with no centrals at all, and others with regularly 2 or 3 centrals per areole arranged in a single vertical row. The specimens from the Hueco and Guadalupe mountains sometimes lack centrals also but more often show a single central like the species except usually to 1 inch long and curving.

Thousands of these large, columnar specimens, usually distinctly reddish of spine and bronze of flower, are shipped by dealers out of the Texas Big Bend every year. They are so obviously different from the little northern form that, since the name *E. viridiflorus* without variety qualification is usually applied to the northern form, these are usually distributed under the name of *E. chloranthus*. However, this southern variety was recognized as a distinct form long ago when it was named *E. viridiflorus* var. *cylindricus* by Engelmann. Coulter, failing to apply Engelmann's name to it, renamed it *Cereus viridiflorus* var. *tubulosus*, basing his description on specimens from Brewster County, Texas. Both men recognized its distinctness from *E. chloranthus*, a distinction which has become blurred in some more recent accounts.

This variety of this cactus was once one of the most common in the Big Bend region. I have been told by older collectors of beds of these cacti extending over many acres in Brewster County, Texas, in which the cacti often stood almost too close for one to walk among them. Their numbers seemed inexhaustible. There are few such stands left today, however, mostly due to the destruction wrought by the cactus dealers whose crews have for years been bringing them out by the truckloads to languish and die in dime-store bins and novelty-shop cactus assortments. I have been on some ranches in the area whose owners have allowed no cactus digging, and there they still grow in quantity; but only a few years ago I watched three big truckloads of them come out as another of these ranches was opened up and swept clean of cacti, and so they appear to be doomed to elimination as surely as the more rare species of the area.

Echinocereus viridiflorus var. standleyi (B. & R.) Orcutt

DESCRIPTION   PLATE 1

STEMS: Similar to the species except becoming cylindrical and growing to about 4 inches tall, while seldom clustering.

AREOLES: As the species.

SPINES: As the species, except that they are a clear, rather translucent yellow, becoming sometimes whitish when old.

FLOWERS: As the species.

FRUITS: As the species.

RANGE. South central New Mexico.

REMARKS. This was described as a species by Britton and Rose, but since they had not seen it flower and their description was very incomplete, it was long uncertain what the plant's relationship really was. After having seen numerous specimens throughout their development and in bloom, I feel certain that it is a form of *E. viridiflorus*, as Orcutt has already suggested. I cannot distinguish its flowers from those of the species by any essential feature. It is close to the variety *cylindricus* in the cylindrical shape of its stems and in the character of its centrals,

but its radial spines are shorter and more like those of variety *viridiflorus*. This leaves it distinct from these other forms only by the clear yellow color of its spines. This is a doubtful character to base even a variety upon, and it surely will not support its being listed as a separate species. It may be that it does not even warrant varietal status, but I list it separately here since anyone reading the literature will be anxious to know what the plant referred to so incompletely by almost all authors actually is.

Echinocereus davisii Houghton

DESCRIPTION   PLATE 2

STEMS: Globular or nearly so and very small. This is a dwarf plant, $1/2$ to $1\frac{1}{4}$ inches tall when mature. Stems occur singly as far as is known. There are 6 to 8 ribs on this tiny stem, which are rather high and broken into nearly completely separated tubercles. The color of the flesh is dark green.

AREOLES: Narrow oval to elongated and $1/8$ to $3/16$ of an inch long, having very little if any wool upon them, even when young.

SPINES: White, with the tips or sometimes the outer one-half dark brown. These spines are all radials and are 8 to 13 in number. The upper ones are shortest, slender, round, and $1/8$ to $1/4$ of an inch long, while the laterals are longer, stouter, usually flattened, and $3/8$ to $5/8$ of an inch long. The spines are straight or often somewhat curved and recurved back against the plant.

FLOWERS: Straw-yellow, about 1 inch long, not opening widely. The outer petals are narrow with midlines reddish to umber and the edges yellowish. They are pointed and entire. The inner petals are straw-yellow, and linear to slightly broadened above, with the tips sharply pointed. The filaments are green, the anthers light yellow. The style is light green and is crowned by 5 light green, heavy, curving stigma lobes. The ovary has about 12 white spines to $1/4$ of an inch long on each areole, but no wool.

FRUITS: Oval, about $3/8$ of an inch long, apparently remaining green.

RANGE. Found on only a few limestone summits a few miles south of Marathon, Brewster County, Texas.

REMARKS. This is one of the two dwarf cacti of Brewster County, Texas, and it is remarkable that it grows on the same few hills as the other, *Mammillaria nellieae*. It even grows in the same situation as that other, underneath the moss in the crevices of the limestone ledges. The tiny plant is rarely visible at all because of its mossy protection, and only sends its flowers up briefly above this layer. It is a real hands-and-knees effort to search for these diminutive plants in the expanse of the Texas hills. The best effort will be useless unless one is on the right hills, and these are restricted to two or three ranches near Marathon.

One would think that the little cactus would be secure in its very limited range, but that is not the case. After Houghton described this plant in 1931 and others wrote about it, collectors and dealers went straight to the spot and brought out hundreds of specimens. This continued for some years, and most collections then sported some of these attractive little novelties. In this way the wild population was reduced steadily until more recently the area in which they grow has come into the hands of owners who allow no one to dig cacti at all. This is fortunate for the survival of the species, but the plant has become more and more rare in collections, and its value on the market has now become rather high.

The problem here, again, is to place this cactus properly in respect to its relatives, and as always this cannot be done with absolute certainty or to please everyone. A. D. Houghton designated it a separate species when he first described it, but W. T. Marshall soon considered its similarities to *E. viridiflorus* too great and called it *E. viridiflorus* var. *davisii*. Anyone may take his choice of these arrangements, since it is a matter of evaluation of similarities and differences which all can see. I choose to leave it distinct from *E. viridiflorus* because it differs from that plant in rib and spine number and spine length, as well as in size. Of perhaps more importance to me in deciding to regard it as a separate species are the facts that the petals of its flowers are more pointed than those of *E. viridiflorus,* and that it has no wool on the ovary areoles while the other does. This matter of wool or no wool has been made the basis for separating others of this genus into entirely different sections, and so it certainly seems significant enough here to separate species.

Although tiny in size, *E. davisii* is not short-lived, as one might expect. I have seen a series of specimens collected ten years ago and grown all this while by a collector who knows how to care for her plants. They have bloomed most years, but have hardly increased in size in all this time.

Echinocereus chloranthus (Eng.) Rumpl.
"Green-Flowered Torch Cactus," "Green-Flowered Pitaya"

DESCRIPTION   PLATE 2

STEMS: Cylindrical, up to 10 inches high by 3 inches thick, occasionally, but not often, producing one or two branches from the main stem. There are 12 to 18 ribs which are low and definitely tuberculate at the areoles, with broad, shallow furrows between the ribs and between the tubercles. The color of the surface is pale green.

AREOLES: Oval to circular in shape and rather large. The young areoles have much short white or yellowish wool. This gradually disappears with age so that old areoles are almost or quite bare except for the floral areole just above the spines which remains as a persistent tuft of wool. The areoles are up to $1/4$ of an inch apart on the mature sides of the stems.

SPINES: There are 12 to 38 radial spines which radiate evenly all around the areole. They are straight and rigid, and interlock with those of adjacent areoles. They may recurve back toward the plant slightly on some specimens, but when young they spread out from the plant before they assume their strictly radiating mature position. The upper 4 to 6 of them are short and weak, $1/4$ of an inch or less in length. There is a gradual increase in size going around the areole, the laterals being about $1/2$ inch long and the lower ones sometimes longer, even up to $3/4$ of an inch. The upper radials are usually white, while the laterals and lower ones vary greatly in color, sometimes being white, yellowish, purple-red, or even variegated with white or light bases and the rest of the spine red.

There is great variation in the centrals in this species. On the typical form there are 3 to 6 centrals on mature areoles. These spread from the center of the areole and are not arranged in a straight line. They are stout and rigid, somewhat translucent, and usually somewhat curved. A typical areole on a typical mature plant will have 1 or 2 upper centrals which are only $1/4$ to $1/2$ inch long and point upward. These are usually red or white with red tips. Then there will usually be 2 centrals spreading laterally, straight or curved, about $3/4$ of an inch long and all red or red with whitish or yellowish bases. Below this is one long central pointing downward and often curved, which is almost always lighter colored, white sometimes with a reddish tip, stout, rigid, and $3/4$ to $1 1/4$ inches long. Some plants have an extra central or two besides these. Young plants do not grow their centrals at all until they are 4 inches or so in height, adding them gradually after that, so that it is easy to find good-sized plants with none or with only a couple of centrals. All of the spines have bulbous bases, but the bases of the radials are usually covered, until they are very old, by the wool of the areole.

FLOWERS: Funnel-shaped, not opening widely, 1 inch in diameter by about $1 1/4$ inches long, very dark green or yellowish-green. The outer petals have brownish midlines and green edges. The inner petals are dark green in the midlines with lighter edges, but are often suffused with brown. The petals are linear, not broadening throughout their lengths, the edges entire, and the tips sharply pointed. The filaments are light green and the anthers cream-colored. The pistil is long, green, and ends in 8 dark green stigma lobes. The areoles of the ovary have white wool and white spines about $1/4$ to $1/2$ inch long upon them. These flowers are produced on the sides of the stems, usually from one-half to two-thirds of the way to the top, but sometimes lower.

FRUITS: Small, greenish, very spiny. They are usually about $1/2$ inch long and almost spherical.

RANGE. A small area of southern New Mexico in Luna and Dona Ana counties, specifically from Cook's Peak and near

Rincon through the Organ and the Franklin mountains into Texas and Mexico. In Texas occurring in scattered mountain areas from El Paso east about as far as Van Horn, apparently being limited to El Paso and Hudspeth counties, except for a separate variety isolated in Brewster County.

REMARKS. This cactus was first described by Engelmann in 1856. Typically, it is a beautiful, tall, and slender column of long, rigid, varicolored spines, these partly obscuring the surface of the stem and spreading in all directions, giving the plant an interesting unkempt appearance in contrast to the usual precision of armament of other Echinocerei. It has small green, yellow-green, or bronze-green flowers produced on the sides of the stems, very similar to those of *E. viridiflorus*. This is a comparatively localized form, however, growing in the mountains from about a hundred miles northwest of El Paso to about the same distance southeast of that city.

E. chloranthus is one of those cacti which are very difficult to distinguish from their relatives, and I find for more confusion among cactus fanciers about it than about any other member of this genus. Somehow the names of this and the previous species were exchanged in popular usage in west Texas many years ago, and even some dealers' lists offer them reversed in this way. In addition, another species has been entirely lost for many years by being included under this one.

The striking similarity of *E. chloranthus* to *E. viridiflorus* is the main cause of the confusion. It is easy enough to distinguish between the typical *E. viridiflorus* var. *viridiflorus*, the northern cactus, and *E. chloranthus*. The northern plant is very small and squat, has elongated areoles with either no central spine or only 1 per areole, and has flowers with rounded petal tips. *E. chloranthus*, on the other hand, is tall and slender, has up to 5 spreading centrals not in a row, rounded areoles, and sharply pointed petals. These differences are plain enough, and the widely different ranges of the two, separated by almost half the length of New Mexico, makes it easy to regard them as very separate forms.

But the trouble lies with the form of *E. viridiflorus* called variety *cylindricus* by Engelmann, which grows in the same range as *E. chloranthus* and on into the Big Bend. This variety is typically cylindrical also, but somewhat stouter than *E. chloranthus*, with elongated areoles and with 1 to 3 centrals in a straight row. These two are close, but they can be told apart by the shape and size of the areoles and the difference in number, length, and arrangement of the central spines on mature specimens. Immature specimens are much alike, but can be recognized by their areoles.

After one has learned to recognize the two forms the possibility of confusion is not yet over, because the names used for them have not remained standard. Marshall and T. M. Bock have proposed the combining of *E. viridiflorus* and *E. chloranthus* entirely as synonyms. Backeberg, on the other hand, chooses to combine this form with the other as *E. viridiflorus* var. *chlo-*

ranthus. Future study may bring a combination of some sort, but there can be no more than conjecture about what the proper relationship of the two is, without new evidence, which is not yet at hand. In the meantime, it seems, any conscientious student of cacti will have to look very carefully at areoles and spines and come to know this interesting little cactus.

Echinocereus chloranthus var. chloranthus (Eng.)

DESCRIPTION   PLATE 2

STEMS: As the species, except growing to only about 8 inches tall.

AREOLES: As the species, except to only about 3/8 of an inch apart.

SPINES: As the species, except always spiny and never hairy, the radials only 12 to 23 in number, and the centrals only 3 to 6 in number.

FLOWERS: As the species.

FRUITS: As the species.

RANGE. Extreme southern New Mexico in Luna and Dona Ana counties, into El Paso and Hudspeth counties, Texas, and on into Mexico.

REMARKS. This is the typical form of the species, but it has a restricted range, and far fewer people have seen it than suppose they have.

Echinocereus chloranthus var. neocapillus Weniger

DESCRIPTION   PLATE 2

STEMS: Cylindrical, up to 10 inches high and 2 1/2 inches thick. It is usually single, but occasionally branches above the ground. It has 12 to 18 ribs, low, with distinct tubercles. The color is pale or yellowish-green.

AREOLES: Oval, about 3/16 of an inch long, covered with much white or yellowish wool when young, bare when old except for a very small tuft which usually remains at the upper end of the areole where the flower is produced. The areoles are up to 1/4 of an inch apart.

SPINES: There are 30 to 38 straight, slender radial spines. These radiate evenly around the areole, being often so crowded that they touch their neighbors most of their lengths, and they interlock with spines from other areoles. The upper ones are very slender and often only 1/8 of an inch long. From this the length increases around the areole, with laterals being up to 1/2 inch long and the lower ones only slightly shorter. They are clear translucent yellow or chalk-white, all of an areole being the same color, this usually forming bands of yellow and white on the older plants. There are 5 to 10 central spines, all heavier and straight. They spread in all directions from the crowded center of the areole. The uppermost ones are $1/8$ to $1/4$ of an inch long, and slender, while the rest of them are heavier and $1/4$ to $3/4$ of an inch long. They may be all translucent yellow, often with a reddish tip, or occasionally all reddish. All spines have bulbous bases. Immature plants or new branches have no spines at all, but have instead a thick covering of white, very fine, flexible hairs from $1/4$ to $1/2$ inch long, about 40 hairs to the areole. When the plant is 1 to 2 inches tall spines begin appearing at the tip of the stem. The juvenile hairs can often be seen on the bases of older specimens.

FLOWERS: Apparently identical with those of the species.

FRUITS: Similar to those of the species.

RANGE. A very small area including only two ranches 5 to 10 miles south of Marathon, Texas.

REMARKS. This cactus was noticed by A. R. Leding in 1932, and he published an article on it in the *Journal of Heredity* in August, 1934, which included pictures of it. At that time he called attention to the unusual form of the juveniles, which are covered with long white hairs instead of spines, but he did not distinguish between the mature form of the plant and the typical *E. chloranthus* or state whether the typical form has hairs when young. He did say that comparison of plants from different localities and the discovery of whether the hairy condition is inherited might show that the form deserves specific or at least varietal rank.

This article by Leding was reprinted in the October–November, 1942, number of the *Cactus and Succulent Journal of America*, with an added note by the author, but no new conclusions were drawn.

The immature plants of this variety are very striking, having no rigid spines at all, but being covered with much long white hair which is $1/4$ to $1/2$ inch long and produced usually 40 or so hairs to each areole. This hair is their only armament until the plants become about $1 1/2$ inches high. At that size they suddenly begin producing the regular armament of yellow or white spines as described above. The bases of plants $1 1/2$ to as much as 4 inches high will often show a belt of this white wool, with the typical spines above, but this hair is gradually replaced by normal spines.

The spines of adults of this form are very similar to those of *E. chloranthus*, but not identical. There are 30 or more radials where the typical form has only 12 to 23. These very numerous radials obscure the surface of the stem much more than do those of the typical form. Also, the centrals of this variety are more numerous and shorter. But the major difference between the two is in the juvenile stage. The young plants of typical *E. chloranthus* never have hairs at all, but are covered from the beginning with rigid spines. There is no possibility of confusing the two in this stage.

E. chloranthus var. *neocapillus* is found growing in a very restricted range encompassing some hills from about 5 to about 10 miles south of Marathon. Where undisturbed the plants grow in quite great numbers, but they have been removed almost entirely from much of their range. Fortunately, some of them are upon ranchland which is closed to all cactus digging, and so they still survive.

Since the nearest occurrence of the typical *E. chloranthus* is about 150 miles northwest, there is little danger of confusing these two in the field. The many more spines, as well as the spine color and the areole shape easily set this variety off from *E. viridiflorus* var. *cylindricus*.

Echinocereus russanthus Weniger

DESCRIPTION   PLATE 3

STEMS: Cylindrical, up to about 10 inches tall and $2 1/2$ inches thick. These stems almost always branch to form clusters of up to a dozen stems. They have 13 to 18 ribs, which are low and narrow with indistinct tubercles. The color of the surface is medium green.

AREOLES: Round at first, then broadly oval. About $1/8$ of an inch long, with white wool when young, situated from $1/8$ to $3/8$ of an inch apart.

SPINES: All spines are very slender and somewhat flexible. There are 30 to 45 slender to very slender and bristle-like radial spines, which are very crowded and which interlock with those of adjacent areoles, giving the plant a very dense spine cover. There is a tuft of small ones at the summit (upper edge) of the areole, which are only $3/16$ to $1/4$ of an inch long. Moving laterally around the areole the radials become longer, the lower laterals being $1/2$ to $5/8$ of an inch long. All radials are white or straw-colored. There are 7 to 12 central spines spreading in all directions from bulbous bases. The upper ones are small, similar to the larger radials in size. The lower ones are from $3/4$ to $1 1/4$ inches long, though still slender and rather flexible. While there is a complete gradation of spine sizes from the smallest radial to the largest central, the centrals are distinguished from the radials not only by their position but also by their color, having at least the tip, often the upper half, and sometimes the whole spine reddish or purplish in color.

FLOWERS: About 1 inch long, funnel-shaped, not opening widely and so only about $1/2$ inch in diameter. They are rust-red in color sometimes with darker midlines. All segments are linear in shape, with the ends somewhat pointed, but not sharply so. The bases of all segments are lighter and the center of the flower is greenish. The stamens are pale yellow. The style is long and yellowish. There are 8 to 10 green stigma lobes.

FRUITS: About $1/2$ inch long, oval to almost spherical. They are covered with clusters of slender white spines, 10 to 12 on each areole.

RANGE. A small area of southwestern Brewster County, Texas, including the northern part of the Chisos Mountains and the country northwest of these to just past Study Butte, but not seen as far west as Terlingua or south to the Rio Grande.

REMARKS. I have often found it rewarding to examine the thousands of specimens which the Texas dealers in cacti have in their bins. Even a slight variation stands out when it is lying among dozens of its supposed fellows. Several times I have found in such places something new to me and have been able to trace it back to its location and discover what it was.

In piles of *E. viridiflorus* var. *cylindricus* from the Texas Big Bend we repeatedly found one or two unusual specimens with far too many and too long and flexible spines to be that cactus. Usually the assortment was being sold as *E. chloranthus*, but the bulk of them were clearly the Big Bend forms of *E. viridiflorus*. These few obviously different specimens were all that could be seen to explain the confusion of names.

These unusual specimens did have the round or oval areoles of *E. chloranthus*, and noting their long central spines I assumed at first that they were that cactus. They have been going under that name for a long time.

But when I saw the actual *E. chloranthus*, which does not grow at all in the Big Bend, it was obvious that the two plants were really very different. All authorities have given the radial count for *E. chloranthus* as between 12 and 23, while this cactus has 30 to at least 45. That cactus has 3 to 6 centrals which are up to ³/₄ of an inch long, while this one has 7 to 12 which are up to as much as 1¹/₄ inches long.

Such differences as these have usually been deemed sufficient to distinguish varieties in this group, and I thought at first that this would prove to be a Big Bend variety of *E. chloranthus*. But when the plants bloomed the new one presented a flower different in most respects from that of the other cactus. These flowers are smaller, with more narrow and linear petals, and are rust or russet-red in color. No flower of *E. chloranthus* ever approaches the color or the texture of these flowers, which are also the smallest I have seen on any Echinocereus. On *E. chloranthus* the flowers are yellow to brown or occasionally almost chocolate brown in color, but never with any reddish coloring, and their petals are firm, opaque, and glossy to the point of being almost waxy. On this Big Bend plant there is no green in the flower beyond the greenish center, the rest of the petals being essentially pale reddish, and these petals are soft, thin, somewhat translucent, and dull of surface instead of glossy. There is no mistaking the two plants when in flower, and these being so different, it seems clear that here is a species entirely separate from *E. chloranthus*.

Once having concluded this, I cast around for what the cactus might have been named, but in all of the species and varieties listed for this group in the U.S. I have found no description of this cactus.

I did discover Engelmann's description of a cactus from northern Mexico which seemed almost identical to this one. It was his *E. longisetus*. His only statement about the flowers of that cactus was "flower…said to be red." When I saw that the type locality of his plant was in the Santa Rosa Mountains, which form the lower end of a continuous mountain chain of which the Chisos Mountains, where our cactus grows, is the northern end, I immediately thought that the two might be the same species and that it might range over this whole mountain chain.

Following up this idea, several of us made trips into these difficult mountains of northern Mexico. We observed and collected *E. longisetus* in its type locality, where it grows in clusters of up to thirty sprawling stems, each up to 12 inches long. On the many plants observed we found the radial number always 16 to 21 per areole and the centrals up to 2 inches long. These differences alone indicate that the plants are not the same. And when the true *E. longisetus* bloomed, there was no further question. It presented beautiful rotate flowers 2 to 2¹/₂ inches in diameter, claret in color with white centers. They looked like a more reddish version of the *E. berlandieri* flowers, surely as different from the flowers of our Chisos Mountain plant as could be.

We were unable to locate *E. longisetus* growing north of its type locality in the Sierra de Huacha or Sierra del Carmen ranges, and assume that it does not grow up into Texas. Neither did we find our cactus growing south of the northern slope of the Chisos Mountains. I assume, therefore, that these two separate species occupy only their respective escarpments of this large mountain system.

E. russanthus is left, therefore, as what appears to be a separate species which, however, has always been thrown in with *E. chloranthus*. It occupies its own small range, where that cactus never grows, and is actually a much more beautiful plant than most of its close relatives.

Echinocereus caespitosus Eng.
"Lace Cactus," "Purple Candle," "Classen's Cactus"

DESCRIPTION   PLATE 3

STEMS: Spherical when very young, quickly becoming oval and then, when mature, cylindrical. These stems occasionally, in some locations, grow to 12 inches tall and 3¹/₂ inches thick, but the typical adult size is 4 to 8 inches tall by 2 to 2¹/₂ inches thick. There is a form which never exceeds 3 inches tall and one inch thick. A plant may remain a single, erect stem all of its life, while its neighbor a few feet away may offset and branch to form a cluster of a dozen or so upright stems. This clustering habit is so common as to provide the basis for the name. There are 10 to 19 ribs which are narrow and definite and divided into distinct tubercles. The flesh is dark green.

AREOLES: Small, rather oval, and quite woolly when young, becoming greatly elongated vertically and bare of wool when older. These areoles are 1/8 to 3/16 of an inch long and almost touching on shrunken, dormant plants, but up to 3/16 of an inch apart on active, well-watered ones.

SPINES: There are 12 to 36 rigid but slender radial spines. They radiate evenly, lying almost flat over the surface of the plant. Crowded around the elongated areole in this flat position, they look, on each side of it, much like the teeth of a comb, and so are often described as being pectinate. Those at the top of the areole are very tiny, often almost bristle-like and only 1/32 to 1/8 of an inch long. The lateral ones are robust and 3/16 to 5/16 of an inch long. The lower 1 to 3 are somewhat smaller again. The spines of adjacent clusters may interlock on the longer spined forms, but do not reach each other on the shorter spined individuals. These spines may be pure white, white with brown tips, yellowish with brown tips, or all brown, or, in one form, have the outer half of each spine shining black or purplish. The plant may be somewhat banded by variations in these colors, but the spines of any single areole are never variegated.

Most commonly there is no central spine, but on many specimens in some locations one can find areoles with 1 central standing straight out or 2 centrals, one above the other in the center of the areole. An occasional plant will have such centrals on the majority or even all of its areoles. These centrals are stout and firm, but only 1/32 to 1/8 of an inch long.

FLOWERS: Very large and colorful on all but the dwarf form, being 2 to 5 inches tall and 2 to 4 inches in diameter, and brilliant purple or rose pink. The flower tube is covered with white, cobwebby wool to at least 1/4 of an inch long and clusters of 10 to 14 very fine, hairlike, white, gray, or black spines, 1/4 to 3/4 of an inch long. Above these the outer segments of the flower lengthen gradually, with greenish or brownish midlines and pink edges. The petals, of which there are 30 to at least 50, arise from usually narrow reddish or reddish-brown bases (which may, however, be bright green instead) to broaden to 1/4 of an inch or more wide above. This upper part of each petal is purple or rose-pink. Its edges are more or less ragged and often notched. The tips vary from erose and rather blunt to almost entire and definitely pointed. The filaments are reddish at the bases, fading above; the anthers, cream-colored. The style is long and reddish or pinkish, crowned by 8 to 22 large, dark green stigma lobes. The dwarf form has the same flower but with a marked reduction in size and number of almost all flower aspects.

FRUITS: Egg-shaped or almost spherical, covered with the slender spines and wool of the ovary. It remains green until it dries and splits open by one or two vertical slits.

RANGE. As Engelmann stated, this is the most eastern of the Echinocerei. Found in hilly, mostly limestone regions from near Ponca City to near Durant, Oklahoma, on the northeast, and from there on south to the edge of the coastal plain just west of the Brazos River. Industry and Cat Spring, Texas, mark its southeastern limit. From this line—which, as Engelmann observed, approximately parallels the 96th longitude—it occurs wherever the proper conditions are found throughout central and western Oklahoma and into southeastern Colorado, as well as over all of northwestern Texas and into a little of eastern New Mexico. The southern limit of its range runs west through Texas just south of San Antonio to Eagle Pass, where it dips into Mexico; from there it curves northwest past the vicinity of Sonora and Big Spring, Texas, to just east of Carlsbad and Roswell, New Mexico. Although it occurs in only widely scattered locations in eastern New Mexico, its western limit runs approximately from Carlsbad north into eastern Colorado.

REMARKS. The lace cactus is probably one of the most collected, most fancied, and best known of all cacti. Almost anyone the world over who grows cacti has this plant, and it is often the favorite of the collection. The high regard in which it stands is well earned by the beauty of the plant body with its truly lacy spines and the exquisiteness of its flowers, which are produced in profusion by a healthy plant. This cactus is well-known because it is very widespread in range and so prolific in its natural habitats as to be readily available to any dime store or nursery which wants to stock it. Furthermore, it is tolerant of the rigors of cactus culture after it is in the collection. It is the common cactus of two-thirds of Oklahoma and all of central Texas. It is not found everywhere in this wide area, but the right sort of limestone or gypsum hill often supports a population of literally hundreds of individuals.

The fact that this cactus has been so commonly seen has not, as one might have hoped, made for less confusion concerning it. Even yet a variety of names are bantered back and forth and each new work on cacti still is unable to make an air-tight case for what the plant really is and what its official name should be. Knowing this, I have made special effort to study thousands of specimens from all possible locations within its range, and have growing before me specimens from each general area in which it is found.

Several quirks of history make for two major problems in dealing with this cactus, and each leads to its own type of confusion. I will attempt here to give as simple an account as possible of what has happened in the past in order to evaluate the conflicting views which exist today about *E. caespitosus*.

The plant was undeniably studied by Engelmann, who wrote up several very complete and detailed descriptions of it between 1848 and 1856. He originated the name *Echinocereus caespitosus* for his cactus. But Terscheck had in 1843 named a plant from Mexico *Echinocactus reichenbachii*. His description was very incomplete and could, as many have since pointed out, fit any one of several cacti in more than one genus.

It is very doubtful whether the two names would ever have been associated at all except that Prince Salm-Dyck, in 1844, referred to some plants in European collections as *Echinopsis pectinata* var. *reichenbachiana*. He wrote Engelmann about the possibility that these might be the same as Engelmann's plant, and Engelmann mentioned this speculation in one account of *E. caespitosus*.

Early writers to and including Coulter all used Engelmann's name, *E. caespitosus*, which is the earliest name with an indisputably adequate description, for the plant. Things might have remained this way and all would have known what plant they were talking about, but in 1893 F. A. Haage, Jr., changed Terscheck's useless *Echinocactus reichenbachii* to *Echinocereus reichenbachii*, and later Britton and Rose adopted this as the name they used when referring to our cactus.

It is true that by the rules of nomenclature the earliest name applying to a plant must be used, but Terscheck's description does not any more link his name to this plant than to a dozen others, while Prince Salm-Dyck's usage of the name as a variety of *E. pectinatus* leads definitely away from our plant. It would therefore seem that the resurrection of Terscheck's name and the adoption of it for our plant was probably not required by the rules. It has certainly led to continuing confusion since that time.

But once done, Britton and Rose's beautiful and popular books carried the name *E. reichenbachii* so well into general use that what cactus *E. caespitosus* actually was has been forgotten by almost everyone. Yet any serious student coming across this name so definitely set forth by Engelmann would have to do something with it. Some merely regarded it as a synonym of the other, but others tried to prove that there were two separate plants for the two names. And here the confusion had its second effect and led to the second large problem encountered in understanding this cactus.

Engelmann pinpointed the eastern range of this cactus almost exactly when he said it corresponded to the 96th meridian, and he very well indicated the western extent of its range in south Texas when he said it goes no farther west than the San Pedro (Devil's) River. But he badly underestimated the extent of its range northward and westward in the northwestern quadrant of its area when he said it occurred only to about the 100th meridian and the Canadian River. In a later note he did add that it grew from the Arkansas River to Saltillo, which exactly corrects the range northward, but he did not ever seem to know that it occurs west of the 100th meridian. Actually, the plant is found well past the western edge of the Texas and Oklahoma panhandles to the last hills east of the Pecos River in New Mexico.

Now, as one might expect, over the huge extent of this range from east to west and north to south there are certain gradients of characteristics in this cactus. And since Engelmann apparently had only eastern specimens to examine—his type came from the farthest southeastern location where it grows—his descriptions are definitely slanted toward the characters most commonly found in the eastern populations and do not allow for extremes found commonly only in specimens from the part of the range he did not know existed. For example, eastern specimens almost always have 20 to 30 radial spines and only extremely rarely—I estimate from my experience maybe in one plant out of a thousand—does one find fewer than 20 radials. Yet in the plants from far western Oklahoma, northwestern Texas, New Mexico, and Colorado, while radial counts of 12 to 32 are found, many localities have a vast majority showing fewer than 20 radials and only a rare plant with more than 20. Throughout central Oklahoma we find all numbers from 12 to 32 commonly on the same hillside. Also, western plants usually have less wool on the growing stem areoles and shorter spines than eastern ones. There are other less obvious gradients as well.

So when students who took the name *E. reichenbachii* for the common eastern forms began to notice the lower spine numbers, shorter spines, and smaller amount of wool of the far northwestern forms, they tended to think they had in these northwestern plants something worthy of a name. Britton and Rose made up some new names such as *E. perbellus* for these forms, but others, by a strange reversal, called them *E. caespitosus*. Boissevain and Davidson seem to have initiated this in ·heir work on the Colorado cacti, and others have followed them. Backeberg, in a 1941 article, made a case for a plant from the Wichita Mountains of Oklahoma as being the true *E. caespitosus* because of its extreme amount of clustering, but in his later works has placed that plant correctly as a form of *E. baileyi*. However, he still keeps *E. caespitosus* as separate from *E. reichenbachii*, saying that the spine clusters of adjacent areoles on *E. caespitosus* do not intertwine, while those of *E. reichenbachii* do. I have checked this character specifically at dozens of locations all over the range of these cacti, and have found growing together, wherever there is a large population of plants, specimens with spines interlocking and specimens with spines not interlocking. Coulter made this variation clear many years ago, saying that on *E. caespitosus*, "Spines may or may not interlock."

It seems obvious, therefore, that we have one definite species with a very large range over which there is gradation. The species description in respect to spine number and so forth is, therefore, broadened in order to include specimens from the part of the range Engelmann did not see. The only question really remaining is which of the two proposed names is legitimate, and since I cannot honestly tell whether Terscheck meant this cactus by his *Echinocactus reichenbachii*, while it is obvious that Engelmann did with his *Echinocereus caespitosus*, I use that name here.

Engelmann noticed that the spine color of individual specimens of this cactus varied from pure white to chestnut-brown or rosy. He called the brown ones *E. caespitosus* var. *castaneus*. This would be the form called by collectors the "brown lace." Later an attempt was made to transfer this variety to *E. pectinatus*, a related species, and then to equate it with *E. pectinatus* var. *rubescens*. However, other characters such as the long wool and the hairlike spines of the flower tube quickly distinguish it from *E. pectinatus* and show this sort of combination to be in error. The fact that almost any large population of *E. caespitosus* studied shows a complete range of colors from white to brown with all sorts of intermediates, and each local population varying only in proportionate numbers of the various colors, indicates that the color of individual plants is only a simple genetic character and not worthy of varietal name at all.

At one time members of the Oklahoma cactus society collected and studied large numbers of these cacti from the Arbuckle Mountains of that state, where this species is very common. In doing this they found several specimens which bloomed with yellowish instead of violet flowers and one plant with white flowers. For these specimens they proposed the variety names *aureiflora* and *albiflora*, respectively. There is no report of these flower colors being seen again, and they are not listed as true varieties.

If we can look beyond all this confusion, we have in this species a beautiful cactus, the lace cactus, white to brown in spine color, which is deservedly a favorite of all. It is most easily confused with *E. pectinatus*. Sometimes individual plants of the two are very hard to tell apart by spine and stem characters, although the spines of *E. caespitosus* are typically not so extremely pressed against the plant nor quite so heavy as those of the other. But for absolute identification of the two one must sometimes wait for the flowers to appear. There are various differences here, the most obvious being that—on the flower tube and remaining on the fruit—*E. caespitosus* has much long wool and extremely thin, flexible, hairlike spines up to ³/₄ of an inch long, while *E. pectinatus* has shorter wool and comparatively thick, rigid spines up to only ³/₈ of an inch long.

Echinocereus caespitosus var. caespitosus (Eng.)

DESCRIPTION   PLATES 3, 7

STEMS: As the species.

AREOLES: As the species.

SPINES: As the species, except that it has 15 to 36 radial spines which are usually long enough to interlock with those of adjacent areoles. In most of its range only a very rare plant has the radials fewer than 20 in number. However in the extreme northwestern part of the range individuals with 15 to 20 radials become the majority in some populations.

FLOWERS: As the species.

FRUITS: As the species.

RANGE. From approximately the 96th parallel in Texas and Oklahoma west to near Del Rio, Big Spring, and Amarillo in Texas and throughout central and western Oklahoma to the base of the Oklahoma Panhandle, but hardly if at all entering the Oklahoma Panhandle itself. The most northwesterly records of this form we have are Alabaster Caverns, Woodward, and Shattuck, Oklahoma, and Sanford and Palo Duro Canyon in Texas.

REMARKS. I take this to be the typical form of the species. It is the form discovered and described by Engelmann, from specimens taken in southeast Texas, as *E. caespitosus*. It is the form of the species which clusters the most, the name applying well for this reason. It is also the largest form the species assumes.

I have broadened the spine count included in this variety from Engelmann's 20 to 30 radials because in populations over the whole of the range given above we find occasional individuals exceeding his limits in both maximum and minimum to the extent we have indicated. Specimens with the lower numbers make up a larger proportion of the population the farther northwest one goes, but individuals falling entirely within his range of spine numbers are found all the way to the edge of the area we have indicated. I feel the plants over this wide area comprise one form varying in a continuous gradient from southeast to northwest. I consider it the typical variety. Those segments of this species which vary from this typical variety I list as separate varieties.

Echinocereus caespitosus var. minor Eng.

DESCRIPTION   PLATE 4

STEMS: As the species, except that it is very much smaller, apparently reaching a maximum of only 3 inches tall and 1 inch in diameter.

AREOLES: As the species.

SPINES: As the species, except that no centrals have been seen.

FLOWERS: Small for the group, being 2 inches tall and 1¹/₂ to 1³/₄ inches in diameter. They are pale lavender-pink in color, and are otherwise as those of the species, except that the petals are smaller and only 15 to 25 in number, and the stigma lobes 8 in number.

FRUITS: As the species, except smaller.

RANGE. Known only from the vicinity of Stockdale, Wilson County, Texas.

REMARKS. Engelmann thought it necessary to set this dwarf form of the lace cactus apart as a variety, and so it seems to be. The diminutive size of its body is striking and the reduction of its flower parts from the typical numbers is consistent.

Warning should be given, however, that not every small lace cactus discovered is this variety. Engelmann spoke about how precocious *E. caespitosus* is in blooming, and it is not unusual to find a 2-inch specimen of the typical variety in bloom. In certain areas, notably around the granitic region of Llano and Ink's Lake, Texas, are found many clusters of very small stems. These, however, all bloom with the typical huge, many-petaled purple flowers, and when grown in the garden will in time take on full stem size.

The cactus meant by variety *minor* is different in that it does not grow larger in any situation, and its flowers are small, with only around 20 petals as opposed to the 30 to 50 of the typical form of the species.

Engelmann gave no range or location for his dwarf form. We have encountered it only in Wilson County, Texas, where it grows in some fields in rather dense stands.

Echinocereus caespitosus var. perbellus (B. & R.)

DESCRIPTION   PLATE 4

STEMS: As the species, except that it is not over 4 inches tall, with ribs numbering 13 to 15.

AREOLES: As the species.

SPINES: As the species, except that the total radial number is only 12 to 15 and the central spine is always missing.

FLOWERS: As the species, except that they are not as large as the flowers of the species sometimes become. They are usually about 2 inches tall and wide.

FRUITS: As the species.

RANGE. The type locality is Big Spring, Texas. Individuals are found occasionally, associated with typical *E. caespitosus* populations north of this point in Texas, along the western edge of Oklahoma as far as Majors County, west into New Mexico as far as the Pecos River, and on into Colorado. A pure population of the form, unmixed with any other, has been found only near Muleshoe, Bailey County, Texas.

REMARKS. This is at best a doubtful variety, and certainly not a separate species. Its existence at all as a separate entity would probably never have been advocated except for that unfortunate failure of Engelmann to have specimens from the northwestern part of its range when he drew up his description of *E. caespitosus*. Limited as he was to specimens from the east, he gave as the radial number for his species 20 to 30, which is the number on almost all examples found in central Oklahoma and Texas. But even here a rare plant will show 15 to 20 or more than 30 radials, giving us a hint that his spread is too narrow. This fact was apparently not realized for many years.

So when Britton and Rose were confronted with small specimens from Big Spring, Texas, with only 12 to 15 radials, they immediately set up a new species, calling it *E. perbellus*, although all of its other characters which they listed equaled those of *E. caespitosus*.

Later authorities appear to have seen no specimens of this form except the originals, and the species has stood as Britton and Rose described it until this time.

In this study I have made great effort to collect this species in its type locality and to study it. Two extensive collecting

trips into the Big Spring area netted numerous specimens of *E. caespitosus* with radials from 17 to 24 in number, but not those with the 12 to 15 of Britton and Rose. Finally, on a third extensive search of the area we collected two specimens, both small plants identical to the previous ones, but both with 12 to 15 radials. We had apparently re-collected *E. perbellus* at last.

But in the process we had established that specimens with fewer than 20 radials but more than 15 were common in the area, as they are in the surrounding countryside. We began to suspect that intermediates could be found linking these two numbers entirely and that we had no separate species here after all. Later collections throughout northwest Texas, western Oklahoma, eastern New Mexico, and Colorado established that the range of radial numbers throughout the area was 12 to 30, the most common being 17 to 26, these latter numbers appearing in the populations at almost any good location.

At one location in Majors County, Oklahoma, we found specimens with radial counts as low as 12 and as high as 23. This was the same location where Caryl, in 1935, reported the first collection of *E. perbellus* in Oklahoma. But what we had here was no separate population of a separate form, but instead just some specimens of *E. caespitosus* with the lower extreme of spine number, mixed with typical specimens. At this discovery we were ready to follow Mrs. Lahman, no doubt the greatest student of Oklahoma cacti, who also in 1935 wrote, "In the meantime, I have crossed *E. perbellus* from my list of Oklahoma cacti until I find someone who really knows what it is." We had about decided that Britton and Rose's taxon had arisen out of Engelmann's failure to realize the scope of his species and that it should be entirely relegated to the synonymy.

This may still be the case, and the name may yet be dropped, but since then we have discovered a population of cacti in Bailey County, Texas, near Muleshoe, in which all of several dozen plants examined have 12 to 14 radials and no centrals. These bloomed with flowers typical, although small for the species, and have no other obvious character to distinguish them from that species. Since this is a pure population of this form, perhaps it should be recognized after all. It certainly cannot be considered a separate species, and may be only a clone. In the meantime, in the complete absence of any experimental evidence concerning any of the relationships of these plants, the most logical way to treat it so that it will not be lost and will be available for future study is to call it a variety of the species.

Echinocereus caespitosus var. purpureus (Lahman)
"Black Lace"

DESCRIPTION   PLATE 5

STEMS: As the species, except that it is smaller in maximum size and clusters more sparingly.

AREOLES: As the species.

SPINES: 14 to 22 radials and 0 to 3 centrals, as the species, except that the outer part of each spine is shiny purplish or glistening black in color.

FLOWERS: As the species, except that they are always purple in color. There were 12 stigma lobes on all specimens seen.

FRUITS: As the species.

RANGE. The Wichita and Glass (Gloss) mountains of western Oklahoma.

REMARKS: This cactus was found at Medicine Park, Oklahoma, on the eastern edge of the Wichita Mountains, and described by Mrs. Lahman, who studied the cacti of Oklahoma extensively. It is very rare and has been seldom seen again. Mr. Charles Polaski of Oklahoma City, who has the finest private collection of cacti I have seen, supplied the first specimen of it which I had the privilege to study. This specimen came from the Glass Mountains about 100 miles north of the type locality at Medicine Park. Mr. Polaski, who grew up in the Wichita Mountains near Medicine Park says he has never seen it there, and I have searched the type locality without finding either it or any form of *E. caespitosus*. A large area of Medicine Park is now under the waters of Lake Lawtonka, and perhaps it grew in this now-flooded area.

The Glass Mountain plants show the strikingly beautiful, purple-black coloring of the spines described by Mrs. Lahman. They show all of the other characters of her plant, except that the variation of radial spines is from 14 to 22, which raises the maximum number 4 spines beyond her report. This does not seem significant in the light of the variations in spine number we have already seen in this group. The large flower is as she describes, a very beautiful deep meadow violet, except that the throat may be reddish instead of green as she described it. This also seems unimportant, since we find other specimens of *E. caespitosus* with flowers with either green or reddish throats. The stigma lobes on all specimens seen were 12 in number, which is strikingly regular for this group.

An evaluation of all the characters of this plant seems to show only the dark coloration of the spines to distinguish it from the typical *E. caespitosus*. Everything else falls within the known range of the species, when it is interpreted in the broad way made necessary by including specimens of all its range. This spine color does not seem sufficient grounds for considering it a separate species, so I place it here as a variety. Whether even this is justified remains to be determined after further study.

The coloring of the plant body is very beautiful, and so conspicuous as to prompt special exclamations when it is seen in a collection. We have no other cactus with this striking coloration. It is so dark that the term, "black lace," arises spontaneously for it. Even this shows how closely it is related to the more common lace cactus. Unfortunately it is very rare. Much ranchland must be covered to discover a single specimen. It would be a good cactus to be distributed by the trade.

Echinocereus melanocentrus Lowry

DESCRIPTION   PLATE 5

STEMS: Almost spherical to oval when young, becoming cylindrical. Single, or when very old, sometimes branching to include two or three side-branches. Each stem may reach a maximum of about 6½ inches tall and about 2 inches thick. There are 10 to 13 ribs of definite, confluent tubercles. The surface color is very deep green.

AREOLES: Practically touching to ⅛ of an inch apart. They are oval when young to elongated when old, and woolly at first, becoming bare.

SPINES: There are 17 to 20 slender radial spines lying pectinate close to the plant surface. The upper ones are only 1/32 to 1/16 of an inch long, the lateral ones gradually lengthening to a maximum in the lower laterals of ¼ to ⅜ of an inch. The lowermost spines are somewhat shorter again. Spines of adjacent clusters may or may not interlock. There is one central spine on each areole standing out, perpendicular to the plant body, or turned slightly upward. It is straight and slender like the radials and rises from a bulbous base, black or mahogany in color. It is 3/16 to ⅜ of an inch long.

FLOWERS: 2 to 3 inches across and tall. They are showy rose-pink in color, with reddish centers. The petals are almost linear or slightly broadening over their upper parts, their ends more or less ragged. They recurve greatly as the flower ages, leaving it open extremely wide by the second day. The style is pinkish, the stigma lobes green and 12 or 13 in number. The ovary has on it cobwebby wool and very black or brown and white, very slender, flexible, hairlike spines ¼ to ½ inch long.

FRUITS: Unknown.

RANGE. Very localized in sections of Jim Wells and Kleberg counties, Texas.

REMARKS: *E. melanocentrus* is one of those rare little cacti we find growing in extremely localized situations here and there. It is found under the extremely heavy brush of the small amount of uncleared territory there is left around Alice and Kingsville, Texas. Even here it is only found in certain spots. Much of this territory is in ranches where the owners are extremely jealous of their rights to keep outsiders out, and so few had seen this cactus until recently. Perhaps this is fortunate, because at the same time that this keeps the plant out of the public eye it preserves it in its natural setting. But the ranchers are using clearing devices and now spraying with brush-killing chemicals more and more, so the plant is not safe in any case. A few Texas dealers have found an accessible location and in the past few years I have seen possibly a hundred of the plants being distributed.

This species is very similar to *E. caespitosus* in general appearance. It looks much like that other species with one conspicuous black central stuck on each areole. However, *E. caespitosus* does not grow anywhere within over 100 miles of the location of *E. melanocentrus,* and the general aspect of the flowers of the two plants are somewhat different.

The flowers of *E. melanocentrus* are apparently identical to those of *E. fitchii,* and there are other similarities to this species found farther west in south Texas, but the two will hardly be confused, since *E. fitchii* has 3 to 7 spreading centrals instead of only one, and its radials are not pectinate.

E. melanocentrus is a little known specialty of an area which, having none of the more common representatives of this group, boasts its own

Echinocereus fitchii B. & R.

DESCRIPTION   PLATE 5

STEMS: Upright and usually single, sometimes putting out only 1 or 2 side-branches when very old. These stems are to 6 inches tall and 2 inches thick, medium to dark green in color, having 10 to 14 ribs of low, confluent tubercles.

AREOLES: Round when young, becoming oval on the sides of the plant. They are small in size, almost touching to $3/16$ of an inch apart, and woolly when young, becoming bare.

SPINES: There are 20 to 25 radial spines which are white with brown tips to tan with reddish-brown or black tips. They are slender and not pectinate, but spreading outward somewhat from the plant surface. The uppers are very short, the lower laterals becoming $1/4$ to $3/8$ of an inch long. There are 3 to 7 slender central spines which are the same color as the radials, rising from slightly bulbous bases, $1/8$ to $3/16$ of an inch long and spreading to the sides instead of standing out in one row.

FLOWERS: Large and showy, pink, always with dark burgundy centers. They are about $2^1/2$ inches tall and 2 to 4 inches across. The flower tube possesses much cobwebby wool and 10 to 17 hairlike, yellowish or white, dark-tipped spines to $1/2$ inch long. There is much variation in petal shape, as there is in this whole group. They run from linear to spatulate, and the ends are blunt or pointed, ragged or entire. Usually the petals recurve when the flower is completely open. The long style is pink, and there are 12 or 13 green stigma lobes. The flowers are fragrant.

FRUITS: Spherical to oval, $1/2$ to 1 inch long. They remain green and covered with white wool and spines.

RANGE. Along the Rio Grande and away from it only a few miles from near Rio Grande City northwest past Laredo to not quite as far upstream as Eagle Pass, Texas.

REMARKS. *E. fitchii* seems to be an immigrant to us from Mexico, appearing as it does just along a stretch of the Rio Grande, but it appears not to be widespread in north Mexico either. I have collected paralleling its whole range about 50 miles within Mexico without seeing one specimen of the plant that far south.

It does occur in Mexico, and there are other forms farther down in that country whose relatoinship to this must be close, but within our own territory it has only a tenuous foothold on gravelly hillsides overlooking the Rio Grande. Much of its territory was flooded by the huge Falcon Lake, and it is now possible to collect this cactus literally from the boat, when that lake is high. It is found to the northwestern edge of Webb County, but hardly farther in that direction, its range stopping almost too abruptly to believe, about 30 miles below the lowermost collection point of *E. caespitosus.*

E. fitchii is easily distinguished from the other cacti of this group by the fact that its spines spread outward instead of lying neatly pectinate. This is a slight difference, but apparently a sufficient one, as one never hears this cactus called a lace cactus. Its numerous spreading centrals also distinguish it.

Its spines are arranged very nearly like those of *E. dasyacanthus,* and it does look much like a small, delicate version of that cactus, but every other character is different, and no one should confuse them.

It also shows a superficial similarity to *E. pectinatus,* but, besides the differences in the spines, the flowers are different. The ovary with its wool and hairlike, flexible spines is entirely unlike that of *E. pectinatus,* which lacks the long wool and has rigid spines.

There is much variation in the spine colors of *E. fitchii,* as indicated in the description, but all spines on any plant are the same, so there is no banding. The difference is from individual to individual. The extreme on one side is almost pure white, with only pale brown tips on the spines; the plant of the opposite extreme has spines all tan or honey-colored below, with the outer half of each spine red-brown or black. Most plants in between these extremes present a sort of salt and pepper appearance over-all.

The species is easy to grow and presents beautiful flowers. These flowers vary remarkably, however, in size and petal characters; there is hardly any variation in their fine, delicate coloring.

Echinocereus baileyi B. & R.

DESCRIPTION   PLATE 6

STEMS: Globose or oblong at first, becoming cylindrical with age. They sometimes remain single, but usually form clusters which may become very dense with up to 30 stems when old. Individual stems measure up to 8 inches tall and $3^1/2$ inches thick. They are medium green in color, with ribs narrow and somewhat tuberculate.

AREOLES: Oval when young, and very woolly, becoming elongated when older. They usually become bare when very old, but may for a long time have a mass of dirty white or tawny wool at the upper edge of the areole, and some plants have been seen on which the areoles remained rimmed with wool. They are ¹/₈ to ¹/₄ of an inch apart.

SPINES: There are 12 to 28 slender but rigid radial spines which are not pectinate, but spreading outward from the plant and interlocking with those of adjacent areoles. The upper ones are very small and weak, the lateral ones become progressively longer until the lower laterals are ⁵/₈ to 1 inch long. There are 0 to 5 centrals, these often very small, sometimes only ¹/₈ to ³/₁₆ of an inch long, but on those plants with well-developed centrals they may be ¹/₄ to ³/₈ of an inch long. When there are several centrals they spread from crowded bases almost lined up vertically in the middle of the areole. The spines vary in color from pure white to yellowish, straw to rust-brown, or even rosy reddish, but all on any given plant will be the same color, giving a fine variety of colors in most stands of the species.

FLOWERS: Large and showy, 2 to 3 inches tall and 2¹/₄ to 3¹/₂ inches in diameter. They are fuchsia in color. The petals arise from narrow red bases and their upper parts are broad and fuchsia in color, with the ends ragged or erose. The stamens are very short, and the style is short for the group. There are 10 to 21, but most commonly 10 to 12, dark green stigma lobes. The ovary surface is covered with a great deal of long white wool and also has 5 to 15 hairlike, white to rusty spines ¹/₄ to ³/₈ of an inch long on each areole.

FRUITS: Egg-shaped, ³/₈ to ¹/₂ of an inch long. They remain green and covered with wool and bristles until they dry and split open laterally to scatter the seeds.

RANGE. Apparently restricted to the Wichita Mountains of southwestern Oklahoma.

REMARKS. This is one of the most attractive of the Echinocerei, yet it is very restricted in its range and, therefore, is not so well known as some of its relatives. It is an inhabitant of the unique granitic region of southwest Oklahoma comprising the Wichita Mountains. There have been occasional reports of its having been collected outside these mountains in adjacent areas of Oklahoma and even in nearby Texas, but those reports which it has been possible to check have all proved to deal with *E. caespitosus* instead. As one enters the Wichita Mountains from the east, near Lawton, Oklahoma, *E. baileyi* is found immediately, growing in beautiful stands, often of hundreds of plants together, upon the undisturbed granite-strewn slopes and ledges. It is found in profusion almost throughout the Wichita Mountains Wildlife Refuge and north of it a few miles, then northwest to Quartz Mountain and its attendant hills. The last of this mountain chain on the northwest is Granite Mountain, arising all alone above the town of Granite, Oklahoma. All over this huge pile of red granite, in the crevices of the main mass and in between the huge boulders, are clumps of *E. baileyi,* but beyond this, as in every other direction from these mountains, stretch the ordinary hills and plains of Oklahoma, where *E. caespitosus* takes over.

E. baileyi is easily distinguished from its relatives by the profusion and length of its spines. These cover the whole plant and stand out from its surface in all directions, giving it a distinctly unkempt appearance when compared with the majority of the Echinocerei. Only *E. longisetus* from far-off northern Mexico has such long and unruly spines, and those are extremely slender and flexible, while these of *E. baileyi* are strong and rigid.

The flowers of *E. baileyi* are similar in many ways to those of the lace cactus, but are not quite as big and flamboyant, and are rose-red rather than purple.

When a whole population of this cactus is viewed on any good mountainside in its range, it presents a remarkable selection of spine colors. There is no variation on the individual plants and, therefore, no banding at all; but individual plants vary greatly from each other in color, the range of colors running from pure white through yellowish, tan, brown, and rusty to rose-red. The effect of all these colors together in a thick stand is very attractive. Also presented is quite a variation in number and length of radial spines, from as few as 12 to as many as 28, and the longest of these from as little as ⁵/₈ of an inch on some plants to as much as 1 inch on others. Central spine number varies also, from none on some plants to 5 on the most heavily armed ones.

All of these variations, with the exception of the radial number, seem to present gradients through the range, the majority of the plants in the east being white or light color and averaging shorter spines and fewer centrals, while on the western edge of the range at Granite, the majority are rusty or reddish, have spines averaging longer, and usually have several centrals in each areole. One cannot set up ranges for these variations within the over-all range, however. These are only averages. For instance, the darkest colored, rosy-tipped spines I have seen were on a plant growing within inches of a pure white neighbor near Medicine Park, at the eastern edge of the range, while the shortest spines I measured were on a white individual on far western Granite Mountain. These variations thus appear to be the result of simple quantitative inheritance within one major unit population.

Britton and Rose first named and described this cactus. Unfortunately they had the benefit of only a few specimens to examine, brought to them by Mr. Bailey; and, therefore, they had no concept of the actual limits of the species' characters. This fact has caused much confusion, especially since most more recent students have apparently seen no more representative series of the plant than they did, and so have attempted to follow Britton and Rose's too narrow description. Backeberg, for instance, goes to quite some trouble, apparently in order to agree with Britton and Rose who say the plant has no centrals, to try to make a case that on older areoles the spines arising in the middle of the young areoles all finally assume radial positions. This is unfortunate, as on every mountainside, even among the predominantly central-less specimens of the east, there is an occasional plant with a distinct central or two, and in the west the vast majority of plants have 2 to 5 unmistakable centrals up to ³/₈ of an inch long. Similarly, Britton and Rose give "about 16" as the number of radials, while the number actually varies from 12 to 28. In the description given above I have broadened the limits to include the whole range of characters found in studying the whole population over its entire known range. This seems the only way to understand it as the continuous entity that it is.

Probably because of Britton and Rose's too limited description, attempts have been made to segregate parts of this population as separate species. Mrs. Lahman, noticing specimens which did not conform to the original description, described and attempted to set off *E. oklahomensis*, distinguished by having 20 to 24 radials only ⁵/₈ of an inch long and 0 to 2 centrals. She also set up *E. longispinus*, with 14 to 16 radials up to 1 inch long. Specimens with both these sets of characters are easily found on almost any undisturbed slope in the Wichita Mountains, and it does not seem that they deserve even varietal designation. They just represent two extremes of the plant, unknown to Britton and Rose.

A more recent attempt has been made by Backeberg to break up the species. In an article in 1941, attempting to show that there was a difference between *E. caespitosus* and *E. reichenbachii*, he turned to some white, very greatly clustering specimens of *E. baileyi* sent him from Oklahoma and described them as the true *E. caespitosus*, rediscovered after all this time. He was impressed by the dense clusters of these specimens and thought Engelmann must have meant something like this in using the name he did for his plant. It is, however, obvious that Backeberg's specimens could not be Engelmann's *E. caespitosus*, since nothing like the Oklahoma plant grows within hundreds of miles of Industry, Texas, which was the type locality of *E. caespitosus*. It is equally obvious to anyone knowing Oklahoma cacti that Backeberg's photo of his plant showed only a short-stemmed, clustering specimen of *E. baileyi*. Backeberg, in his more recent work, *Die Cactaceae*, has recognized this, and now calls this plant *E. baileyi* var. *caespitosus*. It seems unnecessary to maintain even this varietal distinction, as everywhere in the Wichita Mountains the whole range of variation exists together, from single-stemmed, tall specimens to greatly clustering plants. The largest cluster I myself have counted had 30 stems 5 to 6 inches tall, and grew less than two feet from a plant, identical in every respect except that it was a full 8 inches tall and showing signs of old age without offering to ever become more than a single stem.

Backeberg has also set up a set of varieties based almost entirely on spine color, as follows: *E. baileyi* var. *brunispinus* having long, chestnut-brown spines; variety *flavispinus* with soft and pale yellow spines; variety *albispinus* (Lahman) Backeberg having white spines; and variety *roseispinus* having long but soft spines, rose at the tips. This sort of thing appears to be useless in a case of quantitatively varying characters in which there are all possible intermediates. We could as well have eight varieties on color basis as four, once this sort of thing is started.

If one can look beyond the minor differences, he will see whole hillsides of granite boulders in the crevices of which grow beautiful spiny columns and clusters of columns, from as red as the rocks themselves to as white as the snow which covers them here in the winter. This is *E. baileyi*, one of only two or three cacti unique to Oklahoma, and surely one of which the state can be proud.

It is also necessary to report here what appears to be an even more rare and remarkable variant of this variable species. Years ago Oklahoma's outstanding cactophiles, Mr. and Mrs. Charles Polaski, discovered a strange cactus on Headquarters Mountain, near Granite, Oklahoma. Only one individual was found, and much searching of the mountain has never revealed another. But Mr. Polaski is an expert at cactus culture, and he has propagated this individual vegetatively for many years by grafting. He most kindly gave me a cutting of it, as he has to others.

The plant presents real peculiarities. The grafted cuttings have become cylindrical, clustering from the base, some stems up to 2 inches thick. The surface is in very indistinct ribs composed of almost separate tubercles. The areoles have 15 to 20 short, spreading, whitish spines, but are more remarkable for having, besides the spines, a mass of fine, white wool. The whole plant remains covered with this woolly development, under the spines. I puzzled over my cutting of this plant for a number of years, while I tried to persuade it to bloom, but it finally died without responding that much to my care.

In 1965, Curt Backeberg described this form as a new species, calling it *Echinocereus mariae*, and with his article is a photograph of its bloom, which appears much like the typical *E. baileyi* flower.

What actually is this plant? After much reflection, I feel that this individual specimen found upon Headquarters Mountain is only an aberrant, atypical individual of *E. baileyi*, which grows in its typical form all over the mountain. Note that the spines are much like those of *E. baileyi* in everything except length—they are shorter. Note also that the growing tip of *E. baileyi* has the same sort of woolly areoles, the wool later, with maturity, falling off. Add to this the fact that the ribs in the growing tip of *E. baileyi* are, as in most cacti, markedly tuberculate, only flattening out later; that Backeberg's photo shows a flower in no visible character contrasting with those of this species; and that the grafted cuttings greatly surpass the 2.3 centimeters maximum he gives for the stem diameter of the original specimen, and approach the typical stem size of *E. baileyi*. Notice that all of these unique characters of this cactus can be interpreted as a retention of juvenile or immature form. This makes it seem that we have here a plant retarded in some way, and the flower, when it was finally seen, not being unique, I feel it should be considered an atypical individual of *E. baileyi*.

I therefore do not list this as a separate species here. This decision is also influenced by the following consideration. It does not seem proper to erect new species upon only one individual, and I understand that this plant was never re-collected. If the modern concept of the species as a population had been followed in the past, numerous names based upon one atypical specimen only would never have been proposed, and the study of cacti would be much simpler. While the knowledge of this specimen and its existence for all these years in several collections stands as a fitting tribute to the surpassing abilities of Mr. and Mrs. Polaski in collecting and culturing cacti, it seems the one individual can hardly constitute a formal taxon.

Echinocereus albispinus Lahman

DESCRIPTION   PLATE 6

STEMS: Densely clustering. Individual stems are cylindrical and 3 to 6 inches tall, while to only 1 inch thick, with 12 to 14 narrow, tuberculate ribs.

AREOLES: Oval, very woolly when young. The wool persists for a long time, but very old areoles are bare.

SPINES: 14 to about 20 radial spines, not pectinate against the plant surface but deflected evenly outward all around the areole. They are very slender, the uppers the shortest, being only 3/16 of an inch or so long, while the laterals are from 3/8 to 1/2 inch long. There are no centrals. All spines are pure white, or sometimes white with light brown, translucent tips.

FLOWERS: Very pale pink or rose-pink, 1 1/2 to 2 1/2 inches tall and 1 3/4 to 3 inches in diameter. They usually open very widely so that the petals are curved backward. These petals arise from very narrow, brownish bases and broaden only slightly to a maximum width of only 1/4 of an inch. The upper parts of the petals are whitish-pink. The upper edges of the petals are very ragged, but they are pointed at the apex. The style is white, and there are 7 to 11 light green stigma lobes. The ovary surface has much white wool and clusters of 12 or more hairlike spines up to 1/4 of an inch long, in shades of white, grays, tans, browns, to black. These flowers are usually produced below the apex of the plant and may appear well down the sides of the stems.

FRUITS: Almost spherical, 1/2 to 3/4 of an inch across, green, said to be edible. They split open when ripe.

RANGE. The type locality of this species is near Medicine Park, Oklahoma, in the eastern end of the Wichita Mountains. It had not been found outside of the type locality until, during this study, it was collected on a single granite ridge a few miles northwest of Tishomingo, in Johnston County, Oklahoma.

REMARKS. When Mrs. Lahman made her study of the cacti of the Wichita Mountains, she spoke of most of her new forms as variations of *E. baileyi,* even while giving several of them new species names. But two forms which she discovered she set apart

most definitely from that species. After listing her five variations of the *E. baileyi* species, she then said, "Also there are two others which appear to be separate species and are here described as *E. purpureus* and *E. albispinus.*" We have seen that her *E. purpureus* was in fact separate from the *E. baileyi* varieties, since it appears instead to be a form of *E. caespitosus.* Therefore I would assume that her *E. albispinus* is accurately set off from *E. baileyi* also, instead of being just the white form of that plant.

The cactus which fits her description will not be confused with *E. baileyi* by any observer who sees it in a living condition. Its spines are shorter, and while they are not pectinate, they stand out around the areole evenly at the angle found on some specimens of *E. caespitosus.* It has the manicured appearance of that species and none of the disheveled look of *E. baileyi.* In fact, it is much nearer in appearance to a long-spined *E. caespitosus* than to a short-spined *E. baileyi.* Even from Mrs. Lahman's photograph this is clear.

However, it seems distinct from both. Its mature stems are more slender as well as shorter than those of either of the others, and its flowers are different. They are smaller and the most pale in color of any related Echinocereus. The exaggerated way in which they open back until the petal tips almost touch the outside of the ovary is also unique, as well as the low position on the stem from which the flowers usually, but not always, sprout.

E. albispinus is probably the most rare of Oklahoma cacti. We have seen no evidence that this cactus has actually been observed alive by any student since Mrs. Lahman until this time. Her description and photos of it are usually reprinted without any elaboration. Backeberg, however, quickly assumed that she referred to the common white-spined *E. baileyi,* and so appropriated her name for his series of color-dictated varieties, making it *E. baileyi* var. *albispinus.* Not only does this sort of variation based on color alone seem ill-founded, but the use of this name in this way ignores the already-mentioned differences which set this plant off from all the *E. baileyi* forms.

Thanks to the aid of Drs. Bruce Blauch and Claude Gatewood (until recently of the Oklahoma State University), we have collected a number of specimens of a cactus which fits Mrs. Lahman's description very well. We feel that it is distinct from any other and stands best as a separate species between *E. baileyi* and *E. caespitosus.*

It was truly surprising when this cactus turned up on a single one of the many granite ridges near Tishomingo, Oklahoma. The area in which the plant grows in that location is only a few acres and the total population is probably no more than 100 plants. This is fully 100 miles from the type locality of *E. albispinus* or from any known collections of *E. baileyi. E. caespitosus* grows in profusion not many miles away, but is not found associated with this plant. This is one of those surprising turns of distribution found so often in cacti.

Echinocereus chisoensis Marshall

DESCRIPTION PLATE 7

STEMS: Columnar, to 8 inches tall, but remaining rather slender, the greatest diameter seen being two inches. They are almost always simple, but may, very rarely, branch above the ground. They have 13 to 16 ribs composed of very distinct tubercles almost completely separated from each other by broad valleys. The color of the surface is deep green or bluish-green.

AREOLES: Very small for the group, being about 1/8 of an inch or less across. They are circular and woolly at first, becoming oval and naked when older. These areoles are about 1/4 of an inch apart.

SPINES: There are 10 to 15 very slender radial spines which radiate evenly around the areole and lie almost parallel to the plant body. They are white or gray below with the upper part red-brown or maroon. The uppermost ones are very small, only 1/16 to 1/8 of an inch long, and bristle-like. The lateral ones are progressively longer, until the lower laterals are 1/4 to 3/4 of an inch long. There are also 1 to 4 central spines. One is porrect or nearly so and 1/4 to 5/8 of an inch long, while the others are more or less spreading and shorter. They are all very slender and straight, from bulbous bases. They are black or dark red-brown, usually with whitish bases.

FLOWERS: Rose in color, with reddish centers, about 2 1/2 inches long, but never opening widely, and so only 1 to 2 inches in diameter. The petals are long and these would be big flowers of 3 or more inches across if they opened back, but the petals remain almost perfectly upright. They are oblong, the bases deep red and the upper parts rose, with entire, pointed tips. The pistil is short and white. The stigma is composed of 10 small, green lobes. The surface of the ovary has some white wool and clusters of 8 to 14 white to brownish, hairlike spines.

FRUITS: Elongated, 1 to 1 3/8 inches long and about 1/2 inch in diameter. They are red and fleshy when ripe, but covered with wool and bristles. When older they become dry and split open.

RANGE. Restricted to the Chisos Mountains within the Big Bend National Park, Brewster County, Texas.

REMARKS. This cactus was first described by Marshall in 1940. It is an obscure species, perhaps best described as retiring in both habitat and appearance. Even among those living and working at the Big Bend National Park, it is mostly unknown.

The reasons for its remaining so little known are clear. It hides shielded in the middle of clumps of brush and never seems to dare to expose itself on ledges or open spaces. Among the stems of protecting bushes its small, upright column is well camouflaged and so is seldom seen. Even its flowers are strikingly reserved for an Echinocereus. They are as large as many of the flamboyant ones, but discreetly remain almost closed even during the few hours of the afternoon when they are open at all, showing only the pale rose color of the outer petal surfaces. There is bright color within them, but it is deep in the center where only the bees see it and it attracts no one else.

Although almost unknown, the cactus is not rare in its area. Marshall spoke of examining over three hundred specimens, and I found it easy to locate dozens of them, once I knew how to search for them.

The relationships of the plant to other Echinocerei are difficult at best to determine. Marshall discussed its similarity to some forms of *E. fendleri*, but concluded that they were only superficial. On the other hand, characters of the ovary surface, rib and areole arrangement, and spine form all relate it more closely to *E. pectinatus* or *E. caespitosus* than to *E. fendleri*.

E. chisoensis is a delicate cactus, rarely seen, but a unique resident of the Big Bend National Park, where it is, fortunately, protected and so should be with us long after many of its more flamboyant relatives are decimated through a combination of conspicuousness and lack of protection.

Echinocereus pectinatus var. wenigeri Benson
"Comb Hedgehog"

DESCRIPTION PLATE 7

STEMS: Single, or sometimes in old specimens 2 or 3 to one plant. They are egg-shaped to stoutly cylindrical, growing to 10 inches tall and 3 1/2 inches thick. Rows of distinct but confluent tubercles make up shallow ribs on the stems. The number of ribs on Texas plants is 13 to 18.

AREOLES: Broadly oval and woolly when growing at the tip of the plant, but becoming narrowly oval or elongated and bare when older, on the sides of the stem. These areoles are from almost touching to 3/16 of an inch apart.

SPINES: There are 15 to 20 radial spines which are pectinate, spreading over the surface of the plant, the laterals actually to some extent recurved back into the grooves between the ribs. They are medium strength to rather heavy and very rigid. The upper ones are most slender and short and the laterals longer, to between 3/8 and 1/2 inch. There are 2 or 3 central spines standing in a vertical row in the center of each areole. They are stout, but very short, only 1/16 to 1/8 of an inch long. All spines are white with pinkish or purplish tips.

FLOWERS: Very large and striking in appearance, 3 to 5 inches tall and broad. The outer one-half or less of each oblong, broad, blunt petal is lavender pink in color. Below that is an expanse of white extending to the narrow bases of the petals, which are green. This gives a unique, three-colored flower, pink around the edges with a distinct white zone making up sometimes half of the flower, followed by a greenish center. The stigma is whitish and supports 9 to 12 large, dark green stigma lobes. The ovary surface bears some short, white wool and 6 to 18 rigid spines, white or white with dark brown tips and measuring to $3/8$ of an inch long.

FRUITS: Spherical or nearly so, about 1 inch in diameter. Fleshy at first, becoming bronze or brown in color, after which they dry and split open.

RANGE. A local form of a Mexican species encountered only occasionally in Texas, from Del Rio on the east to just beyond Sanderson on the west, in a strip not over twenty miles wide along the Rio Grande. It is not reported from the Big Bend in Texas, but has been reported from the southern edge of New Mexico, although the report has not been confirmed.

REMARKS. The species E. pectinatus grows widely in Mexico, but can be regarded as established in only two areas of the U.S. It is well represented in Arizona, one form coming from that state into the extreme southwest corner of New Mexico as well; and the form just described is rare but can be found in a limited strip of Texas from Del Rio to Sanderson. Strangely, it seems to be missing in the wide expanse of the border between these locations. This leaves the Texas form of it isolated from the rest.

It is never common even in that area. A full day's tramping over the hills just north of the Rio Grande in the vicinity of the lower Pecos and Devil's rivers will yield at best one or two specimens, if the searcher has good eyes and better luck.

The Texas range of the cactus begins just west and south of the southwesternmost range of E. caespitosus and extends west just to the beginning of E. dasyacanthus. It is sandwiched between these its two closest relatives.

The Texas specimens of this cactus have some differences from the typical specimens from Mexico, namely, fewer ribs; more oval, more woolly, and more widely spaced areoles; whiter spine coloring; and a lower maximum number of both radial and central spines, as well as heavier spines. At first, I did not distinguish it from the Mexican E. pectinatus, but after I became familiar with the Texas plants and after I had studied literally hundreds of Mexican specimens coming from that country through our Texas cactus dealers, and had collected the plant in various parts of Mexico myself, without finding one specimen to match ours, I became convinced that we have here our own distinct form. L. Benson erroneously refers my specimens of variety ctenoides from Mexico to this variety and so credits me wrongly with having collected the variety in Mexico as well as in Texas.

The cactus may well be Hooker's E. pectinatus var. texana, but there is no way to know, and, therefore, that name has not been recognized by any recent writers. L. Benson finally described and typified the form, naming it after the author. I feel it deserves varietal rank, as he indicated.

E. pectinatus var. wenigeri can easily be distinguished from E. dasyacanthus because its radials are rigidly recurved and appressed to the surface of the plant instead of spreading outward, and because its centrals are very short, and are always in one vertical line instead of being longer and spreading outward. The typical Mexican E. pectinatus is actually much closer to E. dasyacanthus than is variety wenigeri. It is equally easy to distinguish from the typical E. caespitosus, which also has more outward-standing, finer spines, and often no centrals at all. But some specimens of E. caespitosus have very nearly as recurved radial spines and 1 or 2 short centrals in the middle of the areole. It is then very hard to distinguish the two by the plant body alone. But if one has the opportunity and patience to observe the flowers of the two the distinction is obvious: E. pectinatus presents a flower tube with short wool and short, rigid spines, while E. caespitosus always has long wool and long, flexible, hairlike spines on its flower. The white zone is also always present in the flower of E. pectinatus, while the flower of the other always lacks it, since its darker purple petals deepen to a reddish or greenish center.

Echinocereus pectinatus var. rigidissimus (Eng.) Rumpl.
"Arizona Rainbow Hedgehog," "Cabeza del Veijo"

DESCRIPTION   PLATE 7

STEMS: Thick columnar to 8 inches tall and 4 inches thick. They may be single or rarely branched, with 18 to 23 narrow, tuberculate ribs.

AREOLES: Elongated, and from practically touching to $1/4$ of an inch apart.

SPINES: There are 15 to 23 radial spines which are pectinate and recurved to lie flat on the surface of the plant. They are very heavy and rigid. The upper spines of each areole are small and a translucent tan, amber, or gray. The laterals and lower spines are to $5/8$ of an inch long, tan or amber, amber with red tips, or sometimes all red. The plant usually presents a banded appearance due to successions of these spine colors. There are no central spines.

FLOWERS: Identical to those of previous form except the outer parts of the segments fuchsia and often having 13 stigma lobes.

FRUITS: As those of the previous form.

RANGE. Extreme southwest New Mexico and south Arizona into Sonora, Mexico.

REMARKS. This is now regarded as a variety of E. pectinatus. It presents the same large, white-zoned flowers and the same general appearance, being, however, distinguished from the typical form of the species by its heavier spines and its larger stem size. The spines are always all radials, and are the longest and heaviest of this species. They interlock, and the plant body is usually hidden under this thick, rigid armament lying flat upon it. This seems also to be the only one of this group to present a variegation of the spine color on a single areole. Typically, the upper, smaller spines of each areole are lighter, while the lower ones are more or less red. These characters make it easily distinguishable from the other varieties of the species.

It will be noticed that the pattern of coloration of the spines is almost the same as those of *E. viridiflorus*. Because of this I have seen this cactus confused by beginners with large, robust, short-spined specimens of *E. viridiflorus* var. *cylindricus* of the Big Bend in Texas. If closer observation does not clear up this error, the big purplish flower is surely a surprise when it appears where the little greenish one was expected.

The flower of variety *rigidissimus* is identical with that of the species. It seems, however, to be a more profilic bloomer when cared for, and so is a great favorite of growers. Numerous photographs of this plant in its glory with many of the striking flowers open at once have been printed in various books and magazines.

This cactus seems to be limited in its natural range to the mountains of the southwest corner of New Mexico and southeastern Arizona, coming up out of Mexico in only that one area. Coulter once stated that it was found in west Texas, but this seems doubtful. It is a beautiful form, just managing to enter the corner of our area.

Echinocereus pectinatus var. ctenoides (Eng.)

DESCRIPTION   PLATES 7, 8

STEMS: Single or sometimes clustering to half a dozen stems, each heavily cylindrical and to 6 inches tall by 3 inches in diameter, having 15 or 16 ribs greatly interrupted by tubercles.

AREOLES: As the species.

SPINES: As the species except that the radial number is only 14 to 22 and the centrals always number 2 to 4. The spines are white with very light brown tips. The plants are never purplish or banded with color.

FLOWERS: A large and showy orange-yellow, 2½ to 4 inches long and wide. The petals are almost linear to narrowly spatulate, the ends erose. The upper part of each petal has a bright orange midline. The lower one third of each petal is green, and the center bright green. The style is greenish white, and there are 13 dark green stigmas. The outer ovary surface has a little short white wool and 14 to 16 short, rigid spines, which are white with dark brown tips, per areole.

FRUITS: ½ to 1⅛ inches in diameter, spherical or egg-shaped. They are green, turning to greenish-brown when ripe, and covered with short wool and rigid spines which, however, become deciduous when the fruit ripens.

RANGE. Given originally as from Eagle Pass to the Pecos in Texas and south to near Santa Rosa, Coahuila, Mexico. It is said to exist westward in Mexico into Chihuahua. Apparently it is now extinct in Texas.

REMARKS. It is a real indication of the thoroughness of the early collectors and of Engelmann's studies that this plant was collected and described over one hundred years ago. I am persuaded that none of the more recent students of cacti since Coulter have seen it at all, but this has not kept them from writing about it, and so the confusion is extensive, as can be expected.

Engelmann described the cactus in detail and pictured it well, including the flower. He had specimens from Bigelow, collected at Eagle Pass and near Santa Rosa, Coahuila, and those of Wright, collected by the lower Pecos River, which is not far from Eagle Pass. He stated that the plant "looked distinct enough from *C. dasyacanthus*," and then he stated that "the flowerless plant so closely resembles *C. pectinatus* that it can hardly be distinguished from it except by the fewer ribs."

In spite of this, later students have, probably because of its yellow flowers, tried to link this with *E. dasyacanthus*, and in their enthusiasm they have published some pictures of several different forms under this name. Backeberg finally grew bold enough to come out and call the cactus *E. dasyacanthus* var. *ctenoides*.

In making this study, we recognized that this plant was one of the least known of all in our area and needed clearing up more than almost any other, so we early made attempts to collect and study it. For four years we made field trips regularly to the Eagle Pass vicinity and the area of the lower Pecos River looking for it. In this time I believe that I myself covered almost every undisturbed acreage along the Rio Grande from below Eagle Pass to the Pecos looking for this cactus, and it is not now to be found. We believe the form is now extinct on the north side of the Rio Grande—if indeed Engelmann meant to imply that it was on this side of the river in the first place.

Still wanting to find out what the plant really was, we then extended our field trips into the adjacent part of Coahuila, working down toward the Santa Rosa Mountains, which was the other location where Engelmann reported the plant as growing. We found nothing for many miles below Eagle Pass, but in the rugged mountains northwest of Santa Rosa (now called Ciudad Muzquiz) we suddenly found stands of small, white Echinocerei almost exactly like *E. pectinatus*, except for their whiter spines. We noted that they were much more inclined to cluster than any *E. pectinatus* we had seen, and then, noting the regularly 15 or 16 ribs and 2 to 4 centrals, we began to hope that we had found *ctenoides*. When the plants bloomed, they presented large, light-orange flowers, and we had our confirmation.

It is obvious, as it should have been from Engelmann's description and his illustrations, that this is a form of *E. pectina-*

tus. It bears no characters half so close to *E. dasyacanthus,* except the flower color, and we now know that that species has flowers ranging from yellow to magenta. With this we have the parallel situation of *E. pectinatus* with flowers from orange-yellow to fuchsia.

The question of whether this cactus should even remain listed as a separate variety will doubtless now become the order of business. We do not separate the yellow, pink, and magenta-flowered strains of *E. dasyacanthus* this way. But it seems that this plant has other consistently maintained characters setting it off from its species: such as its greater clustering tendency, its smaller size, its fewer ribs, and so forth.

We apparently are faced here with the first cactus form rendered extinct from our area of the United States in the past hundred years. Very much of the land around Eagle Pass is farmed and the majority of the range areas which look undisturbed have actually been cleared in one way or another in the past, so this is not really surprising. But may we take warning from this and cherish our other cacti found in limited areas more actively?

Echinocereus dasyacanthus Eng.

"Texas Rainbow Cactus," "Golden Rainbow Hedgehog," "Yellow-Flowered Pitaya"

DESCRIPTION   PLATE 9

STEMS: Oval at first, soon becoming cylindrical. They grow to a maximum of 14 inches tall and 4 inches thick. These stems often remain single, but old plants quite often branch to form several heads. They have 12 to 21 narrow, tuberculate ribs.

AREOLES: Round and with tan wool at the growing tip of an active stem, becoming oval or elliptical and bare when older. They are 1/8 to 3/8 of an inch apart.

SPINES: There are 15 to 25 radial spines per areole, all spreading outward at various angles from the surface of the plant and interlocking with those of adjacent areoles, so that the plant surface is heavily covered by them. They are rigid and of medium thickness, the upper ones very short and the laterals to 1/2 or even 5/8 of an inch long. There are also 2 to 5 robust centrals usually 1/8 to 1/2 inch long, but occasionally 3/4 or even 1 inch long. These centrals stand spreading in all directions from the center of the areole, and are not lined up in a vertical row. All spines are white, yellowish, or tan, with their tips reddish or rust-brown. The variations in color shades are often found in zones up and down an individual plant, giving the typical specimen distinct bands of color, although some specimens are of one unvarying color and so are not banded at all.

FLOWERS: Very large and showy. 3 to 5 1/2 inches long and wide, in colors they range from yellow through pink to violet and magenta. The very long petals are spatulate, with the ends ragged and variously notched or pointed. Their bases are green. The style is long and white. There are 12 to 22 large, deep green stigma lobes. The long flower tube has some short wool and 7 to 18 rigid spines to 1/2 inch long and pure white to white with reddish tips upon each areole.

FRUITS: Spherical, 1 to 2 inches in diameter. They are covered with spines until ripe, when these become deciduous and the fruit becomes red-brown or purplish.

RANGE. Southeastern New Mexico through southwestern Texas and the Big Bend. On the east it extends to near Sanderson and Fort Stockton, and into the Guadalupe Mountains of Texas. It follows these mountains a short distance north into New Mexico. It is common in the Big Bend and around El Paso, Texas. It has been said to extend west all the way into Arizona, but I cannot verify this.

REMARKS. *E. dasyacanthus* is the largest member of this group, the most robust in every feature. It likes to stand unprotected by the shade of any other plant on the thin soil of rocky slopes, where its thick spine cover gives it protection from the severe elements as well as from all enemies. A colony of fine old plants on a Big Bend hillside, many of them to at least a foot tall and varying from almost white to reddish or rusty brown, often banded with these colors, is a proud and handsome sight. They bloom with huge flowers, often opening well down on the sides of the plants. These flowers come in all shades from pale yellow to reddish, pink, and even deep magenta.

It seems obvious that no varieties can be set up within this species on the basis of flower color. Other variations found within the limits of this species, such as banding or lack of banding with color, do not seem any more significant. Miss Glover set up the name *E. steereae* for the whitish, nonbanded, violet-flowered population found in the Chisos Mountains of the Big Bend, but this does not seem warranted. Rumpler tried to make this *E. pectinatus* var. *steereae,* but the radials are not pectinate, nor are the areoles elongated. If made a variety, it would have to be *E. dasyacantha* var. *steereae,* as Backeberg lists it, but even this does not seem supportable since we would have only the flower color to distinguish it.

Whether or not the limits of this species have been drawn widely enough is another question. Coulter found a cactus somewhere in southeastern New Mexico which he called *E. dasyacanthus* var. *neo-mexicanus* (note that this is not the same as Wooton's *E. neo-mexicanus*). Coulter described his plant as having areoles 3/8 to 9/16 of an inch apart, with stouter, "spreading radials and 4 stout centrals and larger seeds." He apparently did not see the flowers of this plant.

No one has since been sure what this cactus of Coulter's really was, and the name should probably be eliminated, since it seems impossible to know. Most have found it irresistible to speculate, however, and I would add my own theory. Coulter did not know that *E. dasyacanthus* could have any flower color except yellow. He even used this flower color to key this plant from its relatives. So he automatically set both the species and his variety of it off from all of its red or purple-flowered relatives and apparently never thought to compare characters between the two groups he had set up, yellow-flowered and purple-flowered. Since we now know that this division will not stand, when we disregard flower color, we find that the characters of his *E. dasyacanthus* var. *neo-mexicanus* and those of the red-flowered *E. roetteri* are practically identical. Remembering that they are similar enough so that Engelmann had first called *E. roetteri* by the name of *E. dasyacanthus* var. *minor*, and that Coulter did not know the flower color of his variety, I find it likely that his variety *neo-mexicanus* was nothing but *E. roetteri*. Beyond this sort of speculation we cannot go.

Benson decided to combine *E. dasyacanthus* with *E. pectinatus* as a variety of that other species, and since by the rules of nomenclature, one must use an earlier variety name for such a combination if one exists, he calls our cactus *E. pectinatus* var. *neo-mexicanus* in place of *E. dasyacanthus*. Even in doing this, he commented that this was unfortunate, and so it surely is, as it would leave us for our most well-known rainbow cactus only an obscure name which refers to no one knows what for sure. It seems that the species is distinct enough from *E. pectinatus* anyway, and the combination need not be made in the first place.

Echinocereus dasyacanthus var. **dasyacanthus** (Eng.)

DESCRIPTION   PLATE 9

    STEMS: As the species.

    AREOLES: As the species, except always round.

    SPINES: As the species, except that the centrals are not seen less than 3/8 of an inch long.

    FLOWERS: As the species.

    FRUITS: As the species.

RANGE. Southeastern New Mexico and southwestern Texas east to the Guadalupe and Davis mountains and to near Sanderson, Texas. From these areas it ranges into Mexico. It is also said to range west into Arizona, but I have been unable to confirm this definitely.

REMARKS. This is the common, typical form of the species which is so widely appreciated by almost everyone who looks at cacti at all. It is a dominant part of almost every collection from western Texas or southern New Mexico. However, most specimens grown in gardens come from along the highways instead of from farther south in the nearly inaccessible mountains along the Rio Grande, and so most people see only yellow-flowered individuals.

There is actually a gradient of flower color in the wild population. Nearly all plants growing in New Mexico and around El Paso bloom yellow or orange-yellow. In the Big Bend of Texas pink is more common; and in the lower and eastern part of the Big Bend red and purplish are almost the rule. The full range of colors is found south and west of Sanderson, with some populations there being almost entirely magenta. I saw a beautiful collection of over one hundred local specimens in a rock garden in Sanderson in which all the range of colors were blooming together, but with yellow the most rare. Each specimen I have seen has presented only one color of flower, but Marshall reported seeing a specimen bloom with yellow and purple flowers simultaneously.

Echinocereus dasyacanthus var. **hildmanii** Arendt

DESCRIPTION   PLATE 9

    STEMS: Ovate to tapering cylindrical, single at first but soon clustering to at least 6 or 8 stems, each of these to 10 inches tall and 3 inches in diameter. The flesh is dark green, and the stems have 12 to 16 very tuberculate, narrow ribs.

    AREOLES: Round to oval, woolly when young, then bare. They are 3/16 to 1/4 of an inch apart.

    SPINES: 15 or 16 radials to 3/8 of an inch long, white or gray at the bases with maroon or brownish tips. There are 3 to 5 centrals 1/8 to 5/16 of an inch long, from the same color as the radials to completely maroon or dark red-brown. The spines do not band the plant with color.

    FLOWERS: 4 inches tall, 3 1/2 inches across, deep orange-yellow, with 15 to 19 stigmas. Otherwise they are as the species.

    FRUITS: Not observed.

RANGE. The Davis and Apache mountains of west Texas to near Pecos, Texas.

REMARKS. This form is very close to *E. dasyacanthus*, yet is sufficiently distinct from it to be set apart from it even by amateurs who don't have any name for it. It is never a rainbow, having no banding of colors. The fewer spines do not cover its body so entirely, so the dark green flesh is always visible. Although the individual stems are smaller, the cactus is definitely a clustering one. I have actually yet to see an unbranched specimen, and the largest I have seen had 8 stems loosely clumped in a cluster well over a foot in diameter. This sort of growth is never seen in the typical *E. dasyacanthus*. Yet the flowers of the two are almost indistinguishable, and the other character differences between them are so minor that it seems no more than a variety.

Since Arendt described it in 1892, it has, probably, not been seen by any student until now. Schumann did not mention it, and Britton and Rose seem to have confused it with *E. fendleri* var. *bonkerae,* in which Backeberg followed them. It should be noted that their description when discussing the plant is of specimens collected in the Santa Catalina Mountains of Arizona, and so not of this plant. Arendt described it definitely as a Texas cactus. It is a rare form, and limited to the Davis and Apache mountains and the hills northeast of them to near the Pecos River.

Echinocereus roetteri (Eng.) Rumpl.

DESCRIPTION   PLATE 10

STEMS: Single, at first rather egg-shaped, but becoming cylindrical, up to 6 inches tall and about 3 inches in diameter. The surface is bluish or grayish-green, and there are 10 to 13 ribs which are composed of definite tubercles.

AREOLES: Oval or sometimes round, with some tan wool when young, but naked when old. These areoles are $1/4$ to $1/2$ inch apart.

SPINES: There are 8 to 15 radial spines, the variation due to the plant's frequent addition of very tiny bristle-like radials at the top of the areoles. These upper radials are only $1/8$ to $3/16$ of an inch long. The lateral radials are of medium thickness, straight, and up to $1/2$ inch long. The lowermost radial is a little shorter and weaker than the laterals. There are also 2 to 5 centrals which are stout and straight, $3/8$ to $1/2$ inch long, and spreading in all directions. All the spines are opaque and ashy brown or almost maroon, with the tips blackish, and their bases are bulbous.

FLOWERS: Brilliant purplish in color, but only 2 to 3 inches long and not opening widely.

FRUITS: Almost round to elongated egg-shaped, and small, being only $1/2$ to $7/8$ of an inch long.

RANGE. Originally given by Engelmann as from El Paso, Texas, south in the sand hills, and said by Coulter to range from there west into Arizona and south into Chihuahua. But the only records in recent times have been from southeastern New Mexico.

REMARKS. This is a very obscure and difficult cactus. It has been surrounded by confusion from the beginning. Engelmann first described it as *E. dasyacanthus* var. *minor,* but later withdrew that connection and called it *Cereus roetteri.* Coulter probably studied it more thoroughly than anyone else, having at hand plants from Texas, Arizona, and Chihuahua. Britton and Rose seem to have been misled by Engelmann's first linking of the plant with *E. dasyacanthus.* Their specimen collected at El Paso is a tiny thing only $1 1/2$ inches tall, which seems to have no centrals at all, and appears to be a seedling of *E. dasyacanthus.* Their specimen from Arizona has 1 or 2 very short centrals, apparently in a row, and appears to be one of the *E. pectinatus* group. At any rate, since I have seen living plants of *E. roetteri,*

their preserved specimens do not seem to me to be this plant. This may explain why their description of the cactus is erroneous in several respects. More recently Backeberg has realized the close relationship of this cactus with *E. lloydii,* and combines these two, calling that other cactus *E. roetteri* var. *lloydii.*

It does seem obvious that these latter two are closely related. How closely is not clear. However, on the basis of the very few specimens of this rare cactus I have seen, I feel it is too soon to combine them. *E. roetteri* seems to be a much smaller, nonclustering form with other vegetative characters strikingly similar to the more robust *E. lloydii.* But the flowers and fruits of *E. roetteri* are very much smaller than those of the other, and its flowers show none of the firm, lasting characters of the claretcup group, which those of *E. lloydii* display.

E. roetteri is today an extremely rare cactus. The few known specimens recently collected all have come from southern New Mexico. It is surprising that with the large amount of recent study of Arizona cacti this one has not been reported there since Coulter. It is not so surprising that it is not seen around El Paso, which is its type locality, since the real estate, farming, and military developments there have already greatly reduced several much more common species of the area. For this reason it appears that it cannot be found in Texas today, surviving only farther west, in less disturbed areas.

Echinocereus lloydii B. & R.

DESCRIPTION   PLATE 11

STEMS: Simple at first, but clustering and branching slowly to form clumps of up to about six stems when old, the single stems attaining a large size before clustering. Mature stems grow to 12 inches high and as much as $4 1/2$ inches thick, and are cylindrical and bright green to gray-green in color. The ribs are 11 to 13 in number, broad, interrupted, and extremely tuberculate, being formed of broad thickenings at the areoles. There are deep furrows running down the sides of the ribs between these broad bases of the tubercles. The vertical furrows between adjacent ribs on the older parts of the stem are the deepest I have seen on any Echinocereus, being up to at least $3/4$ of an inch deep.

AREOLES: Medium to large, oval to circular, with much white wool when young, but becoming practically bare with age. They are $1/2$ to $5/8$ of an inch apart.

SPINES: When mature all ashy-gray to reddish-gray, but when young and growing they are a brilliant purplish-red, this color often remaining for many years on the tips of the spines. All spines are of medium stoutness, round, and straight from bulbous bases. There are 14 to 17 radial spines, the lower and lateral ones being $1/2$ to occasionally $7/8$ of an inch long. The upper radials are very much more slender, and much shorter—down to ¹/₄ of an inch long. There are 4 to 8 central spines identical to the larger radials standing perpendicular to the stem and spreading slightly from the crowded center of the areole.

FLOWERS: Large and very beautiful, usually being 3 inches long and 2 to 3¹/₂ inches in diameter. There is much variation in their color. They are most commonly scarlet, but I have specimens with petals coral-pink instead. The outer petals are greenish in the midline with entire edges and pointed tips. The inner petals are long, spatulate, with entire edges although these are sometimes somewhat notched at the tips. There are 9 to 14 green stigma lobes. The filaments are pinkish, the anthers extremely small and pinkish or rose in color. The ovary tube bears some white wool and clusters of 7 to 12 firm, reddish spines which are almost equivalent in arrangement to those on the stem areoles, except that they are more slender.

FRUITS: Egg-shaped and 1¹/₄ to 2 inches long. They are densely covered with spines; when the fruit is ripe, these spines loosen fairly easily, but do not seem to fall unless brushed off. The ripe fruit is greenish-orange in color and fleshy.

RANGE. Known only from the type locality, Tuna Springs, Texas, which is about 20 miles east of Fort Stockton in Pecos County.

REMARKS. This cactus was named by Britton and Rose in 1922 from plants collected by Mr. F. E. Lloyd, in his honor. Mr. Lloyd collected many cacti in the area around Tuna Springs, and there was no other label of location on his plants but that.

Tuna Springs has not existed as a town and is not on most Texas maps, so during all these years it has been impossible for interested people to go and find this cactus. The long period of time in which the plant has been lost has not been completely unfortunate, because this has meant that no one has collected it. Consequently it has grown undisturbed and rather commonly in its small area, when most of our rare species whose locales have been known are nearing extinction. But recently the fact that Tuna Springs was once a stagecoach stop a short way east of Fort Stockton has become known, and dealers have been rapidly bringing out the plants. Its continued survival under these conditions is doubtful.

This is a heavy-stemmed, clustering Echinocereus possessing an interesting set of characteristics, which make it unique. In areoles, spines, and stem shape it is very close to the scarlet-flowered *E. triglochidiatus-E. polyacanthus-E. coccineus* group, and its flowers show certain similarities to these (such as in the pink anthers). Yet there are definite differences from these and the flowers are more purplish and less waxy or long-lasting than those of the claret cups, making it appear rather intermediate between those and the purple-flowered groups. The theorists will surely play with this one, but in the meantime, it is a rare and beautiful Texas cactus recently rediscovered.

Echinocereus triglochidiatus Eng.
"Claret-Cup Cactus," "Strawberry Cactus," "King's Cup Cactus"

DESCRIPTION   PLATES 11, 12

STEMS: Globular to cylindrical in shape with 5 to 9 broad, rounded ribs having wide, shallow grooves between them. These stems may be from 3 to 18 inches in maximum length by 2¹/₂ to 4¹/₂ inches thick. The surface of the stems is very soft, often markedly wrinkled, and from dark to pale green in color. These stems cluster in different numbers in different varieties, usually producing fewer than a dozen heads, but in one form an old plant occasionally becomes a large mat of up to around 50 heads. In all cases, however, the stems are loosely and irregularly clustered, a plant being made up of various-sized stems, standing or partly reclining in an irregular clump.

AREOLES: Circular, varying greatly in size within the species from no more than ¹/₈ of an inch to sometimes over ¹/₄ of an inch in diameter. They also vary in distance from one another. The areoles always have much white wool when young, but usually become bare in age.

SPINES: Yellowish or red when growing, becoming opaque, ashy-gray to almost black when old. They vary within the species in number, size, and shape, the range being as follows: radials from 2 to 9 in number and centrals 0 or 1, all these variously from ³/₈ to 2¹/₂ inches long, from rather slender to very thick, rounded to greatly flattened, angular, or channeled, as well as either straight or curved.

FLOWERS: 2 to 2³/₄ inches long and 1 to 1¹/₂ inches in diameter, rigid, waxy, and remarkable among the cacti for their persistence, often staying open for several days and nights. The stiff, blunt petals are scarlet-red or orange-red from narrow green or whitish bases. The stamens are as long as or slightly longer than the petals, with filaments greenish below, becoming fuchsia above. The anthers are very tiny and fuchsia. They are about the same length as the style, so that they sometimes partly enclose the stigma, which has 5 to 11 green lobes. The ovary surface has small areoles upon it, each with a fleshy scale-like segment, a little white wool, and 2 to 6 slender, white, or white-tipped brown spines.

FRUITS: Varying within the species. They are round or oval and from ³/₄ to 1¹/₂ inches in largest measurement, somewhat tuberculate to practically smooth, with some spines which usually become deciduous with ripening. In color they are from green to green with a pinkish cast or else bright red when ripe.

RANGE. Taken as a species, this plant ranges over a very wide area from near Kerrville in central Texas, west through all of the Texas Big Bend to near El Paso, then north through central New Mexico into Colorado and northwestern Arizona.

REMARKS. There has probably been more confusion about *E.*

triglochidiatus than about any other Echinocereus. It is mostly due, I believe, to the fact that this name is the oldest among the red-flowered Echinocerei. Because of this the descriptions given under the name have been broadened from time to time to include every new form which has been put with it in combination. This process has gone on until the extreme is reached by L. Benson's description in the *Cacti of Arizona*, where he describes *E. triglochidiatus* as having stems from 8 to 24 inches high and spines from as few as 3 to as many as 16 per areole. This sort of description is obviously drawn up to include everything in the red-flowered Echinocereus group. It really has little to do with the *E. triglochidiatus* as it was described by Engelmann. Since we have all degrees between these two extremes in the literature, it is not hard to see why the confusion is so great. There will never be anything but confusion here until we see how this problem came about.

There exists a whole series of Echinocerei all of which have flowers similar in that their firm, long-lasting petals are scarlet-red with no blue pigments in them and their stamens light magenta. They are often called the "claret cups" because of this remarkable flower coloration. The shape of the flower and its parts is essentially the same in all of these forms, with the only difference between their flowers being minor variations in the proportions of some of the floral parts.

In size, manner of growth, and details of stem and spines, however, these forms show easily as much variation as is found between many other recognized cactus species, and far more than between some. To give a general description broad enough to encompass all of them is almost to repeat the broad characteristics of the entire clustering, sparsely ribbed group of Echinocerei.

This problem has caused disagreement as to how to treat these forms from the very start. On the one hand, there have been authorities who have described them all as separate species because of their diversity of stem and spine characters; on the other hand some have placed most of them together as varieties within large species groupings because of their flower similarities. A few have even proposed uniting them all into one large, variable species complex. Almost every authority has his own system at least slightly different from every other, often with different names for the same plants—and sometimes the same author has changed his system from publication to publication.

All of this makes *E. triglochidiatus* one of the most difficult groups of cacti to understand. Synonymous names are often taken to mean different plants, and on the other hand, doubtful combinations have been made where some definite characters or other have been overlooked. This has led to the reporting of some of these forms from areas, and even from states, where they do not really occur. On the basis of this sort of thing, several of them have been almost lost sight of altogether. It has even been maintained by some that they cannot really be distinguished at all, but intergrade entirely.

After much observation of the plants in their habitats and after study of available herbarium materials and the literature on them, I have concluded that, once erroneous and incomplete descriptions and doubtful records based on these are eliminated, most of the major forms long ago described in this group do exist within definite ranges and can be distinguished by constant characters.

What are they then? Most of them are too widespread to be clones. Several of them are found in identical or very similar environments in overlapping ranges, and I have seen them preserve their distinctive characters perfectly in the uniform environments of gardens and greenhouses. Therefore, they do not seem to qualify as ecotypes or environmental modifications of a single taxon. This leaves their differences as rather clearly genetic, and the crucial questions here would be: What are their genetic relationships? Are they close enough genetically to be varieties or distinct enough, after all, to be species? But these are the questions no one can yet answer, because of a twofold lack. First, there is no standard degree of genetic relationship, at least in cacti, one side of which is a variety and the other side of which is a species. The thing has just not been worked out to this degree as yet. And, more important, we know nothing so far concerning the genetic relationships of the Echinocerei. There has been absolutely no biosystematic research reported upon them; not even chromosome numbers are known for these forms. So at the present time no one can say categorically from any research data that these are either species or varieties. Any decision is a purely arbitrary, philosophical one.

So we continue to get different treatments of these forms determined entirely by each author's concept of species. This accounts for the highly confusing spectacle we have today of two leading authorities on cacti so completely at odds that while Benson regards the claret cups all as varieties of one vastly enlarged species, Backeberg treats them just as confidently as separate small species. It is still no more than a philosophical argument.

Faced with the necessity of taking a stand on this question, I am following a middle course. It seems clear that some of these forms are too close to be totally separate species. I am, therefore, following Benson in listing as varieties under the species name, *E. triglochidiatus*, all those forms which are close enough to the typical form that their inclusion does not cause the original species description to be altered basically. But I agree with Backeberg that the lumping of everything with the one characteristic of a firm, long-lasting flower into one species is unnecessary, and so I am leaving separate from that species all of those forms whose vegetative characters are so far removed from the original, typical form that their inclusion would cause the species to become something basically different from the original. This decision, like any made at this time about this group, is arbitrary, and we look forward to the day when someone will be able to give us experimental evidence to decide these questions.

From this position, then, we move on to discover and understand the varieties of this fine species.

Echinocereus triglochidiatus var. triglochidiatus (Eng.)

DESCRIPTION   PLATE 11

STEMS: Clustering or branching only slowly to form small clumps often of no more than two or three stems, with an apparent maximum of a dozen or so stems per plant. The stems are of unequal lengths and loosely clustered, each one cylindrical, dark green, and usually somewhat wrinkled, the largest being up to about 8 inches high and about 3 inches in diameter. There are usually 7 ribs, but occasionally there may be 6 or 8, and they are broad, with slight swellings at the areoles and with very shallow grooves between them.

AREOLES: Circular, but not large for the group, with white wool persisting on them, 7/8 to 1 1/2 inches apart, these being the more widely spaced areoles found in this group.

SPINES: Ashy-gray to almost black, from 1/2 to 2 1/2 inches long. They are very stout, most of them being about 1/8 of an inch in diameter for most of their lengths. They have very much enlarged bases and are very flattened or angled, with distinct ridges or grooves running the length of the spines, the top surfaces of them even being concave in most cases. Some of the spines are straight, but some of them at least are curved, in every specimen I have seen. There are 2 to 6 spines to an areole, all of them radials, but a fair share of the areoles on any plant usually have the 3 spines from which comes the name of the plant.

FLOWERS: As the species, except to 1 1/4 inches long; the petals broadest at the tips and very blunt.

FRUITS: Oval or egg-shaped, 1 to 1 1/4 inches long and 3/4 to 1 inch in diameter. They are tuberculate. Fruits I have watched remained green until about January, when they rotted without coloring. The areoles were on the upper ends of long, broad tubercles about 1/8 of an inch wide at the top and 1/2 inch wide at their bases. Each areole possessed a pinkish, fleshy scale and 2 to 5 stout, persistent spines which showed under magnification the same angled, channeled, and twisted character as the plant's major spines. Britton and Rose, as well as Boissevain, have described the fruits as red, with deciduous spines, but it is worth remembering that these authors had already combined this with other forms known to have red fruits, so their descriptions may be of those other forms. There is no description of the fruits of this form by earlier authorities before the confusion of combinations had begun to enter the picture.

RANGE. Northern New Mexico from near the upper Pecos River west to just beyond the Arizona boundary and north into Col-

orado. Its southern limit seems to be near Albuquerque, New Mexico.

REMARKS. In the process of combination which has been practiced the form originally described by Engelmann as *E. triglochidiatus*—with its stems only up to 8 inches high and its spines very long, very heavy, greatly angled, and all radials—has almost been lost sight of, as witnessed by the fact that its range is often given today as being from Arizona throughout New Mexico and trans-Pecos Texas. When the form originally circumscribed by Engelmann is considered, however, I find it to be the form described above, and this specific cactus has a definite range much less wide than is often ascribed to it, due to the inclusion of other forms under the too-broad descriptions. When this is once understood, the confusion vanishes.

The easternmost report of this plant is still Engelmann's report of it on the Gallinas River just east of the upper Pecos, which would be near Las Vegas or Anton Chico, New Mexico, and the westernmost report of it from Fort Defiance, just within upper Arizona. It seems most common about the mountain slopes from Albuquerque to the Gallup area of New Mexico and north from there into south-central Colorado. Coulter cites a supposed collection of it in Texas by Wislizenus in 1846, and on the strength of that places its range as extending that far into Texas, but it is significant that Engelmann in 1856, having worked over Wislizenus' material, did not mention any collections of it in Texas. This one Texas report may have led later students to mistake for it variety *octacanthus*, which does grow widely in Texas, and may be the reason for the survival of the idea that it grows in Texas. In much collecting throughout far west Texas and in lower New Mexico, I have never seen it growing there, nor found anyone who had, in spite of the fact that thousands of plants have been shipped out of Texas erroneously called by this name.

The plant is a handsome cactus, one of New Mexico's finest. It is very hardy, and its dark green looks its best half buried in a snowbank. It is, of course, most beautiful in the spring when it has its fiery red flowers. Their character, shared with the other red-flowered Echinocerei but unique among other cacti, of staying open for several days and nights at a time, makes the plant a favorite of all.

Echinocereus triglochidiatus var. gonacanthus (Eng.) B. & R.
"Claret-Cup Cactus," "King's Cup Cactus"

DESCRIPTION   PLATE 12

STEMS: Cylindrical, clustering very slowly and sparingly, usually only 2 or 3 stems to a plant and the most I have seen in one cluster being 6. Each stem has 7 to 9 ribs which are somewhat rounded, with shallow grooves between them and with distinct, rounded swellings of the ribs at the areoles. There are two separate populations of this form identical except for size. In the widespread northwestern population the stems are only 3 to 6 inches high and to about 2½ inches thick, but there is a localized population restricted to the vicinity of the White Sands National Monument, where the stems grow to a maximum of at least 18 inches tall by 4½ inches thick.

AREOLES: These are very large for the group, ¼ to ⅜ of an inch in diameter, with a great deal of wool when young, but losing much of it with age. They are about ¼ to ⅜ of an inch apart.

SPINES: The spines of this cactus are most striking. They are as heavy as or heavier than those of variety *triglochidiatus*, and there are more of them. At least some of them are always curved, bent, and twisted, and they are conspicuously angled, ridged, and furrowed—the largest ones often having 6 or 7 flattened surfaces and deep grooves. They are yellowish, mottled or tipped with black, when young, and then gray to almost black when old. There is commonly one very heavy central spine which usually has 6 or 7 angles, and is curved and twisted, 1 to 2½ inches long, and around ⅛ of an inch thick. There are 6 to 8 radial spines, the lower 7 radiating fairly evenly and being the shortest of the spines. The upper radial is usually about equal to the central spine and may be even longer. It is often mistaken for a second central because of its size.

FLOWERS: As the species, except that they are larger, being about 2½ inches long, with the petals widening more gradually from their narrow bases and their tips not as broad as those of the plant's relatives. The ovary surface has slender white bristles at least ½ inch long upon it.

FRUITS: Unreported by anyone except Earle, who describes them as spiny, globose, and green with a pink blush.

RANGE. This cactus is always rare, and is found in a comparatively small area around Zuni and Gallup, New Mexico, extending from there to just within Arizona and into the southwestern corner of Colorado around Cortez and Dolores. There is also a separate population of the variety in southern New Mexico, where it grows in the White Sands region between the San Andres and Sacramento mountains.

REMARKS. This is a very beautiful cactus, yet one rarely seen. Its spines are very remarkable and set it off from any of its relatives. They are heavy enough to be worthy of some massive barrel cactus. It is closest to variety *triglochidiatus,* but the spines are always much more numerous and much more ridged, grooved, and flattened.

Since its discovery, the study of this cactus has gone through a history of confusion. It was named by Engelmann; and, at first, Coulter followed in keeping it distinct. But later Coulter and Nelson broadened their description of it to include characters of variety *triglochidiatus,* and they were followed in this by others. Plants with fewer ribs and spines were then called by

this name, and of course when plants which were really variety *triglochidiatus* were called *E. gonacanthus,* the supposed range of variety *gonacanthus* was enlarged. Britton and Rose then took the step which logically followed from the blurring of distinctions between the two plants and placed *E. gonacanthus* for the first time as a variety of the other. Different combinations were also made. Boissevain and Davidson, in their *Colorado Cacti,* picture and describe a cactus collected near Cortez, Colorado, which appears to be this form, but which they call *E. coccineus* var. *octacanthus.* This confuses the cactus with that very different cactus from a far-off part of Texas. But even today the idea persists that *E. gonacanthus* occurs in Texas.

This seems to be a perfect example of what happens when details of stem and spine structure are regarded as insignificant, for this is a constant form occurring in a definite, small range, which any person interested in cacti would want to be able to identify and refer to specifically. Yet, because of the confusion, I have found typical specimens of it, collected near its type locality, in herbaria under four different names. It is probably best considered as only a variety of the larger species, but unless it is kept distinct no order will be possible in this group.

Throughout its range in northwest New Mexico and Colorado variety *gonacanthus* grows as a small plant with stems only to about six inches tall, precocious only in its spination. But there is a strange quirk in its range and its response to a different environment.

A cactus was collected long ago by Wooton at the White Sands area of southern New Mexico, which had 7 radial spines and one much-flattened central, and which he, therefore, called *E. gonacanthus.* I have seen this specimen, and in its preserved state it certainly could pass for our plant. However, its occurrence so far from the ordinary range of the variety seems strange and might make us doubt that it is our plant. Our doubts are increased when we find that the White Sands cactus grows to a majestic 18 inches tall by 4½ inches in thickness, making it probably the largest Echinocereus in our Southwest.

I went into the study of this White Sands cactus with these doubts. I studied the cacti growing in their natural habitat. They have been fairly common and are still to be found here and there within the White Sands National Monument, but they have for the most part been eliminated in the rest of their territory, which lies mostly within the military's missile range, from wide areas of which the vegetation seems to have been systematically eliminated.

After observing numerous specimens of the cactus I was forced to conclude that they are identical to the much smaller variety *gonacanthus* in every respect but stem size and I wondered how one could explain the great difference in size alone. Fortunately this question was answered when cactophile friends in both Albuquerque and Colorado showed me what had happened to specimens of the White Sands cacti which they had brought out and planted in their gardens. In each case, during one year in their gardens, stems 12 inches or more tall when collected had shrunk to half that size or sometimes even smaller, and then had proceeded with the slow, limited growth and branching seen in the northern wild population.

Obviously, we have at the White Sands a local population of variety *gonacanthus* isolated some way in a very unusual habitat which enables it to grow to sizes it cannot match or even maintain anywhere else. This makes it probably the most remarkable example of environmental effect upon growth of any cactus within our area. Except for this, the variety is a smaller, heavy-spined cactus, a rare and beautiful resident of the northwest corner of our area, where it grows in small clumps under the cedar trees on the higher, sandy hills.

Echinocereus triglochidiatus var. octacanthus (Muehlenpf.) Marshall

"Strawberry Cactus," "Claret-Cup Cactus"

DESCRIPTION   PLATE 12

STEMS: Branching or clustering to form clumps, of from 2 or 3 to sometimes as many as 50 stems in some old plants. The stems are globular to cylindrical, bright green or pale, yellow-green, and plump, with shiny surfaces. They are of varying heights and somewhat loosely clustered within the clump. There is a distinct but gradual increase in the maximum size of the plants from one end of its range to the other, the stems hardly ever exceeding 5 inches in height in the northern part of the range, but often standing 9 to 12 inches high in the southern part, particularly in the eastern Big Bend and along the Devil's River. They are always comparatively thick, the largest ones being 4½ inches in diameter. They have 5 to 9 wide, shallow ribs with slight enlargements at the areoles, but with no—or only slight—cross-furrows between areoles.

AREOLES: Round, about ³/₁₆ of an inch across, and ³/₈ to 1¼ inches apart. At first they have much short white wool on them, but later they become bare and are entirely filled by the swollen bases of the spines.

SPINES: All spines on this plant are slender or medium in thickness, actually measuring from only ¹/₃₂ to ¹/₁₆ of an inch in diameter, always round and straight or nearly so, and having very bulbous bases. When young they are yellowish, often with distinct red streaks and shadings, especially toward the bases. When old they may remain yellowish or darken to gray or almost black. The amount of darkening seems to depend upon how much sun they get: I have collected plants from sunny ledges which had almost black spines, only to have the new spines remain yellowish or gray when grown with some shade. There are 3 to 9 radials, very nearly equal in size on any areole, or with the upper ones only slightly smaller. They are from ½ to 1¼ inches long. There may be one central spine standing out at a right angle

to the stem, ⅝ to 1½ inches long, round and scarcely any heavier than the radials, but many plants lack the central entirely.

FLOWERS: As the species, except for the following limitations: they are smaller, being only 1½ to 2 inches tall, with the petals short and blunt; the ovary tube has almost no wool, but has clusters of 2 to 6 slender spines up to ½ inch long; the stigma lobes are 5 to 8 in number and light green.

FRUITS: Round, smooth, red, edible berries about ¾ to 1½ inches in diameter. They have a few spines which soon fall off, leaving them naked by the time they are ripe.

RANGE. A band of territory about 100 miles wide from central Texas west through the Big Bend, perhaps to near El Paso. Specifically, the northeastern limit of this strip is just east of the Colorado River near Lampasas, Texas, the southeastern limit about Kerrville, Texas. From there it is found quite commonly westward past Junction and Del Rio. The northern edge of the range proceeds on south of Fort Stockton to the Davis Mountains, while the southern limit, after dropping into Mexico at Del Rio, takes in all of the Big Bend. The western limit of the range is not so definitely known, due to confusion of the names and incompleteness of the older records. The most western strictly verifiable reports seem to be from Presidio County on the south and near El Paso on the north.

REMARKS. This plant was first named *Echinopsis octacanthus* in 1848 by Muehlenpfordt, from a plant collected by Dr. F. Roemer in Texas. In 1849 Engelmann described the same Texas plant and named it *Cereus roemeri*. Muehlenpfordt had in the meantime named an entirely different New Mexico plant *Cereus roemeri*, and from here on one can anticipate confusion.

In 1896 Coulter wrote of a plant fitting this description, calling it *Cereus octacanthus*, but stating that it occurred from extreme southwestern Texas around El Paso northwestward through New Mexico into Utah. It seems impossible now to guess what plant he was referring to. But from this time on it was assumed that *Echinocereus octacanthus*, as Britton and Rose called it, occurred in New Mexico. Perhaps the reason lies in the coincidence of both a Texas plant and a different New Mexico plant having been given the same name, *Cereus roemeri*, and in the superficial similarity between the Texas plant and a Colorado and New Mexico cactus called *E. coccineus*. To add to the confusion, Boissevain and Davidson, in their *Colorado Cacti*, mistook for variety *octacanthus* both variety *gonacanthus*, a primarily Colorado cactus which can have the same number of ribs and spines but which is vastly different in most other details, and *E. mojaviensis*, another similar species which reaches from the West into the corner of Colorado, and called their amalgamation of these two *E. coccineus* var. *octacanthus*.

As a start in putting the confusion straight, I will say that I have not seen a plant definitely known to be from either Colorado or New Mexico having the combination of characters set out in the early, carefully circumscribed descriptions and outlined above for this plant. I believe it to be entirely a Texas cactus, except for an extension into northern Mexico.

A further confusion was building, however. In 1856 Engelmann created a name, *E. paucispinus*, for a Texas form with 5 to 7 ribs and 3 to 6 round, slender radials. This form he said usually lacked a central, but might have an occasional round, porrect one.

It was soon noticed that the rib and spine numbers of the new *E. paucispinus* matched those of the New Mexico *E. triglochidiatus*, which also lacks centrals. Soon the differences between the two were overlooked, and the Texas plant was being spoken of as *E. triglochidiatus*. However, when both plants are seen together the difference between them is obvious. The color and surface of the stems are very different. The spines of the so-called *E. paucispinus* are always round and not more than ¹/₁₆ of an inch thick—truly insignificant on the broad ribs; while those of *E. triglochidiatus* are always greatly flattened, ridged or even grooved, and twice to four times as thick—easily the most striking thing about that plant. On these characteristics alone it is easy to separate them.

As I have found no real intermediate between these two plants to confuse them, I have also found no specimens of either of them growing in that wide expanse separating the New Mexico *E. triglochidiatus* from the Texas *E. paucispinus*. There is about 200 miles between their known ranges. However, this difference in ranges means that few people have seen them together and realized the difference, with the result that in Texas this plant is almost entirely known under the name of the other. Britton and Rose are largely responsible for this confusion, since they united the two, but even in doing so they stated their opinion that *E. paucispinus* should perhaps be restored for the Texas plants. And they did us the service of picturing side by side a true *E. triglochidiatus* var. *triglochidiatus* and the Texas plant, even though their Texas specimen appears to be a badly damaged variety *octacanthus*.

And here we may have a clue to unravel some more of the confusion. In erecting the species *E. paucispinus*, the Texas form with fewer ribs, fewer but round spines, and no central spine, Engelmann appears to have merely set apart and given a name to the lower end of variety *octacanthus'* range of variations. For a long time I have tried to keep the two separate, but it just cannot be done. Too many times, on too many hills, the whole range of characters from 5 to 9 ribs, 3 to 9 radials, and 1 or no central have been found growing happily together. The flowers and fruits appear to be identical, and it seems that the two must be combined entirely.

So we have, when we see the whole picture, variety *octacanthus*, an entirely or at least primarily Texas cactus which was once called *E. roemeri* and so was confused with the true *E. roemeri* of New Mexico and Colorado. Then those of its individuals with fewer ribs and spines were called *E. paucispinus*

and immediately confused with the very different New Mexico form, variety *triglochidiatus*.

In the extreme northeastern part of its range, variety *octacanthus* is a small cactus with stems only 3 to 5 inches high, one of the weakest growths of any in this group. However, in this area it is adjusting to the wettest habitat any of the red-flowered Echinocerei succeed in colonizing, and this may be the price. But around Sabinal and Uvalde, Texas, one begins to come across clumps of this cactus much more robust in size of the stems. These specimens grow larger as one goes west through Del Rio, Langtry, and Sanderson, until from Del Rio west to south of Marathon and Alpine one occasionally finds majestic clumps with massive stems to at least 12 inches tall. This appears to be the plant's response to the more arid conditions of this part of its range. If we are correct in our interpretation of the immense effect of the White Sands area's conditions on variety *gonacanthus*, then we should not be surprised at a similar though less extreme and more gradual effect of the environment on this related cactus.

The spines in this western area are more uniformly dark gray, which one would expect, due to the more general exposure to the sun here. I was gratified to find that a specimen taken from a canyon south of Alpine, where it was shaded most of the day, had the same light, reddish-yellow spines as those growing under the shade of the eastern junipers, although it stood almost 10 inches high, completely overshadowing its eastern counterpart in size.

Variety *octacanthus* is definitely more resistant to rot than most others in this genus. I have seen plants of it growing and healthy beside rotted plants of *E. enneacanthus* and *E. caespitosus*, where their ranges all meet around Sabinal, Texas. For this reason it would probably be a better cactus for use in eastern gardens than many others of the genus.

Echinocereus triglochidiatus var. hexaedrus (Eng.) Boissevain & Davidson

DESCRIPTION

STEMS: Few in the clump, each 4 to 6 inches high and 2 to 2¹/₂ inches in diameter, with 6 obtuse ribs having wide, shallow grooves between them.

AREOLES: Only ¹/₁₆ to ¹/₈ of an inch in diameter, which makes them among the smallest in this group. They are about ¹/₂ to ⁵/₈ of an inch apart, and woolly when young.

SPINES: Slender, with bulbous bases, and distinctly angular or flattened. Each areole usually has 6 radial spines, but Engelmann says one specimen had 7 and another 5. The lower radials are the shortest spines, being ³/₈ to ⁷/₈ of an inch long, and yellowish-red in color. The upper radials are longer, about ⁵/₈ to 1¹/₈ inches long, stouter, and darker in color.

The central spine is missing, although there may be one, and Engelmann mentions finding one plant with two centrals. The centrals are ⁷/₈ to 1³/₈ inches long and definitely flattened, but not very thick.

FLOWERS: Unknown.

FRUITS: Unknown.

RANGE. Known only from about 15 miles west of Zuni, New Mexico.

REMARKS: This cactus was described by Engelmann from plants collected by Bigelow in 1853. No one has reported seeing it since that time. Coulter described it many years later from Bigelow's preserved specimens. The writer has not seen these, so the description given above is a combination of Engelmann's and Coulter's.

It is hardly possible to do more than guess about the real relationships of this cactus to the other forms it resembles, since we know so little about it; so I merely list it as did the only two authorities who had it before them. Since then various authors have given it as a form of one or the other related species, but little can be proved.

I do find in the U.S. National Herbarium one specimen collected by Standley in the Tunitcha Mountains of New Mexico, not far north of Zuni, which fairly well fits Engelmann's description of *E. hexaedrus*. It was labeled by Standley as *E. paucispinus*, but that is doubtful, since it has the very flattened spines which *E. paucispinus* (var. *octacanthus*) does not have, and it was collected very far from that plant's area in Texas. It could be the only collection of variety *hexaedrus* since the type.

It would be a real service for someone to rediscover and study this cactus, if it still exists.

Echinocereus coccineus Eng.
"Aggregate Cactus," "Bunch-Ball Cactus," "Turk's Head Cactus," "Heart Twister," "Red-Flowered Hedgehog Cactus"

DESCRIPTION   PLATES 12, 13

STEMS: This cactus always consists of a cluster of short, equal-sized stems tightly packed to form a dense, hemispherical mass 1 to 6 feet in diameter and containing, in old specimens, up to several hundred heads. Each head or stem is from only 2 to 6 inches high and up to about 2¹/₂ inches in diameter, with 8 to 11 ribs which are either practically straight or often composed of pronounced tubercles or projections on the tips of which the areoles are found.

AREOLES: These are large, circular to more or less oval in shape, and only ³/₁₆ to ¹/₂ inch apart—the closest areoles among the clustering, few-ribbed Echinocerei. They are woolly when young, becoming bare.

SPINES: All spines on one variety of this cactus are slender to medium in thickness, often almost bristle-like, straight, and round. In color they are white, gray-white, or straw; sometimes the centrals are brownish when new. On the other form of the species the central is stouter, darker, and definitely flattened. Due to the closeness of the areoles and the length of the spines, the general appearance is of a mass of whitish bristles, from which fact comes the common name, "hedgehog cactus." There are 8 to 12 radial spines, ¹/₄ to 1¹/₈ inches long, which all more or less stand out from the stem of the plant, the upper ones being the shorter ones. There are also 1 to 4 centrals: in the one variety, these are always round, very slender to medium in thickness, ³/₈ to 1³/₄ inches long, and standing out nearly perpendicular to the stem; in the other variety the main central is flattened, a little stouter, directed downward, and 1 to 3 inches long.

FLOWERS: Deep crimson to orange-red in color, around 1¹/₂ to 2 inches long and opening from 1 to 2 inches in diameter. The stamens are fuchsia and shorter than the petals. The stigma lobes are green and 6 to 12 in number. The tube surface has white wool and 8 to 11 slender white spines, ¹/₄ to ¹/₂ inch long, in each areole.

FRUITS: Red, juicy, with deciduous bristles.

RANGE. Growing in a wide territory from Colorado south past Raton, New Mexico, down along the upper Pecos River to about even with Santa Fe and Albuquerque, and from there west into Arizona and Utah.

REMARKS. The "bunch-ball cactus" was among the first collected in our area and is distinctive enough, with its slender, round spines and its manner of growing as a tight, perfectly regular ball of stems that it has not been so much confused with others of the group as some. However, it also has had too many names applied to it. Engelmann first called it *E. coccineus*, and then, later, because of a change of genus name, he called it *Cereus phoeniceus*. He also had once named a plant *Mammillaria aggregata*, which he did not describe in any detail. Coulter, assuming correctly that this was our cactus, called our plant *Cereus aggregatus*. Later authorities got back to the first definite name, *E. coccineus*, until, in an attempt to combine this cactus with others by reducing it to a variety, L. Benson found it necessary to rename it yet again as *E. triglochidiatus* var. *melanacanthus*, resurrecting for it an obscure varietal name once coined by Engelmann but ignored since as referring to no form really distinct from the species.

There has been much confusion of *E. triglochidiatus* var. *octacanthus* with *E. coccineus* because they both have round spines. Since the two do not grow at all in the same areas, the differences between them have been easily overlooked, but they are very different plants, with hundreds of miles and other forms separating their ranges, and when they are closely compared it is hardly possible to confuse them.

Echinocereus coccineus var. coccineus (Eng.)

DESCRIPTION   PLATE 12

STEMS: As the species, except that the ribs undulate by having definite and pronounced tubercles at the areoles.

AREOLES: As the species, except that they are to only ³/₈ of an inch apart.

SPINES: As the species, except that all spines are round, the centrals all slender, spreading, and to only ⁷/₈ of an inch long.

FLOWERS: As the species, except that the stigma lobes number only 6 to 8.

FRUITS: As the species.

RANGE. As the species.

REMARKS. This is the typical form of the species. It was apparently very common in northern New Mexico at one time, growing equally well under the trees on the lower mountains and in grassy valleys, forming huge mounds of dozens of stems. It has been a great favorite in that area because of the beauty of the large, symmetrical clumps it forms, its brilliant flowers, and its hardiness. For this reason many plants were dug up, and most of them were allowed to languish and die in boxes and planters. As a result it is now much easier to find it growing in gardens of the cities of that area than on the range, and one has to search long in remote spots to find an old specimen rounded up into a massive hemisphere. All one usually finds in any easily accessible place are young specimens of only a few heads, which give little clue to the magnificent things they could become if left unmolested.

Echinocereus coccineus var. conoideus Eng.
"Beehive Cactus"

DESCRIPTION   PLATE 13

STEMS: 3 to 6 inches high, 2 to 2¹/₂ inches in diameter, the tips being markedly smaller in diameter, this giving them a conical shape. When old, they form large, rounded mounds of 30 to 40 nearly equal stems, somewhat similar to but larger in individual stem size than those of the typical species form. There are 9 to 11 ribs on each stem, which are almost straight with at most very small swellings at the areoles and with rather deep furrows between them.

AREOLES: Large, woolly when young, later almost bare, ¹/₄ to ¹/₂ inch apart.

SPINES: There are 9 to 12 slender radial spines which are very uneven, the upper 2 or 3 being only ¹/₄ to ¹/₂ inch long, while the lateral and lower ones are larger, up to 1¹/₈ inches long. They are all round, with enlarged bases, and are white to straw-colored. There are 3 or 4 central spines. The upper ones are as the radials in shape and color and not much if any longer than the longest radials. The lower central, however, is directed downward, instead of standing perpendicular to the stem, and is usually somewhat curved. This lower central is a little stouter than the other spines, although still slender for the group, and different from the other spines on the areole in being definitely flattened, often to the point of being quadrangular. It is darker in color, often being yellowish with a brown base, or else ashy-gray. It is 1 to 3 inches long.

FLOWERS: These are a little larger than some in this group, being about the same length and color, but opening all of 2 inches in diameter, and there are 9 to 12 green stigma lobes.

FRUITS: As the species.

RANGE. From along the upper Pecos River in north central New Mexico north into southern Colorado and west into Arizona.

REMARKS. Variety conoideus is very close to variety coccineus, and there seems more justification for uniting these two, as Britton and Rose suggested but did not do, than any of the other forms listed here. Boissevain and Davidson stated that transitional forms existed between these two but kept them as separate species, a position which seems hard to maintain. However, the typical forms of the two are so different that it seems there must be some distinction made between them, so we are going back to Engelmann's first opinion and placing this plant once again as a variety of the other. Variety conoideus has the longer spines and less tuberculate ribs, with more widely separated areoles, and it is a larger, more robust plant in general. In particular, the long, flattened, and darker central spine serves to identify it quickly.

The plant was first named Cereus roemeri by Muehlenpfordt, but Engelmann did not seem certain about Muehlenpfordt's description; and besides he had in the meantime applied the name roemeri to the Texas cactus we know as E. triglochidiatus var. octacanthus, so he was obliged to rename this New Mexico cactus. He used the name Cereus phoeniceus var. conoideus, and later, when he decided to elevate it to species rank, Cereus conoideus. Muehlenpfordt's description seems very clear, however, and his name, being the oldest, is the one which should be used if the plant is treated as a species. The Texas plant cannot go under this name.

But since the plant we are considering seems much more accurately placed as a variety, by the rules of nomenclature it must carry the first varietal name applied to it. This is quite clearly Engelmann's variety conoideus.

Most of what was said about the growth habits of E. coccineus would apply to this cactus as well, except that it seems to grow in higher mountains and on more rocky locations. This one has also been gathered from the field too widely and is now hard to find growing wild.

Echinocereus polyacanthus var. rosei (Wooton & Standley)
"Red-Goblet Cactus," "Pitahaya"

DESCRIPTION   PLATE 13

STEMS: This is another cactus forming flat, loose clumps of unequal stems. The clumps may become large, with up to 50 stems, but this is rare and they are usually smaller, with only a dozen or fewer heads. Each stem is cylindrical, but somewhat tapering over almost the whole length toward the smaller, rather pointed tip. They grow to at least 10 inches long and 4 inches thick at the base, when in ideal situations, but remain much smaller in poor environments. The color is a lighter or paler green than some of its relatives. The number of ribs is variable, from 9 to 11, these broad with very shallow grooves between them on the older parts of the stems, but sharp with fairly prominent tubercles or swellings at the areoles and deep, narrow grooves between them at the tips.

AREOLES: This plant has probably the most conspicuous areoles of the group. When young they are about 1/4 of an inch across, circular, bulging outward, with much white or yellowish wool covering the bases of the new spines. As they get older they become more typical, nearly flat, and lose much of their wool. They are from 3/8 to 1 inch apart.

SPINES: The spines of this cactus are undoubtedly the most variable in size of any in the group. I have seen plants with large centrals over 2 inches long and other plants with no spines over 1/2 inch long. In spite of this variation, the spines are constant in being straight, of medium stoutness, and always round. There are 7 to 10 radials 3/8 to 1 inch long, radiating, the lower ones usually almost twice as long as the upper ones. There are 3 to 5 centrals on mature plants. Young seedlings always have only 1 central per areole, and in some mature specimens occasional areoles will have only the 1 central, but this is never typical of the whole mature plant. These centrals may be 1/2 to 2 inches long, depending upon the specimen, but they are always round, from somewhat enlarged bases, and spreading at various angles from the areole. All spines are reddish, ashy-gray, or occasionally dark, purplish-gray, with the centrals usually somewhat darker than the radials.

FLOWERS: Variable in color, including tints from pale red to orange, these often in the same flower. These shades are unique among the firm, long-lasting flowers of this group. Otherwise the flowers are typical of the group, 1 1/2 to 2 1/2 inches long, with short, rigid petals broadening and blunt at the ends. They have fuchsia stamens and the stigma lobes number 7 to 10. On the ovary are brownish or yellowish spines, 1/8 to 5/8 of an inch long, with reddish tips, plus some short wool.

FRUITS: 3/4 to 1 inch long, greenish-purple when ripe, with deciduous spines.

RANGE. From Mexico northward over west Texas and much of New Mexico, into southern Colorado and southeastern Arizona. The northeastern limit of the known range is near San Antonio, Texas, and so far as is known the northern edge of the range runs past Rocksprings, Texas, to the Davis Mountains and then turns sharply north through the Guadalupe Mountains into New Mexico, where it follows the Pecos River, goes past Las Vegas, New Mexico, and along the eastern edge of the mountains into Colorado. The range seems to come back south out of Colorado east of the Continental Divide, and does not cross this demarcation until near Lordsburg, New Mexico, where it moves into southeast Arizona.

REMARKS: *E. polyacanthus* var. *rosei* is the most common red-flowered Echinocereus throughout southern New Mexico and far southwest Texas. It is easily found on the lower slopes of the Franklin and Organ mountains and in similar places west into Arizona. It is less common but may be found occasionally in the mountains of central New Mexico and north into Colorado. It is even less common, but has also been collected in the Texas Big Bend and the Davis and Guadalupe mountains. Its eastern limit is hard to establish, as occasional specimens which must be referred to this species have turned up in widely separated places over a very large area. I have a living specimen with very short spines but otherwise typical from near Rocksprings, Texas, and there is in the U.S. National Herbarium a specimen labeled as collected by Toumey at San Antonio in 1897, but I cannot find it growing in the area now.

Because of the variability of its spines and its very wide range this cactus has been widely confused with others of its relatives. In northern New Mexico and Colorado it is sometimes mistaken for *E. coccineus*, from which it can be distinguished by the facts that it never grows in the compact, dome-shaped clusters nor has such slender spines as that plant, or for *E. coccineus* var. *conoideus*, from which it can be told by the fact that its spines are never flattened as is the lower central of that plant. In Texas its immature growth and certain stunted, atypical specimens have been called *E. triglochidiatus* var. *octacanthus*, in spite of the fact that Engelmann in his early description was so thorough that he mentioned that the immature plants have only 1 central per areole. The atypical forms can be distinguished by the fact that they have more ribs than variety *octacanthus*.

Engelmann did leave room for confusion to enter by giving two slightly varying descriptions for the plant he named *E. polyacanthus*. His original description was of plants collected in Chihuahua, Mexico, by Wislizenus. This was a narrow description of a very localized cactus found only there. It is unique for the whole group of scarlet-flowered Echinocerei in having long wool on the flower tube. In his later writings Engelmann used the same name, but broadened the description somewhat, as well as the range. In the later descriptions he said the cactus was a common plant at El Paso, and did not mention the long wool on the flower. Since no specimens have ever been collected at El Paso or anywhere in the U.S. with this long wool, its seems clear that, after further study, Engelmann meant to include all of this form, whether having long or short wool, under this name. Coulter took it this way, and so included in the range of the species New Mexico and Arizona.

Wooton and Standley returned to restricting *E. polyacanthus* to the local Chihuahuan form, and set up the New Mexico representatives having only short wool as two new species, *E. rosei* and *E. neo-mexicanus*.

Britton and Rose faced the problem of relating these forms. Dr. Rose made the famous trip to the type locality of *E. polyacanthus* at Cosihuiriachi, Chihuahua, and collected specimens there, establishing to their satisfaction that the original type specimens were actually different from our forms, at least in having the long wool on the flower tube. They, therefore, followed Wooton and Standley in their names, *E. rosei* and *E. neo-mexicanus*, for the two U.S. forms which lack this unique character. Since then no one has used the name *E. polyacanthus* for any U.S. cactus except Benson, who ignores the distinction and calls the plants of New Mexico and Arizona *E. triglochidiatus* var. *polyacanthus*.

Helia Bravo, in her book, *Las Cactaceas de Mexico*, has a good illustration of the true *E. polyacanthus*.

It seems necessary to follow most recent students in separating the U.S. forms in some way from the unique Chihuahuan cactus, which must carry the name *E. polyacanthus*. But it seems equally true that the U.S. forms are very close to it, close enough so that Engelmann had justification in lumping them all together. The best way to show the whole picture appears to be by regarding the U.S. forms as varieties of the species. Our common cactus of such wide range in the U.S. then becomes *E. polyacanthus* var. *rosei*.

Echinocereus polyacanthus var. **neo-mexicanus** (Standley)

DESCRIPTION   PLATE 13

STEMS: As those of variety *rosei*, except to only about 3 inches thick and having 11 to 15 ribs.

AREOLES: As those of variety *rosei*, but closer, being ³/₈ to ⁵/₈ of an inch apart.

SPINES: Radial spines variable in number from 8 to 16, but usually 10 to 13. These are slender; straight; round; white, straw, or yellow; and to ⁵/₈ of an inch long. The spreading centrals number 4 to 6 on mature plants, and are straight, round, slender, and usually ³/₄ to 1¹/₄ inches long. In color they are yellowish below with the outer parts or the tips reddish or blackish.

FLOWERS: As those of variety *rosei*, except usually smaller and of burnt-orange to yellow coloring. The petals are not as wide as those of the other variety and are, as Wooton put it, "*almost* acute," if one emphasizes the *almost*.

FRUITS: As those of variety *rosei*.

RANGE. Fairly common around Las Cruces, New Mexico, and found occasionally at least to Socorro, in central New Mexico.

REMARKS. This plant is very close to the previous variety, but is easily recognized by the more numerous ribs and the more numerous, lighter colored, and more slender spines. Where variety *rosei* presents a gray or purplish-gray appearance, the spine covering of variety *neo-mexicanus* is always yellowish, and sometimes strikingly so. It does not appear to be a separate species, but it does definitely appear to stand in some way distinct from the other more widespread form. Collections made around Las Cruces are easily divisible into the two types.

This is a beautiful cactus, usually large and impressive in growth, with the long-lasting flowers which make it a favorite. Near El Paso and Las Cruces, in the few areas which have been too remote for the casual collector or which have been in some way protected, there are still to be seen whole slopes dotted with the clumps of tall heads covered in April and May with beautiful goblet-shaped flowers, and here and there within the cities transplanted clumps are to be seen gracing yards and gardens most beautifully. Variety *neo-mexicanus* is cold-resistant and would be a good garden cactus in other colder areas, except that it is definitely a desert form and so must be protected from moisture more carefully than some of the other species of this group.

It is worth mentioning, for the sake of any hobbyist who might be growing the plant inside to protect it from the winter dampness of their areas, that this cactus, like many other winter-hardy forms, must have some cold during the winter in order to trigger the blooms. In south Texas I have seen plants which had grown for several years without a suggestion of a flower bloom profusely for the first time after the stimulus of one of those freezes which are so destructive to southern cacti.

Echinocereus enneacanthus Eng.
"Strawberry Cactus," "Pitaya"

DESCRIPTION   PLATE 14

STEMS: 3 to 30 inches long and 1¹/₂ to 4 inches thick, and cylindrical, tapering somewhat over the last one-third of the length to a rather pointed tip. These stems grow in loose clusters of a few to as many as 100 in a large plant. New stems multiply as side branches at or just above the ground level, so their first growth tends to be lateral, after which they turn upward. This results in all of the stems around the edges of a large clump being long and curving, the lower part often lying flat on the ground and the upper part standing erect. In color they are bright green, and the flesh of the plant is soft, even flabby, giving them a more or less wrinkled appearance and causing them to appear actually withered in very dry periods or in the winter. There are 7 to 10 ribs on each stem, which are low and broad with shallow grooves between them and with slight to rather pronounced tubercles or swellings at the areoles.

AREOLES: Circular, about $1/8$ of an inch in diameter, with much gray wool on them when young, some of which remains on the older areoles. These are placed $1/4$ to $1^1/2$ inches apart on mature stems.

SPINES: All spines on this plant are rigid and slender to fairly stout, rise from enlarged bases, and are light-colored, being white to straw-colored or very light brown. All spines are distinctly translucent, having a horny appearance with age. When very young and while still growing, the spines are a delicate pink color which fades quickly as they mature. There are 7 to 12 white radial spines radiating evenly, straight or slightly curved back toward the stem, but varying greatly in length and thickness. The upper ones tend to be shortest, only $1/4$ to $5/8$ of an inch long, while the lateral and lower ones are usually longer—$1/2$ to as much as 1 inch long. There is one stout central spine standing perpendicular to the surface of the stem or slightly deflexed. It has a very bulbous base and is round and white when young, but becomes darker, especially toward the base, and more or less flattened when old. On immature tips this central is very little longer than the radial spines, but with age it usually continues to grow, becoming heavier and longer, up to $1^1/4$ or even 2 inches long. Many plants are found with 2 extra central spines above this main one, these spreading upward and remaining shorter.

FLOWERS: Large and beautiful, opening widely, 2 to 3 inches in height and about the same in diameter, purple-red in color. There are 10 to 20 short outer petals with brownish-green centers and pinkish, crinkled edges. The inner petals are in 1 to 3 rows, 12 to 35 in number and oblong, linear, or spatulate in shape. The edges of these petals are entire or toothed, and the tips pointed or blunt. The stamens are much shorter than the petals, the filaments greenish, and the anthers yellow. The style is white, the stigma lobes green, long and slender, 8 to 12 in number. The tube of the flower has white wool and white bristle-like spines up to $1/2$ inch long upon it.

FRUITS: About 1 inch long, almost spherical, greenish to brownish or purplish, with bristle-like spines which fall off easily. The flesh of the fruit is edible and very delicious.

RANGE. Along the Rio Grande from near that river's mouth to the Big Bend. It has seldom been found west of the Pecos River or more than 50 miles north of the Rio Grande in any area. However, there have been isolated reports of it from near San Angelo, Kerrville, San Antonio, and Raymondville, Texas, which would mark the northern and eastern extremes of its range. Coulter says it occurs west of Texas into Arizona, but I have found no record of it ever having been collected in New Mexico.

REMARKS. This is the common Echinocereus of a wide area of the lower Rio Grande Valley. It is found occasionally farther west, but only becomes common near Del Rio. It is very common from the Devil's River to Eagle Pass, large clumps of it dotting the gravelly ground on the low hills just north of the Rio Grande wherever these hills have not been cleared. It is so common as to be a pest at Laredo and for about 50 miles north and east of there, with clumps under almost every bush on whatever of the range is well-drained and has not yet been cleared. The practice of "rooting" or "chaining" the range with large machinery in order to clear out the brush seems to do away with this, as well as with most other small cacti, although it merely does a favor to the large Opuntias of the region, whose pads are scattered by the machines and immediately take root as new plants. The result is that you now have to hunt for unspoiled range where the pitayas still are allowed to grow and the giant Opuntias have not taken over. Below Laredo this cactus is found commonly to near Rio Grande City, but below there it is found only rarely.

E. enneacanthus was noticed and collected on the very early survey of the Rio Grande area by Wislizenus, and named by Engelmann in 1848. It is a distinct form which has seldom been confused with any other. However, there seem to be more or less distinct varieties within its population, which are listed below.

When its clusters are covered with dozens of its large, lively colored flowers (usually during April), the species is a beautiful cactus, appreciated by almost everyone. It is most appreciated by those who take its common name of strawberry cactus literally, for the greenish-brown fruits have a flavor very similar to strawberries. Where it grows profusely the fruits are actually gathered, the spines brushed off, and the flesh eaten with cream and sugar.

This cactus is fairly hardy, being able to stand a temperature considerably below freezing, but it cannot stand excess moisture. If it is in some way protected from winter rains and allowed to wither in dryness during the winter, it can live quite far north of its natural range. Then, when moisture is given to it again in the spring, the reward will be quick appearance of many large flowers.

Echinocereus enneacanthus var. enneacanthus (Eng.)

DESCRIPTION — PLATE 14

STEMS: As the species, except that they grow to only about 12 inches long, $2^3/4$ inches thick, and are much less flabby, with only slight tubercles at the areoles.

AREOLES: As the species, except that they are to only 1 inch apart.

SPINES: As the species.

FLOWERS: As the species, except with only 10 to 15 outer petals and only 12 to 15 inner petals in one row. These petals are oblong or linear in shape, with edges entire and tips pointed. There are only 8 to 10 stigma lobes.

FRUITS: As the species.

RANGE. As the species.

REMARKS. This is the typical variety of the species which is common over all of its range. Its smaller stems to only 12 inches long are prostrate for only the first part of their length, and the plant tends to form rather tidy, firm clumps.

Echinocereus enneacanthus var. carnosus (Rumpl.) K. Schumann

DESCRIPTION   PLATE 14

STEMS: Becoming at least 16 and sometimes as much as 30 inches long by 3 to 4 inches in diameter. These very flabby stems grow out laterally from the cluster and when large lie fully prostrate on the ground, only the very tips turning upward. There are 8 or 9 broad ribs on each stem, with rather pronounced tubercles.

AREOLES: 3/4 to 1 1/2 inches apart.

SPINES: There are 8 or 9 radials, the uppers only 3/8 of an inch long (often missing entirely), and the laterals 1/2 to 3/4 of an inch long. There is usually only 1 porrect central 1/2 to 2 inches long, but rarely there may be 2 short upper centrals besides. The centrals are round when immature and flattened when old.

FLOWERS: Very large and full. There are 13 to 20 short, greenish outer petals and 20 to 35 inner petals in 3 rows. These inner petals are spatulate, the edges crinkled and toothed, with the tips not pointed. The narrow bases are greenish, the broader upper parts fuchsia or reddish-purple. The style is white and short. There are 10 to 12 green, linear stigma lobes.

FRUITS: As the species.

RANGE. Occurring only about Laredo and Eagle Pass, Texas.

REMARKS. There is no experimental evidence to show the relationship of this form to the typical variety enneacanthus. Its range is entirely within that of the species, and there is no way at present to know how much of its distinctness is due to environment. It does exist as a recognizable form, however, and in its fullest development a very remarkable one. I have seen large plants fully five feet in diameter, their outer stems spreading over the ground like giant starfish arms. The sight of such green snake-like forms nearly a yard long running out from under a mesquite tree is unforgettable. The large, extremely full flowers of this form are as remarkable as the stems. With their several rows of petals they are truly the roses of the cacti.

Small specimens of variety carnosus may be distinguished from the typical form by the excessive flabbiness of the stems, the more distant areoles and, of course, the surpassing flowers.

This form has apparently been known by the name E. enneacanthus var. major Hort.

Echinocereus stramineus (Eng.) Rumpl.
"Strawberry Cactus," "Organo," "Pitaya"

DESCRIPTION   PLATE 14

STEMS: Up to at least 10 inches tall and 3 1/2 inches thick, tapering gradually over most of their lengths to a rather pointed apex. They have 11 to 13 ribs, which are rather sharp, with fairly deep furrows between them and with slight tubercles or enlargements at the areoles. These stems cluster very freely by multiplying from the base, thus forming large, compact clumps of up to 100 or more equal stems. Such a large plant has the form of a hemisphere, often 2 or 3 feet across and nearly as high.

AREOLES: On this cactus they are small, round, white, with much wool when young, and 3/8 to 3/4 of an inch apart.

SPINES: All white to straw-colored and translucent, slender to medium in thickness from thickened or bulbous bases, covering the plant profusely. When very young at the tip of the stem, the spines are a very delicate pink in color, this becoming straw-colored for a while and then fading quickly to whitish. The radials vary in number from 7 to 14, and in size from 3/8 to 1 1/2 inches long, these extremes in size often being found on the same areole with the lower being the longer ones. They are all round and either straight or curved. The centrals vary from 2 to 5 in number and are to 3 1/2 inches long, slender for their length, and round or slightly flattened. They are usually a little darker than the radials, and may be straight or curved. Usually the lower central is perpendicular to the stem surface, while the others spread upward at various angles and interlock with those of other areoles.

FLOWERS: The flowers of this cactus are very large and beautiful, and are produced in large numbers. They are 4 to 5 inches tall by 3 to 4 inches in diameter, and purple-red in color. There are 10 to 15 pointed outer petals with green centers and pink edges. There are 15 to 20 inner petals which are longer than the outer ones, with narrow bases and broadening to 1/2 inch wide or more toward the tips. These bases are a bright red which blends gradually to a bright rose toward the tips. The edges of these inner petals are ragged and toothed, and the blunt ends are sometimes notched. The filaments are short and red. The anthers are yellow. The style is long and red, and on top of it there are 10 to 13 long, green stigma lobes. The tube of the flower is very long, with many white, bristle-like spines upon it.

FRUITS: These are spherical, 1¹/₂ to 2 inches long, purplish to red when ripe, with deciduous bristle-like spines. They are edible.

RANGE. From El Paso almost to the lower Pecos River in Texas, and extending deep into Mexico. It is said to have been collected in southern New Mexico, but I have not been able to verify this.

REMARKS. *E. stramineus* is one of the most beautiful Echinocerei. Its domelike, compact manner of growth is shared by no other cactus within its range, and only by the more western and northern *E. coccineus*. It grows commonly only on the upper slopes of the sandy hills east of El Paso and on the limestone ridges in and around the Big Bend National Park. In these places its large clumps show up from a distance as glistening, whitish, or golden balls on the almost bare crowns of these hills. When it blooms in the spring its flowers form brilliant diadems of color for these otherwise drab rises. Its flowers are among the largest and most numerous of any Echinocereus. I have counted 40 of these brilliant purple blossoms on one clump at one time. Its fruits are also delicious, with a taste similar to and said by some even to surpass that of strawberries.

I have not seen this cactus from anywhere west of the Franklin Mountains near El Paso, and there are no recent reports of its collection west of there, although there are old reports of it from southern New Mexico and even Arizona. It occurs only occasionally east of the Hueco Mountains of Texas, in an area south of Marfa, Alpine, and Marathon, Texas, extending into the Big Bend National Park, where it is once again almost as common as farther west. Near Langtry, Texas, seems to be its eastern limit. It grows widely in Mexico, and is considered by some to be the same as *E. conglomeratus* (Forster) Maths. of Mexico.

This species must have the very dry, rocky conditions of its hillsides. For this reason it seldom survives when transplanted to gardens unless extra care is taken to give it sandy soil and to shield it from moisture.

Echinocereus dubius (Eng.) Rumpl.
"Strawberry Cactus," "Pitaya"

DESCRIPTION   PLATE 15

STEMS: Cylindrical, tapering at the upper end to a somewhat pointed tip. They are up to at least 15 inches long and 3 inches thick, light green in color and very soft and flabby. They have 7 to 10 broad, rounded ribs with shallow furrows between them and very slight enlargements at the areoles.

These stems branch and cluster very slowly to form loose, irregular clumps which I have never seen with more than 8 heads. The stems branch at all angles from about the ground level, and the heavy, flabby stems seem too soft to stand upright, so the clump is usually partly sprawling or semiprostrate—never rounded, compact, and regular as is that of *E. stramineus*.

AREOLES: These are circular, about ¹/₄ of an inch in diameter and 1 to 1¹/₂ inches apart, having much white wool when young, but losing all of it with age.

SPINES: All of the spines are white to light brown and somewhat translucent when young, becoming opaque when old. They grow from enlarged bases. The radial spines are 5 to 9 in number, often very irregular in size, being almost bristle-like to medium in thickness, ¹/₂ to 1¹/₂ inches long, the upper ones shorter than the lower ones and these upper ones sometimes pushed aside or eliminated entirely by the large bases of the centrals. There are 1 to 5 very conspicuous central spines curving or spreading in all directions from mature areoles. They are very large, 1¹/₂ to 3 inches long and from ¹/₁₆ to ¹/₈ of an inch in thickness. They are also markedly flattened and sometimes ridged. It should be mentioned that the development of these centrals is very slow, so that young areoles often have only 1 or 2 shorter, round centrals, which makes them look almost exactly like typical *E. enneacanthus* spines. And when the plant is growing in conditions not entirely favorable to it these spines do not achieve their full development; thus large stems will sometimes have entirely juvenile spines. I have collected such plants, especially near the Devil's River, which I would have taken for the other species except for the more robust, lighter green, and more flabby stems, and only after two full years in better growing conditions have these plants gone ahead to produce the typical large growth of central spines.

FLOWERS: Magenta in color. Otherwise similar to those of *E. stramineus*, but not nearly so beautiful because they are much smaller in size, and because they fail to open widely and are produced in comparatively sparse numbers, each clump having only a few blossoms each year. They are only 2 to 3 inches long and about 2 inches across. There are about 10 outer petals, green in the centers with pinkish edges. There are about 10 inner petals with entire edges, narrow bases which broaden considerably and then end in a broad tip with a prolonged point at the apex. The bases are greenish with an orange area above that shading into magenta on the broader ends of the petals. The filaments are brownish and the anthers yellow. The style is long and white, while the stigma lobes are 8 to 10 in number, and green. The ovary tube has white spines ¹/₄ to ³/₄ of an inch long, and has almost no wool upon it.

FRUITS: Globular, 1 to 1¹/₂ inches long, with many deciduous spines. It is said to be as edible as that of *E. stramineus*.

RANGE. Near the Rio Grande from near El Paso to the mouth of the Devil's River, and extending into Mexico.

REMARKS. *E. dubius* is very closely related to *E. stramineus*, which grows in similar situations, but usually at higher elevations. *E. dubius* can hardly be mistaken for the other cactus, however, since it has fewer branches and ribs and poorer floral development, and it never grows in the huge, dome-shaped masses characteristic of *E. stramineus*. No authority seems to have suggested any combination of the two. *E. stramineus* is much more popular with collectors because only in the size of its spines does *E. dubius* excel; and yet, because it has more ribs and closer areoles, *E. stramineus* appears enclosed in its spines, while the stems of *E. dubius* are not obscured by its heavier, larger ones. Only on the hills just north of the Big Bend National Park have I seen these two species growing together; here the young plants are sometimes hard to distinguish, but the large, mature ones are easily told apart.

E. dubius also is close to *E. enneacanthus* var. *carnosus*, in its stem structure, but it does not ever become so huge as that other form, and the flower developments of the two are the opposite extremes of the group.

This cactus usually grows wherever the rocky hills spread out their lower slopes toward the Rio Grande. Its favorite place is the edge of the sandy river valley at the base of the hills. Just west of Sierra Blanca, Texas, where the highway starts to climb out of the sandy valley into the Sierra Blanca range it is very abundant. Along the Rio Grande below Presidio it is also common to beyond the Big Bend National Park. The specimens east of Presidio have longer, straighter, more stout and ridged central spines than those farther west, until one gets beyond the Park. East of the Big Bend Park it is very rarely seen, and the atypical specimens I found on the lower Devil's River must represent its eastern limit, as well as its weakest spine development.

Borg, in his book, *Cacti*, apparently is in error when he says that it is found in the sandy wastes of southeastern Texas, since there is no record of it anywhere except in the far southwestern part of the state.

Echinocereus fendleri (Eng.) Rumpl.
"Fendler's Pitaya," "Fendler's Hedgehog Cactus," "Purple Hedgehog," "Strawberry Cactus," "Torch Cactus," "Sitting Cactus," "Pink-Flowered Echinocereus"

DESCRIPTION   PLATE 15
STEMS: This cactus grows as a small, loose clump of upright stems which may take various shapes, from short and almost oval to longer and cylindrical, usually tapering and therefore often somewhat conical. These stems are not usually over 12 inches tall, but may reach a maximum of 18 inches tall and about 4 inches thick in one variety. The surface is dark green and soft, often being wrinkled in appearance. There are 8 to 16 ribs, which are broad, somewhat wrinkled, and have rather conspicuous swellings around the areoles.

AREOLES: Circular, not large, with some white wool when young, but later becoming bare. Up to only 1/2 inch apart on mature growth.

SPINES: Rather stout from bulbous bases. This is the only purple-flowered Echinocereus I know within our area which has spines that can be called truly variegated in color. At least some of the spines on each plant have brown and white or black and white coloring in streaks along them. There are 5 to 12 radial spines which are round or sometimes slightly angled and variegated brown and ashy-gray with white streaks. The lower ones are the stoutest and are 1/2 to 1 inch long; the upper lateral ones are bristle-like, usually white and only 1/4 to 1/2 inch long. The radial is missing entirely from the top of the areole. There is usually one central spine which is longer, more stout, round or only very slightly flattened. This spine is from 3/4 to 3 inches long, dark brown or black fading to gray when old, except in one variety where it reaches only 5/16 of an inch long. Some varieties of the species sometimes present 2 additional centrals.

FLOWERS: Large, to at least 3 inches in height and diameter, and a beautiful violet-purple. There are broad, greenish outer petals with violet edges. The inner petals are long, somewhat variable in shape, and violet-purple. The bases of these are narrow and dark purple-red, the petal broadening from this to a blunt or pointed tip. The filaments are green and the anthers light yellow. The style is whitish and only a little longer than the stamens. The stigma has 9 to 16 dark green lobes. The tube of the ovary has some white wool and many spines which are white or white with brown tips and measure to at least 3/8 of an inch long.

FRUITS: Almost spherical, 1 to 1 1/2 inches long, purplish, covered with spines which fall easily from it. It is fleshy and edible.

RANGE. Extreme southwestern Texas, all of western New Mexico and into Arizona, Colorado, and Mexico. Its eastern range apparently stops at a line from near the upper Pecos River in New Mexico to just east of El Paso, to near Presidio, Texas. Within Texas it has been collected only in the Franklin Mountains just within the border of that state and in extreme western Presidio County.

REMARKS. *E. fendleri* is one of the most beautiful Echinocerei. Its flowers are large and of very delicate rose shades which are not matched by any of its relatives within our area. The colors of its spines are also unique for us, being truly variegated. The brown and whitish shadings in them I have not seen elsewhere except in some specimens of the more western *E. engelmannii*. The clumps formed by *E. fendleri* within our territory are not large, and they do not flower as profusely as some, but it is a very worth-while cactus.

Engelmann, in first describing and naming the cactus a hundred years ago, described a form of it with only 5 to 7 radial spines and no centrals, calling it variety *pauperculus*, but said also that on every specimen he had seen of this form some areoles had normal spines, so he suspected it was only an atypical growth. I have seen specimens from both New Mexico and Texas with this atypical spination, but each was a stunted or injured plant which could well have suffered some impairment to the spine growth, and each which I was able to grow under good conditions later put on typical spines. So I feel that this cannot stand as a distinct variety, and I therefore include this in the description of the species.

E. fendleri must be considered as one of the more western Echinocerei, only dwelling a comparatively short distance into our territory. It reaches a great development in Arizona where there are at least four varieties besides the typical one. Our New Mexico plants, however, are mostly the typical form, as would be expected, since its type locality is near Santa Fe, New Mexico. Only in extreme southwestern New Mexico do we find one of these other varieties.

Echinocereus fendleri var. fendleri (Eng.)

DESCRIPTION   PLATE 15

STEMS: As the species, except that the stems are usually around 6 inches tall and reach a maximum of 12 inches, with only 9 to 12 ribs.

AREOLES: As the species.

SPINES: As the species, except that the radials number only 5 to 10, and the single central is 1 to 2 inches long and usually curving upward.

FLOWERS: As the species.

FRUITS: As the species.

RANGE. As the species.

Echinocereus fendleri var. rectispinus (Peebles) L. Benson

DESCRIPTION   PLATE 15

STEMS: Forming small clumps of up to 6 or 8 comparatively firm, columnar stems, up to about 8 inches tall. There are 8 to 11 ribs on these stems, which are narrower than on the typical form and not tuberculate.

AREOLES. Similar to the species.

SPINES: There are 10 to 12 radials very similar to the typical except that they are usually lighter in color. There is 1 main central spine which is often accompanied by 1 or 2 upper accessory centrals. The main one is stout and porrect and straight instead of curving upward. It is $1/2$ to $1^1/4$ inches long. The accessory centrals are only $1/4$ to $3/4$ of an inch long.

FLOWERS: Similar to those of the species, with stigmas numbering 10 to 13.

FRUITS: As the species.

RANGE. Extreme southwestern New Mexico and extreme southeastern Arizona. In New Mexico reported, so far, only from western Hidalgo County.

Echinocereus papillosus A. Linke
"Yellow-Flowered Echinocereus," "Yellow-Flowered Alicoche"

DESCRIPTION   PLATE 16

STEMS: This plant consists of 2 or 3 to sometimes, in one variety, dozens of clustering and branching stems forming a very loose clump. The stems are slender, soft, and weak, apparently unable to entirely support their own weight, and so they lean and sprawl at awkward angles, although seldom being actually prostrate. Each stem is deep green in color, up to 10 inches long, and 1 to $2^3/4$ inches thick. There are 7 to 9 ribs which are extremely tuberculate, formed of series of conical enlargements about $3/8$ of an inch high, with the areoles on the tips of them, these enlargements being separated by deep valleys which almost completely interrupt the ribs.

AREOLES: Small, bare, $3/8$ to $1/2$ inch apart, crowning the tubercles.

SPINES: Slender but rigid, straight, and round, from bulbous bases, white to brownish or yellowish in color. There are 7 to 11 radial spines radiating evenly. They are whitish to yellow-brown, usually with brownish bases. The lower and lateral ones are longest and heaviest, being up to $1/2$ inch long. The upper 2 or 3 are very much shorter and very slender, almost bristle-like. There is 1 central spine about $3/4$ of an inch long, not much more stout than the radials, but having a very bulbous base and standing perpendicular to the stem surface. It is brownish to sometimes bright yellow, often with a dark brown base, a yellow zone in the middle, and a brown tip.

FLOWERS: Large, beautiful, and delicately fragrant, $2^1/2$ to 4 inches in diameter and height. The outer petals are oblong, reddish in their centers to yellowish at the edges—which are ragged. The inner petals lie in 2 to 4 rows, and are long, rising from narrow, bright orange-red bases, giving the center of the flower a striking red color. The upper part of the inner petal is much wider, with ragged edges and a tip either somewhat pointed or blunt. This upper part of the petal is yellow, shading to almost white at the edges. The midline of each petal on the dorsal side has some unique feathery ridges and furrows extending almost to the tip. The filaments are reddish, the anthers light yellow. The style is white, and the stigma lobes are green, 10 to 13 in number, long, and broad, with a furrow running the length of the underside of each. The ovary surface has reddish scales and white spines up to about 1/4 of an inch long.

FRUITS: Greenish, covered with short bristles.

RANGE. A comparatively small part of south Texas bounded by a line from about 20 miles east of Laredo northeast into McMullen County, then southeast to near Alice, and from there south to within a few miles of Edinburg and back to Laredo.

REMARKS. In south Texas is found a cactus unique among the Echinocerei of the U.S. in having large, fragrant, yellow flowers with red centers. The plant itself is insignificant and not particularly attractive in its growth, but it is highly prized for its beautiful flowers. It would undoubtedly be a favorite with cactus collectors except for two facts.

First, it grows in a comparatively small area of south Texas, and this not right along the Rio Grande where most collecting has been done. The center of its range is Duval, Jim Hogg, and upper Starr counties. From there it extends not quite to the Rio Grande Valley at any point on the west and south, and not quite to the coastal plain on the east. This interior country where it grows is dense brush country through which few people travel and in which fewer care to collect. This area presents some of the most difficult brush to move around in that I have encountered anywhere. And even here the cactus is an inconspicuous plant usually well-hidden under the chaparral or the tall Opuntias of the area. So it is seldom found except by the hardy.

The second reason for its being so little known is that the plant is one of the most difficult to grow out of its natural habitat. It is found only on the light, sandy, limestone loam of the area. It cannot tolerate the darker soils of the Rio Grande Valley, or even of the bluffs overlooking the valley. Its range starts where this light sandy loam starts, a few miles to 50 miles from the river, and at the same time it is unable to grow in the soils of the coastal plain on the east. I have the word of an experienced cactus dealer and grower in Laredo that it will not grow unprotected in that city only 20 miles from its natural range, and also that of a long-time grower of cacti in San Antonio that it will not live out-of-doors in that city less than a hundred miles above its range. I know of a grower much farther west who grows it with some success, but it is in desert soil and in real desert conditions. If conditions such as this are not painstakingly provided, the very soft flesh of the plant will rot almost overnight. I find it necessary, myself, to give it the most careful treatment to keep it alive and flowering, but the reward for this sort of care is great when one succeeds in getting a healthy plant to produce its huge yellow and red flowers.

Long ago Hildmann described a variety of *E. papillosus* which he said has spines pink to red, passing to brownish. He called it variety *rubescens*. I have not found this variety, or seen anyone who knows it. Cactophiles might keep it in mind and try to discover whether it is truly a distinct variety.

Echinocereus papillosus var. papillosus (A. Linke)

DESCRIPTION   PLATES 16, 17
    STEMS: As the species, except each plant a clump of only up to 10 or 12 stems.

    AREOLES: As the species.

    SPINES: As the species.

    FLOWERS: As the species.

    FRUITS: As the species.

RANGE. As the species.

REMARKS. This is the typical form of the plant, and it is discussed above. Only in one small area will the dwarf form, described next, be encountered.

Echinocereus papillosus var. angusticeps (Glover) Marshall "The Small Papillosus"

DESCRIPTION   PLATE 16
    STEMS: As the species except that it is markedly smaller, attaining the size of only 3 to 4 inches tall and 1 to 1 1/4 inches in diameter, but occurring in dense clusters of many stems. While 1 to 3 or 4 dozen stems to the plant is common, Miss Glover tells of one specimen containing 95 of these small stems. The stems are sprawling to upright.

    AREOLES: As the species.

    SPINES: As the species, except that they are shorter, the central spine reaching only 3/8 of an inch long.

    FLOWERS: As the species except that they are usually slightly smaller and have a larger number of petals. The petals are usually more blunt at the tips. The yellow coloring is more greenish and the red paler.

    FRUITS: As the species.

RANGE. Northern Hidalgo County, Texas.

REMARKS. While this cactus does not seem to be a separate species, it is definitely recognizable as a separate variety. It is a very interesting, dwarf-like form, found in only the portion of Hidalgo County above Edinburg, Texas, where it grows under mesquite and brush thickets.

Echinocereus pentalophus (DC) Rumpl.
"Alicoche," "Lady-Finger Cactus"

DESCRIPTION   PLATE 16

STEMS: Light green and rather flabby, up to 12 inches long, but usually only 4 to 6 inches, slender, from 1/2 to 1 1/4 inches in diameter. The ribs number 4 or 5 on old stems, and are low, with very shallow furrows between them so that the stem in cross-section is almost a perfect square or pentagon. There are very low tubercles at the areoles. Young growing tips have much more pronounced tubercles and much more distinct furrows between the ribs, and in some specimens the stem does not flatten out much until very old. These slender stems branch and bud off new stems at any point and at any angle, forming an unorganized mass, most of which is prostrate on the ground. Young branches often are upright for a while, but soon bend over unless supported by something. These prostrate branches root at the areoles touching the ground and the whole mass thus grows rapidly, a very old plant becoming 10 or even 15 feet in diameter.

AREOLES: Very small, less than 1/16 of an inch in diameter, with yellowish wool when young, then bare. They are spaced 3/8 to 3/4 of an inch apart.

SPINES: Very short and slender, but rigid, from bulbous bases. There are 3 to 6 radials which are 1/16 to 1/2 inch long, rose-colored when growing, then lightening to brownish with dark tips and finally becoming gray with dark tips when old. There is often no central, but one may be present, which is somewhat stouter than the radials, darker in color, and from 3/8 to 1/2 inch long. This central points upward if present, and sometimes the upper radial assumes this direction without moving from its position.

FLOWERS: 3 to at least 4 inches in diameter as they open widely. The outer petals have greenish midlines and pink edges. The inner petals are about 18 in number and long, their bases rather narrow and the upper part broadening to a maximum of 3/4 of an inch wide toward their tips. The edges are entire, the end of the petal blunt and often somewhat notched, but still having a small point at the apex of the midline. The basal third to one-half of each petal is white shading to yellowish, while the upper part is a light cerise. This results in a beautiful flower, cerise-pink with a large whitish center. The filaments are greenish, the anthers yellow. The style is composed of 10 to 16 linear, olive-green lobes with a yellow furrow on the ventral side of each. The ovary wall has much long white wool and many brown, bristle-like spines, giving it a woolly covering.

FRUITS: Egg-shaped, green, 1/2 to 3/4 of an inch long, covered with white wool and brown spines.

RANGE. Northeastern Mexico, extending across the Rio Grande into its lower valley up as far as Rio Grande City. It nowhere occurs over 15 or 20 miles north of the river.

REMARKS. The most common Echinocerei of deep south Texas and the lower Rio Grande Valley on both sides of the river are several forms of prostrate cacti. These all have very slender stems, usually 1 inch or less in diameter. They branch very profusely, forming masses of these stems, most of which lie entirely or partly on the ground, rooting where they touch the ground, and spreading the plant outward in this way. In some of them there are upright stems or tips of stems when young, but in all at least the old stems are prostrate. They are all known locally as the alicoches.

In spite of the lowly forms of their growth, these are interesting cacti, and are justly famous for the beauty of their large pinkish flowers. These flowers, often 4 inches or more in diameter, are particularly startling when numbers of them appear upon a prostrate mass of these slender stems.

The number of forms in this group is not large, but they were among the very early cacti described, and the differences between them not being strikingly obvious, there has been a history of confusion over them.

E. pentalophus was described very early, in 1826, by De Candolle. At that time he also described three varieties of it, variety *simplex*, variety *subarticulatus*, and variety *radicans*. It is very difficult to know today just what these varieties were, but we can see a hint here that the species is somewhat variable and that identification of these forms will be confusing. In 1837, Pfeiffer ascribed the new names of variety *propinquus* and variety *leptacanthus* to the first two of De Candolle's varieties respectively, and he was followed in this by Salm-Dyck in 1850. Then, in 1898, Schumann dropped the species name and spoke of *Cereus leptacanthus*.

In the meantime, Engelmann had coined a new name for the plants he studied, calling them *Cereus procumbens*. We may perhaps understand why Engelmann did this if we notice a statement he made in his *Synopsis of Cactaceae* in 1856. He said, *C. pentalophus* is "... similar, but an erect plant." Thinking this, he naturally gave the prostrate plants he had before him a new name. But it seems clear that in the variety *simplex* of *E. pentalophus* as described by De Candolle, there is a form with more numerous upright branches and with central spines, and that the variety *subarticulatus* was a more uniformly prostrate plant with no central spines on most areoles, which seems to fit Engelmann's specimens. Accordingly, *E. procumbens* is considered widely to be a synonym of *E. pentalophus*, and perhaps more specifically, of *E. pentalophus* var. *subarticulatus*.

More recently, there has been mentioned a *Cereus runyonii* from near the mouth of the Rio Grande. It has never been described completely, but it seems to have the same characters as *E. pentalophus* except for the fact that it has underground stems with areoles and short spines on them. I do not believe that this species has been validly published, its mention being only in a list published in 1926 by Orcutt, but the area where it was found is one of very sandy coastal dunes, and since these cacti lie prostrate, it seems easy to account for the unusual occurrence of underground stems by the drifting action of wind-blown sand covering up the usual prostrate stems of the ordinary *E. pentalophus*.

This is the cactus called the lady-finger cactus because of the small size of its stems, which are perhaps the slenderest of the genus. But anyone happening upon a clump of these stems, prostrate and spreading over and under each other to cover the ground like a mass of green, intertwining snakes, might think of a less pleasant name for it. However, when this mass covers itself with dozens of large, cerise flowers it is a different matter. It is a favorite because of the beauty of its flowers and because it is among the easiest of cacti to grow. Wherever even a piece of it touches sandy, well-drained soil it roots and grows, and with its prostrate, spreading habit it soon fills a window box or overflows a pot.

Echinocereus berlandieri (Eng.) Rumpl.
"Berlandier's Alicoche"

DESCRIPTION   PLATE 17

STEMS: A sprawling, clustering, and branching plant with the older parts of the stems prostrate, but with the growing tips and sometimes complete stems erect. The stems are deep green to bright green and slender, not flabby, up to about 6 inches long and 1/2 to 1 inch thick, although not usually over 3/4 of an inch thick. There may be 4 to 6 ribs, composed of rows of distinct, conical tubercles at the areoles with rounded notches between them often interrupting the ribs entirely. These rows of tubercles usually spiral about the stem, and often stop and start abruptly, so that the upper part of the stem may have either more or fewer ribs than the lower part of it.

AREOLES: Round, 1/8 of an inch in diameter, having much white wool when young, but becoming entirely bare with age. They are from 3/8 to 5/8 of an inch apart.

SPINES: Slender to rather stout, round, from bulbous bases, very light yellow to white, and rather translucent, with slightly brownish bases and very minutely brown-tipped when young, becoming all gray and opaque when old. There are 6 to 8 radial spines, slender and yellowish white, sometimes with tips and bases brownish. They are 1/4 to 1 1/4 inches long, the lower 3 being longest, and the upper 3 being much shorter and more bristle-like, except on areoles without a central, where the upper radial often is longer and heavier and moved into the areole almost to the position of an upward-pushing central. On typical plants there is 1 central

on most areoles. It is much stouter and longer than the radials, being 1/2 to 1 1/2 inches long, and stands almost perpendicular to the stem or else turned upward. The areoles low on the stems tend to have short, weak centrals or none at all, while those toward the tips have robust, long centrals, which often gives the plant a curious top-heavy look. Some specimens are weaker in armament and on them centrals are found only on occasional areoles, but I have never seen a plant of this species wholly without centrals.

FLOWERS: Said to be 2 to 4 inches in diameter in some descriptions, but all I have seen were 3 to 5 inches across, while only 2 inches tall, opening very widely. The petals are in only one row, always very long and narrow, not usually over 3/8 of an inch wide at any point. They have very gradually tapering, pointed tips with entire edges. The bases, and at least the lower one-third of the petals' length are whitish, while the tips are cerise-pink. The stigma lobes are 7 to 11 in number. The surface of the ovary has very short white wool and many longer, weak, dark spines.

FRUITS: Green, egg-shaped, about 3/4 of an inch long, covered with long, dark bristles, but having very little, and very short wool.

RANGE. Throughout most of south Texas below a line drawn from the Rio Grande just northwest of Laredo to near Uvalde, Texas, then southeast to just below San Antonio and down to Corpus Christi. Most common along the Nueces River and the lower Rio Grande.

REMARKS. Berlandier's alicoche is very close to the true alicoche, *E. pentalophus*, and has often been confused with it. However, it is a more northern form occurring over a wide area of south Texas, while the other is restricted very closely to a small section of the lower Rio Grande Valley. *E. berlandieri* was first discovered and described from along the Nueces River, where *E. pentalophus* never grows. It has flowers of the same color as the other cactus, but they are larger, with fewer, more narrow and pointed petals, fewer stigma lobes, and only short wool on the ovary surface. It also is a more upright-growing plant, never with all stems prostrate and never branching or rooting except near the base of the stems. Its stems are shorter, more slender, more tuberculate, and less flabby. It has longer and more numerous spines, usually with long and robust central spines on most areoles, while *E. pentalophus* usually has no centrals at all and at most sometimes produces a very much shorter and weaker one on an occasional areole.

It must be admitted that there have been found plants which seem to be puzzling intermediates, if only such things as spine character are observed. The secret to this seems to be that it is not uncommon to find immature or stunted specimens of *E. berlandieri* which present only the shorter spines typical for *E. pentalophus*, but when I have grown such plants in good conditions they have, within a year, put on the greater armament typical of this species, as well as shown the narrower, more pointed petals and shorter wool on the flower tube which are a sure sign of this species.

The two forms are so close that some have thought that perhaps they should be combined, but since we really know nothing experimentally about their actual relationship, any combination would be only conjectural at this stage. A combination here would make the nomenclature extremely confusing. It may well be that *E. berlandieri* is the plant referred to as *C. pentalophus* variety *simplex* by De Candolle and variety *propinquus* by Pfeiffer, since that form was supposed to have central spines. This could then be the plant referred to by Engelmann as the "erect" *C. pentalophus*. But if this is so, it is hard to see why he went on to give it a new species name at all.

E. berlandieri has been further confused with the next species we will take up, *E. blanckii*. Britton and Rose went so far as to claim that these two very distinct and different species were synonymous. They even feature a clear photograph of *E. berlandieri* as *E. blanckii*, while at the same time having a correct color plate of *E. blanckii*. We do not know how much Coulter's and even Engelmann's descriptions of *E. berlandieri* were influenced by a failure to distinguish between these two species, since neither of those authors mentions *E. blanckii* at all.

E. berlandieri, when once identified certainly and separated from its relatives, is a handsome plant forming small thickets of slender, sprawling stems standing at least 6 inches high. When blooming, a big clump of it will have dozens of the very large flowers with beautiful, two-colored, sharp-pointed petals.

It may formerly have been common over its wide range, but it now is seldom seen anywhere (and then in only small clusters) except on the low banks overlooking the sandy plains of the Rio Grande delta below Brownsville, where it is still found under almost every bush. Still, an occasional specimen is found much farther north. I found a fine specimen growing 20 miles south of D'Hanis, Texas, which puts it only about 50 miles southwest of San Antonio. I have also found several nice specimens a few miles north and east of Laredo, Texas. These points apparently are near the extreme northwestward limit of its range.

Echinocereus blanckii (Poselgr.) Palmer
"Alicoche"

DESCRIPTION   PLATE 17

STEMS: At first erect, but later sprawling. They are very soft and usually wrinkled, twisted, and contorted when old, bright green in color when in perfect health, but rapidly fading and turning yellowish-red when overexposed to the sun. The stems are $3/4$ to $1\frac{1}{2}$ inches in diameter and to at least 14 inches long. There are 5 to 8 ribs. On young, growing tips these are composed of rows of practically unconnected tubercles, but on older parts of the stems these ribs are continuous, with the tubercles less prominent and with almost no depressions between tubercles or adjacent ribs, making the old stems almost perfect hexagons to octagons in cross sections. These ribs do not usually spiral, but individual ribs may stop or start at any point on the stem, increasing or decreasing the number of them. These stems sometimes branch above the ground, but not profusely. The plant produces most of its stems in clusters from its large underground root. Since they come forth from very small bases often only $1/4$ of an inch in diameter at the ground level, if for any reason the soil is moved away from them, these young stems appear standing on very spindly bases, from which they abruptly widen to the typical size.

AREOLES: Small, less than $1/8$ of an inch in diameter, $1/4$ to $1/2$ inch apart. They have a very little short wool when young, and then become bare.

SPINES: Radial spines 6 to 9 in number, very slender and translucent, $3/16$ to $7/8$ of an inch long, radiating evenly. The 3 radials on each side of the areole are the longest, and are white, sometimes with minute black tips when young. The lower radial is the shortest and is very weak, almost bristle-like. The uppermost radial is very dark brown when young, in striking contrast to the other white radials, and fades gradually to almost gray when very old, usually keeping at least a brown tip. There is 1 stouter central spine with a bulbous base. It stands perpendicular to the stem at first, but then turns downward and often is slightly curved downward. This central spine is from $1/2$ to 2 inches long. It is translucent and variegated when young, with zones of very dark brown to light brown and almost white alternating throughout its length. When old it fades to almost the same gray as the other spines.

FLOWERS: Funnel-shaped, not usually opening widely. About 2 inches tall by $2\frac{1}{4}$ to $3\frac{1}{2}$ inches across in their natural, partly spread state. The ovary surface has pointed, reddish, scalelike segments and clusters of white to brown spines on it, with a little short wool. The outer petals have purple midlines with lavender-pink edges, and are narrow and pointed, with smooth, unbroken edges. The inner petals are about 26 in number, widening a little to $3/8$ or $1/2$ inch across near the tips, their margins smooth and their tips sharply pointed. The upper four-fifths of each of these is light rose in color, while the base darkens to carmine, giving the flower a dark, reddish throat. The filaments match the center of the flower. The anthers are orange-yellow. The pink style is little longer than the stamens. There are 8 to 11 long, slender, and very light green stigma lobes.

FRUITS: Practically unknown. There seem to be no descriptions of them except for the very general statement by Miss

Schulz in *Texas Cacti* that, "The fruit is greenish, globose, and covered with small spines."

RANGE. Northeastern Mexico and southern Texas, particularly in Starr and Hidalgo counties. Reported otherwise only once, and this from near Carrizo Springs, Texas, in Dimmit County.

REMARKS. *E. blanckii* is a very distinct species of prostrate Echinocereus. It was first named and described by Poselger in a German publication in 1853. Strangely, however, neither Engelmann nor Coulter mentioned it in their studies, so it was overlooked for many years. Then, in 1922, Britton and Rose confused it with *E. berlandieri*, stating that the two were synonymous. They published a photograph obviously of *E. berlandieri* as *E. blanckii*, but at the same time also published the best color plate of *E. blanckii* in bloom that I have seen. As a result of this, *E. blanckii* is still confused with the others of this group. I have seen numerous pictures of both *E. pentalophus* and *E. berlandieri* called *E. blanckii* in popular magazines and in catalogs but, due to its rarity, have not seen any good picture of the true species except the one of Britton and Rose, one in Borg's *Cacti*, and one in *Texas Cacti* by Ellen Schulz.

This species is easily distinguished from both *E. berlandieri* and *E. pentalophus* by the thicker stems with more ribs, the more numerous radial spines with the lower one smallest and the upper one dark colored. The downward-turning, variegated central spines are also very distinct from anything found in the others. When the flower is present there is no possibility of mistaking this cactus, as it has an over-all darker color with a dark center where the others have strikingly whitish centers, it opens only partly while they open extremely wide, and its petals are narrower, more pointed, and more numerous than in the other prostrate Echinocerei. Also, it normally blooms in February or March, about a month earlier than the others, but buds on disturbed plants may remain half-formed for more than two months and then open normally much after their usual season.

E. blanckii is primarily a Mexican species, and it occurs in Texas mainly in Starr and Hidalgo counties. The only record I find of its occurrence outside these two counties is a single specimen which is incomplete but which appears to be of this species in the herbarium of The University of Texas. This is labeled as collected 18 miles southwest of the Dimmit-Frio county line, which would be near Carrizo Springs, Texas, well above Laredo. On the basis of this specimen its range would be rather large. Without it the range would be restricted to Starr and Hidalgo counties. But nowhere is it common, and, in recent years I know of only a dozen or so plants being brought in by professional dealers who comb the countryside continually. It is an exceedingly inconspicuous plant in the field, and it cannot stand much sun. The stems quickly turn yellow and red and wilt if exposed to the sun, so it is limited to the shady thickets where it is very hard to find. With the increase in the practice of clearing the brush cover, it will probably be one of the first species to become extinct on our side of the Rio Grande. This is unfortunate, as it is a beautiful cactus producing many fine flowers when given the conditions it requires.

A possible reason for its scarceness may be this plant's apparent inability to produce fruits. These have never been described except for the incomplete description given by Schulz, and the form may be practically sterile. A fine specimen forming a clump all of 10 feet across is fully protected within the Santa Ana National Wildlife Refuge, and over a number of years of observation this has been seen to bloom profusely, but has never set a fruit. The reason for this is unknown.

Genus *Wilcoxia* B. & R.

THE GENUS *Wilcoxia* was erected by Britton and Rose in 1909. Some earlier writers had included its members in *Cereus* and some in *Echinocereus*. Since 1909 the species in the genus have been dealt with in various ways. Berger placed them in the genus *Peniocereus*, while Benson returned both of these genera to the genus *Cereus*, and others have considered each of these a subgenus of that large genus.

Whatever they have concluded about the genus, all recent writers have agreed that while these species seem to form a rather good grouping, the separation of the genus as such from other genera is not as clear-cut as they would like. Most say that any final word on the genus will have to await further investigation. With this word of caution about its status, we use the genus in the way most authorities are using it at the present time.

Five species in this genus are usually recognized. They are almost entirely Mexican, only one species coming into the United States at all, and that one only into southern Texas.

They are also inconspicuous cacti. In form they are very slender-stemmed, sparingly branched bushes. The stems, about ⅝ of an inch or less in diameter, grow very long, but are weak, so the plants seldom attain much size unless they have trees or shrubs to recline upon. If growing in a thicket, they clamber over the other plants, some species then becoming up to three yards or more long. But the slender stems are usually well hidden among the branches of the supporting plants.

Each individual grows from a cluster of tuberous roots which provide the water storage for these cacti, whose stems are too slender to handle that function adequately.

The spines are very short, ¼ of an inch or less long, and are appressed to the stems. There is also more or less hair on the areoles.

The flower is large and beautiful, bell-shaped or funnel-shaped, but with a short tube. It is reddish to purplish in color, and diurnal. The ovary surface is scaly, woolly, and covered with bristly or hairlike spines which remain on the fruits. The seeds are black.

By way of summarizing the differences between the genus *Wilcoxia* and those genera closest to it encountered in our area, we can list the following points: genus *Wilcoxia* differs from the genus *Echinocereus* by having much more slender stems, by its clambering habit, by never being caespitose, by having fascicled, tuberous roots, by producing its flower from within its spine areole instead of from a rupture of the stem epidermis just above the areole, and by the difference of seed form. *Wilcoxia* differs from the genus *Peniocereus* by having even more slender stems with 8 ribs where that genus has only 3 to 6 ribs; by having fascicled tubers while that has a single extremely large taproot; by producing red to purple flowers with short perianth tubes, which open during the day, instead of white or very occasionally rose flowers with long tubes, which open nocturnally; by having fruit with wool and bristles instead of with rigid spines; and by the difference in seed form.

Wilcoxia poselgeri (Lem.) B. & R.
"Pencil Cactus," "Dahlia Cactus," "Sacasil"

DESCRIPTION   PLATE 17
ROOTS: A cluster of dahlia-like tuberous roots usually half a dozen or more in number. Each tuber is rather spindle-shaped, up to about 4 inches long and about 1 inch in diameter.

STEMS: Long, very slender, and sparingly branched to form a very weak bush standing by its own strength sometimes to 2 feet tall, but when supported by the branches of a thicket sometimes attaining a height of 3 or even 4 feet. Each stem is round with 8 very low and inconspicuous ribs and is from $1/4$ to $5/8$ of an inch thick. The upper parts of the stems are green, but the lower parts become brown and woody.

AREOLES: Very small and very close together, with some white wool.

SPINES: There are 9 to 12 very slender radial spines only about $1/16$ to $3/16$ of an inch long. They lie perfectly flat against the surface of the plant and are white or gray in color. There is 1 central spine about $1/4$ of an inch long, which is turned upward against the upper radials. It is white, whitish tipped with brown, or sometimes all dark.

FLOWERS: Borne on the sides of the stems, very near to their tips. The flowers are funnel-shaped and $1^{1}/2$ to 2 inches wide by 2 to $2^{1}/2$ inches long, deep pink in color. The outer petals are narrow with greenish midribs and pink edges. Inner petals are broader but still linear and sharply pointed, deep pink or rose shading to lighter edges. The stamens are pale yellow. The stigma has 8 long green lobes. The ovary surface has reddish scales upon it and has a dense covering of long wool and black-and-white hairlike bristles. Each flower opens about noon and closes before night, usually for 2 or 3 days.

FRUITS: Practically oval in shape, becoming nearly dry and remaining covered with the wool and bristles. The seeds are black.

RANGE. From western Hidalgo County, Texas, along the Rio Grande to slightly beyond Laredo, Texas, and in adjacent Mexico. It has not been reported more than about 30 miles away from the Rio Grande on the U.S. side.

REMARKS: The pencil cactus is a fascinating member of this family, but so inconspicuous and actually camouflaged in its native habitat that few people have seen it. It is rather common in its range, but always grows in thickets where its slender stems lie upon those of the bushes and trees. The support of these thickets seems practically essential to it, since individuals un-

fortunate enough to be growing in the open rarely attain a height of over a foot or so. Within thickets in the same area one finds many individuals 2 or 3 feet tall and sometimes even more. Yet these are extremely hard to see. I have found that almost any good thicket in the area will have one, but about the only way to discover it is just to sit down and study the tangle of branches until it becomes apparent.

Once discovered, the cactus usually prompts exclamations of wonder. It presents the most slender stems of any U.S. cactus except *Opuntia leptocaulis*. These may extend for several feet, and branch, but they do not increase in size with age, remaining almost exactly the thickness of a lead pencil. Its common name is well chosen. But in spite of this slenderness, the plant may reach quite a good size, with a dozen or more branches. And once having gotten so large, it can really amaze us with the production of up to two or three dozen of its large, beautiful flowers at a time.

Each plant grows from a cluster of fleshy roots. It does best in sandy, loose soil, and can be grown quite easily in cultivation if treated much like other cacti of the region. However the individual plants seem to lose vigor after a few years. While they may remain alive for up to ten years or so, they seem to largely stop growing or blooming after the first three to five years. It seems that there must be a maximum size and number of the fleshy tubers and that these are not replaced with age. Mrs. Roy Quillin (Ellen Schulz), long a student of these cacti, always keeps several beautiful specimens of this cactus growing in pots, but she keeps them vigorous by cutting off the upper branches every few years and, after rooting these for her new starts, throwing away the whole of each plant which has passed its prime. Others grow them very successfully to very large size by grafting them upon other cacti.

Wilcoxia poselgeri has been known in the past as *Echinocereus poselgeri* Lem., and as *Cereus poselgeri* Coult. Even earlier it was known under the name *Cereus tuberosus* Poselgr. and *Echinocereus tuberosus* Rumpl. It is the only U.S. species of Britton and Rose's genus *Wilcoxia*.

Genus *Peniocereus* (Berger) B. & R.

THIS IS ANOTHER small genus erected by Britton and Rose. The name means something like thread cereus, referring to the slender stems of all the members.

Before Britton and Rose made this separation, the group had been part of the large genus *Cereus*. It is very hard to show significant characters to distinguish this genus *Peniocereus* from several other closely related genera. Perhaps its standing as a separate genus cannot be well justified, but the old genus *Cereus* has been so subdivided and reduced that it would be impossible to weigh the question of putting it together again without a restudy of many Central and South American genera, and that places the question beyond the scope of this book. It should be noted that Benson, in his 1950 study, placed these small genera back into *Cereus*, but that at the same time Backeberg and others have gone on very rapidly carving new genera out of the territory formerly covered by the original genus *Cereus*. It appears to be a matter which will be decided by the turn of taxonomic philosophy.

One cannot even state the number of species in the genus *Peniocereus* definitely or give an unequivocal set of characteristics for the genus, because these will be different depending upon whose limits to the genus one elects to follow. The number of species will be from two in the case of the most restrictive authors to seven in the case of Backeberg, who places back into this genus such things as Marshall's genus *Neoevansia* and some species from the genus *Acanthocereus*.

Therefore, we can only give characteristics of this genus in a very general way here. We can say that the members of the genus all have a single, extremely large, fleshy taproot, from which grow one to several slender stems which are ribbed at first but then become round. All have fragrant, nocturnal flowers with long perianth tubes, the flowers produced from within the spine areole, and all have very short spines on the stems, and rigid spines on the fruits.

A comparison of this genus with the genus *Wilcoxia* was made in the discussion of that genus. The other genus in our area to which it is most closely related is *Acanthocereus*. The differences between these two genera are as follows: *Peniocereus* has a huge, fleshy taproot, stems ribbed but becoming round when old, very short spines, and more elongated fruits, while members of *Acanthocereus* have fibrous roots, stems always markedly ribbed, much longer spines, and fruits more nearly spherical.

Peniocereus greggii (Eng.) B. & R.
  "Arizona Queen of the Night," "Texas Night-Blooming Cereus," "Deer-Horn Cactus," "Chaparral Cactus," "Sweet-Potato Cactus"

DESCRIPTION   PLATE 18
  ROOTS: Each plant has a single, huge, fleshy taproot. This is roughly carrot-shaped or turnip-shaped, but often takes on the shapes of crevices between rocks and other obstacles through or around which it grows, and so may be greatly distorted. A typical plant of medium age will possess a root 8 to 12 inches long and 3 to 5 inches in diameter at its thickest point, but very old plants have been reported with the root up to 2 feet in diameter and weighing up to 125 pounds.
  STEMS: Slender, erect, and sparingly branched to form a weak

bush, 1 to reportedly at least 9 feet tall. Young branches are dark, dull, grayish-green, quickly becoming reddish when in too much sun. They are from ¹/₂ to 1 inch thick, with 3 to 6 very strong ribs. Old stems do not increase in size, but rather shrink to a smaller diameter, and in the process the surface loses its areoles and ribs and becomes brownish, woody, and circular in shape.

AREOLES: Very tiny and closely situated on tiny tubercle-like prominences crowning the ribs. There is much white wool at the growing tips, some of which remains when the areoles are older. They are round to elliptical in shape.

SPINES: Each areole has 6 to 9 spreading radials and 1 or sometimes 2 centrals. All of these are blackish fading to gray; they are very short, being only ¹/₃₂ to ¹/₈ of an inch long, but stout and rigid, from bulbous bases.

FLOWERS: Strictly nocturnal. Produced from well down on the sides of the branches, these flowers are large and beautiful, as well as extremely fragrant. In size, they are 5 to 8 inches long by 2 to 3 inches in diameter; in color, whitish with the outer perianth segments somewhat tinged with brown; in shape, having a very long, very slender perianth tube, with the inner perianth segments spreading very widely and the outer segments usually recurved. The ovary surface has tubercles, and the areoles on these bear short, rigid spines. The outer surface of the elongated tube has scales and longer, more bristle-like spines. The perianth segments are lanceolate and sharply pointed. The stamens are erect, exserted, with the anthers cream in color. The style is slender; the stigma, white.

FRUITS: These are 2 to 3 inches long, ovoid in form, with the upper end attenuated and ending in the persistent, dried remains of the perianth, which is sometimes referred to as the "beak." Some authors give the size of the fruit as 5 to 6 inches long, but this includes the dried perianth, which is not actually part of the fruit and which usually hangs downward anyway. The surface of the fruit is strongly tuberculate, each tubercle bearing a round, black areole about ¹/₈ of an inch in diameter. These areoles bear short, black, rigid spines. The color of the surface remains bright green until after they are very ripe and the pulp is a beautifully contrasting magenta. Later as the fruits soften and start to disintegrate the surface becomes a brilliant orange-red. The seeds are black, very broadly obovate, and about ¹/₈ of an inch or a little more in greatest diameter.

RANGE. Trans-Pecos Texas, west through southern New Mexico, across southern Arizona, and in adjacent Mexico.

REMARKS. *Peniocereus greggii* is one of the most fascinating of the cacti. It is one of only two "night-blooming cereus" species found in our area. It is justly famous for its large, extremely fragrant, nocturnal flowers—so famous that one finds a rivalry, as seen in its names: both Arizona queen of the night and Texas night-blooming cereus.

These flowers are not the only amazing things about the cactus. The blooms come out on the sides of very slender stems. The branching of these stems creates a spindly bush which always grows up within a thicket of other plants. The other plants about it provide not only the support which is necessary if it is to stand over a foot or two tall, but also the light shade which it likes, and a shield of stems and branches among which it is extremely well camouflaged.

The cactus is always rare in all of its range, and this fact, together with its camouflage, makes it almost completely foolish to start out anywhere looking specifically for it. The chances are overwhelmingly against one's finding a specimen. But the plant has to face the crucial few days when it must expose itself in flower, and this has been the downfall of many a fine specimen. The standard way of searching for it has often been to search the desert at night with good lights, under which the large white flowers stand out like signs. Or, even more simply, some merely follow the wonderful fragrance of these flowers back to the plant. This scent is said to carry sometimes up to one-fourth of a mile in the desert.

Once the plant is located and the searcher sees its slender stems, he has still not seen perhaps the most amazing part, for like the iceberg this plant has most of its bulk underground. The bush above ground may be one foot or several feet tall. This depends almost entirely on the conditions in which it is growing and not on its age, since the stems die back very quickly during severe seasons and are usually destroyed whenever they grow past the limit of whatever chaparral they may be surrounded by. So any specimen of this cactus which is old enough to stand a foot or more high will normally have a taproot 6 inches long and 3 inches thick at the minimum, and without being any taller it may as easily be an ancient specimen with the root weighing dozens of pounds. There is hardly any way to predict the size of this enormous root, where the water storage of this plant is taken care of so that the stems may remain so inconspicuously slender among those of the thicket.

Bearing this in mind and noting the fact that it grows invariably in very rocky or very hard, clayey soil, it is a courageous person who starts to dig up this cactus. The root conforms to the shape of rocks and other roots it has to grow between, and getting it out is usually a good half-day's work for a strong man.

Once acquired, keeping the plant alive is also difficult. The huge root is very vulnerable to fungus if it is kept in soil even a little too damp. If rotting is avoided, the plant seems to decline gradually over a few years' time in greenhouse cultivation or in pots. I have only been able to keep my own specimens healthy, growing, and blooming, even in the climate of San Antonio, when they are planted in outdoor beds shielded from the rain. It is no wonder they are so seldom seen in collections.

Engelmann, at one time, distinguished two varieties of this species, which he called variety *cismontanus* and variety *transmontanus*. Few have since tried to separate them, and we have seen no clear division in any of the material we have studied.

Kuntze, in 1919, described plants of this species collected at Organ, New Mexico, which had light purple flowers instead of white. He established the new variety *roseiflorus* for these, but I will not list this variety separately, for two reasons. We have already seen how unwise it is to erect varieties on flower color alone, and there seems to be no other difference in these plants from the typical. Also, I know of no record since then of the collection of specimens with purplish flowers.

Genus *Acanthocereus* (Berger) B. & R.

Here is a small genus of somewhere around a dozen species carved out of the huge old genus *Cereus.* No one seems to dispute this one. Whether it is so little criticized because it is more of a natural group or because so little is certainly known about it is a question which might occur to anyone reading the numerous but remarkably incomplete and often contradictory statements about its members. From Linnaeus on we have had not a lack of, but actually too many, references to these plants. What we do lack is enough good data on which solid decisions can be based.

The members are more or less shrubby plants. The stems grow upright at first, but usually cannot support their own weight for long, and thus recline upon some support—usually other plants—or else become more or less prostrate and thicket-forming. Supported stems may grow to at least twenty feet tall and branch sparingly, but prostrate stems throw up many upright branches. Stems may be from an inch or so to 4 inches in diameter. Mature stems have 3 to 7 conspicuous ribs. The areoles are not close, and bear strong and rigid spines. The flowers are nocturnal, large, and white, with the perianth tube long and the ovary usually spiny. The fruit is round or nearly so, spiny or with the spines deciduous. The seeds are black or brown.

This is a group of tropical, lowland cacti. They are never found far from a coast, and seem to thrive best on semi-arid coastal plains. However they can tolerate much more moisture than most cacti, and when given it their rate of growth is often amazing. I have had one species, when planted in an outdoor bed where it got sufficient water, produce a 6-foot stem in one summer's growing season. But they are most severely limited by cold, being among the most tender of the cacti. A frost will kill the tips of the stems, and at 32 degrees Fahrenheit the whole of the plant above the ground is killed, although the roots may sprout again.

The combination of conditions these plants need is found in various coastal areas in Central and South America. There are species of Acanthocerei native in eastern Mexico, Guatemala, and Panama, and in northern, coastal regions of Colombia, Venezuela, and Bahia, Brazil. In the U.S. they have a precarious hold along the coast in south Texas and in Florida. Besides these locations, they have been introduced in Cuba, the islands of St. Thomas and St. Croix, and probably in some other areas.

Acanthocereus pentagonus (L.) B. & R.
"Triangle Cactus," "Night-Blooming Cereus," "Organo," "Pitahaya"

DESCRIPTION   PLATE 18

ROOTS: Fibrous.

STEMS: At first upright, later reclining, becoming practically prostrate and rooting to form low thickets unless supported. If supported, it grows to at least 6 feet tall. Such an upright stem may branch once or twice and the branches, if supported, rebranch similarly to attain a total height of at least 20 feet. The thickness of the stems is extremely variable: from $1^{1}/_{4}$ to 4 inches in diameter. Mature stems have 3, 4, or 5 ribs so high and narrow that the stem has only an extremely small central axis and is essentially a triangle, quadrangle, or pentagon with deeply concave sides. These winglike ribs are from about $^{1}/_{2}$ to 2 inches high. Their summits are somewhat tuberculate at first, but become almost smooth. The surface is light to medium green.

AREOLES: Round, $^{1}/_{8}$ to $^{3}/_{8}$ of an inch across, bulging on slight prominences on the summits of the ribs. They are spaced from about ³/₄ to at least 2 inches apart, and have very short, whitish wool.

SPINES: There are 5 to 7 radial spines which radiate rather evenly around the areole; 1 to 3 upper ones are from ³/₁₆ to 1 inch long. There are sometimes 2 upper laterals and always 2 lower laterals, each ³/₄ to 1 inch long. There is always one lower radial which is more slender than the laterals and ¼ to ³/₄ of an inch long. There are also 1 to 4 central spines; 1 is always a lower central, porrect or slightly deflexed and ³/₄ to 1¹/₂ inches long. There may be 0 to 2 laterally directed centrals ³/₄ to 2 inches long, and 0 or 1 upper central 1 to 2¹/₄ inches long. All spines are medium to heavy in thickness, straight and round, from bulbous bases. They are light brown when growing, then rough and gray when old.

FLOWERS: Nocturnal, extremely large and showy, but only slightly if at all fragrant. They are white in color, from 5¹/₂ to 8 inches long, and about 5¹/₂ to 6 inches wide when fully expanded. The ovary is hardly expanded more than the long green tube, which is only ¹/₂ to ³/₄ of an inch in diameter. There are conspicuous areoles on slight prominences rather closely placed on the ovary and becoming very widely spaced as they proceed up the tube. These have white wool in them and one to several rigid spines each; these spines are very short on the ovary but become progressively longer as they proceed up the tube until they are to about ¼ of an inch long on the upper tube areoles. The outer perianth segments are greenish, the inner ones white. All are lanceolate and pointed. The stamens are shorter than the perianth segments, with the filaments white and the anthers straw in color. The stigma is white, with 10 to 12 close-standing lobes.

FRUITS: Oval to rather egg-shaped, about 3 inches long by 2 inches in diameter. They are slightly tuberculate, with 1 to 4 spines per areole, and they are bright red and edible when ripe. The seeds are obovate, about ¹/₈ of an inch (3 millimeters) in size, and bright, shining black in color.

RANGE. In Texas in a few locations only a few miles from the coast in Kenedy, Willacy, and Cameron counties. It is reported to be also a native in southern Florida, along the east coast of Mexico, in coastal parts of and on islands near Guatemala, Panama, Colombia, Venezuela, and Bahia, Brazil, and to have been widely introduced in other places, among them Cuba, parts of the Virgin Islands, and reportedly southern Louisiana.

REMARKS. The triangle cactus is a very beautiful cactus, but a very difficult one to deal with in a study with only the scope of this one. It is clearly a tropical cactus which has at best a precarious foothold in the United States and which never attains its full growth here. There are many questions about it which could only be answered by a wide survey of this genus in several countries of tropical America.

The very name of the cactus is the first of these questions which we cannot evaluate satisfactorily here. Cacti similar to this were seen very early, and we have numerous very old names accompanied only by notes too incomplete to be conclusive and by no type specimens. We are in the embarrassing situation of having too many names which might refer either to this cactus or to some entirely different one.

Linnaeus started this problem. In 1737 he named a *Cactus pentagonus* and gave a very brief description of it. He gave no location for this cactus except, "Habitat in America." The description could apply to this plant, but there are difficulties. A main obstacle is that he describes its stem as being 5-angled, which our plant never is in the U.S. But in a new note in 1753, Linnaeus modified this point a little by saying that the stem was sub-5-angled (*subquinquangularis*).

Haworth, in 1813, applied this name to a Central American plant, but, interestingly enough, no later authorities used the name for many years. Engelmann, in referring to a Mexican cactus which must have been the same as ours, ignored Linnaeus' name entirely and called the plant *Cereus variabilis*, while Coulter refers apparently to the same Mexican plant under the name originated at about the same time by Pfeiffer, *Cereus princips*.

In the meantime there had been a host of other names which some have thought referred to our plant and some have thought were meant for entirely different forms. Among them were *Cactus pitajaya* Jacquim, published in 1761, *Cereus prismaticus* Wildenow, 1813, *Cereus undulosus* DC, 1828, *Cereus acutangulus* Otto, 1837, *Cereus baxaniensis* Karwinsky, 1837, *Cereus nitidus* SD, 1850, *Cereus dussii* Schumann, 1899, *Cereus sirul* Weber, 1904, and so on. Only very extensive study of much material and very astute evaluation of tiny clues could ever determine whether any one of these names is a synonym for the cactus we have in our area or a legitimate name of some closely related form.

It is obvious that there was no agreement on a name for this cactus up to this century. Perhaps the most remarkable fact to be seen from the above list is that all of the authorities seemed to avoid the use of Linnaeus' name, *Cactus pentagonus*. Did they consider the name unusable because the description was so brief and lacked even a type locality for the plant it was supposed to name?

It remained for Britton and Rose, in 1909, to revive the old name and apply it for the first time to our Texas cactus, adapting it to their new genus as *Acanthocereus pentagonus*. They were able to do this by stating that the plant has 3 to 5 ribs, thus enabling it to fit the number mentioned by Linnaeus fairly well. Due to their wide influence, our plant has been known from their time until recently as *A. pentagonus*, and most have happily forgotten, if they ever knew, about the whole 150 years of controversy over names.

We do not want to be blamed for ending a period of pleasant stability by introducing some doubt once again. It was Backeberg who, in his recent great work on cacti, had the courage to restudy the literature and who came up with a disquieting decision. He it is who now tells us that Britton and Rose went back to the wrong name by Linnaeus for this cactus.

Backeberg does not feel that the assumption is warranted that Linnaeus had our plant before him in describing his *Cactus pentagonus*. It must be admitted that this can be no more than an assumption and that for 150 years none of the authorities assumed it. But isn't this better than the maze of names we are faced with without it? What can be offered positively?

Backeberg is ready with an answer. He says that *Cactus pentagonus* L. is "unidentifiable." Then he refers us to Hummelink, who has already stated that the first name, *Acanthocereus pentagonus*, of Britton and Rose could only have been *Cactus tetragonus* L.

The point is that in the same publication in 1753 Linnaeus relisted his *Cactus pentagonus* and also described a new form, *Cactus tetragonus*, with stems 4-sided. This plant is even more inadequately described than the first, but it does have a more proper number of angles to the stem for our cactus. And even more important, Linnaeus pinpoints the location of it as "Curaçao, America." This does give something to work on. Backeberg makes the flat statement that our plant is the same as the one which grows on Curaçao, and so he considers the question of names closed. He lists our cactus as *Acanthocereus tetragonus* (L.) Hummelink.

I have not so far read any discussion of Backeberg and Hummelink's idea, and no doubt there will be rebuttals. In the meantime I am unable to make a choice between the two proposals. I have been able to examine no specimens from Curaçao, and it seems that only a very detailed comparison of specimens from this type locality and our plants can give any basis on which to determine their relationship. In the present state of our knowledge, I feel it best to repeat the use of Britton and Rose's name, at the same time pointing out the question about it and warning any serious cactus student that he may or may not in the future find the tide of opinion turning toward Backeberg's theory.

The triangle cactus is a beautiful one. It seems to be the only U.S. cactus which can outdo the large Opuntias in rate of growth. I have seen well-established plants produce stems 5 and 6 feet tall in one growing season, and since some of these fall over and root where they touch the ground, in a few years such plants become large thickets.

This is its mode of growth in the wild. It grows in the very dense brush just back from the coast in south Texas, sprouting under the trees and bushes which present an almost unbroken cover in this area. Here the large stems start upward, and if they find a tree trunk to lean against or attain a tree limb before they bend of their own weight, they go clambering up the tree and branch sparingly in it. Those branches which do not succeed in remaining upright touch the ground again and by rerooting where they touch, help the cactus to spread. By combinations of this method and seeding, in several Texas locations the cactus forms an understory plant so thick among the trees and bushes that it is difficult to walk through the stands. On summer nights the brush in such a place is so covered with hundreds of the huge white flowers that the sight is glorious.

But often when one goes to such a place the sight is not so wonderful. This cactus is one of the most tender to frost of any I have grown. It is far more tender than most of the larger Mexican Cerei. So if one goes to such a natural stand of it in south Texas in the spring after a winter in which there has been a freeze in the area, one finds the trees draped with the dry, brown skeletons of the stems and only new shoots starting again from the roots. It seems that throughout its range in Texas the plant is killed back nearly to the ground by freezes every few years. The cold limits its range, and nowhere north of Corpus Christi can the plant be grown successfully without protection. It is definitely a tropical species barely hanging on in our area.

All specimens which I have seen growing wild in Texas have been uniform in having the mature stems 3-angled—hence the name, triangle cactus. Only in cultivated specimens have I seen the stems 4-angled, and these I suspect came from Mexico. I have never seen a 5-angled mature stem in a U.S. specimen. However, this is apparently not typical of the species in the rest of its range. Many stems on the plant as it grows in Mexico have 4 ribs and some are seen there with 5, while the plant growing on Curaçao is described as having only 4 or more ribs.

This and other differences may be due to the fact that in Texas we actually have only young sprouts of the plant. Here, in a lucky time when it does not get frosted for several years it may attain 8 feet or so tall, but then comes a freeze and it has to start over again. Only a hundred miles or so south along the Tamaulipas coast, where it never gets frozen, the cactus grows 20 feet or more up into the large trees and is a truly impressive giant.

The largest stand of this cactus which I have seen is in Cameron County, Texas, in the brush about a mile and a half inland from the waterway called Callo Atascosa. It is almost within sight of the Atascosa Wildlife Refuge, and it is unfortunate that it is not within this protected area. Such a stand is a unique extension of the tropical flora into our area.

Genus *Echinocactus* Link & Otto

Most of the cacti in the genus *Echinocactus* live up to the meaning of the name. Some of them present among the strongest, most rigid spines found on any cacti, and most of them are covered with as complete a spine cover as is found anywhere. Their main spines are often made especially troublesome by being hooked at the end, but, because they are never barbed along the shaft they are actually not as vicious as the much more slender spines of the Opuntias. Although these heavy spines are a feature of most of the Echinocacti, a few of them present more slender and flexible spines, and there are even a few spineless members of the group.

These cacti are often known as the "barrel cacti," and this term is a good one if it reminds us of their heavy, fleshy bodies and we do not let it limit our concept of them to something only barrel-shaped or barrel-sized. In size they may actually range from the huge, truly barrel-like species usually thought of under this name and sometimes weighing hundreds of pounds, to miniature forms essentially the same but, in some cases, only a few inches high when mature. In shape they are typically globular, although they may be very flattened, hemispherical, or sometimes heavily cylindrical.

The exteriors of these cacti are typically firm and solid. They are shaped into from 8 to more than 20 vertical or spiraling ribs, which may be broad or narrow, high or low, smooth and even throughout their lengths or undulating, notched, or cross-furrowed, but never completely interrupted. These ribs may be thought of as partly or completely fused tubercles, but with the fusing process always clearly visible. They are never rows of completely separate tubercles. The areoles are on the summits of these ribs.

The presence of these ribs distinguishes the Echinocacti handily from the tubercled cacti, but not from the Cerei. For the characters which set these apart and the characters which a botanist uses to be sure of his genera, we have to look to the reproductive structures. All of the Cerei produce the flowers on the sides of the stems, have a flower tube prolonged above the ovary, and also have a spiny ovary surface. Our Echinocacti, however, produce their flowers at or near the apex of the plant, have no distinct floral tube, and the ovary bears scales and sometimes wool, but not spines.

It is harder to state differences between the Echinocacti and their other relatives. Ribs versus tubercles will usually do it, giving us a handy way to tell them from any of the Mammillarias and the members of the genus *Pediocactus* or genus *Ariocarpus*, but the genus *Lophophora* has what are best thought of as low ribs. These are small, spineless forms, different from the Echinocacti in various ways, but for clearly observable differences one has to look to their ovaries and fruits, which are naked, with no appendages of any kind. Most of the Mammillarias can also be separated from the Echinocacti by having such naked fruits, but several of them may have some scales on their fruits.

The genus *Echinocactus* is used here in practically the old and original sense given it by Link and Otto. It was originally described as a large and complex grouping of ribbed cacti which produced their flowers at or near the apex of the plant, where the blossoms grew out of the upper edges of the young spine-bearing areoles, and whose ovary and fruit surfaces were to some degree scaly. Schumann organized a series of subgenera within it, and later Britton and Rose divided the old genus up into a whole array of separate small genera, leaving the original name, *Echinocactus*, to cover in their system only a few species of large barrel cacti.

The dividing process has continued until we have had at least twelve genera carved out of the old genus, among them *Echino-cactus* (in the sense of Britton and Rose), *Ferocactus*, *Homalo-cephala*, *Hamatocactus*, *Glandulicactus*, *Astrophytum*, *Sclero-cactus*, *Thelocactus*, *Ancistrocactus*, *Neolloydia*, *Echinomastus*, and *Coloradoa*.

Due to the large influence of Britton and Rose's publications these are no doubt the names that most cactus fanciers are familiar with today. Most people probably think of them as distinct and definite groupings, even though almost all would be hard-pressed if they had to try to tell the differences among them. They are annoyed when someone comes along who thinks that what they have known as *Ferocactus johnsonii* is actually *Echinomastus johnsonii*, or that *Ferocactus uncinatus* should have an entirely new genus made for it; and they sometimes make uncomplimentary remarks about taxonomists who bring up such subjects. This is because they are blissfully unaware of the uncertainty of these numerous small genera.

Actually, these genera were erected upon very small differences and these differences are used to divide them so arbitrarily that, for instance, the presence or absence of wool on the ovary is taken to be important enough to divide the woolly *Echino-cactus* (*sensu* B. & R.) from the nonwoolly *Ferocactus*, while the equally woolly ovary of *Homalocephala* is considered of no significance and the single species placed in this latter genus is linked in this system no more closely to *Echinocactus* than to *Ferocactus*. Or *Glandulicactus* is a genus recently erected almost entirely, as the name implies, because of the presence of glands on the plants, even though other plants left in three other genera of the group may have equally obvious glands.

These small genera erected upon this sort of extreme use of the dividing rather than the synthesizing method are so poorly defined that their actual history is one of continual shifting of species from one to another and continual disagreement among the authorities who have tried honestly to define them. *Echinocactus uncinatus*, for instance, has been placed during the fifty years since the move to break up the original genus into five different genera, Britton and Rose placing it in *Fero-cactus*, Knuth putting it in *Echinomastus*, Marshall in *Thelo-cactus*, Buxbaum in *Hamatocactus*, and finally Backeberg making the new genus *Glandulicactus* for it. Various other species have been shifted from genus to genus and the genera themselves have been both combined and redivided from time to time. The result is that the index of any recent book on cacti is used only with difficulty because it either lists many of these forms under different genera from the book last consulted or else is rendered overly long by listing each species repeatedly under the various genera each has been placed into by one authority or another.

This situation looks, on the face of it, like the dividing process gone to excess, and this attitude toward the problem has been taken by one contemporary authority. Dr. L. Benson, in his book, *Arizona Cacti*, has ignored these newer genera and placed them all back into the old genus *Echinocactus*. This greatly simplifies things, and would seem a welcome move, if it can be justified.

Some twenty years have passed since Benson's recombination of these genera and there should be something more to be said on the problem. However, we actually find no more prospect of agreement on how to classify this group today than ever. Backeberg has recently published his large work with the genetic divisions at their all-time extreme. Dr. Benson has published studies on another genus, *Pediocactus*, in which he has applied a similar combining to some other small genera, but he has not dealt again with the Echinocacti themselves. We are left with the two fundamentally opposing views, each with a top expert in the field backing it; thus, we must make a choice for ourselves between them.

To help in doing this we must look about for some newer research which might shed light on the problem. Remarkably little actual research has been reported recently on these cacti, but there has been a little. I do not want to place too much weight upon this small bit of evidence, but we must use it in choosing between the two very different approaches to this group.

The most significant recent research is that of Dr. Norman H. Boke at the University of Oklahoma. He has undertaken very fine anatomical studies, particularly of the shoot and areole formation in various species of cacti. Of particular importance, he has shown that the famous groove which in some cacti extends above the spine areole—in some running a long way upward and in some a shorter distance—is really only an extension of the spine areole itself and so all flowers which come out of the upper edge of an unelongated spine areole or at the end of this groove are essentially coming from the same position in relation to the areole. He has shown that the areole in all such cases is the same in essential development and structure, described by the term "monomorphic," as opposed to the term "dimorphic" for situations where the flower areole is separated from the spine areole entirely. This is important, since it makes all but academic the huge discussions of grooves versus merely elongated areoles and short grooves versus long grooves which have figured in trying to divide the genera within this group. The areole in all of the various members of this large group is uniformly monomorphic, a fact which is of some significance.

On most of the other characters used to divide the Echino-cacti into the many genera proposed, much has been written in the past, but there is no new evidence. Some authorities could be quoted on each distinguishing character proposed; and other, equally eminent students, on reasons why the character is of doubtful value.

However, what little recent research has been done has made it clear that if the theory of dividing into separate genera on the basis of each and every little difference prevails, the familiar genera of Britton and Rose will, for the most part, not stand as generally used today. Instead there will have to be newer and more logical realignments and even some more splittings. Backeberg has already embarked upon that sort of future with his genus *Glandulicactus*. An indication of the future, if this line is followed, can be seen in a statement by Dr. Boke summarizing his research on only three species in the group. He says,

> The anatomical data obtained in this study emphasize the similarities between *Homalocephala texensis* and *Echinocactus horizonthalonius* as well as the difference between these two species and *Echinocactus grusonii*. The combined list of characters suggests to the author that if *E. horizonthalonius* is to be retained in the genus *Echinocactus*, *Homalocephala* should be returned to the same genus. It further suggests that *E. horizonthalonius* could, with equal logic, be referred to the genus *Homalocephala*. The outcome will depend upon taxonomic opinion and also upon the results of investigations on the developmental anatomy of other species now included in the genus *Echinocactus*.

These further investigations have not yet been reported, but since it seems clear that after they are there will probably have to come a very far-reaching and so far unpredictable realignment of the genera already proposed, it seems undesirable to perpetuate genus names in this book which have so little meaning now and which have such unpredictable futures. For this reason I am inclined to follow Benson in a conservative approach, going back to the usage of the older, inclusive genus *Echinocactus*, at least until more work is done. There is a trend toward synthesis as opposed to division in plant taxonomy and the distinct possibility exists that a more complete understanding will show that these recent genera are better thought of as subgenera or tribes, as Schumann first meant them to be. For these reasons I am referring them all back to the genus *Echinocactus*.

The Echinocacti, understood in this way, are especially interesting to cactus fanciers because of their heavy bodies and conspicuous, often beautiful spine covers. They include all of the huge barrel cacti growing within the United States, which inspire such feelings of awe in us—except the huge saguaro. Because they are such favorites, collectors like especially to grow them.

But fanciers must always remember that these are the real old desert rats. If one were to rate the cacti on their adaptation for survival in extreme desert situations, the finest and most beautiful of these Echinocacti would be among the most specialized for the extremes of heat and drought. And one should always remember that this makes the big, tough-looking specimens one most admires among the least capable of surviving in our cool, moist gardens and patios. It is a sad sight to see a venerable old desert barrel turning to mush in an over-watered situation. We feel sorry for a person who has to watch a desert planting of these cacti going to pieces in his yard, but there are unscrupulous nurserymen who will extract large prices for selling and installing fine old plants in places where they cannot possibly live. Many growers have shown that all of these can be grown almost anywhere if they are protected and cared for properly, in which

case their beauty is well worth the trouble they take, but anyone wishing to grow them must go to the trouble of learning their requirements and providing for them properly.

Knowing that some will disagree with the treatment of this group which I am using and will wish to use instead the microgenera of Britton and Rose, and realizing that the decision is at this time largely an arbitrary one, I add with the listing of each species in this group the alternate name which would be the valid one at the present time under that system.

KEY TO THE ECHINOCACTI

1a. Plants spiny—2.
  2a. Central spines never more than one—3.
    3a. Central spine hooked if present, or else absent—4.
      4a. Radial spines 7 or 8 in number, $3/4$ to 2 inches long, the upper 4 or 5 of them straight and flattened, the lower 3 round and hooked; central spine 2 inches or more long; flower red-brown   —*E. uncinatus* var. *wrightii*.
      4b. Radial spines 8 or more, $3/8$ to $1\,1/4$ inches long, all round and straight; central spines absent or less than $1\,3/4$ inches long; flower cream or yellow in color—5.
      5a. Radials 10 to 19; central spine always present and $1/4$ to $1\,3/4$ inches long; flower large and yellow with red throat —6.
        6a. Stem becoming to 5 inches in diameter; radial spines 10 to 13 in number; flowers 2 to 3 inches tall
            —*E. setispinus* var. *hamatus*.
        6b. Stems becoming to only 3 inches in diameter; radial spines 12 to 19; flowers $1\,3/4$ to 2 inches tall
            —*E. setispinus* var. *setaceus*.
      5b. Radials 8 to 11; central usually absent and when present (in rare cases) only $1/2$ inch or less long; flower cream to pale yellowish without red coloring   —*E. mesae-verdae*
                (in part).
    3b. Central spine present and straight—7.
      7a. Mature plants large, 6 to 12 inches in diameter; spines very heavy and cross-ridged; radials 5 to 8 in number; central deflexed—8.
        8a. Ribs 5 to 13; areoles $1/2$ to $7/8$ of an inch apart; stigma lobes 6 to 10; fruits imbedded in much long wool, soon-drying, and not bright colored—9.
          9a. Spines extremely heavy, very flattened and very severely recurving against the plant; stems remaining at most pyramid-shaped instead of cylindrical, with the ribs noticeably tuberculate   —*E. horizonthalonius*
                      var. *curvispina*.
          9b. Spines not so heavy, only somewhat flattened and not recurving against the plant; stems becoming columnar, with the ribs hardly tuberculate   —*E. horizonthalonius*
                      var. *moelleri*.

8b. Ribs 13 to 27; areoles 1 to 1¼ inches apart; stigma lobes 10 to 17; fruits standing exposed beyond the wool, very slow drying, and bright red in color   —E. texensis.
7b. Mature plants not so large, 1½ to 4 inches in diameter; spines rigid but not extremely heavy or cross-ridged; radials 8 to 16 in number; central porrect or turned upward —10.
10a. Central usually present on only some areoles and ½ inch or less long; radials 8 to 11 in number and ½ inch or less long   —E. mesae-verdae (in part).
10b. Central always present, ⅝ to ⅞ of an inch long; radials 10 to 16 in number and to ⅞ of an inch long   —E. erectocentrus var. pallidus.
2b. Central spines more than 1 on mature plants—11.
11a. Lowermost central spine hooked; upper ones straight—12.
12a. Mature plants massive in size; radial spines 12 to 20, all but the lower 3 of them slender, flexible, bristle-like, and white; central spines very heavy and cross-ringed   —E. wislizeni.
12b. Mature plants small to large, but not massive, radial spines all rigid; centrals various but not cross-ringed—13.
13a. Mature plants large, 7 to 12 inches thick; largest central spines 2 to 6 inches long—14.
14a. Ribs very high and broad and composed of massive, rounded tubercles 1½ to 2 inches tall and in diameter at their bases; central spines 4 to 8 in number, all round or nearly so and smooth   —E. hamatacanthus.
14b. Ribs high but acute, composed of indistinct tubercles only about ⅜ of an inch across; central spines 4, all flat and pubescent   —E. sinuatus.
13b. Mature plants small, not over 6 inches and usually 4 inches or less thick; largest central spines 2 inches or less long—15.
15a. Radials brown, yellowish, or tan, fading to gray; upper centrals conspicuous for forming an erect "V" of straight, diverging spines; flowers greenish or yellowish—16.
16a. Radials 12 or more, ribs 13; flowers greenish and not opening widely—17.
17a. Roots fibrous; radials 12 to 14; flowers green suffused with rose   —E. brevihamatus.
17b. Roots composed of a long, fleshy, white taproot; radials 13 to 28; flowers plain green   —E. scheeri.
16b. Radials 7 to 12; ribs 8; flowers yellow and opening widely   —E. tobuschii.
15b. Radials all but the lower one on each side of the areole white; upper centrals not forming a conspicuous, erect "V"; flowers rose, purplish, pink, white, or rarely pale yellowish   —E. whipplei (in part).
11b. All central spines straight—18.
18a. Radial spines predominantly white—19.
19a. Radials 25 to 36; plant small, 3½ inches or less tall   —E. mariposensis.
19b. Radials 7 to 16; plants becoming larger than 3½ inches tall—20.

20a. Radials ½ to 1 inch long; centrals somewhat flattened and 1 to 2 inches long   —E. whipplei (in part).
20b. Radials ¼ to ½ inch long; centrals round and ⅜ to 1⅛ inches long   —E. conoideus.
18b. Radial spines with various strong colors besides white —21.
21a. Ribs 8 in mature plants   —E. bicolor var. schottii.
21b. Ribs 12 to 14—22.
22a. Spines with bright red zones and some of them flattened and 1 inch or more long on mature plants; flowers large and very bright rose-pink   —E. flavidispinus.
22b. Spines gray or yellowish to dull purplish or reddish, but not bright red; all spines round and none over ⅜ of an inch long; flowers small and pale pinkish —23.
23a. Lowermost porrect central only ⅛ to 3/16 of an inch long; ribs ¾ to 1 inch wide   —E. intertextus var. intertextus.
23b. Lowermost porrect central ¼ to ⅝ of an inch long; ribs narrower, only ⅝ to ¾ of an inch apart   —E. intertextus var. dasyacanthus.
1b. Plants spineless—E. asterias.

Echinocactus horizonthalonius Lem.
"Turk's Head," "Devil's Head," "Eagle Claws," "Bisnagre," "Bisnaga de Dulce," "Bisnaga Meloncillo"

DESCRIPTION   PLATES 18, 19
STEMS: Each plant is at first a depressed hemisphere which later elongates to become a pyramid or a short cylinder in shape. It grows to a maximum size of about 8 inches tall and 8 inches in diameter, and is almost always single, but rarely forming 2 or very rarely 3 stems. There are almost always 8 ribs, but reports have been made of 5 to 13 ribs. These are very broad and rounded, with shallow grooves between them, and when old they are more or less interrupted by shallow cross-furrows. They may be vertical or spiraling. The color of the surface is a dull gray-green. Young plants have only a very little short wool at the apex, but old plants have a tuft of long wool filling the apex.

AREOLES: Spherical or nearly so and ½ to ⅞ of an inch apart. Having much long wool when young, but nearly bare when old.

SPINES: There are 5 to 8 radial spines. They radiate rather evenly around the areole, except that there is no lower radial present. In one form the radials are strongly recurved against the plant. Those of adjacent areoles interlock extensively. There is also one central spine on mature plants, which is more or less strongly deflexed and curved downward upon the others. All spines are from ³/₄ to 1¹/₂ inches long, heavy to very heavy from enlarged bases, almost round to distinctly flattened. Their surfaces are rough and more or less cross-ridged. Their color is brownish or reddish fading to grayish or sometimes almost black.

FLOWERS: Very brilliant rose-red in color. They are 2 to 3 inches broad and long. The ovary is covered with small scales and dense white or pink wool. The outer segments are short, narrow, and sharply pointed, sometimes ending in a blackish spine. The inner petals are longer, somewhat lance-shaped, with notched, toothed, or ragged edges, but usually ending in a spinelike point. There are very many short yellow stamens. The style is pink. There are 6 to 10 long stigma lobes which are reddish or pink on the lower side with the upper or inner sides salmon to somewhat orange or even olive.

FRUITS: Oblong, to 1¹/₄ inches long by about ¹/₂ inch thick, with some scales on the surface and enclosed in the long wool at the apex of the plant. This fruit dries from the tip downward so that when it is ripe the lower part is usually reddish and soft while the upper part is brown and dry. This upper, dry part usually breaks off, leaving the base and many seeds imbedded in the long wool. The seeds are about ¹/₈ of an inch long, somewhat irregular and angular in shape, with large, depressed hila. The surface is rough and dark brown.

RANGE. All of trans-Pecos Texas, most of southern New Mexico and on into Arizona and Mexico.

REMARKS. With this species we venture into the fascinating group of the barrel cacti. While this is not one of the largest of the group, it is as tough as they come, its surface almost as hard as leather and its spines so strong, rigid, and spreading that one of its local common names, "eagle claws," is apt.

This little barrel grows on arid, rocky hilltops and slopes where there is no brush and very little grass to shade it. One may encounter it in such exposed places once he has passed westward over the Pecos River anywhere below Roswell, New Mexico. It is especially common in parts of the Davis, Guadalupe, Franklin, and other mountains of southern New Mexico and southwest Texas, where places may still be found with dozens of fine old specimens dotting the hillsides. However, it is much more usual now, over most of its range, to find an isolated plant and to search the surrounding area without finding a companion to this one somehow surviving individual. The most likely places to see this species in quantity today are in the bins of cactus dealers and the beds of nurserymen.

It is hard for us now to imagine the wealth of such plants that our unspoiled deserts once boasted and the mayhem man has visited upon them in a relatively short time. Mr. Ernest Braunton, in an article published in the *Cactus and Succulent Journal* in 1933, tells of counting 500 cacti of this species uprooted and dumped into a ravine during a single clearing and building project that year in El Paso, Texas. He called then for

some sort of conservation of such plants, but was not heard, and now one has to go far into the out-of-the-way places of the mountains to find any of these cacti at all. Such is the situation almost everywhere, and the individuals we do find seem to be only the lucky ones which have so far been missed by the diggers. Since this cactus does not hide under any brush or survive well in thick grass, it is especially vulnerable and the motives for taking it have been several.

As one of its Spanish common names implies, in the past its flesh has been used for the making of cactus candy. It is probably used little if at all for this in the U.S. today, but now it is taken for use in the so-called desert plantings fashionable for yards and gardens. But in this it usually suffers almost as certain a death as in the candy manufacture. It is so strictly a desert plant that it does not thrive well even in the yards of New Mexico or west Texas; only those willing to give it the most specialized situation should try to grow it. In the meantime, it becomes more and more scarce as we are fascinated by the tough old fellows and bring them from their deserts.

This species apparently received two names in the same year. In 1839 it was named *E. horizonthalonius* by Lemaire and *E. equitans* by Scheidweiler; however, the first of these two names has long been the one used for it. Engelmann attempted to set those specimens with central spines apart as variety *centrispinus*, but this division was long ago dropped as unnecessary since it would comprise almost all mature specimens seen and leave out all juvenile ones. However, there do seem to be two recognizable varieties which are consistent.

Echinocactus horizonthalonius var. curvispina SD

DESCRIPTION   PLATE 18

STEMS: As the species, except that old specimens remain short and pyramid-shaped instead of cylindrical and have ribs which are very flat but quite noticeably interrupted by cross-furrows and, therefore, tuberculate.

AREOLES: As the species.

SPINES: As the species, except that they are always very heavy, very flat, and very severely recurved against the plant, with no spines projecting outward.

FLOWERS: As the species.

FRUITS: As the species.

RANGE. Practically limited to west Texas. From the lower Pecos River to the Davis and Guadalupe mountains.

REMARKS. The Texas members of this species are mostly of this form. I have examined hundreds of Davis Mountain specimens without seeing a single plant diverging from this description. In southeastern New Mexico there are less definite examples which appear sometimes as intermediates. Engelmann stated, in "Corrections to the Cactaceae of the Boundary," that these two forms had "entire identity" and could scarcely be called varieties, but that the intermediates seem to require them. Yet when one moves so short a distance from the Franklin Mountains as the Selden and Portrillo mountains he finds all of the specimens there clearly of the next variety.

Variety *curvispina* is, therefore, the eastern form of the species. The extremely heavy, recurved spines on the squat, pyramid-shaped barrel gives us one of the most beautiful forms found in the cacti. It is a plant remarkable for the unvarying tidiness and symmetry of its form and it gives a fascinating expression of unyielding toughness. Still, its spines are so appressed against its surface that one may hold an old giant of this variety in the flat of the hand without getting a prick from it. I have seen workmen unloading a truckload of these plants by casually tossing them down from one to another like balls—all barehanded. This is something one had better not try with the more western variety of the species.

Echinocactus horizonthalonius var. moelleri Haage Jr.

DESCRIPTION   PLATE 19

STEMS: As the species, except that with age it becomes more columnar than pyramid-shaped and taller but not so large in diameter. The ribs are high but with very shallow cross-grooves; the tubercles are more fused and often are hardly visible at all.

AREOLES: As the species.

SPINES: As the species, except that the spines are not so heavy, being only somewhat flattened, and straighter; not recurving against the plant but rather standing out at angles from its surface.

FLOWERS: As the species.

FRUITS: As the species.

RANGE. From the Franklin and Guadalupe mountains west into Arizona.

REMARKS. This is the western form of the species. By comparison to the other variety it is smaller in diameter but taller and more columnar, with sharper, higher, less interrupted ribs. But the most noticeable difference is in the spines, which in this variety show none of the tidiness of the others, but stand out at all angles in chaotic, interlacing masses. Where the one may be handled easily, woe betide anyone who thinks to pick up this variety by other than the roots, as there are spines aimed in every direction and if he seeks to withdraw from a point in one direction he will usually back into an opposing point nearby or even be caught between the spines, which often have a pincers action. These spines are also much less heavy or flattened than those of the other variety.

Echinocactus texensis Hopff.
[*Homalocephala texensis* (Hopff.) B. & R.]
"Devil's Head," "Horse Crippler," "Candy Cactus," "Manco Caballo," "Viznaga"

DESCRIPTION   PLATE 19

STEMS: Very broad. Greatly flattened to sometimes dome-shaped. This cactus grows to a maximum of about 12 inches across, and such large plants rise from only 2 to occasionally 8 inches high. Stems are usually single, but the plants occasionally produce 2 or 3 equal stems. When injured at the summit, they often produce a cluster of small heads on top of the old one. The surface is dark green. The ribs are prominent and acute, normally 13 or 14, 20 or 21, or 27 in number. The apex of the stem is filled with some long, white wool.

AREOLES: Triangular to inverted heart-shaped, $1/4$ to $3/8$ of an inch in greatest diameter, and covered with white or gray wool. They are located about 1 to $1^1/4$ inches apart.

SPINES: Reddish or brownish-gray, becoming whitish when old. Only a little flattened, they are ringed by regularly occurring ridges, and are very heavy and rigid. There are 6 or 7 radial spines from $3/8$ to 2 inches long. There are typically 2 diverging upper radials which are comparatively small and short, 2 lateral radials which are very heavy and long—often the longest spines—and a pair of lower diverging radials which are again smaller. Occasionally there may be one additional radial which is also comparatively small and directed straight upward. All the radials may be straight and spreading to strongly recurved. There is also one central spine which is the stoutest spine, often $1/8$ of an inch thick at the base and sometimes much more than that. It is from $3/4$ to $2^3/4$ inches long, deflexed, and from straight to recurved or sometimes slightly hooked.

FLOWERS: These are bell-shaped, 1 to $2^1/4$ inches in diameter and similar in length, slightly fragrant and very beautiful, each flower displaying an interesting range of shades. The ovary is densely covered with long white wool and many short, sharp-pointed but soft, blackish scales. These scales lengthen as they progress upward, while the wool thins. The outer perianth segments are short, narrow, and sharp-pointed. Their midribs are fleshy and greenish or brownish, ending in a brownish point, while their edges are greenish to whitish, fringed, and more or less covered with a web of wool. The inner perianth segments are narrowly lanceolate from narrow bases. These bases are red. A pale rose midline extends up the petal, darkening noticeably as it nears the apex, where it ends in a pronounced mucro which is purplish or brownish. All of the expanded part of the petal is pale lavender, salmon, pink or sometimes almost white, depending upon the individual plant. The edges of the petals are fringed to the tips, feathery in appearance. The filaments are reddish to pinkish, the anthers pale yellow. The style is yellowish or pinkish. The stigma has 10 to 17 rather long yellowish or pinkish lobes, each often having a red stripe on the lower side.

FRUITS: Spherical to oval, ³/₄ to about 1¹/₂ inches long. They remain fleshy and become brilliant red. After a very long time on the plant they usually split open vertically on one side. Scattered over the surface are the dried and hardened, bristle-like ovary scales, each with a tuft of white wool in its axil. On the top of the fruit clings the dried remains of the perianth. The seeds are black, kidney-shaped, slightly less than ¹/₈ of an inch in length.

RANGE. All of Texas west of a line from approximately the mouth of the Colorado River to near Fort Worth and Wichita Falls, except the Texas Panhandle and the extreme western tip of the state beyond the Guadalupe Mountains. Also in extreme southwest Oklahoma and southeastern New Mexico as far northwest as Roswell. Extending deep into adjacent Mexico.

REMARKS. It is fitting for this plant to carry the name *texensis*, for it has one of the widest ranges of any cactus in that state, and it does not venture far into any other state, barely entering Oklahoma and only penetrating a corner of New Mexico. It is a low, flat, retiring cactus content to stay under the grass, so although it is fairly common over a wide range, many people do not know it. Yet when one has once discovered it, he is not likely to forget the plant.

The impression this cactus gives is one of elemental, even brutal strength. It squats low to the ground, usually only 2 to 5 inches or so high, its surface is hard and unyielding, and it is covered with a loose system of not too many but some of the most robust and rigid spines found on any of our cacti. There it sits, and it seems to dare anyone to come its way. No wonder the ranchers of two nations call it in two languages by the name "Horse Crippler," for it is said that it sits there unseen in the grass, and if a running horse steps on it, the rigid spines will penetrate the tender underside of the hoof and cripple the horse. Its very strength brings its downfall, since most ranchers regularly uproot any of these pests they see on their ranges, and this has greatly reduced the numbers of these cacti found in many areas. However, the species is still very common in certain fields from within sight of the Gulf around Corpus Christi northwest through central Texas and in extreme southeast New Mexico. To either side of this broad southeast to northwest band one finds it less frequently, but it ranges over a wide area.

This species is remarkable because, even though it is one of the toughest of the barrels in structure, it can stand lots more moisture than most others of this group. For this reason it is much better adapted to cultivation than most of its relatives and can also stand more cold than most of them. It is a favorite among collectors and growers.

The species was first described and named *Echinocactus texensis* in 1842. Three years later Engelmann described it again and designated it *Echinocactus lindheimeri*. There were few other names coined for it, but *E. platycephalus* by Muehlen-

pfordt and *Melocactus laciniatus* by Berlandier are two synonyms.

There have been two varieties of this cactus proposed, variety *gourgensii* Cels and variety *longispinus* Schelle. Since it grows over so wide a range it is surprising there are not more localized forms deserving varietal rank, but the species is remarkably stable. There is a general gradient of spine size on these plants as one moves from southeast to northwest over its range. Those specimens from southeast Texas have more slender and usually somewhat shorter spines than those from farther northwest. This is not surprising, and the first of the above proposed varieties seems to be no more than a segment of this gradient which cannot really be set apart.

However, there is one local population which seems to be rather distinct from the rest, and which may deserve varietal rank. In the Big Bend of Texas, in Brewster County, one finds a population of this species which is identical to the rest except for the following points: its surface is more gray-green than typical, and its central spines run from 2 to 2³/₄ inches long on mature individuals. This plant's physiology is also so different from that of the typical specimens from the rest of Texas that while the typical specimens have been growing, blooming, and fruiting each year in my beds, my examples of this form have sat right beside them for five years with a minimum of growth and never a bloom. This may be variety *longispinus* Schelle, but since I have never succeeded in seeing its flowers and fruits and cannot give more details about it, it is not so listed here.

After what looked like a history free of any arguments over its taxonomic place, this cactus caught the eye of Britton and Rose and they took it out of the genus *Echinocactus* and erected a new genus, *Homalocephala*, for it. This has remained a monotypic genus.

There seems to have been little if any discussion of the validity of this new genus. It was accepted as a logical result when the original genus *Echinocactus* was broken up, and so it may be if one is to follow in that step to no one knows yet what fragmentation. However, I have noted in the discussion of the genus *Echinocactus* that some of the most significant recent research on cacti has involved this species. Dr. Boke's summary of his anatomical research results are so important here that we should refer to them again. He says, "The combined list of characters suggests to the author that if *E. horizonthalonius* is to be retained in the genus *Echinocactus*, *Homalocephala* should be returned to the same genus. It further suggests that *E. horizonthalonius* could, with equal logic, be referred to the genus *Homalocephala*."

Faced with this alternative, I choose to return *Homalocephala texensis* to the genus where it was originally thought to belong, rather than to further fragment the original genus and eliminate it from our area altogether by making it a *Homalocephala horizonthalonius*.

I find a great similarity between *Echinocactus texensis* and a plant brought out of Mexico by a dealer. I saw several dozen specimens of this Mexican plant, some of them up to about 16 inches in diameter but still only about 8 inches tall. The ribs, areoles, and spines of this plant are almost identical to those of our plant, except that the spines are longer and more yellow in color, and the centrals stand more upward. The plant was being sold as *Echinocactus victoriensis*, but I have been able to learn little more about it. It does not seem to be *Ferocactus rafaelensis* (Purpus) B. & R. This plant appears to be the most closely related to our Texas cactus of anything I have yet seen.

Echinocactus asterias Zucc.
[*Astrophytum asterias* (Zucc.) Lem.]
   "Sea-Urchin Cactus"

DESCRIPTION   PLATE 19

STEMS: Extremely flat, depressed disc-shaped to sometimes low dome-shaped. Mature plants are from 2 to occasionally 6 inches in diameter by less than 1 to at most 2½ inches tall. This plant body, which is always simple, is divided by very narrow but distinct vertical grooves, into 8 broad, almost flat ribs. These ribs actually form triangular sections of the stem. Up the center of each section runs a line of areoles which are on no projections and separated by no cross-grooves of any kind. The surface of the plant is a dull green, and scattered over it are tiny, less than pin-head-sized clusters of very short, whitish wool.

AREOLES: Circular, a little less than ⅛ to ¼ of an inch across, and filled with dense wool, at first straw-colored, then gray. They are located about ¼ to ⅜ of an inch apart.

SPINES: None.

FLOWERS: Yellow with orange throats. 2 to 3½ inches across and about 2 inches tall. Opening widely. The ovary is densely covered with scales which have blackish, bristle-like points at their summits and much cobwebby wool in their axils. The outer perianth segments are short, narrow and pointed, greenish in color, and covered on their outer surfaces with short fuzz. The inner segments are long, slightly spatulate, from narrow orange bases. The upper parts are clear yellow, the edges entire and the tips from entire and slightly pointed to somewhat erose and irregular. The filaments are orange at their bases and yellow above. The anthers are yellow. The style is yellowish and the stigma has 10 to 12 yellow lobes.

FRUITS: Oval, about ½ inch long. Densely covered with spines and wool. Becoming dry while on the plant and finally breaking off at or near the base. The seeds are black or nearly so, shiny, about 1/16 of an inch long.

RANGE. Entering Texas from Mexico only in the lower Rio Grande Valley, where it is found in a few locations in Starr and Hidalgo counties.

REMARKS. Strange as it may seem, this is a diminutive barrel cactus. It is unmistakably the dwarfed relative of a group of large, columnar barrels found in Mexico and it is still very closely related to the biggest barrels of all. But this one has apparently survived by being small, inconspicuous, and retiring. It even dispenses with the typical heavy covering of spines and shows that survival is possible without these. This is said to be accomplished by having the whole body suffused with some chemical compounds distasteful to all enemies so that it can remain unarmored among them. It also has scattered over its surface to a greater or lesser degree on different specimens a series of clusters of short white wool, said to substitute to some extent for the lack of the shade which other cacti get from their spines.

The form of this cactus is unique and remarkably beautiful. It projects a very short distance above the ground even when plump and water-filled. When water is deficient it shrinks to a mere flat disc which hardly projects above the ground at all and may be almost covered by the sand. Its common name comes from the fact that its broad, nearly flat ribs and its shape make it look almost exactly like the skeleton of a sea urchin denuded of its spines.

The cactus has had at best a precarious foothold on the north side of the Rio Grande. It has been found on the dry hills overlooking the river and never more than about 15 or 20 miles north of that river. And we have in recent times not been kind to this immigrant. The cactus has been a favorite among collectors, partly because it is a beautiful curiosity without spines. Dealers have for many years scoured the counties where it grows for the plant, and have uprooted it by the thousands for the trade. At the present time it takes a very good guide to show one the few locations in Texas where it still grows in numbers, and the chances are rather good that when one gets there a cactus digger will already have eliminated the population. With the widespread clearing of the area which is now going on, this cactus may well be eliminated in Texas, although it is abundant in Mexico.

The species was long ago called *Echinocactus asterias* by Zuccarini. Over a hundred years ago Lemaire separated out some cacti formerly in that genus, including this one, into a new genus, *Astrophytum*. Coulter later thought this unwarranted and returned them to *Echinocactus*. K. Schumann agreed with him, but listed *Astrophytum* as a subgenus of the genus *Echinocactus*.

Most authors since then have treated *Astrophytum* as a separate genus, although very few of the books on U.S. cacti have included it at all, since only this one species is found in the U.S. and that only in a very small region of south Texas. Buxbaum, the great theorizer about cacti, decided that the Astrophytums do not have any close relationship to the Echinocacti at all, but instead he considers them the most northerly of the South American cactus group. He considers the closest relatives to the sea-urchin cactus to be the members of the South

American genus *Frailea*. Others, including Backeberg, have opposed this idea most strenuously, and their arguments show good reasons why it is after all an Echinocactus. It does seem that if this, with its scaly, woolly ovary, is not a member of the Echinocacti then the distinguishing characters of that group are of little validity and the group can hardly exist on any level at all.

Echinocactus wislizeni Eng.
[*Ferocactus wislizeni* (Eng.) B. & R.]
"Barrel Cactus," "Fishhook Barrel," "Candy Barrel,"
"Visnaga," "Biznaga," "Biznaga de Agua"

DESCRIPTION   PLATE 20
STEMS: Spherical at first, then ovate or conical, and finally cylindrical. This plant becomes very massive, up to at least 4 feet tall, and is said to have reached 6 feet tall. It grows about 2 feet in diameter. There are 13 to 25 ribs which are sharp, up to about 1¼ inches high, and a little undulate because of the slight bulging at the areoles. The color of the surface is dark green.

AREOLES: ⅝ to 1 inch long and ¾ to 1¼ inches apart, elliptic to linear. Those areoles which have not produced flowers have the upper end prolonged as a narrow groove; but after blooming this upper part of the areole is permanently broadened and connected to the lower, spinous part by a more narrow neck. It has a short brownish wool which fades to gray and then is mostly lost on old areoles. Some glands are present.

SPINES: There are 12 to more than 20 slender radial spines. The upper and lateral ones are flexible, bristle-like, whitish, and about 1 to 2 inches long. The lower 3 are a little shorter and rigid, approaching the character of the centrals. There are 4 very strong centrals 1½ to 3 inches long, yellowish to red or purplish-red, and all ringed by conspicuous annular ridges. The upper three are straight, spreading upward, and are round to somewhat flattened. The lower one stands porrect or slightly deflexed, is usually hooked downward at the end (but on rare specimens is nearly straight), is much heavier than the other centrals, and is somewhat to greatly flattened.

FLOWERS: Variable shades of yellow, gold, orange, or red, about 2 inches long by 2 to 3 inches across. The ovary is covered with scales which are green, edged in white. The outer segments of the perianth are short, triangular-shaped to ovoid, with pointed apexes, the midlines greenish to reddish or yellowish, and the edges entire and lighter colored. The inner segments are linear and sharply pointed, the edges slightly irregular or erose. They are most commonly orange-red on the midlines shading to conch-shell pink on the edges, but they may be all yellow or all red. The extremely numerous filaments are yellow or red, the very small anthers yellow. There are 18 to at least 26 long, pointed, erect stigma lobes which are in yellow flowers yellow, in red flowers reddish below and yellowish above.

FRUITS: Oblong, 1¼ to 2¼ inches long, practically covered with white-edged scales. They are yellowish and fleshy at first, but remain long on the plants, becoming finally dried and hard. The seeds are nearly ⅛ of an inch long, black, with the surface rough but not tuberculate.

RANGE. From Arizona east through the mountains of southern Hidalgo and Luna counties, New Mexico, to the Organ and Franklin mountains of Dona Ana County, and extending into Texas only in the Franklin Mountains near El Paso. Also in adjacent Mexico.

REMARKS. This is the largest cactus in our area, and the one which is truly barrel-like in its dimensions. An old specimen of this cactus is awe-inspiring for its sheer bulk and the impression of age and strength it presents. It is the tough old patriarch of the exposed mountain slopes in our semidesert regions. Such a mountainside still dotted with its population of old barrels is an unforgettable sight. The effect is much like that of viewing a herd of buffalo or a flock of whooping cranes, and the chance of experiencing it today is almost as unlikely. Each of these is a giant among its kind, formidable to confront—yet today each is, as a species, only a pitiful remnant of what it once was. One is lucky now to find an individual candy barrel, and there are very few places left in our area where one can see a population of old specimens still undisturbed in their natural glory.

There are several reasons why such great, formidable species have fared so badly in the last hundred years, and understanding them can teach us much about this cactus and about ourselves. Some of these reasons arise out of the fact that, taken individually, these organisms are not as invulnerable as they appear. They are all approaching extremes in development and adaptation to very special environments, and while this gives them great survival powers in these special environments, it makes them conspicuous targets for new enemies which enter the community and it renders them ungainly misfits which cannot maintain themselves when the environment is changed or they are pulled out and put somewhere else.

Modern man is the new enemy which has recently entered the environment of each of these, and they have fallen in terrible numbers before his attack. But why did he come before them as such a ruthless destroyer? Precisely because of their size and majesty.

Each of them was so big that an individual presented a mass of flesh usable for food and other purposes. As they slaughtered the buffalo for meat and hides, they slaughtered the barrel cactus to use its watery pulp. The few that were sacrificed to the thirst of prospectors caused no problem. The real inroads upon this plant came with its use for making candy. This became so widespread that it became known by the name, candy barrel.

Man's slaughter of these organisms could be more easily excused if it had been limited by even such uses of them, but it has not been. The very appearance of them apparently invokes a reaction in modern man, and he has turned his weapons upon them in a frenzy of destruction. It is as though before their formidable majesty he developed an inferiority complex which issued in an urge to kill. The extent of this factor in the slaughter of the buffalo is easily seen, but few realize that it has played a big part in the disappearance of the barrel cactus.

One of the few places where I have seen a stand of old barrels was in a small canyon so deep in the Franklin Mountains that a mountain lion shadowed us as we proceeded up it. Here I found myself on a steep slope with several dozen fine old cacti up to four feet tall in view at the same time. But I had arrived there a week or so too late. As I moved from one to another of these old monarchs, each perhaps half a century old, I found that each had been neatly decapitated or else the apex split open by one deft stroke of a machete or some such instrument. The exposed flesh of each one was melting away in the heat. Since then that canyon is a sad place to anyone knowing what was needlessly destroyed.

I did not understand the reason for such a destruction until some time later when I stood and observed people filing through the cactus house of the New York Botanical Garden. Here I saw a man push against the fence which protected the plants and, gesturing excitedly toward a beautiful old barrel cactus, roar for the benefit of his young son, "Look at that big, ugly, ——— ——— thing!! God, if I could only get at it, you'd see how I'd fix it! I'd tear it apart!!" Only then did I realize how such great organisms have been sacrificed to the ego of modern man.

More indirectly, but quite as effectively they have been sacrificed to man's meddling with their environment. When he moves in and tampers with it, they, being so specialized, are usually the first to go. And, finally, the unwise treatment of those who do appreciate the beauty of these cacti takes its toll. Fine old giants are pulled up and planted in lush yards where they cannot live. The extent of this activity is so great that I have seen them arrive by the truckload at nurseries in climates where they cannot possibly be kept alive out-of-doors. Against all of this destruction the buffalo and the whooping crane are now protected, but not the candy barrel within our area.

There have been a few problems about this species' taxonomy. Engelmann first described and named it. He also described and named an *Echinocactus emoryi*, which has been the subject of much confusion since some have thought it was a synonym of this and some have thought not, and he also had an *E. wislizeni* var. *decipiens,* but neither of these forms appears in the area covered by this study and so we do not have to evaluate them here. Apparent later synonyms for *E. wislizeni* were *E. falconeri* Orcutt and *E. arizonicus* Kunze.

Everything was rather stable, taxonomically, concerning this plant until Britton and Rose. These authors, however, in breaking up the old genus *Echinocactus* erected a new genus *Ferocactus* and placed in it this plant, along with various others. It has generally been known since their time as *Ferocactus wislizeni*.

But Britton and Rose's genus *Ferocactus* has not fared very well. A number of species which they included in it have since been removed by other students to other genera, among them their *Ferocactus johnsonii* to *Echinomastus*, *F. hamatacanthus* to *Hamatocactus* and *F. crassahamatus* and *F. uncinatus* to *Glandulicactus*. It is obvious that Britton and Rose's concept of the genus *Ferocactus* was not satisfactory and that the genus has come to be, at best, another microgenus. The only real character which can be cited to set *wislizeni* off from the Echinocacti is the absence of wool on the ovary and fruit. If this is considered a character less essential than it takes to support a genus all by itself, as Link and Otto obviously regarded it, then we would have little if anything else definite to uphold the genus *Ferocactus*. Because of these considerations I am using the older genus name for this plant.

Echinocactus uncinatus var. wrightii Eng.

[*Glandulicactus uncinatus* var. *wrightii* (Eng.) Backbg.]
"Turk's Head," "Cat-Claw Cactus," "Brown-Flowered Hedgehog," "Texas Hedgehog"

DESCRIPTION   PLATE 20

STEMS: Oval, up to 8 inches tall and 4½ inches thick, but usually much smaller. These stems are almost always single, but occasionally they may produce 1 or 2 branches at or near the base. The surface is bluish-green with a gray glaucescence and is formed into 9 to 13 ribs. These ribs are fairly high and conspicuous, separated by broad grooves, and consist of rather distinct but partly fused tubercles. The tubercles themselves are rather remarkable in shape. The areole is on the upper slope of the tubercle, which is prolonged below or ventral to the areole into a chinlike swelling which more or less overhangs the upper end of the areole on the next tubercle. The abrupt drop-off from this prominent chin before the next tubercle produces a sharp cross-indentation of the rib when it is old. On the new tubercles the chin and this cross-indentation are not yet so definite.

AREOLES: Elongated oval, to about ⅝ of an inch long, the upper end prolonged into a narrow extension which has been called a groove. The spines all grow from the broader lower portion of the areole, while the flower is produced from the narrower upper end of it. In the still more narrow neck of the areole joining these two regions there are produced several yellowish glands. The whole areole contains gray or slightly yellowish wool.

SPINES: All spines are very heavy and are at first red, later reddish-brown, straw-colored, or grayish, with the points remaining darker. There are 7 or 8 radial spines which radiate rather evenly. The upper and lateral 4 or 5 are straight, flattened, and from 3/4 to 2 inches long. The lower 3 radials are 3/4 to 1 1/4 inches long, round, or nearly so, more or less curved, and hooked at their tips. There is one central spine from 2 to at least 4 inches long, which stands porrect or turned upward, and is very heavy, angled, usually twisted, and hooked at the tip.

FLOWERS: Maroon to garnet in color. They are funnel-shaped, not opening widely, 3/4 to 1 1/4 inches long, and about 1 inch across. The narrow ovary is covered with short, broad scales with brown centers and broad white, membranous edges. The outer perianth segments are triangular to long triangular with bluntly pointed tips and white, entire, but often crinkled, edges. The maroon to garnet inner segments are linear, their edges sometimes lighter colored and often irregular or toothed above, with the apex slightly pointed, irregular, or sometimes even squared off. The filaments are brown or maroon, the anthers cream-colored. The style is brown, the stigma having 10 to 14 broad, fat lobes which are cream-colored above and maroon below.

FRUITS: Oblong to egg-shaped, 5/8 to 1 inch long. They are for a brief time pale reddish between the whitish scales which very nearly cover them. They soon become dry and colorless, usually remaining on the plant for a long time in this condition. The seeds are about 1/16 of an inch long, curved, and compressed, with the hila basal. The surface of the seeds is finely tuberculate.

RANGE. Southern New Mexico, south Texas, and adjacent Mexico.

REMARKS. Although commonly designated as a hedgehog cactus rather than a barrel, this cactus is a smaller one of the latter group with spines to rival any.

The range given above for this form is less specific than for most. This is because, while the cactus has been found over a huge area, it is apparently common today hardly anywhere, and we suspect that it has been eliminated from some of its former range. It is still to be found in limited numbers on dry hills from El Paso to Van Horn and on down the Rio Grande past Presidio, Texas. This is a far cry from Coulter's statement of 1896 that it was then "abundant from El Paso, Texas, to the Pecos," but it does seem to be the center of this cactus' range and the only area where one can count on finding it today.

From here there are isolated records of the plant for great distances in all directions, even though none of them seem to represent established populations at these faraway points. Coulter stated its range as, "Extending almost to the mouth of the Rio Grande." After several years of extensive observation almost all along that river, the idea of this cactus existing any more below the Big Bend had about become unbelievable to me, when suddenly I found one specimen of the cactus growing happily near Falcon Dam in Starr County, far down toward the mouth of the river from any place I had seen it before. No more could be found in the area, and we have still found no record of the plant in the more than 300 miles between this collection and the Trans-Pecos records. However, this does corroborate to a great extent Nealley's old record of the plant having been taken near Rio Grande City.

In all other directions we find similar very widely scattered records, some of them not duplicated in many years. Northeast of the central range there is Lloyd's record of the plant just east of Fort Stockton, Texas, which I have not been able to duplicate. Going north and west of El Paso there are few and very widely scattered records of the cactus in New Mexico. Very far to the northwest. Wooton and Standley list it as found at Pena Blanca, New Mexico, which is only some 25 miles or so southwest of Santa Fe. While it has been found west of El Paso in southern New Mexico, it apparently does not reach Arizona. We are faced with the fact that there must once have been a very huge area over which this cactus ranged, but that today, everywhere but in the central range as outlined above, it is so rare that if one locates a single specimen he should consider himself very lucky.

Our U.S. form is not the typical form of the species, *Echinocactus uncinatus* Galeotti. That form has 3 or 4 central spines and a difference in the seed form, and seems restricted to Mexico. Engelmann realized the difference in our form and called our variety *wrightii*. There has been no disagreement about this since, except that some authors have not bothered to tack on the varietal name, merely using the species name for our plant. No one has produced any evidence that I have seen of the typical form being found in the U.S. One man, the late Mr. Fred Leasure, an El Paso teacher who for most of a lifetime collected, studied, and dealt in cacti from that area, once told me that he had found a population of the typical form with several centrals, somewhere in the mountains near El Paso. I was never able to learn any details about this.

Most of the disagreement over this plant has been about what genus to put it in, and the history of these arguments is a rather disillusioning one.

Galeotti, in the beginning, placed the species in the old genus *Echinocactus*. There was no question at all through all of the earlier treatments of the cactus until Britton and Rose broke up the large genus. When they did, they put this cactus in their new genus *Ferocactus*. It does have some close similarities to the other species placed in that genus, among them being a very scaly ovary which is bare of wool. But differences can be cited too. Once these small similarities and differences began to be considered significant on the generic level, the gate was down, and the confusion which has resulted has not enhanced the reputation of cactus scholarship.

Knuth, in 1935, was just as certain as Britton and Rose had been about *Ferocactus* that the cactus belonged in the equally new genus *Echinomastus*. He had his reasons also. But by 1941

Marshall published the plant as *Thelocactus uncinatus*, with his set of arguments backing this name. By this time Backeberg had also published his solution of the problem, which was to erect an entirely new genus for the species. He justified this to a large extent by the presence of glands in the areoles of the species, and so his new name was *Glandulicactus uncinatus*.

In 1951 Buxbaum published yet another disposition of the species. He was very sure that it should be in the genus *Hamatocactus*. His reasons were good enough to persuade Marshall, and in 1957 he published his new opinion that the species should really be called *Hamatocactus uncinatus*. However, Backeberg remained unconvinced and in his still more recent large work maintains the genus *Glandulicactus* and adds some other species to it.

One seems to be able to take his own choice of all these genera for this species, with perhaps *Hamatocactus* and *Glandulicactus* having a slight edge in taxonomic opinion at the present time. It would take a long digression to outline the points for and against each genus. They are all very detailed, slight differences of morphology which tend to balance each other off too well, leaving the decision between them at best somewhat arbitrary. I myself feel that these are all no more than microgenera and that the argument may well be left with the theorists while we, by harking back to the old genus *Echinocactus* of Link and Otto, can find a name so usable and stable that it will not be different in every book picked up.

This is a rare species, a tough, desert-loving one, and therefore one which is not very easy to cultivate. It rots very quickly from too much moisture, but if this problem is taken care of, it can grow slowly and produce a number of small but interesting flowers which are very unusual for their brownish hues.

Echinocactus whipplei Eng. & Big.
[*Sclerocactus whipplei* (Eng. & Big.) B. & R.]
    "Devil's Claw Barrel"

DESCRIPTION   PLATE 20
    STEMS: From practically spherical to an ovate or even short-cylindrical shape. These stems are usually single and up to 6 inches tall by 4 inches in diameter, but occasionally forming small clusters of 2 or 3 stems, and said to have reached 12 inches tall and 6 inches in diameter. They have 13 to 15 ribs composed of conspicuous tubercles 1/4 to 3/8 of an inch high. These tubercles are almost completely separated near the stem apex, but are quite fused lower down on the stem. The surface is dark green.
    AREOLES: Circular at first, but the growth of the flower out of the upper edge of each produces a narrower extension of it upward which persists, leaving the areole from then on elliptical ovate, or even narrowly ovate. Areoles range in size

from about 3/16 to slightly over 1/4 of an inch long, and have much white wool.

SPINES: There are 7 to 11 straight, evenly radiating radial spines 1/2 to 1 inch long. They are rather slender, compressed, and all but 1 lower lateral on each side white in color. These 2 lower laterals are gray or brownish in color. There are 4 central spines on matured specimens, although immature ones have no centrals. The lowermost central is porrect to a little deflexed, strong, round to somewhat flattened, hooked at the end, and 1 to 2 inches long. It is gray or tan to reddish-purple, usually streaked with white. The two lateral centrals are similar but straight. The upper central is lighter in color, sometimes whitish, more flattened (sometimes very much so), and straight or nearly so.

FLOWERS: Very beautiful, more or less funnel-shaped blooms of varying colors: mostly fuchsia, but sometimes purplish, pink, white, or even yellowish. They are about 1 to 2 inches in diameter and nearly the same length. The short ovary has a few short, greenish, triangular scales with membranous, crinkled edges and short hairs in their axils. They intergrade into the outer perianth segments, which are almost lanceolate, greenish in the midline with the edges whitish, membranous, and crinkled. The inner perianth segments are fuchsia, pink, white, or yellowish; lanceolate; with their ends pointed and the edges entire or nearly so. The filaments are pink, rose, or yellow, the anthers orange. The style and stigma are greenish or rose, the stigma with 5 to 10 lobes.

FRUITS: Oblong, about 1/4 to 1/2 inch long. Green to pinkish and fleshy at first. The surface has several scales upon it, with small tufts of wool in their axils. When ripe it becomes dry and then opens by splitting all the way around at or near the base.

RANGE. The northwestern corner of New Mexico into northeastern Arizona, the very southwestern corner of Colorado, and on into Utah. In New Mexico mostly limited to San Juan, McKinley and Sandoval counties, but recorded once from upper Socorro County.

REMARKS. This is a beautiful though diminutive barrel cactus which is so retiring in both its appearance and its range that many have never seen it. It looks like just another clump of dried grass and sticks in the field, and although it occurs over a wide area of several states, it is adapted to such extremely arid conditions that one has to go far into the desolate hills and Indian reservations to find it. For these reasons it has not been brought out and sold as commonly as many other cacti. This is probably just as well, since with its adaptation to such extreme conditions it is extra sensitive to moisture and most people are disappointed who try to keep it alive outside of the arid southwest.

The species was first dealt with by Engelmann and Bigelow, who named it *Echinocactus whipplei*. The only change in its name since was that made by Britton and Rose who decided to put it in one of their separate microgenera. They called it *Sclerocactus whipplei*, and this name has been widely used.

The basis for this separation of *Sclerocactus* from the other Echinocacti has always been at best vague, and in 1950, when L. Benson was acting upon his own taxonomic principle of synthesis above splitting, he dropped this new genus and used the original name. But in 1966 Benson published a series of articles in which he resurrected the genus *Sclerocactus* again and broadened it to include species never before in it. This was done, however, without the advancing of any new facts to make the move appear more necessary now than before. The decision either way seems purely arbitrary, and since we have not seen a single new character mentioned since Britton and Rose's doubtful ones to justify putting their little grouping on a par with the genus *Echinocactus* I see no real reason to regard it as more than a subgenus.

In his series of articles Benson distinguishes three varieties of this species. The form he designates variety *roseus* does not grow in our area and so I do not deal with it here. He designates as *Sclerocactus whipplei* var. *whipplei* a form which he says is found only in Arizona, growing to only 3 inches tall, and having the upper central white, flat, and 1/16 to 1/8 of an inch wide at the base, and, so far as is known, bearing only yellow flowers. Then he has a third variety, *Sclerocactus whipplei* var. *intermedius*. This is the one found in all four states which grows to 6 inches tall, has the upper central less flattened and only 1/24 to 1/16 of an inch thick at the base, and has purple, rose, pink, or white flowers. If these varieties are distinct all New Mexico specimens known so far would be the latter, as no one has reported yellow flowers in the state.

I have been unable to follow these varieties in every case. Some New Mexico plants seem to duplicate all of the characters of variety *whipplei* so closely that they would, except for blooming with fuchsia flowers, be that variety. Since I have avoided basing any variety on flower color and the other distinguishing characters of these two varieties seem to intergrade in New Mexico specimens, I am not listing these varieties definitely here. More study of this species will be needed before a final word on them can be given.

Echinocactus mesae-verdae (Boissevain) L. Benson
[*Sclerocactus mesae-verdae* (Boissevain) L. Benson]
  "Mesa Verde Cactus"

DESCRIPTION   PLATE 21
  STEMS: Depressed-globose to short-cylindrical in shape, with mature plants usually from 1½ to 3 inches tall and wide, but said to have achieved 7 inches tall. There are 13 to 17 ribs. On young plants they are indistinct, composed of tubercles almost completely separated from one another, but on older plants these tubercles become confluent, with deep grooves between the ribs and lesser cross-furrows between the tubercles. The surface is pale grayish-green.

AREOLES: Ovate and 1/8 to 1/4 of an inch long, containing much wool at first yellowish and then fading to gray.

SPINES: There are 8 to 11 radial spines spreading irregularly around the areole. They are straight or slightly curved, round or nearly so, tan or straw-colored, about 3/8 to 1/2 inch long, and rigid. Central spines are usually missing, but on very rare individuals are present—then described as being one per areole, 1/2 inch or less in length, gray with a dark tip, porrect to ascending, and straight or sometimes hooked.

FLOWERS: Cream to whitish in color, funnel-shaped, 3/4 to 1 1/4 inches wide and tall. The ovary and tube have a few broadly triangular scales placed high on them, but have no wool. The outer perianth segments are from triangular to oblanceolate and brownish with yellowish, entire margins. Inner perianth segments are cream or whitish from greenish bases, oblanceolate, entire or somewhat erose at the tips. The filaments are green or yellowish-green, the anthers yellow. The stigma has 6 to 8 light green lobes. The flowers are fragrant.

FRUITS: Very small: about 3/16 of an inch long, and cylindrical in shape. They are greenish at first, becoming brownish and dry and finally splitting open with an irregular, transverse opening near the middle of the fruit. The seeds are black, 1/8 of an inch or a little more in the longest measurement.

RANGE. A very small area in the extreme southwest corner of Colorado and the extreme northwest corner of New Mexico, actually comprising a strip of territory only about fifty miles long from near Cortez, Colorado, past Mesa Verde to slightly southwest of Shiprock, New Mexico.

REMARKS. This is one of the rarest of our cacti. It was discovered by Boissevain near Cortez, Colorado. He remarked about its rarity and the fact that it is adapted to drought beyond any other Colorado cactus, so much so that he could not keep it healthy even in his Colorado garden. Actually it is adapted to an extremely alkaline soil, as well as to extreme dryness. The combination of its rarity and the difficulty encountered in trying to grow the plant artificially means that few have ever seen it. Yet it does grow down into New Mexico, and is a most interesting, if rather prosaic cactus inhabitant of our area.

In his first description of the cactus, Boissevain thought of it as representing a new genus. Going all the way with pride of state, he gave it the name *Coloradoa mesae-verdae*, certainly one of the most geographical plant names ever. It seems difficult to justify *Coloradoa* as a genus, and in 1951 L. Benson moved the plant to the genus *Echinocactus*. This would seem to have given the species a place to rest comfortably, but in a recent set of articles Benson has reinstated the genus *Sclerocactus* again, after having himself dropped it, and now he assigns this cactus to that genus. Thus this cactus has begun its journey, following the others in looking for a generic home. We hope it is not as long a journey as it has been for some others of the Echinocacti.

In view of the extreme rarity of this cactus and the great difficulty which is encountered in keeping it alive after taken, it would seem useless and wanton to endanger the species by collecting in the wild specimens which are probably doomed by being taken anyway. Perhaps someone can grow these plants from seeds, and thus condition them to cultivation, after which this rarity can take its place in collections.

Echinocactus brevihamatus Eng.
[*Ancistrocactus brevihamatus* (Eng.) B. &R.]
"Fishhook Cactus"

DESCRIPTION   PLATE 21

ROOTS: Fibrous.

STEMS: Globose, egg-shaped, or, when older, columnar. The maximum size seems to be about 5 inches high by 3½ inches in diameter, and no clustering has been reported. The surface is a very dark, dull green. There are 13 straight or slightly spiraling ribs which are made up of rows of tubercles almost completely separated from each other by deep notches. These tubercles are up to about ½ inch tall from bases nearly as broad, but are compressed from side to side to leave an uninterrupted groove between the ribs.

AREOLES: Almost linear. The lower end of the areole is slightly expanded and contains the spine cluster. Above this is a narrow groovelike portion of the areole containing 1 to several glands. At the upper end of this groove the flower is produced, and after flowering this portion remains a little expanded. The whole areole thus measures ¼ to ½ inch long and runs from three-fourths to all of the way to the base of the tubercle. These areoles are at first filled with white wool, which is mostly lost on old areoles.

SPINES: There are 12 to 14 rather heavy radial spines which spread out slightly from the plant. They are from ⅜ to 1 inch long, the upper ones the longer. They are opaque, tan with dark brown tips at first, then turning gray. There are typically 4 centrals, but occasionally 1 or 2 more. The uppermost is erect in front of the upper radials, slender, straight, its upper surface flat while its lower side is rounded. This spine is ¾ to 1¼ inches long. On either side of it are 2 or more centrals diverging upward and similar except growing to 1¾ inches long. These upper centrals are all colored like the radials except that their flattened upper sides may be rust-colored in some specimens. The lowermost central stands out perpendicular to the plant surface, is heavier, distinctly flattened, and hooked, and measures ¾ to 1 inch long. It is yellowish-brown, rust, or dark brown on its flat upper side, lighter below, with the hook dark brown.

FLOWERS: Green in color, suffused with rose. They are 1 to 1⅝ inches long, but only ½ to ¾ of an inch wide, since they can hardly open because of the spines around them. The ovary of the flower has upon it fewer than a dozen small scalelike segments with fringed edges. Next there are about 8 outer perianth segments which are oblong with bluntly pointed ends. There are slightly over a dozen inner segments which are almost linear, about ⅝ of an inch long, and pointed. These are dark green with a faint rose midline on the outer side and dull rose fading to green edges on the inner surfaces. The filaments are bright rose. The anthers are yellow. The style is short, and there are 10 or 11 rose-pink stigma lobes.

FRUITS: Egg-shaped, green, becoming faintly pinkish when very ripe. They are ⅝ to about 1 inch long. There are several scales upon the surface of each fruit. They do not become completely dry, but remain somewhat fleshy until they disintegrate. The seeds are dark brown to blackish.

RANGE. Along the Rio Grande from near the mouth of the Pecos River to near Eagle Pass, occurring northeast almost to Uvalde and Brackettville, Texas, in the Anacacho Mountains, but not found otherwise more than a few miles north of Del Rio or up the Devil's River.

REMARKS. This species is a member of a very closely related group. However it has remained distinct in almost the whole of the literature since its first description by Engelmann, being regarded as a separate species by all except Weber who reduced it to a variety of the more widely known species, *Echinocactus scheeri*.

This plant is immediately told from *E. scheeri* by its fibrous roots, its darker green body, its fewer and longer opaque radial spines, and its flowers which are suffused with rose. Many take the name *brevihamatus* to mean that it has the lower, hooked central spine shorter than those of its relatives, but this leads them into difficulty, since the centrals of *E. scheeri* are often much shorter. Engelmann coined the name because of "the shortness of the hook," not the shortness of the spine, by which he meant that the hook itself is not curved as far around as in the typical *E. scheeri*. This is still an observation of doubtful value, since I have seen specimens of *E. scheeri* on which the spines failed to hook at all.

The species is limited to a comparatively small area in four counties of Texas along the middle course of the Rio Grande. It is found growing in the scattered clumps of low vegetation on rocky hillsides overlooking the river and on alluvial soil between the hills, never far from the Rio Grande except where it spreads into the Anacacho Mountains.

Engelmann included this species and its relatives in the genus *Echinocactus*. They were left there, a subgenus *Ancistrocactus* being erected by Schumann for them and some other species later put in a number of other genera, until Britton and Rose broke up the genus. When they did this Britton and Rose elevated *Ancistrocactus* to an entirely separate genus containing only this and a couple of other species. Their arrangement is naturally best known today. But if, in order to methodize some of the chaos which has resulted from Britton and Rose's break-up of that genus we go back to the original genus *Echinocactus* these are surely part of it.

Echinocactus scheeri SD
[*Ancistrocactus scheeri* (SD) B. & R.]
   "Fishhook Cactus," "Root Cactus"

DESCRIPTION   PLATE 21

ROOTS: *E. scheeri* grows from a long, fleshy, white taproot which is ¹/₄ to ¹/₂ inch in diameter and may be from a few inches to as much as 3 feet long. This root may occasionally branch to form several the same size.

STEMS: Globular at first, becoming quickly columnar or even club-shaped with the upper end often twice the diameter of the lower half. These stems grow to at least 7 inches tall and 3 inches in diameter, and are single until very old, when they sometimes branch from the base to form clumps of 6 or 8 stems. The flesh is medium to dark green in color. There are 13 straight or spiral ribs which are composed of only slightly connected, almost perfectly conical or only slightly compressed tubercles to ¹/₂ inch tall and the same width at their bases on large specimens.

AREOLES: Broadly ovate on unflowering tubercles. On flowering tubercles the ovate areoles are prolonged by a short groovelike extension above, at the upper end of which the flower appears. There are several glands in this groove. The length of this groove and, therefore, of the areole depends to a great degree on the age of the plant. Typically it extends from the spinous part of the areole at the summit of the tubercle about one-half of the way down the upper side of the tubercle; but in immature plants the groove does not form at all; in young flowering plants it is short; and on old plants it often extends three-fourths or more of the way to the axil. The areoles, therefore, vary from about ¹/₈ to as much as ³/₈ of an inch long. They have much white wool in them at first.

SPINES: There are 13 to 28 very slender radial spines, radiating strictly and tending to recurve toward the plant. They are ¹/₄ to ¹/₂ inch long on young plants, but grow to as much as 1¹/₈ inches long on some very old specimens. They are a very light, translucent yellowish shade, with the tips red-brown. There are also 3 or 4 centrals as follows: 2 straight upper centrals diverge as they stand erect to form a distinct V. They are ³/₄ to 2 inches long, distinctly flattened, the upper side being brown to dark mahogany-brown, while the lower or outer side is tan to whitish. There may or may not be 1 more upper central bisecting the V formed by the other 2 and similar to

them except shorter and more slender. The lowermost central stands out perpendicular to the stem; it is stout, flattened above or sometimes almost round, and almost always hooked. It varies on different plants from ¹/₂ to 1¹/₂ inches long. In color it is variegated, being mostly dark brown or black above and light brown or whitish below.

FLOWERS: Plain green or yellow-green. About 1 inch long, but only ¹/₂ to ³/₄ of an inch wide due to their inability to open farther because of the surrounding spines. There are about 12 fringed scales on the ovary. There are about 8 outer segments of the perianth, which are linear with blunt ends, deep green with yellowish edges. There are about 13 inner segments, to about an inch long and almost ¹/₄ of an inch wide, with pointed ends. These are bright green in some specimens or yellowish in others. The color of the filaments varies. In some plants they are green, in some yellowish, while in a few they are pink or even reddish. The anthers are yellow or pale orange. The style is somewhat longer than the stamens. The stigma lobes vary in number from 5 to 10, in length from ³/₁₆ to ¹/₄ of an inch, and in color from green to yellowish, cream or even brown, sometimes the brown ones having a faint pink flush at the tips.

FRUITS: ³/₄ to 1³/₈ inches long, not including the old perianth which persists upon them. They are club-shaped. There are 12 to 24 scales widely spaced upon each fruit. They remain green for the whole of the summer, but when very ripe they finally turn yellowish tinged with pink. They ultimately disintegrate, sometimes splitting open vertically on one side as they rot. The seeds are about ¹/₁₆ of an inch long, very dark mahogany-brown with the surface dull instead of shining due to extremely fine pitting. They are globular, compressed from side to side, with large, deeply concave hila.

RANGE. In Texas south of a line from approximately Eagle Pass to Pleasanton to near Kingsville, also ranging deep into Mexico.

REMARKS. This species was described before any of its relatives by Prince Salm-Dyck. As Britton and Rose mention, there is doubt as to what specimens the description was originally based upon. Engelmann made his description, the first detailed one, from obviously very immature specimens, since he gave as the maximum size a mere 2 inches tall. His plants also were from Eagle Pass, the northern extreme of their range. Coulter, Britton and Rose, and even Backeberg have descriptions which are essentially repetitions of Engelmann's, although the latter two did increase the maximum size to 4 inches tall.

I have studied literally hundreds of these plants in their habitats and also as they have come to San Antonio dealers before being sent all over the world. I have seen plants from Eagle Pass on the north to Brownsville on the south and numbers from Mexico. As a result I find that I must enlarge the description in several respects.

I have in my collection a plant which consists of a single stem

7 inches tall and club-shaped, being 3 inches in diameter near its top and only 2 inches thick near the ground. I have seen several clusters formed by the branching of such large stems near the ground, the largest with 8 heads forming a cluster about a foot across. This species can be a much larger and more majestic plant than we have been told.

Very early in my study of it, I noticed wide variations in the number of radial spines on different plants—considerably wider than the limits heretofore given. Engelmann's 11 to 18 was narrowed by Britton and Rose to 15 to 18, which number Backeberg repeats. On the other hand, in one group of 50 plants at a single location near Zapata, Texas, I found specimens with all numbers of radials from 13 and 14 on one plant to 28 on all areoles of another. Many plants varied widely in the number on the various areoles of the same plant. For instance, one had 18, 19, 21, 23, and 24 on its different areoles. I must state, however, that every plant I studied in the vicinity of Eagle Pass had between 14 and 17 radials, showing why Engelmann did not give the higher numbers in his description.

I was fortunate to be able to examine much larger specimens than the earlier authorities, and I found the spines on these to be somewhat longer also. For instance, some of these old plants have radials to 1¼ inches long where Engelmann described them as to only ½ inch on his little plants and everyone has dutifully followed him. I found great variation in the lower central spine also, from only ½ inch long on some plants to 1½ inches on others. I have one good big plant 5 inches tall which keeps its short but stout ½-inch centrals and also one 4-inch plant whose centrals are all 1½ inches long, so central length is not entirely related to the size of the plant.

The flowers of the species vary also. The petals may be dark green or green suffused with yellow so as to be almost golden. The filaments may be various colors, and the stigma lobes vary greatly in number, size, and color. All of the several flowers of any single specimen are consistent in these characters, however.

The fruits of the species are all similar, as described, and they are all alike in having the long, white taproot of almost unvarying size over a distance of up to several feet. This root is said to be unique among cacti. Many people, not knowing of it, pull the cactus up instead of digging it out. The root is so slender that it breaks off easily and they may not realize what is missing when they take the plant home or why it languishes so long before it re-establishes its roots.

The species grows over a wide area, including much of Mexico, and it seems clear that this is an aggregate containing several forms which could perhaps be separated out as varieties, if anyone wished to make a complete study of them. Britton and Rose have a form which appears at first glance to be one of these. It is their *Echinocactus megarhizus* Rose, from near Victoria, Mexico. It has the fleshy root, 20 or more radials, and 4 centrals quite like those of *E. scheeri*. However, they describe its seeds as black and shining, which would set it apart from our cactus at once.

I have seen two specimens of *E. scheeri* in which the lower centrals were not hooked at all.

It should be noticed that *E. scheeri* may not be separated from *E. brevihamatus* on the basis of how far down the tubercle the groove extends, as Engelmann seemed to think, since on the large, old plants of *E. scheeri*, which Engelmann's measurements indicate he did not have before him, the groove goes fully as far as on the other species.

The plant has been one of the most common on gravelly hillsides from Eagle Pass south, becoming very common around the area of Falcon Lake. However, dealers have kept after it relentlessly. It is found in almost every box of cacti in dime and curio stores, and more recently large tracts of its territory are being cleared, which spells its doom in those areas. We hope the conspicuous V formed by its upper centrals means victory for it over its enemies and that this attractive little fishhook cactus will be with us a long time to come.

This, along with the last species, will be in the genus *Echinocactus* or the genus *Ancistrocactus* according to the philosophy of the person defining these genera.

Echinocactus tobuschii (Marsh)
[*Ancistrocactus tobuschii* Marsh]

DESCRIPTION   PLATE 22

ROOTS: Short, not too well developed taproots which are turnip-shaped, tapering, and brown rather than white.

STEMS: Low, flattened hemispheres. The largest I have seen was about 3½ inches in diameter and nearly as tall. I have seen only one double plant, but have been told of clusters of 8 and 10 heads having been found. The flesh is dark green. There are 8 broad, flat ribs made up of pyramidal tubercles to almost ½ inch tall from greatly flattened, quadrangular bases to as much as ⅝ of an inch wide.

AREOLES: Linear or very nearly so. From the spine cluster at the lower end of the areole there extends a narrow groove inward and upward usually half to three-fourths of the length of the tubercle to the floral part of the areole. There is some white wool when the areole is young, but this is later lost. There are also 1 or 2 glands in the groove of each areole.

SPINES: There are 7 to 12 slender radial spines which are ⅝ to ¾ of an inch long, equal in length on any given areole, yellowish in color, becoming gray with age, the tips being a little darker. There are 3 to 5 centrals. The 2 upper centrals are always diverging to form an erect V in front of the upper radials. These upper centrals are to 1½ inches long, flattened, and ridged. There may or may not be 1 other upper central bisecting the V formed by the first two. If it is present it is similar to the others, except more slender, growing to only ⅞ of an inch long, and recurving somewhat back toward the plant. Very rarely on some areoles there may be 2 of these erect centrals in the V. There is always 1 lower central standing out perpendicular to the plant or directed upward a little. It is stout, hooked, angled and ridged, and to 1 inch long. All centrals are translucent yellowish to gray in color.

FLOWERS: 1 to 1¹/₂ inches long and to almost as wide, opening almost completely. The ovary and tube have many scalelike segments upon them which are greenish, triangular in shape, with yellowish, entire edges. These intergrade to almost linear outer perianth segments, with blunt tips, midlines greenish tinged with brown, and with yellow, entire edges. The inner segments are about 20 to 25 in number, clear citron or golden yellow, with no variation at midline or edges. They are shorter than the outer segments, almost spatulate, coming to pointed tips often having a very small, soft spine at the apex. The filaments are yellowish, the anthers pale orange. The style is green and up to ¹/₄ of an inch longer than the stamens. The stigma has 5 to 9 yellow or whitish lobes which are very small at first, but when expanded become over ¹/₈ of an inch long.

FRUITS: Elongated egg-shaped, about 1 inch long, greenish in color, flushing pinkish when very ripe. There are numerous small scales upon it. The seed is almost spherical, very dark brown and shiny, with a large hilum.

RANGE. Known only from a very small area in the Texas hill country from just above Vanderpool to near Ingram and Mountain Home, Texas.

REMARKS. This little cactus was discovered by H. Tobusch in 1951 and described by Marsh in 1952. It is one of the rarest forms in the Southwest, known only from an area not more than 30 miles long. I have succeeded in finding scattered plants in the type area, but there appear to be stands of them in only a couple of places and I would estimate that the population does not comprise over a few hundred plants in all. This should be remembered by any who are tempted to take any number of them. They could become extinct very easily.

These plants might at first be mistaken for small specimens of *E. brevihamatus* with fewer ribs made up of broader tubercles and fewer radial spines. The range of that other species comes to about 50 miles southwest of this plant at the nearest point that I could find. Any idea that they might be the same species is dispelled, however, when they bloom. The bright yellow, broadly opening flowers with entire edges on the outer perianth segments and with greenish-yellow filaments, long styles, and 5 to 9 stigma lobes found on *E. tobuschii* are greatly different from the green suffused with rose, hardly open flowers of the other form, with their rose-pink filaments, short styles, and 10 or 11 rose-pink stigma lobes. *E. tobuschii* seems to be a distinct form limited to the environs of the canyons cutting into the edge of the Edwards Plateau.

The author of the original description of this cactus was already a victim of the confusion which exists about the cactus genera. In his description he used the dodge so often resorted to when one is confused and called the cactus *Mammillaria (Ancistrocactus) tobuschii*. Of course a review of the characteristics will make it clear that it is not a Mammillaria. It is definitely one of the group known widely as the genus *Ancistrocactus*, which group is obviously part of the Echinocacti. As this group is returned to the genus *Echinocactus* this species must necessarily follow, and once its relationship to the other Echinocacti is seen, its difference from the Mammillarias should also be clear.

Echinocactus setispinus Eng.
[*Hamatocactus setispinus* (Eng.) B. & R.]
"Fishhook Cactus," "Hedgehog Cactus,"
"Twisted-Rib Cactus"

DESCRIPTION   PLATE 22

STEMS: Hemispheric at first, later egg-shaped, and finally columnar. They may be single or may branch around the base to form clusters of up to 7 or 8 heads. There is great variation in size, some individuals reaching a maximum of 3 inches tall, while others may reach 12 inches. One form never exceeds 3 inches in diameter, while another attains 5 inches. The color of the surface is light green in one form and dark green in another. There are 13 sharp ribs which are about ³/₈ of an inch high, undulating, with shallow cross-furrows between the areoles. On one form these ribs usually spiral, on another they are straight and vertical.

AREOLES: At first elliptic or egg-shaped and about ³/₁₆ of an inch long. They very soon elongate to nearly twice that length and becoming obovate as the floral part of the areole develops above the original spine-producing part. After the flower and fruit are gone, the floral part of the areole remains, with several glands within it. Then, as it gets older this floral part contracts to become a narrow groove running about ¹/₈ of an inch inward and upward from the spine-bearing part of the areole. There is quite a lot of yellowish wool in the young areole, most of which is lost with age.

SPINES: The radial spines are 10 to 19 in number, round, slender, bristle-like to somewhat rigid, and straight or recurved toward the plant. They are from ³/₁₆ to 1¹/₄ inches long, the upper ones the longest. They are dark mahogany, yellow, or whitish in color. There is one central spine which stands perpendicular to the plant surface, is round, weak, hooked, and ¹/₄ to 1³/₈ inches long. This central is translucent yellow fading to gray on one form, while on another it is opaque brown.

FLOWERS: Ivory or cream with red centers and extremely fragrant; 1³/₄ to 3 inches tall and 2¹/₄ to 3 inches wide. The ovary is cylindrical with a few scales on it and the outer perianth tube has many triangular scales which are green, brownish, or reddish-green, with white or yellowish, fringed edges. The outer perianth segments are triangular to oblong with blunt ends, or sometimes with their upper parts much broader than the bases and flaring into earlike projections on each side just below the blunt tip. They have greenish midlines with yellowish, fringed edges. The inner segments are spatulate and ivory or cream with red bases. Their edges are somewhat ragged and often toothed, the tips pointed. The filaments are reddish, weak, and swirled. The anthers are cream-colored or pale yellow. The style is long, thick, and greenish-yellow. There are 5 to 11, but usually 9 or 10 stigma lobes, which are yellow or pale orange, to $1/4$ of an inch long, rough, and blunt. They usually curve in all directions.

FRUITS: Spherical or nearly so, $3/8$ to $3/4$ of an inch across. Bright scarlet in color with a smooth, shiny skin and almost no scales. They remain upon the plants for a long time, often a year, if not disturbed, before they finally dry up and split open down one side, releasing the seeds. The seeds are about $1/16$ of an inch long, black, with a finely pitted surface, somewhat irregular in shape, having been described variously as globose and club-shaped. The large hilum at or near the end of the seed is surrounded by a broad lip with an unpitted, shining surface.

RANGE. Growing over a wide area of central and south Texas and on into Mexico. Known to grow north as far as San Saba, Lampasas, and near Georgetown, Texas. From there the northeastern boundary of its range seems to be approximately the Colorado River. Rare near the mouth of that river, it becomes more and more common going south along the lower Texas Coast all the way to Brownsville. On the west it is not found so far north, but is seen around the mouth of the Devil's River, which seems to be about the limit of its northwestern range.

REMARKS. *Echinocactus setispinus* is one of the most common cacti in south Texas, and also one of the most colorful. It will bloom practically the whole summer if happily situated. It is at the same time one of the most easily grown, being very resistant to rotting, and so is a great favorite for indoor growing as a potted plant. I have seen large specimens which had lived for many years in the windows of business establishments, planted all these years in flat dishes with soil not over two inches deep. I have also seen numerous dish gardens and planters originally planted with an assortment of various cacti, in which, after some months, only this species remained alive. Here at last is the cactus which I can recommend for the amateur grower who cannot provide the specialized conditions other cacti require and who wants to grow a cactus on his windowsill. It does not like the full sun, and it tolerates more moisture than most.

In the extreme western part of its range this cactus is found growing near another species of this genus, *E. sinuatus*, and is often confused with it. The two are readily distinguished, however, by the fact that *E. sinuatus* has broader, not so sharply edged ribs, fewer radial spines, and 4 central spines at least some of which are always flattened.

E. setispinus was originally considered by all authorities as part of the genus *Echinocactus*. When Schumann set out subgenera for that large genus he placed it in his subgenus *Ancistrocactus*. But Britton and Rose segregated this species from the rest in a new genus, *Hamatocactus*. Other species were added to this new genus by other authors, and for a time its favor in taxonomic opinion was at full tide. Then the tide began to turn as they began to subtract from the proposed genus *Hamatocactus*. Buxbaum put one of its members back into *Ferocactus*, while adding *E. uncinatus* to it. Backeberg, of course, took *E. uncinatus* out again as he erected a new genus for it. Meanwhile Hester had decided on the basis of seed characters that all of those species put in *Hamatocactus* really belonged in *Thelocactus*. This sort of confusion has not yet been resolved, and seems to be the result of trying to define the genera too closely. Since no new character has come to light which will separate these microgenera cleanly and no one has managed a combination of characters which will organize them logically, the return to the inclusive old genus *Echinocactus* seems indicated here too, at least until these smaller groups can be redefined in meaningful terms.

Echinocactus setispinus var. hamatus Eng.
[*Hamatocactus setispinus* var. *hamatus* (Eng.) B. & R.]
   "Twisted-Rib Cactus," "Fishhook Cactus,"
   "Hedgehog Cactus"

DESCRIPTION   PLATE 22

STEMS: Hemispheric when young, becoming columnar when old, usually occurring singly, but occasionally branching at the base to form a clump of several stems. The stems grow up to 12 inches tall and 5 inches in diameter. They are dark, dull green in color, and have 13 very sharp ribs which undulate somewhat, but are not interrupted by cross-grooves. These ribs are about $3/8$ of an inch high, and usually spiral by twisting sideways between the areoles. There are hardly distinct enough swellings at the areoles to be called tubercles, but the ribs are slightly higher at each areole than between them.

AREOLES: As the species.

SPINES: There are 10 to 13 radial spines which are very slender, bristle-like, and rather flexible. They are straight and radiate evenly. They are all translucent yellow at first, but when mature they develop as follows: the lower 3 become $3/8$ to $3/4$ of an inch long and dark mahogany-brown on some plants, honey-yellow on others; the lateral 2 or 3 on each side become $5/8$ to 1 inch long and white in color, only the very tips of these sometimes remaining honey-yellow; the 3 to 5 uppermost ones become $3/8$ to $11/4$ inches long, dark mahogany-brown or variegated shades of brown in color. There is 1 central spine which stands out perpendicular to the stem and is hooked. It is 1 to 1³/₄ inches long, round, and very slender, being so weak as to be easily flexible. It is brown, often very dark, but with the tip usually lighter.

FLOWERS: As the species, except that they are 2 to 3 inches tall and 2¹/₂ to 3 inches wide and have the inner perianth segments almost linear, to about ¹/₄ of an inch wide. The edges are crinkled but not toothed or fringed, and the tips are pointed.

FRUITS: As the species.

RANGE. The northern and eastern part of the species range. There is no record of this variety south of Eagle Pass along the Rio Grande until near Brownsville. The southwestern limit of its range seems to be a large arc from Eagle Pass on the north swinging east of Cotulla, Texas, then south to near Alice, and on down to some point in the lower Rio Grande Valley not far west of Brownsville.

REMARKS. The species contains such well marked and constant variations that from its very first descriptions it has been found necessary to speak of varieties. Engelmann set up two of these, but remarked that "many forms" had been collected. It does seem that his two varieties are basic, however. Even though there is variation within each of them, they seem to be the only two consistently distinct and separable varieties.

E. setispinus var. *hamatus* is the larger, more grand form of the species, and it also occurs over much the greater range of the two. At its prime it is a beautiful, bulky plant up to a foot high, dark green, with very slender, flexible spines, the central one of each cluster a perfect little fishhook as round and slender as a real fishhook of its size. When it blooms, which if it gets moisture enough is all summer from April to October, it produces its large, extremely fragrant, yellow and red flowers several at a time, and soon the upper part of the plant is also adorned by the scarlet fruits. Just recently, near San Antonio, I happened upon 13 plants of this variety growing under one mesquite tree, each with 3 to 6 flowers open. As other specimens were under almost every tree and shrub in every direction, both the sight and the fragrance of this unspoiled field was delightful.

The ribs of this cactus are very sharp and not interrupted between the areoles. They almost always spiral by twisting sideways between each pair of areoles. It is from this that the plant gets the name twisted-rib cactus. This twisting becomes more pronounced as the cactus loses water during drought or settles with old age.

This variety grows over much of south-central Texas. It is common along the upper Colorado River and in the hill country of Texas from just north of Austin to some 30 miles or so south of San Antonio and from there on west. It is again very common along the lower Texas coast from Corpus Christi to Brownsville. It does not grow along the Rio Grande any farther than 50 miles or so above its mouth until it is found again near

Eagle Pass, from which point it apparently grows at least as far west as the mouth of the Devil's River. I have also seen beautiful specimens of this cactus which were said to have come from Coahuila, Mexico approximately south of Sanderson, Texas. This is perhaps not surprising since Coulter said it grows in Coahuila and even in Chihuahua. However I have found no verifiable records of it in Texas west of the Devil's River.

In the gap along the Rio Grande where this cactus, variety *hamatus*, does not grow, and limited to that gap, is found the other distinct variety of the species, variety *setaceus*. This is a much smaller form with much more slender stems, straight ribs and heavier, more rigid, as well as more numerous spines. The best means of distinguishing the two varieties will be pointed out after that other variety is described. A good photo of a young specimen of variety *hamatus* is presented by Britton and Rose on page 104 of Volume 3 of *The Cactaceae*, while the other variety is well illustrated on the following page.

Echinocactus setispinus var. setaceus Eng.
[*Hamatocactus setispinus* var. *setaceus* (Eng.) B. & R.]
  "Fishhook Cactus," "Hedgehog Cactus"

DESCRIPTION   PLATE 22

STEMS: Hemispheric when very young, becoming egg-shaped, and when very old often becoming columnar. Some plants branch early to form clusters of up to 7 or 8 heads, while others remain single throughout life. Clustering plants do not usually grow over 3 inches tall, while single plants may become 12 inches in height. The maximum diameter in either case seems to be about 3 inches. The surface is a light green color. There are 13 sharp ribs which are straight, vertical, and shallow, being less than ¹/₄ of an inch deep, but which are interrupted by cross-furrows between the areoles. There are almost no thickenings at the areoles, which could be called tubercles.

AREOLES: As the species.

SPINES: There are 12 to 19 radial spines which are round and rigid, straight or often recurved back toward the plant. The lower 3 or 4 are ³/₁₆ to about ¹/₂ inch long and translucent honey-yellow, sometimes with their bases reddish-brown. The lateral 3 to 5 on each side are ³/₈ to ³/₄ of an inch long and whitish with their tips translucent yellow. The upper 3 to 5 radial spines are ⁵/₈ to 1¹/₈ inches long, translucent honey-yellow, often with dark red-brown bases. There is 1 central spine which stands approximately perpendicular to the stem, is round, hooked, weak but rigid, and ¹/₄ to 1¹/₂ inches long. On some plants this central is translucent honey-yellow becoming gray with age, while on others it is partly or all dark red-brown.

FLOWERS: As the species, except that they are only 1³/₄ to 2 inches tall by 2¹/₄ to 3 inches wide and the inner segments are spatulate.

FRUITS: As the species.

RANGE. Starr and Hidalgo counties, Texas, and south into Mexico.

REMARKS. Although the descriptions of various authors are confusing due to the failure of some to distinguish between this and the previous variety, this plant seems clearly to be *E. setispinus* var. *setaceus* of Engelmann. It can readily be recognized by its straight, shallow ribs, its shiny, pale green color, its more numerous and more rigid radial spines, and its slender stems never observed to be over 3 inches in diameter.

This variety is found in great numbers in a very restricted area of south Texas. It suddenly appears on gravelly hills near Falcon Dam, and is common on such undisturbed slopes nearly to Mission, Texas. On a specimen in the U. S. National Museum collected by Robert Runyon, who no doubt knew south Texas cacti more completely than any other man, I find a note that this cactus occurs in only Starr and Hidalgo counties. This is an area where variety *hamatus* is not found.

It seems almost impossible to discuss variety *setaceus* in any more detail without noting that within it there are two obvious growth forms. They grow together in the same fields, and I have found the two forms actually within inches of each other, in which case the difference between them is striking.

One of them always remains a single stem and becomes when old a very slender column up to 12 inches tall but only 2 to 3 inches thick. This form has the upper radials and the hooked central variegated with brown or sometimes wholly dark brown. The centrals are ¹/₂ to 1¹/₂ inches long.

The other form never grows as a single tall column, but begins branching around the base when about 2¹/₂ inches tall. An old plant will be composed of up to 7 or 8 egg-shaped stems, the largest of which is only 3 inches tall. This form has all its spines shorter and honey-yellow, becoming gray when old. There is no brown in them. The hooked centrals are only ¹/₄ to ³/₈ of an inch long, but they are heavier than on the other form.

These two forms seem to correspond in many ways to two varieties in the literature, the tall one with darker spines to *E. setispinus* var. *cachetianus* (Monv.) Knuth, and the shorter form with yellow spines to *E. setispinus* var. *mierensis* K. Schumann, but there are discrepancies in each case in the descriptions, and it seems impossible to apply the names with certainty to these or any other plants. Even if they were applied to these forms, they could not be other than growth forms or forma.

Two good photographs of the single, columnar type of variety *setaceus* supplied by Robert Runyon are reproduced as figures 113 and 114 on page 105 of Britton and Rose's *The Cactaceae*, Volume 3.

This variety is not nearly so massive and spectacular as the previous variety, and is not as well adapted for the amateur's growing. It is much less tolerant of moisture and shade. Its flesh is much more firm and lighter in color and does not present the soft, deep green, and the luxuriantly massive appearance of the variety *hamatus*. Its flowers are somewhat shorter than those of the other variety, but deeper in the shade of their yellow.

Echinocactus sinuatus Dietrich
[*Hamatocactus sinuatus* (Dietrich) Orcutt]
"Lower Rio Grande Valley Barrel"

DESCRIPTION   PLATE 23

STEMS: Spherical, becoming conical and finally elongated ovate with a definitely pointed tip, and up to at least 12 inches tall and 8 inches thick. It is usually single, but some old plants produce one or two branches at the base. The surface is very dark, dull green or even blue-green. There are 13 ribs which are deep but compressed. They are 1 to 1¹/₄ inches deep, undulating, acute and sharp between the areoles, and raised into indistinct tubercles which are somewhat rounded but only about ³/₈ of an inch across at the areoles.

AREOLES: Round or slightly oval and about ¹/₄ to ³/₈ of an inch in longest measurement at first. The flower comes out of the upper end of the areole, leaving afterward a short groove-like extension of the areole forward which is usually about ¹/₈ of an inch long and so broad as to be almost oval. This has some wool and several large, elongated glands in it. The areoles are about 1 inch apart.

SPINES: There are 8 to 12 spreading radial spines which vary consistently in all specimens as follows: the lowermost 1 is ³/₈ to 1¹/₈ inches long, round or slightly flattened, sometimes slightly hooked, red or purplish with a translucent yellow tip; the spines on each side of this one are similar in color but ⁵/₈ to 1³/₄ inches long, slightly flattened, and also sometimes slightly hooked; the 2 lateral radials on each side are flat, straight, 1 to 2¹/₄ inches long, yellowish, and often slightly banded, becoming gray and rough with age; the upper 1 to 3 radial spines are round, 1¹/₄ to 2¹/₈ inches long, straight, the most slender of the radials, reddish with yellow zones or all yellow, becoming gray with age. There are 4 centrals which are all flat and pubescent. The three upper ones spread upward in front of the upper radials and are 1¹/₄ to 2¹/₂ inches long, straight, yellowish with reddish zones, becoming gray with age. The lowermost central is approximately perpendicular to the stem, hooked, very flat and wide, 2 to 3¹/₂ inches long and to ¹/₈ of an inch wide, reddish, becoming purplish-gray with age.

FLOWERS: 2 to 3 inches long and wide, clear lemon or greenish-yellow without red centers, and hardly fragrant. The ovary has a few rounded and fringed scales. The outer petals are short, greenish with reddish-brown midlines and greenish-yellow, fringed edges. Their tips are pointed, but they are wide and irregular in shape otherwise. The inner petals are long, with entire edges, sharply pointed, all clear lemon yellow with narrow yellow bases. The filaments and anthers are all yellow. The style is yellow and the stigma has 8 to 10 lemon-yellow lobes which are rough and about ³/₈ of an inch long.

FRUITS: Green, oval or egg-shaped, about 1 inch long and ³/₈ of an inch wide at the widest part near the center. There are about 6 to 12 small scales upon each fruit, and the old flower parts persist. When undisturbed these fruits remain on the plant for months, finally rotting, at which time they usually split open and the fermenting pulp containing the seeds spews out. The seeds are about ¹/₂₅ of an inch long, almost globular except compressed and prolonged beaklike at one end surrounding the small, sunken hilum. The surface is slightly shiny, with small but comparatively widely spaced pits all over it.

RANGE. From near Brownsville in the lower Rio Grande Valley in a narrow strip north along the river to Eagle Pass, Texas. Spreading northeast of Eagle Pass beyond Brackettville to the Montell and Camp Wood, Texas, area and west along the Rio Grande to the mouth of the Devil's River.

REMARKS. This cactus has been confused with other forms to a remarkable extent, considering its definite differences from its relatives. Its existence has even been denied by some more recent writers—one of the most strange omissions in all of cactus study.

It was first described as *Echinocactus sinuatus* by Dietrich in 1851. Poselger, in 1853, referred to it as *E. setispinus* var. *sinuatus*, and perhaps also as *E. setispinus* var. *robustus*. Engelmann, a few years later, had no doubt about its standing as a separate species, and wrote an especially full description of it with the stated purpose to show this. Coulter understood the plant well, and followed Engelmann and Dietrich. Weber, however, in 1902, listed an *E. longihamatus sinuatus*, by which he must have meant to place this cactus as a variety of *E. hamatacanthus*. Then came Britton and Rose, who took a cue from Weber but then took one of their long steps and said that the plant was the same as their *Ferocactus hamatacanthus*. They even reproduced a photograph of *E. sinuatus* as their illustration of *Ferocactus hamatacanthus*, the picture in *The Cactaceae*, Volume 3, page 144, figure 152. Marshall, following them, speaks of *sinuatus* as an extreme form of *Hamatocactus hamatacanthus*. Backeberg apparently did not have specimens to study first hand, but recognized from the previous literature that it was probably a separate species, and so listed it with a call for further study to be made of it.

I had found mention by Schulz and others of the big fishhook barrel, *E. hamatacanthus* having been collected near Brownsville and "on the clay dunes near the Texas Coast." I had never understood how that cactus, a native of the Big Bend, could turn up in such a different environment down in the lower

Rio Grande Valley. When I found my first foot-high specimen of *E. sinuatus* near Zapata, Texas, I didn't know what it was, but I knew at a glance that it wasn't any form of *E. setispinus* or *E. hamatacanthus*. I doubt that anyone would confuse them who had actually seen all three together. I have since seen dozens of specimens all the way from the edge of the Gulf to the mouth of the Devil's River, and they are consistently distinct.

As briefly as possible, *E. sinuatus* may be distinguished from *E. setispinus* by the following comparisons: *E. sinuatus* grows to 8 inches thick; has ribs ⁷/₈ to 1¹/₈ inches deep; 8 to 12 radial spines, some of them flattened; 4 centrals, all flattened and more or less pubescent; flowers which are never red-centered and hardly fragrant; fruits ⁷/₈ to 1 inch long, oval or egg-shaped, and green until they rot; and seeds ¹/₂₅ of an inch long, shining, with very fine pits and small hila which have no collars. *E. setispinus*, on the other hand, grows to only 5 inches thick; has ribs ¹/₄ of an inch or less in depth; 10 to 19 radial spines, all round and bristle-like; only 1 central spine, which is round and smooth; flowers which are red-centered and very fragrant; fruits spherical, ³/₈ to ³/₄ of an inch across, and scarlet; seeds about ¹/₁₆ of an inch long, dull with closely set pits and large hila having wide collars.

The following distinguish *E. sinuatus* from *E. hamatacanthus*: *E. sinuatus* grows to a maximum of about 12 by 8 inches; has 13 compressed ribs the summits of which are ³/₈ of an inch wide at the most; 8 to 12 radials, some of which are greatly flattened; 4 centrals, all flattened and more or less pubescent; flowers which are lemon yellow with 8 to 10 stigma lobes; fruits ⁷/₈ to 1 inch long, oval to egg-shaped, and green; seeds ¹/₂₅ of an inch across. *E. hamatacanthus*, on the other hand, grows to at least 24 by 12 inches; has 13 to 17 massively rounded ribs the summits of which are ³/₄ of an inch or more across; 8 to 14 radial spines which are all round or very nearly so, and smooth; 4 to 8 central spines which are smooth instead of pubescent, round or with only the lower one flattened on top; flowers which are entirely straw or pale yellow with or without red centers, with 11 to 14 stigma lobes; fruits 1 to 2 inches long, egg-shaped or oblong, and brownish-red when ripe; and seeds about ¹/₁₆ of an inch long with dull surfaces.

E. sinuatus is a beautiful species first encountered on the first solid ground back of the beach in deep south Texas. It may once have been common around and above Brownsville, but few undisturbed areas in which it can be seen remain there now. It may be found on a strip of territory a few miles wide all along the river up to Eagle Pass, being very common in some areas around Roma and Zapata. It is rare north of Zapata to north of Eagle Pass, but is occasionally seen. In some parts of the Anacacho Mountains and in the hills at the edge of the Edwards Plateau north and east of Brackettville, Texas, it is again rather common, although these northern specimens do not grow nearly as tall as they do farther south, preferring to remain spherical in shape. It is fairly easily found in various hilly areas west of Eagle Pass to the mouth of the Devil's River, which seems to be its westward limit, but it does not grow any distance north along that river. I have also seen numerous specimens collected in northern Mexico, some to almost as far south as Monterrey.

Echinocactus hamatacanthus Muehlenpf.
[*Hamatocactus hamatacanthus* (Muehlenpf.) Knuth]
"Turk's Head," "Visnaga," "Biznaga Costillona," "Biznaga es Pinosa," "Biznaga Ganchuda," "Biznaga Limilla," "Biznaga de Tuna"

DESCRIPTION   PLATE 23

STEMS: Large and heavy, hemispherical or almost spherical, becoming columnar and to a maximum of at least 2 feet tall and 1 foot in diameter. These stems are usually single, but occasionally become double or triple by branching, and when injured sometimes form larger clusters. The surface is dull green or gray-green. There are usually 13, but may occasionally be as many as 17 massive, broad ribs 1 1/2 to 2 inches high and wide. These ribs are divided between the areoles into very distinct, rounded tubercles 1 1/2 to 2 inches tall and the same width at their bases. The rounded tops of these tubercles are about 3/4 of an inch wide on mature plants. The areoles are on the tops of these massive tubercles.

AREOLES: About 1 to 1 1/2 inches apart, oval to oblong, and about 3/8 to 1/2 inch long. There are very wide, felted grooves running inward and upward about 3/8 of an inch from the spinous parts of the areoles on mature plants, but these are not present on young plants which have not yet bloomed. There are very large, elongated glands in these grooves. The flower comes from the end of this groovelike extension of the areole.

SPINES: There may be 8 to 14 radial spines, but usually are 10 or more of them, as follows in appearance: the lowermost spine is 3/4 to 2 inches long and variegated reddish at first, turning gray-brown with age; the 3 laterals on each side are 1 to 3 inches long and the same color or whitish. All of these are round or only very slightly flattened, straight, and radiating evenly. The 3 to 5 upper radials do not radiate, but stand spreading upward. They vary on different plants from as short as 3/4 of an inch to as much as 3 1/4 inches long, are round, or practically so, slender, straight, and reddish or gray, often variegated. There may be 4 to 8 round or somewhat flattened, smooth central spines in each areole. There is one extremely large lower central which stands out approximately perpendicular to the stem, but which usually curves and twists in any direction. It is hooked at the end, entirely round or else round below and flattened on its upper surface, 2 to at least 6 inches long, a heavy spine but some-

what flexible due to its great length. It is yellow mottled with red or else all dull red at first, often indistinctly annulate, becoming gray-brown with age. There are always 3 more upper centrals which stand spreading upward. They are straight, round, relatively slender, reddish often mottled with yellow, later turning gray-brown, and 1 to 3 1/2 inches long. These 4 are all the centrals on young plants, but with age 2 or 3 upper centrals are added which are shorter and more slender, standing erect just back of the previous upper centrals.

FLOWERS: Entirely straw to yellow or the outer parts thus with red centers, 2 1/4 to 4 inches tall, 2 3/4 to 3 inches wide, and very fragrant. The ovary and tube have very many small triangular scales on them; Engelmann, having counted them, said there are 30 to 60 of these. Their centers are reddish or brownish, while their edges are greenish-yellow, crinkled, and may or may not have a few twisted cilia on them. The very many outer perianth segments—Engelmann says there are 55 to 80 of them—range all the way from short, scalelike ones to full-length, oblong ones. They all have reddish midlines, the outer parts being greenish and the edges being yellowish. There are about 30 inner petals which are long, wide, and pointed, the edges entire or often toothed irregularly. These inner petals may be all yellow or yellow with red bases. The filaments will be yellow in all yellow flowers, but reddish in those with red centers. The anthers are yellow. The style is yellow and longer than the stamens. There may be 11 to 14 lobes in the stigma, which are about 1/4 of an inch long, yellow, rough, and usually much curved and twisted.

FRUITS: Egg-shaped to oblong, 1 to 2 inches long, not including the persistent perianth. There are 30 or 40 scales on the fruit, each greenish edged in white. The fruit remains green all summer and fall and then during the winter it ripens, becoming at that time a brownish-red color. The seeds are practically round, about 1/16 of an inch long, black, with the surface pitted.

RANGE. Along and never many miles north of the Rio Grande from the mouth of the Devil's River all the way to El Paso, Texas. Occurring very rarely west of El Paso for perhaps 50 miles along the southern border of New Mexico. Growing very abundantly in Mexico.

REMARKS. *Echinocactus hamatacanthus* is the second largest, second most splendid member of this genus in the United States. It has often been called *E. longihamatus*. Although this latter name may have been coined by Galeotti first, it was used without description and so most have agreed that Muehlenpfordt's *hamatacanthus* has precedence.

This species may be distinguished from its already described relatives by its great rounded ribs composed of massive tubercles swelling around each areole. Both *E. setispinus* and *E. sinuatus* have sharp ribs without these large rounded tubercles. The same characteristic distinguishes it from the only other cactus in our area presenting such a massive size and having hooked spines—*Echinocactus wislizeni*—since that large barrel cactus has very large but uninterrupted, sharp ribs.

Engelmann described three varieties of this cactus. However, since they overlap and there are many intermediates which one cannot assign to any one of them with any certainty, they do not stand distinct as do those of *E. setispinus*. They are no doubt just the extreme variations in spine characters of the species. Variety *crassispinus* Eng. has its central spines when typical relatively heavy and the most flattened of this species. It is the form which Engelmann first called *Echinocactus flexispinus*. He and other authorities consider it to be found only in Chihuahua, but Coulter assigned some Texas specimens to this variety. Variety *gracilispinus* Eng. is the most common form in Texas and Mexico, having its centrals comparatively slender and the hooked one only slightly flattened. Variety *brevispinus* Eng. is the form having the central spines shorter than the others, hardly if any longer than the radials, and all spines round. Almost all young specimens could pass for this variety, and a few mature ones also. Coulter states that this is the form found west of El Paso in New Mexico.

One often finds in the literature the name *Brittonia davisii* applied to this species and credited to Dr. A. D. Houghton. Marshall, in his *Cactaceae* made this *Hamatocactus hamatacanthus* var. *davisii*. However, in an article in the *Cactus and Succulent Journal of America* in 1944, Marshall relates that shortly before his death, Houghton wrote him that he had never published the name at all, and so in this article Marshall agrees with Borg in dropping the name entirely.

E. hamatacanthus is a beautiful cactus, becoming one of the largest in the Southwest. Everything about it grows in grand proportions. This is not a cactus for dish gardens or window ledges, and it should not be dwarfed in a cramped pot. It needs space, in return for which it will grow slowly into a massive barrel with perhaps the longest spines of any in our area. It is not so easy to grow as its relatives from farther east in Texas, being more liable to rot if given too much water. It is more completely a desert species, and one must remember this. Neither is it as resistant to freezing as our other cacti, and it can only at great risk be left unprotected during the winter anywhere north of its range.

This species has been shunted about between genera more than its other close relatives. Of course, it was first described as an Echinocactus. But when Britton and Rosa broke up that genus, they did not assign this species to *Hamatocactus* with the others, but instead to the genus *Ferocactus*. This was because they concluded that this species had enough scales on its ovary to belong there. It was Knuth who finally transferred it to *Hamatocactus*, where it seems most obvious that it would have to remain unless those two microgenera are actually so close as to be merely subdivisions of the one actual genus, *Echinocactus*. But more recently Buxbaum has maintained that it is really a *Ferocactus*,

while Hester shows how impossible it is to keep any of these microgenera separate by asserting that all of the members of *Hamatocactus*, including this one, should be included in *Thelocactus*.

Echinocactus bicolor var. schottii Eng.
[*Thelocactus bicolor* var. *schottii* (Eng.) B. & R.]
"Glory of Texas"

DESCRIPTION   PLATE 23

STEMS: Egg-shaped or conical to almost columnar, sometimes to 10 inches tall and 5 inches in diameter, but usually smaller. These stems are usually single, but very old plants sometimes form small clusters of 3 or 4 heads by branching from the base. There are 8 broad, flat ribs which are composed of wart-like tubercles to about ¹/₂ inch high from almost perfectly square bases up to ³/₄ of an inch wide.

AREOLES: Oval or nearly round with yellow wool at first, later egg-shaped on immature plants. On adult tubercles the floral part of the areole forms a short groove about ¹/₈ to ³/₁₆ of an inch long and often so wide as to make the areole as a whole obovate in shape. In old plants glands are often visible in the areoles.

SPINES: There are 12 to 18 radial spines on each areole. The upper 1 to 4 of these radials are erect, straight, flattened, and ³/₄ to 2¹/₄ inches long. They are yellow when young, becoming gray with age. The lateral and lower radial spines are all round, ¹/₂ to 1¹/₄ inches long, and varicolored, the bases of them being gray, the middle zones dark red, and the ends yellowish. The lower radials often recurve a little back toward the plant. There are 3 or 4 straight central spines. The uppermost stands erect just in front of the upper radials. It is 1 to 3¹/₂ inches long, very flat and broad—often ¹/₈ of an inch wide—and flexible. Standing erect beside this one are 1 or 2 other centrals, flat on some plants but round on others, and not quite so long. These erect centrals are yellow at first, becoming gray. The lower central stands perpendicular to the plant or is turned downward. It is perfectly round or oval, stout and rigid, and ³/₄ to 2³/₄ inches long. It is gray, red, and yellow like the lower radials at first, becoming all gray when very old.

FLOWERS: 2 to 3 inches long, 3 to 4 inches across, opening widely with petals usually recurving backward. They are brilliant fuchsia with scarlet throats and a shining, satiny surface. The sepals vary from short, rounded scales on the ovary wall to more elongated, oblong sepals above. All have greenish midlines and whitish, fringed edges. The inner petals are oblong from narrow bases, about ³/₈ of an inch wide at the widest point, the margins entire but crinkled, the tips pointed and recurving. Their bases are bright scarlet, the upper three-fourths of each one a bright, satiny fuchsia. The filaments are bright scarlet, matching the petal bases. The anthers are yellow. The style is pink and a little longer than the stamens. The stigma has 8 to 11 rough, blunt lobes, light rose to brownish-pink in color.

FRUITS: About ³/₈ to ¹/₂ inch long, becoming dry and splitting open by means of an irregular basal pore. The seeds are about ¹/₁₆ of an inch long, almost globular, with very large hila.

RANGE. Occurring in Texas in two widely separated areas, one near and up to about 20 miles north of the Rio Grande in Starr County, and the other around Lajitas and above Candelaria, Texas, in Brewster County in the Big Bend. No record of collections between these widely separated points comes to light.

REMARKS: This is primarily a Mexican species. We are very fortunate that it steps across our border in two widely separated places, where we can claim it as the glory of Texas. The name is well deserved. The bright-colored, variegated spines are attractive, and when the cactus blooms, it presents undoubtedly the brightest and most exotic flower of any in our area. The fuchsia petals with their scarlet bases are satiny in texture and colorful beyond description. It is unfortunate that they are so sensitive that they will only open in the full heat of the southwestern summer afternoon and close again permanently as the sun begins to fall. They are so sensitive that they start to close visibly when a cloud temporarily covers the sun. I have found that it requires fast action to photograph them, since they close in a short time when taken out of the greenhouse and placed outside where the temperature is 10 degrees cooler, even when the sun is still full upon them. Because of this sensitivity few people have seen these exquisite flowers each one of which is open only three or four hours of only one afternoon.

It is quite common to consider the plants from the two different areas in Texas as different forms, those from Starr County usually being called *E. bicolor* and those from the Big Bend *E. bicolor* var. *schottii* or *E. bicolor* var. *tricolor*. I have examined many specimens from both areas, and although the southern ones are smaller with correspondingly shorter and less colorful spines, there is no essential difference between them. I am convinced that they must all be considered the same form, the western one only being more robust in every respect.

The species was first described from Mexican specimens by Galeotti in 1848, under the name *Echinocactus bicolor*. When Engelmann first described the Texas plants, he found them enough different from the original description that he erected a new variety, calling the Texas plants *E. bicolor* var. *schottii*. He stated that the Texas specimens differed from the species by having more radials and having the upper centrals greatly flattened and the longest spines on the plants.

I have examined many plants from both Texas and the area of the type in Mexico, and find Engelmann's distinction between the Texas specimens and the type of the species partly right and partly in error. There is no consistent difference in number of radials between the two. On Texas specimens I have found 12 to 18 radials, while on Mexican specimens I have found 10 to 18. Engelmann must have seen only examples of the lower number in his Mexican plants. There is, however, a great difference in the length of the radials between the two types. The Mexican form shows lower radials ¹/₄ to ¹/₂ inch long, laterals ⁵/₈ to ³/₄ of an inch, and the upper radials ¹/₂ to ³/₄ of an inch long, while the same spines on Texas plants run lower and lateral radials ¹/₂ to 1¹/₄ inches and the uppers ³/₄ to 2¹/₄ inches long.

In the matter of central spines, Engelmann was quite right, and this is the primary distinction overlooked by many. The Texas plants have a round or oval lower central which is rather stout and ³/₄ to 2³/₄ inches long. Then they have 2 or 3 upper centrals which are erect, the uppermost one being very flat, ¹/₁₆ to ¹/₈ of an inch wide, flexible, and 1 to 3¹/₂ inches long—always longer than the lower central on a mature plant. The Mexican plants of the type area, on the other hand, have this uppermost central round or oval like the lower, very stout, and awl-shaped, not flattened or flexible, and only ³/₄ to 1¹/₈ inches long—never longer than the lower central. In general, the Mexican plant has short, very stout, and rigid spines, while the Texas form is more or less covered by its longer, more slender, more flattened, flexible spines.

The difference between the two forms is certainly not great, but it seems enough that they can be recognized once they are understood. No doubt they are not separate species, but it does seem that Engelmann's variety is valid, even though Britton and Rose, as well as some others, have ignored it. I find no record of the typical *E. bicolor* which occurs in Mexico or any of the several other varieties of it having been found north of the Rio Grande. Variety *schottii*, however, does grow quite some distance down into Mexico.

E. bicolor var. *tricolor* is a name proposed by Schumann for the specimens with the most brilliant red spines. Such extremely red-spined plants show no other differences from the other Texas specimens, however, and are found growing right among the less brightly colored specimens in the Big Bend, so this does not seem a valid basis for a variety, and the name probably should be dropped. Backeberg described a variety *texensis*. After observation of many specimens, it seems to me that plants fitting his description cannot be set off from the variety *schottii*, but intergrade with the others and must be included within that variety.

This species was regarded as an Echinocactus as long as that genus was recognized in its original sense. Later Schumann erected a subgenus *Thelocactus* for it which Britton and Rose elevated to a separate genus. This separation was made because of the few scales on the ovary and its lack of wool, and because of a misinterpretation of the areole. Britton and Rose thought the flower originated in a separate floral areole separated by a groove from the spine areole. It has since been shown that this whole structure is one monomorphic areole and that there is no distinction between the areoles of this plant and those of the most typical Echinocacti. Unless only those species are left in the genus *Echinocactus* which have wool on the ovary, this species must be included along with the rest.

Very large and beautiful specimens of this cactus 8 and even 10 inches tall are now being brought out of the more inaccessible mountains of the Big Bend by resourceful commercial gatherers. They are much larger and have much longer spines than the earlier writers ever saw, but are otherwise the same. Unfortunately this is a very fastidious desert cactus, and these large old specimens grown to such splendid size because of the most perfect desert environment in these very arid mountains will not live and grow further in the less favorable environment of a pot or garden. It is a questionable practice of the dealers to offer for sale these huge old plants which cannot live long. They thrill the collector, but must disappoint him when they soon die. Even the small specimens, which are sold widely, are impracticable for all but the collector who can duplicate the desert conditions for them. There is a saying that they will not live over 3 years in a pot, and in most cases I believe this is longer than can be expected. I have disproved the saying by keeping one in a pot 4 years now, but this must be credited to extremely alkaline, limestone soil and to its position in the full Texas sun in a greenhouse where the temperature climbs to between 110 and 120 degrees every day of the summer. Treated in this seemingly inhumane way, the cactus thrives and shows its appreciation for the heat and sunshine by blooming all summer. Its earliest flower has opened on April 12, and its latest on September 16. It seems cruel to subject such a delicately flowering plant to this kind of treatment, but if it is provided, this plant will show all of its glory.

Echinocactus flavidispinus (Backbg.)
[*Thelocactus flavidispinus* Backbg.]

DESCRIPTION   PLATE 23

STEMS: Hemispherical at first, becoming columnar and sometimes branching at the base or, if injured, at the point of injury. Becoming at least 4 inches tall and 3 inches in diameter. There are 13 ribs composed of rows of conical tubercles to about 3/8 of an inch high. These are distinct in young specimens, but become somewhat confluent on older plants. The color of the surface is light green or even yellowish-green.

AREOLES: Oval at first, but after flowering, ovate, the upper part prolonged into a short groove containing glands.

SPINES: There are 14 to 20 radial spines which are recurved against the plant. They are all yellow at first, or yellow streaked with red. Later the lower and lateral ones remain round, only 1/4 to 3/4 of an inch long, and become bright red in their middle zones with yellow tips, while the uppermost becomes flattened, cream to gray in color, and to 1 inch long. Juvenile plants possess only the radials, and these are all round

at first. When the plant is a little older there appears 1 strong, round central which stands perpendicular to the stem or turned downward; it is pubescent, all yellow or yellow at the base and tip with bright red in the middle, and 3/8 to 7/8 of an inch long. Mature plants add 3 more centrals turned upward: 2 of them are like the radials in all respects, while the uppermost becomes 1 to 1 1/2 inches long, flattened, more or less curved toward the plant, and all yellow, fading to gray with age.

FLOWERS: About 1 1/2 inches tall and 3 to 4 inches in diameter when fully open. The scales on the ovary and the outer perianth segments have brownish-green midlines shading to whitish, entire edges and scarlet bases. The inner segments have very narrow scarlet bases widening to bright rose-pink or fuchsia upper parts, which have entire edges, are very sharp-pointed, and do not recurve. The filaments and anthers are yellow. The style is yellow or pink, and there are 11 stigma lobes which are scarlet at their bases fading to yellowish at their tips.

FRUITS: Not seen.

RANGE. Known only from near Marathon, Texas, particularly in the Pena Blanca Mountains in the upper part of the Big Bend region.

REMARKS. This cactus was first described as *Thelocactus bicolor* var. *flavidispinus* by Backeberg in 1941. Later Backeberg elevated it to a separate species. He apparently had before him only the younger plants, since he described the species as having only 1 central. Examination of many specimens in their native habitat shows that the juveniles have no central, the younger adults for a number of years after flowering have only one, and old plants produce 4 centrals on all areoles, as described above.

This cactus is easily distinguished from *Echinocactus bicolor* var. *schottii* or the typical *Echinocactus bicolor*, neither of which grows anywhere near the very limited range of this form. The 8 ribs of *E. bicolor* and 13 of *E. flavidispinus* are an unvarying difference, and the shorter, more yellow, and all round spines—except for the one upper central on old plants—characterize *E. flavidispinus*.

The flowers of *E. flavidispinus* are basically similar to those of *E. bicolor* var. *schottii*, but differ in details which are obvious if the two are seen blooming together. This flower is a much lighter rose color, its petals are much more pointed and do not open so widely. The filaments are not red, but yellow, and the stigma lobes are more slender and less colorful.

Backeberg did not describe the fruits of this species, and in examining hundreds of specimens in their native locations and in growing examples for several years I have seen many flowers but no fruits. I do not know what if any significance there is to this. The plants in their natural situations suffer very often from some sort of injury to their growing tips, and it may be that some insect rapidly devours the young fruits. At any rate, they do not seem to have been observed up to this time.

In much of its range, I found that fully one-half of the plants had suffered the injury mentioned above. Their growing tips were partly destroyed, perhaps by an insect or by a severe freeze, and they were reproducing at this point 3 or 4 small, spherical branches with short, yellow, juvenile spines upon them. Several of these, when grown in my greenhouse for two years, have now put out the one reddish central heralding maturity, but none of them has yet produced the other 3 centrals obvious on the older, original stem.

The description given for *Thelocactus wagnerianus* Berger, of eastern Mexico, seems very close to this plant. Backeberg discussed the relation of the two in his 1941 article, but did not conclude them to be synonymous. However, he did not realize that the Texas plant has 3 or 4 centrals when fully mature, as does the Mexican one. The relationship between the two needs study, but I have not been privileged to see the Mexican cactus, and so cannot offer anything on it.

Echinocactus intertextus Eng.
[*Echinomastus intertextus* (Eng.) B. & R.]
"The Early Bloomer," "White-Flowered Visnagita"

DESCRIPTION   PLATE 24

STEMS: Always occurring individually and without branching. They are spherical at first, becoming egg-shaped or conical, and when very old, short, thick columns. The maximum size seems to be 4 to 5 inches tall and 3½ to 4 inches in diameter. There are almost always 13 ribs, although 12 and 14 are said to have occurred. These are distinct and broad but low, ⅝ to 1 inch wide and only ¼ to ⅜ of an inch deep on a large plant. The tubercles making up these ribs are distinct, being almost entirely separated by deep cross-grooves. They are conical at first, but on the older sides of the stem the deep cross-grooves separating them make the bases square. The summits of the tubercles are prolonged below the areole into a sharply peaked, chinlike ridge running back so far as to almost overhang the next lower tubercle, and at the cross-groove between them this ridge terminates suddenly with a straight drop into the pitlike depression thus formed for the axil.

AREOLES: The young areoles are rather large, slightly oval, very woolly, becoming bare when old. The mature areole becomes elongated by a woolly groovelike extension which runs inward and upward from the spinous portion all the way to the base of the tubercle, where it meets the cross-groove between the tubercles. The flower is produced from the end of this extended areole in the axil of the tubercle. There is usually left after flowering and fruiting a tuft of longer, yellowish-white wool in this depressed axil.

SPINES: The spines are all round with slightly enlarged bases. They are all dull gray or yellowish at the bases, with the up-

per one-half or so darkening into purplish or reddish-brown tips. There are 16 to 27 radial spines which radiate evenly, recurve slightly and lie tightly against the plant surface on one form and spread outward on another. The upper ones are much the weakest spines, being almost bristle-like and ³/₁₆ to ⅝ of an inch long. The lateral radials are heavier and longer, being up to ⅞ of an inch long. The 3 to 5 centrals are similar to the radials but a little heavier and slightly darker in color. 2 to 4 of these stand erect in front of and against the upper radials in one form or spread upward in the other form. They are ½ to ⅞ of an inch long. The lowermost central stands straight out from the center of the areole. On one form it is heavy, but very short, being only ⅛ to ³/₁₆ of an inch long. On the other form it is not so heavy, but is ¼ to ⅝ of an inch long. Juvenile plants have 16 to 18 strictly radiating radial spines and no centrals. Then 1 central appears and the others follow.

FLOWERS: Salmon to white in color, ¾ to 1 inch long and ½ to 1 inch in diameter, the state of the plant determining how widely they open. On plants growing with a minimum of water the spines will prevent the petals from opening out, but on plants well expanded with water the spines will allow them to open widely. There are about half a dozen small scales on the ovary. The outer perianth segments are from very short to about ¾ of an inch long and ³/₁₆ of an inch wide. They have pink midlines with very pale pink edges, and are pointed, with the edges entire or sometimes somewhat toothed and ragged. The inner petals are about ¾ of an inch long and about ⅛ to ³/₁₆ of an inch wide, whitish at their bases and with a very pale pink midline shading to white edges. They are pointed, often with a tiny, soft spine at the apex, and their edges are usually irregular. The filaments are greenish and the anthers yellowish. The style is greenish, but the stigma has 6 to 12 bright pink to brilliant purple-red lobes.

FRUITS: Small, ⅜ to ½ inch in diameter and globular to somewhat oblong, with the old perianth persistent upon it. It becomes dry and brown without coloring, and then it splits open all around its base and the upper part falls off, releasing the seeds. It has a few scales on its surface. The seeds are about ¹/₁₆ of an inch or slightly larger, black and shining, with a rough surface. They are nearly kidney-shaped and have large hila.

RANGE. From the Texas Big Bend and lower Davis Mountain region west to El Paso and the Franklin Mountains. They occur from there west in a narrow strip along the lower border of New Mexico into the southeastern corner of Arizona, and also in adjacent Chihuahua and Sonora, Mexico.

REMARKS. The white-flowered visnagita is an interesting little cactus venturing into our area from Mexico. Nowhere does it manage to survive very far within our territory. Its deepest penetration is about 100 miles above the Rio Grande around

Alpine and Fort Davis, Texas, where one form has been fairly common in the past, but is now much more rarely seen, due no doubt to the activities of collectors and dealers who have long made Alpine their headquarters. Lower in the Big Bend occasional plants may still be found, but it is nowhere abundant. It may once have existed much farther east in Texas than this, as early reports mention its collection near the mouth of the Pecos River, but no specimens have been reported east of Alpine and the Big Bend National Park for many years. This form is occasionally found along the very southern edge of New Mexico and into southeastern Arizona. Another form of the same species ventures up through the Franklin and Organ mountains as far into New Mexico as Rincon and Lake Valley.

The cactus is well named the early bloomer. So far as I have observed it is the first cactus in its locale to bloom each year. I have had plants bloom in my garden in San Antonio as early as February 13.

Concerning the growing of *E. intertextus* in cultivation I must be discouraging. It is an attractive small cactus, especially for its very early flowers which are unusual in that, while the petals are very pale in color, the brilliance is in the bright colored stigma. But this is one of our most particular cacti in regard to its growing requirements. It cannot tolerate water. It must be kept almost dry at all times or it will rot immediately. Only when given soil which will not hold moisture, and much hot sun will it grow and bloom. It should be remembered that this plant does not grow in partial shade like most small cacti, but is found unprotected in the full sun and heat.

Echinocactus intertextus was first described by Engelmann, and there has been little disagreement about it until recently. The only instance of confusion seems to have been when Coulter apparently mistook an Arizona specimen of it for a Cereus and named it *Cereus pectinatus centralis*. Schumann then called it *Echinocereus pectinatus centralis*. This is of course absurd, as the plant has no real similarity to a Cereus.

Britton and Rose naturally took this species out of the genus *Echinocactus* along with most others, and based their new genus *Echinomastus* on it. While this name has been widely used, there has never been much certainty about this proposed genus among taxonomists. It has been combined with various other genera. Because of the long, groovelike extension of the areole and the tubercles more separated from one another than most of those in the Echinocacti, some have played with the idea of calling this cactus a Coryphantha, but no one has actually done so officially. In his book, *Arizona Cacti*, Benson returned the genus *Echinomastus* to *Echinocactus*, but he is now proposing to merge it with the genus *Neolloydia*. Thus the species seems off on the rounds of the microgenera like so many other species, pausing next as *Neolloydia intertextus*, unless *Echinocactus* in its original sense, the only meaningful genus designation we have had for all these plants is maintained.

Engelmann's description of this species included only the typical form of it and did not include the other variety which he himself originated. The best taxonomical practice would require us to designate this typical form a variety also and to broaden the species description to include both varieties of the species, which has been done here.

Echinocactus intertextus var. intertextus (Eng.)

DESCRIPTION   PLATE 24

STEMS: As the species, except that it grows to only 5 inches tall and that the ribs are broader, being 3/4 to 1 inch wide.

AREOLES: As the species.

SPINES: As the species, except that the radial spines always radiate evenly, recurving and lying tightly against the plant surface, while the upper radials are to only 1/2 inch long, the lateral radials to only 3/4 of an inch long, and the lower radials to only 3/8 of an inch. Also, the upper centrals stand erect in front of and against the upper radials, while the lower, porrect central is very heavy and only 1/8 to 3/16 of an inch long.

FLOWERS: As the species.

FRUITS: As the species.

RANGE. From the Texas Big Bend and lower Davis Mountains west past El Paso in a narrow strip along the lower border of New Mexico into Arizona.

REMARKS. This is the typical form of the species, and it occurs over a wide range. Engelmann's original description of the species was restricted to this form, and most books and articles refer to this only when they use the species name.

This variety appears as a single small hemisphere or short column made of distinct ribs composed of curiously shaped tubercles as described under the species. Its areoles are close together, and the plant is encased in its purplish-red spines, all of which lie flat against the surface, except for the one very short and stout lower central which stands straight out, but which is so short as to be almost unnoticed. The spines meet and interlock over the top of the plant and completely enclose the growing tip, which is very woolly when active. The flowers come out of this woolly summit and often have a terrible time opening because of the interlocking spines.

The effect of the environment upon the form of the flower in this variety was dramatically impressed upon me by one plant which I collected just at blooming time. It had apparently had a very dry winter, and when it bloomed for me the plant was still quite shrunken due to low water content. It bloomed profusely in spite of this, and had as many as 6 flowers at a time on the rather flat summit of the stem. But the spines were so many and so tightly interlocking around them that none of these flowers could open properly. Their petals managed to stand straight up, but that was all, and one had to look directly down into the tube about 3/8 of an inch across which they formed to see the bright purplish stigma. This same plant flourished in cultivation, however, and exactly a year later it bloomed again in my greenhouse. But now it was nicely filled out and plump, and the swelling of the stem had pushed the spines over the summit much apart, so the flowers could now open widely. I was amazed to see the petals open all the way back above the spines until the flowers were rotate and at least 1 inch across.

Echinocactus intertextus var. dasyacanthus Eng.
[*Echinomastus intertextus* var. *dasyacanthus* (Eng.) Backbg.]

DESCRIPTION   PLATE 24

STEMS: As the species, except that they grow to 6 inches tall and that the ribs are somewhat narrower, being only $5/8$ to $3/4$ of an inch wide.

AREOLES: As the species.

SPINES: As the species, except that all spines are longer and more spreading than on the typical variety. The upper radials are $1/2$ to $5/8$ of an inch long and very slender, the lateral radials $5/8$ to $7/8$ of an inch long and heavier, the lower ones $1/2$ to $5/8$ of an inch long and rather heavy. The upper centrals spread upward instead of lying appressed against the radials as in the other form and are $3/4$ to $7/8$ of an inch long. The lower central stands practically perpendicular to the stem, as in the other form, but is no heavier than the upper centrals and is $1/4$ to $5/8$ of an inch long.

FLOWERS: As the species.

FRUITS: Apparently identical with the species.

RANGE. A narrow belt of mountainous territory from near Lake Valley and Rincon, New Mexico, south at least to El Paso and probably into Mexico. Most common in the Franklin and Organ mountains near Las Cruces and El Paso. Apparently not coming into Texas beyond the extent of the foothills of the Franklin Mountains.

REMARKS. This is merely a variety of the species. Engelmann considered it that when he first named it, and it was so considered until Britton and Rose elevated it to species rank, calling it *Echinomastus dasyacanthus*. From that time on collectors have been constantly struggling to distinguish what they were led to believe were two nicely distinct species. It has been a great contribution of Backeberg to return this form to varietal status.

Collectors should not be surprised if they have trouble telling variety *dasyacanthus* from variety *intertextus*. The only real differences are matters of maximum stem size and spine character. The most obvious difference is the length and character of the lowermost, porrect central spine. Near El Paso and in New Mexico just north of El Paso the plants collected in the Franklin and Organ mountain foothills all have the longer, more spreading spines, with the lower central $1/4$ to $5/8$ of an inch long. This contrasts nicely with the typical variety *intertextus* of the Texas Big Bend and the very lower edge of New Mexico with its generally shorter, sharply appressed spines and its lower central very heavy but only $1/8$ to $3/16$ of an inch long. But there are definitely intermediates. They come particularly from the area of Presidio and Candelaria, Texas. As adults some of these are hard to assign to either variety with certainty.

It had seemed to me that even a separate varietal rank for a form merging so closely into the typical was hard to justify, and I might have been tempted to merge them more closely if I had not been shown juveniles of the two forms. These were grown in quantity from seed by Mr. Clark Champie of Anthony, New Mexico-Texas. When 1 inch in diameter both forms were almost hemispherical to slightly conical in shape. But the character of the spines at this stage is completely different one from the other. Variety *intertextus* has all of its 16 to 18 radials heavy, $3/16$ of an inch long, opaque purplish-gray and appressed flat against its surface. One does not feel the spines in handling this cactus, they lie so flat upon the plant. At the same age and size the spines of variety *dasyacanthus* are only about half as heavy, nearly twice as long, translucent yellowish to reddish-rown, and stand spreading well out at all angles from the plant so that it is, indeed, a very dangerous little ball to handle. The difference between them at this age, before they get any centrals at all, is much more striking than it is when they are adults, and no one could look at the flats of seedlings at Mr. Champie's establishment—hundreds of variety *intertextus* consistently the same on one hand and on the other hand hundreds of variety *dasyacanthus* so different—without realizing that here is a difference which must be recognized, even if it is within the one species.

Echinocactus erectocentrus var. pallidus (Backbg.)
[*Echinomastus pallidus* Backbg. nom. prov.]

DESCRIPTION   PLATE 24

STEMS: Single until very old, then occasionally producing several short branches just above the ground. The stem is globose at first, becoming oblong or short columnar and growing to a maximum of 6 inches tall and 4 inches in diameter when old. It has 13 spiraling ribs when young, this number increasing by branching of the ribs to a maximum of at least 21 on large stems. These ribs are up to $5/8$ of an inch deep and composed of definite tubercles which, however, vary greatly in shape on the same plant. Some are compressed from side to side and are only $1/4$ of an inch wide, while others are up to $1/2$ inch broad at their bases. The tubercle is prolonged as a short, sloping ridge running downward from the areole. Often this ridge rises a little to form a second shorter, chinlike projection behind the main tubercle and then ends abruptly by falling to a definite though narrow cross-furrow between the tubercles.

AREOLES: Elongated and very woolly at first, then becoming nearly round and almost bare, except for a woolly groove which extends inward and upward from the spinous portion to the floral portion of the areole in the axil, which is often almost overhung by the chin of the next higher tubercle.

SPINES: Very light straw-colored with pale brown tips when young, becoming darker with the tips sometimes dark purplish-brown on old plants. There are 10 to 16 round, rigid radial spines which all spread out at an angle from the plant surface. The 5 or 6 upper radials spreading erect are the longest spines of the plant, $3/4$ to $7/8$ of an inch long. In front of these at the very tip of the areole or occasionally scattered to as much as halfway down the groove to the axil there will often be 1 to 3 additional very tiny spines to as little as $1/16$ of an inch long. The lateral radials spread outward and are about $3/4$ of an inch long. The lower 2 to 4 radials spread almost perpendicular to the plant surface and are $3/8$ to $3/4$ of an inch long. There is one central spine which is always turned upward to stand in front of the upper radials. It is round and a little heavier than the radials, has a bulbous base, and is $5/8$ to $7/8$ of an inch long.

FLOWERS: 1 to $1 1/2$ inches wide and tall, white in color. There are a few whitish scales on the ovary. The perianth segments on the lower tube are small and scalelike with arrowhead-shaped edges. These gradually lengthen up the tube until they become oblong, blunt-tipped segments about $3/16$ of an inch wide. They have greenish-brown midlines and whitish, entire edges. The inner petals are cream-colored or pure white, only $1/8$ of an inch wide, and pointed, with entire edges. The filaments are green or whitish, the anthers yellow. The stigma has 6 to 10 slender, light green lobes.

FRUITS: Spherical or nearly so, about $1/4$ of an inch in diameter. They are light green, sometimes with pinkish areas when ripening, becoming dry and papery when ripe. The perianth persists and there are a few whitish scales on the fruits. They split open along one side when mature. The seeds are black, finely tuberculate, about $1/10$ of an inch long, with a very large, concave hilum.

RANGE. Known only from lower parts of the Texas Big Bend. Scattered populations occur from near Terlingua, Texas, just west of the Big Bend National Park, to northwest of Ruidosa, Texas.

REMARKS. This cactus was apparently first discovered by J. P. Hester during his wonderfully thorough field study of cacti of the Texas Big Bend region. He published a description of it in the *Cactus and Succulent Journal of America* in 1939, not naming

it however, but assigning it two numbers in his own numbering system—this because he was inclined to think there were two forms here instead of one. No one again took notice of the plant for many years. This is not remarkable, since it only grows in the more inaccessible part of the Big Bend.

The next mention of the cactus appears to be by Backeberg in his *Die Cactaceae*, Vol. 5. He apparently had only a few specimens sent to him in Europe, and his data on them was so meager that he gave the location of them as "U.S.A. (Arizona?)." He had not seen the flowers or fruits. It is obvious, however, from his rather complete description that he was describing this cactus. He showed uncertainty about exactly what to do with the plant, and took care of it by calling it *Echinomastus* sp. (*Echinomastus pallidus* nom. prov.). Its students it seems, have experienced an unusual reluctance to name this cactus, the first one to describe it assigning it only a number and the second one only a provisional name.

It will be clear to anyone who has seen both of them together that this cactus is very close to the Arizona cactus, *Echinocactus* (*Echinomastus*) *erectocentrus* Coult. At a glance the two look alike, and the characteristics of stem and spines are almost alike. The differences are only quantitative. *E. erectocentrus* grows to 8 inches tall, while our cactus has been seen to only 6 inches. The radials of the former are appressed rather tightly against the plant surface, while our Texas plant has its radials more spreading. The centrals are the same, except that on the Arizona plant they sometimes reach 1 inch, while on the Texas plant they have not been observed over $7/8$ of an inch long.

But if the differences of stem and spines are too small to be significant, the flowers and fruits of the two present more definite differences. *E. erectocentrus* has pink flowers and all writers describe it with 8 or 9 pink to deep purple stigma lobes. No one has previously described the flowers of our Texas cactus except for Hester's statement that they were pure white. They are indeed pale cream-colored or pure white, with 6 to 10 light green stigma lobes. The fruits of the two differ in shape, those of *E. erectocentrus* being cylindrical and $1/2$ to $5/8$ of an inch long by $1/4$ of an inch wide, while those of our Texas form are perfectly or very nearly spherical and only $1/4$ of an inch across, but they both split alike along one side to release their seeds.

The differences outlined above do not seem to indicate two distinct species, but neither do I think they can be ignored. I think the plant is best regarded as a separate variety of the Arizona species. Since it is essentially a slightly smaller form of the other and more pale in all of its coloring of spines and flowers, the use of Backeberg's proposed species name for it as the name of the variety seems most appropriate.

Roads have recently been built into the lower Big Bend areas where variety *pallidus* grows. It is never common there, but is found on widely scattered limestone ridges from near Terlingua up along the Rio Grande to beyond Ruidosa, Texas. Where it had been seen until recently by only a very few people, now that the area is opened this has become one of the standard offerings of the Texas cactus dealers, going out under almost every sort of name. Anyone who has searched for this cactus and who knows how scarce it is, when he looks down into a bin of literally hundreds of these specimens in a dealer's stock must realize with sadness how efficient their digging is and in what danger all the cacti lie. This will probably be another in that procession of cacti suddenly sold in every dime store and nursery until its newly opened territory is stripped and the form again becomes unknown except to specialists.

This cactus has all of the characteristics of its relatives, and is like most of them in being very exacting in its requirements of full sun and heat and very little water.

Echinocactus mariposensis (Hester)
[*Echinomastus mariposensis* Hester]

DESCRIPTION   PLATE 25

STEMS: Single, practically globose, egg-shaped, or short oblong. These stems grow to a maximum of 3½ inches tall by about 2 inches in diameter, but are usually smaller. Small plants have 13 ribs, but as they mature the number of ribs increases to 21. These are usually twisted and wrinkled into more or less distinct but small tubercles. The surface is light, often yellowish-green.

AREOLES: At first practically spherical and about ⅛ of an inch across, with much short brownish wool. At maturation the areole extends forward as a narrow groove on the upper side of the tubercle, the flower being produced at the end of this groove in the axil of the tubercle, where it is accompanied by long wool and a tuft of persistent white bristles in the axil.

SPINES: There are 25 to at least 36 radial spines. These radiate evenly, are rigid, and are from 3/16 to ⅜ of an inch long. They are pure, shining white to gray, sometimes tipped with light brown. There are 4 to 7 centrals. The upper 3 to 6 of these spread upwards or are often somewhat appressed against the upper radials, are comparatively heavy, and are ½ to ¾ of an inch long. The lower central is porrect or curving downward, heavy, but only 3/16 to ½ inch long. The centrals are whitish, gray, or pale yellow below, with their distal sections usually light brown or a striking bluish-gray.

FLOWERS: About ¾ to 1¼ inches in diameter and length, opening funnel-shaped or wider. The ovary and tube of each flower have a dozen or so whitish scales. The outer perianth segments have somewhat erose edges. The inner segments are somewhat spatulate, their tips bluntly pointed and sometimes notched or toothed. There are two distinct flower colors found in this species. One has the outer perianth segments with green midribs and white edges and the inner segments with light green midlines and white edges. The other has the outer segments with brown midlines and pink edges and the inner petals pink fading to whitish at the edges. The stamens are cream-colored, sometimes with the filaments pinkish. The style is long and greenish or brownish, the stigma with 5 to 8 green lobes.

FRUITS: Globose or oblong, up to ⅜ of an inch long. They are yellowish-green at first, becoming dry, and then splitting open on one side. They have a few scales upon them. The seeds are slightly over 1/16 of an inch long, ovate, and black.

RANGE. Known only from hills a short distance north and northwest of Terlingua, Texas, in the southwest corner of Brewster County.

REMARKS. This dainty little cactus is the smallest of the barrel cacti in our area—usually little larger than a golf-ball—but it is definitely one of the Echinocacti. It is far from spectacular in any way and, with a very limited range in very rough country, it is not surprising that it was not discovered until 1945 and is still very little known.

J. Pinckney Hester, the tireless explorer of the Texas Big Bend, discovered the cactus and described it in great detail. He found it first on hills overlooking the site of the once famous quicksilver mine called the Mariposa Mine, and named it after that mine. It has still not been reported very many miles from that site. He described it as an Echinomastus, and it is clearly a close relative of those species usually put in that microgenus. It will probably share in whatever decision is finally reached when the question about that group of plants is settled. It also shares most of the growth characteristics of those plants, which means that although it is small and delicate in appearance, it is just as tough a desert species as its bigger relatives. It is not found naturally hiding in any shade, but grows in the open in the thin layer of soil overlying hot, exposed limestone ridges. In cultivation it must be kept drier and in brighter sun than most of the other small species of our area, if it is to survive.

The range of this species is very small and the population must not be great, so specimens should not be taken out in large numbers. In fact, it is a wonder that the population has not already been depleted. It was one of the most terrible experiences of this study to come upon at least a thousand specimens of small cacti, mostly this rare species, gathered by someone and left to die in a pile on a hill only a few miles from the old Mariposa Mine. I was told that this was probably a cache left by a professional cactus-digging crew for the dealer to pick up with a truck—but a cache which he missed. At any rate, the cacti were mostly burned to a crisp by the time I saw them and nothing could be done for them, but perhaps they did not die in vain if my telling of them here makes us a little more conscious of the plight of these little species.

Echinocactus conoideus (DC) Poselgr.
[*Neolloydia conoidea* (DC) B. & R.]

DESCRIPTION   PLATE 25

STEMS: Globular to egg-shaped at first, becoming conical or cylindrical, to at least 4 inches tall and 2³/₄ inches thick. The stem of a plant may remain simple, but it often sprouts near the base, or even from higher on the sides, to produce 2 or 3 branches. The surface is dull gray-green and shaped into 8 or 13 indistinct ribs composed of spiral rows of almost completely separate tubercles. These tubercles are to about ¹/₂ inch long, conical in shape, from bases broad but somewhat compressed horizontally by their crowded, almost overlapping position.

AREOLES: Circular, about ¹/₁₆ of an inch in diameter and with white wool when new. It soon becomes enlarged by the formation of a narrow groovelike extension forward from the spinous part of the areole. On a mature areole this groove extends to the axil of the tubercle, where it broadens into a larger felted area from which the flower comes. After blooming the original circular part of the areole remains as the spine-bearing portion, usually losing its wool, and the felted groove runs upward and inward from this.

SPINES: There are 10 to 16 radial spines per areole, all radiating rather evenly, straight, rigid, white fading to gray, and ¹/₄ to about ¹/₂ inch long. There are also 1 to 4 spreading central spines ³/₈ to slightly over 1 inch long, straight, rigid, blackish when young, fading to gray. The lowest of these is the longest and heaviest one.

FLOWERS: Beautiful violet or violet pink in color, 1 to 2 inches in diameter and about 1 inch tall, opening rather widely. The ovary surface and tube seem most commonly naked of scales, but occasionally the ovary has one or two small, rounded, white-edged scales upon it. The outer perianth segments have pink centers with whitish, entire edges. The inner segments are violet or pinkish-violet all over and are lanceolate, with pointed tips and entire edges. The stamens are bright orange. The stigma has 5 to 7 long, white or yellowish lobes.

FRUITS: Spherical, yellowish or reddish at first, drying and becoming brown, after which they seem to remain until broken open by some outside force. Most of them seem to be naked, but on a few the dried remains of 1 or 2 tiny scales may be recognized. The seeds are about ¹/₁₆ of an inch in diameter, black, tuberculate, with large basal hila.

RANGE. Widely found in central Mexico, extending north into Texas to a distance of about 30 miles or so along the arc of the Rio Grande from near Del Rio west to somewhere near Boquillas.

REMARKS. *Echinocactus conoideus* had long been known from Mexico, where it grows over a huge area, but it was not known at first to be in the United States. Engelmann apparently saw specimens from Texas, but did not seem to connect them with the Mexican species. Instead, he called the Texas plant *Mammillaria strobiliformis*.

When Britton and Rose dealt with it they first erected a new genus, *Neolloydia,* for it, and then described the Texas specimens they saw as a new species separate from the others, calling it *Neolloydia texensis.* This is therefore the name under which it has been most widely known in the U.S.

It was Boedeker who first questioned the correctness of setting off the Texas plants as a separate species, saying that they were actually only the northern form of the original Mexican species, *Echinocactus conoideus.* But it is hard to change a usage so widely followed as this of Britton and Rose. While most authorities since Britton and Rose have not listed the species *texensis* separately, most collectors still use the name.

Being very concerned with what might be the correct name for this plant, we have studied many specimens from both Texas and Mexico. We have found that while the range of variations in the Mexican plants is much greater, it wholly encompasses anything we have found in Texas. Since we have seen duplicated every character of the Texas plants in those from the general type area in Mexico, we do not feel that the Texas plants can even be considered to form a distinct variety.

This species and its close relatives stand at the opposite end of the Echinocacti from the huge barrels. These are the only ones to which it really seems incongruous to apply the term "barrel cactus." Their ribs are indistinct and made up of very nearly separate tubercles and their ovaries have at best very few scales upon them and often none at all. They are undeniably the nearest to the next large group of cacti, the Mammillarias.

Because of this position, these cacti have been classified in almost all possible ways. In its original description it was named by De Candolle *Mammillaria conoidea.* In a few years it had also been saddled with a remarkable number of other names, among them *M. diaphanacantha* by Lemaire, *M. inconspicua* by Scheidweiler, *M. echinocactoides* by Pfeiffer, who must already have noticed its similarity to the Echinocacti, *M. scheeri* by Muehlenpfordt (1845 non 1847), and *M. strobiliformis* by Engelmann. When the large genus *Mammillaria* was divided up, it then naturally had to be given the name *Coryphantha conoidea,* since it has grooved tubercles, and Orcutt took care of that.

But there had been another line of reasoning about its proper relationship, and Poselger had already renamed it *Echinocactus conoideus,* soon followed by Kuntze with *Cactus conoideus.*

As if these weren't already genera enough to choose from, Backeberg more recently took some of the relatives of this cactus and some formerly called Thelocactus species and created a new genus, *Gymnocactus,* for them. But now the most recent move is to revitalize the genus *Neolloydia* by returning these to it and by adding to them other species formerly in the genera *Thelocactus* and *Echinomastus.* Once again we seem to see the splitting process gone to its extreme, giving us more and more unstable microgenera until lately a move has begun to recombine these again.

The main point seems to be the question of which major group this cactus and its close relatives belong in, Echinocactus or Mammillaria. On this the decision seems to have been made some time ago. It is many years since anyone has considered this form a Mammillaria. While it is admittedly the more doubtful of them, all recent students seem to have placed it among the Echinocacti. This is because the ovary has at least one or two scales in at least some specimens, the fruit becomes dry, and it is possible to speak of ribs on at least most of the species involved. Beyond this, little can be said except that the recent move to combine the much more clearly Echinocactus species in *Thelocactus* and *Echinomastus* with these in their own microgenus, *Neolloydia*, draws these more solidly than ever into the Echinocactus group.

Considering this species as an Echinocactus, then, I choose to use the name of that large genus for it—at least until the microgenera are a little more stabilized.

Echinocactus conoideus is not ever very common in Texas. Where it occurs it is usually in stands of several dozen speci-

mens, but these stands are in widely scattered locations. It grows on rocky hillsides, more or less in the open.

Its range does not go at any point very far north of the Rio Grande. It is most easily found around Sanderson, Texas, and in the very eastern edge of the Big Bend. Our knowledge of the eastern limits of its range were changed by finding a nice stand of the cactus on a hillside overlooking Goodenough Springs, which is just north of the Rio Grande south of Comstock, Texas. This is the most eastern record of this species of which I know personally, although there are reports of it from near Del Rio. The cactus has been eliminated at beautiful Goodenough Springs and its whole surrounding area has been submerged with the filling of the lake behind Amistad Dam.

I have no knowledge of this cactus west of the eastern Big Bend. Although I have seen a herbarium specimen labeled "near El Paso," I have been unable to confirm that the species grows that far west.

This is a fairly easy cactus to grow, not quite so badly affected by moisture as are most of the other members of this group. It is not a vigorous grower or a prolific bloomer, but the flowers it does produce are of a very beautiful shade and rather large.

Genus *Lophophora* Coult.

We come here to one of several cactus genera which seem to lie between the Echinocacti and the Mammillarias. Although there have been attempts in the past to submerge them in first one and then the other of these larger groups they seem to defy either combination. The reasons for this may seem rather technical to the nonspecialist, but they are the stuff out of which cactus taxonomy is constructed.

Although some of its members were first described by Lemaire as Echinocacti, the significant points which seem to rule the Lophophoras out of the genus *Echinocactus* are the facts that the ovary and fruit on them are entirely naked and that the fruit remains always fleshy. These characters would put them in agreement with the Mammillarias, but they are even more clearly set apart from that genus by the facts that their stems are ribbed and that their monomorphic areoles produce the flowers from the apexes of young tubercles rather than from the axils. So this small genus is left by all recent students to stand alone.

There are only a very few species in this genus, and as yet little agreement exists as to exactly how many they number. Most authors list two and some three or four, but there is no standardization of species and varietal arrangement, so no definite figure can be given.

The members of *Lophophora* are small, globose, or depressed globose cacti growing from comparatively large, carrot-shaped taproots. Usually the stem of the plant is to about 3 inches in diameter, and although one form sometimes reaches to about 5 inches, they stand no more than 2 inches above the ground. The stems of an individual may be single or may sometimes branch from the base to form large clusters.

The surfaces of these cacti are blue-green, usually with much gray glaucescence. There are no spines at all after the early seedling stage. The very broad and flat ribs are composed of some of the broadest, flattest, most confluent tubercles seen anywhere. The areoles are small and round, with long white to yellowish wool which tends to persist. The flowers are small, bell-shaped, and pink, pale rose, white, or rarely pale yellowish. The fruits are club-shaped and rose-pink or reddish.

The insignificant little members of this genus have been famous out of all proportion to their size and appearance as far back as we can trace them. They are the sacred plants of the Indians best known by the ancient Indian name, *peyotl*, which has become the peyote of common usage. This is all because these plants contain in their flesh a group of alkaloids which, when taken into the human body, have remarkable effects upon the nervous system.

The history of man's use of and society's reaction to these alkaloids is a fascinating study in itself. From ancient times to the present, Indians of Mexico and the U.S. Southwest have eaten these cacti specifically for the effects they have on their senses. An idea of how ancient and how widespread the practice has been can be grasped by noting that these plants have been called in different cultural periods and different Indian societies by all of the following names: *peyotl, teonanacatl, tlalcoyote, uocoui, xicorl, seni,* and *hicore* or *jiculi.* All during the history of the area, the Indians have given the cactus a very special veneration, eating it in very special religious ceremonies. This was because it gave them remarkable sensations which they were convinced came from their Great Spirit and marvelous visions which they were certain were glimpses—granted them by the Great Spirit—of ultimate reality itself.

In the meantime others who did not venerate its visions as quite so god-given discovered peyote and came to enjoy its relaxing effect. Many Mexicans came to relish a little of it now and then, just for the relaxation and sense of well-being it brings, and in central Mexico most good markets will include among the herbs a stock of the mescal buttons, as the plants have also come to be called after mescaline, the most famous of its alkaloids. In the U.S. and in Europe many years ago word of its effects got out, and for years now some people have experimented with it, there being an extensive literature built up through the years on its effects.

Cactus dealers, particularly in southern Texas, where the plants have been easily available, have sold the mescal buttons in quantities for at least 40 years.

But very early, in the U.S., this ran up against the typical American suspicion of anything so mystical and strange as the experiences produced by eating the peyote button. Moves were made long ago to outlaw the sale and even the possession of these cacti, and for a while they were declared narcotics and prohibited by edict. But these moves failed for two reasons. In the first place it was found impossible to maintain that they were narcotics under any meaningful definition of that term. And in the second place it was found a direct breach of the principle of religious freedom to deny the Indians this key part of their religious ceremony. Peyote could no more be denied to these Indians than sacramental wine could be denied the Christians. This move therefore soon collapsed, and peyote again became legal in all but California, where a state prohibition of it has hung on to the present, although it has been only sporadically enforced.

This was the fascinating peyote cactus, then, eaten for millenniums by the Indians as their means to induce and intensify the mystical experience, relished casually as a harmless relaxing agent by many a humble Mexican, and beyond that tried occasionally by the curious all over the world in order to experience its strange effects—until the past few years.

Then suddenly, only a few years ago, our little cactus was catapulted into the limelight, where it is now discussed in everything from the most technical medical and psychological journals to the best art and literary magazines to the most lurid sensation-promoting newspaper.

This spurt of interest in the cactus seems to have been touched off by the success of chemists in synthesizing some of the alkaloids found in the peyote. The most famous of these synthetic products similar to the compounds in peyote is the now well-known LSD. This synthetic compound is extremely potent and does very strange things to the nervous system of the user.

Knowledge of LSD has been general among psychologists and a few others for some years, but it was treated as a dangerous drug and used sparingly for research until recently. However, the accounts which did appear concerning LSD stimulated much interest, and many turned to the comparatively very mild, natural, unconcentrated, layman's version of this sort of agent—peyote. Their motives in eating peyote were various, including a desire to share in the mystical experience many have always invoked by all sorts of means, from fasting to Zen, a desire among artists to profit from the heightening to the visual and auditory senses which it is well-authenticated that peyote brings,

a desire to gain the feeling of cleansing and well-being which it is universally testified that peyote leaves in the user, and, of course, a good share of just plain curiosity.

All this boded only ill for our little cacti. These little species which had foregone the use of spines to protect themselves from their enemies and instead saturated their flesh with a set of alkaloids unpalatable to most animals in order to survive, suddenly found themselves taken by the hundreds and thousands just for these unique protective agents they had developed. The demand became so great that the countryside was systematically sacked of all its peyote. Five or six years ago I knew thousands of acres in the lower Rio Grande Valley where peyote grew in profusion under almost every shrub, but visits to one after another of these locations now show them barren of even a surviving specimen after the crews of gatherers have been through. The plant now only survives north of the Rio Grande in a few small areas.

For all of these years dealers have sold peyote openly to anyone who wanted it, with the full knowledge of the authorities. In the past few years I have been at establishments where hundreds of the plants were being shipped when governmental agents visited and observed the business and heard them assure the cactus dealers that they were doing nothing wrong. This was because various court cases had established that the active substances in these plants were not narcotic or intoxicating substances and because there was no evidence of ill effects from the eating of the plant.

But very recently the picture has changed dramatically. LSD has escaped the laboratory and is being indulged in indiscriminately by all sorts of people. This synthetic substance is very powerful, has sometimes very violent effects, and a case can easily be made that it is a danger when misused. Moves for its control appear justified, and are under way. But how does that involve peyote, which does not even contain this dangerous synthetic substance?

Fuzzy thinking seems to be indicated when peyote is involved at all. LSD, the alkaloids in peyote, and those found naturally in various other plants are all lumped together under the suddenly very emotion-charged term "hallucinogens," because all of them are capable of producing hallucinations in the user. There is little, if any evaluation of these various substances. Every magazine and paper making any attempt to follow the trends has had articles on one of the prime subjects of discussion today, the hallucinogens. In almost all of these articles little or no effort is made to differentiate among them and deal with the subject of their possible good and bad qualities, their potential or lack of potential for harm, and the question of whether each one in its own right should or should not be prohibited to the public. They are all lumped together as hallucinogens and they seem destined to stand or fall with LSD.

The Food and Drug Administration recently invoked the 1938 Federal Food, Drug, and Cosmetic Act and ruled that the sale or use of any of them is the illegal sale or use of drugs. Under this new ruling you may not dig our little cactus, sell it to be eaten, or eat it yourself—unless you are a member of the Native American Church, the legal name of the Indian religious group in the U.S. using it in their ceremonials. Note that the naturally occurring peyote or the substances in it in their naturally occurring concentration have never been ruled narcotic, incapacitating, or even intoxicating, and that it has never been stated to have harmful effects either mental or physical. It has apparently suffered from illogical association in the minds of the authorities with the man-made substances LSD and mescaline, which undeniably can be dangerous, and the 1938 Food and Drug Act, which could as easily be applied to aspirin or wine as this, has been used to suppress it. Because the distinction between peyote and LSD has been overlooked, we are once again in the hard-to-maintain position of prohibiting the use of a substance as too bad for the general public which we allow a chosen group to use as a supreme good in their religious services. Can this position be maintained now any more than it was before?

Of course, this prohibition clearly works for the good of the cacti themselves. Without it the species of this genus which grows in south Texas would soon have become extinct in the U.S., but now the wholesale digging has stopped and the cactus has been granted a reprieve. From the standpoint of the cacti, this is good.

But the cactophile is faced with a peculiar situation. While it is specifically made clear that in all of the United States but California—and most recently some other states also—he may acquire and grow a few peyotes as garden or pot plants, if he should eat one of his plants, or if he should allow someone else to eat one of them, he would be guilty of violating a federal drug control act. This special dispensation for him (no doubt granted to avoid raising his ire) is appreciated, but he must weigh carefully the question of whether, under this sort of ruling a bed of peyotes is not too dangerous to have around. Perhaps, if he wants to keep his collection complete, including the peyote species, he should join the Native American Church—just to be safe. The cactus dealer is, of course, in double jeopardy. He is assured that he can sell a few peyotes singly or in small numbers to those who wish to grow them, but that he is a lawbreaker if anyone eats any of the peyotes he sells. Faced with being prosecuted as a "pusher" at any moment if he sells peyotes, most dealers I know have stopped handling these plants entirely.

We are, of course, happy at the prospect that these interesting cacti may be saved from almost certain extinction by the new ruling, and are not primarily concerned here with whether or not anyone should be free to use them to "expand his consciousness." But we do note that if the present rulings had gone into effect a few years earlier and put these species beyond the pale of respectability at that time, the research which has gone into these plants would have been well-nigh impossible. This is undoubtedly the most peculiar situation that has ever arisen concerning any cactus.

It has been said that somewhere among the cacti you will find almost every kind of strangeness, and that this is the secret of the interest cacti generate in people. There is truth in this, and here, in the genus *Lophophora* we have another kind of strangeness. Here we have our "notorious" cacti, and with them the study of cacti acquires all the exciting elements of mysticism and sinister intrigue and danger. These are the cacti for those who thrive on such things.

Lophophora williamsii (Lem. in SD) Coult.
"Peyote," "Mescal Button," "Whisky Cactus," "Dry Whisky"

DESCRIPTION   PLATES 15, 26

ROOTS: Each plant grows from a large carrot-shaped taproot the same diameter at its top as the stem and tapering slowly below, being usually 3 to 5 inches long.

STEMS: Each plant begins as a single stem and sometimes remains so, but often clusters greatly to form in one variety sometimes up to 50 stems to one specimen. These stems, hemispherical or usually depressed-globular, grow to about 5 inches in diameter, but not over about 2 inches tall. The flesh of the stem is soft and flabby, the surface blue-green, usually with a gray glaucescence. There are 5 to 13 very broad, very low ribs separated by narrow grooves. These ribs may be straight or sinuous. Each rib is more or less divided into tubercles. At the apex these tubercles are fairly distinct, but lower on the stem they are only very slight projections or almost entirely obliterated, with or without small wrinkles to indicate their limits.

AREOLES: Round, or nearly so, and small, only about $1/8$ of an inch in diameter and located $1/4$ to $1\,1/4$ inches apart on the summits of the tubercles. At first each areole is filled with much long white or yellowish wool, so that the usually depressed summit of the stem is more or less filled with the wool of the close-standing young tubercles. With age the wool usually turns gray and may or may not be worn off to leave the areole with merely a tuft of short wool. The flowers are produced from within these areoles at the summits of the young tubercles.

SPINES: The plant is spineless after the very young seedling stage.

FLOWERS: Small, usually pale pink or whitish, but said to be rarely rose or pale yellowish. They are bell-shaped and $1/2$ to 1 inch in diameter. The small ovary is naked. The outermost perianth segments are greenish with entire edges. The inner segments are almost linear and are pale pink to rose, white, or yellowish. The filaments are whitish, the anthers yellow. There are 3 to 7 reddish or yellowish stigma lobes.

FRUITS: Club-shaped, $3/8$ to $3/4$ of an inch long, pale pink or very pale rose in color when ripe, and remaining fleshy and indehiscent. The seeds are $1/16$ of an inch or slightly less in length, with basal hila.

RANGE. Extending from a very wide range in Mexico across the Rio Grande a short distance into south and southwest Texas. In south Texas it occurs in Hidalgo, Starr, and Zapata counties; in west Texas it occurs in a few locations in Brewster County in the Big Bend. There are records of many years ago of the species having been taken near Laredo and near the mouth of the Pecos River, but the plant does not seem to be in these areas now.

REMARKS. This is the famous peyote. Individual stems are often called mescal buttons. Some plants remain single until very large, while others sprout new heads or buttons all around them almost from the beginning. I once collected an old plant of the latter type which was 18 inches across with almost 50 heads. Since it is said that a button 2 or 3 inches in diameter takes around 10 years to grow, it is easy to see that such old plants are very venerable. With the great interest in peyote of recent years it is almost impossible to find such old plants in the wild any more.

There is much variation in the rib shape, number, and size, and some in flower features. This plant has been greatly studied for a long time, and a confusing series of taxa have been set up for it. After observing many of the plants in the field and thousands of them in dealers' bins and markets from our area all the way to Chihuahua and central Mexico, and after growing and flowering them ourselves, we have come to the conclusion that many of the proposed varieties are unnecessary and that the species found in the U.S. needs to be divided into only the following two taxa.

Lophophora williamsii var. williamsii (Lem. in SD)

DESCRIPTION   PLATE 26

ROOTS: As the species.

STEMS: As the species, except that they grow to only 3 inches or less in diameter and the tubercles are less distinct than in the other form, being smaller, only about $5/8$ to $3/4$ of an inch across their bases. They cluster, usually quite early and extensively when old.

AREOLES: As the species, about $1/4$ to $5/8$ of an inch apart.

SPINES: As the species.

FLOWERS: As the species, except that the sepals and petals each grow in fewer than 3 series and the stigma lobes are 3 to 5 in number.

FRUITS: As the species.

RANGE. Central Mexico to south Texas. In Texas it is restricted at the present time to Hidalgo, Starr, and Zapata counties.

REMARKS. This is the typical form of the species. Since it was described too narrowly in the early accounts, a whole series of variety names grew up around it. These include the following: *Anhelonium lewinii* Hennings, which became *Lophophora williamsii* var. *lewinii* (Hennings) Coult.; *Lophophora williamsii* var. *typica* Croiz.; var. *pluricostata* Croiz.; and var. *caespitosa* Y. Ito. I have found specimens falling within the limits of all of these proposed varieties within single populations of both Mexican and Texas plants, and they all intergrade, so it seems most logical to broaden the description of the typical form to include all limits found together and stop trying to interpret simple genetic traits as varieties.

This is the form of the species growing in south Texas, the form which has smaller stems but which forms large clusters of these smaller stems when old. It is the more tender form, preferring to grow under the partial shade of the brush, shrubs, and trees, and rather easily damaged by frost. Two or three degrees below freezing will usually kill it. It does not now appear north or west of southern Zapata County, but old records suggest that it may have once grown in Webb County.

There was also described by Fric as variety *texana* a form with 14 ribs, but the locality of it is not known and I can find no record of another collection with 14 ribs. A variety *lutea* (Rouhiers) Croiz. has been proposed for specimens with yellowish flowers, but we have long ago seen that it is very risky to base even a variety on flower color alone.

Lophophora williamsii var. echinata (Croiz.)

DESCRIPTION   PLATE 26

ROOTS: As the species.

STEMS: As the species, except remaining single or at most dividing to form 2 or 3 heads in very old specimens. These stems are larger than in the typical form, growing to at least 5 inches in diameter. The tubercles are more conical and larger, the bases being $3/4$ to $1^1/4$ inches across.

AREOLES: A little larger than the typical form, with more wool, but otherwise the same.

SPINES: Spineless after the seedling stage, as the species.

FLOWERS: As the species, except that the sepals and petals are more numerous and usually in 3 series each.

RANGE. Northern Mexico, extending from Chihuahua and Coahuila into the Texas Big Bend in lower Brewster County.

REMARKS. This is a larger, tougher form of the species. There is little difference in the structure of the two except that in all respects the stems of this form are heavier and larger, although not clustering to any marked degree. This form is found growing on dry, exposed hillsides of the Big Bend where the lower

Rio Grande Valley form would be burned to a crisp. It can also survive the much more severe cold of the Big Bend. I have several times had the smaller form from south Texas freeze in San Antonio, while this form growing in the same bed showed no ill effects.

This form does seem distinct enough to be recognized, and it has been called a separate species, but this hardly is warranted. It seems at best a variety of the species, but a stable one. It is *L. williamsii* in the sense of Schultes (*Cactus and Succulent Jour-*nal, 1940). Britton and Rose's description of the species seems to include this form along with the typical form.

This is clearly the form which grew nearest to the Indians of Arizona, New Mexico, and northwestern Mexico, and is the one they originally hunted and used for their religious experiences. It has been noted that this form seems to have more of the alkaloids in it than are in the typical variety, since a small plant of this form when consumed will give more effect than the same-sized button of the typical variety.

Genus *Ariocarpus* Scheidweiler

This is a small genus containing about half a dozen very strange cacti, one of which is found in Texas, the rest in Mexico.

The body of an Ariocarpus consists of one or occasionally a cluster of low, flattened stems from only about 2 inches in diameter and not projecting above the soil level at all in some forms to as much as 10 inches across and 5 inches tall in one form. This stem sits on top of a large, carrot-like taproot.

The surface of the stem does not have ribs, but is divided into very distinct, usually imbricated but noncoalescent tubercles. These are very firm, often have a horny, rough epidermis, and are of peculiar shapes, usually more or less triangular and flattened above. There are no spines after the first seedling growth.

The members of this genus are unusual among cacti of our area because they flower in the fall of the year, usually from September to December. The flowers come from the woolly axils of the young tubercles at the center of the plant. They open widely, are diurnal, and are white, yellowish, or purplish in color. The ovary and fruit are both naked; the fruit is fleshy at first, becoming dry at maturity and disintegrating, leaving the seeds in the wool at the center of the plant.

This genus was described and named *Ariocarpus* by Scheidweiler in 1838. The next year Lemaire redescribed it, calling it *Anhalonium,* and many students, including Engelmann and Coulter, thought that Lemaire's name had precedence, so for many years there was confusion over these names.

This is another genus which falls into the gap between the Echinocacti and the Mammillarias, or rather, which has some characters typical of each of these major groups but will not rest easily in either.

The members have fruits which become dry, as do those of the Echinocacti, and some of them have monomorphic areoles also, but they have never been considered Echinocacti. This is partly because they have no ribs and because they have naked ovaries.

They actually seem to be closer to the Mammillarias. In fact, for most of his life Engelmann persisted in including them in the genus *Mammillaria.* This is because they have a tuberculate surface and naked ovaries, and some species of them have dimorphic areoles with the nonproducing spinous portion of the areole at the tip of the tubercle and the floral portion separated from it at the base. However, the tubercle characters are very different; the flowers come from the apex of the stem instead of from older tubercles away from the apex; the fruits become dry and open; and there are differences of seed structure; all of which seems to separate these plants from the Mammillarias as well. Coulter remarked with obvious relish in 1896 that Engelmann had "finally come" to the opinion that these must be kept distinct from *Mammillaria.*

The confusion over this sort of thing had no more than subsided when in 1925 Berger noted an obvious difference between certain members of the genus. Most have no groove on the upper surface of the tubercle, but two have a woolly groove on it. Berger seized upon this difference and proposed that those with grooves should be removed from the genus *Ariocarpus* and put into a new genus, *Roseocactus.*

Since that time there has been a history of disagreement over Berger's proposal. In brief, Marshall did not think that the difference was fundamental enough to warrant completely separating the plants into different genera, and proposed that *Roseocactus* be put back into *Ariocarpus* as a subgenus. Buxbaum seemed to agree with Marshall. The main recent champion of Berger's view was Backeberg, who backed it vociferously in his large work on cacti.

Only very recently was detailed study of the mode of development of the tubercles and areoles carried out and the information acquired, together with other factors, applied to the problems. However, it seems already to have brought some welcome clarification, as well as results of significance to the classification of some other cactus groups. Edward F. Anderson made these studies and reported on them in a series of articles beginning in 1961.

He found that in all of this group there is a single original growing point for the areole development which is located near the base of the tubercle instead of at its tip. From this single point develop all areolar structures, including the spinous portion (if represented), groove (if present), and floral portion. But there are differences in the different species in the way these develop from the original growing point. In *Ariocarpus (Roseocactus) fissuratus,* the floral development is at the base, with elongation of the tubercle occurring beneath the vestigial spinous part of the areole and thus drawing that part of the areole out into the already mentioned groove. In *Ariocarpus retusus,* the type species of the genus *Ariocarpus,* the rudimentary spinous part of the areole soon separates from the floral part and elongation between them then leaves the floral part in its basal position, while it pushes the spinous part to near the tip of the tubercle, where it persists as a woolly spot. In *Ariocarpus trigonus* the elongation occurs ahead of the spinous portion and never allows it to separate from the floral part at the base at all.

The usual interpretation of these events requires us to call the elongated, groovelike areoles of *A. fissuratus* and also the short, basal areoles of *A. trigonus,* whose meristems do not divide, monomorphic. At the same time the areoles of *A. retusus,* where the floral and spinous parts separate, are entirely dimorphic.

Essentially this same difference has, since Britton and Rose, been made the reason for separating the Coryphanthas out of the genus *Mammillaria,* and if it is so fundamental a difference as some have thought, it should also make mandatory the division of the genus *Ariocarpus* as well. But Anderson carried on many other investigations of seedling development, seed structure, other aspects of stem anatomy, fruit composition, and hybrid reactions, and concluded from these that they should all make up one genus, *Roseocactus* being at most a subgenus. The lack of importance of those details of areole structure which have been used so much in separating cacti is further indicated by Anderson's report of *A. fissuratus* individuals without the groove and *A. retusus* individuals which have no spinous portion of the areole at all. This means that in at least *A. retusus* both the monomorphic and the dimorphic areoles occur in the same species, a situation which Dr. Boke has found also in certain Coryphanthas. This study has far-reaching implications for the taxonomy of other groups, where, it seems, too much emphasis has been put on grooves or their absence.

The members of *Ariocarpus* are retiring species, often not rising above the ground level at all, with usually horny and discolored surfaces which make them almost invisible. They are very difficult to find in their native haunts, but this is the point of their method of growth. They have no spines, and they depend instead upon being so insignificant as to be overlooked, upon camouflage, and upon some unpalatable alkaloids in their

flesh for their survival. They are so unusual in their appearance that most people find it hard to believe they are cacti at all.

Ariocarpus fissuratus (Eng.) K. Schumann
"Living Rock," "Star Cactus," "Star Rock," "Sunami," "Chautle," "Peyote Cimarron"

DESCRIPTION   PLATE 26

ROOTS: A carrot-like taproot.

STEMS: Entirely flat to somewhat rounded and depressed-globose, usually level with the ground or rising to only 1 inch or so above it. Covered with very crowded and overlapping tubercles which have bases broad and flattened and upper surfaces flattened and triangular in shape and 1/2 to about 3/4 of an inch long. These upper surfaces are crossed by numerous small fissures which give them a warty appearance. The epidermis of the plants is always very firm and is gray-green when young or well-watered, but in the older plants or in the usual desert situation it is yellowish or brownish and, over most of the surface, hard, horny, and dead-appearing. The apex of the stem has long wool often almost entirely covering the younger tubercles. Plants usually have a single stem, but occasionally they branch to form a cluster of several to as many as a dozen stems.

AREOLES: Each areole is at first circular and at or near the base of the young tubercle, filled with a dense mass of woolly hairs, but by the time it is easily visible on the elongated tubercle it is stretched into a conspicuous woolly groove running from the axial floral part to the tip of the tubercle on the upper surface. Mature areoles are thus linear and 3/8 to about 5/8 of an inch long, except on very rare individuals on which the areoles do not elongate, remaining instead in the axil of the tubercle.

FLOWERS: From the axils of young tubercles at or near the center of the stem, where they arise out of the long wool. They are 1 to 2 inches broad, opening rather widely, but only about 1 inch tall. In color they are from almost white to pink or magenta. The ovary is naked and short; the outer perianth segments are almost linear with pointed tips, brownish or greenish with whitish, entire edges. The inner segments are pinkish or purple with whitish edges and are rather oblong from narrow bases, the tips with small, hairlike points at the apex. The filaments are white, the anthers bright orange. The style and stigma are white, with 5 to 10 lobes.

FRUITS: Oval, about 1/4 to 5/8 of an inch long, pale green or whitish at first, becoming dry and disintegrating while still mostly buried in the long hair at the apex of the plant. The seeds are about 1/16 of an inch long, black, with rough surfaces.

RANGE. Northern Mexico into Texas. In Texas it is found along the Rio Grande from the mouth of the Pecos River to near Presidio, but never penetrating more than a few miles into the state except in the Big Bend, where it occurs almost as far north as Alpine.

REMARKS. This is the plant to which the name "living rock" truly applies. It likes to grow on barren, rocky slopes where it survives burning up by hardly if at all projecting above the ground level and by having its surface covered with a thick, horny, brownish epidermis. It appears that its water storage is in the thick taproot on which the stem merely forms a flattened cap, and that the result of desiccation during the dry seasons is the shrinking of this root. This in turn seems to pull the stem down into the ground as it shrinks, so that it has even less surface to suffer from the cruel elements in these most exposed of all habitats in our region. The result is that the plants do not project any higher than the rocks all around them, and the brown, horny epidermis, broken into irregular warts by the many fissures from which the plant gets its name, looks just as dead and mineral as anything on the slope. I have repeatedly had the experience of walking around on what I thought was an unoccupied slope until I saw the first one of these cacti and then realized that I had been treading all over them, never knowing they were anything but rocks. Fortunately they are so hard that stepping on them does not damage them.

The species is most interesting for its unusual appearance—quite uncactus like—and it blooms with a fine flower at a time of the year when most other cacti are through blooming. It interests people greatly, but I do not often advise it for growing in the usual cactus garden. Most people cannot keep it alive because it is one of the most extreme of the desert-adapted. It grows on the most exposed brows of the most arid ridges in west Texas, and cannot tolerate much moisture at all, or any amount of shade. Few people have the courage to "mistreat" this cactus with enough sunlight, heat, and dryness to keep it alive, healthy, and blooming. They want to pamper it until it is nice and soft and green, but *A. fissuratus* is a hard, rocklike thing, and it will not change, except to melt into rot if it is not kept in a situation approaching its desert home.

As mentioned in discussing the genus, Engelmann long thought that this cactus was a Mammillaria: his first name for it was *Mammillaria fissurata*. Later Lemaire used the name *Anhalonium engelmannii* for it. K. Schumann first put it in *Ariocarpus*. The only other name applied to this species was Berger's *Roseocactus fissuratus*.

There is a form known as *Ariocarpus fissuratus* var. *lloydii* (Rose) Marshall. It is characterized by having the stems higher, more rounded, and larger in maximum size, the tubercles more rounded and with less distinct fissures. This variety is apparently found only in Mexico.

The living rock may have been more common in the past in the eastern part of its Texas range, but it is now very difficult to find east of the Big Bend. There it is still fairly common.

Genus *Pediocactus* B. & R.

ORIGINATED FOR one species of cactus, this genus has grown through the years until it now contains at least seven species. The increase has come about in two ways. Four of its species have been discovered and described only within the past twenty years, and three of these less than ten years ago. This is, therefore, the only group of cacti in the United States which has had major additions to it in the last few years. New understanding has come with these new species. They have tended to fill gaps, and this has resulted in the combining under the over-all genus *Pediocactus* of four small genera: *Pediocactus* sensu B. & R., *Utahia* B. & R., *Navajoa* Croiz., and *Toumeya* B. & R. This action has been taken by Dr. Benson only in the last few years, and since there has not yet been time for any opposing interpretations to appear it may be regarded as still somewhat tentative. However it seems to be the best system to take into account all the newer forms.

This enlarged version of the genus *Pediocactus* would be characterized as follows: the stems are either single or branching sparingly; flattened, spherical, or cylindrical; usually very small but in one form up to 6 inches in diameter and height. The surface of the stem is covered with small but prominent, noncoalescent tubercles, spirally arranged. Areoles are small and entirely on the tips of the tubercles, sometimes with glands present. The spines are variable. The flowers are bell- or funnel-shaped. The ovary is naked or with 2 or 3 small scales, sometimes these having a few hairs or bristles in their axils. The outer perianth segments are fringed to entire. The fruits are green at first, often changing to tan or yellowish, and then becoming dry. They are naked or have several small scales. In shape they are from nearly spherical to almost club-shaped. The fruits are dehiscent, opening by a ring around the apex, by a lateral slit on the upper side, or sometimes rather irregularly by both of these. Seeds are black or gray, the surfaces rough or shiny, but always textured when seen under the microscope.

The members of this genus are once again cacti which fall between the major groups, the Echinocacti and the Mammillarias, overlapping each to some extent. Most technical discussions of these cacti have become involved with trying to balance the characters in which they coincide with the one group against the characters in which they agree with the other. This began even with Engelmann, who had the type species of this genus as an Echinocactus, but who said that this species, with some others, "forms a small section of Echinocacti with the appearance of Mammillarias named by Prince Salm *Theloidei*." Although he insisted that they were still "true" Echinocacti, he repeated that they ". . . constitute the closest and most imperceptible transition to *Mammillaria* subgenus *Coryphantha*."

To show the reasons for the divergent opinions over these cacti in the past, and the way they overlap both adjacent major cactus groups while actually falling outside of either one, we will mention here the most significant of the characters involved. They share with the Echinocacti the following points: the areoles are monomorphic with the flower coming at or near the tips of the tubercles; the flowers are similar to those of the Echinocacti, the ovary often with 2 or 3 tiny scales and occasionally these with a few bristles in their axils; the fruit becomes dry and splits open—but they differ from the Echinocacti by having no ribs and by having mucilage cells, which are not found in any recognized Echinocactus. On the other hand they share with the Mammillarias the following characters: the stems are tubercled instead of ribbed; the ovary is sometimes naked or has only 2 or 3 scales—while differing from them by producing the flowers from a monomorphic areole at the tip of the tubercle and by having dry, dehiscent fruits. In possessing mucilage cells, as Dr. Boke has pointed out, they look toward the Echinocerei. The result of all this is that this genus is left standing with those few others which are somewhat alone, outside of any of the major groups. Buxbaum has considered it significant, because of its peculiar combination of characters, as an ancestor of other groups, but other scholars have disputed his theories on this.

The members of this genus can be as exasperating to the ordinary cactophile as to the taxonomist. If it is difficult to view them in the proper systematic niche, it is even harder to view them in their native habitat. They are all extremely retiring cacti. They are usually so well camouflaged in their natural environment that there are places where it is more rewarding to hunt for them by feel than by sight. And it is not easy to find their locations. With the exception of one species, they all occupy very small ranges, several only a few miles in extent, and some are noted more for their rarity than for anything else. Each is restricted to a particular soil type or geologic formation, and some are associated with one other specific plant. The one species which is more widespread is usually a high mountain inhabitant where only the hardy collectors will come across it.

So these are especially challenging little cacti not seen by many people and perhaps fully appreciated by only the specialist. However, they are part of the huge group known as cacti and they contribute to its amazing diversity.

Pediocactus simpsonii var. simpsonii (Eng.) L. Benson
"Mountain Cactus"

DESCRIPTION   PLATE 27

STEMS: Globose or sometimes even a little elongated in the growing season, but usually depressed and often almost flat in the winter. These stems are up to 5 inches in diameter and 1 to 6 inches tall. They are almost always single, but on rare occasions clustering. The surface is covered with spirally arranged tubercles which are conical or sometimes somewhat pyramidal, 1/4 to 5/8 of an inch long. The color of the surface is light green.

AREOLES: The areoles, situated on the tips of the tubercles, are circular or nearly so. When young, at the apex of the plant, they are large, to 3/16 of an inch in diameter, with much long white wool, but when older they shrink to 1/8 of an inch or so and lose most or all of their wool.

SPINES: There are 15 to 30 radial spines which are white or whitish, rigid and straight, but very slender, radiating, and 1/4 to 1/2 inch long, the shortest and most slender of them being at the top of the areole. On mature plants there are 5 to 11 widely spreading central spines. These are heavier than the radials, rigid, straight or nearly so, and 3/8 to 3/4 of an inch long. They are whitish, cream, or pale yellow below, with the outer half of each darkening to brown or red-brown.

FLOWERS: Bell-shaped, opening rather widely. They are 5/8 to 1 inch in diameter and length, and are pale pink, pale purplish, whitish, or yellowish in color. The ovary has several small scales near its top. The outer perianth segments are broadly rounded, greenish with pink to whitish, somewhat fringed, ragged, or notched edges. The inner segments are pink, pale purple, whitish, or yellowish, almost linear, with pointed tips and entire edges. The stamens are yellow, the stigma with 5 to 7 yellowish lobes.

FRUITS: 1/4 to 3/8 of an inch long. Almost spherical to short-cylindrical. The fruits are green, sometimes suffused with reddish, later becoming dry. When ripe they split open somewhat irregularly along the upper side. The seeds are gray or black, the surface rough, 1/16 to 1/8 of an inch long in largest measurement.

RANGE. Occurring far north of our area in Idaho, Montana, Nevada, Utah, and Colorado. From these states it enters Arizona and the northern mountains of New Mexico.

REMARKS. This cactus is a mountaineer. It is seldom if ever found below 6,000 feet in altitude, and ranges happily up to 10,000 feet in the high Rockies. There are reports of its having been collected even above that altitude, but I have not been able to verify them. However, one thing is certain. This cactus scorns the extreme cold and the snow of the high mountains. Give it a sunny south slope for light and warmth in the summer and it will gladly sit all winter in the snows. It can stand an amazing amount of cold and moisture such as would kill most other cacti almost over night.

The adaptation which this cactus has made to the high mountain climate is all gain in those mountains. Yet with every such gain something is usually lost, and this cactus has almost completely lost the ability to live where most of its fellows reside, in the hot, dry desert below the mountains. It can be kept alive and healthy in gardens in central New Mexico, but this is about its limit. It languishes and dies in two years or so in the low altitude and greater heat of San Antonio, even when kept more moist than its relatives. Those trying to grow this cactus should remember and try to simulate its mountain habitat, or they will have trouble.

This species was first discovered and named by Engelmann. He observed it as a result of several expeditions over many years and described it very fully. However, he was from first to last convinced that it was an Echinocactus, and called it always *Echinocactus simpsonii*.

Coulter followed Engelmann entirely, but in 1893 the plant was called by M. E. Jones *Mammillaria simpsonii*, this indicating that already its position between the two major groups was becoming noticed. K. Schumann found a plant in Colorado which he called *Mammillaria purpusii*, and this is thought to have been the same plant.

In 1913 Britton and Rose first set this species off from both the Echinocacti and the Mammillarias. They originated a new genus for this species alone, calling it *Pediocactus simpsonii*. The genus name is not at all apropos to this mountain cactus and seems to have been prompted by a doubtful report that the cactus was once found on the plains of Kansas. However, it has remained as the valid name for this cactus, and a whole group of others have joined this species in the genus.

Engelmann's very complete description of the species is that of what, to be taxonomically correct, we must call variety *simpsonii.* Besides this Engelmann described a smaller variety which he called variety *minor,* and Coulter added a variety *robustior* from Nevada, Oregon, and Colorado.

Although everyone has mentioned it, variety *minor* has not ever been described very completely. It appears to be a smaller form of the species found in Colorado, but there are few definite characters to establish it. It has been said that some specimens found in northwestern New Mexico might be this form, but as there are doubts about them, the variety is not listed as definitely one within our area. It should be noticed in this connection that a young, immature specimen of *Mammillaria borealis* which has not flowered and on which the grooves of the mature areoles have not yet formed fits the description of variety *minor* very well. This may be the explanation of some of the specimens of variety *minor.*

Be that as it may, the typical variety of the species is found in the mountains of northern New Mexico. It is a beautiful cactus and one of our most hardy forms for cold climates.

Pediocactus knowltonii L. Benson
"Knowlton Cactus"

DESCRIPTION PLATE 27

STEMS: Very small, 1/2 to 1 inch in diameter. These stems are depressed-globular or globular, a fraction of an inch to a maximum of 1 1/2 inches tall. Individuals usually have single stems, but sometimes they form small clusters. Each stem is covered by small tubercles only 1/16 to 1/10 of an inch long.

AREOLES: Almost circular at first, becoming elongated oval. These areoles are very small, being only about 1/24 of an inch in length. They have much white wool at first, which becomes shorter with age, but is quite persistent.

SPINES: There are 18 to 24 radial spines, which lie pectinate or even recurve somewhat and are 1/24 to 1/16 of an inch long. They are somewhat flattened and magnification reveals fine hairs upon them. In color they are white, pinkish, or reddish-tan.

FLOWERS: Opening widely and when fully open about 3/4 of an inch across by about 3/8 of an inch long. They are pinkish in color, with the ovary naked. The outer perianth segments are entire and blunt, the inner segments somewhat pointed. The stamens are yellow. The stigmas are 4 in number and rose-purple.

FRUITS: Egg-shaped or somewhat club-shaped, about 3/8 of an inch long, becoming tan, dry, and dehiscent. The seeds are black and about 1/16 of an inch long.

RANGE. Known only from one area in northwestern New Mexico, near the Los Pinos River just south of the New Mexico-Colorado border.

REMARKS. This is one of the very small, very inconspicuous new species in this genus which have only recently been discovered. It was first described in 1960 by Dr. Benson from plants discovered by the late Mr. Fred G. Knowlton.

The cactus is quite clearly a Pediocactus. Very small, with nothing outstanding in stem, spine, or flower development, it has no special interest because of any feature except its rarity. However, for those who are intrigued by this, it is rare enough to make up for all it lacks otherwise, because it is definitely in the running for the most rare cactus of our area. It has been found so far only on gravelly hills near the Los Pinos River in New Mexico. Its population is apparently small, even there, and collectors should avoid decimating the species.

Pediocactus papyracanthus (Eng.) L. Benson
"Paper-Spined Cactus," "Grama-Grass Cactus," "Toumeya"

DESCRIPTION PLATE 27

STEMS: Ovate or nearly so when young, becoming cylindrical. Most often the stem remains single, but old plants sometimes give off several branches by proliferation of several areoles on the sides of the stem. The surface of the stem is covered by dark green tubercles 1/8 to 3/16 of an inch long when mature.

AREOLES: Round or nearly so, very small on immature stems, but up to 3/16 of an inch long on robust stems. With yellowish wool at first, this becoming gray and short, but persisting. Sometimes active areoles have 1 to several pinkish glands on the upper edge of each.

SPINES: There are 6 to 9 radial spines which are straight, rigid, and flattened, and which radiate evenly. They are from less than 1/8 of an inch to as much as 1/4 of an inch long; the lowermost is heavier, wider, and longer than the others. They are white or gray in color, often snowy white. There are also 1 to 4 central spines. The lowermost central, which seems always to be present after the very early stage, is greatly flattened, up to 1/10 of an inch wide at the base, flexible, papery in texture, and always to some extent twisted and curved. On young areoles it tends to stand at least somewhat upward, but lower down on the sides of the stem it may be aimed in any direction. It is from 3/4 to 1 1/4 inches long, usually mottled brown at first, fading to pale gray or whitish. Mature plants usually have 1 to 3 upper centrals, curving upward. They are similar to the main central except shorter and very much more slender, as well as usually less flattened.

FLOWERS: Bell-shaped, not opening very widely, whitish in color. They are ³/₄ to 1 inch long and wide. The ovary usually has a few small, toothed scales upon it, but may be bare. The outer perianth segments are triangular in shape with their edges entire or ragged, but not fringed. Their midlines are dark brownish, the edges whitish. The inner perianth segments are practically white. The stamens are cream-colored. The style and stigma are also cream-colored, with 4 or 5 stigma lobes.

FRUITS: Almost spherical, ³/₁₆ to ³/₄ of an inch long, becoming tan and dry at maturity and splitting open by a dorsal slit and a ring at the top. They are with or without a few scales. The seeds are black, shiny, but with a fine texture under magnification. These seeds are up to about ¹/₈ of an inch long.

RANGE. A limited area in north-central New Mexico and an even more limited area in northeastern Arizona. In New Mexico it is found in a few scattered locations from near Santa Fe to the Sandia Mountains near Albuquerque. The range in New Mexico and the range in Arizona are not continuous.

REMARKS. This has long been regarded as perhaps the rarest cactus in our area. It is not profitable to try to decide which of several species actually is that, but P. papyracanthus certainly is one of the least seen of them all.

The rarity of its collection is partly due to its scarcity, but also to its excellent camouflage. This species grows in open grasslands where it appears to be almost always, if not always, associated with the grama grasses, from which comes the common name, "grama-grass cactus." It usually grows in or near clumps of these grasses, and in this situation the broad, papery central spines look just like dried grass leaves and the cacti themselves like clumps of grass.

Engelmann first described this cactus as a Mammillaria. Later, after closer examination, he observed that the flowers arose from the unelongated areoles at the tips of the young tubercles, and so observed that the plant was really an Echinocactus, as the genus was then understood. Coulter, therefore, classified it in the genus *Echinocactus*.

We have already discussed in the introduction to the genus *Pediocactus* why this cactus and its relatives could not very logically remain in the genus *Echinocactus*. Britton and Rose appear to have been correct in separating it from that genus. They erected a special new genus, *Toumeya*, for this species alone. It has stood there, all alone, until recently.

The very recent study of these plants by L. Benson has shown what appear to be good reasons for expanding the genus *Pediocactus* to include this cactus. New species only recently discovered are in several respects intermediate between the two original species, *Pediocactus simpsonii* and *Toumeya papyracantha*, and it seems that at best *Toumeya* should be reduced to a subgenus or section of *Pediocactus*.

Genus *Epithelantha* (Weber) B. & R.

THERE SEEMS TO BE but one species of this genus in the United States. It is a very small, but distinctive cactus.

The whole stem of this cactus is covered with very many, very tiny tubercles—apparently the smallest tubercles of any United States cactus. Hiding these almost entirely from view are very many tiny spines. The growing tip of the stem is in the form of a rather distinct depression which is filled with a great deal of hairlike wool and covered over by the converging, later deciduous tips of the longer spines. This makes it very difficult to observe the formation of the tubercles, areoles, and flowers, but the way these are formed has assumed much importance and has been studied very closely. This is because taxonomically almost everything hinges upon them.

Originally Engelmann described this cactus as *Mammillaria micromeris*. In most of its characters it is a perfectly good Mammillaria. Later, however, something unusual was noticed about the cactus. It produces its flower not in the axil of the tubercle, but at the top of it. Mammillarias otherwise produce their flowers from halfway down the dorsal side of the tubercles to deep in the axils.

When this was noticed it was assumed that the flower was produced from within a single, unlengthening, monomorphic areole on the tip of the tubercle. This is the situation in the Echinocacti. Because of this difference, Weber seemed unable to come to a real conclusion about this cactus, listing it once as a Mammillaria, once as *Echinocactus micromeris*, but also coining a new name, *Epithelantha*, for it. He apparently did not officially describe this latter as the name of a new genus, however. Britton and Rose then took the name *Epithelantha* and applied it to a new and separate genus. This genus, because of the supposed production of the flower from within the spine areole, has usually been placed in the subtribe *Echinocactanae*, although

its other features, such as the naked fruits and lack of ribs, seem to point more toward the Mammillarias.

Recently Dr. Norman H. Boke has done most thorough studies of cactus anatomy and development, and studied this species very carefully. In the course of his studies he has discovered that this cactus does not produce its flower from within a monomorphic spine areole after all. The blossom is, in fact, produced after a division of the meristem into a determinate spinous portion and a separate, indeterminate floral or vegetative meristem. This gives essentially a dimorphic areole, very different from those of the Echinocacti. It is actually more removed from the Echinocactus arrangement than is that of the many Mammillarias often set apart as Coryphanthas because they usually have monomorphic areoles elongating toward the axils instead of dimorphic areoles. The situation in this cactus can be interpreted as good dimorphic Mammillarian areoles in which the floral meristems merely remain at the tops of the tubercles. Dr. Boke notes Moran's remark that for many years no one has linked *Epithelantha* to *Mammillaria*, but Boke's conclusion is that a strong case for doing just this can be built.

This possibility is very attractive, since the cactus is in so many ways a better Mammillaria than many of the Mammillarias themselves. It does seem that the work of Boke has made it impossible to classify it any longer with the Echinocacti, and that it points it toward the Mammillarias. Yet the fact remains that its flower is produced at the top of the tubercle, which is a trait not found in other members of that genus, and this difference in itself may be justification for keeping the cactus separate from the genus *Mammillaria*.

As a separate genus based upon this cactus, *Epithelantha* seems, like *Lophophora* and *Ariocarpus*, to fall somewhere between the two major genera, *Echinocactus* and *Mammillaria*. It is worth noting in this connection that the Epithelanthas possess alkaloids similar to those of *Lophophora* and *Ariocarpus*, which seems to link them in some way.

I, therefore, leave this genus in this difficult middle area. Buxbaum has made elaborate schemes in attempting to relate these plants phylogenetically, but others have pointed out that entirely different schemes from his could be devised which would appear just as logical as his, if different assumptions were made to start with. I am not primarily interested here in such phylogenetic schemes, so I merely list this as a small genus because it seems in some way a separate entity among the cacti.

Epithelantha micromeris (Eng.) Weber
"Button Cactus," "Mulato"

DESCRIPTION   PLATE 27

STEMS: Spherical or spheroid, usually with a depressed top. Usually only $1/2$ to 1 inch in diameter, but sometimes to $1 3/4$ inches. Plants usually consist of a single stem, but are occasionally seen with double, and rarely with triple stems. These stems are covered with tiny, wartlike or somewhat conical tubercles about $1/20$ of an inch long.

AREOLES: Dimorphic. The spinous areole is at the tip of the tubercle, is small and at first has much long hair, which is later lost. The flower comes from a separate floral areole which appears adjacent to the spinous areole, also at the top of the tubercle.

SPINES: There are about 20 to 40 slender but rigid spines per areole. They are in one series on immature plants, but in several series on mature areoles. The outermost series on mature plants are the stronger, and the upper ones of these are often $1/4$ to $5/16$ of an inch long when first produced, with the outer half of each swollen in diameter until they are somewhat club-shaped, but with the tips acute. These form an incurving tuft of long spines over the shorter spines and hairs of the new growth in the more or less depressed top of the mature plant. The enlarged outer sections of these spines break off with time, however, and the hairs are shed, leaving the sides of the plants with only short spines about $1/16$ to $1/8$ of an inch long. All spines are white, sometimes with faintly gray tips.

FLOWERS: Very small, only about $3/16$ to $1/4$ of an inch long and $1/8$ to $3/16$ of an inch wide, only partly rising above the long wool and spines in the top of the plant and only partly opening. They are pale, whitish-pink. The ovary is rather clavate, greenish-yellow, and naked. There are 3 to 5 outer perianth segments which have greenish-brown or pinkish midlines and pinkish-white, somewhat notched or eroded edges, in some specimens bearing a few short cilia. There are 5 inner petals which are whitish-pink with entire edges. The stamens are greenish-white. The style and stigma are greenish-white, with 3 or 4 stigma lobes.

FRUITS: Club-shaped and $3/8$ to $3/4$ of an inch long by $1/8$ to $3/16$ of an inch in diameter, red, fleshy, and naked, with the perianth remains persistent upon them. The seeds are black, about $1/16$ of an inch ($1 1/2$ millimeters) long.

RANGE. In the U.S. forming a large arc with the east end in Medina County, Texas, near San Antonio, running west from there, barely remaining within Texas at the mouths of the Devil's and Pecos rivers and perhaps leaving Texas briefly before turning northward through Brewster County in the Big Bend. From there following the Davis and Guadalupe mountains northwest into New Mexico, passing through the Sacramento Mountains to have its northwest end in the Capitan Mountains of New Mexico. The western limit in Texas seems to be the Hueco Mountains just east of El Paso.

REMARKS. The tiny, tidy little button cactus reminds me of a very spherical button indeed, and even more of a white, fuzzy marble or ping-pong ball. It sits on exposed ridges and hillsides, a little white globe among the whitish limestone rocks. It is also the only cactus I have ever seen growing in a river bed. I have on several occasions found populations of dozens of specimens growing among the water-piled rocks in the almost always bone-dry beds of west Texas streams. Once, however, I found them within ten feet of perpetually running water in the bed of a major stream. Specimens in this sort of situation have extensive root systems running for several feet in all directions through the loose rocks and pebbles among which they stand. These roots anchor them against the rushing water which must entirely cover them at times, so long as the whole rock jam is not dislodged. The almost perfect roundness of the plants is what usually betrays their presence on hillsides and ledges where the surrounding rocks are almost never rounded, but in a deposit of water-rounded rocks they are doubly hard to see. This may be why they have not been reported from such a habitat before.

There seems to be only a single form of this genus in the U.S. A separate form of this species, variety *greggii*, was also described by Engelmann but it is a larger form found only in Mexico. Many have regarded this as merely a synonym, but I have concluded that this larger and distinct form does exist. Beginning about 100 miles south of the Rio Grande on the road to Saltillo, I have seen this other form, which is unlike anything I have seen in Texas. I have often found stems of this form to 3 inches in diameter. Dr. Boke, in the report of his study of *Epithelantha*, gives some interesting details of anatomical differences he found between this Mexican form and our U.S. cactus.

H. Bravo, Marshall, Backeberg and others have described a whole list of other Epithelantha forms found in Mexico. I have seen some of these, and I am sure that some of them are distinct from our U.S. cactus, but as they do not enter the United States, I will not deal with them here. Perhaps it should be stressed that they do not grow in the United States, since some of them do from time to time enter the country in the trade. Because of this fact, one should be careful about assuming that any plant he buys as *E. micromeris* is actually the U.S. form. I have often seen the densely clustering Mexican form, with clumps of 10 to 20 heads and beautiful rose-colored flowers 2 to 3 times as large as those on our cactus, sold simply as *E. micromeris*, when in reality it is quite different. No specimen like this has ever been recorded from within the U.S.

Genus *Mammillaria* Haw.

THE MEMBERS of this genus are for the most part comparatively small or sometimes extremely tiny cacti. The plant stems vary in different species from depressed and almost flat to globular or sometimes even columnar in shape, and are often referred to as "heads." In some species these remain single, while in many others they multiply from the base to become caespitose, one individual thus sometimes forming a large clump of these "heads." In a few species the stems may branch sparingly from higher up on the stem.

Each stem is entirely covered by a system of nipple-like projections called tubercles. These are usually arranged in spiral rows, but in a few cases are more loosely organized. These tubercles are usually cylindrical or conical, but sometimes may have more or less quadrangular bases and sometimes are mildly keeled below.

Very early the knowledge of cacti progressed to the point where it became obvious that the huge assortment of forms they present could not be left in the one catchall genus *Cactus* L. By the middle of the eighteenth century Miller felt it necessary to divide the lot. By using the four old names of Turnefort, he separated out many cacti into *Pereskia, Opuntia,* and *Cereus,* leaving the rest in the genus *Cactus.* By 1812 even this narrowed genus *Cactus* was too broad, and Haworth abandoned it entirely, erecting five new genera out of it, one of which was *Mammillaria,* including all of the unjointed, tubercled cacti.

Discoveries of new species continued, and as even this genus came to include a myriad of forms, the process of subdivision began all over again. Engelmann proposed two sections of the genus *Mammillaria.* He had section *Coryphantha,* which he characterized as having grooved tubercles, green fruits, and yellow or brown seeds, and section *Eumammillaria* with groove-

less tubercles, scarlet fruits, and black or blackish seeds. Lemaire very soon elevated the section *Coryphantha* to a separate genus. Many concurred—although not all, as for instance Berger, who left this group as a subdivision which he rechristened *Eu-coryphantha.*

This was the situation, rather uneasy and not wholly satisfactory to anybody, when Britton and Rose presented their major study, and they swept it all away by dividing the old genus *Mammillaria* into a whole spectrum of new and much smaller genera. Their names are in constant use and are most familiar to us today. The old section *Coryphantha* became the genera *Coryphantha, Escobaria, Neobesseya,* and others, and the old genus *Mammillaria* was eliminated as the rest of its forms were separated out into new genera such as *Dolichothele* and *Neomammillaria.* It seemed that the process of subdivision had been carried to its logical conclusion by this courageous leap of Britton and Rose, and almost the whole cactophile world adopted their array of new genera with surprising speed and many sighs of relief.

But the genera of Britton and Rose were not to go unchallenged for long. They were assaulted from two directions. As early as 1931 Fosberg questioned the basis for separating *Escobaria* from *Coryphantha* and concluded that the two should be recombined. This was an early expression of a desire for simplification by recombination. Many people had already found the genera of Britton and Rose so hard to tell from one another that it was often more difficult to determine the genus of a specimen directly than it was to determine its species first; and some had noted that the distinguishing characteristics of these genera were not always consistently present.

But at the same time the trend to still more subdivision was continued by various students. J. Pinkney Hester conducted very detailed studies of the seeds of cacti, and concluded that their variations did not well uphold the alignment of Britton and Rose's genera, but actually, if regarded as diagnostic characters, would require a new realignment. As a result, in 1941, he shifted some species from one to another of these genera and erected such new genera as *Escobesseya*.

Backeberg had already started subdividing further with his subgenera *Subgymnocarpae* and *Neocoryphantha*. Buxbaum conducted large studies of the cacti and proposed his own new subgenera, such as *Pseudocoryphantha*. He also proposed major theoretical schemes of cactus evolution which would appear to indicate radical new alignments of the species in this group. Thousands of words have been written concerning Buxbaum's phylogenetic theories, but we do not need to study them here, because no one has yet actually followed his lead and there has been no essentially new scheme for classifying this group since Britton and Rose.

What we do have at the present time are two opposing philosophies of classification giving two different concepts of this group, the same as they do of the Echinocacti. One considers very small differences in plants to be adequate bases for establishing genera and this results in lists of very slightly varying microgenera. This attitude is well expressed in Backeberg's major work, where all of Britton and Rose's genera are perpetuated and even some new ones added. The other attitude is the more conservative one that a genus should be a major group based upon some rather obvious and very fundamental differences. This attitude regards the newer genera based on very small differences as no more than sections or subgenera, or at most microgenera of an entirely different level from such larger plant genera as for instance *Euphorbia*. This approach had recent expression in L. Benson's *Arizona Cacti* where all of these proposed genera were recombined once again into the original genus *Mammillaria*.

Every serious cactus student is faced today with the battle between these opposing views, and even the amateur is affected by it, since, in order to be conversant, he often has to remember two or even more names for each of his cacti.

It cannot be said that either view is established at this time. The present study does not presume to answer a major taxonomic question such as this. It is not even addressed to such a purpose. I would have preferred to avoid the issue entirely, but under the circumstances even to list a series of species is to take sides.

Since a decision was thrust upon me, I wished to make it as intelligently as possible, so before making my decision I have studied the arguments for each view and then applied to the problem the most recent evidence to come to my attention. After the most exhaustive study of which I am capable, I feel constrained to follow here the recombination of these cacti under the genus *Mammillaria* and to consider this genus in the older

and larger sense. The results of research reported since the publication of the last major work on these cacti has figured largely in my decision, so it may be of value to mention that newer evidence here.

Most significantly, the old distinction between those plants with grooved tubercles and those with grooveless tubercles which prompted Engelmann to make the first division of the group into two sections and which is still so much emphasized that all artificial keys use it, seems to have failed us. Dr. Norman H. Boke, in a series of very detailed studies of cactus shoot form and development, has recently shown that both *Coryphantha erecta* and *C. clava,* two common Mexican species, may have grooved and grooveless tubercles on the same mature heads at the same time, or may change the form of their growth back and forth from the one to the other. This would appear to make it impossible to classify these particular species in either the proposed genus *Coryphantha* or *Neomammillaria* and to make it possible for a given specimen to fulfill the characteristics of both of these genera at once, which would seem to cast real doubt upon the divisions themselves.

In terms more technical but more meaningful to the botanist, the grooved group have areoles monomorphic, which means producing from a single meristem not only both vegetative structures (leaf primordia and spines) but also the later reproductive structures (flowers and branches), while the grooveless forms have areoles dimorphic, with two separate meristems, one producing only vegetative structures at the summit of the tubercle and the other producing only reproductive structures, usually at the axil of the tubercle. This distinction appeared at first to be an essential one, dividing the whole group handily, but here again Dr. Boke was able to show that in the two species mentioned above, the areoles may be either monomorphic or dimorphic on the same adult head of the same specimen.

Since these distinctions have broken down, there apparently remains no character by which the large group formerly known as genus *Mammillaria* can be divided into two major subdivisions. Such things as sepals fringed versus sepals entire, fruit green at maturity versus fruit red at maturity, fruit with a few scales versus fruit naked, and details of seed form all show exceptions on one side or the other in all major subdivisions which have been proposed.

But what about the status of the array of small genera erected within this large group of tubercled cacti? As already mentioned the division into *Coryphantha* and *Escobaria* was challenged almost immediately by Fosberg. The distinguishing characters usually given of green fruit on the one hand and red fruit on the other obviously does not work, because the fruits of some Coryphanthas become brownish or reddish when very ripe and those of several Escobarias remain green barely flushed with apricot on the sunny side. Nor is seed color always reliable to separate these two proposed groups. One searches in vain for a valid reason why Fosberg has not been followed and why these two groups have been allowed to stand so long in most of the literature.

To make a long story short, all other distinguishing characters proposed for these microgenera have proved as uncertain. We have, therefore, been left with only such quantitative characters as long tubercles versus short tubercles, tubercles grooved all the way versus tubercles grooved more or less of the way, flowers predominantly yellow versus flowers brownish through pink to purple, and so on, which hardly seem adequate to distinguish genera—and there are exceptions to all of them anyway. Attempts to separate on this sort of basis have resulted in a constant shifting of species from one to the other genus and finally in the proposal of *Escobaria* subgenus *Pseudocoryphantha* Buxbaum and subgenus *Neocoryphantha* Backbg., as well as of genus *Lepidocoryphantha* Backbg., for those which burst out of the closely drawn genera.

The other genera which Britton and Rose proposed for this group fare little better. We have seen that monomorphic versus dimorphic areoles and grooved versus ungrooved tubercles will not divide them. Neither will flower color, since we have the whole range of colors in the proposed genus *Coryphantha*, in *Neobesseya*, and in Britton and Rose's strictly drawn *Neomammillaria*. Fringed versus nonfringed sepals and even various degrees of fringing in the same species are found in both *Coryphantha* and *Neomammillaria*. Seed form fails also, with both *Escobaria* and *Neomammillaria* showing the whole range of seed coats, shapes, and hilum positions so completely that Buxbaum has to theorize parallel evolution within each of these groups because of it.

It seems that there are no characters left strong enough upon which to erect genera and that the whole group is best considered one genus, as originally conceived. Dr. Boke's judgment after his research would seem justified:

> In any event, it is my opinion that the discovery of a combination of areole monomorphism and areole dimorphism in *Coryphantha clava* and *C. erecta* weakens one of the principal distinctions between the Mammillarias (sensu lato) and other tubercled cacti. I think that it also indicates a cautious, conservative approach in delimiting genera in these cacti.

He who can take the larger view will find in the genus *Mammillaria* a rich and diverse group of cacti presenting almost every sort of interesting variation on the theme of the small, tubercled cactus body. As a group they present all of the challenges to his abilitiy at collecting, classifying, and culturing cacti which the most ardent cactophile can desire.

For those who are fascinated by the Britton and Rose type of genus divisions and who want to concern themselves with this sort of thing, as well as for those who may be familiar with only those plant names, I have added for each form described here the name which seems to be the most valid one under the microgenus system.

KEY TO THE MAMMILLARIAS

1a. Diameter of stems on mature plants 2 inches or more and the length of the tubercles 1/4 of an inch or more—2.
  2a. Stems on mature plants hemispherical to flattened, always as broad as they are tall on normal specimens and usually much greater in diameter than in height—3.
    3a. Areoles always dimorphic, with the spinous portion at the tip of the tubercle and the floral portion in the axil of the tubercle and having no groove connecting them—4.
      4a. Central spines 1 or 2 per areole, short and always straight; outer perianth segments entire—5.
        5a. Color of the plant surface deep green or blue-green; tubercles firm and their bases quadrangular and more or less keeled; flowers whitish, rose, or pinkish—6.
          6a. Radial spines 5 to 9; tubercles strongly keeled and to 7/8 of an inch long; plant to 12 inches in diameter
            —*M. meiacantha.*
          6b. Radial spines 9 to 26; tubercles with bases quadrangular but not so strongly keeled; plants to about 5 inches in diameter—7.
            7a. Radial spines 20 to 26   —*M. heyderi* var. *heyderi.*
            7b. Radial spines 9 to 20—8.
              8a. Radial spines 14 to 20   —*M. heyderi* var. *applanata.*
              8b. Radial spines 9 to 13   —*M. heyderi* var. *hemisphaerica.*
        5b. Color of plant surface light yellowish-green; tubercles flabby and egg-shaped to cylindrical; flowers brightly yellow   —*M. sphaerica.*
      4b. Central spines 1 to 4 and at least some of them hooked; outer perianth segments fringed—9.
        9a. Radial spines 8 to 15; flowers bright purple with about 20 inner perianth segments and 11 yellow stigma lobes   —*M. wrightii.*
        9b. Radial spines 14 to 22; flowers paler pinkish-purple with about 40 inner perianth segments and 5 to 9 green stigma lobes   —*M. wilcoxii.*
    3b. Areoles normally and predominantly monomorphic and prolonged into a groove extending halfway or more toward the axil of the tubercle on mature stems, with the flower produced in the end of this groove—10.
      10a. Tubercles equal in size or nearly so on a given stem and arranged regularly; central spines 0 or 1 per areole and 1/4 to 5/8 of an inch long; flowers greenish-yellow, brownish, or pink; fruits scarlet when ripe—11.
        11a. Flowers greenish, greenish-yellow, or brownish, sometimes streaked with pink; the outer perianth segments fringed   —*M. similis.*
        11b. Flowers pure pink without stripes or zones of various colors; the outer perianth segments not fringed, but entire   —*M. rosiflora.*
      10b. Tubercles unequal in size and shape on a given stem and arranged irregularly; centrals 1 to 4 per areole and 3/4 to

2 inches long; flowers purplish or rose-pink; fruits remaining greenish when ripe   —*M. runyonii.*

2b. Stems on mature plants spherical to columnar, usually taller
than they are broad and often markedly so—12.

12a. Having at least one and often several hooked central spines;
areoles dimorphic with the spinous portion at the tip of the
tubercle and the floral portion in the axil of the tubercle,
the two never connected by a groove   —*M. microcarpa.*

12b. Without hooked centrals; areoles mostly or entirely monomorphic, the flower always produced at the end of the un-
divided areole which is prolonged into a groove running at
least part of the way down the tubercle—13.

13a. Having fleshy taproots and 2 to 8 central spines to 2¼
inches long; flowers purplish   —*M. macromeris.*

13b. Having no fleshy taproots and having central spines not
over 1⅝ inches long—14.

14a. Having one brownish gland in the groove formed by
the elongated areole   —*M. bella.*

14b. Without glands—15.

15a. Centrals 0 to 4 on mature plants—16.

16a. Centrals present—17.

17a. Centrals not hooked—18.

18a. Flowers yellow, orange-yellow, or yellow with
red centers—19.

19a. Stems single or very sparingly branched;
flowers yellow or orange-yellow, sometimes
reddish when fading, but not yellow with
red centers; radials and centrals to at least
¾ of an inch long—20.

20a. Plants large and robust, to at least 6
inches tall and 4 inches or more in diameter when old; tubercles ½ to 1 inch long
—21.

21a. Radials 6 to 16; outer perianth segments lacerated and more or less fringed
—*M. scheeri* (in part).

21b. Radials 14 to 28; outer perianth segments entire and smooth
—*M. scolymoides.*

20b. Plants small, to a maximum of 3 inches
tall or wide; tubercles ⅜ to ½ inch long
—*M. echinus* (in part).

19b. Stems greatly branching by new heads arising from the grooves in old tubercles all
around their bases to form large masses of
often dozens of stems; flowers yellow with
red centers   —*M. sulcata* (in part).

18b. Flowers pale pink to deep rose-purple
—*M. ramillosa.*

17b. One central hooked   —*M. scheeri* (in part).

16b. Centrals absent—22.

22a. Tubercles over ½ inch long; radials ⅜ to ⅝ of
an inch long; flowers yellow with red centers
—*M. sulcata* (stunted or atypical plant).

22b. Tubercles ½ inch or less long; flowers not yellow with red centers—23.

23a. Radials ⅜ to 1 inch long; flowers yellow
—*M. echinus* (stunted or atypical plant).

23b. Radials only ⅛ to ½ inch long; flowers light
purple   —*M. hesteri.*

15b. Centrals 4 to 17 on mature plants—24.

24a. Fruits green or greenish when ripe, sometimes becoming brownish or apricot on part of the surface
when very ripe, but never bright red—25.

25a. Radial spines 12 to 20—26.

26a. Flowers rose-purple to deep purple and 1 inch
or more long and wide; stigma lobes 7 to 12;
at least some of the spines over ½ inch long
—27.

27a. Tubercles ⅜ to 1 inch long; centrals pale
mottled, and brown-tipped, but never
blackish over half or more of their lengths;
flowers 1½ to 2½ inches across when fully
opened; seeds 1½ to 1¾ millimeters long
with ventral hila—28.

28a. Radials to only ⅝ of an inch or so long;
stigma lobes 7 or 8 in number and rose-
purple in color; seeds about 1½ millimeters long, dark brown, with the hila
small   —*M. vivipara* var. *vivipara.*

28b. Radials to around 1 inch long; stigma
lobes 8 to 10 in number and white in
color; seeds about 1¾ millimeters long,
light brown in color, with the hila large
—*M. vivipara* var. *arizonica.*

27b. Tubercles ½ inch or less long; centrals very
dark brown or purplish black over one-half
to all of their lengths; flowers 1 to 1½
inches across when fully opened; seeds 2
millimeters long with subbasal hila
—*M. vivipara* var. *borealis.*

26b. Flowers white, pink, or very pale rose in color
and about ¾ of an inch long; stigma lobes 5
or 6; all spines ½ inch or less long
—*M. varicolor.*

25b. Radial spines 20 to at least 60—29.

29a. Flowers 1 inch or more in length and width;
spines strong and somewhat flexible; seeds 1½
to 2½ millimeters long—30.

30a. Flowers deeply and brilliantly purple or
else reddish-purple; radial spines white or
white tipped light brown—31.

31a. Flowers 2 inches or more long and broad;
radials 20 to 30; seeds dark brown—32.

32a. Tubercles about ¾ of an inch long;
centrals 4 to 7 and straw-colored or
whitish; flowers deep purple with 7 to
9 rose-colored, blunt stigma lobes; seeds
oval, brown, 2 to 2½ millimeters long,
with the surfaces very finely pitted
—*M. vivipara* var. *radiosa.*

32b. Tubercles about ½ inch long; centrals
6 to 12 and purple-black or dark

brown; flowers reddish-purple with 6 to 10 pure white or slightly pinkish, somewhat pointed stigma lobes; seeds 2¹/₂ to 3 millimeters long, markedly reniform and much flattened, with their surfaces shiny smooth and un-pitted —*M. fragrans.*

  31b. Flowers 1 inch or only slightly more in width and length; radials 20 to at least 60; seeds light brown —*M. vivipara* var. *neo-mexicana.*

    30b. Flowers yellowish suffused with purple; radial spines straw-colored with reddish tips —*M. vivipara* var. *deserti.*

      29b. Flowers less than 1 inch in length and width; spines heavy but very brittle and glassy, breaking at slight pressure; seeds 1 millimeter long —*M. albicolumnaria.*

24b. Fruits bright red or scarlet when ripe—33.

  33a. Stems hardly over 2 inches in diameter; length of radial spines ¹/₈ to ³/₈ of an inch; 4 to 7 centrals with one conspicuous, heavy central standing porrect or turned downward a little; flowers over 1 inch in diameter, opening widely, lavender-white or very pale purplish in color, with 5 or 6 white stigma lobes —*M. tuberculosa* (in part).

  33b. Stems to 2³/₄ inches in diameter; radials ¹/₂ to 1 inch long; 7 to 17 centrals without a conspicuous, heavy, porrect one; flowers ³/₄ of an inch or less in diameter and not opening widely, pinkish in color streaked with brown and with 4 or 5 very green stigma lobes —*M. dasyacantha.*

1b. Diameter of stems on mature plants less than 2 inches and length of tubercles ¹/₄ of an inch or less—34.

34a. Radial spines 13 to 18; all spines club-shaped, remaining thick almost their whole length and coming to a point very suddenly —*M. nellieae.*

34b. Radial spines 20 or more; spines not club-shaped, but awl-shaped, bristle-like or hairlike—35.

  35a. Centrals present—36.

    36a. All spines rigid—37.

      37a. Having a fleshy taproot—38.

        38a. Single or sparingly clustering; radials 24 to 36 in number; tubercles grooved all of the way from the tips to the axils by the greatly elongated, monomorphic areoles; stigma lobes bright yellow —*M. duncanii.*

        38b. Densely clustering with dozens of heads in a typical plant; radials 40 to 85 in number; tubercles either ungrooved or grooved to around ¹/₂ of their lengths; stigma lobes pure white —*M. leei* (in part).

      37b. Roots all fibrous—39.

        39a. Stems single to sparingly branching; 1 to 2 inches thick and standing well over 3 inches tall when old—40.

          40a. Centrals from very bulbous bases; flowers coming from the sides of the stems, ¹/₂ inch or less in diameter and dark red in color; tubercles not grooved —*M. pottsii.*

          40b. Centrals not conspicuously bulbous; flowers produced at the summit of the stem, an inch or more in diameter and clear lavender or very pale purplish in color without darker midlines —*M. tuberculosa* (in part).

        39b. Stems branching greatly into large masses, but each stem no more than 1¹/₄ inches thick or 3 inches tall—41.

          41a. Radial spines 20 to 30, gray or straw-colored tipped with brown; centrals 5 to 10, ³/₈ to ⁵/₈ of an inch long and dark brown, red-brown, or black for most of their lengths; stigma lobes green —*M. roberti.*

          41b. Radial spines 24 to 85 and all white in color; centrals 6 to 22, ³/₈ of an inch or less in length; stigma lobes white—42.

            42a. Radials 24 to 45 —*M. sneedii.*

            42b. Radials 40 to 85 —*M. leei* (in part).

    36b. Radial spines soft, flexible, and hairlike —*M. multiceps.*

  35b. Centrals absent; radials 40 to 80 in number, slender and bristle-like but rigid—43.

    43a. Spines pubescent under magnification —*M. lasiacantha* var. *lasiacantha.*

    43b. Spines smooth and naked under magnification —*M. lasiacantha* var. *denudata.*

Mammillaria scheeri Muehlenpf.
[*Coryphantha scheeri* Lem.; *Coryphantha muehlenpfordtii* (Poselgr.) B. & R.]
"Long-Tubercled Coryphantha," "Needle 'Mulee'"

DESCRIPTION   PLATE 28

STEMS: Spherical at first, becoming egg-shaped or somewhat conical when old. These stems grow to 9 inches tall by 5¹/₂ inches in diameter. They are usually single, but sometimes have one or two branches at the base. The surface is bright green or even yellowish-green. It is formed into large, rather soft, spreading tubercles. These arise from broad bases often ³/₄ of an inch or more across, becoming cylindrical above and reaching an over-all length of ³/₄ to 1¹/₂ inches.

AREOLES: Monomorphic. When young the areoles are very woolly. Upon maturing they consist of a roundish spinous portion at the tip of the tubercle and a long, narrow, deep, groovelike portion running part or all of the way down the upper side of the tubercle. In the groove are often one or more brownish glands.

SPINES: 8 to 16 stout to very stout radial spines radiating or slightly spreading outward. These are from ¹/₂ to about 1¹/₄ inches long, the lower ones the heaviest and longest. They are round and proceed from slightly bulbous bases. There are also 1 to 5 central spines ³/₄ to 1¹/₂ inches long, stouter than the radials. One is very stout and stands porrect. This spine may be straight, curved downward slightly over its whole length, or in some individuals straight with a hooked tip. The other centrals are more nearly like the radials and spread upward in front of them. When growing, all spines are reddish or brownish with blackish tips. On some specimens they remain for a long time yellowish—especially the main central—but on others they very soon become ashy-gray.

FLOWERS: About 2 inches long and wide. Orange, bronze, or bronzy-yellow at first, darkening to reddish as they wilt. The outer perianth segments are lacerated and sometimes this effect on their edges approaches a true ciliated fringe. The 20 or so inner segments are narrow below, widening to their broadest near the tips, which are often somewhat pointed and also toothed. The stamens are orange, the style short and with 6 to 10 yellowish or flesh-colored stigma lobes.

FRUITS: Egg-shaped to almost club-shaped, 1 to 1¹/₂ inches long. The surfaces are smooth. They remain greenish. The seeds are dark red-brown with shiny, smooth surfaces. They are about ¹/₈ of an inch long and are flattened ovate.

RANGE. Extreme west Texas and the southern edge of New Mexico into Arizona and Chihuahua. Specifically, from the Pecos River near where it enters Texas to the Davis Mountains, Marfa, and Presidio, Texas, and west. In New Mexico apparently not north of the Organ Mountains, but found from there west into Arizona.

REMARKS. This cactus was well described by Engelmann as a "stately plant." It is the largest in bulk of the Mammillarias in our area. A fine old specimen actually gives more of an impression of a barrel cactus than of this group. But unless we are aware of the size which is attained by some of the Mammillarias in Mexico we may have an erroneous concept of the Mammillarias as all small, delicate cacti. It is fortunate that this large species enters our area to set things straight.

However it is unfortunate that so few people see this fine cactus. Although it has quite a large range in the United States it is nowhere common. I have collected it numbers of times in widely distant places, but I have never seen a stand of this species, and, in fact, never collected more than one plant at any given location. The small number of specimens of this species in any dealer's stock makes it seem likely that the plant nowhere grows in quantity. So it remains a little-known species highly prized by the cactophile who happens to possess one.

Perhaps the scarcity of the plant has led students over the years to write about it from insufficient observation. Certainly, the naming of this species has been royally confused—with the confusion persisting right down to the present.

Muehlenpfordt apparently started things off in 1847 by describing a Mexican plant and naming it *Mammillaria scheeri*. Unfortunately the type of his plant is unknown. When Engelmann studied the cacti of Texas and wrote up this cactus he was

not at first sure that he had the same plant, but knew that he had something very similar, so he called the Texas plants *M. scheeri* var. *valida*. However, after he had seen Mexican specimens he became convinced that there was only one form involved and stated in "Corrections to the Cactaceae of the Boundary" that the variety agrees exactly with Mexican specimens of *M. scheeri*, and so seems to have withdrawn the idea of a separate variety.

Even before this, however, in 1853, Poselger had redescribed the cactus as an Echinocactus. By an interesting coincidence he used the name of the original describer for it. Poselger's name, therefore, came out *Echinocactus muehlenpfordtii*. This name Engelmann, Lemaire, Coulter—everyone in that century, and even Wooton and Standley in this—ignored. They all regarded the original name of *M. scheeri* as valid and used it. Lemaire very early split this cactus off from the Mammillarias as a Coryphantha, but even in doing this he called it *Coryphantha scheeri*.

But when Britton and Rose made their big break with tradition they broke cleanly. They resurrected Poselger's name (when he mistook the species for an Echinocactus) and rechristened the cactus *Coryphantha muehlenpfordtii*. This is therefore the name for the cactus which these great popularizers of the cacti have caused to be the most familiar in recent years.

But the return of this species to the genus *Mammillaria* cannot be merely a shifting to *Mammillaria muehlenpfordtii*, since Forster, in 1847, used that name in a way that makes it a synonym for *Mammillaria celsiana* Lem., a Mexican species. We see no problem in returning to the first name of all, which was *Mammillaria scheeri*, but L. Benson did. He returned this species to its original genus, but in his 1950 work on Arizona cacti he chose to use still another obscure name for the species, a name which had been coined by Cory and which Marshall had mentioned. It was *Coryphantha engelmannii*, and Benson's name for the plant, therefore, became *Mammillaria engelmannii* (Cory) Benson. The reason for this latest substitution may be the fact that the type of Muehlenpfordt's *M. scheeri* is lost, but if we drop all original names for all species of which the type is lost, the roster of botanical names will be greatly altered.

One may take his pick among all of these names and have the cactus as a memorial to any one of those early cactus students he wishes, but whichever name finally prevails, the plant is a large, beautiful, and proud cactus which must have a dry, sunny situation, but which if treated properly contributes a spate of remarkably beautiful flowers of a color unusual among the cacti.

A closely related form is *Mammillaria robustispina* Schott. This is very well named, since it has the stoutest spines of any Mammillaria in the United States. Its spines actually equal those of many *Echinocactus horizonthalonius* specimens in thickness. Benson's 1950 description of *M. robustispina* is so broad that some Texas specimens of *M. scheeri* could fit it, and Earle has recently fallen into this trap, combining it with our species as *Coryphantha muehlenpfordtii* var. *robustispina*. Benson's distribution map of *M. robustispina* implies that its range enters New Mexico, and Earle states its distribution to include southwestern New Mexico. I do not know whether there has been a referral of some ordinary New Mexico *M. scheeri* specimens to this other form or not, but I do know that the real Mexican *M. robustispina* specimens which I have seen are very different from our cactus, and I can find no record of that form's having been collected in New Mexico.

Mammillaria scolymoides Scheidweiler
[*Coryphantha scolymoides* (Scheidweiler) Bodeker]

DESCRIPTION   PLATE 28

STEMS: Single, spherical to conical, and to at least 6 inches tall and 4 inches in diameter. The surface is deep bluish-green, with some grayish glaucescence. The tubercles are to 1 inch long, tapering from bases as wide as the length, firm, and overlapping upward.

AREOLES: When mature the areoles are prolonged beyond the spinous part into deep grooves extending all the way to the bases of the tubercles. These grooves are bare except for a tuft of wool at the base of each, in the axil of the tubercle.

SPINES: Radial spines 14 to 28 in number, 3/4 to 1 1/8 inches long, evenly radiating except at the top of the areole where they are so crowded together as to be bunched into a bundle. There are 1 to 4 heavy central spines, usually 3 of them turned upward and spreading in front of the upper bundle of radials and the lower one standing out conspicuously and curving downward from the middle of the areole. These centrals are all about 1 inch long. All spines are yellowish and hornlike when young, then gray with dark tips.

FLOWERS: About 2 inches long, clear yellow at first and later darkening to a reddish color, but not having a red center. The outer petals are short, pointed, with entire edges, and total about 20 in number. The inner petals are similar except longer, wider, and about 35 in number. The filaments are pinkish, the anthers pale orange-yellow. The stigma has 9 rough, yellowish lobes about 1/4 of an inch long.

FRUITS: Not seen. They failed to develop during the four years that a number of the plants bloomed in my garden.

RANGE. Some of the higher elevations of the Big Bend of Texas: most common in the Glass Mountains near Alpine. There was an early collection made near the lower Pecos River which was referred to this species.

REMARKS. This form has been a source of much confusion, and its position in the classification is still not settled, but it does appear as a definitely recognizable form separate from anything else found in Texas, and so must be listed here. Scheidweiler first described it in 1841 from specimens collected in Mexico, and Engelmann followed him. Then later a small plant

was collected on the Pecos River in Texas which Engelmann classified as *M. scolymoides*. Coulter saw plants from various locations in Texas, New Mexico, and Mexico which he put under this name. Both Engelmann and Coulter, however, felt enough uncertainty about their classifications to suggest the possibility that their plant might be only a form of *Mammillaria cornifera* DC, a species which occurs in Mexico. Schumann relegated it to *Mammillaria radians* DC, another Mexican species. Britton and Rose took Engelmann's and Coulter's suggestions as certainty and merely listed it as a synonym of *Coryphantha cornifera* without describing it, so it is almost unknown since their time. This may be proper, or perhaps it may end up as *Mammillaria cornifera* var. *scolymoides*, but regardless of the name, this is a cactus which west Texas collectors are bound to find and wonder about.

The cactus is fully as near to *Mammillaria echinus* as to any other species. Small specimens are almost indistinguishable from that cactus except for their longer and heavier spines and tubercles. Many have been distributed under that name. But anyone who has ever seen a large, mature specimen cannot but recognize the difference between them. *M. scolymoides* grows at least twice as large as *M. echinus* and in its prime is fully as tall and as impressive as *M. scheeri*, only remaining a little smaller in diameter than that species. In regard to maximum size, my description exceeds that of Engelmann, which has been the one copied by most other students, because Engelmann apparently saw only a small specimen and had no idea of the size it can attain.

All specimens I have collected have come out of the Glass Mountains, a small range of mountains northeast of Alpine, Texas. Although I have seen many specimens in dealers' stocks which apparently came from other mountains deeper in the Big Bend, I have been unable to trace them any more exactly, since they were brought out of these mountains by crews of laborers who roam these areas digging cacti for the trade.

I have collected two specimens of this cactus which, although showing all the other characters of the species, lacked the central spines. One of them had been badly damaged and was recovering from a serious wound on one side. Later, under cultivation, both of them put on normal centrals on new growth. I believe, therefore, that this is an abnormal growth form reverting to the immature condition under bad situations. As such it would be parallel to the same sort of reversion which occurs in the species *M. echinus* and which was the basis for the supposed species *M. pectinata*.

Mammillaria echinus Eng.
[*Coryphantha echinus* (Eng.) B. & R.]

DESCRIPTION   PLATE 28

STEMS: Usually spherical, but sometimes becoming egg-shaped

or conical when old. The plants almost always consist of single stems, but sometimes branch at the base when old to form small clumps of up to about 6 stems. These stems are 2 to 3 inches tall when mature. They are covered with very firm, conical tubercles about ³/₈ to ¹/₂ inch long, which turn upward and somewhat overlap those above them.

AREOLES: At first nearly round, remaining so on some specimens until the plants are very large. But when matured normally the areoles of the plants are elongated by a groovelike extension which may extend only part of the way or all of the way to the base of the tubercle. The flower is produced from the end of this groove. There is white or brownish wool in the grooves at the tip of the plant where they are growing, but on the sides of the plant the grooves are bare except for a tuft of wool remaining at the base of each groove.

SPINES: There are 16 to 30 radial spines growing around the edge of each areole. They are ³/₈ to 1 inch long, and radiate evenly all around the areole except at the upper edge, where they are more numerous and bunched. They lie flat against the plant or even curve back toward the plant a little, interlocking with spines of neighboring areoles. They are slender, but very rigid, round or sometimes slightly flattened from side to side. When young they appear yellowish and partly translucent like the material of horn, and when old they become gray. They usually have black or dark brown tips. There are also 3 or 4 much thicker central spines growing from the center of the typical adult plant areole. These have enlarged bases, are round, and extend about ¹/₂ to ³/₄ of an inch in length, usually being gray with black tips; but a plant is occasionally found on which these centrals are black almost all the way to their bases. Two or three of these spines are turned upward so that they lie directly upon the upper radial spines. The lowest central spine always stands straight out from the center of the areole. It is thick and conspicuous, usually perfectly straight, but sometimes curves downward. Immature plants lack the central spines entirely, having only the radial spines, and sometimes poor growing conditions will keep a plant from growing centrals when it is otherwise mature. An injury or a reversal of good conditions will sometimes cause new growth on a typical plant to be without these centrals.

FLOWERS: At least 3 inches across and to 2 inches tall, the color a very clear sulphur yellow. The outer petals are narrow and brownish-green, with yellowish, smooth edges. The 20 to 30 inner petals are about ³/₈ to ⁵/₈ of an inch wide, pointed, with the edges slightly ragged toward the tips. They are clear yellow in color. The filaments are rose-pink. The anthers are bright orange. The style is about the length of the stamens. The stigma is made up of 10 to 12 rough, cream-colored lobes about ³/₁₆ to ¹/₄ of an inch long.

FRUITS: Oval or egg-shaped, to nearly 1 inch long, light green in color. The remains of the flowers stay upon them. The seeds are dark brown, smooth surfaced, kidney-shaped, and about 1¹/₂ millimeters long.

RANGE. An area of southwest Texas from near the mouth of the Pecos River up to about the level of Fort Stockton, and from there southwest into the mountains of the lower Big Bend area. I find no record of its occurrence west of Marfa, Texas.

REMARKS. This is a very common little cactus in a rather limited area of west Texas. It seems to be confined to the eastern part of the Big Bend. Early students collected it as far east as the lower Pecos River, but it seems not to have been seen that far east for many years.

The cactus, when typical, sits as a small sphere or cone only 2 or 3 inches high. Its spines cover it and enclose it completely. On each areole there is one heavy central spine up to 1 inch long standing straight out, perpendicular to the surface of the plant, or nearly so. This gives the cactus a striking resemblance to the Echinoderm called the sea urchin, and for this reason Engelmann gave it the name it bears.

Early descriptions of the species always listed it as not clustering, but dealers have been bringing many specimens out of the more inaccessible mountains of the lower Big Bend where they must have better conditions, and these are sometimes branched around their bases to form small clusters of up to half a dozen heads.

A hundred years ago, when Engelmann first studied these cacti, he described *Mammillaria echinus* very plainly. At the same time he also described another form identical in every way to this one, except having no central spines. He called this form *M. pectinata*, from the comblike appearance of the radial spines. From that time on there has been discussion by every student of these two forms, some stoutly maintaining them to be separate species and others trying to combine them as varieties.

As a result of growing these cacti and observing them over a period of years, I have satisfied myself that the form called *M. pectinata* is only an immature or abnormal growth form of *M. echinus,* and that the names are, therefore, synonymous. Immature specimens of *M. echinus* under about 1 inch in diameter always lack central spines and are identical to *M. pectinata* in armament. Central spines normally appear gradually on new areoles of these plants as they grow past 1¹/₂ inches or so in size.

But what about larger specimens and even blooming specimens described by Engelmann as having no centrals, on which he based his *M. pectinata*? This sort of thing has been seen by any student who has looked over any number of these plants, since it is fairly common among them. But I have found that a normal *M. echinus* with large centrals can often be caused to put out new growth lacking centrals merely by inflicting an injury on it, or giving it poor growing conditions. For example, I have a plant which I bought from a dealer as *M. pectinata*. It had 3 spherical heads, each about 1¹/₂ inches across, and on no areole was there a central spine. But upon looking closely I could see that these three heads grew from a single short base. This was the remains of what had once been a large *M. echinus* which had suffered so severe an injury to its upper part that only this short section had been left. But it had unmistakably been *M. echinus,* since the old spines of it, when dug out from under the edges of the new growth, had a full set of centrals in each cluster. The new growth it had put out after its injury consisted of 3 perfect miniature heads with no centrals. Now, two years later, these new heads have reached a size where they are maturing, and the first centrals are showing up upon them, proving that when grown they will form a triple-headed *M. echinus* which has grown from the one form to the other twice in its lifetime.

In confirmation of this, I have a specimen of typical *M. echinus* collected near Marathon, Texas. It has been growing in a pot for several years. Something in the transplanting or the lack of some necessary materials since has caused this one plant to put out growth entirely without centrals for the past two years. In other words, the base of this plant is now *M. echinus* and its summit is now *M. pectinata.* It has been blooming every year, proving that this growth without centrals, although typical of the immature, can also occur on mature, flowering plants. It seems obvious, then, that the two forms are one and the same cactus.

Mammillaria sulcata Eng.
[*Coryphantha sulcata* (Eng.) B. & R.]
"Nipple Cactus," "Finger Cactus," "Pineapple Cactus"

DESCRIPTION   PLATE 28

STEMS: Rapidly and densely clustering, new stems growing from the grooves on old tubercles around the base of the plant. Old plants are often masses several feet across, and made up of dozens of heads. Individual stems are spherical, usually with somewhat flattened tops, and often wider than tall. Mature stems will be 3 inches across and about 1¹⁄₂ to 3 inches tall. The surface is dark green and soft, divided into tubercles which are nearly cylindrical, the bases on old ones becoming somewhat broadened. They curve upward to overlap slightly on old specimens, but it is more common for them to stand out from each other. Because they are very soft, when the plant is shrunken from lack of water they often sag downward and give the plant an untidy, irregular appearance. Mature tubercles are to about ³⁄₄ of an inch long.

AREOLES: Practically round and very woolly at first and remaining so on immature growth. On mature growth they are elongated by the formation of groovelike extensions which reach to the axils of the tubercles. These grooves are filled with much white or yellowish wool when young, making the top of the plant woolly, but they are almost bare when old.

SPINES: There are 8 to 15 radial spines ³⁄₈ to ⁵⁄₈ of an inch long, which radiate evenly from the edge of the areole. They are round and rather heavy, yellowish and partly translucent at first, then gray with black or dark red-brown tips. There may be no central spine, or to as many as 3 per areole, this much variation often being found on the same plant. If the central is single, it usually stands perpendicular to the stem. If two are present, one is usually perpendicular or turned a little downward, while the other is turned upward. When three are present the one is still in the perpendicular or down-turning position, while the other two spread upward, sometimes almost against the upper radials. The centrals are the same length as the radials, but heavier. They are usually the same color, but on occasional plants they will be streaked with black almost to their bases on only the upper sides.

FLOWERS: 2 or 3 inches across and 1 to 2 inches tall. They vary from a greenish-yellow to a dark golden-yellow. The centers are usually very bright red, but on rare specimens this red is a paler brownish-red or even almost nonexistent. The outer petals are short and greenish with yellowish, smooth edges. There are 20 to 30 of them. The inner petals are long and rather narrow from narrow, red bases, the upper part being golden and the same width as the outer petals, tapering gradually to a definite point. The upper margins may be entire or sparingly ragged and toothed. There are about 25 inner petals. The filaments are bright red, except in the rare flowers almost without red, where they are greenish. The anthers are yellow. The style is equal in length to the stamens on some plants and somewhat longer on others, greenish, and ending in 7 to 10 yellow, greenish-yellow, or cream-colored lobes.

FRUITS: Oblong, green, about ³⁄₄ of an inch long. The seeds are light brown, about ¹⁄₁₆ of an inch (1¹⁄₂ millimeters) long, with the surface pitted.

RANGE. South-central Texas within a triangle the points of which lie just north of Houston on the east, near Fort Worth on the north, and near the Pecos River on the west.

REMARKS. This cactus does not present any striking form of growth. Its stems are not large, and even the old clumps which may be up to two feet or more across are low, uneven clusters presenting no particular beauty of appearance. It likes to grow under the junipers, oaks, and brush plants of the limestone hills at the edge of the Edwards Plateau. It is rarely found in the more open country farther north, but there are a few records of its having been collected to near Fort Worth. It apparently never grows on the coastal plain or in deep south Texas.

If undistinguished ordinarily, this cactus shows its beauty when it blooms. Its flowers are large and usually of a satiny, golden color unmatched by any other species I have ever seen. With the red centers and sheaves of red filaments these make some of the finest blooms on any of our cacti.

Very rarely one comes across a plant of *M. sulcata* which has a more greenish-yellow flower with the red center almost completely lacking and only represented by a faint brownish-red shading at the very base of the petals. I believe that this is the cactus which was at hand when early students described it first as *Mammillaria similis robustior* Eng., later as *M. wissmannii* Hild., and still later as *Neobesseya wissmannii* (Hild.) B. & R. I therefore present the probability that these names are all synonyms of *M. sulcata*. See the discussion under *Mammillaria similis* for my reasons for this suggestion.

The beauty of its flowers, together with the fact that it is not strictly a desert species, should make this cactus the logical choice for dish gardens and windowsill growing. It does not rot so easily as most, and so can stand much more water in the soil and humidity in the air. If given a limestone soil it should do well and bloom in almost any situation.

After giving this cactus the name *M. sulcata* in his original description, Engelmann later renamed it *M. calcarata*, but it must be called by its earliest name.

Mammillaria ramillosa (Cutak)
[*Coryphantha ramillosa* Cutak]

DESCRIPTION   PLATE 29

ROOTS: Entirely fibrous.

STEMS: Single or very sparingly clustering, to 3½ inches in diameter, spherical or nearly so. The tubercles are about ¾ of an inch long, tapering from very much flattened bases which are wider than the tubercles are tall. These tubercles are firm, are arranged regularly, and overlap upward very much. The color is dark green.

AREOLES: Monomorphic, becoming linear and extending as grooves to the axils of the tubercles. Woolly at first, but bare when mature except for a small tuft of wool at the end of each groove in the axil of the tubercle.

SPINES: There are 14 to 20 slender radial spines ⅜ to about 1 inch long. They radiate evenly around the areole, are flattened, usually curving and twisted, and gray in color, often with darker tips. There are 4 central spines which are also slender, but which are round, 1 to 1⅝ inches long, gray mottled with brown, and spreading and curving in all directions. The radials are pinkish when growing and the centrals wine-colored.

FLOWERS: Varying from pale pink to deep rose-purple in color. They are about 2½ inches long and 2 inches wide, often unable to open so fully because of the long spines around them. The outer petals vary from small, green scales on the flower tube to greenish-purple, linear, unfringed segments. The inner petals are about 1 inch long and to ³/₁₆ of an inch wide, the lower half white, while the upper half is pink to rose-purple. The filaments are white, the anthers pale orange. The style is

about the length of the stamens. There are 6 or 7 stigma lobes ⅛ to ¼ of an inch long.

FRUITS: ¾ to 1 inch long, oval or egg-shaped, green, covered with minute white or silvery, hairlike scales which give them a silvery sheen. The old flower parts remain upon them. The seeds are brown, less than ¹/₁₆ of an inch (1 millimeter) long, very broad above with flattened sides below and a long, narrow point of attachment toward the end of the ventral side.

RANGE. The southeastern corner of Brewster County, Texas, from near the Stillwell Ranch along the Rio Grande to below Sanderson, Texas. Also found in a very small area close to the Rio Grande within the Big Bend National Park, just downstream from Mariscal Canyon.

REMARKS: This cactus presents a dilemma to those who would subdivide the genus. By all of its vegetative characters it is a relative of the large, yellow-flowered Mammillarias just listed, which are often called Coryphanthas, yet its large flower is definitely purplish and reminds one of *Mammillaria macromeris*, which is placed by Backeberg in a separate genus, *Lepidocoryphantha*. Most have been inclined to regard it as a closer relative of the latter cactus, but if two separate genera are made here, this cactus will hardly fit into either of them: the purple flower looks odd in the one and the plant lacks the fringed sepals and the taproot of the other. When one recalls that the yellow-flowered *Mammillaria scheeri* of the first group has more or less fringed sepals anyway, the only conclusion seems to be that any division on the basis of fringed or entire sepals or of flower color is certainly less than generic in significance.

M. ramillosa is distinguished from the purple-flowered *M. macromeris*, which grows close by it, by the facts that *M. ramillosa* forms firm, compact, spherical, squatty stems, while *M. macromeris* is more cylindrical in shape, with longer, looser, flabbier tubercles. The spines of the former are more slender, especially the round centrals. It has only small fibrous roots, instead of the large taproot of the other, and never forms the large carpets of plants which that other species does, even in its most favorable locations. Most specimens I have seen of *M. ramillosa* have been single stems, but sometimes it clusters sparingly.

The significance of the minute hairs on the fruit surface has not been determined. The fruit was not seen by the original describer, and so far as I know these hairs have not been noticed before. They are too tiny to be easily visible to the naked eye except by the silvery sheen they impart to the whole surface of the fruit. They are, however, so numerous that the surface of the fruit approaches the condition described as being hirsute. I have seen such a covering of hairs on no other cactus fruit. Because they are so tiny I find it hard to think of them as scales or hairs in the same sense as those on the fruits of the Echinocacti. If one did equate them with those this would open up a whole new realm of speculation for the theorists.

M. ramillosa was discovered in 1936 by Mr. A. R. Davis, a

great collector of the Big Bend cacti. It was described by Ladislaus Cutak in 1942. It grows on the limestone hills along the Maravillas and Reagan canyons of southeastern Brewster County and along a few other smaller canyons farther east. This is very inaccessible territory, and very few of the cacti have been brought out, so that the plant is almost unknown even today. It can be most easily seen in a small location in the Big Bend National Park where it is fortunately protected. This seems to represent a second location for the plant and is perhaps the second and discontinuous range mentioned by Davis.

The cactus is a rather attractive one, presenting a tidy and symmetrical growth. Its slender spines, however, are extremely untidy, curving and spreading at all angles, and making it look much like a bunch of dead, gray grass stems, which must be its particular form of camouflage.

Mammillaria macromeris Eng.
[*Coryphantha macromeris* (Eng.) Lem.]
"Long Mamma"

DESCRIPTION   PLATE 30

ROOTS: Adult plants have long, fleshy taproots.

STEMS: Usually short columns to about 4 inches tall, but sometimes to 8 inches; to about 3 inches thick. These stems may remain single, but usually cluster by the formation of new stems from the grooves on the lower tubercles. The clusters often form flat mats of stems, but occasionally round up to form hemispherical mounds. Seeds often germinate and grow close around the bases of mature plants. This, with the branching, sometimes produces masses of the plants up to several feet across. The stems are made up of very soft, flabby, long tubercles, arranged regularly and standing upright at the top of the stem, but usually flattened and either curving upward or curving and standing out at various angles on the sides of the stems. These tubercles are 3/4 to 1 1/2 inches long, cylindrical, and dark green in color.

AREOLES: Each tubercle on an adult plant is grooved with a deep groove which usually runs about halfway down the tubercle length, but sometimes goes all the way to the axil. This groove is almost entirely bare when old, but has a little short white wool in it when young. It is the linear extension of the areole forward from the spinous portion, and the flowers, or lower on the stem the new shoots, arise from within this groove.

SPINES: There are 10 to 18 slender radial spines. They are 5/8 to 2 inches long, the upper ones tending to be the longer ones. They are gray in color, sometimes mottled with pale brown. They are flattened and ridged and usually twisted and curved. There are also 2 to 8 heavier central spines on mature plants, these 1 to 2 1/4 inches long, spreading in all directions

from the center of the areole. They are mottled brown, dark brown, purplish, or black. They grow angled and often ridged, either straight or twisted and curved, from bulbous bases.

FLOWERS: Light purple or pinkish in color, 2 inches tall and wide. These flowers would usually open wider if they were not prevented from opening fully by the long spines around them. The green ovary has several white-edged, fringed scales upon it. The 20 to 30 outer petals are short, narrow, and greenish-brown with pink, fringed edges. The 20 to 25 inner petals are about 1 1/4 inches long and 3/16 of an inch wide, the midlines deep pink and the edges almost white. These edges are rough and often fringed, and the ends, while pointed, are also toothed and notched. The filaments are rose-colored, the anthers pale orange. The style is a little longer than the stamens. The stigma has 7 to 10 rough, white lobes about 3/16 of an inch long. These lobes are slender, and each has a smooth, pinkish point like a soft spine on the end.

FRUITS: Almost round or broadly egg-shaped, 5/8 to 1 inch long, greenish in color. The seeds are practically spherical, light brown in color, and smooth.

RANGE. Southern New Mexico into Mexico and southeast along the Rio Grande in Texas to Rio Grande City.

REMARKS. This cactus is very common around Las Cruces, New Mexico, and is easily found around Presidio, Texas. Otherwise it occurs sporadically over a large area, including the area along the course of the Rio Grande where it becomes rather common again as far as Rio Grande City, Texas. It grows on the stony crests and sides of low hills, where it is almost always found under the light shade of shrubs and trees. In such places it sometimes forms mats of closely standing plants extending over a number of square feet.

M. macromeris is remarkable for its long, soft, loosely standing tubercles. These, however, give it a rather untidy appearance, just the opposite of the neat, symmetrical body we admire in most cacti, and cause it to be less of a favorite with cactus fanciers than some others. It does have a beautiful flower, however, and can be a very fine pot plant.

This cactus shares with many others the habit of budding new stems from the grooves of old tubercles. There is nothing unusual about this, since the vegetative meristem is in these monomorphic areoles located at or near the end of this elongated areole. But the grooves usually extend only halfway or so down the long tubercles in this plant, and the new little stems appear quite out of place bursting out of the grooves only a short distance below the ends of the tubercles instead of out of the axils. There have been attempts to make much of this peculiarity, even to using it to set this species off in its own new genus, this called by Backeberg genus *Lepidocoryphantha*. But sober reflection makes it seem obvious that this is no really essential difference from any of the other Mammillarias having monomorphic areoles. In fact, *Mammillaria sulcata* sometimes has similarly short areoles and in this case branches in the same way.

There have been described some varieties of *M. macromeris*, but the cactus is very variable, and it is hard to separate forms exactly. Specimens with light central spines, longer and straighter than the average, seem to be the basis for the variety *longispina* of Schelle, and specimens with black or very dark, shorter, and more twisted and curved centrals may be his variety *nigrispina*, but they both grow together, and the differences seem of doubtful significance. The plants do seem to become smaller in their maximum size in the eastern part of their range, and also to average fewer centrals than those farther west, but the flowers are identical, and no varieties have been set up for this difference.

Engelmann stated that *Mammillaria dactylothele* Labouret was a variety of this species, but Britton and Rose consider it a synonym.

M. macromeris will grow very well if given perfect drainage and enough heat and sunlight. It blooms well when healthy, but one should remember that it needs room to develop its long taproot, so will not do well in a shallow pot. When specimens are collected the long roots are often broken off, as they grow deep into very hard and rocky soil. The plants may live after this, but will usually sit without growing or flowering for years until they can replace their taproots. This is why large plants of this species are often so disappointing in performance after being brought in.

Mammillaria runyonii (B. & R.)
[*Coryphantha runyonii* B. & R.]
"Runyon's Coryphantha," "Dumpling Cactus"

DESCRIPTION   PLATE 30

ROOTS: Having a large, succulent, carrot-shaped taproot.

STEMS: Highly caespitose by producing many irregularly sized and shaped stems from the top of the taproot, the whole mass of these stems sometimes up to 18 inches or more across. The tubercles are so irregularly arranged on most specimens that one can hardly speak of separate stems at all, but on other plants the mass of tubercles is divided roughly into irregular heads up to about 2 inches tall and 1$\frac{1}{2}$ inches thick. The tubercles, which stand at almost any angle, vary in size on the same plant, but most of them are around $\frac{3}{8}$ of an inch long with the maximum being about $\frac{3}{4}$ of an inch long. They are very soft, tapering from very broad bases which are often wider than the tubercle is long.

AREOLES: The spinous portion of the areole is small and practically circular, but the mature areole is prolonged from this in the form of a groove running about halfway down the tubercle, but never to the axil. The flower is produced from the end of this short groove which is naked after completion.

SPINES: Usually there are 6 to 11 radial spines, but there is a tendency for some individuals to produce very many very small tubercles, each having as few as 3 radials. The radials are usually $\frac{1}{4}$ to $\frac{1}{2}$ inch long, but may occasionally grow to 1 inch long. They are evenly spaced around the areole, are straight and round, and yellowish in color at first, then turning gray. There may be 1 to 4 straight, round central spines $\frac{3}{4}$ to 2 inches long, which spread in all directions from the center of the areole. These are gray mottled with brown.

FLOWERS: Purplish or rose-pink, 1$\frac{3}{4}$ inches tall and 2 inches in diameter, opening widely, the petals sometimes even recurving. The outer petals are greenish or purplish, covered and fringed with white hairs. The inner petals are about $\frac{3}{16}$ of an inch wide, long and pointed, the edges smooth except for being somewhat toothed toward the tips. The filaments are pinkish, the anthers pale orange. The style is a little longer than the stamens, and pale pink. The stigma has 6 to 10 lobes which are white, $\frac{1}{8}$ to $\frac{3}{16}$ of an inch long, fairly thick, and not pointed.

FRUITS: Green, $\frac{1}{2}$ to $\frac{3}{4}$ of an inch long, oval. The seeds are brown.

RANGE. The lower Rio Grande Valley from near Roma, Texas, to near Brownsville, and into adjacent Mexico.

REMARKS. This is probably the most untidy and ill-organized of all cacti with normal growth. It sometimes takes on the appearance of a cristate or monstrous growth. Assuming that it starts from a single stem, branching must occur very quickly, since I have never seen a plant so small that it was not already a cluster of tiny heads. These heads branch so fast and so irregularly that it is typical for the larger plants to present a completely disorganized mass of small tubercles at all angles. The whole thing is very low to the ground, not over 2 or 3 inches high, but may be quite broad. Mr. Runyon, its discoverer, said that a large plant, with its fleshy root, might weigh 50 pounds. One should hardly look for such huge specimens now, however, as all of these old clumps seem to have been uprooted long ago, and one should be thrilled to find any specimen over 6 inches in diameter today.

M. runyonii grows on gravelly hillsides overlooking the Rio Grande, and to a few miles north of the river. It may have grown in the lower flats of the valley also, but very little of the valley proper is still uncultivated, so its locations are now few and far between. It always prefers partial shade, and will not do well in full sun.

The plant was first described by Britton and Rose after their break-up of the genus *Mammillaria*, so it has been almost universally known as *Coryphantha runyonii*.

In 1934 Werdermann described a *Coryphantha pirtlei* found in Starr County, Texas. The description of that plant does not present any character which lies outside the descriptions already given for *M. runyonii* or which would enable one to distinguish it from that species, except that his plant was said to occur sometimes as a single stem. Starr County is the area where *M. runyonii* is most common, and I have not been able to find there any specimens which I could separate from the rest of the population and designate as a separate form. At the same time I must admit that I have not found there any individual with a single stem. Since *M. runyonii* is rather variable, I am inclined to consider this name as a synonym, or at best a possible variety of *M. runyonii*, but there can be no certainty about the plant until it is re-collected.

Mammillaria similis Eng.
[*Neobesseya similis* (Eng.) B. & R.]
"Nipple Cactus"

DESCRIPTION   PLATES 30, 31

ROOTS: Fibrous.

STEMS: Occasionally growing individually, but usually clustering, often to form large, irregular masses up to a foot or more across when old. Each stem is spherical, usually wider than it is tall, growing up to 4 inches in diameter, but the average being 2 or 3 inches. The stem is covered by tubercles up to 7/8 of an inch long on large plants. These are cylindrical on the upper part of the plant, but the older ones on the sides of the stem become somewhat flattened and overlap upward a little.

AREOLES: On immature plants round or oval. On mature growth each tubercle is deeply grooved its whole length on the upper side with a groove which is an extension of the areole into or nearly to the axil. The whole areole is at first filled with white wool, but it later becomes bare except for a tuft which persists at the base of the groove in the axil, where the vegetative meristem is.

SPINES: There are 10 to 17 slender radial spines. They vary in length with the size and age of the plant, from 1/8 to 1/2 inch long. They are fairly equal on any one areole, except that the 1 or 2 uppermost ones are usually much more slender than the others. There is often no central spine, but about as often there is one central which is very slightly longer and heavier than the radials. It either stands straight out, perpendicular to the plant surface, or else is turned upward sharply in front of the upper radials. All of the spines are gray to white, sometimes with brown tips, and when young are covered with tiny white hairs or scales only visible under a magnifying glass, but these hairs are soon worn off and the spines then often appear smooth, yellowish, and hornlike.

FLOWERS: 1 to 2 inches tall and the same in diameter, with very narrow, linear, sharply pointed petals. The color of these flowers varies from plant to plant from greenish, bronze, gold, gold streaked with pink, or pale, almost clear yellow. Most commonly all of these shades are mixed in the same

flower. There are 15 to 20 outer petals which are greenish with fringed, yellowish or whitish edges. There are 20 to 25 inner petals which are even narrower than the outer, about 1/8 of an inch wide near their bases and tapering very gradually to a sharp point. These are clear yellow, gold, chartreuse, or bronze, often with pinkish midlines, and with unfringed, smooth edges. The filaments may be white, light green, or yellow. The anthers may be yellow or pale orange. The style is very much longer than the stamens and green or yellowish in color. The stigma has 4 to 6 green or yellowish lobes, which are 1/8 to 1/4 of an inch long and which in some plants are slender and smooth, while in others they are thicker and rough.

FRUITS: Spherical to oval in shape, 3/8 to 3/4 of an inch long. They remain green and below the spines of the plant between the tubercles for nearly a year. The second spring they turn bright scarlet. They then remain where they are and shrivel and harden unless plucked out from their protected places by birds or animals. The seeds are approximately 1/16 of an inch (1 1/2 to over 2 millimeters) across, are almost spherical in shape, and black in color, with pitted surfaces.

RANGE. Generally, Kansas and eastern Colorado south through Oklahoma and north Texas to near San Antonio. More specifically, I have found records of this form's occurrence in a long but narrow belt from south-central Kansas through central Oklahoma into Texas, including the Dallas and Fort Worth area and on down to near San Antonio and Columbus. I find no record of it west of a line from San Antonio to approximately Oklahoma City, and must regard the Colorado specimens as either an isolated population or else an extension of the Montana and Idaho population, which is a form separate from ours.

REMARKS. As most people have met with this cactus, it is a small, irregular clump of spherical stems producing flowers with narrow, sharp-pointed petals of a curious greenish-yellow color often striped with browns and pinks. It has appealed mostly as a curiosity, growing in areas where few if any other cacti are found. Only a few people have seen it in its glory, an old clump a foot or more across, made up of dozens of little heads, and covered with 20 or 30 flowers in its blooming period. When seen this way it is recognized as a beautiful cactus to be cherished.

The cactus grows equally well in loamy places on the central plains or on calcareous hilltops. It does not like the full sun in the summer, shrinking up and even dying when totally unshaded. In its native habitat it is shaded just enough by the prairie grass growing over it on the plains and by shrubs and brush on the hills. It is much more tolerant of moisture than most cacti, but will still rot quickly if placed in poorly drained, heavy soil.

It is rather common in the hills on all sides of Austin, Texas, and is met with occasionally in a band of territory about 100 miles or so wide which includes Waco, Fort Worth, and Dallas, Texas. It may be found, but is not at all common, north of this in a band of about the same width through central Oklahoma, until it becomes rather common again between Ponca City and Tulsa, Oklahoma. From there north rare populations have been found in Kansas, mostly near the Arkansas River and below Hutchinson, Kansas. I find no record of it north of this.

There has been much confusion about *Mammillaria similis* from the beginning, and it is not all cleared up even today. The first cactus of this sort described was a plant from the upper Missouri River area. It was described very briefly by Nuttall in 1818, called *Cactus mammillaris*. In 1827 Sweet renamed this plant *Mammillaria missouriensis*.

In 1849 Engelmann secured this plant from Fort Pierre on the upper Missouri, which is near Pierre, South Dakota. He also felt it necessary to rename the cactus, and called it *Mammillaria nuttallii*, after its discoverer. But Engelmann already had a very similar cactus discovered in central Texas. In 1845 he had named this Texas cactus *Mammillaria similis*. So we have had from this early time two forms, one commonly known as *M. missouriensis* (Engelmann's *M. nuttallii*), discovered in the far north, and the other, *M. similis*, found deep in central Texas. No doubt every serious cactus student has struggled with these two, with the questions of whether they are different or not, how they are related, and what to call them.

We must credit Engelmann with wrestling with these problems himself. By 1856 he had studied many more specimens from wide areas, and by then he must have concluded that these two forms were very close to each other, for he came up with a new naming system for them. The northern *M. missouriensis* he now called *M. nuttallii* var. *borealis*, and said that it grew from Montana and South Dakota to Nebraska, western Kansas, and eastern Colorado. The southern *M. similis* he now called *M. nuttallii* var. *caespitosa*, ranging, he said, from the Kansas River to New Braunfels, Texas. The point is that he made them varieties of the same species.

From this time on some chose to call them two separate species and some to call them varieties of the same species, while at the same time placing them in almost every conceivable genus. The result was that Poselger in 1853 used for our Texas form the name *Echinocactus similis*; Small in 1903 used *Cactus similis*; Britton and Rose in 1913 and again in 1921, Schulz in 1930, and Backeberg in 1960 used *Neobesseya similis*; while Watson in 1878 used *Mammillaria missouriensis* var. *caespitosa*; Coulter in 1896 used *Cactus missouriensis* var. *similis*; and Schumann in 1898 used *Mammillaria missouriensis* var. *similis*. Whether it is correct to place this form as a separate species or as a variety of the other form seems impossible to state categorically even today. I list it here as a separate species, mostly because the recent studies have been rather consistent in doing this, but I summarize the actual known differences between the two so that the reader may come to his own decision.

There is no actual difference of stems or tubercles between the two except that the southern *M. similis* usually grows to a larger maximum size, but this may well be due to the better growing seasons in the south. The spines are essentially the same in number and character in both, except that, once again, the maximum length is slightly greater in the southern form. The flower diameter and length of the northern *M. missouriensis* is about 1 inch, while *M. similis* flowers vary from 1 inch across and long in its extreme upper range in Oklahoma and Kansas to 2 inches in central Texas, with climate seeming definitely to make the difference, since plants from Kansas brought to San Antonio and grown in my collection doubled the size of their flowers the second year.

One flower character is given as definitely different in the two forms. *M. missouriensis* is stated to have 2 to 5 stigma lobes which are very short, about $1/12$ to $1/20$ of an inch long, while *M. similis* has 4 to 6 lobes $1/8$ to $1/4$ of an inch long. This does not seem to be influenced by environment. The size of seeds, which are only about one-half as big in the former as the latter, also seems significant. But these things are about all that can be definitely given to divide them—a fact which leaves them so close that a good case can be made for calling them mere varieties of the same species.

Anyone collecting in the Southwest need not worry about distinguishing between the two, however, as it seems certain that the northern form does not come into Oklahoma or Texas. From southern Kansas down all of them appear to be the same southern *M. similis*.

Most books repeat the listing, as either a variety of this species or as a closely related separate species, of a cactus which I do not believe exists as a separate form at all. Engelmann first described this most doubtful form as a variety, *Mammillaria similis* var. *robustior*, and then later as *M. nuttallii* var. *robustior*. Others, such as Watson and Coulter, followed him in this, calling it *M. missouriensis* var. *robustior*, but did it on the strength of nothing more than Engelmann's preserved specimens, which were collected in 1845 and 1847 by Lindheimer and by Bigelow. In 1898 Hildmann elevated it to a species for the first time, calling it *Mammillaria wissmannii*. Everyone has followed him since then, and the species is listed in all the books on the Texas area, although most of the authors have failed to collect the plant and have merely followed Britton and Rose, who copied the earlier description by Engelmann, reproduced a drawing said to be of the form from *Blühende Kakteen*, and called the cactus a Neobesseya. The only new material on this cactus since Engelmann's time is a photograph in Backeberg's 1960 work purported to be of the plant and credited to Thiele.

Over a period of years I have searched for this cactus throughout central Texas, where it is supposed to be found. I have not been alone, as a perennial project of most Texas cactophiles is the unending search for the "yellow-flowered Neobesseya" having the large flowers with the unfringed outer petals. I have followed many leads, only to find everything *M. similis* with the smaller flower having the fringed outer petals and fewer stigma lobes than *M. wissmannii* is supposed to have. I have never found, nor do I know of any collector who has found the Neobesseya with the gold-yellow flowers having 7 or 8 stigma lobes and unfringed outer perianth segments, although I have seen many specimens of typical *M. similis* called this.

I had puzzled over this situation for a long time, when I was shown some plants of *M. sulcata* from near Kerrville, Texas, which were not quite typical. The flowers on these specimens were more greenish-yellow than the pinard-yellow I had seen before in that species, and the red of the center was almost entirely lacking, only represented by a faint brownish stain in the very center of the flower. Their collector gave me an idea when he speculated that he had in them a cross between *M. sulcata* and *M. similis*. This I doubt. They were quite clearly *M. sulcata*, but his speculation presented a new possibility, which I entertain reluctantly, but which I cannot ignore. It seems highly likely that all of the *M. similis* var. *robustior* or *M. wissmannii* found by Lindheimer and Bigelow in this same area and described by Engelmann were really only these somewhat atypical *M. sulcata*, lacking or nearly lacking the red centers in the flowers.

In support of this theory it should be noted that the size and shape of the two are the same, the number and size of the radial spines fall within the same range, and the 0 to 3 centrals are the same in all respects in both. Add to this the gold-yellow color of the flower which is stressed for both, the unfringed petals and 7 or 8 stigmas described for both, and the case could easily be considered closed. Another remarkable coincidence is that *M. wissmannii* is expressly stated to sprout new stems from the grooves of old tubercles, a character which is very striking in *M. sulcata* but not noticeable in *M. similis*.

I can cite no clear-cut differences noted so far which could separate *M. wissmannii* from *M. sulcata*. The fruit character should do this, since, if *M. wissmannii* is so closely related to *M. similis*, its fruit would be red, while the other's fruit stays green. But there has never been a description of the color of the fruit on *M. wissmannii*, so we can settle nothing there. The seeds of the two are both described, however, but are practically the same size. Since those of *M. wissmannii* are merely described as "dark," we cannot know whether they were actually black like those of *M. similis* or dark brown like those of *M. sulcata*.

In short, I can find no proof that anyone has ever seen anything other than some *M. sulcata* in which the red was lacking in the flower, and which were, therefore, thought to be another cactus. When I put the specimens preserved in the United States National Museum under the name *Neobesseya wissmannii* side by side with specimens of *M. sulcata* I could not separate them by any character showing in the preserved state. Since the range in which the two plants are supposed to grow is practically the same, the evidence seems to point to the assumption that they are one and the same. This would make *Mammillaria (Neolloydia) wissmannii* merely a synonym of *M. sulcata*. It should at least clear up the situation for collectors, in whose gardens I have so many times seen the more brightly yellow-flowered specimens of *M. similis* arbitrarily labeled *M. wissmannii* merely because no one can find anything else to bear this label.

M. similis is an eastern cactus, not strictly a desert habitant. It is, therefore, much better suited to the ordinary cactus collection or window garden than most. It also has the fine feature of being able to take most ordinary winter temperatures over a wide area of the U.S. without protection, so long as it is growing in a well-drained situation. It is probably the best cactus to be grown by the amateur who does not want to bother with the intricacies of cactus culture.

Mammillaria rosiflora (Lahman)
[*Neobesseya rosiflora* Lahman]

DESCRIPTION

STEMS: Identical to those of *M. similis* except reaching a maximum of only about 2³/₄ inches across and clustering more sparingly to form only small clumps.

SPINES: There are 13 to 16 radial spines to ⁵/₁₆ of an inch long, equal around the areole except for the uppermost 2 of them, which are very short and so slender as to be almost bristle-like. They are gray with brown tips, and have minute white hairs on the spines when they are young. There is apparently always one central spine which is about ¹/₄ of an inch long and turned upward.

FLOWERS: About 1¹/₂ inches across and tall. They are a pure pink, without the stripes and zones of various colors found in the flowers of the plant's relatives. The outer petals are narrow, but thick and fleshy, and they are not fringed. The inner petals are so narrow as to be almost threadlike. They are very weak and limp, spreading and bending in all directions. The filaments are deep pink, the anthers yellow. The stigma has 4 to 6 white lobes.

FRUITS: Round to egg-shaped, crimson, ³/₈ of an inch long. The seeds are almost circular, black, pitted on the surface, and less than ¹/₁₆ of an inch (1¹/₂ millimeters) long.

RANGE. Known only from an area about 80 miles long from near Tulsa to near Ponca City, Oklahoma.

REMARKS. This form was discovered by Mrs. Marion Sherwood Lahman, a great student of Oklahoma cacti, and described by her in 1939. She found it in only one location, a prairie just west of Tulsa, Oklahoma. Professors Blauch and Gatewood of Oklahoma State University collected it again near Ponca City, Oklahoma, in 1962, and graciously supplied me with information about it, as well as with a cutting of the plant. I am very sorry to admit that what ability I may possess at cacti culture failed me in this case. I was unable to grow my cutting to blooming stage, or even long enough to secure an adequate photograph of it. I find no recorded collection of it between Tulsa and Ponca City, but it must be assumed that it grows as a rare form in the area.

There is hardly enough information concerning this cactus to decide definitely its relationships to other species. In both instances mentioned above there were found numerous plants of *M. similis* growing within a matter of feet of the *M. rosiflora* specimens. No character of plant body or growth has been found to distinguish the two. Without the flowers one cannot segregate them at all, but *M. rosiflora* has flowers of clear pink, unadulterated by any other colors, with extremely narrow, weak, entirely unfringed petals, which set it apart when in bloom from even the pinkish-flowered *M. similis,* with its petals striped and streaked with browns, grays, greens, or yellows, and its outer segments fringed. The flowers of *M. rosiflora* are strikingly beautiful, about the same shade of pink as a typical flower on *Echinocactus texensis.* They remind one somewhat of those of *Mammillaria vivipara,* but there seems no close relationship here. The same peculiarities of flower which set this form apart from *M. similis* also set it apart very clearly from the pinkish-flowered populations of *M. missouriensis* found in Montana and called by Britton and Rose *Neobesseya notesteinii.*

It will be a worth-while achievement when someone can again locate and collect this very rare form so that more may be learned about it. Unfortunately a very large proportion of the flat prairies of Oklahoma where it is found have been turned to cultivation, reducing greatly the chances that this cactus will get adequate study.

Mammillaria vivipara (Nutt.) Haw.
"Spiny Star," "Ball Cactus," "Pincushion"

DESCRIPTION   PLATES 31, 32, 33

STEMS: Spherical to columnar and single to greatly clustering by offset heads from around the base. Individual stems measure from about 2 to at least 5 inches tall and wide. The surface is deep green in color and is divided into many cylindrical or tapering tubercles which are regularly arranged and spreading or slightly overlapping upward.

AREOLES: Round or nearly so on immature plants, but the upper part of the areole elongated on mature plants into a narrow groove running from the spinous portion of the areole at the tip of the tubercle to the reproductive part in the axil of the tubercle. When young these areoles are filled with much white or yellowish wool, but when old, on the sides of the stems, the wool is usually worn off and they are bare.

SPINES: Various forms have from 12 to at least 60 radial spines. These are slender, straight, radiating rather evenly around the areole. They are firm, 3/8 to about 1 inch long, white, white-tipped dark, or grayish with brown tips. There are also 3 to 12 central spines which are straight, spreading, rather slender to medium in thickness and 1/4 to 1 1/4 inches long. These centrals are from whitish or yellowish with dark tips through mottled brown to partly or completely dark brown or purplish-black.

FLOWERS: Purple, violet, or rose, usually very bright in color, but one form has pale purplish coloring. From about 1 to 2 1/4 inches in length and diameter. The perianth segments are lance-shaped to linear, the outer ones greenish and fringed and the inner ones purple and entire. The stigma has 5 to 10 white to rose-purple lobes which are obtuse in some forms and pointed or even mucronate in others.

FRUITS: Oval in shape, 1/2 to 1 inch long, not including the dried perianth, which persists, remaining green or in some cases becoming brownish when very ripe. The seeds are approximately 1/16 of an inch (1 to 2 1/2 millimeters) long, almost spherical to oval or curved ovate. They are light or dark brown and with the hila ventral or subbasal, concave or convex, and oval to linear in the different forms.

RANGE. Including for the species as a whole a huge area of the North American continent from the Dakotas, Nebraska, Kansas, Oklahoma, and Texas on the east through all the states southwest to California and deep into Mexico.

REMARKS. It seems almost impossible for any but taxonomists to think of this species as a single unity. Collectors of cacti rarely get to collect in more than a fraction of its vast range and rarely see all of the forms together at one time, and so they usually pick up one or two of this species' varieties and then go to the verge of distraction trying to determine which forms they have. This is often hard to determine even with all of the stages of all of the varieties before one, and is almost impossible when one has only the vegetative stages of one or two varieties to study.

Perhaps because of this difficulty of getting an overview of the whole wide-ranging species, its various forms have more often than not been thought of as separate species themselves, even though Engelmann, the original describer of most of them, recognized that they were merely varieties of one large unity and his first descriptions list them that way. Subsequent writers could not conceive of them that way, and soon they were all listed as separate species. The listing of these supposed species by most authors over a long period as though they were completely and obviously distinct has been a great disservice to cactophiles, many of whom have been turned into feuding rivals over these forms, thinking of them as separate species. It was clearly of prime importance to be able to identify them correctly, and yet they are so closely related that with only limited material to study, mistakes were bound to be made. I have even heard of cactus clubs being split over the interpretation of some of these forms. If only the fact could be remembered that this is one very large and variable species and that the different forms, which we can all notice but which are so close that we can only understand them after a great deal of study, are no more than very close and perhaps to some degree even intergrading varieties, then perhaps cactophiles would be less concerned about placing a given specimen exactly.

It would no doubt be better if those who can collect only a

form or two of this species would content themselves with knowing that they have *Mammillaria vivipara*. However, knowing the marvelous inability of the cactophile to be satisfied with this sort of halfway identification, I am following this species description with an account, as clear as I can make it, of each of the varieties of this species occurring in our area. But I must warn those who would follow to the varietal level that here they are embarking upon some of the most stormy seas of controversy in all of cactus study, that all of the winds of argument about these forms are still not spent, and that there are those who will maintain that even in these varieties which seem the most certain we have no secure harbors. But no doubt this, which is one of the most common little cacti over a huge part of this continent, deserves the effort it takes to understand its confusing varieties.

It is important before going any farther to understand that *Mammillaria vivipara* (Nutt.) Haw. is not to be equated with *Cactus viviparus* Nutt., which became the *Coryphantha vivipara* (Nutt.) B. & R. The former is from the beginning an inclusive taxon, taking in, as described by Haworth, all of the then-known range of spine numbers, plant sizes, amount of clustering, and geographical area of the plant. On the other hand the latter, in the sense used by Nuttall and Britton and Rose, is only a very strictly delimited northern form of the species, one segment of the total species, and in modern taxonomic usage should be called *Coryphantha vivipara* var. *vivipara* (Nutt.) B. & R., if one follows their generic scheme, or *Mammillaria vivipara* var. *vivipara* (Nutt.) if the species is returned to this genus.

Mammillaria vivipara var. vivipara (Nutt.)
[*Coryphantha vivipara* (Nutt.) B. & R.]

DESCRIPTION   PLATE 31

STEMS: As the species, except that the stems are always practically globular or even depressed-globular, never columnar, and they grow to only about 2½ inches in diameter.

AREOLES: As the species.

SPINES: There are 12 to 21 radial spines on each areole. These are slender, ⅜ to ⅝ of an inch long, and very white, sometimes with brown tips. There are 1 to 8 central spines which are usually ½ to ¾ of an inch long, and only slightly heavier than the radials. There will always be 1 to 3 centrals directed outward and downward. These are the heaviest spines. The rest of the centrals will be standing upright at the top of the areole, spreading fanwise in front of the upper radials, and varying in thickness, some of them being almost as fine as the radials themselves. There is variation in the color of these centrals from plant to plant. Most commonly they are light brown or honey-colored, often mottled with whitish, and

often with darker tips or other darker zones, but never with blackish coloring.

FLOWERS: Deep magenta or purple in color, not opening widely, 1⅛ to 1¾ inches tall and 1½ to 2 inches across, having very narrow petals. The outer petals are greenish or brownish with pink edges fringed part or all the way to the tips by long, pink cilia. The petals are about ⅛ of an inch wide near the base, tapering gradually to a sharp point. The inner petals are ¾ of an inch long and 1/16 to ⅛ of an inch wide, with edges smooth or sometimes very finely toothed, tapering over their length to a sharp point. There are at least 30 outer petals, about 17 to 20 of them elongated and the rest so short as to be almost like fringed scales. There are about 30 to as many as 47 inner petals. The filaments are green at their bases, the upper parts becoming pink. Anthers are bright orange. The style is the same length as the stamens, or sometimes slightly longer. The stigma has 7 to 10 dark rose-purple lobes, which are slender and about 3/16 of an inch long. They are always somewhat pointed, and may have spinelike mucrones on the ends, but do not always have these.

FRUITS: Oval in shape, ½ to ¾ of an inch long, light green in color, becoming brownish when old. The seeds are light brown in color, their surfaces finely pitted. They are approximately 1/16 of an inch (1 to 1½ millimeters) in length and very thick so as to be almost round, except for the concave hila.

RANGE. From Canada south through Montana, the Dakotas, Nebraska, and Kansas across the northwestern corner of Oklahoma into extreme northwestern Texas, and across eastern Colorado into northeastern New Mexico.

REMARKS. *M. vivipara* var. *vivipara* was discovered very early, its first description having been made by Nuttall in 1813 under the name *Cactus viviparus*. It is the small, northern cactus found in parts of Canada and the northern plains where few other cacti grow. Apparently it is immune to freeze damage, so it grows anywhere in the north where there is not too much moisture and where the soil is right for it. It is quite easily rotted by continued dampness in the wrong soil, its requirement of alkaline soil no doubt keeping it from growing any farther east than the western Great Plains.

Within our area of study it is limited to the northwest, as though it cannot survive the severe heat in which its relatives revel. It is found in scattered locations over all of Oklahoma northwest of a diagonal line running from near Enid to the southwest corner of the state. It is the form of the species found in the upper Texas Panhandle, but the Red River and its upper tributaries seem to mark the southern edge of its penetration in Texas. It grows in the northeastern corner of New Mexico, particularly around Raton, and down nearly as far southwest as Santa Fe. This large area of Oklahoma, Texas, and New Mexico is its home, where it grows on sandy hills and plains; it is not a mountain species, and its range stops short of the high mountains in both Colorado and New Mexico.

The close relatives of *M. vivipara* var. *vivipara* with which it is often confused will be described in detail following this discussion. It may not be distinguished from them by any one characteristic, and from some of them it can hardly be told at all when it is not in flower or fruit. It can be said that it has fewer radial spines than most other forms of the species, but this fact alone will not always separate it from all of them. Part of the confusion over these varieties has arisen from attempts to distinguish them on radial number alone.

When it blooms, variety *vivipara* can be recognized by the 7 to 10 stigma lobes which are long, slender, and pointed, sometimes to the extent of having spinelike tips, as well as being very beautiful dark carmine to pink in color, but never white.

For still more certainty about the identification of his plant, the collector must nurture it further until it forms its fruits. He can then check the seeds it produces, and here find what appears to be the most certain character to distinguish it. Variety *vivipara* has medium brown seeds which are egg-shaped to almost round except for concave, oval hila, and which have roughly pitted surfaces. They are approximately $^1/_{16}$ of an inch (1 to $1^1/_2$ millimeters) long. This distinguishes the variety from its close relatives, all of whose seeds are different in size and detail.

Within itself the variety varies. The description mentions that the color of the centrals varies from plant to plant. However, they never have blackish zones, and they are always some shade of brown, usually predominantly honey-colored. Neither does the amount of clustering the plants do have any significance, as this varies greatly. The first descriptions cautioned us that it grows either singly or profusely clustering; nevertheless, the two types of growth appear so different that all through the years there have been attempts to separate them as two forms, the simple and the clustering. Yet I have plants taken from only a few feet of each other, identical in every respect except that one specimen has grown a single stem while its neighbor has grown as many as 7 heads.

Perhaps the most ambitious attempt to divide up the species on this sort of character was made about 25 years ago by Mrs. Marion Sherwood Lahman, one of the most ardent collectors and students of Oklahoma cacti. She described a total of 6 species of this group in Oklahoma, including 2 new ones, but all of them fall within the limits of the species *M. vivipara* in the sense used by Haworth, and as she separated them on only such general and variable characters as amount of clustering, it appears that her taxa have only doubtful significance.

When dealing with this cactus it must always be remembered that the name, *Mammillaria* (*Coryphantha*) *vivipara* has been and still is used with two very different meanings. Some use this name to refer specifically to the cactus which grows in Nuttall's type locality on the upper Missouri River. This is the exact form which grows, as Engelmann well stated in his earliest writings,

from the Yellowstone and Missouri rivers down to Santa Fe and no farther southwest, and which has only 12 to about 20 radial spines. But as new, very similar forms were discovered, they were all designated by Engelmann as merely varieties of one big species, so they were listed as *M. vivipara* variety or subspecies *borealis, neo-mexicana, radiosa,* and so on. So as the name *M. vivipara* came to mean the species encompassing all of these varieties, writers—Haworth started it, followed by Engelmann himself in his later writings—began to give a description under this name so broad as to take in everything (as for instance saying *M. vivipara* had 12 to 36 or more radials). It is obvious that here the name is being used to refer to a different entity than the limited northern form. The practice of keeping the original, typical form separate by calling it *M. vivipara* var. *vivipara* would have minimized the confusion which resulted, but this practice was not followed at that time, so the form we are discussing here got lost among its own relatives as its name was applied to them all.

When understood in this sense, the variety *vivipara* is a small, retiring cactus which is content to huddle unseen in the prairie grass of the northern plains, but which is amazingly hardy and which produces very beautiful flowers in their season. It is seldom common, and as the grass of northwestern Texas and western Oklahoma has been trimmed ever shorter by overgrazing, these little plants more and more lose their protection and are carried home as curiosities, thus becoming more and more scarce. I observed this order of events myself on the outskirts of Amarillo, Texas. Some years ago I searched for the plant in a particular area there without success. Then, a few years ago, as that city was increasing in size, homes were built in the area where I had unsuccessfully searched, and the ranchland became small lots for ponies. After their intensive grazing, when I visited in one of the new homes, I saw from the window several specimens of the cactus in the almost table-bare lot. Even more recently I noticed that all of these specimens had been taken. With this process and with the cultivation of so much prairie, one has now to look for this cactus in rough places.

Mammillaria vivipara var. radiosa Eng.
[*Coryphantha radiosa* Rydberg]

DESCRIPTION   PLATE 32

STEMS: As the species, except always ovate to columnar when mature and very rarely and sparingly clustering. These stems grow to 5 inches tall and about 3 inches in diameter. The tubercles are cylindrical and to about $^3/_4$ of an inch long.

AREOLES: As the species.

SPINES: As the species, except that the radial spines are always white, sometimes tipped with brown, very slender, to $^1/_2$ inch long, and 17 to 30 in number. The central spines are 4 to 7 in number, spreading from the center of the areole in no set pattern. Most commonly there will be 1 or 2 rather heavy downturning centrals and the rest will stand erect almost against the upper radials, but I have seen some specimens with only 4 centrals and all of them erect—the lower ones lacking entirely. These centrals are light in color, honey- or straw-colored, often with large zones of white.

FLOWERS: About 2 inches across and 2¹/₄ inches tall, very deep violet in color. The petals are 1 to 1¹/₄ inches long and very narrow, being about ¹/₈ of an inch across. The outer ones are 40 to 50 in number, with about 17 of these elongated, and are greenish in color and fringed; while the inner ones are 30 to 40 in number and violet with entire edges. The filaments are deep violet, while the anthers are deep orange. The style is at least ³/₁₆ of an inch longer than the stamens, and pink. The stigma has 7 to 9 rose-colored lobes which are ³/₁₆ to ¹/₄ of an inch long and fairly slender, but not pointed.

FRUITS: About ³/₄ of an inch long, oval, and green in color. The seeds are rather dark brown with a finely striated surface, more than ¹/₁₆ of an inch (2 to 2¹/₂ millimeters) long, and oval, with the ventral surfaces convex and the hila linear in shape.

RANGE. From the southern slopes of the Arbuckle Mountains in Oklahoma south to a line from near Austin, Texas, west past Fredericksburg to Sonora, Texas. The area comprises a triangle with its three points near Springer, Oklahoma, and Austin and Sonora, Texas.

REMARKS. This is a form which usually passes for *Mammillaria vivipara* var. *vivipara*. Admittedly it differs from that variety only in minor characters of the plant body, and very careful observation alone will separate them. Variety *vivipara* always has globose stems and 12 to 21 radials, while the stems of variety *radiosa* become elongated and columnar and it has 17 to 30 radials. The difference of flowers is also minor, the flowers of variety *radiosa* being larger—in fact definitely the largest and most deeply colored of the various forms in this species found in our area—but beyond that about all that can be said is that the stigma lobes of variety *radiosa* are never pointed as they are in variety *vivipara*.

I would surely not blame anyone for thinking we were splitting spines here if we listed these as two separate species: they are difficult even as varieties. It would be much easier to consider these two cacti the same and be done with it, but a hundred years ago Engelmann saw a consistent difference in the seeds of the two cacti, and we must recognize it. The seeds of variety *radiosa* are unmistakably different, almost twice as large in each direction as those of variety *vivipara;* they are full and convex on all surfaces, as well as darker brown, and their surfaces are very finely pitted, where the seeds of variety *vivipara* are small, flattened, and concave, and lighter brown with more coarse pitting. There is more difference between these two than among the seeds of all the various and otherwise vastly differ-

ent Echinocerei, and this species provides the only instance I know where cacti almost identical in other respects have such basically different seeds.

Amazing confusion has arisen out of Engelmann's changing schemes to relate all the forms in this species. In his *Plantae Lindheimerianae* in 1850, before he was combining, he had *M. vivipara* described as it is still found in Nuttall's type locality, and at the same time he described as a separate species a *Mammillaria radiosa* with the type locality, "Sterile, sandy soil on the Pierdenales" (the Pedernales River in central Texas). This plant he described as having 20 to 30 radials, being columnar and having different seeds from *M. vivipara*. It is a very distinct form, treated very fully later by Coulter, and is exactly the form we are discussing here.

But in trying to combine forms, Engelmann later confused an originally clear picture. First, in the *Synopsis of the Cactaceae*, he reduced *M. radiosa* to a variety of *M. vivipara* and put some newly noticed forms, *borealis, neo-mexicana*, and *texana* as subvarieties under it, in so doing expanding his description of *radiosa* and no longer reserving this name for the Texas form. But at the same time he did not lose the identity of the Texas form, since it remained as the subvariety *texana*. Then, still later, swinging back a little the other way, in the *Cactaceae of the Mexican Boundary* he elevated *radiosa* to a subspecies and the three taxa under it to varieties.

Coulter even later returned *M. radiosa* to species status again, and added to it numerous other varieties found all the way to California, giving it the broadest definition of all.

This name, therefore, has many meanings in the literature, but in the present study I use it in the sense of the original description in the *Plantae Lindheimerianae*. It is in no way a synonym of *M. vivipara*, as many have thought, but is a definite Texas and Oklahoma form not found anywhere west of Texas, and its only synonym among Engelmann's names is the subvariety name, *texana*.

It is one of the largest forms of this species, has large, loose-standing tubercles, and extremely fine flowers. It is a localized form of the species and, since no other variety of this cactus grows in its area, identification of field-collected plants should not be a problem.

This may possibly be the Oklahoma form called *Coryphantha radiosa* by Lahman, but her description is so incomplete that it is hard to be certain.

Mammillaria vivipara var. neo-mexicana Eng.
[*Coryphanta neo-mexicana* (Eng.) B. & R.]
   "Spiny Star," "Pincushion," "New Mexico Coryphantha," "Estria del tarde"

DESCRIPTION   PLATE 32
   STEMS: As the species, sometimes growing as single stems, but

usually forming small clusters. Individual stems are spherical at first, becoming short columns when old. The maximum size seems to be 3^1/$_2$ to 4 inches tall by 2^1/$_2$ inches thick. The tubercles measure to ^{1}/$_2$ inch long and are cylindrical or sometimes somewhat flattened from top to bottom and crowded close together.

AREOLES: As the species.

SPINES: Each areole has 20 to 40 slender radial spines to ^{3}/$_8$ of an inch long, white, sometimes with brown or purplish tips. These form a fringe of spines around each areole and interlock with those of neighboring clusters to hide almost completely the flesh of the plant. There are also 6 to 15 central spines on each areole of the adult plant. These are white or yellowish with purplish to light brown tips, grow to ^{3}/$_4$ of an inch long, and spread out in all directions and at all angles from the center of the areole.

FLOWERS: About 1 inch tall and broad, and violet in color, sometimes shading at the center to deep rose. The outer petals are narrow, pointed, and fringed. The inner petals are also very slender and sharp pointed, having smooth edges, and are very deep violet in color. The filaments are green at the bases, becoming pink above. The anthers are orange. The style is as short as the stamens and reddish in color. The stigma lobes are 7 to 10 in number, pure white, short, fat, and not pointed.

FRUITS: Green, oval in shape, and ^{5}/$_8$ to 1^5/$_8$ inches long. The medium brown seeds are approximately ^{1}/$_{16}$ of an inch (about 2 millimeters) long, ovate or almost reniform, with the bodies curved around the ventral, concave, linear hila. The surfaces of the seeds are pitted.

RANGE. The mountain areas of central Colorado and New Mexico, south into Mexico, west into Arizona and east into Texas from El Paso and the Guadalupe Mountains to near Fort Stockton. The plant is very rarely, if ever, found in Texas south or east of Marfa.

REMARKS. This is a comparatively distinct member of this closely knit group. It is fairly easily distinguished from its relatives by the more numerous spines, the more closely crowded and smaller tubercles and the smaller flowers with the short, heavy, white stigma lobes only about ^{1}/$_8$ of an inch long. Its seeds are also distinctive.

Mammillaria vivipara var. *neo-mexicana* is the mountain member of the species. Engelmann once remarked that it was found in the Sandia Mountains at a 13,000-foot altitude. I do not know that it has been seen since at this extreme altitude, but it grows on the hills, and its range takes in all of the high mountains of New Mexico and the Guadalupe and Davis mountains of Texas.

At first, Engelmann called this form subvariety *neo-mexicana* of his *Mammillaria vivipara* subspecies *radiosa*, and later he spoke of it as a variety of the species. He apparently never did consider it a separate species. Small was the first one to elevate it to a separate species, calling it *Cactus neo-mexicanus*, and Nelson

then placed it back into the Mammillarias as a full species. Britton and Rose followed, but called it *Coryphantha neo-mexicana*. It is clearly one of the spiny stars most removed from the typical *M. vivipara* var. *vivipara*, but since the earliest studies concluded it to be part of that species and recent usage seems to have come back to that opinion, we list it here as a variety.

It also became common to list Engelmann's other two subvarieties, *borealis* and *texana* as synonyms of *neo-mexicana*. To do this is to be so superficial as to overlook the differences which Engelmann noticed and outlined carefully when he first separated them, differences of spine numbers and colors, stigmas, flowers, and seeds. To insist on their existence as separate forms is not to deny that there may be intermediate specimens—as Engelmann cautions—nor to state flatly that they are all entirely separate species. The latter position obviously cannot be maintained successfully, and no doubt it was this problem, arising when all of these forms were assigned species rank, that caused the attempt on the part of some students to dismiss them as synonyms. But each of these forms has a separate, continuous range within which it presents consistent characteristics, and we feel constrained to list them as distinct varieties rather than enlarging the description of this form and making it almost meaningless in an attempt to contain them.

Mammillaria vivipara var. borealis Eng.
"Sour Cactus"

DESCRIPTION   PLATE 32

STEMS: As the species, but usually single and only rarely found in small clusters. Individual stems are usually spherical, but when old become more or less egg-shaped. The maximum size seems to be about 3 inches tall by 2 inches in diameter. The tubercles grow to about ^{1}/$_2$ inch long, are closely crowded, and overlap upward.

AREOLES: As the species.

SPINES: Having 12 to 22 white, slender, short radial spines and 3 to 6 central spines which are arranged much like those of the typical variety *vivipara*, one usually turned downward and the other 3 to 5 spreading upward just in front of the upper radials. These centrals, or at least the upper halves of them, are wholly purplish-black or maroon.

FLOWERS: Small, only about 1 to 1^1/$_2$ inches tall and the same in diameter. The petals are ^{3}/$_4$ of an inch or less in length and ^{1}/$_8$ or more in width. The outer petals, about 20 in number, are brownish and fringed; the inner ones are lavender, deep pink, or pale violet, and entire. All petals are sharply pointed. The filaments are pink and the anthers pale orange. The style is about the same length as the stamens, and the stigma has 8 to 12 rather long, slender, pale pink lobes, which are blunt.

FRUITS: Egg-shaped, to about ³/₄ of an inch long, greenish, often becoming brownish or even faintly flushed with brownish red when very ripe. The seeds are very light brown or straw-colored, approximately ¹/₁₆ of an inch (2 millimeters or so) long, oval in shape, with the surface finely pitted. The hilum is near the end of the seed and is round, or nearly so.

RANGE. New Mexico from northwest of Santa Fe past Zuni northwest into Colorado, Arizona, and Utah.

REMARKS. This small cactus of the northwestern New Mexico mountains is apparently limited to the western side of the Continental Divide. It has been generally overlooked by students, and we usually find it included in their files of several other forms, while their descriptions of those other forms have therefore usually been broadened to include it, leading to much confusion.

Engelmann first called this cactus *Mammillaria vivipara* var. *radiosa* subvar. *borealis*. A number of later writers ignored it entirely, but Britton and Rose listed it as a synonym of their *Coryphantha neo-mexicana*. Backeberg seems to leave it as a synonym of that form, which, however, he reduced to a variety of the species. How it ever got so closely connected with variety *neo-mexicana* is hard to understand. It seems to be the nearest relative west of the Continental Divide of the typical northeastern form, variety *vivipara*, even as variety *radiosa* can be regarded as the nearest southerly relative of that typical variety. It is much further removed from variety *neo-mexicana* by several characters. It is closer to variety *radiosa* than to any of the southern or western varieties; but it remains a much smaller plant in over-all size and in size of tubercles; it has fewer radial spines, darker-colored centrals, and probably the smallest flowers of the group, while variety *radiosa* has the largest. The size of seeds is about the same in these two cacti, but otherwise they differ.

Its relationship to the other western forms of this complex species is more difficult, and since the variety *borealis* has almost universally been ignored, we find almost no attempts to deal with it in any recent works on these cacti. The reason for this fact is quite interesting.

First of all, in trying to see the reason for resurrecting this all but forgotten name and to understand in general the western forms of this species, which venture into the area covered by our study far more than most people realize, we must face and deal with one of the most remarkably persistent errors in all of cactus study. Almost throughout the literature on cacti we run across the name *Mammillaria aggregata*. Britton and Rose thought there was a plant of this group in New Mexico which they listed under the name *Coryphantha aggregata*, and Mrs. Lahman even had it growing in Oklahoma. There are whole files under this name in most herbaria. It persists to the present, Benson listing *M. vivipara* var. *aggregata* (which apparently included the form variety *borealis*) in his scheme, while Backeberg used *Coryphantha vivipara* var. *aggregata* for a clustering

form of New Mexico and on west. We will never understand the western forms until we understand this persistent name *aggregata*.

Engelmann coined the name in 1848 in *Emory's Report*, for a plant observed on the Gila River. His description of this plant was very incomplete, as he did not see its flowers or fruits. He said it made hemispherical clusters of several feet across with up to 100 to 200 heads. He started the whole misunderstanding by a simple speculation that *Mammillaria aggregata*, "appears to be allied to *M. vivipara*." How the plant he saw on the Gila ever reminded him of the small, flat clusters of the species *M. vivipara* in the first place is hard to see, but it did, and the name has been applied to that species very often, even down to the present.

Engelmann had made a snap judgment on this plant without even seeing flowers or fruits. He was wrong, and as soon as he knew he had made an error he corrected it manfully. Concerning this report, he wrote in the *Report of the Ives Exploration* in 1861, as follows: "*Cereus phoeniceus*, Pacif. Rail. Rep. Synop. Cact., *Echinocereus coccineus* Wisliz. Rep. N. Mex., note 9. This is *Mammillaria aggregata*, Emory's Report, 1848, and the 'Aggregated Cactus' of the explorers of the western parts of New Mexico and the Gila regions."

How anything could be more clear than the above statement is hard to see. Engelmann is stating that the name is an error, actually a synonym of *Echinocereus coccineus*, and that there is no Mammillaria which should bear the name *aggregata* at all. Early students such as Coulter, Rydberg, and Wooton were aware of the true identity of this plant and did not list the name among the Mammillarias. But Britton and Rose apparently overlooked the retraction of the name and set up a species, *Coryphantha aggregatus*. What their plant of this name was apparently cannot be known for sure.

Engelmann would no doubt be astounded could he know that one hundred years after his retraction of the name it is still listed in the most respected works on the cacti of the area. This illustrates the harm that can be done by the easily tossed-off speculation, and should certainly prompt authors to restrain themselves from casual speculations.

Since all modern accounts of the *M. vivipara* complex in New Mexico and Arizona which I have examined still list this defunct name, usually as a vague catchall, it becomes our task to sort out the specimens filed under the name and place them in the valid taxa in which they really belong. When we do that we find that they all settle into the valid taxa comfortably, but that the process resurrects some almost forgotten varieties and that it extends the known range of some others much farther east than is usually recognized.

How variety *borealis*, which hardly clusters at all, was included in a supposed variety *aggregata* of hemispherical masses to 200 heads is hard to see, but once we look for it we find it there. Or specimens may be classified under several other names. For instance, Boissevain's *Coryphantha radiosa* is mainly variety *borealis*, but his description of it is skewed a little to include *M. vivipara* var. *arizonica*. He never suspected that variety *arizonica* grew in Colorado, but some of the specimens upon which he based his *C. radiosa* were clearly this form.

If we can clear away the accretion of the years of confusion over such errors, we find growing, never profuse but surprisingly widespread, here and there upon the hills and lower mountains of northwest New Mexico and southwest Colorado and into northeast Arizona as well as Utah, a small, usually single-stemmed spiny star with few and very weak radials and few but very dark-colored centrals. It has small flowers, pale by comparison with most of its relatives, and very light brown seeds. It is retiring in habit and appearance, and probably does not mind greatly being overlooked so generally or else being merged with its more robust neighbors. Its name is rather fitting, as it is the most northern form of this species other than the typical variety *vivipara*.

Mammillaria vivipara var. arizonica (Eng.)
[*Coryphantha arizonica* B. & R.]
"Sour Cactus," "Arizona Coryphantha"

DESCRIPTION   PLATE 33

STEMS: Simple or occasionally clustering sparingly to form to 3 or 4 stems. The individual stems are spherical to ovate or conical and robust, becoming sometimes to 4 inches in diameter and as much as 5 inches tall. The tubercles are cylindrical and rather loose-standing, and to 1 inch long.

AREOLES: As the species.

SPINES: With 13 to 20 radial spines which are slender but rigid and long, varying from about $5/8$ to $3/4$ of an inch as a rule, but said to have reached $1 1/4$ inches in length. They are whitish, but not pure white, usually with brown tips. The centrals are 3 to 6 in number, spreading, rather stout, about $5/8$ to $7/8$ of an inch long, and yellow or gray below with deep brown or purplish-brown above.

FLOWERS: Large and showy, about 2 inches in diameter and length, rose-pink to rose-purple in color. The 30 to 40 outer segments are slender and fringed and greenish-brown. The 40 or so inner segments are linear and entire and sharply pointed. The stigma has 7 to 10 white, blunt lobes.

FRUITS: Oval and green. The seeds are approximately $1/16$ of an inch (about $1 3/4$ millimeters) long, broadly egg-shaped, curved, and beaked around the short, oval, greatly concave, ventral hila. They are light brown in color, and pitted.

RANGE. Widely in the far West, and east from northern Arizona into the extreme northwestern corner of New Mexico. Apparently restricted in New Mexico to the area bounded by an arc drawn from near Gallup past Blanco Trading Post and into Colorado near Farmington.

REMARKS. One of the reasons the New Mexico members of this species complex have been so hard to understand is that it has been assumed that this variety does not grow in that state, but that it is strictly an Arizona specialty. Such may be the effect of a name.

But Engelmann in his original description gave no limit to this plant's eastern penetration, saying only, "from the Colorado eastward," and the detailed maps of its range, such as that in Benson's *Arizona Cacti* show it covering the whole of northeastern Arizona right up to the border. Since we know that cacti do not respect state boundaries, it is only logical to expect it to spill over into neighboring New Mexico. This it does, from about Gallup northward, and when we recognize this fact and take the specimens which really fit this taxon from the collection of various forms put under the erroneous name, *Mammillaria aggregata*, as well as from where they have been deposited under other names, we have a nice array of records for the cactus over the extreme northwestern corner of New Mexico.

M. vivipara var. *arizonica* is a robust form of the species in stem size, spination, and flowers. Although it clusters only sparingly, its stems are large and strong, with long tubercles. Its spines are not numerous as in some forms, but are stouter than those of any form yet discussed under this species. The spines, together with the loose-standing tubercles, give it the appearance of a bold, open-growing, well-protected plant which contrasts in appearance with the smaller, more delicate, more retiring variety *borealis* and variety *vivipara*. It more resembles variety *radiosa* of Texas, but has much more rigid and darker-colored spines. Its flowers are also the only other ones approaching in size and brilliance those of variety *radiosa*. However, they are more pinkish than the deep violet blossoms of the Texas form. On the other hand, the seeds of variety *arizonica* are the closest in size and shape to those of variety *vivipara* of any other form, but they are much lighter in color.

Mammillaria vivipara var. deserti (Eng.) non L. Benson
[*Coryphantha deserti* (Eng.) B. & R.]

DESCRIPTION

STEMS: As the species, except apparently always simple and unbranched. These stems are at first globose, later becoming oval or egg-shaped and growing to a maximum of about 4 inches tall by $3 1/2$ inches thick. They have short, cylindrical tubercles to about $1/2$ inch long which are close-standing and compact, but not overlapping.

AREOLES: As the species.

SPINES: Having 22 to 35 radial spines which are $3/8$ to $3/4$ of an inch long, spreading almost pectinate and interlocking with those of adjacent tubercles. The upper and lower radials are rather slender, but the lateral ones are stout and rigid.

They are all gray, the larger ones usually tipped with brown. There are 5 to 10 central spines, the lower 3 to 5 of these being porrect or spreading outward, heavy, awl-shaped, and 1/4 to 3/8 of an inch long. The upper 2 to 5 of them spread upward, are more slender, and are 1/2 to 5/8 of an inch long. All centrals are straw- or honey-colored below with red-brown tips.

FLOWERS: Small, about 1 inch long and wide. In color these flowers are pale pinkish suffused with cream or tan. The outer segments are brownish and fringed; the inner ones are entire and often described as straw-colored with pinkish tips. There are 5 or 6 whitish stigma lobes.

FRUITS: Short, oval, about 1/2 inch or so long. They remain green in color for a long time, but are sometimes suffused with brown or even faint maroon when very ripe. The seeds are 1/16 of an inch (1 1/2 to 2 millimeters) long, dark brown, pitted, obovate, and somewhat curved around the round or oval, convex or flat, ventral hila.

RANGE. Entering New Mexico from southern Arizona. Found in the strip of New Mexico west and south of Silver City.

REMARKS. Originally described as a California cactus, but soon known from Nevada, this form was later traced east across Arizona. Now we find a population along the Arizona border and a short distance into New Mexico which seems clearly this plant, marking another penetration into our area by a western form and giving this cactus a very wide range.

The cactus as it grows in New Mexico and as described above is not to be confused with another plant described under this name in many accounts of the western cacti. Borg and Boissevain equate this cactus with *Mammillaria alversonii* Coult., a larger, clustering form restricted to southern California. Benson gives for *M. vivipara* var. *deserti* (Eng.) L. Benson a description almost totally unlike that of either Engelmann or Coulter and with limits which would appear to exclude the type itself, listing 15 to 20 slender white radials and only 3 to 5 centrals— white, tipped with brown. Only the small, straw-colored flower of his description is the same as in the earlier descriptions, and it seems obvious that whatever his plant may be it is not the same as what Engelmann and Coulter meant by *M. deserti*— nor is it the cactus we see in southwestern New Mexico.

Be that as it may, we have a cactus with a definite range in New Mexico which duplicates the more western form originally described as *M. deserti*. It is a robust but single-stemmed cactus whose short, compact tubercles are almost completely covered by its very numerous, interlocking spines. Only variety *neomexicana* has such a profuse covering of spines, and the spines of that cactus are white and much more slender. This cactus, with its ashy-gray radials and its brown centrals which are all relatively heavy, gives quite a different impression. It most resembles, of any form in this species, variety *arizonica*, but is much more squat and compact, with much shorter tubercles, and many more and much more appressed, more stout spines than

on that relative. The form, spines, and general appearance of variety *deserti* are similar enough to those of *Echinocactus intertextus* var. *dasyacanthus* Eng. that I have several times felt very foolish for at first mistaking it for that cactus of an entirely different genus.

Originally treated as a separate species, this cactus has been incorporated, along with others, into the broad species complex of *M. vivipara*. If this placement is correct, it is the most distant from the typical form of that species, both in its characters and its range. The population of this cactus found in New Mexico forms a distinct entity there, and must be taken into account in gaining any adequate concept of this complex as it occurs in that state. Whether or not one sees it as the same cactus as the California variety *deserti*, which I believe it to be, no collection of New Mexico cacti is complete without it.

Mammillaria fragrans (Hester)
[*Coryphantha fragrans* Hester]

DESCRIPTION   PLATE 33

STEMS: Almost always occurring singly, very rarely with one or two branches from the base. Becoming conic to cylindrical when older, and growing to a maximum of 8 inches tall by about 3 inches in diameter. The tubercles are 3/8 to 5/8 of an inch long, usually being around 1/2 inch on typical plants. They are soft and oval in shape, being flattened dorsally and somewhat broadened above the base to about 3/8 of an inch wide before they taper toward the tips.

AREOLES: Monomorphic, mature areoles lengthening to form grooves extending nearly to the bases of the tubercles, with white wool in the grooves when they are young, but later bare.

SPINES: There are 20 to 30 slender radials to 1/2 inch long, and white in color. There are 6 to 12 centrals to 5/8 of an inch long, which spread at all angles from the center of the areole. They are mostly purple or very dark brown, only the bases of them being gray; with age they usually become entirely black.

FLOWERS: About 1 1/2 to 2 inches across and tall, cup-shaped or even bell-shaped, magenta or reddish-purple in color. The outer petals are greenish with pink edges fringed with long white hairs. The inner petals are narrow, pointed, reddish-purple shading to light pink at the edges from greenish bases, with edges entire or very slightly ragged near the tips. The filaments are greenish below to pink above. The anthers are orange. The style is about the length of the stamens or a little longer. The stigma has 6 to 12 pure white to pinkish lobes which are long and more or less pointed, but rather thick.

FRUITS: Greenish, becoming yellow-green when ripe, oval in shape, and to 1 inch long. The seeds are kidney or bean shaped, approximately 1/8 of an inch (2 1/2 to 3 millimeters) long, and much flattened. Their translucent surface is rich red-brown and shiny smooth, with no pitting, but with a pattern of minute checks showing through from inner layers when viewed with a microscope. The hilum is ventral or nearly so, oval or oblong.

RANGE. The Big Bend of Texas, from near Sanderson on the east to the Rio Grande west of Alpine, but apparently not north of the southern slopes of the Davis and Van Horn mountains.

REMARKS. Here is yet another form which only the closest observation will reveal to be separate from the complex group just listed. It apparently was not distinguished from *M. vivipara* var. *neo-mexicana* by any of the earlier students, which is not surprising since its armament of spines comes within the range of that variety, and the accounts of some other students can only be understood by assuming that they failed to distinguish it from *M. vivipara* var. *radiosa*. For these reasons it was overlooked until described as a separate species by Hester in 1941. Mr. Hester carried on extensive studies of the seeds of cacti, and no doubt his discovery of this plant with seeds so much larger than those of *M. vivipara* var. *neo-mexicana* and different in almost every detail of shape and surface first caused him to notice its other less marked differences from that plant. It was in the same way, by noticing the remarkable seeds, that I first learned that my supposed variety *neo-mexicana* specimens from near the Rio Grande in the Big Bend were different from those collected farther northwest. Much later I learned that I had stumbled upon Hester's cactus.

There are few definite or measurable characters of the plant body by which to recognize the cactus before it fruits. It is a much larger cactus than variety *neo-mexicana*, growing double the height of that species when at its maximum, and it also differs in that it almost never branches. Its tubercles are also unusual in that they broaden out above their bases and are flattened on their upper sides, this giving them a curious ballooned appearance which seems unique in this form, but which is not always obvious in specimens suffering from drought or winter shrinkage. Its central spines are very dark, the dark coloring extending farther down on them than on any other relatives except perhaps some of the northwestern specimens of *M. vivipara* var. *borealis*.

The flower of *M. fragrans* differs from its relatives in several minor ways. Its petals are shorter. Its stigmas are intermediate in length between those of the eastern *M. vivipara* var. *radiosa* and the western variety *neo-mexicana*, but are usually pure white, and only sometimes a light pink. Its flowers are very fragrant with a sweet scent from which comes its name, while those of variety *neo-mexicana* have almost no scent and those of the eastern *M. vivipara* forms have a very strong and pungent, but very green scent which is not sweet.

Hester seems to have failed to distinguish sometimes between his own new form and the old form, *M. vivipara* var. *radiosa*, and as a result he gives the range of *M. fragrans* as extending almost to Fort Worth, Texas, and into southern Oklahoma. In actuality *M. fragrans* differs almost as completely from variety *radiosa* as it does from the other *M. vivipara* varieties, and the range of variety *radiosa* stops just northeast of where the range of this plant begins.

This cactus may also be part of the *M. vivipara* complex. It is similar enough to it so that the assertion would be easy. Yet with no real evidence for the combination, and with the seeds so different, such a combination seems premature.

This is a rare cactus restricted to the lower Big Bend of Texas, but on some hillsides or in some alluvial valleys it may grow in fairly extensive populations. Perhaps it extends into Texas from Mexico, but this is not known. During some limited trips into the very rough mountains across from the Texas Big Bend I did not observe the cactus.

Mammillaria tuberculosa Eng.
[*Escobaria tuberculosa* (Eng.) B. & R.]

DESCRIPTION   PLATES 34, 35

STEMS: Globular to egg-shaped at first, becoming upright cylinders 1 to 2 inches thick, said to grow to 7 inches tall, but not usually exceeding 5 inches and often much shorter. The stems are single until large, then sprout slowly around their bases to form small clusters. The color of the surface is a dull gray-green. The stem is composed of many separate tubercles usually about $3/8$ of an inch long, but sometimes not over $1/4$ of an inch. These tubercles are practically cylindrical when young, but their bases broaden horizontally so that they become somewhat rhomboid and about as wide as they are tall when old. They are somewhat crowded, and mature tubercles turn upward so that they overlap each other.

AREOLES: Small and round on immature stems. On mature stems a groove runs all the way to the base of each tubercle on its upper side, as the linear extension of the areole from the spinous portion at the tip of the tubercle to the floral part of it in the axil. When young, this groove is filled with wool, but when old only a tuft of this white wool remains in the axillary end of the groove.

SPINES: On each areole there are 20 to 30 radial spines, which are slender but stiff, radiating in all directions around the areole. They are white and vary in size, those at the top of the areole being very small bristles, while those around the sides and bottom of the areole are to $3/8$ of an inch long and rather firm. There are 4 to 9 central spines which are gray-white with purplish ends; 4 of these are always much heavier than the radials, with 3 of them spreading upward and to $5/8$ of an inch long, while the lowest of these 4 always stands abruptly outward or turns a little downward. This lowest central is the heaviest spine of all, and is conspicuous. On young plants there are only these 4 centrals, but with age there may be 3 to 5 more centrals added above the others, standing upright with the earlier upper ones; they are never quite as heavy or as long as the first and are intermediate between those and the radials. There is a definite tendency for the spines to be shed from the older part of the stem, leaving the base bare of spines.

FLOWERS: 3/4 to 1 3/8 inches across and 3/4 to 1 inch tall; opening widely. The color of the flower is a very delicate lavender-white or extremely pale purple. The outer petals are greenish-brown with almost white, fringed edges. They are to 3/4 of an inch long and 1/8 of an inch wide, and there are 16 to 18 of them. The inner petals are 10 to 15 in number, 3/4 to 1 inch long, and only 1/8 of an inch wide, very pale lavender fading to almost white at the edges. The filaments are cream, while the anthers are cream or pale yellowish. The style is white, the same length or just longer than the stamens. The stigma is made up of 5 or 6 white lobes which may be short and thick or slender and to as much as 3/16 of an inch long.

FRUITS: Egg-shaped to oblong, about 3/4 of an inch long, and bright red. The seeds are very small, usually around 1/2 millimeter long, and brown in color, with the surface pitted.

RANGE. The mountains of the Big Bend region of Texas, and from there southward into Mexico, westward across southern New Mexico, and into southern Arizona.

REMARKS. *Mammillaria tuberculosa* is usually spoken of as one of the most common cacti of far west Texas and southern New Mexico. In the trade, plants are shipped by the hundreds from this area under the name *Escobaria tuberculosa*. However, it appears that the species is actually much less common than is usually thought, at least today, and that most of those specimens now in collections under this name are actually another species.

The reasons for this confusion are several, and we must understand them if we are to understand this species. There are several plants known commonly as Escobarias which are very close in most of their characteristics. They are small plants with many spines and small flowers, and it requires painstaking work, usually with a magnifier, to recognize the characters which divide them. We are often reluctant to go to this trouble, and the one thing seized upon to distinguish *M. tuberculosa* from its relatives with a minimum of effort—indeed, the character for which it is named—is an unfortunate choice, since at least two other forms show this fully as much as it does. This is the tendency of these cacti to shed their spines on their older tubercles at the bases of the stems. These old tubercles then become corky and dead-appearing, rather unsightly bumps. Perhaps my own experience with these plants should show the problem, as well as illustrate the differences between the confusing forms.

I remember well when I collected plant after plant, mature specimens of which showed this naked, rather ugly base—so, knowing no better, I had to call them all *M. tuberculosa*. Many of these specimens bloomed, and I thought I had the species. They matched those my collector friends called by that name

and the bins of dealers were full of the same plants under the same name.

But what about its relatives—*M. dasyacantha*, for instance? Try as I might, I couldn't find this closely related form. Everyone was vague about it, and finally I was persuaded that it was merely a minor variation of *M. tuberculosa*, for all practical purposes the same.

During all of this time I had one specimen which appeared slightly different from the others. I was dissatisfied with it because, year after year, it refused to bloom, even when growing beside all of the others which put out their small brownish-pink flowers in numbers. Finally, one June, this plant bloomed—not with flowers like the others, but with flowers nearly twice as large and opening out widely where the others remained at best bell-shaped, and with a clear whitish color where the petals of the others were pinkish with definite brown midlines. Its 5 or 6 white stigma lobes contrasting with the 5 very green stigmas of the common plants emphasized the difference.

Only after discovering these differences did I get my magnifier and compare the spines of these plants, and to my delight I found that my newly flowered specimen had 5 centrals with the upper ones standing upright against the upper radials while the lower one stood out and slightly downward and was especially heavy. Examination showed that my common, brownish-flowered plants all had 7 or more comparatively slender centrals spreading irregularly. Much later I was able to observe that my reluctant bloomer had brown seeds, while my other plants had black seeds. I had *M. tuberculosa* and *M. dasyacantha* side by side, both with naked, corky bases.

M. tuberculosa, when known from its relatives, is apparently a plant much less often seen than it is thought to be, while that similar cactus coming in such numbers out of the Big Bend and called so widely by this name is really its relative, *M. dasyacantha*. *M. tuberculosa* is easily distinguished when in bloom by the details of its larger and much more delicately colored flowers, but it blooms reluctantly in cultivation. It is much more difficult to distinguish without the flowers, but the arrangement of the central spines—particularly the presence of the stout lower central standing out by itself—is the best clue. In general, it is a smaller plant than *M. dasyacantha*, its spines having purplish ends instead of brown, and not as completely obscuring the stem as do those of its relatives.

This cactus has also been referred to by the name *Mammillaria strobiliformis*, and this name still persists in some authors, making it necessary for us to review the origins of these names so that we may evaluate them.

In 1850 Scheer described what most agree was this cactus, giving it the name *M. strobiliformis*. His description, however, was vague, and in 1856, when Engelmann first studied the plant, he thought he had a different cactus and originated a new name for it, *M. tuberculosa*. Later, realizing his mistake, Engelmann tried to retract his own name, stating, in the "Corrections to the Cactaceae of the Boundary": "*M. tuberculosa* is clearly identical with *M. strobiliformis* Scheer in Salm. Hort. Dyck (1850), as I have ascertained by a careful examination of the original specimens (now dead) in the collection of Prince Salm. Mr. Scheer's name, having the priority, must be substituted for mine."

It would seem that nothing could be more clear, and the periodic return to the use of the name *M. strobiliformis* even to today is based upon this statement. But the ways of taxonomic priority often lead through mazes of cross-references, and it was soon noted that the name *M. strobiliformis* had already been twice used before Scheer's use of it. In 1848 Muehlenpfordt had applied the name to what is generally agreed to be the already described *M. sulcata* Eng. Then, also in 1848, in the Wislizenus Report, Engelmann himself had described a plant under that same name. There has been rare agreement through the years since that Engelmann's *M. strobiliformis* of 1848 is actually *Echinocactus (Neolloydia) conoidea*, first described by De Candolle in 1829. This leaves it of little interest to us here, but all of this does render the *M. strobiliformis* of Scheer twice a homonym and, therefore, an invalid name for the plant we are discussing, and it leaves Engelmann's *M. tuberculosa* as, after all—unless there is another turn to the maze which we have missed—the first name for this plant valid under taxonomic rules.

Borg repeats Quehl's list of five varieties under this species, but the descriptions of these are very general and seem almost impossible to distinguish in actuality. Several of them appear to indicate the two forms listed next in our study, seeming to show characters clearly outside the limits of this species. However, I have noticed that the New Mexico specimens of this species are often slightly different from the Texas ones, being smaller, with more rounded, often almost spherical, fruits. Further study of these differences might lead toward some of Quehl's varieties or might show these differences as only environmental.

The name *Escobaria orcuttii* appeared in a catalog, without description, in 1925. In 1926 Rose mentioned a *Neolloydia orcuttii*. It was said by him to have 15 centrals, but a rose-colored flower and 6 long, white stigmas. These characters would seem to give a curious intermediate between *M. tuberculosa* and *M. dasyacantha*. But no location for the plant was ever given except "U. S. A. (Texas?)." The plant has not been reported by any recent students, and it seems best to dismiss it entirely, at least until it can be found and described exactly.

Mammillaria dasyacantha Eng.
[*Escobaria dasyacantha* (Eng.) B. & R.]

DESCRIPTION   PLATES 34, 35

STEMS: Practically spherical when young, becoming elongated and cylindrical when older. The young plants consist of single stems, and they often remain this way all their lives, but occasionally old plants sprout at their bases to form small clusters of several stems. They sometimes grow to a maximum of 8 inches tall and 2³/₄ inches thick. Their tubercles are cylindrical and straight in young plants, but become definitely flattened, somewhat overlapping, and ³/₈ to ¹/₂ inch long on old plants. The oldest tubercles on the bases of the plants usually become bare of spines and remain as discolored, dead-appearing bumps.

AREOLES: The spine-bearing portions of the areoles are at the tips of the tubercles, the floral part in the axils, and the tubercles are marked all the way to their bases by grooves, woolly when young but nearly naked when old, which are the narrowed portions of the areoles connecting the two extremities. Immature areoles consist of merely the small, rounded spinous portion.

SPINES: Radial spines 25 to at least 35 in number, radiating all around the areole. These are white in color, usually about ¹/₂ inch long, but sometimes to almost a full inch in length. They are very slender, the upper ones being almost bristlelike. There are also from 7 to as many as 17 centrals which fill the center of each areole and spread irregularly in every direction. These are slender, some of them being almost as slender as the radials. They vary in length, most being about ⁵/₈ of an inch long, but occasionally some are as short as ³/₈ of an inch, and some—particularly the upper ones—sometimes grow to a full inch. The lower parts of them are white, while the tips are reddish-brown.

FLOWERS: 1 inch tall and ¹/₂ to ³/₄ of an inch across, not opening widely, whitish to pale pink in color. The outer petals are ¹/₂ to ⁵/₈ of an inch long, ³/₁₆ of an inch wide, and pointed, with the edges fringed. The midlines of these are greenish-brown, fading to whitish at the edges. There are 8 to 10 of them. There are 13 to 16 inner petals, which are the same width and length, and taper gradually to pointed tips. They have brownish midlines; the edges are tan, whitish, or pink. The filaments are pale pink or cream, the anthers bright yellow. The style is bright green and ends in 4 or 5 very short, very green stigma lobes which are deeply grooved on their ventral sides.

FRUITS: The fruits of this plant are egg-shaped to somewhat elongated, ¹/₂ to ³/₄ of an inch long, and dark red or scarlet. The seeds are small, practically round, about ¹/₂ to 1 millimeter long, pitted deeply on their surfaces, and a shiny black color.

RANGE. The mountains of the lower Big Bend region of Texas, extreme southern New Mexico, and south into Mexico.

REMARKS. In extreme southwestern Texas this is the common species of the group often called Escobarias. It is also the largest species of the group. It is found on slopes and ledges in the mountains, and even on the summits of the higher mountains, often being found growing in the moss-filled crevices of high, exposed rock surfaces. In fact, some of those locations show many young plants without any mature ones, apparently because the seeds have germinated where there is too little soil to support them to maturity. I had to bring home some of these miniature specimens from rocky crevices near the summits of the Chisos Mountains and grow them several years before they put on mature spination, bloomed and fruited, and I knew they were this species. It is interesting to speculate about the means by which seeds are distributed to these high locations. I would suspect that birds deposit them there after eating the fruits of lower-growing mature plants.

The distinguishing characters of *M. dasyacantha* were discussed in connection with the preceding species, the other species with which this one is so widely confused, and under whose name I have seen scores of these cacti being distributed. Without flowers *M. dasyacantha* is recognized by its comparatively thicker stems, its numerous, slender central spines spreading irregularly and without a conspicuous, heavier central standing outward or downward in the areole. With its flowers it is easy to distinguish, because its flowers do not open widely, and they have conspicuously green stigmas, fewer outer petals, and more as well as broader inner petals than the flowers of *M. tuberculosa*. When fruited it may be told by its shiny black seeds which are so different from those of *M. tuberculosa* that Hester felt it necessary to propose a separate genus, *Escobesseya*, with this species as its type species.

It seems important to note that the juvenile plants of *M. dasyacantha* are so markedly different in almost all characters from the adults as to be taken for other forms. These young plants are spherical, sometimes even with depressed tops. When very young their tubercles do not possess any grooves, they have 18 to 22 white, translucent radial spines 1/8 of an inch long, and they have uniformly only 2 central spines per areole, one pointing directly upward and one downward, each 3/16 of an inch long. By the time the plants get to be about 1 inch in diameter, the new tubercles begin to have short grooves, the radials begin to be up to 1/4 of an inch long, and there begin to be 4 centrals to the areole arranged as points of a cross and to 1/2 inch long. When the plant is about 1 3/4 inches in diameter and height more centrals start to appear, and soon the plants begin to lengthen out and take on their adult appearance.

Although this cactus is fairly common, it is a plain one in all of its stages, and the extent to which both this and the previous species have been ignored by almost everyone may be seen by the fact that neither of them seems to have been given a common name, even in the local area.

Mammillaria duncanii (Hester)
[*Escobesseya duncanii* Hester]

DESCRIPTION   PLATE 35

ROOTS: Having one, or often several fleshy, carrot-like tap-

roots 1/4 to 1 inch in diameter and sometimes to as much as a foot long before tapering.

STEMS: Practically spherical to broadly ovate or somewhat conical, to about 2 inches tall by 1 1/4 inches in diameter. The stems are usually single, but a few double- or triple-stemmed specimens have been seen. The stem is covered by small tubercles about 1/8 of an inch long.

AREOLES: Monomorphic, being elongated into a groove from the spinous portion on the tips of the tubercle to the floral portion in the axil, with some white wool in the axillary portion at first.

SPINES: There are 24 to about 40 radial spines which are slender, straight, 3/16 to 3/8 of an inch long, and white or white with very slightly brownish tips. There are 3 to 16 central spines, although the usual number is about 8. These spread very widely and are around 3/8 of an inch long, white, tipped with light brown.

FLOWERS: 5/8 to 3/4 of an inch long and about 1/2 inch wide, not opening widely. They are pale pink, or whitish with pinkish zones. The ovary is smooth and rounded. The outer perianth segments are pointed, the outermost with a few cilia on their margins. They are pinkish with whitish edges. The inner segments are entire, pointed, their midlines pink and their edges whitish. The filaments are whitish, the anthers pale orange. The stigma has 4 to 6 yellow or sometimes almost chartreuse lobes.

FRUITS: Club-shaped, 1/2 to 3/4 of an inch long and about 3/16 of an inch wide, not including the persistent perianth, becoming bright red when ripe. The seeds are practically spherical, black in color, with the surface pitted and the hila basal.

RANGE. A small area of Brewster County, Texas, a few miles west and north of Terlingua, Texas. Said to have been collected also in New Mexico, but this fact has not been verified.

REMARKS. This obscure little cactus was described in 1945 by the very meticulous observer of Big Bend cacti, J. Pinckney Hester. He described it under the name of *Escobesseya duncanii*. It has hardly been seen since.

I was fortunate to receive a number of specimens of this species from Mr. Homer Jones, a dealer friend in Alpine. He had gotten them from the type locality a few miles north of Terlingua, Texas, and was so good an observer himself that he recognized he had something unusual. Although both Mr. Jones and I have searched in the area since that time, we have not been so fortunate as to collect the cactus again. Neither has it appeared in the large number of cacti from the general region passing through his business. I believe that it is extremely rare.

Along with the giving of the type locality in Brewster County, Texas, in his original description of the plant, Mr. Hester added that it was also found "in a low range of mountains a few miles west of Hot Springs, New Mexico." This has prompted much searching for the species in New Mexico. I have searched for it there myself without success. Some have reported finding it in New Mexico, but the two or three of these plants from New Mexico labeled thus which I have been privileged to examine in herbaria have definitely not been this form. They appear to be the smaller form which *M. tuberculosa* often takes in New Mexico; one of them with brown seeds which prove this identification. Therefore, I think that the question of whether the plant grows in New Mexico is still in doubt. Hester may have overstated the range of the cactus because of misidentifying some New Mexico specimens, as he did that of *M. fragrans* by including with it some specimens of *M. vivipara* var. *radiosa*. Another interesting possibility is that the New Mexico in his article is a misprint and he meant to refer to Hot Springs, Texas, which is in Brewster County. However this may be, it seems necessary to doubt the existence of this cactus in such a discontinuous range in New Mexico until obvious specimens of it come forth from that state, and there seem to be none so far.

In the general characteristics of its spines, its flowers, its fruits and seeds, the cactus is very close to *M. dasyacantha*. Except for certain peculiarities, it might pass for a dwarf form of that cactus. Its seeds are so close to those of *M. dasyacantha* that Hester placed it with that species in his proposed new genus, *Escobesseya*, apart from all others. It is, however, set off from *M. dasyacantha* by the unusual fleshy taproot, by its smaller size and its yellow stigma lobes. It is a most interesting, but very unobtrusive little rarity.

Mammillaria albicolumnaria (Hester)
[*Escobaria albicolumnaria* Hester]
"The White Column," "The Silverlace Cactus"

DESCRIPTION   PLATE 36

STEMS: Oblong or cylindrical almost from the beginning, nearly always single, only a few plants having been seen with 2 or 3 stems. These stems are said to grow to 10 inches tall, but are rarely seen over 5 inches. The maximum diameter seems to be about 2½ inches. The tubercles of the stem are about ⅜ of an inch long, tapering to points from rhomboid bases about as wide as they are tall. The bases of old plants become naked of spines in most cases.

AREOLES: Monomorphic, but elongated on mature stems to run the whole length of the tubercle, the spinous part at the tip, the floral part in the axil, and the rest of the areole a narrow groove connecting the two. On younger specimens the areoles usually extend only part way down the tubercles. There is white wool in the grooves when they are young, but most of this disappears with age.

SPINES: Each areole has 25 to sometimes at least 35 radial spines, which are fine and some of them almost bristle-like but which are very rigid and brittle. They are to ⅜ of an inch long, are very white in color, and are somewhat translucent. There are also 11 to as many as 17 central spines to ⅝ of an inch long. They are heavier than the radials and fill up the center of the areole, spreading in all directions. They are pink or very light red when growing, then translucent white with red-brown tips. The spines are all very brittle.

FLOWERS: Small, not opening widely, but remaining funnel-shaped. They are pink in color and are usually only ⅜ to ⅝ of an inch wide and ¾ to 1 inch tall. The outer petals are greenish-brown in the midlines with whitish edges fringed all the way to the pointed tips. There may be 16 to 26 of them. The inner petals are 25 to 26 in number, pale pink to whitish, narrow, and pointed in shape, and their edges are not fringed. They are about ⅛ of an inch wide. The filaments are white and the anthers yellow. The style is shorter than the stamens and pink in color. The stigma is made up of 3 to 7 white or pale pink lobes which are short and thick.

FRUITS: On this cactus the fruits are oblong or club-shaped, to ⅝ of an inch long and ¼ of an inch thick. The lower half of the fruit remains greenish in color when ripe, but the upper half becomes a pale yellowish or apricot color. The seeds are brown, pitted on the surface, and about 1 millimeter long.

RANGE. Found only in the extreme southwestern corner of Brewster County, Texas, near the localities of Terlingua and Lajitas.

REMARKS. This little cactus was not found by the early students who hunted cacti in Texas, probably because of the limited size and the ruggedness of the area in which it grows, one of the most inaccessible locations in the Big Bend. It was first described in 1941, and very few people saw it for some years after that. In recent years, however, dealers have had crews of men combing the mountains of the Big Bend for cacti, and hundreds of this species have gone into the trade, mostly under the name of *Mammillaria (Escobaria) dasyacantha*.

Some students would like to combine this cactus with the three just listed into one species, but it is impossible to do this without ignoring the differences in their seeds which are great enough so that Hester, who no doubt observed more of them alive than any other student, felt it necessary even to place them in different genera. And this cactus is the one of the four which has spines and flowers most like *M. dasyacantha* but seeds like *M. tuberculosa*, so that it cannot well be placed as a variety of either.

In general plant and spine characters this form seems very much like *M. dasyacantha*. It never grows as large, however, and usually does not cluster. It is set off from that species by the translucent whiteness and the brittleness of its spines, which break easily upon handling, rather than by their numbers or arrangement. I have often demonstrated this character by breaking spines off a specimen with the pressure of a finger. This may seem a small point upon which to base a species, but there are other confirming characters. Its many more numerous petals, white stigmas, greenish-apricot fruits, and brown, different shaped seeds set it apart effectively from *M. dasyacantha,* with its fewer petals, green stigmas, scarlet or deep red fruits, and black seeds.

Backeberg, on the other hand, considers it as synonymous with Quehl's variety *durispina* of *M. tuberculosa.* However, the spines themselves very easily show it is not *M. tuberculosa,* as it has too many of them and lacks the heavy lower central which is characteristic of that cactus. Add to that the great difference in flower form, size, number of petals; the pale color of our plant's fruits as compared with the rich red of those of *M. tuberculosa;* and the size of its seeds, which are up to twice those of that species, and it seems it cannot be put under that species either.

So *M. albicolumnaria* seems to stand, a charming little "white column" from the very wildest mountains of the Texas Big Bend, which has become such a favorite with collectors as to be the only one of these four to possess a generally used common name.

Mammillaria varicolor (Tieg.)
[*Escobaria varicolor* (Tieg.) Backbg.]

DESCRIPTION   PLATE 37

STEMS: Apparently single except when injured, in which case they branch to form several heads. Normal stems are egg-shaped, to 5 inches tall and nearly as broad with tubercles to about $1/2$ inch long, conical from broadly flattened bases, turning upward to overlap greatly when old.

AREOLES: On mature stems the areoles are elongated to run as narrow grooves from the spinous portions at the tips of the tubercles to the floral portions in the axils. They are naked except for large tufts of white wool at the floral region. This wool makes the growing tips of the plants very fuzzy, and it persists on old tubercles, making the axils woolly.

SPINES: There are 15 to 20 very slender, white, semitranslucent radial spines. Some of them are to $1/4$ of an inch long, but many of them, especially the upper ones, are weak bristles as short as $1/8$ of an inch long. There are usually 4, but occasionally 5 centrals, which are to about $1/2$ inch long, heavier than the radials, and yellowish at the bases, with the upper part of each central brownish or purplish. They are semitranslucent and hornlike. The lower central stands out, perpendicular to the plant body or downward, while the 3 or 4 upper centrals spread fanwise in front of the upper radials.

FLOWERS: Almost pure white, pink, or very pale rose in color. They are $3/4$ of an inch long and $1^{1}/4$ inches in diameter. The outer petals are 11 or 12 in number, $3/4$ of an inch long, fringed all the way on their edges, and brownish with pinkish edges. The inner petals are 26 or 27 in number, 1 inch long

and $1/8$ of an inch wide, pointed, their edges smooth, and various in color, as above. The filaments and anthers are bright yellow. The style is a little longer than the stamens and white. The stigma has 5 or 6 white lobes which are about $1/8$ of an inch long and slender.

FRUITS: Ellipsoidal or sometimes slightly curved club-shaped, with the wilted perianth persistent. Approximately $1/2$ to $5/8$ of an inch long by only $3/16$ to $1/4$ of an inch in diameter. In color, when ripe, they are a medium bright rose-red. They ripen in August.

RANGE. Originally given only as southwestern Texas. I have collected specimens from only a small range running from near Marathon, Texas, to about 12 miles north of Alpine, Texas.

REMARKS. This is a very obscure little cactus which has no doubt been mistaken many times for other forms. It takes a keen eye to recognize it from the stem characters alone. When it blooms, however, the differences of the flowers from all other forms are obvious. Tiegel says that the flowers vary from almost white to carmine rose, for which variation he named it. Most which I have seen were very nearly pure white to a very pale rose in color. This is vastly different from the magenta or purple of the other forms most similar to it. Beyond this the yellow filaments and less numerous stigma lobes distinguish it from them.

In his original description of it Tiegel called it *Coryphantha (Escobaria) varicolor,* apparently not wishing to commit himself as to which of these no doubt too strictly drawn genera it really belonged with. There was good reason for doubt as to which of these microgenera it really belonged to, since the fruits are practically the only means of distinguishing the two microgenera, and the fruits of this species were never described. Backeberg, however, considered it an Escobaria. Since I have observed the fruits, which proved to be red in color, if I thought it necessary to place it in either of these microgenera, I would have to agree with Backeberg and place it in *Escobaria.*

Tiegel described the cactus as always consisting of a single stem, which seems to be correct in its normal growth. However, the finest specimen I have is a very large old plant which was apparently injured after reaching a diameter of about 3 inches, and which then put out a cluster of five new heads. I have observed numerous specimens with such form in the undisturbed wild population, but each of them shows clearly an injury to the original growing tip.

Tiegel only lists the range of his plant as southwestern Texas. This takes in an immense territory, and is of little value in trying to locate the cactus. It has been so seldom reported since his description that little by way of more specific range can be given. Even Backeberg remarks that he had one specimen sent to him from Texas, but does not locate its place of origin.

The only specimens I have seen have been those I collected in a small area from the Pena Blanca Mountains southeast of Marathon, Texas, to the hills just north of Alpine. Whether the range is any larger than this remains to be seen. It must be rare in all of its range.

Mammillaria hesteri (Wright)
[*Coryphantha hesteri* Wright]

DESCRIPTION   PLATE 37

STEMS: Spherical to egg-shaped, to 3 inches tall and nearly as wide. They may occur singly, but usually cluster very rapidly to form irregular clumps up to more than a foot across. Each stem is covered by tubercles which are cylindrical when young, then tapering and turning upward from broad, flattened bases and up to $1/2$ inch long when old.

AREOLES: Roundish on immature stems, then on mature stems elongating to form grooves running almost all of the way to the axils, with the flowers produced at the ends of these grooves. Maturing stems show all degrees of the lengthening of the areoles. There is only a very small tuft of wool in the base of the groove at first, which usually soon disappears.

SPINES: On mature heads there are 14 to 20 radial spines. They radiate evenly around the areole, but the upper ones are much longer and heavier than the others, the lower ones being only $1/8$ to $1/4$ of an inch long, while the upper ones are often $1/4$ to $1/2$ inch long. In each areole there is one spine markedly heavier than the rest and standing upright against the more slender upper radials behind it. This has been considered just a heavier radial by all who have described the cactus, but I have known people to think it a central spine and so misidentify the plant. The distinction here is very fine, as the spine does seem to arise from the interior of the areole within the circle of the radials. On young stems there are only 12 or 13 short, equal, radiating spines. On plants from the type locality all spines are very white and translucent at first, later developing gray opaqueness with tips of red or purplish-brown. However, specimens from near Sanderson, Texas, all have gray or tan bases, with the upper two-thirds of each spine red or purple-brown. All spines are more or less flattened.

FLOWERS: Mauve, 1 to $1^1/2$ inches across and tall. The outer petals, about 8 in number, grow to about $3/16$ of an inch wide, are greenish to pinkish, and are fringed with long, white hairs. The inner petals, about 22 to 27 in number, grow to about $1/2$ inch long and $3/16$ of an inch or slightly less in width, are bluntly pointed, and have edges smooth or slightly ragged. They are mauve, darkest at the tips. The filaments are white to rose, and the anthers are orange-yellow. The style is slightly longer than the stamens and greenish or yellowish pink. There are 4 to 6 short, stout, rough, cream-colored or white stigma lobes.

FRUITS: Unknown.

RANGE. A small area a few miles southeast of Alpine, Texas, and another small area a short distance west of Sanderson, Texas.

REMARKS. This and the next species are two of several diminutive cacti occurring in very limited areas just south and southeast of Marathon, Texas. Each of these areas is so small as to be only a few miles across, and is all included in only two or three ranches.

M. hesteri was first discovered by J. P. Hester, and he wrote briefly of it in 1930. It was officially described by Wright in 1932 as *Coryphantha hesteri*. Immediately, even though it is a small and rather insignificant cactus, it became a sought-after novelty. The large clusters which used to be available all seem to have been removed, and now one has to search well to find even a small specimen. Since it occurs in such limited areas, it would be very easy for it to be exterminated by too much gathering. I am glad to learn that one of the ranches on which it grows is now closed by the owner to all cactus digging. This should give it an opportunity to increase its sadly depleted population.

Only within the past three years a new stand of this cactus was discovered a short distance west of Sanderson. The plants from this location are identical to those of the type locality except that their spines are much darker in color and the stems are more egg-shaped and thus taller.

In spite of the fact that I have grown this cactus for six years and it has bloomed most of these years, my specimens have never set fruit. Neither have I been fortunate enough to find fruits on wild plants. Therefore I cannot contribute the description of the fruits of this species, which apparently has never been given.

Mammillaria nellieae (Croiz.) Croiz.
[*Coryphantha minima* Baird, *Coryphantha nellieae* Croiz.]

DESCRIPTION   PLATE 37

STEMS: Egg-shaped or cylindrical and very small, usually under 1 inch tall and to $3/4$ of an inch in diameter, but occasionally to as much as $1^3/4$ inches tall. The stems are usually single, but sometimes branch above the base. The tubercles covering the stem are conic and up to about $1/16$ of an inch long.

AREOLES: Each tubercle has a broad, deep, naked groove running the full length of its upper side, which is the linear, monomorphic areole running from the spinous portion at the tip of the tubercle to the floral portion in the axil.

SPINES: There are 13 to 15 definite radial spines which are $1/16$ to $1/8$ of an inch long and which lie flat against the plant all around the areole. They vary from rather slender to fairly heavy. Besides this there are 3 other spines, much heavier and to about ¼ of an inch long which stand upright in front of and curve slightly backward to lie directly upon the upper radials. Two of these are heavy and spread upward, forming a rather distinct V. The third is always somewhat smaller, and bisects the V formed by the first two. Some authorities have called these 3 spines centrals and others have considered them only extra-heavy radials, this latter reckoning giving a maximum of 18 radials. All spines are pinkish when growing, then becoming yellowish until fading to gray. All spines are also unique in shape, being round and maintaining their full thickness from the bases to the very tips, these tips being then suddenly sharp-pointed. This gives the spines somewhat of a club-shaped appearance.

FLOWERS: Rose-purple in color, about ¾ of an inch tall and ⅝ to 1 inch in diameter. The outer petals are short and greenish with pink, fringed edges. The inner petals are about ⅜ of an inch long and about ⅛ of an inch wide, rose-purple, and bluntly pointed, with smooth edges. The filaments are greenish and the anthers pale orange. The style is short, and the stigma has 8 green lobes.

FRUITS: Egg-shaped and very small, being usually ⅛ to ¼ of an inch long, green in color, sometimes with a faint yellowish blush, with the dried perianth remaining upon them. The seeds are about ½ millimeter long, blackish, with smooth surfaces.

RANGE. Known only from the type locality a few miles south of Marathon, in Brewster County, Texas.

REMARKS. This is another of the dwarf cacti found in Brewster County, Texas. It grows in crevices of limestone ledges on a few hills just south of Marathon. It is often so imbedded in the moss of these crevices that the plant itself is almost wholly covered. In such situations it is surprising to see the beautiful purplish flowers rising up above the moss from the wholly unseen cactus below. There are only a few slopes upon which the plants grow openly and exposed.

These little cacti are interesting to see when grown in proper surroundings so that they are healthy, but this is not easy to arrange. They need very good drainage so that they do not rot, but also must have frequent waterings, since these tiny plants cannot store much water within themselves. They need heat and sun, but appreciate being shaded with something which breaks the direct rays of the sun just a little. I know of no collector who has succeeded in keeping specimens of this species alive more than a couple of years, yet the life-span of the plant must be much longer than that.

This cactus is tiny, but the problems with its names are large. It has become almost universally known by the name, *Coryphantha nellieae*, but the name *Coryphantha minima* was given to it in its first description and has precedence. The first of these names was given to it in a description written by Croizat in the January and February, 1934, issue of *Torreya*. Strangely, Croizat seemed totally unaware that Ralph O. Baird had already described the cactus under the name *Coryphantha minima* in

the *American Botanist*, 37 (4), 150–151, 1931. Unaccountably, all authorities since that time have omitted mention of this earlier description by Baird and used only the later name. Baird's description is in every way more complete and official than Croizat's, except that it lacks the Latin description, but this cannot disqualify it, as 1931 antedated the rule requiring Latin descriptions.

Most recently, Backeberg transfers the species to *Escobaria*, calling it *Escobaria nellieae* (Croiz.) Backbg. He says the fruit is unknown. This error would have been avoided if he had referred to Baird's description where the fruit was accurately described as being green, which is a *Coryphantha* characteristic.

Croizat himself had already made the standard argument over whether the cactus is a Coryphantha or an Escobaria unnecessary by writing, "In the course of a recent study of the Cactaceae I have come to the conclusion that the following transfer may be desirable: *Mammillaria nellieae* (Croiz.) comb. nov.— *Cory. nellieae* Croiz. in Torreya 34: 15. 1934." His conclusion here is in line with our approach to this group, but it would seem that under this combination the name of this cactus should by the rules be rather *Mammillaria minima*. This would be true except for one fact, and because of this Baird must lose even in this combination. There had already been a previous *Mammillaria minima* put forth by Reichenbach in Terscheck, Supp. Cact. Verz. 1, for a Mexican cactus. Reichenbach's cactus is now listed as a variety of *M. elongata* DC., but since the name has been used once, it cannot be used again for another plant, so we are left after all with Croizat's *M. nellieae* as the name for our diminutive Texas plant.

The species is easily recognized by the remarkable appearance of the spines, which lie tight against the surface of the plant and preserve their thickness right up to the points, so that they appear very thick for their length and are more like tiny clubs than ordinary spines.

Mammillaria roberti (Berger)
[*Escobaria runyonii* B. & R., *Coryphantha roberti* Berger]
"Runyon's Escobaria," "Junior Tom Thumb Cactus"

DESCRIPTION   PLATE 38

STEMS: Spherical at first, becoming oblong and to about 3 inches tall by 1¼ inches thick. Branching very fast and irregularly to form large, low clumps of dozens of stems. The tubercles covering the stems taper from cylindrical bases and are from 3/16 to ¼ of an inch long.

AREOLES: Round and at the tips of the tubercles on immature stems. On mature stems they develop from oval to almost linear by being prolonged from the spinous portion at the tip of the tubercle into a very narrow, very woolly groove running from halfway to all the way down the upper side of the tubercle. Flowers and new branches are produced from the end of this groove, at or near the axil of the tubercle.

SPINES: There are 20 to 30 slender radial spines which are ³/₁₆ to sometimes almost ¹/₄ of an inch long, white in color, usually barely tipped with brown. There are 5 to at least 10 central spines filling the center of each areole and spreading in all directions. These are ³/₈ to ⁵/₈ of an inch long, the upper ones being much the longer, and are slender. These centrals have white bases, but the upper three-fourths of each one is dark brown, red-brown, or black.

FLOWERS: Very inconspicuous in color, ³/₄ of an inch in diameter and ⁵/₈ of an inch tall, but opening widely. All petals are slender and pointed, buff or tan, with midlines of reddish-brown. The outer ones are fringed and the inner ones may be either with or without fringes. The filaments are pink and the anthers yellow. The style is about ¹/₈ of an inch longer than the stamens and reddish-brown. The stigma has 5 or 6 short, thick lobes which are green, sometimes yellow-green or even brownish-green.

FRUITS: Spherical to egg-shaped, ¹/₄ to ³/₈ of an inch long, scarlet in color.

RANGE. The Rio Grande Valley and its overlooking hills from near McAllen, Texas, to the mouth of the Pecos River. Also found along the west side of the lower Devil's River.

REMARKS. This is undoubtedly one of the most perfectly camouflaged of the cacti. Even large clumps a foot or more in diameter are only a couple of inches high, and the dark-tipped spines blend perfectly with the rocky soil around them and the grasses usually growing up through them and partly covering them. Even the flower is a blending color and gives no aid in locating the plant. Only the scarlet fruit is allowed to advertise, no doubt so that birds and rodents will come and eat them in order to scatter the seeds.

The cactus was discovered by Robert Runyon, a fine student of the cacti of the lower Rio Grande Valley, and it was first described by Britton and Rose as *Escobaria runyoni*. It grows upon the rocky hills overlooking the Rio Grande, being most common near Rio Grande City and around the lower part of what is now the Falcon reservoir. It is still fairly common there, partly because it takes a real search to find it, and partly because it is too insignificant in size and appearance to appeal to those who take home the more beautiful cacti.

While searching along the lower parts of the Devil's River in West Texas for another cactus, we were very surprised to find, growing on the west side of that river, numerous specimens of a cactus identical to this one in all respects. It is clearly the same cactus, and represents a large increase of the known range of this cactus. But this left a large gap between this Devil's River location and the old locations known on the lower Rio Grande, where there was no record of its having been seen. This prompted careful searching, and we have now located the cactus growing all the way past Laredo to Eagle Pass and near Del Rio, so there is in reality one continuous range, much longer than at first thought.

There have been problems over the name for this cactus, all because of the confusion which has existed over genera. In an article in 1929, Berger sought to transfer the whole genus *Escobaria* to *Coryphantha*. In so doing he met a problem with *Escobaria runyoni*, as there already existed a *Coryphantha runyonii*. He attempted to solve the difficulty by re-naming this cactus *Coryphantha roberti*, using the first name of Mr. Runyon for it instead of his surname.

In 1931 Fosberg attempted to do the same thing again and met with the same problem. He coined another new name, *Coryphantha piercei* for this plant.

This system of combination has not caught on, however, perhaps because it did not go far enough. We feel that a combination cannot be avoided, and Britton and Rose's name cannot be preserved, no matter what form this combination takes. Under our proposal to return both of these microgenera to the original genus, *Mammillaria*, this species becomes *Mammillaria roberti*, since this was the first substitute name suggested. This seems especially fitting since it preserves the reference to Dr. Runyon, as was intended.

Mammillaria sneedii (B. & R.)
[*Escobaria sneedii* B. & R.]

DESCRIPTION   PLATE 38

STEMS: To only about 2 inches long and ³/₄ of an inch thick. These small cylindrical stems branch and cluster very greatly to form masses of as many as 100 heads on old specimens. The individual stems are composed of many tiny, cylindrical, green tubercles ¹/₁₆ to ³/₁₆ of an inch long.

AREOLES: Round or nearly so on immature stems, lengthening somewhat on mature stems to form short grooves running from the spinous portion of the areoles at the tips of the tubercles to at most one-third of the way down toward the axils. Flowering or branching occurs at the ends of these short grooves. There is a little white wool in the groove.

SPINES: The tubercles are almost entirely obscured by the many white spines. There are 24 to 45 radiating outer spines, which are about ¹/₈ of an inch long and very slender, but rigid. There are 13 to 17 central spines, which are slightly heavier than the radials and ¹/₈ to ⁵/₁₆ of an inch long. These centrals are all spreading and lie against the radials, except for the middle one out of the center of the areole, which often stands outward and downward at an angle. All spines are white when mature, but pinkish when growing, giving the tip of a growing stem a pinkish color.

FLOWERS: Small—about ¹/₂ inch tall and broad—not opening

widely, and pink to pale rose in color. The outer petals are narrow, with fringed edges. The midlines are rose and they are edged in very pale pink. The inner petals are the same color, but paler. Their edges are fringed at least half of the way to the pointed tips. There are also sometimes notches in the otherwise entire margins of these petal ends. The filaments are pink, the anthers bright orange. The style is longer than the stamens. The stigma has 3 or 4 slender, white lobes.

FRUITS: About 1/4 of an inch thick, almost spherical, but a little longer than they are thick. They become a deep pink when ripe. The seeds are brown, pitted on the surface, and less than 1/16 of an inch (about 1 millimeter) long.

RANGE. Known only from the Franklin Mountains between El Paso, Texas, and Las Cruces, New Mexico.

REMARKS. The tiny, white stems of this little cactus are insignificant individually, but in an old plant made up of dozens of them, the whole may be a clump up to a foot or more in diameter, which is very impressive. Unfortunately, very few persons have ever seen such mature plants, and it is unlikely that anyone will see such a sight in the future unless he grows the plant himself.

The cactus was brought down out of the higher elevations of the Franklin Mountains and shown to Britton and Rose in 1921. They first described it in their large work, saying it was known from only a single station in those mountains, and that only five plants had been found. Immediately many went up looking for it, and no doubt dozens of specimens were brought down, dispersed to gardens, and never heard of again. Some photographs of large clusters were published in various journals, but it is doubted that any of these large plants still survive, and in recent years even small specimens growing wild have been almost impossible to find. The species is no doubt another of those well on the way to extinction, and the future for it would look very dark, except for the work of Mr. Clark Champie of Anthony, New Mexico-Texas. He is the first dealer propagating these Texas and New Mexico species from seed instead of relying upon stripping nature's gardens for his stock. Located as he is at the foot of the Franklins, he has secured mature plants and has many seedlings of *M. sneedii*, so collectors can continue to have the plant from his nursery.

Mammillaria leei (Böd.)
[*Escobaria leei* Böd.]

DESCRIPTION   PLATE 39

ROOTS: Fibrous on young individuals and mostly fibrous when older, but usually with a single definite taproot developed from the original center of an old clump. This taproot is about 3/16 to 1/4 of an inch thick and usually runs for some inches before reducing.

STEMS: Almost spherical at first, later becoming mostly club-shaped, but sometimes cylindrical, to a maximum of about 3 inches long and about 1 1/8 inches thick, but ordinarily only about 1 to 1 1/2 inches tall and 3/4 of an inch thick. These small stems branch and proliferate very rapidly, forming irregular clumps of up to several hundred very tightly packed stems, such clumps a number of inches across, but only about 2 inches high. Each stem is covered with cylindrical tubercles up to about 3/16 of an inch long, although often smaller.

AREOLES: Consisting on many stems of only circular or elliptic areoles on the ends of the tubercles. Whether this represents nonflowering, immature stems was not observed, but this condition sometimes persists on some of the larger stems. On other stems, more or less regardless of stem size, the areoles are elongated into grooves extending from the spinous portions at the ends of the tubercles to around half of the distance to the tubercle bases. The flowers and branches observed came from the ends of these grooves. The whole areole is at first very woolly, and the wool remains in the grooves. The center of the spinous part of the areole is often, but not always, very convex and bulging outward. In such cases the spines are mostly pushed back in position, where they radiate around and form a sort of frame for this convex areole center, this giving the stems in such cases a unique, knobby appearance.

SPINES: There are very many, very tiny, white radial spines. Counting them is difficult, but there seem to be from 40 to at least 90 per areole. These are appressed against the surface of the plant and often recurve between the tubercles. There are also 6 or 7 stouter central spines, white or sometimes white with pale brownish tips. These spines are irregular in length, usually about 1/8 of an inch long, but sometimes a few may be longer. One of these centrals stands perpendicular to the plant body in the center of the areole, but it may be a very short one. The rest radiate in front of the radials.

FLOWERS: Not opening widely. They are about 3/4 of an inch long and 1/2 inch wide. In color they are deep pink suffused with brownish. The outer petals are brown or greenish-brown with light edges fringed by white cilia. The inner petals are deep pink in the midlines, the edges lighter and entire. The stigma lobes are 4 to 6 in number, short, and white.

FRUITS: Oblong or somewhat club-shaped, about 1/2 inch long by 1/8 to 1/4 of an inch thick. They remain greenish tinged with brownish or faintly pinkish when ripe. The seeds are more or less pear-shaped, dark brown, and less than 1/16 of an inch (slightly over 1 millimeter) long.

RANGE. Known only from several canyons about 30 miles southwest of Carlsbad, New Mexico.

REMARKS. This is a very peculiar little cactus. It was apparently first collected in 1924 by W. T. Lee, whose name it bears. Since that time specimens of it have lain in the U. S. National Herbarium, two peculiar, unnamed little specimens to tantalize anyone working through that collection. One of those specimens is a whole cluster with about a hundred stems, most of them hardly thicker than a lead pencil in their dried condition.

Several have dealt with these herbarium specimens to some extent, but only recently does it appear that the cactus has been re-collected. Dr. Rose, in 1925, labeled one of them *Neomammillaria leei*, which would have been its earliest name, but he apparently never wrote up the description of this new species. It therefore fell to Bödecker to make the first description of the cactus in the literature. He did this in 1933, calling it *Escobaria leei*. His description was very incomplete, based apparently upon only these two dead specimens.

Within the past few years several of us have tracked down the plant and collected it in the type locality. In 1966 Castetter and Pierce published an article on the species, giving the first at all complete description, and showing that the plant grows quite a bit larger in stem than Bödecker thought. Castetter and Pierce, however, in spite of the fact that the fruits remain essentially green, leave the cactus as an Escobaria.

We find this form especially interesting and feel that, in the light of the genus problem, it is worthy of much more study. On many stems it remains with unelongated areoles. What is an immature condition in all cacti seems to persist sometimes throughout the life of the stem in this cactus. We have never been able to observe whether such ungrooved stems flower, only having seen flowers on those with elongated, obviously monomorphic areoles. It seems difficult to believe that so many stems would remain immature and never bloom. If they do bloom, it might be significant to know where the flowers are produced, since the groove is absent.

The cactus is close to *M. sneedii*, and the ranges of the two are not far apart. I was at first tempted to think of them as two manifestations of the same cactus, but knowledge of their details seems to put this out of the question.

M. leei comes from a very limited area, so far as is known consisting of only a few canyons. The population cannot be large. It has been fortunate, no doubt, in being practically overlooked until very recently. Let us hope that collectors do not now descend upon it and eliminate it, as they seem to have done to *M. sneedii*.

Mammillaria bella (B. & R.)
[*Escobaria bella* B. & R.]

DESCRIPTION (adapted from Britton and Rose)
STEMS: Clustering, the heads about 2³⁄₈ to 3¹⁄₄ inches long and cylindrical. The tubercles are ⁵⁄₈ to almost ⁷⁄₈ of an inch long, marked by a hairy groove, near the center of which there is a brownish gland.

AREOLES: Not known.

SPINES: Radial spines said to be several, whitish, and less than ¹⁄₂ inch long. The central spines are 3 to 5 in number, brown, and the longest to at least ⁷⁄₈ of an inch long.

FLOWERS: To ³⁄₄ of an inch across, petals pinkish with pale margins, narrow and pointed, the outer ones fringed. The filaments are reddish, the stigma green.

FRUITS: Not known.

RANGE. Collected "on hills of Devil's River, Texas."

REMARKS. This cactus was collected by Rose and Fitch before 1914, and described by Britton and Rose in 1922. There is no record of its having been collected again. Numerous searches along the Devil's River have turned up no plant with the unique characteristic which Britton and Rose emphasize for this one— the possession of the gland in the groove of the tubercles—in conjunction with so small a stem size, such large tubercles, and a smallish, pinkish flower. The nearest I have come to it were some specimens found in the area, which roughly approach these characters but which turned out to be seedlings of *Mammillaria macromeris*.

This being the situation, the plant can only be listed upon the authority of Britton and Rose as a cactus once collected in Texas. There is not even any way to restudy the form. But it seems that their authority requires us to list the cactus, and I repeat their description here in case—and in hope—someone may yet succeed in finding it where all of us have failed.

Mammillaria pottsii Scheer

DESCRIPTION   PLATE 39
STEMS: Cylindrical, to about 1¹⁄₄ inches in diameter and to at least 8 inches tall, although usually only 4 to 5 inches high. It was reported by Coulter to grow to 12 or 14 inches, but this is doubtful. These stems may remain single, but sometimes branch above the ground to form small, irregular clusters of 3 or 4 heads. The tubercles covering the stems are conical to egg-shaped, ¹⁄₈ to ¹⁄₄ of an inch long, rather closely crowded, and somewhat overlapping.

AREOLES: Dimorphic. The spinous portion on the tip of the tubercle is small, round, and especially filled with spines because of the enlarged bases of the centrals. It at first contains much rather long, white wool, but is later bare. The flower develops in or near the axil of the tubercle, together with long wool and sometimes a bristle or two, which remain as an axillary tuft.

SPINES: There are 30 to 40 radial spines which are white, very slender, but straight and rigid. These are about ³⁄₁₆ of an inch long and remarkable for being entirely equal in size as they radiate around the areole. The number of central spines may vary from 6 to 12 from plant to plant, but the number seems to be identical in all areoles of any one plant. These centrals spread evenly in all directions from greatly enlarged, bulbous bases. The lower and lateral ones are all ¹/₄ to ³/₈ of an inch long and straight, but the upper ones are ¹/₂ to ⁵/₈ of an inch long and curve upward. The lower ones are gray with their very tips brownish. The upper ones are gray with as much as the outer half of each dark brown, purple, or a peculiar bluish color; this color, as they curve upward, gives the tip of the plant over which they converge a purplish color.

FLOWERS: Small, ³/₈ to ¹/₂ inch long and wide, bell-shaped, the petals not opening widely, but then recurving toward the tips. They are deep red, maroon, or rust red in color. They develop around the upper sides of the stem instead of at the summit of it. The outer petals are very broad, but with pointed tips, the margins usually ragged or irregularly toothed, but not fringed. These outer segments are red or maroon with pale, cream-colored edges. The inner petals have red to rust-red midstripes with rose to pinkish, smooth margins, and pointed tips. The stamens are cream-colored. The style is reddish, and there are 4 or 5 cream-colored or yellow stigma lobes.

FRUITS: Club-shaped, up to ⁵/₈ of an inch long, pale or light red. The seeds are blackish, pitted, almost oval, and less than ¹/₁₆ of an inch (not quite 1 millimeter) in length.

RANGE. The U. S. range is limited to the mountains deep in the Big Bend region around Terlingua, Texas, but the plant is widely distributed in Mexico.

REMARKS. This is a distinctive cactus unlike anything else found in the United States. Its appearance readily distinguishes it from all the other Mammillarias we have in this country, and when it blooms we have no other cactus with a flower even remotely like this one's small, bell-shaped, red blossom. It seems to be our only representative of the large group of Mammillarias found in Mexico, with small, bell-shaped flowers. In the United States, therefore, it should be one of the most easily recognized of all; yet it has a history of serious confusion with other forms.

It seems that this cactus was first described by Scheer in the Salm-Dyck publication of 1850. Perhaps the uncertainty started there, as that description mentions wrinkles and a very slight groove on the tubercle. This, once the distinction between grooved and grooveless had become paramount, would of course make one think it something else instead of a Mammillaria in the narrow usage of that term. Poselger, in 1853, collected a plant with a groove, which Britton and Rose think must have been *Mammillaria (Escobaria) tuberculosa*, but which Poselger himself thought was our cactus, although he called it *Echinocactus pottsianus*. But when, in the same year, he apparently collected our plant which does not actually have a groove, he thought he had a new species and renamed it *Mammillaria leona*.

From that time the confusion spread. Engelmann seemed to have had a different plant in mind when describing *M. pottsii*, since he said that it has large flowers and grows on the Rio Grande below Laredo. Coulter and others more or less followed him in this, their descriptions, therefore, being confusing. All

the way to the present the confusion has remained. Berger, followed by Borg, finally called some Mexican plant with a "narrow groove" *Coryphantha pottsii*, and so the plant has been put into three different genera. Backeberg has only extended the confusion when he says that *Mammillaria pottsii* was an Escobaria, and so uses for our plant the name *Mammillaria leona* Poselgr. once again.

Britton and Rose seemed to have been among the first to realize the source of the confusion. They got back to our cactus again in their description, but they were very limited, having only one Texas record of this cactus to work with.

Craig states most clearly the cause of the difficulty in saying that the tubercles of this cactus become wrinkled and shrunken when dehydrated—as do most—and that since the original description mentions both a slight groove and many wrinkles, Scheer must have had before him a shrunken, atypical plant, and thus the groove he mentioned to start the whole confusion was not the natural one of an elongated areole. Through this overemphasis on a groove, then, the original name became applied to other grooved cacti of the *Coryphantha* and *Escobaria* microgenera, while the Texas plant, although seldom seen at all, was known under Poselger's name of *M. leona*. This seems to have been the situation until Britton and Rose reapplied the original name to the plant again. Since both Craig and Marsden, two of our greatest authorities on the Mammillarias, see no difficulty in using Scheer's name, I follow them here.

Be that as it may, the plant which grows in Texas and which we will call by the name of *M. pottsii* is a beautiful cactus of one to several slender, whitish columns over which is thrown a peculiar bluish cast by the unusual coloring of the upper centrals. It most nearly resembles *M. tuberculosa*, but is much more beautiful because of its more regular and tidy spines. The greatly enlarged bases of its central spines are a quick clue for recognizing this plant. When it blooms its flowers are fine little bell-shaped, deep-red blossoms produced in a ring around the upper part of the stems. They are small flowers, but they are charming, showing that cactus flowers can be small and demure as well as large and flamboyant.

Because of the confusion about *M. pottsii* which has reigned for so long, many of the older accounts of its range cannot be trusted. It does not, for instance, grow in Texas below Laredo, as Engelmann and Coulter thought. Britton and Rose also make the peculiar statement that it comes from the "highlands of the Rio Grande." No doubt the mountains of the Big Bend, where it does grow and through which that river flows, are highlands, but it does not grow in the mountains of northern New Mexico, the "highlands" in which the Rio Grande actually arises. To be specific, all specimens of which I know came from the mountains deep in the Big Bend around Terlingua, Texas.

The cactus grows well in limestone soil which is well-drained, and is often used in dish or windowsill gardens. It is, however, a desert species, and needs much sun and cannot tolerate much dampness.

Mammillaria lasiacantha Eng.

DESCRIPTION   PLATES 39, 40

STEMS: Usually single, but sometimes forming small clusters of 2 or 3 heads. Each stem is spherical, conical, or egg-shaped and small, the maximum appearing to be about 2 inches in diameter and only slightly taller. The plant is covered by many small, cylindrical tubercles to about ³/₁₆ of an inch long and ¹/₈ of an inch in diameter. The axils between these are bare.

AREOLES: The spinous portions of the dimorphic areoles are on the tips of the tubercles and are small and somewhat egg-shaped. The floral portions of the areoles remain in the axils of the tubercles, the flowers thus being produced in the axils.

SPINES: Each areole produces 40 to 60 or more white radial spines which lie flat, interlocking with those of the neighboring areoles and covering the surface of the plant. These spines are so numerous that they cannot all lie in one plane around the areole, and so they are produced in several series forming 3 or 4 concentric rings in the areole, one radiating layer of them lying upon the next. They are from about ¹/₁₆ to ³/₁₆ of an inch long. They may have rough, even pubescent surfaces caused by varying numbers of almost microscopic white hairs upon them, or they may be smooth of surface.

FLOWERS: ¹/₂ to ³/₄ of an inch long and the same diameter, opening widely. The color is whitish with each petal marked by a conspicuous tan, red-brown, or purplish-red midstripe. The outer petals are slender, with the ends either rounded or bluntly pointed, their margins usually somewhat irregular. The inner petals are oblong, rather wide, being ¹/₁₆ to ¹/₈ of an inch wide over most of their lengths, and the tips are smooth and rounded or else ragged. The filaments are long and yellowish, the anthers yellow. The style is greenish and slightly longer than the stamens. The stigma has 4 or 5 small, greenish or yellowish lobes.

FRUITS: Bright scarlet, club-shaped, and ³/₈ to ⁵/₈ of an inch long. The remains of the flower persist upon them, and the surfaces of the fruits are naked. The seeds are oval in shape, black with pitted surfaces, and less than ¹/₁₆ of an inch (about 1 millimeter) in length.

RANGE. Entering the U. S. from Mexico along a stretch of the Rio Grande from south of Sanderson, Texas, west to El Paso, and growing from Sanderson northwest past Fort Stockton through the Guadalupe Mountains west of Carlsbad, New Mexico, and from the Rio Grande at El Paso into the Sacramento Mountains near Almagordo, New Mexico, which seems to be the northern limit of the range.

REMARKS. This is another of our tiniest cacti. It usually grows as a little ball up to an inch or two in diameter, and is perfectly white due to the huge number of white spines entirely covering its surface. Very rarely it clusters, but to only 2 or 3 heads. It is found growing on the tops of hills where the soil is thin, often wedged in between limestone rocks, and it will not prosper un-

less there is much limestone in its soil. It is usually more or less covered by surrounding grasses, but does not seem to require shade, as I have collected plants which were totally unprotected from the sun and have grown them this way for several years. No doubt the huge number of its spines provide its flesh its own partial shade.

It is a real indication of the thoroughness of the early explorers that they even noticed this tiny cactus, and remarkable observation on Engelmann's part that he separated this species into two other very similar varieties. I have met few cactophiles or even dealers who have taken the trouble to do this, since it involves using a magnifying glass to distinguish them.

As a species, *M. lasiacantha* has had a comparatively uneventful taxonomic history. Only one dissenting voice seems to have been raised concerning its position as a Mammillaria. In 1951 Buxbaum, because of seed characters and the fact that the axillary, floral part of the areole develops first instead of the spinous part—this the reverse of many others in the genus—separated this cactus and some of its relatives into a new genus which he called *Ebnerella*, but he has not so far been followed in this.

There has perhaps been enough confusion over the varieties of this cactus to make up for the unanimity concerning the species. Much has been written about *M. lasiacantha* which is confusing because different authors using this name may be referring to different forms. Britton and Rose, for instance, mean by this name the form which should more accurately be called variety *lasiacantha* of the species. On the other hand, some authors have clearly seen only the variety *denudata* and write of the species from knowledge of only this variety. Ranges given are particularly confused because of this sort of thing.

The species is another one of that large variety of tiny cacti which we find growing in west Texas and southern New Mexico, in the most exposed and unlikely places for such small, delicate-appearing plants. It is these inconspicuous forms for which one has to search carefully which give this area such a surprising array of cactus species.

Mammillaria lasiacantha var. lasiacantha (Eng.)

DESCRIPTION   PLATE 39

STEMS: As the species, except to only about 1 inch in maximum diameter and height.

AREOLES: As the species.

SPINES: As the species, except that the average number is in the upper number range for the species, and that the surfaces of the spines are always roughened by at least some to very many almost microscopic cilia or trichomes. Many specimens have the spines wholly pubescent.

FLOWERS: As the species, except about ³/₄ of an inch in length and width, the main petals about 1/8 of an inch wide, and the stigmas more yellowish than greenish.

FRUITS: As the species.

RANGE. From near Fort Stockton, Texas, and the Davis Mountains north in the Guadalupe Mountains west of Carlsbad, New Mexico, to between Carlsbad and Alamogordo, New Mexico.

REMARKS. This form appears to have been the type for the species. Then later, when he described the two varieties within the species, Engelmann called this form *M. lasiacantha* var. *minor.* His name for the variety would be most appropriate, but the rules of taxonomy, if this is the type form, require it to be called instead variety *lasiacantha.*

The spines of variety *lasiacantha* have on them a growth of almost microscopic "hairs" which give them a fuzzy appearance under a lens. Individual specimens vary in the amount of this hair, but it is always there to some extent, and in some plants it is so thick as to be a velvety covering on the spines. Specimens of the other variety, *M. lasiacantha* var. *denudata,* lack this hair entirely or have only a few scraggly cilia, and their spines are, therefore, smooth and shiny.

If this matter of pubescent versus smooth spines were the only difference between these two forms, it would seem that the various students who have combined them would be justified, but there are also other differences. As indicated by Engelmann's name for it, variety *minor,* the rough-spined form is smaller in maximum size. Its maximum observed size is about 1 inch, while specimens of the smooth-spined form 2 inches in diameter are rather easy to find. The smallness of the over-all size probably keeps us from evaluating this difference properly. It is a difference in maximum size of double—which would be very noticeable in two giant barrel cacti. At the same time, the flowers of this smaller form are larger, with wider petals, than those of the larger variety.

Admittedly these differences may intergrade. There are very clearly a few cilia on some specimens of variety *denudata.* This would certainly preclude calling them separate species, as did Britton and Rose, but this is not an obstacle in varietal relationships. When I note that I have found no specimen of the small, truly pubescent, large-flowered variety *lasiacantha* from south of the Davis Mountains, and that in hundreds of specimens from the bins of Big Bend dealers collected in the lower Big Bend which I have examined with a magnifying glass, and even among those doubtful specimens from that area which I have grown and flowered not a one has been other than variety *denudata,* I feel that we have here two legitimate varieties which should be recognized.

At present, however, dealers and collectors alike, knowing only that there are supposed to be two forms, seem to be separating their plants by some sort of magic into two supposed categories, and the lots I see under one name or the other usually have little meaning. Actually, I know of no way to separate the two varieties without using a magnifier, and even beyond that,

in some borderline cases, growing the specimens to flowering to compare the flowers.

The failure to do this makes for much confusion. In general, most people have seen the next variety and very few have actually had variety *lasiacantha.* Huge numbers of variety *denudata* have been and still are being sold out of the lower Big Bend, where they are abundant, while few dealers have worked out of the more northerly range of variety *lasiacantha,* where that variety is relatively rare anyway. The study of these two forms by Britton and Rose suffered from this same situation. Although they listed the plants as two separate species, they admitted that they had not themselves seen the more rare *M. lasiacantha.*

Dr. Boke, in his very valuable anatomical and developmental study of *M. lasiacantha,* did not distinguish between the two varieties at all. His specimens were collected in several locations, all but one of which were in the lower Big Bend, where all he would presumably have collected were variety *denudata,* so the bulk of his work must have been done with this form. But some of his plants came from a ridge 9 miles east of Alpine, Texas, where he could conceivably have picked up a few specimens of variety *lasiacantha.* This possibility becomes interesting because he mentions that he found mucilaginous areas in all but 2 or 3 of the many specimens which he examined. He could suggest no reason why 2 or 3 of his specimens lacked this mucilaginous system. Could it be that these 2 or 3 without it were his only specimens of variety *lasiacantha,* and that this is another difference between these varieties? Restudy would be necessary to determine whether this is true.

Mammillaria lasiacantha var. denudata Eng.

DESCRIPTION   PLATES 39, 40

STEMS: As the species, except with the maximum size at least 2 inches tall and wide.

AREOLES: As the species.

SPINES: As the species, except smooth and shiny, with usually no cilia or trichomes upon them, and at most on some specimens a few scattered "hairs" upon the spines.

FLOWERS: As the species, except to about 1/2 inch in diameter, petals almost linear and only about 1/16 of an inch wide, and stigma with more greenish than yellowish lobes.

FRUITS: As the species.

RANGE. From Mexico into the mountains of the Big Bend in Texas, along the Rio Grande from near Sanderson to Canutillo, Texas, just beyond El Paso. It also occurs north past Alpine and Marfa, Texas, into the southern part of the Davis Mountains.

REMARKS. This is the more common southern form of the species. It is very common in parts of the Big Bend region, and thousands of the plants come out of that area into the trade every year. On the west it has been collected at Sierra Blanca and at Canutillo, Texas, but I find no record of it in New Mexico. On the east, Orcutt once reported it from Langtry, Texas, but it does not seem to have been found there since.

Although these two varieties are very close, this is a larger plant when grown, and has smaller flowers. The two are certainly not separate species, as some have maintained.

Mammillaria multiceps SD
"Hair-Covered Cactus," "Grape Cactus"

DESCRIPTION   PLATE 40

STEMS: Spherical to egg-shaped or sometimes short-columnar. Matured, blooming heads measure from ¹/₂ to almost 2 inches in diameter and 2 inches tall, producing off-sets extremely rapidly so that a typical plant consists of a dozen to more than a score of different-sized heads forming a large, low, matlike clump. The tubercles are conical or cylindrical, spreading, and up to ³/₈ of an inch long.

AREOLES: Dimorphic. The spinous portion on the end of the tubercle is round, with white wool at first, later naked. The floral or vegetative portion in the axil of the tubercle produces with the flower some wool and usually several long, twisted, white, hairlike bristles which persist.

SPINES: Radial spines number 30 to more than 60, and are said to have sometimes reached 80. These are produced in several series. The outer ones are white, hairlike, very fine, entirely flexible, and usually curved and twisted. When straightened they are ¹/₄ to ⁵/₈ of an inch long. The inner series become progressively shorter and heavier until the innermost are straight, rigid bristles spreading in all directions, white or light yellow in color, and usually somewhat pubescent. In the center of the areole are 4 to 9 comparatively heavy central spines with bulbous bases. They are straight, rigid, ¹/₄ to ³/₈ of an inch long, and spreading in all directions. In color they are white to yellow or brown at their bases, the upper parts and tips of them varying on different plants from whitish or light honey-yellow to dark red-brown or almost black. These are more or less pubescent under a lens. There is also an outer series of centrals which are lighter in color and more slender than the inner ones, and sometimes approach so closely to the heaviest inner radials that on some plants the point of transition from one to the other is not clear. Counting these, there may be up to 12 centrals.

FLOWERS: About ³/₄ of an inch long and the same diameter, brownish-yellow or almost tan in color, with pinkish to mauve-rose streaks. The petals have cream or tan edges shading into pinkish or dull rose midlines. They are usually unfringed, but the outer ones may occasionally have a few cilia on their edges. The filaments are yellowish or white, the an-

thers yellow. The style is cream-colored and short. There are 3 to 8 cream-colored to yellow stigma lobes.

FRUITS: About ¹/₂ to ³/₄ of an inch long, scarlet, egg-shaped to club-shaped, the old flower parts persisting upon them. The seeds are black, pitted, approximately ¹/₁₆ of an inch (about 1¹/₂ millimeters) long.

RANGE. Entering Texas from Mexico all along the Rio Grande from its mouth to the mouth of the Pecos River, extending north along the Gulf Coast of Texas to near Rockport, but growing only in a narrow band of coastal plain extending not over a few miles from the beach. Up the river from Brownsville, Texas, it never grows north of the sandy hills overlooking the Rio Grande Valley anywhere below Eagle Pass, but near that city it leaves the vicinity of the river to grow on the summits of the limestone hills of the Edwards Escarpment past Brackettville and Uvalde, almost to Bandera and Rocksprings, Texas.

REMARKS. This little cactus can be recognized easily by the flexible, hairlike radial spines which cover its surface and from which it gets its name, the "hair-covered cactus." No other small, unribbed cactus in the Southwest has such spines.

The individual stems of this cactus are small, usually around an inch or only a little more in diameter and height, but they multiply very rapidly by branching. Often a head an inch in diameter will surround itself with as many as a dozen little off-sets. The result is soon a low clump sometimes more than a foot across, made up of many heads.

In Texas this cactus grows in two widely differing habitats. It grows in or near the Rio Grande Valley, usually in rich, deep, lowland soil where it seems to prefer the shelter of thickets, or else between the clumps of coastal grasses on the low, flat coastal plain almost within sight of the Gulf. It is a far cry from such places to its other habitat, where it grows on the crests of rocky hills, usually wedged into crevices of limestone ledges, often where there hardly seems soil enough to support it, and often even on the undersides of the ledges, where it is shaded by the rocks. It loves the highest brows of the Edwards Escarpment north of Uvalde and Brackettville, Texas, but it is handicapped here by its susceptibility to freezing. During the years when the winters in this area are mild its clumps proliferate and become large, but after one of the colder winters which occasionally visit this area, the plants are a sad sight, severely frozen back and often half dead. The plant seems to be able to survive almost as far north as Rocksprings, Texas, but no farther.

Even though it sometimes produces clumps up to more than a foot across, *M. multiceps* is always an inconspicuous cactus. Even though produced in profusion, its flowers are small and not highly colored, Engelmann calling them "dirty yellow." Its red fruits provide the only real color it has. However it is interesting for the large clusters it forms, and a clump of the little, hairy heads is attractive. Because of its habit of growing from shallow crevices of rock ledges, it makes fine, healthy growth in little pockets of soil in rock gardens and on the sides of irregular rock patio walls, wherever the temperature does not get too cold for it.

This particular little cactus of Texas and northern Mexico was first described by Prince Salm-Dyck in 1850, and he called it *Mammillaria multiceps*. It would have seemed that it could have had a history unconfused by name troubles, since no one has doubted that it is a Mammillaria of the best form, but such was not to be the case.

Very much earlier, in the beginnings of cactus study, a similar cactus had been found and described in Cuba and some other West Indies islands. Miller first named this other cactus *Cactus proliferus*, way back in 1768. Lamarck renamed it *Cactus glomeratus* in 1783, and De Candolle in 1803 called it *Cactus pusillus*. In 1812 Haworth placed it more properly as *Mammillaria prolifera*.

This already discovered West Indian cactus is very close to our form, and this fact was soon noticed. When Engelmann saw our Texas plant and wrote of it in 1856, he said that it "seems scarcely distinct" from the West Indian one, and so he called our Texas cactus *Mammillaria pusilla* var. *texana*. Since then the Texas form has been called in the literature almost every possible combination of variety *texana* or variety *multiceps* with each one of the various names already given for the West Indian cactus. At the same time there have always been others who have maintained that the two are separate, and so used simply *Mammillaria multiceps* for our cactus.

It seems that the first thing necessary in trying to arrive at the correct name for this cactus is to establish once and for all how close to the West Indian cactus it is. Although this would seem to be simple, it is in reality not easy to do. It is almost impossible today to get specimens from Cuba and the islands in that area. I have not had the good fortune to observe living plants from the islands, and herbarium material from there is very scarce. This means I can only rely upon the statements of other students concerning the similarity or differences between these cacti.

Looking back into the statements of these students, we find that the early students, who seemed to have observed the West Indian plants enough that Engelmann called it "well-known" all agree that it has only 12 to 20 radial spines. Coulter states that it differs from our mainland form "only in the very much fewer (12 to 20) radial spines, although numerous specimens, both dried and living, were examined for additional characters. This difference, however, is so constant and striking that, taken together with the wide geographical separation, it should stand as varietal." He therefore agreed with Engelmann in making our form a variety of the other.

Since that time it seems that students have not been able to decide whether this difference between 12 to 20 radials on one hand and 30 to 80 on the other hand is justification for two different varieties or two different species. There has, altogether, been a hundred years of discussion of this problem, and there still is no agreement. I am choosing to list our form as a separate species. However this decision, I wish to make clear, is not on the basis of any first-hand observation or any new data, but only on the strength of its being listed this way by Britton and Rose, Craig, and Backeberg. These are the most thorough students to have dealt with it recently.

There remains still another problem concerning this cactus. There seem to be two rather distinct growth forms of it in Texas and northern Mexico. The two forms seem identical except that one of them has the outer parts of the centrals dark brown, red-brown, or black, while the other has the centrals all whitish or else translucent, honey-yellow. Plants of these two different colorings seen side by side are conspicuously different, and the difference has been noticed by several authors.

Engelmann, Coulter, and Britton and Rose seem none of them to have seen both forms. The descriptions by the first two do not include characters of the yellow-spined form at all. Of course, Britton and Rose's very broad description of the West Indian *M. prolifera* would include it, but they apparently knew nothing of that species being in either the United States or Mexico. Schulz and Runyon only listed *M. multiceps*, but stated, "There are two distinct varieties. The most common has brown spines. The other has gray or nearly white spines. The flowers and fruits of the two varieties are very much alike." This was probably the first recognition of the existence of the two forms.

Borg was probably the next to refer to the two forms. He described the yellow-spined one briefly but clearly, but he sadly confused things by calling this so far unnamed, yellow-spined form *M. prolifera* var. *texana* Eng., while he reserved for the dark-spined form the name *M. prolifera* var. *multiceps* SD.

It seems that Borg makes an error here. It is unfortunate that he equates Engelmann's variety *texana* with the yellow-spined form of this species, because Engelmann expressly stated the plants he meant by that name to have "Interior spines . . . in young or weakly specimens whitish with dark tips, in robust ones yellow at base, brown upwards, and almost black at tip." It seems clear that variety *texana* is the same plant as Salm-Dyck's *M. multiceps*.

Is there then a reason for describing the yellow-spined form as a separate variety at all? When I first discovered it I thought that there was. All of the specimens I have seen from the summits of the high hills in the Texas hill country are of this coloring, and as I had seen only the dark-spined form from the very different coastal and Valley habitat, I thought that this could be a separate form with its own northern range. But this idea proved to be wrong. I was very surprised to find the two forms growing together in Potrero Canyon in the Santa Rosa Mountains of Coahuila, Mexico. This showed that the dark-spined form could also grow in high, rocky situations, and I soon confirmed this in other Mexican locations. When I later saw the yellow-spined form, formerly seen only on high hills, growing in a habitat about as completely the opposite as could be found, on the coastal plain only a short distance from Copano Bay and the Gulf of Mexico, I realized that the ranges and habitats of these two cannot be separated. They actually grow together on the same hillsides, in a few cases. They appear to be merely growth forms, perhaps simple phenotypes of the same variable population. They are much like the two color phases found in the same populations of *Echinocereus caespitosus*.

Given the kind of care used on any but the most extreme desert forms of cacti, even in a small pot, this little cactus will grow and proliferate its small heads into an interesting cluster. It blooms freely for many weeks at a time, and for months after that its brilliant, scarlet fruits will be popping out to decorate it.

Mammillaria microcarpa Eng.
"Fishhook Cactus," "Pincushion Cactus," "Sunset Cactus"

DESCRIPTION   PLATE 40

STEMS: Single until old, then clustering at the base or sometimes branching above the base to form small clumps of several stems. Each stems grows to at least 6 inches, but usually to only about 3 inches tall; each 1 to 3½ inches in diameter and practically spherical, conical, or somewhat cylindrical in shape. The tubercles are cylindrical when young, then conical from more or less quadrangular bases which are sometimes flattened from side to side when old; the younger tubercles up to about ¼ of an inch long and the same width at their bases, the old tubercles up to nearly ½ inch long.

AREOLES: Dimorphic. The spinous portion, at the tip of the tubercle, is small, round or oval, with some white wool at first, but later bare. The floral or vegetative part, in the axil, is without wool, and so the axils are bare.

SPINES: There are conspicuous, slender, white radial spines and dark-colored, hooked central spines. There are 20 to 30 radials radiating evenly from the areole, lying flat upon the surface of the plant, and interlocking with those of neighboring areoles. They are very slender, but stiff, often slightly hairy under a magnifying glass, and ⅛ to ½ inch long. The upper and lower spines of each areole are the shortest, usually about ¼ of an inch long, with an occasional one only ⅛ of an inch, while the lateral spines are the longer. Each areole has 1 to 3 centrals. The lowermost one of these centrals stands out perpendicular to the plant surface, is ¼ to ¾ of an inch long, red-brown to almost black, with the base the lightest color and the dark point strongly hooked. The upper centrals stand upright just in front of the upper radials, forming a V if there are two of them, but there may be only one. These are never hooked, are usually whitish over the lower half, with the upper half red or yellow-brown.

FLOWERS: Rose-purple in color, ¾ to 1⅛ inches long and wide. Usually there are a number of these flowers forming a ring around the new growth of the plant. They open widely. The outer petals are short, oblong or conical, having brown-ish midlines and pink, fringed edges. The inner petals are longer, about ¾ of an inch long, slender (being about 3/16 of an inch wide at their widest), with smooth edges and either bluntly pointed or sharply pointed tips. These petals may be solid pink in some specimens, or in others have deeper midlines fading to almost white edges. The filaments are pink, the anthers pale orange. The style is very long, easily ¼ of an inch above the stamens, making the pistil about equal to the length of the longest petals. There are 6 to 10 slender, light green stigma lobes about 3/16 of an inch long.

FRUITS: Scarlet when ripe, oval to club-shaped, ¾ to 1 inch long, with the dried flower parts remaining upon them. These fruits develop rather slowly, there is a long blooming season, and those started late in the summer remain as small, green, oval structures under the spines of the plant until during the winter they dry up without ripening properly at all. For this reason the fruits have sometimes been called dimorphic. The seeds are black, pitted, almost round, and less than 1/16 of an inch (1 millimeter or less) in diameter.

RANGE. Extreme western Texas from the very northwestern corner of Presidio County to the Franklin Mountains near El Paso, and across the extreme southern part of New Mexico into Arizona and Mexico.

REMARKS. This is the dainty little fishhook cactus we so often see in dimestore bins and dish gardens. It is rather common in the places where it grows, and its white, spine-covered surface with the slender, dark brown centrals standing out for all the world like fishhooks makes it a sure seller for the novelty it presents. Those who succeed in providing it the perfect drainage and hot sun it needs will have the added reward, quite without warning some day in the summer, of a whole ring of fine, rose-purple flowers circling the crown of the plant.

Mammillaria microcarpa was first mentioned in Engelmann's *Emory Report* of 1848. Engelmann at that time only had a drawing of a plant seen on the expedition in Arizona. Because this drawing showed extremely tiny fruits only about ⅛ of an inch long, Engelmann remarked that the species should be called *M. microcarpa*, as no other cactus has so small a fruit. This drawing, incidentally, shows no hooked central spines.

In his later studies, Engelmann examined many specimens of our cactus, and in his writings described it completely. However, he apparently did not ever connect it with the cactus of Emory's report, since he named it *Mammillaria grahami* and only referred to it under this name.

The cactus was known by this name, *M. grahami*, by all writers up to Britton and Rose. In their large work on cacti, they went back to the earlier name, *M. microcarpa*, for this species. This was because, in 1922, at Dr. Rose's request, a Mrs. Ross visited the locality in Arizona which was thought to be the same spot where the cactus figured in the drawing made on Emory's expedition was said to have been abundant, and there she found our cactus growing. This was taken by Britton and Rose as conclusive evidence that the drawing was of this plant, and they resurrected the old name, *M. microcarpa*, to replace the one which had been used for the past 70 years.

There were naturally many who objected. They pointed out that the 1848 drawing and description does not show or mention the most conspicuous feature of the plant, the hooked central spines—a remarkable omission—and that the ⅛-inch fruits of that description are surely not the ¾- to 1-inch fruits of our cactus. These were undoubtedly the reasons why Engelmann felt it necessary to give this cactus the different name of *M. grahami* when he came across it. In reply to Britton and Rose's argument that since our cactus grows at the location where Emory's plant was collected, the two must be the same, it was argued that since Mrs. Ross's determination of the exact spot 70 years later was at best a guess, and since in many cases moving only a few hundred yards from a location gives a different cactus, we have too little reason indeed to maintain from the supposed identity of location that our plant with the long, dark, hooked centrals and fruits nearly an inch long is *M. microcarpa* of the early report, which lacked dark, hooked spines and which had tiny fruits. But such was the veneration in which the work of Britton and Rose was held, that soon everyone was using the name *M. microcarpa* for this species; I have not found an author in the past 30 years going back to the other name. It is, therefore, in spite of my own suspicion that the original *M. microcarpa* was some entirely different plant, but in deference to the unanimous use of this name by all other writers of recent years, that I list this cactus under that name.

This cactus grows in abundance in the Franklin Mountains near El Paso, Texas. Occasionally it is found in the mountains northwest of Presidio, Texas, particularly near Candelaria, Texas. In New Mexico it is encountered in the mountains across the very southern part of the state, particularly in the Tortugas and Selden mountains near Las Cruces, and in the Peloncillo Mountains in the southwestern corner of the state.

This cactus has very close relatives in *M. pellosperma* Eng., of Arizona, California, and Utah, and *M. sheldonii* B. & R., of Sonora, Mexico. *M. milleri* B. & R. is considered to be a synonym.

Mammillaria wrightii Eng.

DESCRIPTION   PLATE 41

STEMS: Solitary, the part above the ground 1½ to 3 inches in diameter and varying in shape according to environmental conditions. When moist and growing it is hemispherical or even spherical, when desiccated and dormant it is very much flattened and even depressed on top. The stem is prolonged below the ground into a tapering, top-shaped base which is similar to a short taproot, but which has never been interpreted that way. The surface above the ground is covered by coni-

cal or almost cylindrical tubercles ¼ to ⅞ of an inch long, whose bases are round and whose axils are naked.

AREOLES: Dimorphic. The spinous portion on the tip of the tubercle is round, with short white wool. The floral part is in the axil.

SPINES: There are 8 to 15 radial spines which lie flat upon the surface of the plant, or very nearly so. They are 3/16 to ⅝ of an inch long, and vary in color. They may be all white, or they may be white with brown tips. There is a tendency for the uppermost of them to be darker, and sometimes these are all brown. The bases are somewhat bulbous, and the spines have more or less of a fine, hairy pubescence upon them visible only with a lens. There are 1 to 4, but usually 2 or 3 central spines. These are red-brown or blackish, slender, ⅜ to ½ inch long, usually all hooked, although it is said that sometimes the upper one may be straight. These spines also have some fine pubescence upon them.

FLOWERS: Bright purple in color. They are about 1 inch long and the same in diameter when open fully. There are about 13 outer segments which are somewhat triangular in shape, about ⅜ of an inch long by 3/16 of an inch wide, pointed, purplish-green, with light-colored, fringed edges. The inner petals are about 20 in number, almost linear, about ¾ of an inch long by ⅛ to 3/16 of an inch wide, pointed, and purple. The filaments are greenish at their bases, pinkish above. The anthers are pale orange. The style is greenish, becoming pinkish above. There are 11 lemon-yellow stigma lobes.

FRUITS: About ¾ to 1 inch long, oval to broadly obovate, about ⅝ of an inch in widest diameter, dull purple in color. These fruits often occur well to the sides of the plant. The seeds are large, more than 1/16 of an inch (about 2 millimeters) long, almost round, and black, with pitted surfaces.

RANGE. Reported from several points in a narrow strip of south-central New Mexico, the northernmost of these points being near Anton Chico, New Mexico, another in the mountains east of Carrizozo, and others in the Organ Mountains near Las Cruces, New Mexico.

REMARKS. This cactus and the next are always surrounded by confusion. The reason for this is easy to understand when it is realized that they are very similar in all of their characteristics—so much so that it is extremely hard to know which of them one has if he sees only one of them by itself. Since they are so rare that few have seen them at all, and very few students have actually seen both species together for real comparison, the descriptions of them have sometimes been inconsistent and they have sometimes been mistaken for each other so that the limits of their ranges are blurred. We will discuss their relationship after they have both been described.

It can be said that *M. wrightii* is a very rare little cactus of the lower mountain slopes in south-central New Mexico. It is so rare that mass, organized searches for it have, on several occasions, failed to turn up a single specimen, but at the same time, individuals looking casually over the hills in its territory have occasionally stumbled upon a specimen or two. Besides the fact of its rarity, another reason for this sort of thing happening is, no doubt, the fact that the cactus has a large base underground, and in the late summer, when it goes dormant, it protects itself by shrinking down almost to ground level, becoming very flat. It is very hard to see in this shrunken condition in which it stays throughout the winter.

Hallenbeck, after a most concerted hunt in 1934, involving many people and covering a huge territory, finally found a stand of nearly fifty specimens of what may have been this cactus near Anton Chico, New Mexico. He promptly took them all, explaining his action by saying that he believed those were all that existed and he felt bound to take every one in order to preserve the species. I think no better criticism of this sort of wholesale gathering of rare plants need be made than to note that no one of his collected plants or any of their offspring can be traced today, but that there have been a few specimens collected in the wild in the years since then, proving that nature is the best preserver of her children after all.

As a result of this sort of thing, *M. wrightii* is more than ever a very rare little cactus of the mountains and hills of south-central New Mexico. As far as I know, the species is not on the market, and fortunate is the cactophile who ever gets to see one. I want to express my appreciation to Mr. Ed Nadolney of Albuquerque, New Mexico, for letting me have several fine specimens of this cactus from his living collection, as I have not been fortunate enough to collect the species myself.

Mammillaria wilcoxii Toumey

DESCRIPTION   PLATE 42

STEMS: Solitary, rounded to nearly spherical without a large underground base, to 6 inches in diameter, but often much smaller. The tubercles are $3/8$ to $3/4$ of an inch long, conical from somewhat flattened bases about $1/4$ of an inch wide. The axils are naked.

AREOLES: Dimorphic. The spinous portion on the tip of the tubercle is oval and very small, with some short wool. The floral portion is in the axil.

SPINES: There are 14 to 22 radial spines which are $3/8$ to $5/8$ of an inch long, slender and straight, white with light brown tips or sometimes the whole spine light brown, these radiating from the areole or spreading outward slightly, interlocking with those of neighboring areoles to almost obscure the view of the tubercles. There may be 1 to 5 spreading centrals, at least one of which is hooked, but in most cases there are 2 or 3 of them and they are all hooked. These are brown, slender,

and $1/2$ to $1 1/4$ inches long. Under a lens all spines show a variable amount of downlike pubescence.

FLOWERS: Pink, pale rose, or very pale purple in color. They are 1 to $1 1/4$ inches long, about $1 5/8$ inches wide when open fully. There are about 20 outer perianth segments which are brownish-green, almost linear, $3/4$ of an inch long by about $1/8$ of an inch wide, pointed, and fringed with white hairs. There are up to about 40 inner petals in two rows, which are long and narrow, usually to $1 1/4$ inches long by $1/8$ of an inch wide, and pointed, and have pink midlines and cream-colored edges. The filaments are white, the anthers light orange. The style is greenish and the stigma has 5 to 9 green lobes.

FRUITS: Pink to greenish-purple, obovate, $5/8$ to 1 inch long and to about $1/2$ inch thick. The seeds are black, pitted, almost round, and to $1/16$ of an inch (about $1 3/4$ millimeters) long.

RANGE. Southeastern Arizona and Sonora, into southwestern New Mexico. It is certain that this plant is found in the mountains along the extreme southwestern edge of New Mexico, but how far east it extends is uncertain due to the failure of authorities to agree on the identity of several specimens. It seems certain it has been collected as far east in New Mexico as Silver City and near Deming, and it has been said to have been seen as far as the Franklin Mountains, but this location is doubtful.

REMARKS. *Mammillaria wilcoxii* is a more western form than *M. wrightii*, Arizona being its main locale. It does grow in New Mexico, but it is so rare there as to be an oddity anywhere it is found.

The rarity of these two forms has made it difficult to study them, and they have been often confused. It is hard to establish ranges upon the records of only a few collections, yet this is all that have been made of either of these two cacti in New Mexico. They are so rare that few people have been fortunate enough to see the two forms side by side. This makes for such confusion as must have occurred in Wooton's study, since he lists only *M. wrightii*, and then says his specimens came "from the mountains of the western side of the state, but it is reported from the upper Pecos region east of Santa Fe." We must assume that he did not distinguish the two forms, thought he was seeing only *M. wrightii*, and so stated that this species occurred along the western edge of New Mexico, where no one else has ever collected it.

W. Taylor Marshall became convinced that the cacti collected by Hallenbeck near Anton Chico were *M. wilcoxii*, and so would extend the range of this species that far northeast, although all he had were Hallenbeck's photographs, and Hallenbeck's own descriptions of his plants seem to contradict the theory. Marshall also maintained that some specimens collected in the Organ Mountains were *M. wilcoxii*, although their collector, Dr. H. V. Halladay, as well as Ladislaus Cutak, who studied them, were equally certain they were *M. wrightii*. In this way the ranges of the two have both been overextended and confused. Since there is no real evidence to the contrary, it seems most logical that *M. wilcoxii* is restricted to the southwestern corner of New Mexico, while *M. wrightii* is found only in the south-central mountains of the state.

The difference between the two cacti can be summarized as follows: *M. wrightii* has an enlarged underground base, 8 to 15 radials, and short centrals, while its flowers are about 1 inch across, have 13 triangular sepals, about 20 inner petals, and 11 yellow stigma lobes. *M. wilcoxii* has no such enlarged base, has 14 or more radials, and longer centrals, while its flowers are at least 1 inch and usually more in diameter, with about 20 linear sepals, up to 40 inner petals, and 5 to 9 green stigma lobes. The general appearance of the two has not been better shown and contrasted than by a fine photograph of the two forms sitting side by side which is on page 183 of Marshall and Bock's book, *Cactaceae*.

It may be, as some have suggested, that these two forms are mere varieties of the same species. If that is so, there may be intermediate forms, but his has not been demonstrated so far.

Mammillaria heyderi Muehlenpf.
"Nipple Cactus," "Biznaga de Chilitos," "Little Chilis"

DESCRIPTION   PLATES 42, 43

STEMS: Each plant consists of a single stem which is a flattened hemisphere up to 5 inches in diameter and up to about 2 inches tall. It grows from a heavy base under the ground which is not prolonged into a taproot, but which abruptly issues in fibrous roots. The stem is covered by firm tubercles neatly arranged in spiral rows, the axils between them being very woolly when young. This wool disappears on most plants on the older sides of the stem, but on an occasional specimen it persists and sometimes seems to become even thicker between the old tubercles. The mature tubercles are up to about 1/2 inch long, the tips round and conical from pyramidal, quadrangular bases about 1/4 of an inch wide. The ventral side of this base is definitely keeled. The sap of this plant is milky.

AREOLES: Dimorphic. The spinous portion on the tip of the tubercle is round, small, with a little white wool at first, then naked. The floral portion is in the axil, with much white wool at first.

SPINES: There are 9 to at least 26 radial spines radiating evenly like the spokes of a wheel from each areole. They are 3/16 to 1/2 inch long, the lower being longer and stouter than the upper ones, although all of them are slender and weak. The small upper ones are whitish with red-brown tips, while the larger lower ones are all red-brown on most specimens. There is usually only one central spine which stands straight out from the center of the areole and is short—only 1/8 to 3/8 of an inch long. It is all dark reddish-brown, or reddish-brown

at base and tip with a zone of lighter brown in the center. On rare specimens there are found two identical central spines, one turned upward and the other deflexed.

FLOWERS: Often occurring a number at a time arranged in a circle around the newer growth at the center of the plant. Each is 3/4 to 1 1/2 inches tall and wide, brownish, pinkish, or very pale purple shading to white. The outer petals have a greenish or brownish midline which shades into whitish, smooth, unfringed edges and a pointed tip. The inner petals have brownish-pink to pale rose midlines with whitish or pink edges which are entire to slightly ragged toward the pointed tips. The filaments are whitish to deep pink. The anthers are yellow. The stigma has 5 to 10 light green, cream-colored, or tan lobes.

FRUITS: Bright carmine red in color, club-shaped, and 1/2 to 1 1/2 inches long. They usually ripen about a year after their inception, so there is often a ring of them on the plant at the same time as the flowers. The seeds are less than 1/16 of an inch (about 1 millimeter) long, reddish-brown, and pitted.

RANGE. As a species ranging north out of Mexico over a huge area. The northern definitely known limit runs from near Corpus Christi on the Texas Gulf Coast to near San Antonio, then almost straight north to Jackson and Greer counties in the extreme southwestern corner of Oklahoma. From there it seems to turn back southwest, running somewhere near Carlsbad, New Mexico, and from there west through southern New Mexico into Arizona. There are old reports of the cactus from the Oklahoma Panhandle and from southeastern Colorado, but I could not verify these reports.

REMARKS. The cactus described as *Mammillaria heyderi* by Muehlenpfordt was the nipple cactus. He originally described it as having 20 to 22 radial spines, but it soon became apparent that the number of these radials is much more variable than that. Because of this there has been confusion. Engelmann handled the specimens having radial numbers outside these limits at two different times in two different ways, once as separate species and once as varieties of one larger species. Authorities have differed on this point until this day.

It seems to be rather clear now, however, that we have here one large, wide-ranging species within which are several very close forms which can hardly be considered more than varieties, and that is the way I am handling them here.

This cactus grows as a more or less flattened hemisphere of very regular tubercles always arranged tidily in spirals. It never grows as large in diameter as *M. meiacantha*, its nearest relative in our area, but it is often less flattened and, therefore, taller.

It is usually found under the partial shade of trees, shrubs, or tall grass, and cannot do well in the full, unbroken sunshine. It can tolerate more water than many cacti, and so is more easily grown out of its normal environment than many species. When it blooms, with its pinkish or brownish-white flowers—on healthy, big plants, often a dozen or more of these form a flowery diadem around the top of the plant—it is a beautiful sight. If another ring of the carmine red fruits from last year's flowering is also present outside the ring of flowers, as is often the case, then the sight is truly spectacular.

The Spanish common name for the plant, *biznaga de chilitos*, and its English equivalent, little chilis, refer to the fruits, which are edible and flavorful and greatly relished by the knowing natives of its locality, as well as by the birds, which will even enter my greenhouse to get at them.

There is quite a bit of variation in the color of the flowers in this species. Often there seem to be two main flower colors, one a pinkish midline of the petals fading to white edges, and the other a brownish or even greenish-brown midline with white edges to the petals. There have been attempts to separate the varieties on this basis, but this cannot be done, since one often finds identical plants in a single population blooming side by side with the two flower colors.

I must mention here a few specimens collected in central and northern Texas which present a peculiarity of armament for this species. These were fairly large plants and typical *M. heyderi* in every characteristic of stem and tubercles. They were remarkable for having all radials pure white instead of more or less colored and tipped with brown. Also, the number of the radials varied from 20 to 26 per areole, with many areoles having 23 or 24. Even more remarkable on these plants was the fact that about one out of five of the areoles had two centrals instead of one. These two centrals were the same as the ordinary single central spine found standing perpendicular to the stem on the other areoles, but where there were two, one was turned sharply upward and the other as sharply downward. Neither of these was a misplaced radial, since the ring of radials was unbroken around them. Both the number of radials and the possession of two centrals in some areoles put these specimens beyond the limits so far given for *M. heyderi*.

It is impossible to be sure from these few specimens whether this represents an extreme form of *M. heyderi* and the species should be expanded to include these characters, or whether they represent a new form. But since I have other specimens of *M. heyderi* var. *heyderi* on which occasional areoles have 23 or 24 radials, indicating that the maximum in the usual descriptions is too low, and I also have a single specimen of *M. heyderi* var. *applanata* on which a few areoles possess the two centrals, indicating that this may be a seldom expressed character carried in all of these forms, I am inclined to assume the former. So I have expanded the description of the species to include these characters. These specimens cannot be equated with the Mexican *M. heyderi* var. *waltheri* (Bödecker) Craig, although they do in some ways link that form more closely with the other varieties of the species.

Expansion of the limits of this species there has had to be, and it is hard to know where this should stop. It must not go on until the concept of the species is meaningless. L. Benson lists *M. heyderi* as occurring in very small areas of extreme southeast Arizona. His description, however, does not agree with any previous description of the cactus. He describes it as having conical tubercles, 2 to 15 radial spines, and 2 or 3 central spines. This combination of characters is not given for any previously described U. S. species in the literature.

Mammillaria heyderi var. heyderi (Muehlenpf.)

DESCRIPTION   PLATE 42

STEMS: As the species.

AREOLES: As the species.

SPINES: As the species, except radials 20 to 26 in number.

FLOWERS: As the species, except only ¾ to about 1 inch long and broad, and the stigma lobes 6 to 8 in number.

FRUITS: As the species, except ¾ to 1½ inches long.

RANGE. From near Brownsville, Texas, south and west into Mexico and north to the west of a line running past San Antonio to near Fredericksburg, Texas, occurring from this northeastern limit west through Texas to near Carlsbad, New Mexico, on the north, and past El Paso over all of southern New Mexico and into Chihuahua on the south.

REMARKS. This was the first one of this exceedingly close group to be described. It was the form actually described as *M. heyderi* by Muehlenpfordt, and so is the typical variety of the species. It also seems to have the widest range of the three U. S. varieties in the species.

There should be little difficulty in recognizing this variety. It is the only cactus occurring in the southwest U. S. with milky sap and more than 20 radial spines.

Mammillaria heyderi var. applanata Eng.

DESCRIPTION   PLATE 42

STEMS: As the species.

AREOLES: As the species.

SPINES: As the species, except the radial spines 14 to 20 in number.

FLOWERS: As the species, except to only about 1 inch in size, and having stigma lobes 5 to 10 in number.

FRUITS: As the species.

RANGE. From near Austin and Fredericksburg, Texas, south over most of south Texas and west into the Big Bend. Also collected in numbers in extreme southwestern Oklahoma in Harmon, Jackson, and Greer counties. It is the form which has been reported from Cimarron County in the Oklahoma Panhandle and from southeastern Colorado, but I cannot verify these reports.

REMARKS. This cactus was considered a separate species and then again called a variety of *M. heyderi* by Engelmann, who first described it. Then Coulter, Wooton, and others considered the two synonymous. Since that time most students have listed it as a separate species, following Britton and Rose, although most have followed them also in appending a note that the two may represent only races or varieties. This seems much more likely. The cactus has also been known in the past under the name *M. texensis* Lab.

Everything mentioned concerning the manner of growth of *M. heyderi* applies as well to this cactus. It cannot be separated from the typical variety except by counting spines. In part of their range they may grow together. However, the extents of their ranges are different. Variety *applanata* grows farther east in south Texas, since variety *heyderi* has not been found on the Texas coast and variety *applanata* has. One of the peculiarities of variety *applanata* is the apparently isolated population of it found in at least three counties of southwestern Oklahoma. There is no record of the cactus having been found anywhere in the approximately 300 miles separating this Oklahoma population from the regular range of the cactus in central Texas.

Near Roma, Texas, a large number of large variety *heyderi* and variety *applanata* were found growing together. Among these plants was one specimen of variety *applanata* with 18 and 19 radial spines in all areoles and usually with one typical central, but on 6 areoles of the plant there were 2 equal centrals ³/₈ of an inch long, one pointed upward and one exactly opposing it in a downward direction. It is impossible to collect more specimens in this interesting area, as irrigation wells were already completed at the time, and a square mile of territory upon which these and almost the whole list of other cacti native to that area were growing was being cleared when the collection was made.

Drs. Claude W. Gatewood and Bruce Blauch of Oklahoma State University have written me of a specimen collected by them at Mangum, Oklahoma, which has 14 to 16 radials and on a few areoles the same arrangement of 2 centrals. The possession of 2 centrals on at least a few areoles is obviously a character which can crop up at any place in this species, but which has not been mentioned in connection with it.

Mammillaria heyderi var. **hemisphaerica** Eng.

DESCRIPTION

PLATE 43

STEMS: As the species.

AREOLES: As the species.

SPINES: As the species, except radials only 9 to 13 in number.

FLOWERS: As the species, except almost always pinkish white instead of purplish or greenish white and somewhat larger than in the other forms, being 1 to 1¹/₂ inches tall and wide. Stigma lobes 5 to 8.

FRUITS: As the species, except averaging smaller than those of the other forms.

RANGE. From eastern Mexico along the Texas Gulf Coast from Brownsville to the vicinity of Corpus Christi. Extending inland in south Texas not over 30 to 50 miles, but extending northwest from the upper end of its coastal limit as far as Atascosa County, Texas. Also collected in numbers in Jackson and Greer counties of southwestern Oklahoma, and reported from the Organ Mountains of New Mexico, although this latter record is not certain.

REMARKS. *M. heyderi* var. *hemisphaerica* is in certain respects different from its relatives within the species, but the similarities are much more obvious. It has, however, never been considered synonymous with them. Even when Coulter was calling variety *applanata* the same as *M. heyderi,* he found it necessary to list *hemisphaerica* as a separate cactus.

Variety *hemisphaerica* has the smallest number of radials of the *M. heyderi* group. This provides the main clue for recognizing it, as any cactus with milky sap, the single short central, and only 9 to 13 radials found in our 5-state area is likely to be this variety, although there are two other cacti which at least come close to this area and show the same features.

Among the things which separate this plant from variety *applanata* and variety *heyderi* are the facts that the flower is noticeably larger and the fruits usually smaller than those of its relatives. This conflicts with Backeberg's statement that the flowers of *hemisphaerica* are smaller than those of its relatives, but among many specimens from United States and also from the type locality in Mexico which I have examined I have always found the flowers larger. Engelmann also states that the seeds are smaller, but Craig gives their dimensions as the same, and I have not been able to notice any difference in the seeds of the three varieties. Neither is it true that the stem of this variety is more rounded and hemispherical than those of variety *heyderi* and variety *applanata,* as its name would imply. The shape of the stem in this variety, as in the others, depends entirely upon whether the environment is favorable or unfavorable. The tallest, most rounded specimen of this species I have seen is a luxuriant, large specimen of variety *applanata,* while the flattest specimen I have seen was a desiccated plant of variety *hemisphaerica* found on the dry bluff just back of the beach near Corpus Christi.

The main locality for variety *hemisphaerica* is the Gulf Coast from its type locality within Mexico north to Corpus Christi.

Here it grows to the very edges of the sand dunes along the beach, as close to the water as the bushes grow which it must have over it to protect it from the full sun it can hardly tolerate. As you go west from the Gulf into the south Texas brush country you soon lose this species, except in a narrow strip extending along the Nueces River and into Atascosa County.

It is a real surprise, therefore, to collect this same cactus growing rather commonly, along with variety *applanata,* in Jackson and Greer counties of extreme southwestern Oklahoma, but there it is, having skipped over all of Texas between these widely discontinuous ranges.

There have been supposed collections of variety *hemisphaerica* in the Organ Mountains of New Mexico. This is indeed a greatly different environment from the south Texas coast, and if this is our cactus, makes for one of the most curious distributions of all cacti. I cannot either confirm or deny this occurrence of the variety in New Mexico, since all I have seen are the herbarium specimens from New Mexico, and these lack the flowers. It should be remembered, however, that there grow in Arizona and nearby Mexico two species of Mammillarias very similar in most respects, with the same number of radial spines as variety *hemisphaerica.* Merely counting spines would not separate this variety and those two: *Mammillaria macdougalii* and *M. gummifera.* The best means of distinguishing these from our cactus is by the fact that *M. macdougalii* and *M. gummifera* have the outer perianth segments of their flowers fringed with cilia, while variety *hemisphaerica* has smooth edges on these segments. The fruits of *M. macdougalii* also fail to become bright red, remaining greenish with only the upper parts turning rose. Without having seen the flowers and fruits of these Organ Mountain specimens, I feel that it is at least as likely that they are one of these more southwestern forms as that they are variety *hemisphaerica,* since finding one of those in the Organ Mountains would prove far less an extension of their known ranges and environments than to find the Gulf Coast cactus there. Perhaps the reader may be fortunate enough to secure this New Mexico form and, seeing its flowers, be able to settle the question, which I feel must stand unanswered at present.

Mammillaria meiacantha Eng.
"Biznaga de Chilitos," "Little Chilis"

DESCRIPTION   PLATE 43

STEMS: Each plant consists of a single circular stem up to as much as 12 inches across, but greatly depressed so that it rises to a maximum of 1 or 2 inches above the ground. This is the top of a large underground base which might be interpreted as an extremely short taproot. The almost flat surface of the stem above the ground is covered by firm, dark green or blue-green tubercles arranged in spiral rows. These tubercles are pyramidal from quadrangular bases having their ventral angle exaggerated into a keel. They vary from about 1/2 inch long and 3/8 of an inch wide at the base on small specimens to a maximum of about 7/8 of an inch long and 5/8 of an inch wide on large plants. A milky sap is exuded at any wound.

AREOLES: Dimorphic. The spinous portion on the tip of the tubercle is nearly round and about 1/8 of an inch across, with white wool at first, but later bare. The floral portion is in the axil of the tubercle, with white wool at first, which is later lost.

SPINES: There are 5 to 9 stout radial spines which instead of lying flat upon the surface of the plant stand more or less spreading. They are 1/4 to 1/2 inch long. The lower ones on each areole are the longest and heaviest. They are pinkish at first, fading to gray or yellowish, and always having black or dark brown tips. There is one central spine which is similar to the radials except often a little darker and only about 1/4 to 3/8 of an inch long. It stands out almost perpendicular to the surface of the plant, or quite often is turned upward almost with the upper radials.

FLOWERS: Opening widely, 1 to 1 3/4 inches long and wide, often a number of them forming a ring of blooms just outside the newer center of the plant. The 12 to 14 outer segments of the perianth have reddish-brown midlines with pinkish, entire edges. The 14 to 16 inner petals have purplish midlines and pink or white edges. These are to 1/4 of an inch wide, with pointed tips and edges often very lightly notched toward the tip. The filaments are white or pink, while the anthers are cream or yellowish. The style is longer than the stamens. There are 6 to 9 light green stigma lobes.

FRUITS: Elongated and club-shaped, deep rose or scarlet in color. They are about 7/8 to 1 1/4 inches long. The seeds are reddish-brown, less than 1/16 of an inch (less than 1 millimeter) long, and pitted.

RANGE. From northern Mexico throughout southwestern Texas west of a line running from near Sanderson, Texas, along the eastern edges of the Davis and Guadalupe mountains to near Carlsbad, New Mexico, and throughout about the lower one-fourth of New Mexico into Arizona.

REMARKS. This is the largest Mammillaria found in the U.S., but certainly not the most conspicuous. Although most specimens are about 5 to 8 inches in diameter, it is still possible to find old plants up to 12 inches across—that is, if one has eyes sharp enough to find this cactus at all. Although growing easily to pie-plate size, *M. meiacantha* is usually so flat as to be near the shape of an inverted pie-plate, and in very dry seasons its large fleshy base shrinks and literally pulls the plant into the ground so that it is common for its tubercles to be level with the soil or only slightly above it. The surrounding grass and weeds then make its discovery a real accomplishment.

This species has numerous close relatives from which it is not easily distinguished. Various characters have been tried as distinguishing ones, but most of them can be matched by the extreme forms of its relatives. *M. meiacantha* has sharply quadrangular and keeled tubercles, but the bases of the tubercles of *M. heyderi* and *M. melanocentra* are also somewhat quadrangular. It has milky sap, but so do those other species, although on them one must often pierce the base of the stem itself to get a flow of this white sap, while in *M. meiacantha* it flows from any pin-prick on any tubercle. The flowers and fruits are quite similar to those of the other species, except a little larger than those of the western varieties of *M. heyderi*.

For distinguishing *M. meiacantha*, then, it seems we must come back to its spines. It has only 5 to 9 stout radials, which number distinguishes it from all the *M. heyderi* group, as well as from *M. macdougalii* and *M. gummifera*, all of these having from 9 to more than 20 slender, almost bristle-like radials. Only *M. melanocentra*, a Mexican species, has spines similar in number and thickness, but here the length of spines distinguishes, as *M. meiacantha* has radials only 1/4 to 1/2 inch long and centrals only 1/4 to 3/8 of an inch long, while *M. melanocentra* has radials 3/4 to 1 1/2 inches long and the central 3/4 to 1 1/4 inches long, making separation easy.

With only such details of spines to separate these closely related forms, it is natural that there has been a history of uncertainty about how they should be classified and how closely they should be linked in the taxonomy. Engelmann, who first described a number of them, remarked that *M. meiacantha* might be only a variety of *M. heyderi*, but this idea did not appear likely enough to any of those who studied these plants after him to be followed by any of them. All left it as a separate species until 1945, when Craig, in his *Mammillaria Handbook*, combined *M. meiacantha* with the long-spined Mexican species, *M. melanocentra*, as *M. melanocentra* var. *meiacantha*. This seems a more likely relationship, and he was followed in this by Marsden. Backeberg, however, more recently leaves the cactus as a separate species. What future taxonomists will do, and whether the cactus will be called a variety, or remain a species does not yet seem possible to predict.

At any rate, *M. meiacantha* is a definite resident of west Texas and southern New Mexico which anyone will want to recognize. It is more specifically a desert plant than is *M. heyderi*, with which most are more familiar. It can stand the full sun better, and often grows totally unshaded except for the sparse grasses of the Big Bend hillsides, while *M. heyderi* grows only under bushes and shrubs and suffers in full sun. But being more of a desert cactus, it also rots more quickly than the others if watered too much. This must be kept in mind when it is cultivated.

There seems some confusion about the range of *M. meiacantha*, or else it is not now growing over large parts of its former territory. Engelmann said it was found throughout New Mexico, and Coulter, another student of the past century, stated that it grew then from the Guadalupe River of Texas on west. I can find no evidence of its having been seen east of the Big Bend and the Davis Mountains in Texas, or north of approximately the southern one-fourth of New Mexico since their times.

Mammillaria sphaerica Dietrich
[*Dolichothele sphaerica* (Dietrich) B. & R.]

DESCRIPTION   PLATE 44

ROOTS: A thick, soft, fleshy taproot sometimes up to 1 inch thick.

STEMS: Light green in color, spherical, often depressed at the top. These heads usually produce new ones on all sides rapidly, so that a mature plant usually consists of a low mass up to nearly a foot in diameter composed of irregularly clustering stems. The tubercles making up the stem of a vigorous plant are very soft, spreading loosely, and ranging from 1/2 to 1 1/4 inches long. They are cylindrical, usually tapering toward the end, and are not grooved and not broadened at the base. When a plant suffers from insufficient water or too much sun, however, these same tubercles will shrink to as little as 1/4 of an inch long and become firm, regular in size, and closely packed, giving the plant a very different appearance.

AREOLES: Dimorphic. The spinous portion on the tip of the tubercle is small and circular, with some short wool at first, becoming bare. The floral portion in the axil of the tubercle has some hairs which may or may not persist after the flower.

SPINES: There are 12 to 15 radial spines which are slender and weak. They radiate evenly around the areole, but on the same areole they will usually vary in length from the three lower ones which are as short as 3/16 of an inch to the thicker lateral and upper ones which are 3/8 to 5/8 of an inch long. They have brownish, enlarged bases, and the upper parts are smooth, hornlike, and yellow in color, becoming gray with age. There is one central standing out perpendicularly to the plant, it being similar to the radials except slightly thicker and 3/8 to 1/2 inch long.

FLOWERS: Clear lemon-yellow in color, about 2 to 2 1/2 inches in diameter and height. The ovary is cylindrical, light green, and naked. There are a total of about 25 petals. The outer ones are short, narrow, linear, and pointed. The next ones are long—the longest on the flower, broadening toward the point to about 3/8 of an inch wide, with brownish midlines and yellow, smooth edges. The innermost petals broaden from very narrow bases to about the same width, but are shorter. They are lemon-yellow. The filaments are pale orange and swirled in position, the anthers of the same color being tucked in around the style. There are 8 long, rough stigma lobes which are yellowish. The flower is fragrant.

FRUITS: Seldom seen, as the plants do not seem to set many fruits even in the native habitats. When produced they are egg-shaped, about 1/2 inch long, persisting on the plant as green structures between the tubercles until at least the following winter, when they turn maroon, although they have usually been eaten by animals and disappeared before this. The seeds are black, with pitted surfaces.

RANGE. South Texas below a line from near Laredo to approximately Corpus Christi, and on into Mexico.

REMARKS. This cactus grows under the bushes in the thickets of the south Texas brush country. Its low clusters are rather common, wherever the brush has never been cleared, below the longitude of Laredo on the west and Corpus Christi on the east, but it is much more often found, at least today, in the western part of its range than nearer the coast. Where the brush has at any time been cleared and then has grown back again, as in vast areas of this territory, the vegetation may look the same, but there is little use searching for our cactus, as it cannot survive the sun without its protecting shrubs, and it does not seem to be able to reestablish itself under the new growth.

Mammillaria sphaerica can most quickly be distinguished from the other Mammillarias of Texas, which it superficially resembles, by its color. Its surface is a very light, almost sickly yellow-green, even when most healthy, while all of the other Mammillarias we have are dark green or even bluish-green.

When growing in its habitat or with perfect conditions, *M. sphaerica* has large, soft, loose, spreading tubercles. The looseness of these and the variation in their sizes on the several heads of a robust clump make it hard to distinguish the individual heads of such a clump. It often looks like one disorganized stem. But if water or shade is withdrawn from such a plant, or if it is transplanted, the tubercles will shrink to less than one-half their former size and be pulled together until the plant appears entirely different, being now a cluster of small, spherical, compact heads of short, firm tubercles. This latter appearance seems to be the condition from which all of the early descriptions were made.

The flowers of this species are large, a beautiful, clear yellow in color, and produced in large numbers, on a healthy specimen. It is not uncommon for a good specimen to have a dozen blooms at a time, covering it entirely. I had trouble photographing this species, trying to get a good specimen in bloom with few enough flowers so that the plant body would still be visible.

Because of its beautiful flowers plus the liking of this species for shade and its rather good tolerance of coolness and moisture, this should be a much better cactus for growing in northern and eastern climates than the strictly desert species. One must remember, however, that it cannot stand freezing, and so would have to be well-protected when grown in the north.

M. sphaerica has a very close relative in northern Mexico, called *M. longimamma*. The two are very similar, and might even be considered varieties of the same species. The latter, however, is larger in most respects than our Texas form, its tubercles to 2 inches long, its spines to 1 inch long, and its flowers about the same size. The two may easily be confused, and two characters only are usually given by which to distinguish them. *M. sphaerica* has smooth spines and the filaments of its flowers are swirled, while *M. longimamma* has rough or hairy spines and straight filaments.

These cacti have, since Britton and Rose's fragmentation of the genera, often been considered to make up a separate genus called *Dolichothele*. The validity of this separation is still the subject of much discussion.

Through the years of discussion of this problem, the reasons given for the separation of these plants from *Mammillaria* have boiled down to only one real one. It is undeniable that the flowers of these plants have a longer and more constricted flower tube than the typical Mammillarias, and this is the whole reason upon which Buxbaum, for instance, insists the genus *Dolichothele* should be kept separate. He insists that in these plants the tube is a solid, closed column, and that this is essentially different from the more hollow tubes of other cacti.

The evaluation of this character is a very technical job for a botanist. Suffice it to say here that while Buxbaum considers this "column-building" of the tube an essentially distinct character isolating these plants from all other cacti, others have noted that there are degrees of lengthening and closing of the tube among cacti, and that these cacti are not the only ones showing this feature to at least some degree.

Backeberg states flatly that Buxbaum erred in saying that this character fully isolated the Dolichotheles from all others. He devotes several pages of very technical discussion in *Die Cactaceae* to this problem, and there is no reason to repeat his points here, but he concludes with statements that, strictly speaking, all arguments for the separation of these cacti are removed, and that after the inclusion of the genus *Phellosperma* and *Krainzia* into *Mammillaria* again by Buxbaum, there exists no ground for separating *Dolichothele* from *Mammillaria* either. His argument is so effective, in my opinion, that I fail to see why, after making it, he has gone ahead and listed the genus *Dolichothele* anyway in his own account. I only differ from him by acting upon his arguments and placing these cacti back into *Mammillaria*. The whole point of his discussion seems to be that opinions can at this stage differ, and that the final solution of "the *Dolichothele* problem" cannot even yet be presented. With this I heartily agree. I only differ in feeling that much confusion would have been avoided if separations had not been made until the evidence for them had been definite in the first place, and that, since the evidence for this particular separation is not clear even yet, the best thing for the service of clarity would be to drop the separation which has always stood, at best, on doubtful grounds. If cactus genera are to be meaningful it seems they should be based on something more tangible than this, or taxonomy will always remain the bugaboo it is now for the cactophile, and we will continue to be the target of jokes about "cactusization," defined by C. V. Morton as "the process of fragmenting or even pulverizing large genera of plants . . . a popular sport among numerous fanciers of the Cactaceae."

Genus *Opuntia* Miller

Placed last in this account is the large genus, *Opuntia*. Those who deal in matters of primitive versus advanced and theories of development tell us it should really be the first United States genus considered. The Opuntias are generally regarded as more primitive than the cacti we have already enumerated, and they also certainly deserve first place for their success. In over half of our states Opuntias are the only cacti found, and it is these cacti which enable us to say that cacti grow over almost the whole of the U.S. It is also the Opuntias which have escaped and flourished when introduced in such faraway parts of the world as the Mediterranean and north African countries, where they have become in many places a common part of the scenery, and Australia, where they have become the classic examples of plant invaders.

But in spite of all this I am putting the genus *Opuntia* at the back of the book. This is in deference to the fact that most people find them the least interesting of the cacti, and many people associate them too strongly with unpleasantness to be able to appreciate them at all. Even many cactophiles lack interest in them. It is not at all uncommon to find a fancier with a large collection of almost all other types of cacti, which includes not a single Opuntia, or only a few of the more exotic forms of the genus. Some collectors will travel hundreds of miles to get a new barrel cactus and on the way pass by twenty species of Opuntias all in sight from the highway without even stopping to study them.

There are very real reasons for this lack of interest in or actual avoidance of the Opuntias. I do not deny that. These cacti bring it upon themselves. The Opuntias make no attempt to please, and actually seem to be the experts in every means of antagonizing other organisms. They have several built-in features not shared by other cacti, which lose them friends.

No doubt their most effective feature in provoking our dislike is one of their most obvious distinguishing characteristics—their possession of glochids. Glochids are special spines produced by this genus, usually in great numbers. They are distinct from the ordinary spines, which these cacti usually have in profusion as well, although there may be intermediates.

The ordinary, larger spines of a cactus are dangerous enough, may inflict real injuries, and in cases where they are hooked or positioned at opposing angles on the plant, may hold one all too firmly, but they are not ordinarily barbed, and so they can usually be extracted from clothing or flesh rather easily if one is careful to remove them at the same angle they went in. But not so the glochids. These are comparatively very slender, often almost invisible they are so thin, and during development the cells covering the surface of each glochid loosen on their posterior edges so that on the completed glochid they stand as hundreds of firm, scalelike structures, each aimed obliquely to the rear—literally forming hundreds of tiny barbs to hold this tiny spear in whatever soft tissue it may pierce with its sharp point, and to rend and tear if there is an attempt to remove it. Add to this the fact that glochids, instead of being solidly attached to the plant like the other spines, become when mature so loosely held that they come off the areole at the slightest touch, and you have here instruments of torture parallel to and equally as diabolical as the spines of the porcupine. Man or beast usually comes away from a brush with an Opuntia bearing in his flesh whole clusters of these tiny, almost invisible glochids, which may not have been felt at all when they pierced the flesh, but which are firmly imbedded there—not deep, not even through the skin—but each one well set and with its shaft projecting so that any slightest touch to it or pressure on it makes the tiny barbs tear, and produces a pain like a needle prick. They are especially maddening because they are often so tiny that you can hardly see what is causing all the pain, and so delicate that if you do find them and take hold of them to remove them, their ends usually break off, leaving the tips imbedded, with only the stumps to be bumped and cause continual pain. If one cannot get the maddening things out at once before they work in and set their barbs, the only really effective thing to do for a mass of tiny glochids in the flesh is to shave them off with a close-shaving razor. Once the projecting ends are removed this way, the tips in the skin will not be felt again and will soon work out.

Some Opuntias make use of barbs on their larger spines as well, and on some of them a whole branch comes off and remains stuck to animal or human which has touched it, hitching a ride to a new location this way. It is an extremely unpleasant task to pull one of these branches off when its spines are well imbedded.

So who can blame the person who wouldn't touch an Opuntia with a ten-foot pole, let alone have it in his greenhouse, especially when many of them have a habit of spreading out into good-sized bushes and so taking up much room? Add to this the fact that they are the most difficult of all cacti to classify, the most variable and, therefore, difficult to recognize, and you have reasons enough for avoiding them.

Yet there is much to be said for the Opuntias as well. They have many quite interesting features, may be very beautiful, and are also the most widely used for food of any cacti. And then they are undoubtedly the most challenging of the cacti. So there are those most dedicated of cactophiles who wade right into the thickets of the Opuntias, so to speak, and study them out. When to these people who are dedicated to understanding *all* cacti are added all of the people who are more likely to see an Opuntia in the back pasture or by the roadside than any other cactus, and who would like to know something about it, there must be a large number who will find interest in the admittedly difficult account of this complex, creeping, sprawling group, whose relationships are sometimes almost as hard to understand as its thickets are to penetrate. We offer them here, at the end of our account, as the final challenge in cactus study.

Usually mentioned characteristics of the Opuntias are the possession of jointed stems; cylindrical or conic leaves on young stems; the presence of glochids; the production of spreading, rotate flowers with more or less sensitive stamens and with areoles, which often produce glochids and spines, on the ovaries; fruits with thick rinds; and seeds comparatively large, rounded in one plane and flattened in the other, while covered by hard, bony, light-colored arils.

There is usually little difficulty in recognizing an Opuntia and telling it from the cacti of the other genera. One or another of the features just listed is almost always so obvious that one could hardly miss it. So we do not need to dwell here on the characteristics of the genus.

But once a person knows he has an Opuntia, bis problems have only begun, if he wishes to classify it further. This is because the process of sorting out the Opuntias within the group is one of the most difficult in all taxonomy. Several things contribute to this difficulty.

One of these is the fact that the Opuntias seem to react to differences in their environments more quickly and with more drastic growth-form changes than do other cacti. In the Echinocacti or Echinocerei the plant usually grows much the same as any other of its own species as long as the environment is tolerable at all, and then ordinarily, if the environment becomes so changed that it cannot put out typical growth, it just fails to grow at all. On the other hand, the Opuntia in a bad situation will grow on, but grow in a form often so radically different from the typical that one would hardly suspect the environmentally modified specimen to be of the same species as a typical one.

As a result of this fact, where, for instance, in the former genera one can list maximum and minimum spine numbers, spine lengths, and spine characters within definite, rather narrow, and unvarying limits, and often use these to recognize species, one has to list the spines of Opuntias within widely varying limits and one must be very careful in any attempt to delineate species of Opuntias by their spine characters. A simple experiment, if only once carried out, would keep a person from ever again depending on Opuntia spines remaining the same. It is easy to take half a dozen different, typically spiny Opuntias and by growing them a few years in a very shady, moist situation, end up with half a dozen very nearly indistinguishable, spineless or only weakly spined specimens. All too often such an atypical plant has been given a separate name or has been mistaken for a normally weak-spined species. The literature is, therefore, a morass of conflicting reports.

Other characters of the Opuntias, such as stem size or even stem shape, flower and fruit size, and so on, are also capable of being influenced by the environment. Where an Echinocactus or a Mammillaria either puts out a standard-sized flower and fruit or else just waits to make the effort until the environment is more favorable, an Opuntia in a poor situation usually does not mind at all putting out a flower half as big as typical, and may go ahead to ripen a fruit also half as big as it should have been. Great care must be taken to allow for this variability.

Perhaps the only effort to approach this problem properly was made by Dr. David Griffiths, who, with U. S. experiment stations at his disposal, once started an ambitious program of growing all the Opuntias of the Southwest in identical situations and of raising seedlings of them all in uniform and differing environments in order to discover what really are the constant characters of these cacti. But this sort of a program would take many years to yield really definite answers, and although Dr. Griffiths was able to gain some hints in the years he carried it on, no one continued his fields of Opuntias, and no such attempt has been made again. We are therefore left to work out indirectly what the solid characters of these species are, and it is no easy task.

To the foregoing must be added the fact that some of the Opuntia species cover huge ranges of territory and within these huge territories show various different forms not directly due to environment. It seems clear, for instance, that the large prickly pears of the U.S. can only be understood if a few very broad species are recognized. One of these, *Opuntia engelmannii,* with its range running from at least Louisiana—and some would say even from Florida—to California, would be one of the widest ranging of any U.S. cactus. And within this huge entity are a number of varieties which have caused great confusion, as some have described them as separate species, and others have ignored them entirely, assuming them to be the mere results of local environments. It is hard to find agreement as to how to interpret such a situation, and experimental evidence is so far almost totally lacking.

In this study, when faced with this sort of situation, I have taken the attitude that no described form can be ignored and relegated to the synonymy without investigation. So we have made great efforts to locate and study each one described for this area, no matter how obscure. And wherever we have found a form which exists as a population with a definable range, which does not seem to be due to a local environmental factor, but which does not seem distinct enough to be clearly a separate species, I have listed it as a variety. Only by keeping these forms thus in sight can we keep them available for the biosystematic studies which are long overdue and which will someday give us a clearer understanding of the Opuntias.

The genus *Opuntia* is an old one, and it has been subdivided. The system for the U.S. members has usually taken the form of a division into 2 or 3 groups based mostly on the forms of the stems and partly on spine characters. These groupings were some of them made very early and the divisions called subgenera or sections of the genus. The earliest divisions were into subgenus *Cylindropuntia* Eng., with stems tending to be cylindrical and more or less tuberculate, and subgenus *Platyopuntia* Weber, having the stems to some degree flattened. *Cylindropuntia* was then divided and those members of it which had cylindrical stems were left under that name, while those which had more or less club-shaped stems were placed in a subgenus called variously *Clavatopuntia* by Fric, *Clavatae* by Berger, and most recently *Cornyopuntia* by Knuth. This arrangement would give 3 groups of Opuntias in the United States, and there are several others in Central and South America.

Little fault can be found with these groupings. They seem natural groups within the genus. But granting that, we are soon faced with the old genus problem, since some authors have recently elevated these groupings, originally sections or subgenera of the genus *Opuntia* to the level of genera themselves, thus doing away with the old genus entirely, or like Earle, limiting the genus *Opuntia* to the forms which made up the former subgenus *Platyopuntia*.

What are we to do about the newer system which divides this genus into several genera? Here once more it seems I must make a decision based almost totally upon my own philosophy and my concept of a genus. It seems rather clear that there is a natural grouping into cylindrical and flat-jointed Opuntias, although

a few species are close to intermediates even here. The division between cylindrical and club-shaped is not as clear. There are some forms which show an ability to adopt somewhat of either stem form, and are difficult to place definitely in either. Other differences which have been searched out between these two groups—such as spines sheathed or not sheathed—have not proved too reliable either.

After much study of this problem it seems to me that while these groupings represent something natural, and have some significance, they hardly represent essential enough differences to be the bases for different genera. To use the worn, but it seems important, analogy from the genus *Euphorbia* once again, the stems of *Euphorbia obesa, Euphorbia grandicornis,* and *Euphorbia prostrata* seem every bit as essentially different as do those of our three Opuntia groups. We have also, in our laboratory, run a series of chromatographic studies on Opuntias and found no evidence of chemical groupings to parallel these divisions, as one would expect if the differences were generic. So we have concluded that while these groupings may be useful, and may form the basis for subdividing the old genus *Opuntia*, they should probably not supplant it.

I am not concerning myself here with the long lists of series or sections into which this genus has been divided by various authors. Each series published so far contradicts the others, and I have found enough faults in those of Britton and Rose and also in those of Backeberg, for instance, that I feel such detailed classification of the group is still premature. We just don't understand the genetics of these plants, the way they vary, and the significance of their various characters well enough yet. Perhaps, if their many forms are not lost sight of, after experimentation is carried on it will then be possible to set up meaningful series of the Opuntias.

Those hardy enough, and possessing enough of the true botanist's curiosity which will let him pass up no plant, however thorny, will find a huge opportunity in the study of the Opuntias. In sheer numbers of their populations and extents of their ranges they excel. Nor does one have the disappointing experience with these, that he all too often has with the other cacti, of traveling to a spot where a species is supposed to grow profusely only to find that some collector or dealer has stripped the area bare of every specimen which once was there. So few bother to bring home Opuntias that one can travel through country most ruthlessly sacked of cacti and still find the Opuntias untouched. Even the inroads of agriculture have not adversely affected the majority of them. Root-plowing, chaining, and most of the other practices used to clear the range of the chaparral have usually, while exterminating the other cacti, merely torn the Opuntias apart and distributed their stems widely, each one of which then rooted, and the Opuntia population has, therefore, multiplied. So the opportunity for studying them is perhaps greater today in our area than ever before. Only a few obscure species limited to very small ranges have been reduced by clearing of fields and agricultural practices, although in the future the picture will probably be very different. All the big guns of the chemical industry are being aimed at the chaparral, and the mass spraying of the range with some of the newer herbicides, barely started now, clearly could reduce these plants to a vanishing point. But the student of the Opuntias can take heart in knowing that, tough as these plants are, they will be among the last wild plants to go, and he will be one of the last students of wild plants to survive.

The flat-stemmed Opuntias are known almost universally as prickly pears. Tough and thorny as they are, these are the main food-producing cacti. Tons of their stems are fed to cattle, particularly in Texas and Mexico, where sophisticated methods are used to burn the spines off so that the flesh is available to the animals. And these plants are used extensively for human consumption as well. The young pads, before their tissues have hardened or their spines been produced are relished. Called *nopalitos,* these are eaten widely in Mexico, where they are usually breaded with cornmeal and fried, and in Texas, where they are more often boiled and added to a sort of omelet. In the spring they are often on sale at markets in San Antonio and the rest of south Texas, and in San Antonio they are served in some Mexican restaurants, as well as being sold canned in some supermarkets. But the most widely used part of the Opuntia is probably the fruit, called tuna. Certain species producing large, sweet fruits are cultivated as crops in Mexico, and this was one of the reasons for these plants being introduced into some other parts of the world where they have become such pests.

The large, upright, cylindrical-stemmed Opuntias are known collectively as chollas. I do not know of any use of these chollas for food. They are far too woody and tough, and their fruits are not edible. But certain species of them make very large and beautiful bushes, and are widely grown as ornamentals. Almost any inhabited area of the Southwest will have some specimens of these species planted just for their beauty. They may be prized highly in places where almost no other shrubs or trees will grow. And anyone who has looked over the typical curio store knows well the lamp bases and other trinkets made of the curious, reticulated wood of these chollas.

So, whether regarded as friends or enemies, the Opuntias are easily some of the most strange, fascinating, and challenging of plants.

KEY TO THE OPUNTIAS

1a. Joints flattened; spines not covered with papery sheaths (Platyopuntias)—2.

2a. Plants upright and bushy, 2 to 7 feet tall, sometimes spreading and forming thickets, but with no branches prostrate, and with upright branches attaining a length of three pads or more—3.

3a. Areoles $3/4$ to $2^1/2$ inches apart, with the majority on any pad one inch or more apart—4.

4. Possessing spines—5.

5a. Spines all round   —O. *stricta* (in part).

5b. At least one spine of each areole flattened—6.

6a. Pads conspicuously tuberculate by raised areoles; fruits spiny, with 1 to 5 rigid spines up to 1 inch long on at least each upper areole, and these fruits becoming dry when ripe   —O. *spinosibacca.*

6b. Pads not markedly tuberculate; fruits naked or nearly so—7.

7a. Spines when mature whitish, yellow, red-brown, or mottled, but with no part of any spine black—8.

8a. Pads circular or variously shaped, but not over twice as long as broad—9.

9a. Seeds $1/16$ to $3/16$ of an inch ($1^1/2$–$4^1/2$ millimeters) in diameter—10.

10a. Spines on old areoles on old pads not increasing in number beyond the normal 10 or so of mature pads—11.

11a. Areoles and glochids normal in appearance and not exaggerated in development when old—12.

12a. Fruits spherical, oval, or broadly pear-shaped, with little or no constriction below, with the umbilicus not constricted but flat or nearly so and as broad or nearly as broad as the widest part of the fruit; flowers yellow to red, but never yellow with red centers—13.

13a. Fruits 2 to $3^1/2$ inches long, deep burgundy in color when ripe; seeds $1/8$ of an inch or a little more (3–4 millimeters) in diameter; stigmas green—14.

14a. Spines deep brown at their bases, becoming white or whitish toward the tips; leaves $1/4$ to $3/8$ of an inch long; fruits edible
—O. *engelmannii* var. *engelmannii.*

14b. Spines and glochids all bright yellow or yellow with the bases to sometimes all but the tips red-brown; leaves $1/4$ to $1/2$ inch long; fruits not pleasant to the taste
—O. *engelmannii* var. *texana.*

13b. Fruits 1 to 2 inches long, bright red to purplish-red when ripe; seeds $1/16$ to $3/16$ of an inch ($1^1/2$–$4^1/2$ millimeters) in diameter; stigmas white to greenish—15.

15a. Spines heavy and rigid, the longest spine usually about $1^1/2$ inches long and only rarely reaching $2^1/2$ inches; fruits purplish-red—16.

16a. Fruits spherical or nearly so with no constriction below and always spineless; seeds about $3/16$

of an inch (4–4¹/₂ millimeters) in diameter; spines red-brown or with at least the bases red-brown; flowers small with dark green stigmas　—*O. engelmannii* var. *cyclodes.*

16b. Fruits not spherical, but broadly egg-shaped with some slight constriction below and having numerous glochids and often a few spines ¹/₄ to ⁵/₈ of an inch long on them; seeds extremely small, being ¹/₁₆ of an inch or slightly more (1¹/₂–2¹/₂ millimeters) in diameter; spines entirely yellow; flowers large with stigmas light greenish-white
　—*O. engelmannii* var. *alta.*

15b. Spines slender and long, as well as somewhat flexible, the main spines being 2 to 3 inches long; fruits not so purplish, but more bright red; stigmas either dark green or white —17.

17a. Pads thick and light or yellowish-green; main central spines all sharply deflexed and very flexible and ¹/₂ to 3 inches long; fruit broad egg-shaped to club-shaped, with some constriction below; seeds about ¹/₈ of an inch (3–3¹/₂ millimeters) in diameter; stigmas dark green
　—*O. engelmannii* var. *flexispina.*

17b. Pads thin and blue-green in color; main spines porrect, 2 to 3 inches long and conspicuously longer than the other spines; fruits spherical to oval with no constriction below; seeds between ¹/₁₆ and ¹/₈ of an inch (2–3 millimeters) in diameter; stigmas white —*O. engelmannii* var. *cacanapa.*

12b. Fruits elongated and club-shaped, with the base definitely constricted and the umbilicus also constricted, much narrower than the widest part of the fruit and deeply to very deeply pitted; stigmas yellowish—18.

18a. Spines bright yellow or yellow with light brown bases; flowers all yellow; fruits purplish or plum in color; seeds ³/₁₆ of an inch or less (3¹/₂–4¹/₂ millimeters) in diameter
　—*O. tardospina.*

18b. Spines brown below with whitish

above, never bright yellow; flowers orange-yellow with red centers; fruits bright scarlet-red in color; seeds ³/₁₆ of an inch or more (4–5 millimeters) in diameter
　—*O. phaeacantha* var. *major* (in part).

11b. Areoles and glochids exaggerated in development when old—19.

19a. Areoles enlarging to ¹/₂ inch in diameter on old stems and bulging outward to form a sort of cylindrical projection to ¹/₂ inch high, with a compact tuft of short glochids on the summit of it; pads large, mostly round, and blue-green in color　—*O. engelmannii* var. *dulcis.*

19b. Areoles large and bulging outward noticeably, with glochids very long and scattered loosely throughout the areole, forming starlike clusters almost covering the surfaces of the mature pads; pads smaller and more obovate and with the color more dull dark green than is typical for the species
　—*O. engelmannii* var. *aciculata* (in part).

10b. Spines on old areoles on old trunks increasing greatly to 20 or 30 per areole, covering the older parts of the plants with a complete covering of spines　—*O. chlorotica.*

9b. Seeds more than ³/₁₆ of an inch (4¹/₂ millimeters or more) in greatest diameter
　—*O. phaeacantha* var. *camanchica* (when unusually large and ascending).

8b. Pads greatly elongated so that at least some of them on a normal plant are at least twice as long as they are broad　—*O. engelmannii* var. *linguiformis.*

7b. Spines when growing black or bright orange, when mature black or dark blackish-brown, at least at the base—20.

20a. Fruits ³/₄ to 1¹/₂ inches long, oval or ovate, with no noticeable constriction below and the umbilicus rather deeply pitted, yellowish to scarlet when ripe; seeds ¹/₈ to ³/₁₆ of an inch (3–4¹/₂ millimeters) in diameter; spines heavy, rigid, very angular, and 1 to 6 per areole, found on most areoles, but to only 2 inches or less in length; glochids becoming long and average in number on edge areoles; pads thin and blue-green to yellow-green in color, not becoming reddish　—*O. phaeacantha* var. *nigricans.*

20b. Fruits 1¹/₄ to 2 inches long, elongated oval or egg-shaped, with some slight constriction below and a shallowly pitted umbilicus; seeds more than ³/₁₆ of an inch (about 5 millimeters) in diameter; spines heavy, rigid, almost round to somewhat flattened, 2 to 4 per areole in only the upper areoles, but to 3 inches long; glochids few at first, becoming *very* many and *very* long in the edge areoles; pads thick and pale green, often reddish in color or spotted with reddish around the areoles   —*O. phaeacantha* var. *brunnea.*

4b. Spineless—21.
   21a. Pads elongated obovate to elliptic or even spindle-shaped; surface of pads smooth and shining, not glaucous; leaves only 1/8 to 1/4 of an inch long; ovaries narrow and elongated; fruits elongated, pear-shaped, constricted at the base and with deeply pitted umbilicus   —*O. stricta* (in part).
   21b. Pads round or oval or even broader than long, surface dull and glaucous; leaves 3/8 to 5/8 of an inch long; ovaries short and stout; fruits spherical to broadly pear-shaped, with little or no basal constriction and umbilicus flat or only slightly concave—22.
      22a. Surface blue-green; areoles small; glochids very few and short   —*O. engelmannii* var. *subarmata.*
      22b. Surface bright green or dark green, but not blue-green; areoles enlarged and bulging; glochids very long in loose, spreading clusters   —*O. engelmannii* var. *aciculata* (when spineless).

3b. Areoles 1/4 to 1 1/4 inches apart, with the majority on any pad less than 1 inch apart—23.
   23a. Spineless—24.
      24a. Pads pubescent; glochids very many but very short and minute, hardly exceeding the wool in the bulging areoles; fruits remaining greenish and rather dry when ripe   —*O. rufida.*
      24b. Pads not pubescent; glochids few but larger; fruits bright red or orange-red and fleshy when ripe   —*O. macrocentra* (in part).
   23b. Spines present—25.
      25a. Spines black or brown, sometimes with gray but never with yellow coloring, to 4 per areole in a few of the upper areoles only, 2 to 5 inches long, somewhat flexible, and at least one spine flattened; pads usually purplish in color; seeds 3/16 to more than 1/4 of an inch (4 1/2–7 millimeters) in diameter   —*O. macrocentra* (in part).
      25b. Spines yellow in their outer zones, with black or brown bases, not flexible, from 3/4 to 4 inches, but usually less than 2 inches long; pads sometimes reddish, but not distinctly purplish in color; seeds around 1/8 of an inch (2 1/2–4 millimeters) in diameter—26.
      26a. Spines 1 to 3 on a few upper areoles only, 1/2 to 2 inches, but said to have attained 4 inches long; bases of spines brown; spines round; pads usually with reddish coloring; glochids many but very short   —*O. gosseliniana* var. *santa-rita.*
      26b. Spines 3 to 16 on many or all areoles; never over 1 3/4 inches long; bases black or dark red-brown, at least when young; pads yellow-green without purple or reddish coloring; glochids many and long—27.
      27a. Spines 6 to as many as 15, consisting of 1 to 5 rigid

main spines which are either round or flattened and 3/16 to 3/4 of an inch long, plus up to 10 lower, bristle-like spines 3/16 to 3/4 of an inch long   —*O. strigil.*
      27b. Spines 3 to 6, consisting of about 2 rigid, round main ones 1/2 to 1 1/4 inches long and 2 or 3 lower, bristle-like spines 3/16 to 5/8 of an inch long   —*O. atrispina.*

2b. Plants growing prostrate or sprawling, or if ascending, never standing upright over 2 or 3 pads or 12 to 20 inches tall—28.
  28a. Pads 6 to 10 inches long in maximum size—29.
     29a. Areoles 3/8 to 7/8 of an inch apart; fruits more or less spiny and becoming dry when ripe—30.
      30a. Spines 1 to 10 per areole; fruits 1 1/2 to 2 inches long and broadly club-shaped, spiny above or spineless—31.
         31a. Spines 1 to 4 in only the upper areoles of the pads   —*O. rhodantha* var. *rhodantha* (in part).
         31b. Spines 4 to 10 in all or nearly all areoles of the pads   —*O. rhodantha* var. *spinosior.*
      30b. Spines 10 to 15 in all or nearly all areoles; fruits 7/8 to 1 1/4 inches long and obovate to broadly club-shaped, spiny   —*O. hystricina* (in part).
     29b. Areoles 3/4 to 2 inches apart; fruits remaining fleshy and spineless—32.
      32a. At least some areoles with more than one spine; pads almost circular to broad egg-shaped; seeds thin or average in thickness—33.
         33a. Spines 1 to 5, slender to medium thickness, round or nearly so with no lower bristle-like spines present—34.
            34a. Fruits 1 1/2 to 3 1/2 inches long, club-shaped, with pronounced constriction at the base and with the top narrow and deeply pitted; seeds about 1/8 of an inch (2 1/2–4 millimeters) in diameter, with narrow rims and the body of the seed rather thick   —*O. leptocarpa.*
            34b. Fruits 1 1/4 to 2 3/8 inches long, broadly club-shaped, with the base constricted and the umbilicus somewhat pitted; seeds about 3/16 of an inch (4–5 millimeters) in diameter   —*O. phaeacantha* var. *major* (in part, when stunted).
         33b. Spines 1 to 8, main spines heavy to very heavy and flattened, often with lower bristle-like spines present; fruits 1 to 2 inches long, oval to very broadly egg-shaped, with little or no constriction at the base and with broad, flat, or shallowly pitted umbilicus; seeds 3/16 to 1/4 of an inch (4 1/2–6 millimeters) in diameter, with wide rims   —*O. phaeacantha* var. *camanchica* (in part).
      32b. Spineless or with only one spine in a few areoles; pads elongated egg-shaped to spindle-shaped; seeds very thick   —*O. compressa* var. *allairei.*
  28b. Pads 2 to 6 inches long—35.
     35a. At least some areoles of the pad more than 1 1/4 inches apart—this is a stunted, abnormally small specimen of some larger species, and it will probably be impossible to identify it with this key.
     35b. Areoles 3/16 to 1 1/4 inches apart—36.

36a. Pads solidly attached to each other and not detaching to come away from the plant at a touch—37.

  37a. Spines to 5 or more per areole and found on ¹/₂ or more areoles of mature pads; stigmas bright green —38.

    38a. Fruits remaining fleshy when ripe and oval or oblong in shape; seeds not thick for their diameters —39.

      39a. Pads thin with definitely constricted or even attenuated bases; spines round or nearly so, slender and flexible and mostly deflexed; glochids red-brown and short; seeds slightly over ¹/₈ to ¹/₄ inch (3¹/₂–6 millimeters) in diameter, with narrow to medium rims —*O. phaeacantha* var. *tenuispina*.

      39b. Pads thickish, round or nearly so with no definite constrictions at their bases; spines at least somewhat flattened, medium to thick and always rigid, glochids long and yellow or light brown; seeds ³/₁₆ to just over ¹/₄ inch (4¹/₂–6¹/₂ millimeters) in diameter, with wide rims —*O. cymochila*.

    38b. Fruits dry when ripe, various in shape—40.

      40a. Pads elongated oval to clavate, less than half as broad as they are long, and very thick; roots stolon-like; seeds about ¹/₄ of an inch (6–7 millimeters) in diameter —*O. arenaria*.

      40b. Pads round or oval to broadly egg-shaped or oblong, always more than half as broad as they are long and not unusually thick; roots normally fibrous—41.

        41a. Pads more or less prostrate, sometimes with young pads ascending, but with older ones reclining; at least main spines rigid and stout —42.

          42a. Surface of pads noticeably tuberculate and often wrinkled; glochids few to average and short; main spines 0 to 5 per areole and porrect to deflexed, 2 inches or less long, all rigid or often becoming greatly elongated, soft, flexible, and hairlike, particularly toward the bases of the pads —*O. polyacantha* (in part).

          42b. Surface of pads not noticeably tuberculate or wrinkled; glochids many and often long; main spines 1 to 8 per areole, spreading, heavy, but moderately flexible, and to 4 inches long —*O. hystricina* (in part).

        41b. Pads all erect or ascending, with not even old pads reclining; spines slender, to 4 inches long, and moderately flexible —*O. erinaceae*.

  37b. Spines 0 to 4 or rarely 5 per areole on only the upper edge areoles or at most on those of the upper one-half of the pad—43.

    43a. Fruit remaining fleshy; stigmas yellow or whitish —44.

      44a. Fruits egg-shaped to club-shaped with the bases noticeably constricted—45.

45a. Pads ascending from a central trunklet, blue-green or gray-green in color, usually with some purplish blotching around the areoles; root a large central taproot ¹/₂ to 1¹/₂ inches in diameter and 12 inches or longer, not tuber-like enlargements on otherwise fibrous roots; flowers deep red to purple—46.

  46a. Plants standing 6 to 12 inches tall; pads medium thickness and to 4 or 5 inches long, glabrous, blue-green in color, the surface flat without raised areoles; glochids numerous and yellow in color; fruits 1¹/₂ inches or more long; seeds just over ³/₁₆ to ¹/₄ of an inch (5–6 millimeters) in diameter —*O. pottsii*.

  46b. Plants standing less than 6 inches tall; pads thin and to only 2¹/₂ inches long, glaucous gray-green in color, the surface tuberculate by raised areoles; glochids numerous and bright red-brown in color; fruits ⁵/₈ to 1 inch long. Seeds ¹/₈ of an inch or a little more (3–4 millimeters) in diameter —*O. plumbea*.

45b. Pads prostrate or sprawling, not ascending from a central trunklet, thick, yellow-gray or deep green, but not blue-green in color; roots fibrous or fibrous with tubers on them, but with no central taproot—47.

  47a. Pads gray-green or yellow-green and glaucous—48.

    48a. Pads to 5¹/₂ inches long; spines to 2¹/₄ inches long and slender to medium in thickness; glochids greenish-yellow to straw or light brown, average in number, and to ¹/₄ of an inch or less long; flowers large and yellow in color; fruits 1¹/₂ to 2¹/₂ inches long; seeds ³/₁₆ to ¹/₄ of an inch (5 millimeters plus) in diameter —*O. compressa* var. *stenochila*.

    48b. Pads to 4 inches long; spines to 2³/₄ inches long and thick to very thick; glochids bright yellow, very numerous and conspicuous, and to ¹/₂ inch long on old pads; flowers small and reddish in color; fruits ³/₄ to 1 inch long and very slender; seeds ¹/₈ of an inch or a little more (about 3¹/₂ millimeters) in diameter —*O. ballii*.

  47b. Pads deep green, surface shining—49.

    49a. Plant entirely prostrate, with all pads reclining by the end of their first season; pads very thick, very wrinkled when dehydrated, but not tuberculate by elevations at the areoles; spines 0 to 3 per areole on the upper areoles and 1 inch or less long, heavy, straight, and round; inner petals 10 to 14 in number —*O. compressa* var. *humifusa*.

    49b. Plants sprawling, with very old pads

sometimes reclining, but most pads ascending, pads not so thick as the last, somewhat to extremely tuberculate by raised areoles; spines 0 to 5, often some of them over 1 inch long and often the main spine somewhat flattened; inner petals 5 to 9 in number—50.

50a. Spineless; flowers very large (4 to 5 inches in diameter); fruits 2 inches or more long; pads very tuberculate
—*O. compressa* var. *grandiflora*.

50b. Spines 1 to 5; flowers average size (2 to 3 inches in diameter); fruits 1 to 2 inches long—51.

51a. Seeds about ³/₁₆ of an inch (4–5 millimeters) in diameter—52.

52a. Glochids brown or yellowish; surface only somewhat tuberculate; spines 1 to 5; inner petals 7 to 9 in number   —*O. compressa* var. *macrorhiza*.

52b. Glochids bright red-brown; surface very tuberculate; spines 1 to 3; inner petals 5 to 7
—*O. compressa* var. *fusco-atra*.

51b. Seeds only around ¹/₁₆ of an inch (1¹/₂–2 millimeters) in diameter
—*O. compressa* var. *microsperma*.

44b. Fruits oval with no constriction below
—*O. phaeacantha* var. *camanchica* (when stunted).

43b. Fruits becoming dry when ripe; flowers yellow, pink, or rose; stigmas bright green—53.

53a. Stigma lobes 4 to 6; fruits ³/₄ to 1³/₈ inches long, spineless, and without constriction below—54.

54a. Fruits spherical to oval; seeds slightly over ³/₁₆ of an inch (5 millimeters) in diameter, thickish, with narrow, acute rims
—*O. sphaerocarpa*.

54b. Fruits oblong; seeds from ¹/₄ to just over ⁵/₁₆ of an inch (6–8 millimeters) in diameter, flat and not thick for the size, with wide rims
—*O. polyacantha* (in part, when sparcely-spined).

53b. Stigma lobes 8 to 12; fruits 1¹/₂ to 1³/₄ inches long, broad club-shaped with some tapering constriction below; upper areoles spiny or else entirely spineless   —*O. rhodantha* var. *rhodantha* (in part).

36b. Pads loosely attached so that they separate at a touch; pads small, thick, and almost cylindrical when young —55.

55a. Fruits fleshy, elongated, and club-shaped, 1¹/₄ inches or more long; seeds just under ³/₁₆ of an inch (4 millimeters) in diameter; pads to 4¹/₂ inches long, stigmas yellowish   —*O. drummondii*.

55b. Fruits dry, oval or broadly egg-shaped, ¹/₂ to 1 inch long; seeds just over ³/₁₆ of an inch (5 millimeters) in diameter; stigma lobes bright green   —*O. fragilis*.

1b. Joints not flattened but cylindrical or club-shaped; spines with either conspicuous or rudimentary papery sheaths—56.

56a. Joints club-shaped or egg-shaped and very tuberculate; plants prostrate or ascending but 12 inches or less in height; spine sheaths rudimentary on tips of immature spines only and usually not present on adult spines (Cornyopuntias)—57.

57a. Joints elongated club-shaped, prostrate to ascending, usually curved; spines to more than 1¹/₄ inches long—58.

58a. Main central spine very heavy, flat, wide, and roughly cross-striated—59.

59a. Joints 3¹/₂ to 6 inches long; tubercles 1 to 1³/₄ inches long   —*O. stanlyi*.

59b. Joints 1 to 3 inches long; tubercles ¹/₂ to ³/₄ of an inch long   —*O. schottii*.

58b. Main spines round or nearly so, slender to medium thickness, not striated   —*O. grahamii*.

57b. Joints short club-shaped or egg-shaped; main spines to only 1¹/₄ inch long   —*O. clavata*.

56b. Joints cylindrical; plants upright or ascending, never prostrate, bushy, and 1 to 12 feet tall; spine sheaths conspicuous, at least on newly matured main spines (Cylindropuntias)—60.

60a. Width of current year's joints ³/₄ to 2 inches—61.

61a. Tubercles ³/₄ to 1¹/₂ inches long; color deep green at all times—62.

62a. Fruits globose and about 1 inch in diameter, always tuberculate—63.

63a. Main spines ³/₄ to 1¹/₄ inches long; spine sheaths whitish or straw-colored; fruits spineless when mature—64.

64a. Flowers purple or reddish (reported as rarely yellowish or white); growth treelike and 3 to 8 feet tall   —*O. imbricata* var. *arborescens*.

64b. Flowers pale greenish with lavender shading; a small bush 1 to 3 feet tall   —*O. imbricata* var. *viridiflora* (in part).

63b. Main spines 2 to 2¹/₂ inches long, with glistening silvery sheaths; flowers greenish yellow; growth low, 1 to 2 feet tall; fruits with sheathed spines to 1 inch long   —*O. tunicata*.

62b. Fruits obovate to globose, 1 to 2 inches in diameter, becoming nearly or entirely smooth when ripe; main spines to no more than ⁵/₈ of an inch long
—*O. imbricata* var. *vexans*.

61a. Tubercles ³/₈ to ³/₄ inch long—65.

65a. A large bush 3 to 12 feet tall; spines 6 to 25 in number, mostly ³/₈ of an inch or less long and only rarely to ⁵/₈ of an inch, spine sheaths inconspicuous and soon falling off; color of plant surface often purplish in severe conditions   —*O. spinosior*.

65b. Low spreading or mat-forming bushes 1 to 2 feet tall; spines 3 to 12 in number, maximum spine length ³/₄ to 1¹/₄ inches, spine sheaths loose, persistent, and conspicuous; color of plant surface light green   —*O. whipplei* (in part).

60b. Width of current year's joints ³/₄ of an inch or less—66.

66a. Plants low-growing, 1 to 3 feet tall; width of current

year's joints ³/₈ to ³/₄ of an inch, with distinct tubercles —67.

  67a. Largest spines 1¼ inches or less long (usually less than 1 inch)—68.

    68a. Erect, more or less trunked plants; joints strictly cylindrical; spine sheaths not conspicuous and shining; flower greenish-purple or lavender with reddish stigma lobes —*O. imbricata* var. *viridiflora* (in part).

    68b. Ascending or spreading, but without real trunks, often mat-forming plants; joints slightly clavate by being constricted at the bases. Spine sheaths conspicuous and shining; flowers pale yellow; stigmas greenish   —*O. whipplei* (in part).

  67b. Largest spines 1½ to 2 inches long; tubercles ⁵/₈ to 1 inch long   —*O. davisii.*

66b. Plants bushy and growing 3 to 6 feet or more tall; width of current year's joints ⅛ to ½ inch; tubercles indistinct or sometimes actually absent—69.

  69a. Joints ¼ to ½ inch thick, with tubercles indistinct to distinct, but always present—70.

    70a. Joints ³/₁₆ to ½ inch in diameter; flowers greenish-purple and 1 to 1¼ inches in diameter; fruit red and with indistinct tubercles or else smooth when ripe, ³/₄ to 1 inch long; spines to 1 inch long —*O. kleiniae.*

    70b. Joints ³/₁₆ to ³/₈ of an inch in diameter; flowers unknown; fruits yellowish and distinctly tuberculate when ripe, ⁹/₁₆ to ³/₄ of an inch long; spines 1 to 2½ inches long   —*O. vaginata.*

  69b. Joints ⅛ to ¼ of an inch thick, with tubercles at best indistinct and often absent; flowers yellow or greenish-yellow and ½ to ⅞ of an inch in diameter; fruits red or orange-red and smooth when ripe   —*O. leptocaulis.*

Opuntia stricta Haw.
"Pest Pear"

DESCRIPTION   PLATE 44

STEMS: An erect plant, but much branched and diffuse instead of treelike. Usually 2 to 3 feet tall, having elongated, ovate to elliptical or even spindle-shaped pads usually 6 to 9 inches long, but sometimes to 14 inches in length. These pads are of medium thickness, bluish-green and glabrous when young, but becoming light green and somewhat glaucous when old. Its leaves are ⅛ to ³/₁₆ of an inch long.

AREOLES: Very elongated in young pads, becoming oval when older. They are ¼ of an inch or a little more in length, and situated 1¼ to 2½ inches apart.

SPINES: Variable. These plants are often entirely spineless, but some specimens have 1 to 3 spines per areole. When present the spines are porrect or spreading, ³/₈ to 1³/₄ inches long, straight, stiff, and of medium thickness. They are round in cross-section, yellow in color, sometimes becoming slightly mottled with brown, but not having brown bases.

GLOCHIDS: Few and very short on young pads, becoming more with age, but never becoming conspicuous. Remaining comparatively short, growing to a maximum of about ³/₈ of an inch long. They are yellow or straw-colored.

FLOWERS: About 3 to 4 inches in diameter, clear lemon-yellow in color. The ovary is slender club-shaped and 1½ to 3 inches long, with a few glochids in its areoles. The perianth segments are pointed spatulate, greenish at their bases, and clear yellow above. The filaments are greenish below, becoming yellow above, and the anthers are yellow. The short, greenish-yellow style has 6 to 8 fat, white or very pale greenish-white stigma lobes tipping it.

FRUITS: Light pinkish-red to rather bright carmine-red when ripe. In shape elongated club-shaped and 1½ to about 2³/₄ inches long by ³/₄ to 1 inch thick at the broadest upper part. The umbilicus on the summit of the fruit is deeply pitted. The flesh is sweet and edible. The seeds are about ⅛ of an inch (2½–3 millimeters) in diameter, thin, regular, and with very narrow but fairly thick rims.

RANGE. This is primarily a Caribbean species, found on Cuba, Haiti, and the West Indies, but widely spread to South America and Australia. It is found in the United States in south Florida, at Houma, Louisiana, and at the entrance to Galveston Bay.

REMARKS. This was one of the earliest of our Opuntias to be studied. It was first described under the name, *Cactus strictus* in 1803, and then again as *Opuntia stricta* in 1812, both by Haworth. It has often been called *Opuntia inermis.* This is because of a picture, apparently of this plant, which was published by De Candolle in 1799 labeled *Cactus opuntia inermis,* but this is not generally taken to have constituted an official description.

The cactus grows widely in the Caribbean Islands and the West Indies, which seem to be its native location, but it has been cultivated on the west coast of South America, and was taken to Australia. It is the cactus which ran wild over millions of acres of New South Wales and Queensland and became perhaps the most famous of plant invaders in modern times. There it took over huge tracts of both agricultural and grazing lands, making them unfit for any use, and earned its designation as the pest pear. Huge programs were instituted to control it, and it has more recently been brought under a measure of control in Australia.

It is most fortunate that this cactus has not been so successful in the U.S. It has been found at scattered locations in Florida, at one location at Houma, Louisiana, and at one location in Texas, this being at the lower end of Galveston Bay. It is not known whether it was introduced to these places in modern times or not, but the places where it has been found, at least in Louisiana and Texas, are both precisely the places where early shipping came ashore, and thus it looks like the cactus was brought, either knowingly or as a stowaway, on early boats from its Caribbean home. Anyway, the plant did not spread and invade to any extent anywhere in the U.S., and in fact it seems to have practically failed here. It has not been re-collected in many years in Louisiana, and can now be found only on Galveston Island and the Bolivar Peninsula in Texas.

The Galveston Island specimens, which comprise the only population of other than isolated individuals we know of in our area, is found as a solid row of thickets along the top of the high sea-wall embankment between the city of Galveston and Fort Point at the north end of the island. Here it grows near the massive concrete bunkers and gun emplacements thrown up to guard the entrance to Galveston Bay, and looking at it ranged near the ruins of these fortifications it is easy to imagine that it might have been planted there by the defenders as one more barrier to deter invaders. It would at least make the route of infiltrators more difficult. It does seem strange that anyone planting such a barrier would use this cactus instead of the native, larger, and much more spiny *Opuntia engelmannii* var. *texana* which must have been growing nearby, as it is today, but the defenders probably knew little about the country beyond their island and might well have brought the pest pear they had seen in the Caribbean here for this use.

Opuntia stricta must be compared carefully with two varieties of *O. engelmannii* which grow on the eastern Texas Coast, and with which it is often confused, variety *texana* and variety *alta*. When they are all in flower or fruit these three are easily told apart. *O. stricta* is distinguished from both of the others by its elongated, club-shaped ovary, since that of the others is obovate or inverted cone-shaped and is usually as broad or nearly as broad as it is long, and also by the resulting fruits which in *O. stricta* are elongated club-shaped with deeply pitted summits and light red or carmine-red in color, while those of the *O. engelmannii* varieties are broad obovate to almost spherical with the umbilici flat or practically so and the color deep purplish or burgundy-red. The fruits of *O. stricta* are sweet and edible, which also distinguishes it from *O. engelmannii* var. *texana*, whose fruits are insipid and unpleasant, but this will not distinguish it from *O. engelmannii* var. *alta*, whose more rounded fruits are also sweet.

The most clear difference between *O. stricta* and these other two cacti which can be seen when only vegetative characters are present, is the elongated ovate, elliptical, or spindle-shaped pads, which contrast rather clearly with the circular to very broadly ovate pads of all *O. engelmannii* forms in normal growth. *O. stricta* also has many fewer spines, and these always completely round, while at least the main spines of any normal *O. engelmannii* form are flattened at least at the bases.

O. stricta is admittedly close to *O. engelmannii* var. *alta*, which grows profusely almost all along the Texas coast, but careful observation can separate them. We have been interested to find in our laboratory that *O. stricta* presents a basically different chromatograph map from any of these other forms.

This is one cactus which we are not especially happy to have

to include in this account. We believe it to have been an introduction to our area, and it seems fortunate that it has not spread.

Opuntia engelmannii SD
"Nopal," "Tuna," "Engelmann's Prickly Pear," "Flaming Prickly Pear"

DESCRIPTION   PLATES 44, 45, 46, 47, 48
STEMS: Always growing upright, forming a bush which may be compact with a definite central trunk or open and diffuse without a main trunk. These bushes commonly attain a height of 3 to 6 feet, and some varieties sometimes stand over 10 feet tall when in optimum environments. Individual pads are thick and circular to broadly egg-shaped. They are 8 to 12 or even 14 inches long when mature. The surface is medium green or sometimes slightly blue-green, often becoming pale yellowish-green with age. It is covered more or less thickly with a whitish bloom which easily rubs off. The leaves are about $3/16$ to $1/2$ inch long.

AREOLES: Small and oval or oblong at first, usually becoming round and enlarging to $1/4$ of an inch or more with maturity. Sometimes they produce much wool and other tissue to form a hemispherically bulging or even columnar structure when very old.

SPINES: Very variable. Typically there are 1 to 5 per areole on newly matured pads, but sometimes the number increases to as many as 10 or 12 during the second year. The main spines are heavy and rigid on typical forms, but on some forms they are more slender and more or less flexible. The larger spines are always flattened to some degree, often greatly so, and often also somewhat twisted and curved, but these are usually surrounded by smaller spines which may be round and straight. The several main spines are heavy and spreading and curving downward and outward, $3/4$ to $2\frac{1}{2}$ inches long, except for one form on which they are porrect and to 3 inches long. The rest of the spines spread in all directions around these and are shorter, as well as more slender. All the spines are variable in color, ranging on different specimens from entirely yellow, yellow with only slightly brownish bases through yellow mottled with brown, whitish with dark brown bases, to deep reddish-brown only slightly yellowish above. They always show more or less of an annular pattern.

GLOCHIDS: Tending to be few in number on the sides of the pads, but often becoming rather numerous on the edges of old pads. They are coarse and rigid, almost like the smaller fixed spines, $1/8$ to sometimes $5/8$ of an inch long, spreading loosely, and in one form having an exaggerated development of them, becoming a large raylike cluster. They may be all yellow, yellow mottled with brown, or all red-brown.

FLOWERS: Large and showy and produced in profusion. They are 2¹/₂ to 4 inches tall and wide, clear yellow, orange, or bright red in color, the whole perianth one color on any one flower and never variegated. The ovary is variable in length from 1 to 3 inches, but is always thick for its length, obovate or inverted cone-shaped, often as wide at the top as it is long. The outer perianth segments are short and varying in shape. The inner segments are 8 to 10 in number, long, to about 1¹/₂ inches wide with the tip the broadest part, entire, blunt, but usually with a slight point at the apex. The filaments are long and cream-colored. The anthers are the same color. The stamens are very sensitive, moving at the slightest touch. The style is whitish, the stigma made up of 5 to 10 heavy lobes ranging from dark green to pure white in the different varieties.

FRUITS: Varying within the species. Dark red, usually becoming dull purplish or burgundy when very ripe. They are completely spherical to broadly pear-shaped, with no constriction or else with a slight one at the base, but with the umbilicus perfectly flat or nearly so. Ranging in size from 1 to 3¹/₂ inches long in the different forms of the species. Also differing in the character of the fruit pulp, this in some varieties being edible and in some not, as noted in their descriptions. The seeds small to tiny, ¹/₁₆ to ³/₁₆ inch (1¹/₂–4¹/₂ millimeters) in greatest diameter and comparatively thin, with narrow rims.

RANGE. When all of its varieties are included, *O. engelmannii* is apparently one of the widest ranging cacti of our continent. In this broad sense, it grows from the Gulf Coast all the way to the Pacific and deep into Mexico; more specifically, in our area, from Brownsville all along the Gulf Coast into southwestern Louisiana, then back northwest past Dallas, Texas, to extreme south-central Oklahoma, which is its northernmost penetration. From there its range dips down to the vicinity of Abilene, Texas, after which it turns northwestward again into New Mexico, passing near Santa Fe, and from there going slightly southwestward into Arizona. It is found almost universally south of this line into Mexico.

REMARKS. Almost every student writing about this cactus has prefaced his remarks with something about this being a most misunderstood species or some such warning of difficulty to be expected. The warning is worth heeding, as only the more persistent cactophile will ever achieve any satisfactory understanding of this species. Its relationships are so subtle that no brief survey will ever reveal them and no one can ever identify all of its forms at a glance.

Most descriptions of *O. engelmannii* have started, "Originally described as . . ." and then gone on to show necessary broadening of the original descriptions. This is because the plant was originally described by Prince Salm-Dyck and later by Engelmann from a few specimens out of Chihuahua. Immediately

the broadening began. Engelmann himself first extended the species to include some California material, and later stated that it grew east all the way to the mouth of the Rio Grande and included those forms found there. Our description above is the broadened one very similar to the later ones of Engelmann and that of Britton and Rose.

In this huge range, spanning over half the lower width of the continent, it is not surprising that there are many local populations which are different enough one from another to have been taken at one time or another for separate species. There have been various grand theories as to why so much variation occurs, most of them hinging upon assumed hybridization of an original, lately invading stock with various already existing local cacti. The first difficulty with these theories is in answering the question of what the original, invading stock was, where it came from and how it managed to invade so wide a territory. One of the pet ideas these days is that it was one of the hardy, edible prickly pears from Mexico, and that it was carried north throughout the area by early Spanish missionaries and settlers, after which it escaped and commenced the hybridizing procedure. This is an interesting and ingenious theory, but there is no actual evidence for it at all. Nor has there been shown any actual hybridization experiment to prove that this process could give the results this theory would require. It is not within the scope of this work to pass on such theories, the attempt here being, rather, to enumerate the forms we do find growing so that others may explain them if they will, but it does seem after studying them that such elaborate theories are unnecessary. Although the genetics of the cacti is still largely unknown, modern genetic principles would lead us to expect just such variation of any such widely ranging species as we find this one to be, due to the simple segregation of local populations in different environments. One must be prepared for finding these variations whenever he goes into the widely different locations where this plant grows, and must do something more than close his eyes to them or explain them away if he is to make any sense out of the cactus world.

In general, *O. engelmannii* is the largest and strongest of our U.S. prickly pears. While in some severe locations it remains a straggly bush of hardly more than 3 feet in height, in much of its territory it is not unusual for it to become a giant of 6 feet tall, and a south Texas variety occasionally stands more than 10 feet tall. Each plant is a whole thicket of giant pads comparable in size and shape to skillets, and seeming almost as indestructable. The strength of the plant is expressed also in its numbers. It is not unusual for it to take over a stretch of rangeland, and in much of south Texas there are thousands of square miles where it grows to the exclusion of almost everything else. Most of the ranchers hate it with a fury and work hard to destroy it, but for all their efforts they hardly affect it. This cactus can be imagined reacting with glee to the widespread rooting and chaining of the range, which eliminates much of the competing brush and most other cacti, since all of its branches and pads torn apart and scattered by the machines only root where they are distributed and thus the cactus is multiplied while its competitors for space are being eliminated.

At those drought times when the ranchers have nothing else left to feed their cattle, they suddenly look at *O. engelmannii* with a new appreciation, and move upon it with everything from common blow-torches to huge gas flame-throwers on wheels, burning off the spines which are the plant's only protection. The hungry cattle soon catch on, and it is not an uncommon sight in south Texas and northern Mexico to see herds of cattle eagerly following the burner and jostling each other to get at the juicy pads while they are still hot from the torch which seared away their armor. But even this does not long affect our indestructable giant. Almost immediately new pads start rising from the old stump, and soon it is back to its old size.

The newer technique of herbicide broadcasting could change this picture completely, as not even this giant cactus can survive the chemicals which destroy trees and all the rest of the range brush. At the time when this means is used widely enough to eliminate our giant prickly pear, however, there will be no flora of the Southwest left except grasses, and most ecologists doubt that even the animal life or the climate of the region could survive such an impoverishment.

This cactus is so commonly seen over much of its range that people hardly think of it, or else so dislike it—almost everyone in the area has his own story of most painful injury from it—that many cannot appreciate its beauty even when that does appear. But the tough giant does have its tender moments, and then, for usually a month of the spring, it produces every day a new crop of large, roselike flowers, to the delight of bees and all others who can evade the spines and appreciate the blooms. These flowers vary greatly in color, those of some individuals being clear yellow, those of others deep red, and there are found all intermediate shades of orange between these two extremes. While all shades are sometimes found together in the same field, there seems to be a gradient in this color distribution, the red being very common in south Texas, while it is more rare and most specimens bloom yellow or orange in New Mexico.

The burgundy or deep red fruits resulting from these flowers are large and juicy, but vary in quality of the pulp, those of some of the varieties being very flavorful, while those of others are unpleasant. This probably is one reason why in some areas the fruits have all disappeared soon after they ripen while in other areas they remain on the plants so long that ripe fruits are often found nearly all winter.

O. engelmannii as it occurs in southern New Mexico is very much like the original descriptions, since those were based on plants from neighboring Chihuahua. These plants usually have very heavy and whitish spines with dark brown bases. As one moves away from that locality either west or east he finds some differences in the specimens he sees. Both in Texas and California the predominant color of the spines becomes more yellow

than white, and there are other differences in the various local populations.

In Texas, particularly, we find many different variations to confuse us, as we might expect in the widely differing environments of that state's huge area, and added to that we find one major mistake made very early in the study of this cactus which still affects us and distorts our understanding of the plant today.

After describing *O. engelmannii* from Chihuahuan specimens and before understanding its wide range, Engelmann was sent specimens of cacti from New Braunfels, Texas. They were sent by Mr. Lindheimer, an early botanist living there. Some of these pads were from plants Lindheimer described to him as 6 feet tall with trunks, others from plants he said grew low and spreading. Unfortunately he sent Engelmann only fruits of the low-growing plants, and these were slender club-shaped with a deeply pitted umbilicus, very different from the fruits of the Chihuahuan *O. engelmannii* already described. Knowing no more than this about the New Braunfels plants, Engelmann described the whole thing as one variable new species growing either tall or low and spreading, and called it *O. lindheimeri*.

Engelmann was too hasty in this, and, with his usual honesty, he admitted it later. In his *Synopsis of the Cactaceae of the U.S.* he stated without reservation: "*O. lindheimeri* Eng. Pl. Lindh., is partly this same plant [*O. engelmannii*, which he had just been discussing], partly a hybrid form between it and perhaps *O. rafinesquii*, with narrow clavate fruit." So he who erected the species, *O. lindheimeri*, himself abolished it, stating clearly that the large plants of New Braunfels are *O. engelmannii* and the low form with the clavate, deeply pitted fruits which threw him off in the first place, is a different plant which he regarded as some sort of hybrid form. This low-growing form was later called a separate species and named by Mackensen *O. leptocarpa*.

The point of all this is that there is nothing left to be referred to by the name *O. lindheimeri*. That has resolved naturally into *O. engelmannii* and the then yet unnamed smaller species, incidentally extending *O. engelmannii*'s range far across Texas where Engelmann in his earlier works did not state it to be.

All this seems perfectly clear, yet the name, *O. lindheimeri* still persists in usage among Texans so much that all large prickly pears in the state are usually called by that name. Harder yet to understand, most botanical works still use that name for the Texas specimens of this species, just because they are from Texas. Britton and Rose show no consciousness of *O. lindheimeri*'s synonymy with *O. engelmannii*. While they discuss its variableness at length, they seem never to have read Engelmann's renunciation of the name, made within a few years of his having coined it.

And as the error persists it compounds. Backeberg, most recently, knows well the reference to the upright, trunked form and the low one, but chooses not only to ignore Engelmann's statement that the New Braunfels plant is *O. engelmannii* and to keep the name *O. lindheimeri* for it, but then insists that the two forms found at New Braunfels are all one dimorphic species. Then, on this already discredited, supposedly dimorphic species, he erects a whole new section of the genus, section *Lindheimeriana* Backbg., into which he places together this already evaporated species and the reportedly polymorphic forms of the Galapagos Islands, merely because they are supposedly very variable. Before he is through, then, his *O. lindheimeri* has also become polymorphic and has taken in all the forms found at the mouth of the Rio Grande which Engelmann had already stated were *O. engelmannii*.

Because *O. engelmannii* was for so long thought of as a practically unvarying species inhabiting only southern New Mexico and perhaps some of adjacent Arizona, the slightly differing forms found in Texas and the far West were constantly given names as new species. Engelmann started this himself, and others have continued it until we have a whole series of supposed species difficult to distinguish and place logically. Griffiths contributed a long list of these.

Dr. David Griffiths, sent here by the Australian government, was associated with the U.S. Department of Agriculture for some years, studying the prickly pears all the way from Texas to California in order to try to find some natural enemies of them which could be introduced into Australia to aid in the fight against those which had established themselves and become such a scourge there. He collected scores of specimens and grew them in the U.S. Experiment Stations in Texas and in California, which were at his disposal. He took this wonderful opportunity to carry on detailed taxonomic studies of the Opuntias. His was undoubtedly the most extensive study of this group made to this day. As a result he published many papers upon them and described numerous new species, apparently producing a new species name for nearly every variation of pad, fruit, or even flower color he found.

Britton and Rose published their large work on cacti soon after Griffiths' work, but they apparently did not have the patience to study through all of his forms, and it seems they chose to list a few of them, selected almost at random, and relegated all the rest, with hardly a mention, to synonymy. Since then most others have followed in ignoring them, which is all that can be done unless a great deal of time is spent in the field recovering them, much of this time in quite inaccessible areas.

I was happily following this easy path, until the ranchers brought me up short. I was calling all of the big prickly pears the same name, when some of the ranchers with whom I was looking over the pastures objected and even took offense, pointing out that this one was good and tender cattle food, while that one was so tough and fibrous the cattle could not eat it even after the spines were burned off, that this one grew only on one ranch while that one was only on a neighbor's, and so on. I felt acutely the derision aimed my way when I had no separate names for the various forms the ordinary cowboys could distinguish at a glance. This sort of prodding made me dig up the original descriptions of all these ignored forms from Engelmann through Griffiths. I studied the original Griffiths collection in the U.S. National Museum, and then headed into the hills to try to locate them. It has taken much effort over several years, but usually they were where they were supposed to be, and many of them were distinct, once the effort was made to understand them. I can now name my rancher friends' different prickly pears to everyone's satisfaction.

Of course, the taxonomists will not be satisfied until the exact relationships of all these forms are understood, and I do not pretend to have any final word on that. Griffiths made a great start which could have led to that, but unfortunately all he was able to do was grow these forms together in the experiment stations a few years and report on the stability of their characters in these uniform situations, proving these characters more than just environmental adaptations. There is no record of anyone having done any breeding experiments or of any other such studies on them at all since then. In fact, many of these forms have probably not been collected again until this time. It is exactly for this reason that they are all dealt with here and the most specific data possible concerning them is given: otherwise they were all but lost. It is hoped that this will interest some of the newer experimental taxonomists in them and make it possible for them to find the exact forms for their detailed modern studies. Then and only then can we know exactly how to deal with them taxonomically. In the meantime it is my conviction after observing them widely that some of them more accurately deserve varietal status than species rank, and so they are listed that way here. Some of them, such as those based upon flower or spine color alone seem clearly to be only synonyms or at best forma, and these will be mentioned here, but not listed as separate taxa.

Those readers desiring only a general knowledge of the Opuntias and who are satisfied with knowing what "that big prickly pear is that we see all over the desert," and who are not worried about the detailed differences encountered within that wide ranging plant, need go no further into these varieties. The large, upright prickly pear they see all across the southern expanses of the U.S. is for the most part Engelmann's prickly pear.

Opuntia engelmannii var. engelmannii (SD)

DESCRIPTION   PLATE 44

STEMS: As the species, except usually only 3 to 5 feet tall.

AREOLES: 1 to at least 2 inches apart. They are larger than in some forms of the species, being 3/16 to 3/8 of an inch across during the first year and sometimes enlarging even further when older. They are oval to round and more or less bulging, with brown wool.

SPINES: As the species, except that the main centrals are less than 2 1/2 inches long, heavy, and much flattened, and all spines are at first brown or deep red-brown at their bases, shading to lighter above, until the outer parts are an opaque, chalky white or pale straw-colored, the whole spine usually fading entirely to a plain gray with age.

GLOCHIDS: As the species, except yellow, brownish, or mottled yellow and brown in color and often increasing greatly to form conspicuous, open, spreading clusters on the edges of older pads.

FLOWERS: As the species, except mostly yellow and only occasionally orange or reddish, having the ovary only 1 to 1^1/$_2$ inches long and the stigma of 8 to 10 dark green lobes.

FRUITS: 2 to 3 inches long, globose to sometimes broadly pear-shaped, with little or no constriction below and a flat, wide umbilicus on top. In color they are deep, dull burgundy when ripe. The pulp is juicy and edible. The seeds measure ^{1}/$_8$ to not quite ^{3}/$_{16}$ of an inch (3–4 millimeters) in diameter, with narrow rims.

RANGE. From Chihuahua and western Coahuila, Mexico, into southwestern Texas, southern New Mexico, and southeastern Arizona. Specifically, in our area, west of a line running from near Eagle Pass, Texas, to near Austin, and then on into extreme south-central Oklahoma. From there south of a line to Abilene, Texas, and on into New Mexico between Hobbs and Clovis, to the vicinity of Santa Rosa and Anton Chico, New Mexico. Beyond this the northern boundary retreats rapidly southwestward, passing near Santa Fe, but then apparently crossing into Arizona in the mountains west of Silver City, New Mexico.

REMARKS. This is the form of the species which was first described, and which is meant when the name is used in the narrow sense, as by all those who separate from it the primarily Texas forms—nowadays lumping these together under the name O. lindheimeri—and the far western forms which are given various other names. This description attempts to make it possible to distinguish this typical form of the species from all of its related varieties, although it must be remembered that the distinction between these forms is not a distinction between separate species, and that there are possible intermediates which will be hard to place. This is the reason why it has seemed more logical to place this, even though it is the originally described form, as a varietal subdivision apart from and under the broader, all inclusive species description. By this method the confusion over these plants is reduced, at least for me.

If any one character can be mentioned which will serve to set this variety apart from all the rest to follow, it is the whiteness of the spines, usually set off against their distinctly brown bases. This whiteness is usually conspicuous and only rarely and in young spines shades into a straw-color toward the tip, while in all the other varieties which stand separate in not only this but various other ways, the predominant color is a distinct yellow which does not even bleach to a real white.

Earle, in his recent book, *Cacti of the Southwest,* refers to this variety and recognizes one of the interesting distinctions between it and some of its related varieties when he states, "A tasty jelly can be made of the fruits from southeastern Arizona, those in other parts of its range have a 'flat' taste." Those from other areas with the "flat" taste do not belong to this variety. It is interesting that tenderness of pads does not accompany this tastiness of fruit in this variety. Its supporting tissues are too tough for cattle to master, so in the areas where this variety is the only one growing, it is not the custom to "burn pears" as it is in those areas inhabited by some of its relatives.

There have been proposed at various times, as varieties or even species, some segregates which seem to actually fall within the limits of this variety. These seem to represent one or another of the extremes it takes under various conditions, but they do not have consistent, qualitative differences from it. It seems best to regard them merely as synonyms of this variety, but still to mention them so that further study of them may be made by interested workers. I add a short discussion of those found in the area of this study.

O. *valida* Gr. seems to represent the most spiny extreme of the variety. There seems to be no way to distinguish it from the typical specimens except that the spines average a little longer and a few more numerous per areole. Some specimens in most any large population of the variety will be apt to show this armament.

On the other hand, Griffiths proposed two species which seem to be only specimens of this variety with minimal size of pads and numbers of spines. They are O. *gregoriana* and O. *gomei.* The first he found near El Paso, and the second in the Platt National Park in south-central Oklahoma. This latter is, I believe, the most northeasterly record of the plant, and its smallness as well as its paucity of spines seems a natural stunting. I have more typical specimens of the variety collected not far from the Platt Park.

A particular problem is presented by a form growing in the San Andreas Canyon of the Sacramento Mountains just south of Alamogordo, New Mexico. Griffiths, with his usual thoroughness, called our attention to it and, as was his habit, erected a new species on it. He called it O. *dillei.*

As seen growing in the type locality, a very small area where it comprises only a small population (Griffiths said he saw a dozen plants only, and there are few more in evidence today) this certainly seems a distinct cactus—more so than some others. The yellow-green pads are massive, often 12 or 14 inches long, as wide or wider, and up to 1 inch thick. These huge, cart-wheel pads are often completely spineless, only occasionally having 1 or 2 spines up to 1 inch long scattered here and there. It only remotely suggests a huge, bald O. *engelmannii,* and for this reason there has been more of a tendency for writers to treat it separately from the typical form than in the case of some others of Griffiths' many species. However, a special factor enters here which seems to change the picture.

Griffiths mentions that all of the specimens he saw of this description were growing in places inaccessible to livestock, and his published photo of the plant shows it growing out of the sides of steep canyon walls. Observations in the area seem to confirm that all of the population are restricted to such rocky ledges, which constitute a rather special environmental situation. As was his habit, Griffiths took some cuttings of these plants and grew them in his experimental plots. He found that, "Under cultivation the species becomes much more spiny than indicated above." This sort of change did not take place with many of his other forms when they were cultivated, and it should make us suspect that we have here only an environmentally caused growth form instead of a genetically different plant. We should perhaps already have suspected this from the knowledge that growing out of vertical or nearly vertical rocky cliffs has the effect of reducing spines on other Opuntias as well. For instance, spineless *O. macrocentra* specimens are sometimes found on cliffs, with typical, spiny specimens above or at the base of the same cliffs. And there is *O. laevis* Coult., said to be restricted to cliffs in southern Arizona and southwestern New Mexico. While its presence only upon cliffs is generally interpreted as the result of livestock having eaten the individuals growing in the accessible places because they were unprotected by spines, I take this to be the same effect of cliff-hanging working on the normally spiny *O. phaeacantha*.

Be that as it may, Griffiths himself says, "*O. dillei* is most closely related to *O. engelmannii*, from which it differs in rarity of its spines, which are very conspicuous on that species." It seems obvious that when, in cultivation, this difference is wiped out, we lose the real basis for making this a separate form. He does further state that the fruits and seeds are also different, but in typical *O. engelmannii* var. *engelmannii* I have found fruits and seeds which seemed in every essential detail identical with both his description and his photograph of those organs given for *O. dillei*.

It seems best, therefore, since we want to avoid listing environmentally induced aberrations as taxa, to consider *O. dillei* here as merely a synonym of the typical variety. I take the space to discuss it in the hope that this will prompt someone to do ecological and genetic studies on it which will give us definite answers as to why the small population in that particular canyon develops differently. This might clear up other such problems for us at the same time. Engelmann, for instance, mentioned another growth form collected by Mr. Wright on Limpia Creek in the Davis Mountains of Texas, which he noticed but apparently did not think distinct enough for naming. I have seen and collected that form still there in Limpia Canyon, 100 years later. Far better, no doubt, to leave it nameless in this group which has already had too many names, but it will be wonderful when someone discovers why in the Opuntias we have so many and such confusing forms. Until they do we must keep track of even such apparent synonyms as *O. dillei,* and

require everyone to make plain whether he is referring broadly to the species *O. engelmannii* or precisely to the more closely limited *O. engelmannii* var. *engelmannii* when he refers to Engelmann's prickly pear.

Opuntia engelmannii var. cyclodes Eng.

DESCRIPTION

STEMS: As the species, except that it is a much spreading bush only 3 to 5 feet high and usually wider than it is tall, without a well-defined central stem. The individual pads are as those of the species, except only 6 to 8 inches long, usually circular, but sometimes very broad oval or egg-shaped. The surface is bright green or yellow green with some glaucescence.

AREOLES: As the species, except never quite as large in maximum size as in some forms, and only 1 to $1^1/_2$ inches apart.

SPINES: As the species, except for the following details. All spines are deflexed, relatively slender, and pale yellow or straw-colored with or without red or reddish-brown bases. There are usually 1 or 2 spines per areole on the upper half or so of the pad, but sometimes up to 6 spines. A typical areole's armor consists of 1 large, flattened spine $^3/_4$ to $1^3/_4$ inches long, plus occasionally an additional shorter spine below which is only $^3/_8$ to 1 inch long; but some specimens show up to 4 of the larger spines spreading downward and 2 of the lower, shorter ones.

GLOCHIDS: As the species, except on current growth usually missing entirely. On older pads side areoles show few and very short glochids, if any, but edge areoles produce some yellow glochids up to $^1/_2$ inch long.

FLOWERS: As the species, except smaller, being usually only about 2 inches in diameter and length, with bright orange anthers and 6 or 7 dark green stigma lobes.

FRUITS: As the species, except always spherical or practically so, only 1 to $1^3/_4$ inches in diameter, purplish when fully ripe, but not very juicy and not pleasant to the taste. The seeds are about $^3/_{16}$ of an inch (4–$4^1/_2$ millimeters) in diameter, the largest found in this species, and with broader rims than is typical for the species.

RANGE. From the Chisos Mountains in the Texas Big Bend to near Anton Chico, New Mexico, and back down to Stein's Pass, where the northern limit passes into Arizona.

REMARKS. This variety of the species was the first recognized of all which were to follow, having been set up by Engelmann as early as he listed the species, but it has suffered varying fortunes at the hands of later authorities. Engelmann encountered it at

Anton Chico, New Mexico, at the northern edge of the species' range. Coulter, in the next serious study, said that the variety ranges over all of southern New Mexico from El Paso to Stein's Pass. This would have left us with a clear idea of the plant in New Mexico, at least, but then Wooton unaccountably stated "the fruit of the New Mexico plant is never globose but ellipsoid to slightly obovoid, about twice as long as broad," and also stated that he had never seen the variety. Britton and Rose, on the other hand, do not doubt the existence of spherical fruits, but state that the characters of the variety are not constant and render it a synonym of the species. All since have ignored it entirely, except perhaps Benson, who mentions that there is a possible segregate of *O. engelmannii* with circular joints, smaller flowers, and spines of this color; but he says the status of the plant is undetermined and he never actually links it with this name.

It is not surprising, then, that when Miss Anthony found, not in New Mexico, but in the Big Bend of Texas a plant of almost exactly this description, she did not connect it with this old variety, but erected a new taxon for it. There is a common failure to relate Texas and New Mexico cacti. No doubt because it was in Texas and because it had yellowish spines, she related it to the old, defunct name for the Texas forms of the species, and called it *O. lindheimeri* var. *chisoensis*. I have studied the preserved specimens of Miss Anthony's type, as well as the plant growing in all stages of flower and fruit in the Chisos Mountains, her type locality. I have also studied both preserved specimens and the living plants from Engelmann's type locality of his variety near Anton Chico, New Mexico, and I cannot but think them the same. Various other specimens have been seen from widely scattered points in southern New Mexico, bearing out the existence of the plant in exactly the range Coulter claimed for it. The Big Bend material, classed with it, only extends its previous range 250 miles or so down along the Rio Grande from its previously known existence at El Paso.

As for the question, raised by Britton and Rose and most others since, of whether this form is distinct enough from the type of the species to deserve varietal rank, a reading of Backeberg's unequivocal statement of how far Miss Anthony's variety is from the type of *O. lindheimeri*, which we have seen is more properly *O. engelmannii*, should answer that. With him the question would seem to be instead whether this should not be set up as a separate species entirely. Charting a middle course between these opposing views, I choose to leave it here as Engelmann first represented it, a recognizable variety occurring, it is true, wholly within the range of typical *O. engelmannii* var. *engelmannii*, but separate from it by several definite characters.

Variety *cyclodes* grows, so far as has been seen, always on the lower slopes of high mountain ranges, where it often forms large populations. Although in several situations I have seen it growing within a few miles of the typical variety *engelmannii*, I have never seen the two mingled in one stand.

Opuntia engelmannii var. texana (Gr.)

DESCRIPTION   PLATES 45, 51

STEMS: As the species.

AREOLES: As the species, except with less wool than in some of the other varieties.

SPINES: As the species, except usually somewhat more slender than those of the typical variety and always yellow instead of white in their lighter color. That color varies from entirely bright, translucent yellow to yellow with brown bases or even sometimes almost entirely red-brown with only yellowish mottling or yellowish tips. The number of spines varies from 1 to 8 per areole on the upper areoles of the pad.

GLOCHIDS: As the species, except perhaps fewer in number than in the typical variety.

FLOWERS: As the species, except usually around 3 to 4 inches in diameter. The stigma lobes number 6 to 9 and are dark green.

FRUITS: Within the range of the species, but always 2 to 3½ inches long, globose to sometimes broadly pear-shaped, with little or no constriction below and a flat, wide umbilicus. They are a deep, dull burgundy in color when fully ripe. The pulp is juicy but flat and rather unpleasant to the taste. The seeds measure ⅛ to not quite 3/16 of an inch (3–4 millimeters) in diameter, with narrow rims.

RANGE. All of south and central Texas east into western Louisiana. Extending north to about Tyler, Texas, and the Dallas area, then southwest to the Texas Big Bend and southeastern New Mexico, as well as into Mexico.

REMARKS. Certainly the difference between this form and the typical *Opuntia engelmannii* var. *engelmannii* is slight. It is hard to see how the two could ever be considered as separate species, yet this is the plant which is today almost universally referred to as *O. lindheimeri*, in opposition to *O. engelmannii*. Remembering Engelmann's own denial of this, I am glad to be free to recombine the two and be done with the tedious arguments for leaving them two species. This plant is much more understandable in its proper place within that large, variable species complex, and only thus can we understand Engelmann's statement that *O. engelmannii* grows all the way to the Gulf Coast.

But can we merge it entirely with the typical form and forget it as a synonym? Although it is close to the typical variety and there may be some intermediates hard to assign between the two, when we make the separation between them varietal instead of specific, this need not hinder us, and there do seem reasons to assign this plant a separate place beside the other variety. Summarized, the distinctions between the two are as follows: variety *texana* has translucent yellow instead of opaque white as the dominant spine color; it has more slender spines, larger leaves, somewhat larger flowers and fruits, fruit pulp flat and unpleasant to the taste instead of tasty, pads with soft enough supportive tissues to be edible by grazing animals instead of so tough as to be unusable in this fashion. Admittedly these differences are all minor, and it is largely in deference to my rancher friends that I first took the distinction seriously, but in the area where both forms grow together, a rancher will often know the two varieties at a glance. This one is the widely used cactus cattle food of south Texas and northern Mexico.

It is hard to establish the exact range of this variety because many reports and herbarium specimens are too incomplete to make determination exact. I have not been able to collect the variety myself east of the lower Brazos River in south Texas, but it apparently has extended much farther east. O. *anahuacensis* Gr., from Griffiths' description, would seem to have been this variety growing near the mouth of the Trinity River, but repeated searching of that area has not revealed it growing there today. A related variety, O. *engelmannii* var. *alta*, is in profusion in the area, but it does not fit his description. Assuming that the name Griffiths gave to his plant meant that he found it near the town of Anahuac, I have searched that immediate vicinity repeatedly, but all around that town the land has long been farmed, and no cacti survive except variety *alta* growing on waste islands nearby. Griffiths' plant may have been growing in what is now the cultivated area.

Engelmann and others mention such a plant as this from western Louisiana, and I have seen one good specimen, definitely variety *texana*, from Cameron, Louisiana, although I do not know whether it was native there or introduced. I also have had a specimen which appeared to be this variety from the piney woods just north of Alexandria, Louisiana, but it was extremely stunted and unhealthy, and did not survive for me long enough that its true form could be determined beyond question.

On the western side of its range, it is equally hard to establish an exact limit to this plant's range. It has been so long the rule to call all western forms O. *engelmannii* and eastern ones O. *lindheimeri*, that few have thought to look for more subtle distinctions. For this reason the descriptions of O. *engelmannii* have been broadened enough to include any of this variety which might have appeared in the West—this being the reason for the statement found in more recent books that the spines of that species are either white or yellowish. Herbarium specimens in O. *engelmannii* folders from New Mexico show specimens which I would suspect are actually variety *texana*. The variety is fairly common in the Big Bend of Texas, particularly in the mountains all the way from the Chisos to the Guadalupes, occasionally growing together with the typical variety *engelmannii*. I have also seen it in the Sacramento and Organ mountains of New Mexico. From his descriptions and keys, I believe what Wooton called O. *lindheimeri*, collected by him in the Guadalupe Mountains of New Mexico was this variety, and it also appears to be the plant of the Organ and Tortuga mountains in southern New Mexico generally called O. *wootonii* Gr. This latter form is supposed to have a special shape of the pad, but it seems to come

within this variety, as I have duplicated its shape in Texas specimens growing in typical populations of the variety. It must be noted here that Miss Anthony's O. *engelmannii* var. *wootonii* cannot be the same cactus.

In the territory from San Antonio (which is the type locality) to Laredo, Texas, variety *texana* is very common, and here it often has spines almost wholly red-brown, with only the tips slightly yellowish. This coloring formed the basis for Griffiths' O. *ferruginispina*, but it seems only a minor color variation of the same plant. Upon the more typically colored specimens in this same area Griffiths once erected another supposed species, O. *sinclairii*, but it also is only a synonym of this variety. Mackensen also tried to separate this variety further, taking the extremes of the population as it is found at San Antonio and calling them O. *convexa*, O. *griffithsiana*, and O. *reflexa*, but the differences between these are minor, and after living at San Antonio for 6 years, I have seen so many intermediates between them that it does not seem they represent more than individual variations.

Although it is another species which is generally known by the name, pest pear, this variety is the worst pest pear of south Texas. Only in a few local situations and along the Texas coast do other varieties take its place as dominant in the brush which has developed from the overgrazing of the range. Its increase in recent times has been dramatic.

I have seen isolated specimens typical of this variety in all ways except with fruits very large and strongly clavate. I suspect that they may be diseased fruits, as are the extremely large and clavate ones sometimes found on O. *compressa* var. *fuscoatra* which were the basis for the supposed species, O. *macateei*. There is a strong temptation to say that this form of variety *texana* with the elongated fruits is Griffiths' O. *pyrocarpa*, but his description does not otherwise fit this plant and does not seem to indicate a member of this species at all. I have not seen any plant which does conform to his description under that name, even in the type locality.

Opuntia engelmannii var. alta (Gr.)

DESCRIPTION   PLATES 45, 46

STEMS: As the species, except usually forming a more definite trunk, and averaging taller than the typical variety, being commonly 3 to 6 feet tall and sometimes growing to more than 10 feet. The pad surface is more yellow-green than on most of the other varieties, and the surface is somewhat irregular, often giving the pad edge an irregular outline. This latter effect is not marked enough, however, to be considered a tuberculate surface.

AREOLES: As the species.

SPINES: As the species, except for the following differences.

On the average the spines are more numerous, being 1 to 6 on most areoles of new pads, and ordinarily 8 to 10 or occasionally even 12 on very old pads. All spines are always pure translucent yellow in color, with no brown at the bases. The spines stand more porrect in the areole, not spreading so widely. The main spines are flattened, but not so greatly as in the typical variety, often only the bases showing this character; the smaller ones are usually round. On new growth the spines are usually about 1 inch long, but on older pads the main ones may sometimes elongate up to a maximum of 2¹/₂ inches long.

GLOCHIDS: As the species, except always bright yellow in color.

FLOWERS: As the species, except even more variable in color than those of most of the other varieties. They may be found from very pale cream through yellow, orange, and red to dark purplish-red. The stigma lobes are pale green, sometimes almost white. The ovary is noticeably tuberculate.

FRUITS: Purplish-red in color, as the species. 1 to 2 inches long. In shape they are broadly oval or egg-shaped, usually with some slight constriction below and having the umbilici flat to shallowly pitted, but narrower than the widest part of the fruit. There are usually numerous glochids and often a few slender spines ¹/₄ to ³/₄ of an inch long on these fruits until they are fully ripe, when they fall off. The pulp is deep red and edible. The seeds are quite small, being from less than ¹/₁₆ of an inch to only slightly more (1¹/₂–2¹/₂ millimeters) in diameter, with almost no rims.

RANGE. All along the Texas Gulf Coast, entering the state from Mexico, and found in almost continuous stands on the islands, just above the salt flats or back of the dunes all the way to the Sabine River. Said to be native in coastal Louisiana also, but not so numerous there, and also said to have been introduced all the way to Florida. Found inland in the Rio Grande Valley about as far as Mission, Texas, but nowhere else more than about 20 miles or so from the Gulf.

REMARKS. We have here a variety easily confused, if only spines are considered, with the more spiny individuals of *O. engelmannii* var. *texana,* but clearly different, if we will take the trouble to observe such things as fruits and seeds.

O. engelmannii var. *alta* grows in huge thickets around the mouth of each river entering the Gulf on the Texas coast. Such places are often most easily approached by boat—an unusual experience in cactus hunting—for the numerous islands in the bays and the first clayey rises above the salt flats are often so covered with huge thickets of this cactus, many individuals standing 6 to 10 feet tall, that one can hardly set foot on them. The cactus often grows so close to the water that one can reach it from the boat itself. Or some may prefer to observe it where it grows as smaller and more scattered individuals just back of the beach sand dunes or spotted here and there on the coastal plain a few miles from the baysides. Large stands of it may be easily and comfortably observed in the Santa Ana National Wildlife Refuge by the lower Rio Grande and in the Aransas National Wildlife Refuge on the Gulf.

When students of cacti have been faced with these huge populations of this cactus they have reacted variously to what they saw. Engelmann, in *Pl. Lindh.,* lists "*O. engelmannii* . . . at the mouth of the Rio Grande, with almost globose fruits, innumerable small seeds and very luscious deep red pulp." He obviously had this variety before him, and we notice that he had no hesitancy in assigning it to the species *O. engelmannii,* not feeling it necessary to set it apart from the western type in any way.

The next person to study the coastal cacti was Dr. Griffiths. He evidently spent much time with them, and he got thoroughly entangled in trying to work out the variations he found on the Gulf. He had no way to indicate each form he came across except by describing it as a new species, and where in some other areas he did us great service this way, here his method seemed to carry him too far. He soon had a whole list of supposed species growing in this same strip along the Texas coast.

When Britton and Rose were faced with this profusion of species, they made short work of it, writing as follows:

Dr. Rose has examined all this region and is of the opinion that only one species of this series exists there, and this we believe is to be referred to *O. lindheimeri.* It is very common about Brownsville and Corpus Christi, where it forms thickets covering thousands of acres of land. It is very variable in habit, being either low and widely spreading or becoming tall and tree-like, sometimes 3 meters high, with a definite cylindric trunk. Plants from these two extremes, if studied apart from the field, might be considered as different species, but in the field one sees innumerable intergrading forms . . . Decided differences in the flower colors have been pointed out in the original descriptions, and we have observed them in greenhouse specimens, but they do not correlate with other characters.

It seems to me that Britton and Rose were right in reducing the bulk of this coastal form to only one taxon, but I follow Engelmann in referring it to *O. engelmannii,* since *O. lindheimeri* is an invalid name for type material from two different species. Yet I am not ready to regard this Gulf Coast form as identical with the typical variety *engelmannii,* nor even with variety *texana* which sometimes grows near it. When considered together as one entity, this form presents definite and constant characters which set it off enough from all others of the *O. engelmannii* complex to make it one distinct variety within that species.

In order to help serious students who may want to follow the many segregates of this variety which Griffiths recognized and check them themselves, I add a list of the more important of his species here included as synonyms of this variety, together with the most outstanding character he gave for each one:

O. cyanella Gr. Flower brick-red, fading to purplish. Growing at the mouth of the Rio Grande.

O. gilvoalba Gr.   Flower very pale, being yellowish-white or cream-colored. This rare form was collected about 30 years ago by Mr. Fred Lawson, the well-known cactus dealer of San Antonio, Texas. His original plant still is growing in San Antonio, and is now a huge, treelike specimen about 12 feet high and broad and with several trunks oval in shape and about 2 feet in circumference. Countless cuttings from this specimen have been distributed worldwide. I have heard it referred to as *O. lawsonii,* and have been told that the name was once published, but have failed to find this publication. Found near the mouth of the Rio Grande.

O. deltica Gr.   Flower yellow, fading to reddish. Spines not quite so numerous as in some specimens of the variety. Fruit broader and more spherical than average. Found here and there in almost the whole range, but the type locality was near Brownsville.

O. laxiflora Gr.   Flower orange-red to purplish-red. From near Brownsville.

O. bentonii Gr.   Spines usually fewer and shorter than typical for the variety, but ordinarily 1 to 5 on each areole. Pads usually darker green. Flowers yellow. Fruit oval to rather elongated obovate. The more elongated of these fruits are the most nearly like those of variety *texana* found in the area, but the same plant at the same time will display oval fruits more typical of variety *alta*—as shown in Griffiths' own photograph. Said by Griffiths to grow from the Brazos River into southwestern Louisiana and to be in cultivation in Florida. This form has been listed as a synonym of *O. stricta* by Britton and Rose and also by Backeberg, but it is much larger and more spiny than that plant and does not have its narrow, club-shaped, constricted, and deeply pitted fruits. The whole question of the relationship of our variety to those large Opuntias of the eastern Gulf Coast has hardly been explored. It is my suspicion that once our Texas coastal variety is looked at carefully as an entity separate from the more western varieties, and this form is compared with, for example, *O. dillenii* (Ker-Gawler) Haw., we may find the relationship very close.

O. engelmannii var. *alta,* taken to include all of those listed above, is probably the largest and most robust of the Texas cacti. A strictly coastal species, it surprises many people by growing so near the water. It is not useful in any stage. Its fruits are edible, but smaller than those of the more western edible varieties and full of a huge number of very small seeds. Its large pads are too woody and tough to be fed to cattle.

Opuntia engelmannii var. cacanapa (Gr.)

DESCRIPTION   PLATE 46

STEMS: As the species, except usually more profusely branching, forming a broader, more bushy plant which is usually a whole thicket in itself. The pads also remain more bluish and glaucous than those of the other forms, and are usually smaller and more regular in shape than in some of the others, being normally round or only slightly oval and usually only 5 to 8 inches in diameter, rarely larger than 10 inches. These pads are also thinner than is typical for the species.

AREOLES: As the species, except a little smaller than is typical.

SPINES: Fewer in each areole than the typical variety usually shows, having commonly only 1 on each upper side areole of the pad with 1 to 3 and rarely to 6 on the edge areoles. These spines are usually all bright yellow, only occasionally showing brown coloring in the bases. The main spine is sharply and rigidly porrect, flattened, and 1 to 3 inches long. The other spines are 3/4 to 2 inches long, slightly flattened or round, and also nearly porrect.

GLOCHIDS: As the species, except very few, the sides of the pads often showing none, and the edge areoles only boasting a few scattered ones.

FLOWERS: As the species, except apparently always yellow, and in all examples observed with the stigma lobes white or yellowish instead of green. The blooms come several weeks later than the other varieties of the same species in the same area.

FRUITS: Spherical to very broadly obovate with no constriction at either end. They are small for the species, being only 1 to 2 inches long, averaging slightly over 1 inch. In color they are dark red, with less purple in the hue than is typical for the species. The umbilicus is large and perfectly flat. The fruit pulp is juicy, but tasteless and apparently is not eaten by animals, since these fruits remain on the plants long after those of other varieties are gone.

RANGE. Along the Rio Grande in northern Zapata County and over the whole western half of Webb County, Texas. It also occurs in the Chisos Mountains of Brewster County, Texas. Both of these populations represent only small invasions into the U.S. from northern Mexico.

REMARKS. If we were to apply the appealing but too simple suggestion that we should separate only Opuntia forms different enough to be recognizable from the moving automobile, this would still be a separate form. Once it is noticed, the more bushy growth of smaller, more bluish pads with their long, porrect, bright yellow spines can be picked out of a mixed stand at a glance, even when one is riding by at good speed. The difference from the other *O. engelmannii* varieties with which it often grows in the same thickets is so constant that it must be listed separately, yet the fact seems clear that it also falls within the larger species. The plant is very common around Laredo, Texas, where it makes up in some places, particularly very near the Rio Grande, half of the population of large Opuntias covering the uncleared range.

The collection of this form in the Chisos Mountains of the

Texas Big Bend was a real surprise and very confusing until we observed this plant growing rather widely in northern Coahuila, Mexico. We found it as far south as Sabinas, Coahuila. It was then easy to see that our two Texas locations represent extensions of its territory northward at the two ends of its range where the Rio Grande dips south, while it apparently does not grow to the river along its northward arc between these two points.

O. engelmannii var. *cacanapa* is closest to variety *cyclodes*, from which it can readily be distinguished by its longer and more slender, more porrect spines, larger flowers with white instead of green stigmas, brighter red fruits with much smaller seeds, and thinner, blue-green instead of thick, bright green or yellow-green pads.

Dr. Griffiths first encountered this form early in his studies near Encinal, Texas, which is at the extreme northern edge of its range. He gave a rather sketchy but clear enough description of it then under the name, *O. cacanapa*. Several years later he redescribed it as he found it in the center of its U.S. range around Laredo, Texas, with a new name, *O. tricolor*. The two are clearly the same, and although the plant is more commonly known under the second name, the original one should be applied to it.

This is one of the most beautiful of the *O. engelmannii* varieties, striking along the roadside with its round, frosty bluish pads and long, perfectly porrect, bright yellow spines.

REMARKS. This is one of Griffiths' forms which, while certainly not a separate species in the current concept, does appear in a definite area among the regular population. It seems possible to distinguish it from the typical *O. engelmannii* only on spine characters, which are never stable enough in Opuntias to be the sole basis for separating species.

I list this form here as a variety only because its unique spination is obviously not environmentally caused, and this seems the best way to retrieve it from the synonymy where it has been all but lost, so that the newer techniques of taxonomy may someday be used upon it. This might reveal its true relationship to the typical form of the species and to other varieties in the midst of which it grows.

The spines on this plant are much more slender than is typical for the species, and this is all the more striking since they are longer. The main spines become 2 to 3 inches long. These spines are slender enough to be somewhat flexible to the touch, hence the name of the plant. If anyone wonders about listing this form separately from the other varieties, let him try to imagine an *O. engelmannii* with flexible spines, and I think he will realize that this plant requires some sort of separate treatment. These spines become markedly deflexed as they mature, and on old pads all lie pressed downward almost against the surface of the pad.

The cactus is encountered occasionally on the dry hills overlooking the Rio Grande both above and below Laredo, but is never abundant.

Opuntia engelmannii var. flexispina (Gr.)

DESCRIPTION   PLATE 46

STEMS: As the species, except smaller than some forms, growing only to about 4 feet tall and spreading, without a truly central trunk. The pads are mostly yellow-green, with a minimum of glaucescence, often becoming quite shiny.

AREOLES: As the species.

SPINES: As the species, except averaging longer, the main spines being 2 inches or more long, as well as more slender to the point of being somewhat flexible. All spines are yellow with or without brown bases, and all slope sharply downward or recurve tightly against the surface of the pad.

GLOCHIDS: As the species.

FLOWERS: As the species, except apparently always yellow and with the stigmas dark green.

FRUITS: 1½ to 2 inches long, broad to rather elongated egg-shaped, with some constriction below. The seeds are about ⅛ of an inch (3 millimeters) in diameter.

RANGE. Known only from Webb and Zapata counties, Texas, where it is never common, but may be found occasionally from near Zapata to about 40 miles northwest of Laredo, always near the Rio Grande.

Opuntia engelmannii var. aciculata (Gr.)

DESCRIPTION   PLATE 47

STEMS: As the species in growth except not observed becoming over about 4 feet high. The pads are typical, except smaller, being 5 to 8 inches long. They are also a deep, vivid green seldom seen in the other varieties.

AREOLES: As the species, except more closely set than typical, being from only ½ to 1¼ inches apart, and with somewhat more brown wool. The young areoles on the sides of the pads are not as small as is typical and seem more round, but the edge areoles are typical in size, all seeming, however, much more conspicuous than ordinary because of the exaggerated glochid formation.

SPINES: Often completely lacking. However, many plants produce 1 to 3 spines on the upper and edge areoles. Only occasionally a plant will produce a full armament of 3 to 8 spines on old stem pads. These spines are typical for the species, except more slender and all more strictly deflexed or spreading downward. They are brown with yellow tips or mottled.

GLOCHIDS: Very conspicuous and formidable. They are bright

red-brown or mottled or bright brown with yellow tips, and vary in length from $^1/_8$ to $^1/_2$ inch in the same areole and spread outward from all parts of the areole so as to form a large, loose, starlike cluster up to $^1/_2$ inch across. These pronounced clusters are found on all areoles, not just on the edges of the pads.

FLOWERS: As the species, varying from clear yellow through orange to brick-red, and sometimes almost magenta. The stigmas have dark green lobes.

FRUITS: Oval to broadly pear-shaped with a little constriction below and with the umbilici flat or nearly so. They are deep purplish-red in color. The seeds are $^1/_8$ of an inch or slightly more (3–3$^1/_2$ millimeters) in diameter.

RANGE. Apparently limited to Webb County, Texas, northwestward along the Rio Grande to about 50 miles above Laredo. It has been observed also in Nuevo Leon, Mexico, southwest of Laredo.

REMARKS. This has been a much misunderstood cactus. Originally discovered by Griffiths, it would probably have remained unnoticed like most of his other finds except that Britton and Rose chose to list it as a separate species instead of lumping it with his other forms in the synonymy of *O. engelmannii*. Kept in this way before the public while the other forms were overlooked, the striking beauty of the spineless specimens with their areoles like stars of which the widely spreading glochids are the bright rays made it a favorite of growers. It has been cultivated almost around the world by collectors, and has recently been the only strictly Texas Opuntia cultivated and listed for sale in the catalogs of the large California dealers. All this testifies to its uniqueness, and when a spineless specimen of the darker flower color is crowned with its deep red blooms it is certainly one of the most beautiful of the Opuntias, worthy of a place in any cactus collection.

This spineless form, which is the one cultivated, is seldom linked in the minds of cactus growers with the common, spiny *O. engelmannii*. Griffith seemed to have had only this or specimens with an occasional short spine before him, so his original description does not reflect the whole range of spination in the form. Britton and Rose mentioned that it may have several spines, but that they were deciduous. Observation in the type locality, however, shows some specimens with up to 8 long, deflexed spines on older pads. These are quite like the spines of the *O. engelmannii* complex in character and nearest to those of *O. engelmannii* var. *flexispina*. When it is observed that the flowers and fruits are practically identical to those of some other members of this group, it seems clear to us that we have here another variety of that complex with only minor differences from the typical form except for the exaggerated glochid formation.

Backeberg's *O. aciculata* is this form, but the plant he describes and pictures as *O. aciculata* var. *orbiculata* is another cactus entirely, clearly of the *O. phaeacantha* species.

O. engelmannii var. *aciculata* is encountered a few miles east of Laredo, Texas, and north of that city along the Rio Grande, where it grows only on the tops of the gravelly hills. It is most common in the vicinity of the Dolores Ranch. Formerly one could drive north of Laredo on the river road and find it growing rather profusely on the shoulders of that unimproved road where it passes the Dolores Ranch, but recently that road was widened and paved, and the shoulders scraped bare of all vegetation in the process. Now one can only catch glimpses of the cactus through the ranch's very high deer-proof fence and must drive on 40 to 50 miles above Laredo, where it is not nearly so common, to observe or collect it. I know of no other place where it can be found without a rather strenuous expedition into rough rangelands. It has been reported to me by some Texas collectors that it has been found southeast of this area below Hebbronville, Texas, but I have been unable to verify this.

Opuntia engelmannii var. dulcis (Eng.) Schumann

DESCRIPTION   PLATE 47

STEMS: As the species, except growing more low and spreading than typical. The tallest plant observed was about 3$^1/_2$ feet tall.

AREOLES: As the species at first, but becoming very large, often to $^1/_2$ inch in diameter when old and containing a large amount of gray wool in the form of a raised doughnut with spines and long glochids on the outer edge of it and a tuft of short glochids in the center. This wool proliferates with age until on older pads each areole contains a raised doughnut of wool which becomes a columnar growth extending outward sometimes up to $^1/_2$ inch, with spines and long glochids on the edge of it and the tuft of short glochids in its center. At a touch the whole structure of a mature areole dislodges from the surface of the plant as a unit, instead of glochids being dislodged individually, the whole cluster of spines and glochids with the woolly center sticking to clothing or flesh like a burr and leaving the surface of the plant with a small pit where the areole had been.

SPINES: As the species, except usually 1 to 3 and never over 6 per areole in number. In color they are brown at the base, the upper parts whitish to pale straw-yellow, all fading to dirty tan.

GLOCHIDS: Mottled brown and yellow or all yellow in color. Arranged in a unique way as follows: around the lower edge of the young areole is a semicircle of scattered, spreading glochids which are coarse and formidable, becoming with age almost bristle-like and up to $^1/_4$ of an inch long. With age the upper part of the areole is nearly ringed with these also. The center of the new areole contains the bulging gray wool, at first with a mass of short, very fine glochids growing out of it. The wool seems to overtake these smaller glochids and grows over them except in the center of the areole, where it remains depressed, forming the doughnut of gray wool. Out of this depressed center there continues to grow the tight cluster of very fine, short glochids not at all like the heavy ones on the edge of the areole. These center glochids seem to stay just ahead of the wool as it grows outward to form the curious projection in the middle of the areole.

FLOWERS: As the species. Yellow and orange colors have been seen. The stigmas are dark green.

FRUITS: Egg-shaped with a slight constriction below and the umbilici broad but slightly pitted. They are 1¼ to 1¾ inches long, and purplish in color, and are said by Engelmann to be sweet and more edible than most others of this group, a statement which is borne out by the fact that they are so soon removed from the plants by animals that fully ripened fruits are seldom seen in the field. The seeds are ⅛ of an inch or a little more (3–4 millimeters) in diameter.

RANGE. Originally said by Engelmann to have been collected at Presidio del Norde and Eagle Pass, Texas. Collected in this study only about 50 miles southeast of Eagle Pass, Texas, growing on the hills overlooking the Rio Grande and again about 20 miles southeast of Anahuac, Nuevo Leon, Mexico, which is about 60 miles southwest of Laredo, Texas. Although we were not able to find it there, a specimen said to have been collected somewhere near Presidio, Texas, is growing in the garden of Mr. Homer Jones, the cactus dealer at Alpine, Texas.

REMARKS. It is another testimony to the thoroughness of the early students of cacti that a hundred years ago they found and described carefully this unusual form. Engelmann made the first description from Bigelow's specimens. Coulter also worked with the same preserved specimens and with the living plants which, remarkably, were still growing at the Missouri Botanical Garden 30 years later. He was the first to recognize that it was actually only another form of our large species; so, using the other name for the species, he called it O. lindheimeri var. dulcis. Schumann studied it also, and first made the combination of names I am using.

Wooton still later claimed our plant as growing in southeast New Mexico, but his description and picture shows an entirely different cactus, and to our knowledge it has not yet actually been found in New Mexico.

Britton and Rose, perhaps seeing that Wooton's plant seems nothing but a rather typical O. engelmannii, ignored the form completely, calling it a synonym of their O. lindheimeri. Everyone has followed in this since, as the plant is rare and was apparently not seen again. Even Griffiths makes no mention of it.

We happened upon the cactus growing rather sparingly in the very small areas described above. The areole structure with its remarkable wool and glochid formation is most striking on old plants and surely warrants listing the plant so that it is not overlooked entirely as it has been in all the studies since Britton

and Rose. Other than in the unique areole structure, however, the plants characters are all similar to those of the species to which it belongs. Something like this remarkable areole structure is found again in quite another plant, however. On old pads of O. atrispina there usually develops something like the doughnut-shaped elevation of wool, but in that plant the edge areoles then proliferate the growth centers until they finally have several of these elevated circles in each areole.

Opuntia engelmannii var. subarmata (Gr.)
"Flap-Jack Cactus"

DESCRIPTION   PLATE 47

STEMS: Growing as a large, upright, compactly branching bush to at least 6 feet high and often as broad. Individual pads are round to obovate or often broader than they are long. They are to at least 12 inches long and wide, blue-green with much white glaucescence on them at first, changing when very old to yellow-green. They are firm and heavy, sometimes up to 1 inch thick.

AREOLES: As the species, except smaller than in some forms.

SPINES: None on young, active pads. On very old pads which have enlarged to form a trunk or main branch there may occasionally be one spine on some areoles. It is ½ inch or less long, mottled brown or gray, slender, and flattened, as well as deflexed in position.

GLOCHIDS: As the species, except very few in number.

FLOWERS: As the species.

FRUITS: Very broad egg-shaped with a slight constriction below and the umbilicus flat or nearly so. They are 2 to 2½ inches long, and dark red to almost purple in color. The seeds are a little more than 1/16 to just over ⅛ of an inch (2–3½ millimeters) in diameter, with wider rims than are found in most other varieties of the species.

RANGE. Never common, but encountered occasionally along the Rio Grande from near Laredo, Texas, to the Devil's River.

REMARKS. Here is a large, robust O. engelmannii, standing sometimes higher than a man's head, and displaying huge, smooth pads, yet totally without spines except some small ones on old trunks. These pads are so broad and round that they naturally evoke the name, flap-jack cactus, long used for them. The question naturally occurs to one, how can a plant which appears so luscious stand perfectly spineless but untouched in a pasture where the animals eat any ordinary O. engelmannii to the very ground as soon as its spines are burned off? The ranchers answer that the flap-jack cactus survives because it is so tough that the animals can't chew it. And a person's first attempt to lop off a branch of the plant confirms this assertion very quickly. The skin of the pads itself is very tough and the supporting vascular tissue is the most rigid I have seen in any U. S. Platyopuntia. One has to go to the large chollas to equal its strength. It takes a hatchet or some similar tool to sever even a young pad from this giant. Spines are rendered unnecessary by the toughness of this plant's tissues.

The cactus is never common, and there is no indication that it grows in stands anywhere. It is encountered here and there within its range as a proud individual usually towering over the lower *O. engelmannii* forms around it. These occasional individuals have been found along the Rio Grande from the Devil's River on the northwest to within about 25 miles of Laredo, Texas, on the southeast.

The listing of the plant here as a variety of *O. engelmannii* does not imply that all about its relationship is known, any more than about the other forms of this species listed as varieties. If anything, it really implies the opposite. The cactus does present general plant body, flower, and fruit characters so similar to those of *O. engelmannii* as to make it difficult to let it stand as a separate species. Yet it does not seem proper to lose it in that species by synonymy. Its unique features are more than just the one of spinelessness—they include its manner of growth, its robustness, the firmness of its tissue mentioned above, and so on, so that it seems it has to be regarded as more than a simple genetic form emerging here and there. The varietal status seems best until it is further studied.

We find no real intermediates between *O. engelmannii* var. *subarmata* and the other varieties of the species. Griffiths, as we have seen, described what would sound like an intermediate, calling it *O. dillei*. But that was from canyons of the Sacramento Mountains of New Mexico, where we do not find our form, and its character of having few spines appears definitely to be an environmental one so that it seems necessary to regard it as a synonym of the typical variety. The spinelessness of our present form is not due to environment, as it often is found in the field surrounded by extremely spiny examples of the species, and it puts on no additional spines in cultivation. The point is also made that *O. dillei* survives only where it is inaccessible to livestock which eat it otherwise, while variety *subarmata* scorns such enemies.

Opuntia engelmannii var. linguiformis (Gr.)
"Cow's Tongue Cactus," "Lengua de Vaca"

DESCRIPTION   PLATE 48

STEMS: Growing upright or sprawling, often 3 to 5 feet high. Individual pads narrowly ovate to linear, varying often on the same plant from a minimum of about 8 inches long by 6 wide to a greatly exaggerated length of sometimes as much as 36 inches long by only 4 inches wide at the widest point at or near the base of the pad. Otherwise these stems are as the species.

AREOLES: As the species.

SPINES: As the species, except often shorter than typical.

GLOCHIDS: As the species.

FLOWERS: A weak bloomer. Some plants fail to bloom at all and are reproduced only vegetatively, but other plants bloom fairly well in good situations. The flowers are identical to the species. All observed, however, were orange or red in hue with dark green stigmas.

FRUITS: As the species in both fruits and seeds.

RANGE. Originally found and definitely known to grow wild only in Bexar County, Texas. The original location was near the southeast quadrant of San Antonio's Loop 13 and Loop 410, just south of the small towns of China Grove and Sayers.

REMARKS. The cow's tongue cactus has long been a favorite with gardeners. The strange shape of the exaggerated pads is very striking, and countless yards in South Texas have somewhere in a corner a bush of this cactus. It grows well in the whole area and reproduces itself vegetatively by the rooting of dislodged pads, but it is not grown for its flowers, as many people have never seen it bloom, and some specimens, it seems, cannot even be pampered into blooming.

The striking shape of the pads is obviously due to the continued activity of each pad's growing tip. It appears that this growing tip somehow escapes the biological restriction which would normally stop growth early in the pad development on most cacti, and thus the pads of this form continue to lengthen, perhaps as long as they live. There is reason to believe that the more healthy the plant is the more rapidly the growing tip proliferates in relation to the lateral growth, and so the more exaggerated the shape becomes. Nothing is known of the internal physiology or the genetic basis for this unusual growth pattern, but the plant seems to put all its energy into the lengthening of the pads at the expense of flowering. Fruits with seeds are occasionally produced, but the seedlings have never been observed. This may represent some mutant form of *O. engelmannii* which reproduces itself entirely vegetatively. There is an accompanying loss of strength, as the form is more damaged by insect pests than the species, as well as more easily killed by frost.

The original plants came from southeastern Bexar County, Texas. In the type locality most of the land is now farmed, and few of the wild population have survived. Only an occasional specimen may still be found persisting in a fence-row. But innumerable examples are in the yards of San Antonio and most of South Texas to as far north as the vicinity of Austin, beyond which the cold will hardly allow it to be grown.

It is hard to know now whether the form ever grew wild in other than the Bexar County location. San Antonians like to believe it is their own unique contribution to the cactus world, and it may well be. I have been told of the plant's growing wild in various other places, but all of these I have been able to check have been near old farm sites or in some such situations where they could well have escaped from some old cultivation. Britton and Rose mention having seen similar plants from near Brownsville, Texas, but do not indicate whether they were native there.

Opuntia chlorotica Eng. & Big.
"Clock-Face Prickly Pear"

DESCRIPTION   PLATE 48

STEMS: Erect, bushy, becoming 6 or 7 feet tall in good situations, but often smaller. They form a definite, rounded trunk quite early, often when only 2 or 3 feet tall. The individual pads are circular to very broadly obovate, with little or no constriction below, 6 to 12 inches long, pale yellowish-green with some whitish glaucescence when young.

AREOLES: Small to medium-sized and spaced about 1 inch apart on young and growing pads, but on the very old pads increasing in size, often to 1/2 inch and until the trunk is almost entirely covered by these enlarged areoles. In the old areoles much wool appears, producing on the trunk a thick layer which has sometimes been called a tomentum.

SPINES: Pure yellow in color, 1/2 to 2 inches long, more or less flattened, medium in thickness, and mostly deflexed. There are 1 to 6 spines per areole on young, growing pads, but they continue to be produced on older pads, until on the main stems and trunk the total may run 20 to 30 per areole, these large clusters of deflexed spines often almost wholly covering the trunk with a formidable mass of spines unique in the Platyopuntias.

GLOCHIDS: Few and short on new pads, but also increasing greatly with age until becoming a spreading mass of rigid bristles, many up to 1/2 or 3/4 of an inch long, in each enlarged areole. They are always yellow or straw in color.

FLOWERS: Clear yellow in color, 1 1/2 to 3 inches in diameter. The ovary is 1 1/8 to 1 1/2 inches long and very wide, usually 1 inch or more in diameter, tuberculate, with each areole having a cluster of short, brown glochids and occasionally 1 or 2 bristles up to 1/2 inch long. The stamens are yellow, and the stigmas have 10 or 12 fat greenish-yellow lobes.

FRUITS: Spherical to ovate, 1 1/2 to 2 inches in length, with a shallowly pitted umbilicus. In color they are reddish-purple. The seeds are around 1/8 of an inch (2 1/2–3 1/2 millimeters) in diameter.

RANGE. The mountains of southwestern New Mexico west of the Rio Grande on into Arizona and said to extend into California and Sonora, Mexico.

REMARKS. This cactus is very close to some forms of *O. engelmannii*, so close that there is a temptation to reduce it to the status of a variety of that species. As far as I know, however, no authority has yet actually done this, although several have discussed the possibility. I have found no one expert enough to tell the 1-year-old pads of this cactus, when removed from the bush, from those of some specimens of *O. engelmannii* var. *texana*, for instance, in every case. There seems to be little difference except that the areoles of *O. chlorotica* are closer together on the average. And the 2-or 3-year-old pads of *O. chlorotica* are almost identical with those of some *O. engelmannii* var. *flexispina* specimens. But after that, the older, trunk-forming parts of this cactus go on in the growth of their areoles and the production of spines beyond anything seen in the *O. engelmannii* forms. The flowers are practically identical in all visible aspects to those of *O. engelmannii*, and the seeds are essentially the same. The fruits of *O. chlorotica* seem more consistently round and they have more areoles with more glochids on them, as well as a little more deeply pitted umbilicus.

This cactus is a beautiful inhabitant of the high mountains in southwestern New Mexico, being especially common and robust on the slopes of western Sierra, Grant, and Hidalgo counties, where the massive covering of bright yellow spines on the lower parts of old plants rivals in shining brilliance those of some of the chollas.

Opuntia tardospina Gr.

DESCRIPTION   PLATE 48

STEMS: An erect cactus, diffuse and spreading instead of bushlike. Lacking any central stem or trunk, it produces many ascending branches, forming a small thicket 2 to 3 feet tall when mature. The pads are round to broadly pear-shaped, 6 to 12 inches long, medium in thickness. The surface is glaucous and bright to yellowish-green.

AREOLES: Conspicuous from the first, being almost round and 3/16 of an inch or more long when young, often increasing to round and 3/8 of an inch in diameter when old, bulging with much wool. They are situated 3/4 to 1 5/8 inches apart.

SPINES: As observed in the field, 1 or 2 per areole in number, in only a few upper areoles of the pad. The main spines are 3/4 to 1 1/2 inches long, rather heavy and flattened, deflexed or even recurved tightly against the pad. The second spine, when present, is a small lower spine also deflexed and only 3/16 to 7/8 of an inch long. The spines are all translucent yellow with or without brown bases. *O. tardospina* is said by the discoverer to become much more spiny under cultivation.

GLOCHIDS: Few at first, soon becoming many to very many in all areoles, 3/16 to 1/2 inch long, yellow or sometimes yellow mottled with brown.

FLOWERS: 2 1/2 to 3 inches in diameter and pure lemon-yellow in color. The ovary is 1 3/4 to 2 inches long, club-shaped, 3/4 of an inch wide, with a few very short glochids on it. The style is shorter than the stamens. The stigma has 7 white or yellow-white lobes.

FRUITS: Broadly egg-shaped to club-shaped, with rather noticeable constriction of the base and with the umbilici pitted fairly deeply. They are $1^1/_2$ to $2^1/_4$ inches long and purplish-red when ripe. The pulp is not very juicy, is slow ripening, and is unpalatable. The seeds are $^1/_8$ to $^3/_{16}$ of an inch (3–$4^1/_2$ millimeters) in diameter.

RANGE. In the hills along the Colorado River in central Texas from near Austin to Llano and Lampasas, Texas, and southwest to upper Uvalde County.

REMARKS. This is one of Griffiths' numerous discoveries which has been very difficult for students to confirm, but which has seemed from his description unique enough that, although we can tell from their handling of it that most scholars never saw the plant, they have consistently retained the species with little comment.

The amount of living material which Griffiths had before him when he made his description must have been small. He, in fact, states that the description is mainly from the type plant. This plant was collected near Lampasas, Texas. Griffiths' reliance on so little material, the failure of more recent students to show evidence that they had their own material, and the difficulty we encountered in this study in finding it, all show that the cactus is rare in its type locality. Perhaps this is because the type locality is the most northerly location at which it has been found.

The fact that Griffiths based his description upon a plant from the extreme edge of its range, where the soil and water conditions are not severe, and even there upon a plant from the "valley lands," may explain why it has been so hard to recognize the plant again. Even in that area it has been impossible to rediscover specimens with pads and fruits quite as big as his maximum, and farther southwest, where the conditions are much more rocky and arid, the specimens found are much smaller.

But the species has truly outstanding characteristics, and once a person realizes that the size descriptions given are for a seldom-attained maximum and starts looking for these characters in a smaller plant, he will find O. *tardospina* here and there in the hills from the type locality southwest along the edge of the Edwards Plateau.

The most remarkable things about the cactus are the large, bulging, dark-colored areoles, the conspicuous, loose clusters of uneven glochids, and the yellow and deflexed, but late-appearing and soon discolored spines. Griffiths did not describe the flowers, but they seem always to be clear yellow, fading to pinkish. I have always found them appearing early in the spring, being over and gone before those of the other species growing in the same area arrive.

Neither did Griffiths describe the seeds of the plant. Britton and Rose erroneously state them to be 5 millimeters (over $^3/_{16}$ of an inch) broad, and Backeberg follows them in the description. But then, Britton and Rose give a description almost completely different from the original and ignore all of the most conspicuous details of areoles, glochids, and spines. Their whole description, including seeds, would fit an O. *phaeacantha* var. *camanchica* with minimum armament, and they show to represent their plant a drawing of a plant from north of Dallas, Texas, where that other cactus is the main large Opuntia to be found. Seeds produced by the specimens collected in this study were rather smaller in diameter, very different from those of O. *phaeacantha* var. *camanchica*, and in the range of those of O. *engelmannii*, which is its nearest relative. Our plant also shows some similarities to O. *atrispina*, another of Griffiths' species, whose range begins just beyond where that of O. *tardospina* stops on the southwest.

Opuntia spinosibacca Anthony

DESCRIPTION   PLATE 49

STEMS: A strictly upright bush, its base becoming more or less trunklike by much thickening of the old pads. Many branches arise from this short base, each composed of rows of pads small for so large a cactus. These branches standing close together make this a compact, tidy shrub up to at least 4 feet tall. The pads are usually pear-shaped with rather pronounced constrictions at their bases, but occasionally they are almost round. They are from 4 to 7 inches long and 3 to 6 inches wide, of average thickness for their size, but conspicuously tubercled so that each areole is on the summit of a small elevation. This gives the edge of the pad an unusual, slightly notched outline. The color of the pads is a light green or yellowish-green.

AREOLES: Situated $^3/_4$ to $1^1/_2$ inches apart, the areoles are oval to round, small on the faces of young pads, but to $^1/_4$ of an inch in diameter on the edges of older pads.

SPINES: There are 1 to 8 spines per areole, with all or almost all areoles spiny. As is common in Opuntias, lower areoles have fewer spines and the number rises in areoles toward the upper edge of the pad. A fully spined areole has 1 to 5 main spines $^3/_4$ to $2^3/_4$ inches long spreading in all directions. These spines are heavy to very heavy, slightly or greatly flattened, often twisted and curved. They are red-brown or dark brown over the lower two-thirds of their lengths, then gray above, with the tips yellow and translucent. Below these main spines are 1 to 4 lower spines spreading downward, straw-colored mottled with brown. These range from $^3/_8$ to $^5/_8$ of an inch long, and are very slender bristles.

GLOCHIDS: Very few on this cactus. There appear to be none on the sides of most pads and only 6 to 12 in each areole of the upper edge. These few, however, are up to $^1/_2$ inch long and light brown in color, often with yellow tips.

FLOWERS: Standing about 2 inches tall, but not opening widely, so normally 2 inches or less across. In color, they are bright orange-yellow with red centers. The ovary is 1 inch long, broadly vase-shaped, slightly tuberculate, and 3/4 of an inch across at its top, which is its widest point. The petals are very wide, the edges usually somewhat ragged, but with a tiny point at the apex. They are orange-yellow, with their bases bright red, and this red may flush up the midline most of the way to the top. The stamens are very pale yellowish. The style is long and white. The stigma is composed of 7 to 9 light yellowish lobes.

FRUITS: 1 to 1 3/4 inches long, 1/2 to 1 inch thick, oval or egg-shaped, and slightly tuberculate. There is no constriction at the base, which is broadly rounded. There is a rather pronounced constriction at the top, above which the upper edge flares widely to enclose the broad, very deeply concave flower scar. All of the areoles on the edge and a few down farther on the sides of the fruit have 1 to 4 spines on them. These are 1/4 to 1 inch long, rigid, round to slightly flattened, colored much as are the spines on the pads. Spreading straight out from the upper edge of the fruit or turning slightly downward, they surround the whole upper part of it with a formidable armament. When mature the fruits take on a very light greenish-yellow color. They never show any red or purple shading. Almost at once after yellowing, the fruits begin to dry out. This starts below and proceeds upward, the skin becoming tan and papery in appearance and wrinkling slightly, but not enough to change the shape or reduce the over-all size. When opened, the dried fruit presents a mass of very tightly packed seeds with the outer skin of the fruit resembling a peanut hull. The seeds are remarkably irregular. They may be almost any shape from perfectly round to elongated and from a little less than 3/16 to just over 1/4 of an inch (4–6 1/2 millimeters) in diameter. They are usually thin or very thin, but may be flat or sometimes greatly twisted. The rim is from medium width to very broad, 1/2 to 1 1/2 millimeters wide, varying on its way around the seed.

RANGE. Known only in the small area extending a few miles from near the ranger station at Boquillas toward the Hot Springs, all in the Big Bend National Park, Brewster County, Texas.

REMARKS. It is remarkable that this unique cactus was not described until 1956. It presents a set of characteristics truly amazing when all combined in the one cactus. It is no wonder that theorists have not yet decided where its relationships lie. It has a tall, upright, bushy manner of growth found in the O. engelmannii group, but the compactness of its form and the smallness of its pads contrast sharply with those upright but spreading Opuntias with their large pads. It has a very yellow-green color of the surface, which I have seen otherwise only in O. chlorotica and a few specimens of O. engelmannii. Its spines appear more similar to those of some O. phaeacantha forms. It has a tubercled surface unique to itself, or equaled only on some of the small, crawling Opuntias. And most unusual of all, it has fruits which do not ever color any shade of red or purple like

our other large forms and which are similar to those of the small, dry-fruited Opuntias and the Cornyopuntia by being truly spiny, by becoming faintly yellowish when mature, and then by becoming dry and hard and papery. This is undoubtedly the platypus of the Opuntias. Miss Anthony discovered O. spinosibacca during her study of the Opuntias of the Big Bend, and it is clearly the greatest achievement of her study.

The reason for the late date of its discovery no doubt is the fact that this prickly pear seems to grow only on a few remote hills bordering the Rio Grande in the very deepest tip of the Big Bend. Until comparatively recently there would have been no way to enter its area except by the most strenuous expedition. But fortunately for the cactus fancier, the Parks Department's new paved road to Boquillas Canyon runs right through this area, and one may see ranks of these tidy, compact bushes drawn up stiffly on the limestone ledges of the hills he skirts without even leaving the asphalt. Fortunately also, the range of this cactus is within the Big Bend Park, where it is protected and will no doubt be flourishing when many of the desert species are gone the way of the bulldozer and the herbicide.

Opuntia rufida Eng.
"Blind Pear"

DESCRIPTION   PLATE 49

STEMS: Growing erect and bushy with a definite trunk, and 2 to 6 feet tall. The pads are 4 to 8 inches long, round to broadly egg-shaped, or sometimes wider than they are long. They are thick, with flat surfaces, pale gray-green to somewhat yellowish-green in color. The surface appears dull due to being covered with a very short pubescence.

AREOLES: Conspicuous, being round and large, 3/16 to 1/4 of an inch in diameter, and crowded, being 1/2 to 1 inch apart.

SPINES: None.

GLOCHIDS: Very many, but very short and extremely slender. They are only about 1/16 of an inch long, and so crowded in the areole as to form a dense hemispherical tuft. This is red-brown to light brown, often fading to grayish with age.

FLOWERS: 2 to 2 1/2 inches in diameter, orange-yellow in color. The outer petals are almost linear or at least lanceolate, the inner ones obovate, with the ends erose or notched. The stamens are whitish. The style is somewhat longer than the stamens, and there are 5 to 11 dark green stigma lobes. The ovary is 1 to 1 1/8 inches long and about 5/8 of an inch across at the top, which is its widest part. It is tuberculate.

FRUITS: Almost spherical. They are about 1 to 1 1/4 inches in length, and greenish-red in color. The pulp is greenish. The seeds are between 1/16 and 1/8 inch (2–3 millimeters) in diameter, irregular in shape, with narrow rims.

RANGE. Crossing from Mexico into the United States only in

Texas, and there growing only on rocky mountainsides along the Rio Grande from near Presidio, through the Big Bend National Park.

REMARKS. This is a large, beautiful, and distinctive Mexican species which enhances our flora by crossing into our territory. However, it does not venture far into the United States. Only along a stretch of the Rio Grande something over a hundred miles long beginning near Presidio and ending at about the eastern edge of the Big Bend National Park is it to be found on our side of the stream, and nowhere is it found over about 20 miles north of the river.

This narrow strip of territory comprises the most rugged and inaccessible mountains of the Big Bend, and in them *O. rufida* is to be found growing on rocky mountainsides and high ridges. Most typically it is seen as proud bushes growing out of almost vertical cliffs far above one, where it would take hours at least to climb up for a close look. In the past a full-scale expedition was needed to get to its area, but more recently, in the Big Bend National Park, some roads and trails lead past good stands of the cactus. And only very recently the very beautiful new road constructed from Presidio down along the river to the Park has opened up most of its U.S. range to all. Along this road there are several places where the cactus can be found close enough to the road to be accessible to hardy cactophiles. The best stands I have observed which are readily accessible are near Boquillas and just off the highway west of Terlingua, Texas.

Because of its inaccessibility, early students had few specimens to refer to, and their descriptions of *O. rufida* were far from complete. This led to confusion. It was particularly confused with another smaller Mexican cactus, *O. microdasys* (Lehmann) Pfeiffer, because both of these have pubescent surfaces and lack spines. It does relate to that species, but *O. microdasys* is a low, spreading, or at best only a partly erect species without a trunk and with everything in miniature as compared to *O. rufida*. *O. microdasys* was and still is the most commonly cultivated Opuntia. Almost every dime store has starts of it for sale. So often was it taken for our larger cactus that Griffiths stated that in his time specimens of *O. microdasys* were still being distributed for *O. rufida* in American collections. Working from these specimens and probably never having seen the real *O. rufida* alive, Schumann called the cactus *O. microdasys* var. *rufida*, and this name has hung on for the form of *O. microdasys* with red glochids. This is, however, a completely different thing from the real *O. rufida* which grows in Texas—and yet, at the beginning of this study it was only this *O. microdasys* with red glochids which I found in the few existing Texas collections and which I naturally took for *O. rufida* until I saw the real thing growing in the wild. I have still never seen the real *O. rufida* in cultivation. All cultivated or herbarium material going under that name should be checked carefully before being accepted as the real thing.

It is also very easy to confuse the true *O. rufida* with a cactus found growing in Mexico, which Griffiths named *O. macrocalyx*. This cactus grows around Saltillo, Coahuila, and I have seen it as far north as Monclova, Coahuila. It might be taken for a low, spreading, trunkless variant of *O. rufida*. Its pads are fully as big and very similar, except that they are darker green in color. Its growth form is mostly ascending, but is spreading and diffuse in its branching, without any central trunk, forming thickets usually about 2 to 3 feet in height. Its areoles are even closer together than those of our cactus, more like those of *O. microdasys* in spacing. Its flower is similar to that of *O. rufida*, but its fruit is elongated and 2 inches or more in length. It is not necessary here for us to evaluate its relationship to *O. rufida*, but the two should not be confused.

Griffiths considered that *O. rufida* resembled *O. glosseliniana* var. *santa-rita* (Gr. & Hare) Benson more closely than any of these, except for the lack of spines. No one has studied this relationship. Anthony, in her study of the Big Bend Opuntias, describes a new variety, *O. rufia* var. *tortiflora*, which Backeberg does not regard as valid. It is interesting that on seeing her actual preserved specimen of this plant, I would have called it a spineless example of *O. glosseliniana* var. *santa-rita*. Whether future studies can link the two more closely will be interesting to watch.

Opuntia macrocentra Eng.
"Purple Prickly Pear"

DESCRIPTION   PLATE 49

STEMS: Upright, forming a small bush up to 2 or 3 feet high, but without any trunklike main stem. The pads are 4 to 8 inches in length, round, broader than they are long, or sometimes broadly egg-shaped. These pads are comparatively thin, being often only $1/2$ to $5/8$ of an inch thick. They may be medium green to yellowish-green when shaded and well watered, but more often they are purplish over-all or at least spotted and streaked with purple. In the winter and in the heat of the summer this purple coloration is usually very pronounced.

AREOLES: Small and inconspicuous on the sides of the pads, enlarging to about $1/4$ of an inch in the edges. They vary in the distance of their spacing, on some smaller plants being only $3/8$ to $3/4$ of an inch apart, while on larger, more robust plants they may be $3/4$ to $1^1/4$ inches apart.

SPINES: Few in number, being limited to the very upper and edge areoles, but these long and conspicuous. There are only 1 to 4 spines as a maximum, with 1 or 2 per armored areole being most common. Of these, 1 to 3 are very exaggerated spines 2 to 5 inches long, the upper round and the lower one flattened or often even grooved. They are so slender for their length that they are flexible and usually are twisted and bent.

They are all black or else blackish below with usually gray or brown zones at the center and tips. There is sometimes 1 lower deflexed spine ³/₄ to 1¹/₂ inches long.

GLOCHIDS: Very few to average in number, short, ¹/₁₆ to ³/₁₆ of an inch long on the sides of the pads and not increasing in number but sometimes increasing in length to ¹/₂ inch on the edges. They are brown or red-brown in color.

FLOWERS: Approximately 3 inches in diameter, light yellowish with red centers. The ovary is short and egg-shaped, with some glochids on it. The stamens are yellow, and the stigma has 5 to 11 yellow or light greenish-yellow lobes.

FRUITS: ³/₄ to 1¹/₂ inches long, spherical to broadly vase-shaped, with no constriction at the base and with the apex deeply pitted. They become bright red or orange-red in color when ripe. The seeds are about ³/₁₆ of an inch (4–5 millimeters) in diameter, flat but twisted and irregular, with a wide, undulating rim.

RANGE. West of a line from Brewster County in the lower Big Bend of Texas northwest through the Davis Mountains to near Van Horn, Texas, and from there north to near Roswell, New Mexico. In New Mexico all south of a line from near Roswell northwest at least as far as Socorro, then back southwest where it enters southeast Arizona.

REMARKS. O. macrocentra is one of the most striking Opuntias. The sight of this bushy prickly pear with the beautiful purple pads and extremely long, blackish spines is one of those desert visions which remain so visibly in a visitor's memory. And it is remarkable that the more severe the desert climate the more vivid the coloring of the purple prickly pear becomes. Actually, the beautiful hue is merely the means this cactus uses to survive severe conditions, whether they be heat or cold or desiccation. It survives by building up large amounts of these bright pigments at its surface to shield its tender flesh. This means of protection is widely used by cacti, as many of them turn reddish in severe conditions. This cactus only excels in the amount and richness of its coloration, but that is enough to render it memorable.

The spines of this cactus are few in number, but among the longest of this genus, being normally 2 to 4 inches but sometimes to 5 inches long. They are, however, slender for their length and flexible. At least one of them is always flattened, which seems to set this form off from O. gosseliniana var. santa-rita (Gr. & Hare) Benson, with which it is often confused. Benson's insistence, strange in the light of all early descriptions, that the spines are round contributes to this error.

O. macrocentra is very common, even forming the dominant Opuntia in much of the lower Big Bend of Texas. In the area of the Big Bend National Park it grows profusely, the small bushes often standing on rocky slopes where almost nothing else can survive, burnt purple by the sun in summer and frozen as purple in the winter, but still erect and unvanquished. Here in the Big

Bend, in the most severe exposures, the pads are often smaller with closer areoles than typical, but nearby, where there is a little protection and moisture will be the larger, greener pads with areoles farther apart. Miss Anthony, in her study of Opuntias of the Big Bend designated the specimens she found with everything in miniature as O. macrocentra var. minor, but it does not seem this is other than the typical form stunted by environment.

In the Hueco Mountains on the Texas–New Mexico border there has been noticed another population smaller than typical and having lighter colored spines than typical. This form, which has not been proved distinct either, has been referred to as O. macrocentra var. castetteri, but I have not found this name's official publication.

In southern New Mexico and Arizona O. macrocentra grows typically, as in the Big Bend, but as one goes farther north anywhere in its range, where the heat and aridity is not so severe, the species often has larger pads than farther south and presents much less of the purple coloring in the summer. Spination is also less heavy here, occasionally reduced to none. In the Davis Mountains of Texas, on a protected ridge where moisture oozed out of the rock ledges most of the time, I collected specimens with broad, fan-shaped pads, bright green in the summer and perfectly spineless. This would no doubt be the extreme effect of easy conditions on the species. But these northern plants get their turn to deck out in color when winter hits them, often standing beautifully purple against the white snow.

There is so much variation in the shape and color of the fruits and the size of the seeds in various individuals of this species that I suspect the variations might fall into definite segregates within it, but so far I have not been able to correlate these differences with any other constantly varying characters or any definite populations. This would bear much more study.

The species is very close to and often confused with the cactus O. phaeacantha var. brunnea Eng., which grows with it in the Big Bend and around El Paso. This other form often shows reddish coloring, sometimes almost as purple as O. macrocentra, and also has long, blackish-based spines. Almost every herbarium collection I have seen contains a scattering of this form in its O. macrocentra file, and some descriptions of O. macrocentra, beginning with those of Britton and Rose who did not recognize variety brunnea, have been broadened to include characters of that other plant. Before being satisfied that he knows the purple prickly pear one should study the description of that other form and be sure he can distinguish the two.

Opuntia gosseliniana var. santa-rita (Gr. & Hare) Benson

DESCRIPTION   PLATE 50

STEMS: An erect, bushy shrub 2 to 5 feet high with a distinct, though short trunk. The pads are thin and mostly circular but varying occasionally to be very broadly egg-shaped or sometimes broader than they are long. Their surfaces are glaucous blue-green, with reddish coloring around the areoles and along the edge; this coloring is more pronounced during winter.

AREOLES: Oval to round and only $1/8$ of an inch or slightly more in diameter when young, but increasing with age to about $1/4$ of an inch. They are bulging when young, with much wool and many short glochids. The growth of the wool and glochids on old stem pads sometimes produces an elongation of the areole structure outward somewhat like that seen to an extreme degree in *O. engelmannii* var. *dulcis*. The areoles are spaced about $1/2$ to 1 inch apart.

SPINES: Not numerous, new pads often being spineless or with 1 spine present on only a few edge areoles. Older pads may have up to 3 spines in the upper areoles only. These spines are brown or red-brown at the bases with the upper parts yellowish or mottled with yellow. In shape they are cylindrical, in position spreading or deflexed, in size slender and $3/4$ to 4 inches long, although usually about $1 1/2$ to 2 inches.

GLOCHIDS: Many on all areoles, but very short, being usually only about $1/8$ of an inch long, forming with the wool a compact, bulging mass in the areole. They are yellow to brown in color.

FLOWERS: Yellow, with white or yellowish-white stigma lobes.

FRUITS: Oval to oblong, said to often be curved, 1 to $1 3/8$ inches long, $3/4$ of an inch or a little more in diameter, with little or no constriction below and with a pitted apex. They are purple or purplish-red in color. The seeds are $1/8$ of an inch or less (2–3 millimeters) in diameter, flat, with narrow, acute rims.

RANGE. Long known to extend out of Sonora, Mexico, into extreme southeastern Arizona. It has been found more recently in extreme southwestern New Mexico, where it is probably limited to Hidalgo County. It is found again in Texas near the Rio Grande between Presidio and the Big Bend National Park.

REMARKS. Everyone has been cautious about declaring this a New Mexico plant, although it has seemed it should enter out of adjacent Arizona into that state. Now, however, it is definitely known to be there, having been collected a number of times. I am even more reluctant to claim it as a Texas plant, but I have found a few specimens growing on the mountains near the Rio Grande below Presidio, which I have followed all the way through fruiting and cannot distinguish from plants I have which were gathered in the Santa Rita Mountain type locality itself.

O. *gosseliniana* var. *santa-rita* shows similarities not just to one, but to several other cacti. The reddish coloring of its pads makes it seem at first to be close to *O. macrocentra*, but in almost everything else it is very distinct from that cactus, growing more arborescent, having a similar number of spines but these very different in shape and color, having different color of both flowers and fruits, and having entirely different, much smaller seeds. In these seeds, as well as in its size and manner of growth it is somewhat like *O. engelmannii*, this and *O. rufida* being the only other Opuntias in our area equaling *O. engelmannii* var. *alta* and var. *tricolor* in the smallness of their seeds, but it is different from that species in various other ways. However, the seeds, almost identical to those of *O. rufida*, give us another link, and it is a strong one. In all main appearances this cactus is very much like a spiny *O. rufida*, and the discovery of variety *santa-rita* growing in that plant's range in Texas requires us to take a second thought about this. Of course, there are differences besides the spines between them, variety *santa-rita* not being pubescent and having a different hue of pad, not having its glochids quite so fine, having white instead of green stigmas and different colored fruits, but, nevertheless, it may be the most closely related to *O. rufida* of any cactus in our area.

Originally, in the first description of this cactus, Griffiths and Hare emphasized another similarity which they thought so strong that they named the plant *O. chlorotica* var. *santa-rita*. About the same number of similarities and differences separate *O. chlorotica* and variety *santa-rita* as the others. Britton and Rose were heroic enough, if it may be called that, to ignore all these and let the plant stand as *Opuntia santa-rita*, without comment. Marshall followed them. But more recently Benson has chosen to link the form up with yet another species, *Opuntia gosseliniana*. This is a much more spiny cactus found in Sonora near the Pacific. I do not know that plant, and since all of the students from Arizona and California who should know both forms best now choose to make this combination, I will trust that the reasons for it are even stronger than the ones which could be given for combining it with any of the above.

This cactus is beautiful, but seems to be more affected by environmental factors than most large Opuntias, suffering quickly from both extreme drought or too much moisture, unusual cold, and so on. Perhaps for this reason it is never common and only isolated individuals are encountered anywhere in the U.S.

Opuntia strigil Eng.

DESCRIPTION   PLATE 50

STEMS: Erect, growing as a diffuse shrub without trunk, usually about 2 feet tall. The pads are 3 to 8 inches long, round to broadly egg-shaped, medium in thickness with no constriction at the base. The surface is pale green or yellow-green in color.

AREOLES: $1/4$ to $3/4$ of an inch apart and therefore appearing crowded on the sides of the pads, but often running together on the edges. They are round or oval, $3/16$ to $3/8$ of an inch across, and often become elevated by the addition of much gray wool.

SPINES: Possessing an array of 5 to 10 very slender, almost bristle-like spines ¼ to ¾ of an inch long around the lower half of each areole. These are dark brown at their bases, fading to red-brown and finally, toward the tips, becoming yellow or whitish, or else they are all whitish. Some plants have 1 to 3 central spines on each upper and edge areole, but many individuals lack these. When present they are ¾ to 1¾ inches long, slender to medium strength, round or somewhat flattened, straight and erect on the edges while more or less deflexed and bent in various directions on the sides of the pads. They are dark brown below, medium or red-brown and rather translucent in the middle zone and translucent yellowish beyond that, the three colors contrasting conspicuously.

GLOCHIDS: Each mature areole has a loose, spreading cluster of slender yellow glochids in the upper part of it. They are from ⅛ to ½ inch long, the largest ones standing upward from the upper part of the areole opposite the lower radiating spines and almost equaling them in length, contrasting sharply with them in color.

FLOWERS: Small to medium in size, being 1½ to 2½ inches across and 1¼ to 1½ inches tall. The ovary is short, with leaves and a few long bristles on its areoles. The petals are lemon-yellow to cream-yellow, with a slight orange cast to the midline, their ends 1 inch broad, blunt, and entirely erose or with a very slight point at the apex. The stamens are cream-colored; the stigmas with 6 cream-colored or very pale greenish-white lobes. The flowers fade to pinkish or salmon as they wilt.

FRUITS: Spherical or practically so, and very small, usually only ½ to ⅞ of an inch long. They have a few very slender, brown bristles on them, and broad, flat or slightly depressed umbilici. They are bright red in color. The seeds are ⅛ of an inch or slightly larger (3–4 millimeters) in diameter, regular, and flat, with narrow, acute rims.

RANGE. A comparatively small, triangular area of Texas from just west of Fort Stockton on the northwest to near Ozona on the northeast, and narrowing to the vicinity of Longfellow, Sanderson, and Dryden on the south.

REMARKS. There has long been a lack of specific information about this cactus. It is so unusual in appearance that all students have given adequate descriptions of it, but none seem to have known where it actually grows. This was probably because Engelmann, in first describing it, said simply, "In crevices of limestone rocks, between the Pecos and El Paso, Texas." This was repeated by Coulter and by Britton and Rose, all of whom apparently saw only the type specimens.

Much time spent in the huge area covered by that statement has enabled me to pinpoint its range rather closely. It does not occur in far west Texas at all. It first appears as one leaves the mountains of west Texas traveling east. At the edge of its western range it will be found as compact little upright bushes standing on the flat tops of limestone ridges and buttes just west of

Fort Stockton on the north and near Longfellow, Texas, on the south. In these locations it is fairly common, but only on the tops of the hills. East of Fort Stockton it is found here and there on the hills or high ground, but less and less commonly all the way beyond the Pecos River to its easternmost collection just a few miles west of Ozona, Texas, this giving an east-west range at this latitude of about 100 miles. The range is much narrower south of this, running only from near Longfellow to about Dryden, a distance of only about 30 miles. It has never been seen on the Pecos River beyond a few miles from the site of the old Fort Lancaster, which must have been the type locality where Wright first found it in 1851.

Over all of its range *O. strigil* is always found associated with *O. phaeacantha* var. *nigricans*, the two forms contrasting beautifully in almost all characters as they stand together on the tops of the hills.

O. strigil is one of the most unusual of the Opuntias. Its close-set areoles with their numerous, very slender bristles give it an appearance of gracefulness and an entirely misleading aspect of delicacy which make it among the most attractive in any collection of Opuntias. Its fruits are among the smallest of any Opuntia in the Southwest. Its small, compact bushes are only at home on the very thin soil overlying limestone outcrops. It seems never to form thickets, probably because no arm of the bush ever touches the ground so there can be no rooting of still attached parts of the plant. It doesn't spread from the original base.

The relationship of *O. strigil* to other Opuntias is not clear. It has small seeds similar to those of the *O. engelmannii* complex, but is unlike those forms in almost all other characters. On the other hand, *O. phaeacantha* var. *nigricans*, which grows with it over all of its range, has seeds hardly larger, and some specimens of variety *nigricans* approach rather closely to *O. strigil* in the character of their smaller spines and glochids. However, this cactus has very different flowers and fruits. Near Dryden, Texas, the extreme southeastern edge of *O. strigil*'s range is close to the extreme southwestern tip of *O. atrispina*'s range. In this area are found some specimens which are almost intermediate between these two closely related forms. The relationship between the two is worthy of more study.

Opuntia atrispina Gr.

DESCRIPTION   PLATE 50

STEMS: An ascending, spreading plant 2 to 3 feet tall, with joints round to broadly egg-shaped, 4 to 7 inches long by 3½ to 6 inches wide, with pads thin to medium thickness, and with the areoles usually somewhat raised. The surface is rather shiny and bright or yellow-green, occasionally with some reddish color around the areoles on specimens growing in severe exposure.

AREOLES: Slightly elongated oval and ¹/₈ to ³/₁₆ of an inch long when young, to egg-shaped or almost round and ¹/₄ of an inch or more in diameter when older. Situated ¹/₄ to 1¹/₄ inches apart on the pad. The areoles on this plant have the peculiar habit of proliferating when old until each areole contains 2 to as many as 6 or 8 circular growing centers, the glochids arranged in these bunches and the areoles then becoming very big and bulging. After this sort of growth the edge areoles become to ¹/₂ inch in diameter and almost touch each other.

SPINES: 3 to 6 in number on the upper ¹/₂ to ²/₃ of the pad, the main spines with black or very dark red-brown bases shading into a zone of brown followed by yellow toward the tips. The smaller spines are similar except lighter in color. There are usually 1 or 2 main spines ¹/₂ to 1¹/₄ inches long, heavy and rigid, round, porrect or deflexed, and bent downward, but in some specimens these main spines may be missing entirely. There is below them another central ³/₈ to 1¹/₈ inches long, identical to them except strongly recurved downward. There will then be 1 to 3 lower, deflexed and spreading, thin and bristle-like spines ³/₈ to ⁵/₈ of an inch long. All of these spines seem to fade to a dull gray-brown or blackish within a year or so and often the old spines seem to become brittle so that many of them are broken or missing entirely on old pads.

GLOCHIDS: Yellowish or brownish or mottled at first, becoming dull blackish-brown when old. There are average to many on young pads, ¹/₈ to ¹/₂ inch long, in irregular, untidy clusters, becoming very many and filling the areoles on old edge areoles.

FLOWERS: Deep chrome-yellow with a somewhat greenish center when first open. Soon fading to flesh-color or apricot. They usually stand only 2 to 2¹/₂ inches in diameter, but are sometimes smaller, down to 1 inch in diameter. The ovary tube is small, ³/₄ to 1 inch long, slightly tuberculate, with some glochids on it. The stamens are cream-colored; the style white. The stigma has 7 or 8 yellow or slightly greenish-yellow lobes.

FRUITS: Bright red or yellowish-red in color, with pulp rather dry and greenish. In shape they are almost round to broadly pear-shaped, with little or no constriction below and with the umbilici from almost flat to sometimes quite deeply pitted. Extremely variable in size, ripe fruits having been measured which were from ³/₈ to 1⁵/₈ inches long. The seeds are ¹/₈ of an inch or a little more (3–4 millimeters) in diameter, comparatively thick, with narrow rims.

RANGE. A narrow strip of southwest Texas about 20 miles wide from the Anacacho Mountains in the southwest corner of Uvalde County west past Del Rio, the mountains of the Devil's and Pecos rivers, to near Dryden, Texas. We have collected it again in some hills just east of Sabinas, Coahuila, Mexico, which indicates that the range extends on into Mexico for an unknown distance.

REMARKS. This is another of Griffiths' Texas discoveries, first found near the Devil's River, where we find it today only near the mouth of that river. This is the center of that narrow strip along our border in which it grows.

I believe the knowledge of this cactus has been clouded for most by an unfortunate lack in the original description and a subsequent misunderstanding. Dr. Griffiths described the spines of his plant very completely as to color and size, but unaccountably failed to make any statement at all about their shape. Britton and Rose apparently put great reliance on the color of spines, stated by Griffiths to be for this species, "Jet black to reddish brown at base with yellow tips." One would think that this would be striking enough to distinguish any plant, so when Dr. Rose, looking over the type locality, found a plant with jet black spine bases, he thought he had *O. atrispina*. This plant had heavy, very flat spines, and Britton and Rose, therefore, incorporated into their description the statement, "Principle ones [spines] . . . flattened." Once added in this way to the description, the supposed trait of flat spines has remained in all subsequent write-ups, even being featured in Backeberg's description of the plant and his key.

It is easy to see how this idea of *O. atrispina* having flat spines got started and persists. There is a cactus at the Devil's River with very heavy and very conspicuously flattened, often even triangular black-based spines, their upper parts whitish. It is the cactus one would probably notice first when one visits the type locality. I thought it was *O. atrispina* and grew it in my own collection for some time for that species. This plant grows quite commonly from Del Rio west to at least the Davis Mountains and thence northwest into New Mexico. I even tried at one time to persuade some New Mexico cactophiles that they had *O. atrispina* in their state, fortunately with little success. However, I would have been right if this were Griffiths' cactus.

At this time I already had a cactus for which I could not find a name, which I kept finding on the higher elevations along about a hundred miles of the Rio Grande. It had spines blackish below with yellow tips, but these spines were always round. When it bloomed and fruited, it fitted Griffiths' description exactly. Only when I began to suspect that this was the true *O. atrispina* and that Britton and Rose had seen the wrong plant, did I check everything on their plant with flat spines against Griffiths' description, and when I did I found that its areoles were too far apart to fit *O. atrispina*, it had larger orange-yellow flowers with bright red centers and much too large fruits. It couldn't be the plant Griffiths described. I then understood why their figure illustrating *O. atrispina* looks so little like it as to be no better than misleading.

The true *O. atrispina* has been virtually unknown all these years while the other plant has been taken for it. This other cactus, also unknown by its right name all this time due to the confusion, is actually *O. phaeacantha* var. *nigricans* Eng. *O. atrispina*, as rightly known, has no trait of flower, fruit, or pad relating it to the *O. phaeacantha* group. It is actually closest to *O. strigil*, whose range adjoins that of this cactus on the west. As I have mentioned in discussing that species, there are some specimens which appear almost intermediate between these two around Dryden, Texas. It also has some characters in common with *O. tardospina*, whose range almost but not quite meets its own on the northeast.

A remarkable peculiarity of this cactus, noted by Griffiths, is the way its fruits differ so widely in size. Healthy, well-watered plants produce fruits 1 to 1⅝ inches long, yet one often sees in the field specimens having fruits ¾ of an inch or so in length. Quite by accident I learned that this variation is due to the environment. A pot containing one of these plants once got moved back in my garden by mistake, just after flowering, to where it got almost no water for the rest of the summer. I first noticed it when its fruits ripened to a beautiful red when only ½ inch in length. Experimentation since then has shown that by witholding water at flowering and fruiting time I get on this plant as many flowers as usual, but these reduced to as little as 1 inch in diameter, and I have had these small flowers produce tiny fruits only ⅜ of an inch long yet ripening normally and containing 1 or 2 normal seeds. This is very different from most Opuntias, which in my experience either fail to bloom at all under such conditions or have regular-sized flowers which either manage to produce normal-sized fruits or abort them entirely.

Opuntia leptocarpa Mackensen

DESCRIPTION   PLATE 51

ROOTS: Usually tuberous, but in some whole populations they are fibrous.

STEMS: Large, robust pads which stand upright at first, but are too weak to support each other, so that when a branch attains the length of 2 or 3 pads it falls over and lies on the ground, thus keeping the plant a low, sprawling one at most 1 to 1½ feet high. The pads are broadly oval or egg-shaped to sometimes almost spindle-shaped, with a gradual but not pronounced constriction at the base. They are 4 to at least 10 inches long and to 7 inches wide, but thin for the size, which probably accounts for their being so often bent over by the weight of new pads sprouting from them. They are bright, deep green with a shiny surface when healthy, but somewhat glaucous and yellow-green when suffering from drought or sunburn.

AREOLES: Small and oval or round on the sides of the pads, enlarging somewhat, but not conspicuously on the edges. They are located ¾ to 2 inches apart.

SPINES: 1 to 5 per areole, found on upper and edge areoles only. Occasional plants are almost spineless. The main spines are yellow or straw mottled with brown, the lower and smaller spines gray. All spines are slender to medium thickness, round or only slightly flattened. A fully armed edge areole will present 1 main central ½ to 1¼ inches long, porrect or slightly deflexed; 1 to 2 upper spines standing at any angle, ½ to 1 inch long; and 1 or 2 slender, deflexed lower spines ¼ to 1 inch long.

GLOCHIDS: Brown to red-brown in color, few and short, 1/16 to ⅛ of an inch long on the sides of the pads, to medium in number and sometimes to ¼ of an inch long on the edges of the pads. They are never conspicuous.

FLOWERS: 2½ to 3 inches across, yellow or orange with maroon to bright red centers. The ovary is 1½ to 2 inches long, narrowly club-shaped, and tuberculate, with short red glochids on it. The petals have a more pronounced point at the apex than on most Opuntias. The anthers are cream in color. The stigmas consist of 6 to 8 white or greenish-white lobes.

FRUITS: Very large, being 2 to 3½ inches long and 1 to 1⅝ inches thick. They are club-shaped with a pronounced or even exaggerated constriction of the base and narrow and deeply pitted umbilici. They become old red when fully ripe, but the flesh often remains greenish and sour until late fall, when it finally becomes red and sweet. The seeds are less than ⅛ to not quite 3/16 of an inch (2½–4 millimeters) in diameter. They are regular in shape, flat but rather thick bodied, with narrow, acute rims.

RANGE. An area of south Texas bounded, so far as is presently known by the following points: Langtry, Texas, and the vicinity of the mouth of the Devil's River on the west, near Austin on the north, Flatonia on the east, Mustang Island in front of Corpus Christi Bay to near Brownsville on the southeast, and Laredo on the southwest.

REMARKS. Mackensen, in originally describing *O. leptocarpa*, stated that it was intermediate between *O. macrorhiza* and *O. lindheimeri* [*O. engelmannii*]. His remark was one of those purely subjective pronouncements which contribute nothing but confusion, and much confusion has entered here.

Having the combination of such large pads and fruits with such small seeds and growing, as it does around San Antonio, in the same fields with *O. engelmannii*, the careless observer, encouraged in this direction by Mackensen's statement, sees it as just a low, prostrate form of that upright, bushy giant. On the other hand, to some such observers casually alerted by Mackensen's statement, its flowers and fruits may seem essentially only oversized versions of those of *O. macrorhiza*, while its often tuberous roots will surely strengthen this idea. I find people about equally divided as to which of these other species to call it. This is unfortunate. Closer observation will show that its flowers, fruits, and roots are essentially different from those of *O. engelmannii*, while its pad character and size, glochids, spines, and seeds put it clearly outside the limits of *O. macrorhiza*. Natural hybrid or what have you though it may turn out to be, although it is somewhere between the two, yet it is neither of them, and in the preoccupation with relating it to those two, the fact has not been mentioned that its closest similarity is actually to the *O. phaeacantha* group. But it seems clear that with our present knowledge such speculation gets us nowhere.

This plant probably figured in Engelmann's confusion which resulted in his contradictory description of his now long-defunct *O. lindheimeri* as "erect, robust or low and prostrate," and accounts for his attempt to set that off from *E. engelmannii* at all. He said in *Plantae Lindheimerianae,* "the fruit which Lindheimer has sent as belonging to this species *[O. lindheimeri]* resembles very much that of *O. vulgaris,* 2–2½ inch long, slender, with a deep umbilicus, very different from that of the following species *[O. engelmannii]*." It should be noted that the plants sent him by Lindheimer were from New Braunfels, Texas, within the range of *O. leptocarpa.* Later, after gaining more knowledge of the New Braunfels plants, Engelmann said, "*O. lindheimeri* Eng. Pl. Lindh. is partly this same plant *[O. engelmannii],* partly a hybrid form between it and perhaps *O. rafinesquii [O. compressa],* with narrow clavate fruit." While the low, prostrate form referred to above, that first caused Engelmann to set up a species *O. lindheimeri,* could conceivably have been *O. phaeacantha* var. *camanchica,* which is found about New Braunfels also, that plant does not have the long, narrow, clavate fruits he mentioned. These are found on *O. leptocarpa,* and we still find in the area in question the large, upright *O. engelmannii* with large but broad and flat-topped fruits and the low, sprawling *O. leptocarpa* with large but narrow and deeply pitted fruits. Both have similar large pads and small seeds, but they have different flowers and roots, and so, as Engelmann discovered and admitted long ago and as any careful observer will verify, they cannot be combined into the one nonexistent species *O. lindheimeri.*

Speculation about this plant's relationship to *O. phaeacantha* var. *major* might prove to be more fruitful. A careful checking of the characters of the two show few really clear differences between them. About all that can be demonstrated to distinguish them is *O. leptocarpa's* lower maximum height and much more sprawling, almost prostrate aspect, its fruits being larger and its seeds smaller. While *O. leptocarpa* has tuberous roots in most specimens seen and *O. phaeacantha* usually fibrous, we know from other species that this seldom if ever can be a diagnostic character. There have been found *O. phaeacantha* specimens in New Mexico with tuberous roots. At this writing I am leaving the two separate, but further study is needed to see if they are really more closely related.

In few places in its whole range does *O. leptocarpa* exist in large stands. It is most widespread and common in Comal County, Texas, which is the type locality, and in Bexar County. Outside of these counties we find scattered small populations with many miles between them, the main ones being just west of Falls City, Texas; near Devine and Flatonia; in the sand

dunes at Port Aransas on Mustang Island; in the sandy river bottoms at Laredo, Texas; and in the flats from Del Rio to Langtry.

Opuntia phaeacantha Eng.
"New Mexico Prickly Pear," "Brown-Spined Prickly Pear," "Tulip Prickly Pear"

DESCRIPTION   PLATES 51, 52, 53

ROOTS: Almost always fibrous, but some specimens have been found with tuberous roots.

STEMS: Growing either as a large, robust, ascending cactus 2 to 3 feet or more high, trunkless, and forming dense thickets sometimes up to 6 or 8 feet across, or else as a low, prostrate plant with most of its pads resting their edges on the ground and so only 1 to 1½ feet in height. The pads are flat, almost spherical to broadly egg-shaped or sometimes even club-shaped from 4 to 9 inches long and 3 to 7 inches wide. The surface is glaucous and bluish-green or deep green when young, usually becoming bright shiny green or yellow-green when older, and sometimes taking on a purplish cast around the areoles and pad edges during the winter.

AREOLES: Small to medium and oval to round when young, becoming round and enlarged to ¼ of an inch or so when older. They vary from ¾ to 2 inches apart.

SPINES: 1 to 8 spines per areole on only the very upper areoles of the pad or sometimes on the upper ¾ or more of each pad. In length the spines vary from ¾ to 3 inches long. They spread in almost all directions from the areole, with the upper spines large and heavy, the uppermost of these usually round and at least the main porrect or deflexed central flattened. There are usually some small, weak spines below these main ones. All spines are yellow, gray, or mottled toward the tips, with the bases brown, red-brown, or black.

GLOCHIDS: Few to average in number and short on young pads, becoming usually quite numerous to very many on the edges of old pads and ½ to ⅜ of an inch long. In color they are pale brown to red-brown.

FLOWERS: 2 to 3 inches in diameter, bright yellow or orange with red to maroon centers. The ovary varies from only ¾ of an inch long in some forms to as much as 1¾ inches in others, always with some short red-brown glochids on it. The stamens are yellowish or cream in color. The style is long and pinkish or whitish. The stigmas have 6 to 10 short, fat, whitish, yellowish, or very pale greenish lobes.

FRUITS: Variable within this large complex: from oval or goblet-shaped with little or no constriction at the bases and the umbilici somewhat pitted to flat, to pear-shaped or even club-shaped with pronounced constriction of both the bases and umbilici. In size they range from 1 to 2¹/₂ inches long; in color, from yellowish-red to bright scarlet or cherry-red to deep purplish-red. The seeds measure from ¹/₈ to ¹/₄ of an inch (3–6 millimeters) in diameter.

RANGE. A very large area covering many states. In our area it grows over approximately the western halves of Oklahoma and Texas and all of New Mexico.

REMARKS. This is the second major complex of U.S. Opuntias. It includes a number of forms so different as to require separate treatment. Their existence renders any general description like the above almost useless, and yet they intergrade so often that they have caused much confusion. Most of them have been described at one time or another as separate species, yet they hardly seem that distinct, and there have been many schemes for grouping them. At the present time there is no agreement as to how they should be treated, the writings of the authorities ranging all the way from those who would give most of them species rank to those who speak of O. phaeacantha in general terms such as the above and would forget almost all of the segregates. The method followed here is to give the above general description, beyond which anyone satisfied with merely knowing O. phaeacantha in this general way need not go, but then to describe below the segregates which we find definite and distinguishable with known ranges, listing them as varieties. In this way we hope to satisfy the serious student and also to keep the knowledge of these forms alive until more about their real relationships can be learned.

O. phaeacantha, all of these forms included, may equal or even exceed O. engelmannii in the amount of territory it covers in the United States. While it does not venture as far into the southeast as does that other species, it does range practically to the Pacific, and extends its territory far north through Nebraska, Colorado, and Montana. It is an extremely hardy, often very conspicuous cactus over most of the western United States.

Opuntia phaeacantha var. major Eng.

DESCRIPTION   PLATE 51
STEMS: Ascending and spreading. Growing without a central trunk to at least 3 feet tall. The pads are round or nearly so, only rarely being very broadly pear-shaped, and 4 to 8 inches long. Their surfaces are flat, deep green to yellow-green in color, often with some purplish around the areoles, and with only very slight glaucescence, usually becoming shiny when older.

AREOLES: As the species, except smaller and more elongated oval when young than some phaeacantha forms, and spaced 1 to 2 inches apart.

SPINES: Fewer, shorter, and lighter in color than most forms of the species possess. There are typically 1 to 3 spines on only

the upper edge areoles, with only a few individuals showing to 4 spines on the areoles of about the upper half of the pad. The 1 or 2 main spines are porrect or spreading, ³/₄ to 1⁷/₈ inches long, averaging about 1¹/₄ inches, flat or round, with usually the uppermost one round and the lower one flattened. These are gray, whitish, or straw with brown or red-brown bases. There may or may not be 1 or 2 lower, deflexed, bristle-like spines, ¹/₄ to ³/₄ of an inch long and grayish in color.

GLOCHIDS: Very few and short, or even none on the sides of the pads. The edges of old pads develop an average number of them to ¹/₄ of an inch or longer and yellow or brownish in color.

FLOWERS: As the species, except that the ovary is usually 1¹/₄ to 1³/₄ inches long.

FRUITS: 1¹/₂ to 2¹/₂ inches long, club-shaped, with noticeable constriction of the bases, and constricted, pitted umbilici. In color, they are light red to purplish-red. The pulp is juicy, but sour to the taste. The seeds are about ³/₁₆ of an inch (4–5 millimeters) in diameter.

RANGE. From at least as far north as the vicinity of Santa Fe, New Mexico, south and east over the southeastern corner of New Mexico into far west Texas from El Paso to at least Fort Stockton.

REMARKS. Engelmann felt it necessary after describing O. phaeacantha in very general terms to break the species up into varieties, and one of these was his variety major. He described this variety rather poorly, merely stating that it had suborbiculate pads to 8 inches long and spines fewer, shorter, and paler than typical for the species. Coulter, working from the same specimens as Engelmann, while abandoning all of Engelmann's other varieties of the species, felt this one alone was so distinct as to require listing. Wooton apparently means this variety only and is eliminating all of the lower, very spiny, and very common New Mexico forms of the species when he writes of O. phaeacantha, since he says it grows to 1 meter tall and "is the common sub-erect species of the north and central part of the state of New Mexico, but nowhere very abundant." Britton and Rose, on the other hand, were the first to eliminate all of these varieties and spoke of O. phaeacantha only in the most general way.

Early in this study, after we had seen many small, very spiny plants of this species with fat, hardly constricted fruits, we began looking for the reason why Engelmann and Coulter in their descriptions of the species both called the fruits "slender," "Pyriform," with "base much constricted," and so on, as well as why Wooton described it as so large and so uncommon. We sensed something more than meets the eye in the usual present-day accounts of the species here, and began looking for some special form.

In this search we finally found the form described above growing in a garden collection in New Mexico. It was a large, spreading plant 3 feet high and had grown in the few years it had been in the garden to an impenetrable thicket over 6 feet across. The gardener could not remember where he had collected it, beyond the fact that it was in the mountains near Santa Fe, which is exactly the type locality given by Engelmann for his variety *major*. It was the first *O. phaeacantha* we had seen with actually club-shaped fruits, deeply pitted at the apex. The fruits were up to 2¹/₂ inches long. In studying this plant, we soon realized that we must have the form which was the basis for Engelmann's variety *major*.

Wooton was certainly correct in stating that this form is not abundant anywhere, as much searching has never enabled us to find it growing wild anywhere in northern or central New Mexico. The nearest to that area where we have ourselves found it growing is west of Roswell, New Mexico, where we have found numerous individuals growing on the eastern foothills of the Capitan Mountains. We have also found isolated individuals of this form growing near Lovington and southeast of Carlsbad, both in the southeastern corner of the state. Griffiths' herbarium specimens in the United States National Museum appear to increase the southeastern range of the variety still more, as he has what appear to be this same plant from near Fort Stockton, Texas, and from El Paso. We have not been able to collect it in Texas ourselves, however.

The true extent of the range of this variety is very hard to discover, since, because of the general tendency to submerge any brown-spined Opuntia under the catch-all name *O. phaeacantha* and dismiss it, there are too many incomplete descriptions in the literature, and herbarium collections are hopelessly mixed. There are specimens from Arizona which may be this variety, but one can hardly be sure from a single pad, and we hesitate on this, since we have not found it anywhere in western New Mexico. In Texas the relationship between this variety and *O. leptocarpa*, which has almost identical flowers and fruits, but which does not grow so robustly and which usually has tuberous roots as well as smaller seeds, should be considered. While we have not seen variety *major* in far northern New Mexico, we do find a form of *O. phaeacantha* rather intermediate between this and *O. phaeacantha* var. *camanchica* in Colorado, growing at higher elevations and farther north than variety *camanchica* does in that state. It has spines, fruits, and seeds much like variety *major*, but is much smaller and more low-growing than this variety appears farther south. We do not know whether this difference is due to the environment and variety *major* should actually be considered to range into Colorado or whether this is another segregate, but we assume this is the cactus from Colorado described by Coulter as *O. mesacantha* var. *oplocarpa*, which might, therefore, be a synonym of variety *major* or might be a very closely related Colorado form. It is our opinion that *O. expansa* Gr. is a synonym of variety *major*.

This is a rather rare variety of *O. phaeacantha*, but an important one to the understanding of the species. The ignoring of it in most recent accounts of the species has made much of the early literature on this species hardly understandable. We do not pretend to know the details of its relationship to the other forms of this complex, but the knowledge of it must be kept alive until all this is worked out. The tendency to overlook it entirely or to casually dismiss it as a hybrid between *O. phaeacantha* and *O. engelmannii* without presenting any evidence that this hybridization actually occurs will surely not satisfy any thorough student.

Opuntia phaeacantha var. **nigricans** Eng.

DESCRIPTION PLATE 51

STEMS: A large bush 2 to 3 feet high when mature. The branches are upright but without any central stem and so it spreads outward to form small thickets. The pads are normally 4 to 8 inches but sometimes to 10 inches long, round to broadly egg-shaped, with little or no constriction below. These pads are thin to medium thickness. In color they are at first a very glaucous blue-green, but when older become yellow-green. The two colors often contrast sharply between the upper and lower pads of the same plant.

AREOLES: ³/₄ to 1⁷/₈ inches apart. They are oval to round and small to medium sized on the sides of the pads, increasing to ³/₈ of an inch and becoming round on the edges of the pads.

SPINES: There are 1 to 6 spines per areole on the upper ¹/₂ to almost all areoles of the pad. There is 1 main central spine which is only rarely missing, ¹/₂ to 2 inches long, porrect to deflexed in position, medium thickness to very heavy, very flattened or even triangular in shape. This spine is mostly black or blackish-brown, with usually a zone of gray or purplish-gray above and then a dark tip. There will usually be 2 lateral spines very similar to this one, spreading and often curving outward. There will usually be 1 upper spine (which, however, may be missing) the same length as the others, erect or porrect in position, and similar to them except apparently always round. Below these main spines will be 0 to 4 lower, deflexed, slender, often bristle-like spines ¹/₄ to ³/₄ of an inch long, usually gray with bases and tips somewhat blackish.

GLOCHIDS: Red-brown, brown, straw, or mottled in color. They are very variable in number, from almost none to very many on the sides of the pads, but almost always becoming many to very many and ¹/₄ to ³/₄ of an inch long on the edges of the pads.

FLOWERS: As the species, except that the ovary is only ³/₄ to 1 inch long.

FRUITS: Oval to goblet-shaped, with some slight constriction at the base and a rather deeply pitted apex. In size they are ³/₄ to 1¹/₂ inches long. They become deep purplish-red. The seeds are ¹/₈ to almost ³/₁₆ of an inch (3–4 millimeters) in diameter, flat, but usually very irregular in shape.

RANGE. Apparently comprising a narrow but very long strip of territory entering Texas from the south, where we have collected the plant in Coahuila, Mexico, and proceeding far north into New Mexico. The eastern and western boundaries of this strip are approximately as follows: entering Texas between Del Rio on the east and the Chisos Mountains on the west, proceeding northward past Fort Stockton on the east and Alpine on the west, then to the eastern foothills and the western slopes of the Guadalupe and Capitan mountains in southern New Mexico, and finally to the sides of the abrupt escarpment just east of Mosquero, New Mexico, in Harding County, which is its most northeasterly known range, and to the hills between Albuquerque and Cuba, New Mexico, which is its most northwesterly known penetration.

REMARKS: This cactus often forms dense thickets on the sides and tops of rocky ridges or steep slopes. It is a beautiful plant in the spring of the year when its pads are new and a wonderful bluish-green color, their smooth, glaucous surfaces contrasting with the heavy, blackish spines. But later in the summer, when the extreme heat and dryness have had their effect, one would hardly recognize it as the same plant, for its pads have become by then a yellowish-green from which they will not change for the rest of their lives.

Because it grows in the type locality of that plant and because both have blackish coloring in the spines, this form has been widely mistaken for *O. atrispina* Gr., particularly since Britton and Rose seem to describe this plant under that name. However, any careful reading of Griffiths' description of *O. atrispina* will show that this cannot be the cactus he had in mind, and even a casual comparison will separate the two.

When we come to establish what this cactus really is, we find only one account in the literature which will fit it, and that is Engelmann's description of *O. phaeacantha* var. *nigricans*. Admittedly his description of this form is so incomplete that we can only guess at what he had before him, yet we cannot ignore the statements of a botanists of his stature, so when we find a cactus fitting his description perfectly as far as it goes and still existing in the area of his type, we must presume that we have in this cactus the plant he meant. When we notice that the flowers, which he did not describe, are on our plant the large, orange-yellow blooms with red centers of the *O. phaeacantha* complex, and that the fruits fall within the limits of that species, then I feel that we can be certain we have before us the *O. phaeacantha* var. *nigricans* of Engelmann, and that it is a wide-ranging variety of this very large and complex species.

It has been the fashion for many years to regard this variety as merely a synonym of the species broadly considered, yet any reasonable amount of observation will show how different this form is from the other varieties here listed. The flower has a remarkably short ovary (about $3/4$ of an inch long), which is distinctly different from the $1^1/4$- to $1^1/2$-inch ovary of some others in this complex. Its spines are as others in the group in having the main central flattened and the uppers round, and so

on, but only variety *nigricans* has such dark colored, such heavy and such greatly flattened lower centrals, and no other form of the species has the heavy, flat, spreading laterals of this variety. It is interesting to note that almost every recent work which has dropped *O. phaeacantha* var. *nigricans* has then described this plant separately under the name of *O. atrispina*.

After studying both her description and her preserved specimens, I believe that Miss Anthony's *O. engelmannii* X *phaeacantha* of her Big Bend study is this cactus. I have heard it called such a hybrid by others, and if one likes to speculate on hybrids, this would be a likely candidate. The bluish-green of its young pads, the possession of heavy, curving lateral spines, the grayness instead of yellowness of the upper parts of its spines, much about its fruits and seeds all remind one of *O. engelmannii*, but no form of *O. engelmannii* has red-centered, yellow flowers. Here again experimental work with these plants to establish something of their genetics is all that would clarify things further, and renaming various forms as hybrids before we even know whether the species involved can interbreed would not seem really to advance our understanding.

On the tops of many limestone ridges from just west of Fort Stockton, Texas, to around Sanderson, this plant grows together with *O. strigil,* the two such contrasting Opuntias making a strikingly beautiful sight together.

Opuntia phaeacantha var. brunnea Eng.

DESCRIPTION   PLATE 52

STEMS: To about 3 feet tall, consisting of upright branches without a central trunk. Pads 4 to 8 inches long, round or even wider than they are long, usually with no constriction below, but sometimes broadly egg-shaped with some lower constriction. Their color is slightly blue-green when very young, when older glaucous yellow-green, usually with some purplish-red mottling on the edges of the pads and these often suffused with this color in winter. The pads are rather thick.

AREOLES: Small to medium and elongated to almost round on the sides of the pads, enlarge to about $3/16$ of an inch or so and become almost round on the edges of old pads. They are spaced $3/4$ to $1^5/8$ inches apart.

SPINES: 1 to 5 per areole on only the upper edge or to at most the upper third of the pad. The main central spine is 1 to 3 inches long, porrect or deflexed, straight or often twisted and bent, medium to heavy, and round to slightly flattened. There will usually, but not always be 1 to 3 upper spines, 1 to $2^1/2$ inches long, erect or spreading upward, medium to very heavy, round to very flat and twisted. These main spines are all blackish, chocolate-brown or red-brown at the bases, their upper parts tan or grayish. There may be 1 or 2 lower, deflexed, slender, and often bristle-like spines, $3/16$ to 1 inch long. These are either round or flattened, and gray in color.

GLOCHIDS: Brown to straw in color, almost none to an average number but very short on the sides of the pads. On the edges there are few at first, later often increasing to very many and growing to $^3/_4$ of an inch long.

FLOWERS: As the species.

FRUITS: $1^1/_4$ to $2^1/_2$ inches long, oval to club-shaped with some constriction below and a shallowly concave umbilicus above. They are dull red in color. The seeds measure $^3/_{16}$ of an inch or a little more ($4^1/_2$–$5^1/_2$ millimeters) in diameter.

RANGE. Southwest Texas from the Anacacho Mountains east of Del Rio along the Rio Grande through the Big Bend at least to El Paso, Texas. Also northward from the Big Bend through the Davis Mountains to the southern parts of the Guadalupe and Organ mountains, where it enters New Mexico a short distance.

REMARKS. Engelmann had an *O. phaeacantha* var. *brunnea* from El Paso, which was never redescribed after his time and which was apparently never taken seriously by anyone except Griffiths. In Griffiths' preserved collection I find very good specimens of this form collected at El Paso and at Fort Hancock and labeled by him with this name, but relabeled otherwise since then by others. I find the variety quite abundant in the Anacacho Mountains, growing here and there around Langtry, Texas, and on into the eastern Big Bend. It becomes quite numerous again west of Terlingua, Texas, and continues all along the Rio Grande to El Paso. There are some fairly good stands of it in the Davis Mountains and scattered individuals along the Texas-New Mexico line at the Guadalupe, Hueco, and Franklin mountains, where it enters New Mexico for a short distance.

Engelmann described the form very incompletely, but did mention most of the important features which distinguish it from the other varieties of the species. The greater glaucescence, thicker joints, and purplish-red winter coloring he mentions are all important points in recognizing it. He remarks that the spines are longer than typical for the species, and with the spines usually to 3 inches long this is important. He calls the spines greatly angled, which is true of most of the main ones, but in this cactus one notices that it is the upper centrals which are the most greatly flattened instead of the lower central—a reversal of the usual order in the species. Beyond this he does not go, but the flowers and fruits are typical for the species, and the seeds larger than those of most of the other varieties.

The coloring this plant assumes in severe weather, when linked with the 3-inch spines, misleads many observers into thinking it is *O. macrocentra*. When I first realized the existence of this form, I checked back through those of my own specimens which I had called *O. macrocentra* and found that I had included several of this cactus under that name. I am convinced that herbarium collections filed under *O. macrocentra* often contain specimens of this cactus, and that some descriptions of that plant have been overly broadened and made almost useless because of this confusion.

To distinguish these two cacti from only vegetative parts is not always easy, but one clue is that the coloring of *O. phaeacantha* var. *brunnea* is not ever actually purple, as is that of the other, but really a dull, dark, purplish-red. In gardens of west Texas collectors I have several times had my attention called to the fact that one of a collector's *O. macrocentra* specimens will be a beautiful purple while the other one beside it will be a very different purplish-red. This is because they have collected for that plant a specimen of this variety which is all but unknown today after reposing in the synonym of *O. phaeacantha* for 100 years.

There are other differences besides differences of hue, but they take close observation. The pads of variety *brunnea* are thick, while those of the other are thin. While the areoles of this variety are $^3/_4$ of an inch or more apart, with an average over 1 inch apart, those of the other species are always less than 1 inch apart. The spines of this variety are long, but never as long as the maximum on *O. macrocentra*. Although they easily equal in length those on some less robust specimens of that other species, they are more brown than black, and are rigid rather than flexible like those others. The flowers of the two are very similar, but the fruits are different. *O. macrocentra*'s fruits are to only $1^1/_2$ inches long, with no constriction below, deeply pitted above, and bright red to orange-red. Those of variety *brunnea* are to $2^1/_2$ inches long, with some constriction below, shallow umbilicus, and dull, dark red color.

It is my opinion that when Britton and Rose gave for *O. macrocentra* fruit to $2^3/_8$ inches long and purple, they did it because they had included in their specimens some which were actually of this variety. This idea seems to be borne out by the figure they featured to illustrate *O. macrocentra*. I could never visualize *O. macrocentra* from their figure, while it is a passable representation of an *O. phaeacantha* var. *brunnea* pad. More recently both Backeberg and Earle have followed in giving such overly broadened descriptions of *O. macrocentra*.

Anthony's *O. tenuispina* from the Big Bend also appears to be this cactus. There are reasons to think that Rose's *O. chihuahuensis* may also have been this variety, but it is so incompletely described that one cannot be sure what it was. Wooton and Standley considered the plants of the *O. phaeacantha* complex found in the Organ Mountains just within New Mexico to be *O. chihuahuensis,* saying that they exactly match the type specimens of Rose's plant. They also say that a specimen from that location classified by Coulter himself as his *O. mesacantha* var. *oplocarpa* is the same. Specimens that I have collected in this area exactly match the description given above for variety *brunnea,* and the evidence seems good that both of the above are this variety. These plants are certainly different from the Colorado plants called variety *oplocarpa* by Coulter. If that is a valid variety at all it apparently does not enter New Mexico from Colorado.

The question of how far variety *brunnea* ranges into New Mexico is a hard one. Assuming that the above-mentioned plants are synonyms, Wooton mentions them from only the Organ

Mountains, but Britton and Rose talk as though they were more widespread over southern New Mexico, extending north out of Chihuahua. I have seen this variety in New Mexico only in the Guadalupe and Organ mountains, and this not over 40 miles or so from the border. I have never seen this plant west of El Paso, but recently I was sent a specimen from the Santa Rita Mountains of Arizona which appears to be it. Whether further study will enlarge its range westward remains to be seen.

Opuntia phaeacantha var. camanchica (Eng.)

DESCRIPTION   PLATE 53

ROOTS: Although in most cases the roots are fibrous, occasional specimens have tubers upon their roots.

STEMS: Growing as a low, semiprostrate, spreading cactus. It produces large pads, but these usually lie on their edges by the second season to form chains of reclining pads. By the rooting of these pads there are formed clumps sometimes 3 to 5 feet across. The pads are often 8 or 9 inches in length, so a leaning branch may rise to a foot or even a little higher, but this is about the maximum height. The pads vary from perfectly round through egg-shaped, to occasionally broad club-shaped with constricted bases. They vary from 3 to 9 inches long, with slightly less width. The average size would be about 6 inches long by 5 inches wide. The surfaces are flat and the thickness medium, which is slightly less than $1/2$ inch thick. They are rather deep green in color with some glaucescence, sometimes taking on a reddish cast around the areoles and on the edges during the winter.

AREOLES: These are oval or oblong to round. They are about $3/16$ of an inch across on the sides of the pads, enlarging to about $1/4$ of an inch on the edges. They are from $3/4$ to $1 1/2$ inches apart.

SPINES: There will be from 1 to 8 spines on the upper $3/4$ or more of the areoles, only the lowest areoles not bearing spines. The lowermost spine-bearing areoles usually have one spine, with the number increasing upward until the very upper and edge areoles have 3 to 8 spines. A fully armed areole will contain 1 to 5 straight upper spines $3/4$ to 3 inches long. These spread in all directions upward and outward, are of medium thickness, entirely round on some specimens, flattened on others, their bases and usually the lower half brown, red-brown or blackish-brown, followed by a zone of tan, gray, purplish-gray, or whitish, and ending in yellowish, semitranslucent tips. It will also contain 1 to 5 lower spines turning or spreading downward from the lower part of the areole. The largest one of these may be up to $1 1/4$ inches long, flattened, and rather heavy, but the rest of them will range smaller in size and thickness until they are hardly more than deflexed

bristles. All of these lower spines are whitish or gray with brown tips.

Plants not vigorous for some reason, such as those growing in shade, may put out pads as big as those on normal, robust plants, but will be deficient in spines. It is common then for only the upper third of the areoles to bear spines at all, and for these to have only 1 to 3 spines. In this case there will be 2 lower, deflexed spines $3/8$ to $3/4$ of an inch long, gray with lighter tips on most of the armed areoles, and only an occasional areole on the very edge may have 1 of the heavier, brown upper spines to about $1 1/4$ inches long.

GLOCHIDS: Somewhat variable. Some specimens will have almost none, some an average number, and sometimes on old pads of the same plant they may become very conspicuous. From $1/8$ of an inch or nearly that short on the sides of the pads to at least $3/8$ of an inch long on the edges of old pads. They are straw, tan, or brownish in color.

FLOWERS: As the species, except longer, with the ovary $1 1/4$ to $1 3/4$ inches long.

FRUITS: Bright cherry-red to dull plum-red when ripe, with juicy, pleasant-tasting flesh. Oval in shape, not constricted at the base, 1 to $2 1/2$ inches long by $3/4$ to $1 1/2$ inches wide. The umbilicus is a rather narrow surface which is flat or only very shallowly concave. The seeds are $3/16$ to $1/4$ of an inch ($4 1/2$–6 millimeters) in largest measurement. They are very irregular in shape, perfectly flat and thin, or much twisted and thicker, round to square or even sometimes almost triangular. They have conspicuous rims 1 to $1 1/2$ millimeters wide, but sharp. These rims are usually wavy and irregular.

RANGE. Out of Kansas and Colorado to the north over western Oklahoma, Texas, and all of eastern New Mexico. More specifically, it occurs in Oklahoma west of a line running approximately from Blackwell to Ardmore, and in Texas west of a line from near Fort Worth south to the Balcones Fault in the vicinity of San Antonio. It is not known to grow south of San Antonio, and occurs rather commonly east of the central mountains in New Mexico, but is seldom if ever seen west of central New Mexico.

REMARKS. This is the smallest, most prostrate, most spiny version of the species. It occurs primarily east of the more upright, bushy varieties' mountain ranges, preferring to grow on the high plains and hills east of the mountains. In their healthy, robust, typical forms these varieties are easy to tell apart. In immature, stunted, atypical conditions it is often impossible to distinguish them one from the other. This is, however, true of most Opuntias, even separate species. When he undertook the study of our cacti, Engelmann found it necessary to distinguish this form. He listed it as a separate species, but he remarked that it differed from O. phaeacantha "only in habit." This is essentially true, but exactly what that means and what significance there is to it cannot really be told even yet, 100 years later.

It is true that the upright growth of the other varieties and the prostrate growth of this variety are hardly definite enough characters upon which to separate species. Shade or poor growing conditions will render them all almost identical in a couple of seasons. This smaller cactus called variety *camanchica* is also normally more spiny than its larger relatives, but the same poor conditions will cause it to develop fewer spines. Fruit shape seems a minor point also, yet minor as these things may be individually, when taken together they add up to two clearly different cacti. No matter how closely they may coincide when they can't grow normally, when they are grown side by side in the same good environment, they are separate entities. I have seen this in a well-arranged old garden, where on one hand was upright *O. phaeacantha* var. *major* 3 to 4 feet high and lightly spined, while 6 feet away a plant of prostrate *O. phaeacantha* var. *camanchia* made an impenetrable mat, about 1 foot high covered with its much more numerous spines. Fruits were characteristically different on these two plants also.

So there is a difference, even though, beginning with Britton and Rose, numerous authorities have made these and the other forms listed here as varieties synonymous. Borg has stood almost alone in setting this cactus off from the others in the species as a separate subspecies. No one quite knows, even yet, the basis for these differences or what their significances are. The kind of differences we see do not seem great enough to fit our modern ideas of separate species, and so we agree in the downgrading of such as this form from that of species rank. But then what is it, if not a species? Is *camanchica* an intermediate of some kind? Is there a hybridization, and if so between what forms? Or are these merely individual variations within a species? There is even yet not one particle of evidence, no breeding records, no hybridization experiments, no genetic studies on these plants, so we cannot answer such questions as these. We only know that we are faced with the separate forms and need a way to refer to them. Hesitating to call them species, suspecting that they are in some way more closely related than that, we use the only other rank currently in vogue for such close relationships, and our cactus becomes *O. phaeacantha* var. *camanchica*.

This then, is the prostrate but large-jointed, heavy-spined prickly pear which Engelmann found growing on the Llano Estacado, which we know is common in western Oklahoma, northwestern Texas, the panhandles of both these states, and into New Mexico, and which Coulter stated grew "from southern Colorado through western Texas, New Mexico and Arizona."

As might be expected in any form with such a wide range, there are many minor variations in local races. There have been attempts to give various of these species or varietal rank, but it does not seem they can be maintained. Much confusion has resulted. Some of these local forms which can best be regarded as synonyms but which are often referred to separately should be mentioned here to help a beginner past the confusion.

In central Texas a form with somewhat fewer spines than typical and more often having tuberous roots, but otherwise indistinguishable from this variety was described and named by Rose *O. mackensenii*. Because of its occasional tuberous roots he seemed to associate it with *O. compressa* rather than the *O. phaeacantha* group, but otherwise it is clearly of this complex. It is the form seen commonly around Austin, Texas, and west through the Texas hill country on the southern edge of the variety's range. Perhaps its fewer spines may be due to marginal growing conditions on the edge of the range.

O. phaeacantha var. *camanchica* has often been called. *O. tortispina*, a name coined by Engelmann for a form with spines lighter-colored and more twisted than is typical. The two cannot be separated, and I have a number of times, in northwestern Oklahoma, seen the two supposedly different forms growing together along with all sorts of intermediates between them. The lighter form is more common in northern Oklahoma and Kansas. Miss Anthony unaccountably uses this name for the variety with the regular dark spines as it is found in the Big Bend.

There grows in Colorado the nearest thing we have seen to an intermediate between variety *camanchica* and the upright varieties of *O. phaeacantha*. These Colorado plants have the low-growing form of this variety, but far fewer spines as well as elongated, clavate fruits and small seeds such as it never has. Most of the characters of this Colorado plant are like those of variety *major*, except that it lacks the size and erectness of that variety. It seems to be the form described by Coulter as *O. mesacantha* var. *oplocarpa*, but may represent only the effect of the severe northern climate and altitude on variety *major*. At the same time, variety *camanchica* grows very spiny and very typical up along the east side of the Colorado mountains. However, we have seen a few specimens from Oklahoma and northwest Texas of variety *camanchica* which approached this Colorado form by having longer than typical fruits. Although it is so incompletely described that no one can be sure, *O. pyrocarpa* Gr. may have been such a variety *camanchica* with minimum spines and long fruits.

Indistinct and problematical as variety *camanchica* may be to a taxonomist, it is very real and very much a plant to be taken into consideration over huge areas of the high plains. Here it is the largest Platyopuntia to be found, and often quite a pest. The grass it protects from grazing animals often grows up to practically hide it, but everything moving must be alert for it or suffer the consequences of blundering into it.

Opuntia phaeacantha var. tenuispina (Eng.)

DESCRIPTION   PLATE 53

ROOTS: Previous accounts did not describe the roots, except for Wooton, who said they were sometimes tuberous. Roots of those living plants examined in this study were fibrous.

STEMS: A low, semiprostrate, spreading plant. Occasionally the most ascending branches of the plant may extend to about 1 foot high. The pads are 3 to 8 inches long and to 4 inches wide, pear-shaped, with the bases noticeably constricted. The pads are rather thin, smooth, and dark blue-green or bright, shiny green in color.

AREOLES: The areoles are oval to practically round, and from slightly over $^1/_8$ to about $^3/_{16}$ of an inch across. They are closely set on the pads, varying from $^3/_8$ of an inch apart low on the pad to one inch apart higher up. Some full-sized pads have no areoles over $^3/_4$ of an inch apart.

SPINES: There are found 1 to 6 spines on all but the very lowest areoles of the pad. Areoles up to about the middle of the pad will carry 1 to 3 slender, whitish spines from a mere fraction of an inch to as much as 1 inch long. These all grow downward and lie spread almost against the pad surface. The most fully armed areoles around the upper edge of the pad will carry 1 or 2 main spines 1 to $2^1/_2$ inches long, usually white or gray, always with brown tips and often with pale brownish bases. They are usually turned severely downward, but occasionally one may stand fairly erect on the edge of the pad. These main spines are straight, slender, round or practically so, firm instead of bristle-like, but slender enough to be easily flexible. Below them in the areole will be 1 to 4 shorter, deflexed spines like those found lower on the pad.

GLOCHIDS: Bright reddish-brown fading to dirty brown, rather numerous, forming a dense tuft in the center of the areole, but very slender and short, being only $^1/_8$ of an inch or slightly longer on any areole. They hardly extend beyond the brown wool of the areole. The effect of this is to give the areoles the appearance of bulging outward.

FLOWERS: As the species, except only $2^1/_2$ to 3 inches across, and when old fading gradually to a pale pinkish. There are 6 to 8 green stigma lobes.

FRUITS: Bright red in color, oblong or elliptic, with little if any constriction at the base, but with a very deeply pitted umbilicus. From 1 to $1^5/_8$ inches long and about $^3/_4$ of an inch thick. There are usually brown glochids on the areoles of the fruits, and sometimes the upper edge areoles have 1 to 3 slender, whitish spines, tipped brown and up to $^3/_8$ of an inch long, on them. The seeds are very irregular in outline, sometimes round and almost even, but more often elongated in one axis, twisted, or otherwise unevenly shaped. This gives quite a variation in measurement, individual seeds from the same plant ranging from hardly more than $^1/_8$ to $^1/_4$ of an inch (3–6 millimeters) in greatest diameter. They are of average thickness.

RANGE. Originally stated to be limited to the sandhills around El Paso, from the village of Dona Ana, above Las Cruces, New Mexico, to the village of San Elizario below El Paso, in Texas. In spite of numerous claims to a broader range, there seem to be no indisputable records of the plant outside of this limited area.

REMARKS. In his study of cacti 100 years ago, Engelmann described and named a small prickly pear growing on the sandhills around El Paso. It had several distinctive characters, namely its constricted pads, its rather numerous, light-colored, and slender, flexible spines which were mostly pointed downward on the pads, its bright brown or reddish-brown but short glochids, its close-standing areoles, and its oblong, deeply-pitted fruits. Engelmann considered it a separate species and called it O. tenuispina.

Coulter repeated Engelmann's description and range for the plant, apparently no other specimens of it having come to light in the 40 years intervening before his own study but those first seen by Engelmann. It appears from this that it was a rare plant limited to the habitat of the Rio Grande Valley sands around El Paso and Las Cruces.

In his own accounts a little later, however, Wooton made a strange statement which opened the gates to much confusion, saying, "This is the most common species in the lower Rio Grande Valley on the heavier soils." How he transferred the cactus from the sand hills to the heavier soils is unknown, and the photograph he reproduced for the plant is so poor that it does not tell us whether he was confusing this plant with another or not.

At any rate, Britton and Rose apparently did become so confused. Although they saw the real thing and give us probably the best picture of the cactus so far existing, their description shows that they also included with it something quite different, something with fewer spines. Having brought in some other plant, they included this other plant's range and said the species even grows west into Arizona.

Following them, the range has been enlarged by other writers until the plant has sometimes been considered a common cactus of all southern New Mexico and Arizona. Finally Anthony called a rather large, bushy cactus of almost entirely different description growing in the Big Bend of Texas O. tenuispina. We have concluded that her plant was instead O. phaeacantha var. brunnea.

Nothing can be definite until the question is decided: is O. tenuispina the rare plant of very limited habitat it at first appeared to be, or is it really a common plant of wide range? Is the broadening of range and description a natural result of wider study or is there another cactus close enough in general characters to have become confused with it and so explain the increase of range?

A partial answer to the question can be found by looking at Rose's own specimens as they are still preserved. Upon searching them out, we find that all of the specimens he called by this name from outside the original small range have been redetermined by other students since as ordinary O. tortispina. This is the white-spined form O. phaeacantha var. camanchica sometimes takes, and I believe some of the confusion has arisen because of mistaking this cactus for O. tenuispina.

There is an even better explanation for the trouble with this cactus. One of the problems of Opuntia study is the fact that most Opuntias, when immature or not growing in conditions very favorable to them, fail to put on their complete spination. The very characters of spines upon which so much depends in recognizing them do not show at all on such stunted specimens. Anyone who has tried to collect and grow Opuntias knows that all too often his various beautiful types, painstakingly gathered, end up in a few years of cultivation practically indistinguishable. And he will find that all of the *O. phaeacantha* group show in this imperfect growth form a few slender, whitish, rather deflexed spines and lack their main and heavy upper spines. If too little light is part of the trouble there is also a tendency for the pads of all of them to lengthen and produce narrowed bases.

Now this imperfect form of all these varieties happens to fit somewhat nearly the description of *O. tenuispina*, especially the very general and simplified descriptions of Wooton and Britton and Rose, which have been the ones most widely copied by recent writers. The details of areoles and so on, having been left out of their descriptions and so not being referred to, it has been easy to imagine that many weakly spined specimens of the other *O. phaeacantha* varieties were this cactus. In this way, we believe, the supposed range of *O. tenuispina* has grown and grown, while the conception of the plant has become diluted so that more and more plants have been taken in.

The actual *O. tenuispina*, however, when properly recognized, is one of our rarest prickly pears, and it is now probably very near extinction. Most of the sandy strip along the Rio Grande where it had grown is now included in the remarkable megalopolis which is fast fusing Las Cruces, El Paso, and Juarez, and most cacti there are already gone or appear doomed as the build-up proceeds across the sands toward the slopes of the Franklin Mountains. It may be that in the future there will be no further opportunity to study the problem of this form.

I have not been so fortunate as to collect this cactus myself, in spite of quite a lot of wandering around the sands of its area. However, I am indebted to Mr. Charles Polaski, the remarkable collector and grower of cacti who has been the source of most of the Oklahoma specimens in European collections, for making it possible for me to describe and photograph the plant. He has a whole bed of the variety grown from a collection he made, "west of El Paso." We feel most certain it is the plant in question, and it may represent the only living specimens in cultivation today. It represents what we feel to be at least a very distinct variety with definite form not due to stunting or other environmental influence. It has kept its characteristics unchanged both in Mr. Polaski's yard in the rather severe Oklahoma climate, and in my garden in San Antonio. I feel most fortunate to be able to include it in this study at all, even though I cannot give any further data on presently existing wild populations. Perhaps this will prompt someone to locate and study them further, if they still exist at all.

It is my opinion that this form is the smallest, most low-growing of the *O. phaeacantha* complex, and so I list it here as a variety of that species.

Opuntia cymochila Eng.

DESCRIPTION PLATE 53

ROOTS: Described as fibrous, and usually so, but occasional examples with tuberous roots have been found.

STEMS: Prostrate. Growing as a spreading mat of small pads rooting where they lie either flat on the ground or resting on their edges. The height of the clump will be the height of the most upright pad, which may be 6 or 8 inches, while the width of the clump is usually 1 to 4 feet. Pads are usually round or sometimes even wider than they are long, but occasionally become slightly egg-shaped. These pads are rather thick for their size, averaging about 1/2 inch thick. They are from 2 1/2 to occasionally 6 inches long and to 4 inches wide. In the dry season or in the winter the pads are much shrunken and take on a very wrinkled appearance, but in a moist growing season they fill out and become flat. They are deep glossy green when filled with moisture, but when dry or suffering from freezes, they become lighter green often suffused with a reddish color.

AREOLES: These are oval or round, small or medium in size, and usually 3/8 to 3/4 of an inch apart, but have been found 1 inch apart.

SPINES: Robust plants will have a total of 1 to 7 spines on almost all areoles or sometimes on those of only the upper half of the pad. Of these spines, 1 to 3 are main central spines which are 1 to 2 3/4 inches long, fairly heavy, round to flattened and often twisted, but straight. Most of these spread in a downward direction, but sometimes one or two of them may stand straight out from the areole or even ascend. From the lower part of the areole there will spread downward 1 to 5 small spines 3/16 to 1 inch long. These are slender, almost bristle-like to fairly stout and very slightly flattened. All spines are white or gray with the very tips light brown and translucent, and the bases brownish. Occasionally the brownish coloring extends up most of the length of the spine. Less healthy plants growing in excessively dry or exposed places and all new pads before maturity will lack the main upper spines entirely and will present only the lower, deflexed spines, these 1/4 to 1 inch long, slender and bristle-like, and pure white with brownish tips.

GLOCHIDS: Yellow, straw, or dirty brownish-yellow in color. They are not too numerous in young areoles, but usually increase to very many in old areoles. They stand out in a compact cluster in the middle of the areole and are comparatively long, ³/₁₆ of an inch at first, becoming often ¹/₂ inch long on old pads.

FLOWERS: About 3 inches in diameter and 2¹/₂ inches tall. Usually wholly chrome-yellow in color, but sometimes with the center golden-brown. The outer petals are short and pointed, the inner ones broad at the ends with a tiny point at the apex. The stamens are very pale yellow, the style long and pale green. There are 9 green stigma lobes.

FRUITS: Purplish-red in color, oval or broadly egg-shaped, 1 to 1¹/₂ inches long and ³/₄ to 1 inch in diameter at the thickest point. The base is not constricted at all, or only very slightly so on some plants. The umbilicus is narrow and forms a deep pit. The seeds are large, a little over ³/₁₆ to just over ¹/₄ of an inch (5–6¹/₂ millimeters) in diameter, of medium thickness, irregular in shape. In the same plant there will be seeds practically round, elongated, and almost triangular, and sometimes they are greatly twisted. The body of the seed is depressed in its center with a ridge around its edge. The rim of the seed is wide to very wide (1–2 millimeters), but very sharp. It often undulates, but there is no notch at the hilum.

RANGE. The whole of the Oklahoma and Texas panhandles and adjacent New Mexico west to the mountains and south into west Texas. Extending east from the panhandles about as far as Cheyenne, Woodward, Alva, and Manchester, Oklahoma, and north into west and central Kansas and eastern Colorado. It also grows south in Texas to a line running from near Abilene approximately to Big Spring and Pecos, then dipping sharply south past Fort Davis to just south of Marfa, the southernmost point at which the cactus has been recorded. From there the range retreats northward abruptly, entering New Mexico east of the Sacramento Mountains.

REMARKS. O. cymochila was first described and named by Engelmann as a small cactus of the Comanche Plains. When he later erected his large species O. rafinesquii he included this plant in it as O. rafinesquii var. cymochila. When Coulter substituted mesacantha for rafinesquii, he left our cactus as O. mesacantha var. cymochila. These men would, therefore, connect this cactus with O. compressa, which is the presently accepted name for that widespread Opuntia complex.

Wooton, in his study of New Mexico cacti, says instead that the cactus, except for its having succulent instead of dry fruits, resembles O. polyacantha.

Britton and Rose, in their study, made O. cymochila a synonym of O. tortispina Eng. and were followed in this by Borg. Backeberg connected the two, but still distinguished between them and so has O. tortispina var. cymochila. Since both Boissevain and Benson consider O. tortispina closely related to or even a variety of O. phaeacantha, a view with which I agree, this gives us yet another way of relating this plant.

There are plausible reasons for each of the above combina-

tions, yet obviously they can't all be correct. The cactus remains recognizably distinct from them all, and since there seem to be about as many reasons for one combination as for another, it is probably better not linked any more closely to any one of them than to the others. We therefore leave it standing separate among them until we have better evidence for one relationship or another.

The mature and robust O. cymochila is easily distinguished from the actual O. compressa and all the varieties of that cactus, some of which may grow in its range, by the possession of spines on all or nearly all areoles. O. compressa and its varieties have spines only on the upper parts of the pads. This seems a simple distinction, but a chance for confusion enters with the fact that young or stunted specimens of O. cymochila often lack the major spines, and the appearance of this weakly bespined growth is almost identical to that of some forms of O. compressa. I have collected plants, particularly just north of Big Spring, Texas, which seemed perfectly good examples of O. compressa until grown for a couple of years in good conditions, when they put forth more numerous spines than that cactus ever has. These plants, by then, had also displayed the fruits of O. cymochila, rather oval fruits with little or no constriction of the bases and with very large, relatively thin seeds. These features are greatly different from the narrow, clavate fruits of the other plant, with its much smaller, very thick seeds.

It is obvious that O. cymochila is distinct from the dry, spiny-fruited O. polyacantha, and I do not believe that Wooton ever meant they should be combined, but it is surprising how closely a stunted plant of O. cymochila with pads all shrunken and with only depressed, white spines can approximate this other species when seen on some dry Canadian River bluff. Here again, a chance to grow well and put out its real spination as well as its purplish, naked, fleshy fruits will show it as so entirely different from the other with its dry, spiny fruits that in one's garden it is hard to believe they could ever have looked alike.

The problem of relating this cactus properly to the O. phaeacantha group is more complex. It might have fallen in line neatly as a smaller relative of O. phaeacantha var. camanchica, much of whose range it shares, except for the interjection of another name and description which has brought nothing but confusion for this area.

At the same time and in the same publication in which he first put forth O. cymochila, Engelmann also described an O. tortispina. He gave the same range for the two, the Comanche Plains. Coulter repeated the description of the latter, but said that O. tortispina grows all the way to Nebraska. Significantly, he did not combine it as a variety of his O. mesacantha (O. compressa), as he did O. cymochila. Wooton ignored O. tortispina entirely, but Britton and Rose took this to be the proper name for the common cactus growing from Wisconsin and Dakota all the way to New Mexico, and decided O. cymochila was the same plant. They were followed in this by others. We must take time to see what *O. tortispina* was before we can determine if it is our plant or how they are related.

Engelmann's description of *O. tortispina* had some characters in common with *O. cymochila*. He said it was a practically prostrate cactus with round or nearly round pads. It had straw-colored or brownish glochids. It had upper spines 1¹/₂ to 2¹/₂ inches long and white or white with yellowish tips and bases. Its fruits were oval and not constricted. All this is similar in the two plants. But in size of pad *O. tortispina* was said to be larger than *O. cymochila*. Engelmann had before him pads 6 to 8 inches long with areoles 1 to 1¹/₂ inches apart. This larger plant also had a total of 6 to 8 spines, 1 or 2 more than a robust *O. cymochila* has. Much has been made of the fact that Engelmann said his *O. tortispina* had spines compressed, angled, sometimes even channeled and twisted, and named the plant for this feature. Its fruits were also longer, being 1³/₄ to 2 inches long, with at most a shallow depression at the top.

Everyone remembers the twisted-spine character, but most of the other characters Engelmann gave for that plant have been ignored. I believe a careful reading of the description shows that Engelmann's *O. tortispina* has characters found quite often in *O. phaeacantha* var. *camanchica,* but except for the whitish spine color, its characters really give us a much more robust plant with larger pads, more widely spaced areoles, and fruits and seeds more similar to that cactus than to *O. cymochila*.

This leaves us with *O. cymochila* as a distinct form occurring over a vast area of the high western plains. Where it grows in more hilly country it still is usually found on the flats of the valleys rather than on steep slopes. It often dots the flat plains of the panhandles where the sod has not been broken. It has kept its hold through the dust storms of the area, often now perched on top of low mounds formed by the drifting dust which was held by its older pads and through which its newer ones have grown. In more grassy places and especially on the rough breaks along the Canadian and other rivers of the area, it is often very hard to find, as the grass grows up in the clump and entirely shields the low pads from view. One can learn to spot it by looking for the mounds of longer grass here and there on the prairie caused by the protection from grazing animals the grass gets from the unseen pads between which it grows.

Opuntia compressa (Salisbury) Macbride
"Low Prickly Pear," "Smooth Prickly Pear"

DESCRIPTION   PLATES 54, 55, 56

ROOTS: Fibrous, often entirely so, but often with spindle-shaped to spherical tubers upon these fibrous roots. The plant never has a central taproot.

STEMS: A low-growing species with pads entirely prostrate or spreading upward at first and then reclining on their edges with age. The height of the plant thus is usually 1 foot or less, but occasionally in some forms it grows to 18 inches tall. The pads are round or even broader than long to egg-shaped or sometimes spindle-shaped, some with and some without constriction below. They are typically 1 to 6 inches long, by 1 to 5 inches wide, but occasionally in some forms they may be to 7 or 8 inches long on exceptionally robust specimens. They are of average thickness to very thick for their size, tuberculate by raised areoles or smooth and flat, dark green to pale or yellowish-green, some forms with purplish spots at the areoles in the winter.

AREOLES: Small and inconspicuous, ¹/₁₆ to ¹/₈ of an inch in diameter and elongated oval to circular at first, becoming with age more circular and sometimes to ¹/₄ of an inch across. They are spaced ³/₁₆ to 1¹/₄ inches apart.

SPINES: Entirely spineless or with spines on less than the upper half of each pad. Areoles of the lower half to two-thirds of each pad are always spineless. The armed areoles with 1 to 5 spines are arranged as follows. There may be 1 or 2 straight main spines which stand porrect, somewhat deflexed or erect, ¹/₄ to 2¹/₄ inches in length, rather slender to heavy, round or flattened, their color from almost pure grayish-white to yellowish or mottled above with the bases brown or red-brown, or occasionally the whole spine brown. There may be present, but more often will be lacking, one lower, deflexed spine ³/₁₆ to 1 inch long, slender, similar in color. Some forms have occasionally, besides these, 1 or 2 bristle-like spines spreading downward, only ¹/₈ to ³/₈ of an inch long, and white in color.

GLOCHIDS: Few, short, and fine at first, comprising a compact tuft in the middle of the areole, but usually increasing greatly in number on old pads and becoming to ¹/₄ or even ³/₈ of an inch long. As numerous on the sides of the pads as on the edges, or even more numerous. They are greenish-yellow, straw, brown, or bright red-brown in color.

FLOWERS: 2 to 5 inches in diameter, pale yellow to orange-yellow, or orange-yellow with red centers. The ovary is elongated obovate to clavate and is 1 to 2¹/₄ inches long. The anthers are cream-colored. The stigma lobes are 4 to 9 in number, white or yellowish in color.

FRUITS: Clavate with constricted or greatly prolonged bases and narrow, noticeably depressed to deeply pitted umbilici, red-brown in color. The seeds are round, flat, but thick-bodied, with narrow, acute rims. They are ¹/₈ to ¹/₄ of an inch (3–6 millimeters) in diameter and 2 to sometimes 4 millimeters thick.

RANGE. Including all of the forms at least tentatively assigned to the species, ranging over the entire U.S. except approximately the northwest third and the state of Maine.

REMARKS. When all of its varieties are considered together, this small, prostrate, inconspicuous prickly pear is no doubt the leading candidate for the most wide-ranging cactus in the U.S. It is known to occur from New England southwest through all states to the Rocky Mountains, and from there on west through New Mexico and Arizona probably into California. It is said to be absent only from the state of Maine and those states west of the Continental Divide and north of Arizona and California.

This wide-ranging, adaptable cactus was naturally among the earliest noticed, and should be the easiest to recognize and name, but it actually presents the greatest confusion to serious students of cacti. Even finding the proper name for the species is enough to discourage the hardiest cactophile. It was first christened *Cactus opuntia* by Linnaeus, and shortly thereafter *Cactus compressus* by Salisbury. Soon it was called *Cactus humifusus* by Rafinesque. By the rules of nomenclature, after the genus *Opuntia* was erected, its name could not remain *Opuntia opuntia*, although some books have called it that, so Salisbury's name, as revised by Macbride into *Opuntia compressa* is now accepted as valid, although Prince Salm-Dyck had in the meantime coined yet another name, *Opuntia vulgaris,* for it.

But this is only the beginning of the naming problem. Any plant growing over so huge an area is likely to present various localized forms, and whatever level of relationship they represent, few will be satisfied with a view so general that it ignores them. I know from experience that few collectors who have side by side two of the widely differing forms this species can show are satisfied when I tell them they are both *O. compressa.* They want to know more exactly what they have. So from the first these differing forms had to be studied and named, and here the real confusion enters. We will deal with these variations which come within our area of study one by one.

Rafinesque seemed to be the first to notice these different variations. He treated them all as separate species, erecting first of all a species, *O. humifusa,* for the western, Mississippi Valley form. Later he broke down even this, his original western species, into several others, *O. humifusa* (in a more restricted sense), *O. caespitosa,* and *O. mesacantha,* plus others, but his descriptions of these latter variations were so vague that no one can really identify plants from them, so that Engelmann, in exasperation with him and failing to go back to the earlier names, proposed instead to start over, calling the whole complex *O. rafinesquii.* This seems an illogical solution, and most students have returned to the name *O. compressa* as the valid one for the species, with mostly newer names having been proposed for the varieties.

The description given above is a broadened one drawn to include all of the varieties presently assigned to the species complex. It is not the description of the form restricted to the eastern seaboard, which was the type variety and which is still commonly referred to as *O. compressa,* but which, under the modern system, should be given a varietal rank. This typical variety does not enter the area of this study, and so is not described separately here. The question of what forms to include in the species complex is at present a very arbitrary one, with very little solid evidence for or against the inclusion of some forms. I am drawing the species boundaries as they seem most

understandable to me. Future study may very well revise the limits of this species further.

Opuntia compressa var. humifusa (Raf.)

ROOTS: Usually fibrous, but occasionally with peanut-shaped or spindle-shaped tubers on these fibrous roots. The plant never has a fleshy taproot.

STEMS: Prostrate, never ascending over 1 or 2 pads high. The pads are round to broadly oblong, usually 2 to 4 inches long, but sometimes reaching 5 inches. The pads are thick and flat when healthy, becoming wrinkled when desiccated, but never being tuberculate by elevations at the areoles. The surface is dark or bright green and shining, sometimes having some purplish coloring at the areoles in winter or drought.

AREOLES: Small, being only $1/16$ to hardly $1/8$ of an inch long and enlarging little if any with age. They are elongated oval to round in shape, and the opposite of being bulging outward with wool, they are usually rather concave, pitlike depressions on the surface of the flat pad. They are spaced $1/2$ to 1 inch apart.

SPINES: Most often the plant is spineless. If spines are present they will be found in only a few upper edge areoles and will number only 1 to 3 per areole. They ordinarily consist of 1 or 2 spreading spines up to 1 inch long. Rarely there will be 1 lower, deflexed, and very small one. The main spines are round, straight, and heavy, whitish to brownish in color.

GLOCHIDS: Few and short at first, comprising a small, compact tuft of minute bristles less than $1/8$ of an inch long in the small areoles. Often they do not increase at all on old pads, but in some specimens they lengthen to $3/16$ of an inch or so with age. They are red-brown to yellowish in color.

FLOWERS: Yellow, usually, but not always, with red centers or else streaked with red. They are 2 to 3 inches in diameter and $1^3/4$ to 3 inches tall, including the relatively long, slender ovary. On the ovary there are some glochids. There are 10 to 14 broad inner petals. The filaments are orange, often conspicuously so, and the anthers are cream-yellow. The style is short, and there are 4 to 8 white or very pale greenish-yellow, fat, grooved stigma lobes.

FRUITS: Elongated club-shaped or oval above, always with a constricted, slender, and markedly elongated base and deeply pitted apex. They are $1^1/8$ to 2 inches long, $1/2$ to $3/4$ of an inch thick at the thickest part, which is near the top, the whole lower one-third at least being only $1/4$ to $3/8$ of an inch thick. These fruits are greenish for a long time, but tardily become apricot or plum-red or brownish red, the pulp remaining greenish and sour in poor growing conditions, but when growing in the best conditions becoming reddish and sweet. The seeds are ³/₁₆ of an inch or just under (3¹/₂–4¹/₂ millimeters) in diameter, thick to very thick, with narrow rims.

RANGE. Entering our area from the north and east, coming into Louisiana from Mississippi, into Arkansas from Mississippi, Tennessee, and Missouri, and extending throughout Arkansas and northern Louisiana into Texas and probably into Oklahoma. Its southwestern limit seems to be a line running approximately through Alexandria, Louisiana, to the vicinity of Silsbee, Texas. From there its known range turns sharply north, remaining east of the Trinity River until it nears Dallas. From there it seems to retreat back toward Arkansas, except for an apparent occurrence of it near Madill, Oklahoma, which opens up the possibility that it ranges widely over eastern Oklahoma.

REMARKS. There has been continuous discussion for 150 years about how different the O. *compressa* of the eastern seaboard is from that found in the Mississippi Valley. One thing is apparently agreed upon from Rafinesque through the last article treating the problem. All seem to agree that there is a difference between the two forms, although it is frustrating to find so little anywhere by way of a concrete statement of how they actually differ.

The early students regarded the two as entirely separate species. The eastern one, apparently found only east of the Appalachian Range, is usually called O. *compressa*. It is the type form of the species, and considered as part of the bigger complex, would be the typical variety of it. But how do we treat the form of the Mississippi Valley, which is the one concerning us directly? Rafinesque divided it into his several separate species before he was through. It was his inability to identify these by their descriptions that caused Engelmann to abandon them all and rename the Mississippi Valley form O. *rafinesquii*. Engelmann then added new names for what he regarded as new species he found farther west.

Coulter, regarding this as an unsatisfactory dodge, and working from the fact that Rafinesque said his O. *mesacantha* grew from Kentucky to Louisiana, took this name, O. *mesacantha*, for what he considered a major western species in opposition to the eastern O. *compressa*. He ended up with nine named subspecies in his western complex under that name.

More recently it has been regarded as improbable that all of these forms are separate species and even as doubtful that many of them are separate forms at all. It has come to be considered more correct to regard those which are separate forms as varieties of the one huge species, O. *compressa*. This has caused the most recent works to eliminate all the names of Rafinesque and most of those of Engelmann and of Coulter. The change has made for greater clarity, except when one turns to various floras and handbooks which still often use the different names of the above authors, apparently at random. There has been no standardization of the varietal names. The result is that most beginners, not knowing which are synonyms, go into the field with twice as many names as there are cacti, and are soon frustrated when they can't find them all. With the aid of the above admittedly over-simplified summary and the following discussion of our form, it is hoped some of this can be avoided.

In the geographical territory we are considering we are not concerned with the typical, eastern variety. However, we do have throughout Arkansas and much of Louisiana and coming into Oklahoma and Texas what appears to be the midwestern or Mississippi Valley variety of the cactus. We need the correct varietal name for it. The first person to deal with this particular form was Rafinesque. However incompletely he described it, it seems clear that he meant this cactus by his O. *humifusa*. Engelmann described our form, but, as already mentioned, his solution of renaming it entirely to O. *rafinesquii* is unsatisfactory. Coulter, who next described it, returned to a Rafinesque name, but chose a more obscure one, O. *mesacantha*, which we cannot pin down to anything we know at all. We are left with Rafinesque's first name for the Mississippi Valley form. Regarding it now as a variety instead of a species, we get as a name for the low prickly pear of this area O. *compressa* var. *humifusa*.

By whatever name, this is an inconspicuous little prickly pear found mostly in sandy places or on the drier hillsides jutting out of the piney woods. In such places it sometimes forms mats covering the ground. Occasionally plants are found on wooded hillsides under the trees, but here they are more straggling and pads tend to be somewhat etiolated, in which case they become larger and more elongated than typical, but still remain fat and thick.

I have plants from various locations in Arkansas. In Hempstead County, near Tokio, they grow in sandy bottoms. There are fine examples to be seen in Benton County in the northwest corner of the state, growing east of Rogers, Arkansas. They are not as common in the eastern part of the state, but have been found near Batesville in the north and Warren in the south.

In Louisiana the plant is less common and only a few records of it there have been found. It appears to grow best in the northwest part of the state, having been found just north of Alexandria, near Winnfield, and near Minden.

The variety enters Texas from Louisiana, but only grows along the eastern edge of this state. The southwesternmost record of it is from near Silsbee, Texas, in Hardin County. It does not progress farther to enter the coastal plain or the central Texas limestone hills, being restricted almost entirely to the eastern piney woods. It grows quite profusely under the trees at Woodville, Texas, and has been found again at various places north of there. It is rather common at Longview, Texas, this being the apparent basis for Griffiths' O. *nemoralis*.

The question of this variety's occurring in Oklahoma is still an open one. Engelmann and Coulter both state that, when they wrote, it had not been found west of the western boundary of Missouri and Arkansas. We have seen that it progresses farther west than that in Texas, but there have not been any good records of it from Oklahoma cited in more recent works, although Waterfall, in his "Catalog of the Flora of Oklahoma," lists O.

rafinesquii as well as *O. macrorhiza,* and must mean this variety. Not having found it in many trips into Oklahoma, I would be inclined to doubt its growing there, except for one population of plants which I found growing in the Tishomingo Wildlife Reservation near Madill, Oklahoma. These seem to be referable only to this variety, even though they are growing so far west. Perhaps future study will show that the variety is found in very scattered spots over the eastern hills of Oklahoma.

O. compressa var. *humifusa* has small, shiny, dark green pads which are very thick. They become very wrinkled in winter or drought, in which case they also often get purple blotches at the areoles, but the pads are smooth-surfaced and never appear tuberculate by elevation of the areoles. In fact, more often the small areoles actually seem to be in slight depressions of the surface. In this and in the fact that neither the areole nor the glochids increase noticeably in size with age or on the edge of the pad, as do those of most of its relatives, it is like the more eastern, typical variety. It is also a very prostrate form. When it is growing in the same garden bed with them, the difference is striking between this form with its pads all reclining once they have reached maturity and variety *macrorhiza,* variety *fusco-atra,* and variety *allairei,* all of which have arms more or less turning upward from old pads that much prefer to touch only their edges to the ground.

It has often been stated that this variety always has fibrous roots. In fact, these roots have been used as the main character to distinguish it from the more western forms. Britton and Rose separate this form from *O. macrorhiza* in their key by roots fibrous versus roots tuberous alone. But handy as this would be, it just isn't true that variety *humifusa* always lacks tubers. While fibrous roots are the most common, I have found small, peanut-shaped tubers up to about ³/₄ of an inch in diameter and 1¹/₂ inches long on specimens in Arkansas and in Louisiana, as well as in Missouri. The character of the roots cannot be used to separate forms in this species.

Opuntia compressa var. macrorhiza (Eng.) Benson

DESCRIPTION   PLATE 54

ROOTS: Having a basically fibrous root system without a central taproot, but these slender fibrous roots often having spherical to spindle-shaped tubers on them. These tubers may be from a fraction of an inch up to sometimes 3 inches in diameter. They may occur in clusters on the various branching roots, or may sometimes be found in a series of several one after another along the same root. Plants lacking tubers completely are not uncommon.

STEMS: Prostrate or nearly so, with old pads mostly leaning on their edges on the ground, and with newer pads only temporarily upright, the whole plant being 6 inches to 1 foot high. The pads are almost round to elongated obovate, often with some constriction at the bases, but this not pronounced. These pads are medium in thickness to rather thick; the surface is quite tuberculate by raised areoles when growing, and these elevations remain more or less noticeable on old pads, which may also become wrinkled. In color they are medium, shining green when young, becoming dull, dark green when old. The pads are normally 2 to 5 inches long, but when growing under shading vegetation they sometimes become etiolated to 6 or even 8 inches long.

AREOLES: Oval or almost round and ¹/₈ of an inch or so across at first, enlarging to ¹/₄ of an inch or more on old pads. They are ¹/₂ to 1¹/₄ inches apart.

SPINES: Spines are present on the upper one-fourth of the pad or less, but the pads are occasionally but not often totally spineless. The most common spination is 2 to 3 spines per areole, but very robust plants present up to a maximum of 5 spines on some edge areoles. On young or weak plants all spines are round or with only the bases somewhat flattened, but robust specimens have the main spine conspicuously flattened. Completely armed areoles present 1 main central spine which is porrect or a little deflexed, slender to medium thickness, straight, round if weak but flattened if robust, and ¹/₄ to 1³/₄ inches long. There may be, but will not always be, 1 or 2 upper spines porrect to erect, ³/₈ to 1 inch long, slender, weak, and always round. These main spines are gray or whitish, with often the bases and sometimes the tips brown or red-brown, fading to all gray and rough when old. On robust specimens there will sometimes be 1 or 2 lower spines spreading below which are very slender, thin, whitish bristles ¹/₈ to ³/₈ of an inch long.

GLOCHIDS: Bright red-brown to dirty straw in color, medium in number, and ³/₁₆ to ¹/₄ of an inch long, in a compact clump at each areole at first. On old pads they often grow to ⁵/₁₆ of an inch long and form large clusters.

FLOWERS: Orange yellow with red centers. They are 2¹/₂ to 3 inches in diameter and 3 to 3¹/₂ inches tall, the ovary being 1¹/₄ to 2¹/₄ inches long, with some reddish-brown glochids on it. There are 7 to 9 inner petals which are very broad from narrow, red bases. The stigma has 4 to 9 yellowish, fat stigma lobes.

FRUITS: Elongated club-shaped, 1¹/₄ to 2¹/₂ inches long and ³/₄ to 1 inch in diameter at the thickest part. The base is greatly constricted and prolonged. The top is shallowly to deeply pitted. These fruits become light red to purplish-red, often however remaining greenish very late in the season. The pulp is greenish and tasteless until fall, finally becoming colorless or slightly reddish and sweet to the taste. The seeds are from just under ³/₁₆ to just under ¹/₄ of an inch (4–5¹/₂ millimeters) in diameter. They are thick or very thick, their rims of medium width but acute.

RANGE. Western Arkansas on the east through all of Oklahoma

and all of Texas west of a line from near Tyler to near Houston. The plant grows almost throughout New Mexico and on into Colorado and Arizona.

REMARKS. This is a very wide-ranging plant, but, being small and marked by no unique feature, it is usually ignored or actually avoided even by cactus fanciers. Over a huge area it is the common prostrate prickly pear that lies in the grass or under thickets and, except for a few days each year when it has beautiful flowers, has little to offer to anyone except thorns for those who don't look before they step.

Information about the exact range of this plant and its relationships is hard to be sure about even today, because it so nearly approaches other forms in appearance and because the name has been so often misapplied that printed records of it and even labeled herbarium specimens are often actually something else. One has to wade through a mass of extraneous material to assemble a picture of the true form. Also, the early descriptions were largely taken from too few and often stunted specimens, and so there has had to be a broadening of the original concept almost from the beginning, a broadening which has threatened to go on until it seemed almost all prostrate prickly pears would be herded under this name. Only by a tracing of the history of the form can its present status be understood.

When Engelmann made the first concerted study of the western forms of this species, he found in the west, beyond the *O. compressa* forms he had seen in the east, several small, prostrate cacti. Almost without exception he set each one of these up as a separate new species. One of them was a plant sent him by Lindheimer from the upper Guadalupe River at New Braunfels, Texas. Engelmann described it from Lindheimer's specimens and called it *O. macrorhiza*. These specimens were, by any character he gives for them—size of pad, number of spines, character of spines, length of spines, size of fruits—less than robust. I have seen some of these Lindheimer specimens, and they are small, weak examples such as one can find in the type locality, but which one has to search out on the most exposed, dry, rocky ledges. The plant usually attains a much greater size and development even in the type locality. I cannot but conclude that these type specimens are atypically underdeveloped individuals with characters nearer to those of the more eastern *O. compressa* var. *humifusa* than are found in more typical individuals. But all of Engelmann's specimens from New Braunfels happened to have tuberous roots, and he seized upon this as a distinguishing feature, actually stating that the plant is really different from the eastern form mainly by the roots.

Taking Engelmann's limited description and following his statement, some students have had real trouble with these two forms. For instance, Britton and Rose happily keyed them: roots fibrous = the eastern form, roots tuberous = *O. macrorhiza*. It would be wonderful if it were that simple, but following this in the field gives difficulty. In numerous fields in Texas, Oklahoma, and Arkansas, I would be forced by this to say that I have the

two forms growing as close as 6 feet apart and all intermixed over the whole population. Even in the type locality of *O. macrorhiza* both kinds of roots are found together. So, if this were true, not only would we have variety *humifusa* growing all the way into New Mexico when all have stated that it hardly goes west of Arkansas and Louisiana, but we would in honesty be required to combine the two. The only conclusion is that either plant can have either wholly fibrous roots or roots with tubers present, the western form, it is true, having tubers more often than not, while the eastern one usually lacks them. But the character of the roots obviously cannot be used to separate the two cacti.

If this is true, then why not combine the two forms entirely? It seems remarkable that this has never been attempted. But perhaps the fact that the western form so often surpasses Engelmann's original description in other characters has enabled all to see that it is actually different in other ways.

Coulter was quick to see that the description of this form had to be broadened, and he set about it, raising the spination maximums in number, length, and stoutness, but still not realizing the maximums of fruit size sometimes attained, or the fact, unnoticed until Griffiths observed it, that the main spine could be flattened when fully developed.

Because the plant, as originally described, was a less than robust thing, more robust specimens were sometimes described as new species when they were noticed. Engelmann himself started this, for instance, with his *O. fusiliformis* of Kansas and Nebraska. All students since have considered this merely a synonym. Only the very long fruits, said to be sometimes 2 to 2¹/₂ inches long distinguish it from the other, and I have collected variety *macrorhiza* from a dozen places, including the type locality, with fruits this size. More recently Mackensen called some long-spined examples he found at Kerrville, Texas, *O. roseana*, but I find nothing in this locality outside the limits of variety *macrorhiza* as it grows in its own type locality not very far away.

But the broadening of the characters of the plant cannot go on indefinitely, to include everything. I have given in this description the full maximum of each character that we have found in and near the type locality close to which we have lived and in which we have observed constantly for 7 years. I have excluded from consideration any described or preserved materials from any other place which do not, in all their features, fall within the limits attained in that type area.

This gives us in *O. compressa* var. *macrorhiza* a very widely distributed plant. Its easternmost record would be that mentioned by Coulter of near Fayetteville, Arkansas, and Demaree's collections from near Bismarck and from Magnet Cove, Hot Springs County, Arkansas. We also have the plant collected near Jasper, in Newton County, and near Little Rock, Pulaski County. These records give us a range of the whole northwestern part of that state. It has apparently not been collected in Louisiana, and the known collections of it in Texas give as an eastern limit excluding the whole eastern edge of the state, it first appearing along a line roughly from Tyler—where Griffiths collected it and dubbed it O. *sanguinocula*—to Houston. It apparently ranges practically all of the rest of Texas, being very common in the central and northern parts, but occurring in scattered, usually very sandy, localities elsewhere. I have collected it on the Bolivar Peninsula—where, however, it was growing only on and around the grounds of old Fort Bolivar, and one is tempted to assume it may have been introduced—in the Corpus Christi area, as well as near Harlingen in the southern extremity of the state. At the other end of the state, in the Chisos Mountains and near Muleshoe, Texas, well up toward the northwestern edge of the state, I have come across isolated populations which seem clearly to be this cactus. It ranges practically all, if not all of Oklahoma, being very common as far west as Alva and Woodward. It occurs in scattered localities in New Mexico, becoming quite common in the northern mountains of that state, and I have seen good specimens of it from both Arizona and Colorado.

It will be noticed that this range does give us both variety *macrorhiza* and variety *humifusa* in an overlapping area in western Arkansas and probably some of Oklahoma. When the two are so close, how, without the roots to decide for us automatically, can we tell them apart? Admittedly in weak specimens without blooms it can sometimes be almost impossible, and everyone should be honest enough to admit that he can't identify an incomplete or atypical specimen with certainty. This would reduce the confusion. Also, if we think of these two as varieties instead of separate species, we need not be surprised if there are specimens apparently intermediate. But in identifying typical specimens there is little difficulty. The salient differences between them are as follows: variety *macrorhiza* has tuberculate surfaces to the pads, up to 5 spines with the main spine flattened and to 1³/₄ inches long when spination is completely developed, flowers with only 7 to 9 inner petals. On the other hand, variety *humifusa* has a flat surface to the pad, a maximum of 3 spines which are heavier but always round and to only 1 inch long, and flowers with 10 to 14 inner petals. The two are very close together, and there may be intergrading. They surely do not warrant being considered separate species. This form seems most logically considered, therefore, as the more western member of the O. *compressa* complex, and so is known today by most taxonomists as O. *compressa* var. *macrorhiza*.

Opuntia compressa var. **microsperma** (Eng.) non Benson

DESCRIPTION   PLATE 54

ROOTS: Mostly fibrous with small tubers on them, but sometimes entirely fibrous.

STEMS: Prostrate, 6 to 8 inches high, with most pads resting one edge on the ground. The pads are broad to elongated egg-shaped, 1 to 4 inches long by ³/₄ to 2¹/₂ inches wide, rather thick, with the surface very tuberculate by elevations of the areoles. The color is medium green with purplish shading around the areoles.

AREOLES: Small, round or oval, ¹/₁₆ to ¹/₈ of an inch long, on top of distinct elevations. They are situated ¹/₄ to ³/₄ of an inch apart.

SPINES: Sometimes spineless, but more often with 1 to 3 spines on the upper areoles of the pad. The one or two main spines are very slender, round, and all white, or with the bases brown and the upper parts white. Occasionally there is 1 lower, deflexed, bristle-like spine, ¹/₈ to ³/₄ of an inch long besides the main spines.

GLOCHIDS: Greenish-yellow or straw color, many in all areoles, at first to ³/₁₆ of an inch long, but when older becoming to ¹/₄ of an inch long.

FLOWERS: Identical with those of the previous variety.

FRUITS: Very elongated club-shaped. They are 1 to 1¹/₄ inches long by ³/₈ of an inch thick at the widest part, which is near the top, the base being very constricted. The apex is deeply pitted. The fruits on my specimens remain green all summer and through September, after which they dry without turning color. The seeds are from just under ¹/₁₆ to just under ¹/₈ of an inch (1¹/₂–2¹/₂ millimeters) in diameter, smooth, and thick, with almost no rims.

RANGE. Collected 10 miles north of Campbellton, Atascosa County, Texas, growing in deep sand near the Atascosa River.

REMARKS. Engelmann originated this variety over 100 years ago, but he gave almost no description of it except to emphasize its extremely small seeds. He also neglected to give any location for it. Coulter, working with Engelmann's materials before him, both the preserved specimens and living plants still being cultivated at that time at the Missouri Botanical Garden, was impressed enough by the tiny seeds to continue listing it as a separate form. But after that all authorities dropped it into the synonymy.

Most recently the name has been revived and used in an entirely new sense. When Benson decided to treat the common, prostrate, Mississippi Valley Opuntia—until then always regarded as a separate species and called O. *humifusa*, O. *rafinesquii*, or O. *mesacantha*—as a variety instead of a species, he, in an attempt to be taxonomically proper, called that form O. *compressa* var. *microsperma*. His stated reason was that this was the earliest varietal name in existence under that species. This is true, but in using it thus he ignores the fact that Engelmann erected it for the very special form with the tiny seeds and meant it to refer to that form alone, as the meaning of the name clearly shows. To use this name for the ordinary, larger seeded, common form is to say that this seed difference is of no significance, and to apply this name to the large-seeded form is an error which every person who can tell the meaning of this simple name can recognize. It blurs a distinction which was considered significant by those earlier students of cacti.

In the course of this study many collections of the species O. *compressa* were made over several states. Time and again the ordinary forms with seeds 3 to 5 millimeters in diameter were found, and we had only wondered vaguely about Engelmann's variety *microsperma* with the tiny seeds. Since we knew the seeds of the species well, it was a real surprise when Mr. Kim Kuebel, an interested friend and cactus collector, brought in a plant of the O. *compressa* complex which had tiny seeds only $1^1/_2$ to $2^1/_2$ millimeters in diameter. They equal in size the smallest Opuntia seeds we have seen, but are very thick. It was obvious to us that we must have the plant referred to by Engelmann, but probably not collected again until this time.

We studied the plant carefully, trying to discover the details of its relationship. It is certainly only a variety of the large O. *compressa* complex. Within that, however, its closest affinities are to the more western O. *compressa* var. *macrorhiza* rather than to the eastern variety *humifusa*. This is shown by the tuberculate surface of the pads, the more numerous glochids, more slender spines, and so on. The fruit is remarkable for never turning red, but then many others of this species only turn light red or apricot, and sometimes this is only a blush on the sunny side of the fruit.

It is impossible to give a range for this form, as Engelmann's specimens carried no location at all. We have so far found this plant in only one location, as given above. Typical variety *macrorhiza*, with seeds $4^1/_2$ to 5 millimeters in diameter was growing nearby.

Listing the variety *microsperma* as a separate form on the basis of only one population would not ordinarily have been justified, but this is a form which we know existed somewhere a hundred years ago. Whether the unique, small seeds are an environmentally induced or a genetically stable character, which has occurred only in this location or, as seems more likely, crops up here and there, no one knows. By listing the form instead of ignoring it and appropriating the name for one of its relatives, we hope that we may prevent its again being lost, with no one ever knowing more about it, and that we may alert collectors to be on the watch for it. Thus we may someday learn what its true significance is.

Opuntia compressa var. fusco-atra (Eng.)

DESCRIPTION   PLATES 54, 55

ROOTS: Either fibrous or about half of the time with small tubers upon the fibrous roots.

STEMS: Prostrate, usually resting at least one edge of each pad on the ground, only to 6 or 8 inches high. The pads are almost round to broadly club-shaped with some constriction at the base, usually 2 to 4 inches long and 2 to 3 inches wide, but rarely to at least 6 inches long and 4 inches wide. They are thin or of medium thickness, noticeably tuberculate by elevations of the areoles. The surfaces of the pads are shiny and bright green to deep green or sometimes rather blue-green.

AREOLES: Small and elongated when young, becoming round and larger to about $1/_4$ of an inch in diameter on old pads. They are spaced $3/_{16}$ to $1^1/_4$ inches apart, varying with the size of the pads; both extremes have been observed on the same plant.

SPINES: Usually having 1 to 3 spines on only upper areoles of the pad, but rarely having a total of 4 or 5 by the addition of one or two very small, bristle-like spines at the lower edge of the areole. There is 1 main spine porrect or nearly so, slender to medium thickness, round or practically so, $1/_4$ to 2 inches long. There may be 1 or 2 upper spines above this and similar to it except only $3/_8$ to 1 inch long, and sometimes 1 lower spine deflexed below and $3/_8$ to $5/_8$ of an inch long. Spreading below these are occasionally 1 or 2 very slender bristles $1/_8$ to $1/_2$ inch long. All spines are yellowish when growing, but when hardened become completely dark brown or gray with brownish bases.

GLOCHIDS: Many, in erect, compact clusters in all areoles, becoming very many and to $1/_4$ of an inch long when old. In color they are very bright, shining red-brown when young, fading to dark, dirty brown when old.

FLOWERS: Completely sulphur yellow or yellow with red centers. They are very variable in size, depending upon environmental conditions, from $1^3/_4$ to 4 inches in diameter and 2 to 3 inches tall, with very slender ovaries $1^1/_8$ to $1^3/_8$ inches long, having some brown glochids on them. There are very few but broad inner petals, usually only 4 or 5, the total number of perianth segments usually being only 9. The stigma has 3 to 5 white lobes.

FRUITS: Elongated club-shaped with constricted bases and deeply pitted tops. They are typically 1 to $1^1/_2$ inches long, but sometimes to 2 inches, and $5/_8$ to $7/_8$ of an inch in diameter at the thickest point. The seeds are about $3/_{16}$ of an inch (4–5 millimeters) in diameter, fairly thick, with narrow, acute rims.

RANGE. The coastal plain, sandy areas near the beaches and on islands of the Texas coast from the western edge of present-day Houston to beyond Brownsville. The plant is never found more than a few miles from the Gulf, except in the valleys of the Colorado and Brazos rivers, where it occurs inland at least 75 miles, its known range in this area running from Houston west to Sealy in Austin County, and to Altair in Colorado County.

REMARKS. This is almost certainly only an extreme form of the O. *compressa* complex, but, although it was noticed and described over 100 years ago by that amazingly thorough student, Engelmann, it has been so rarely collected since then that little has been known about it. It is very close to *O. compressa* var. *macrorhiza,* which is found occasionally in most of its range and sometimes, as just west of Houston, grows side by side with it. Still, the two are rather distinct, and there is no reason to confuse them. Variety *fusco-atra* can be recognized at once by its combination of numerous brilliant red-brown glochids, very marked elevation of the areoles, and extreme reduction in number of flower segments.

In the type locality, stated to be the "sterile prairies west of Houston," which begin approximately where the pine trees leave off, at about the present western city limits of Houston in the vicinity of U.S. Route 90, and extend past Addicks and Katy, the plant is very common. However, this very flat territory gives all the appearance of being very arid, in spite of the high rainfall of the area, and here the plants appear stunted, the pads usually only 2 to 3 inches long. This no doubt accounts for the tiny size given in the original description. Where growing near the beaches the cactus becomes much larger.

Although the cactus is to be encountered here and there along most of the Texas coast south of the type locality, it is never common anywhere else except around Copano Bay in the Rockport area. At Fulton Beach, particularly, it grows in profusion right down to the water's edge. And here it appears to develop a remarkable environmental form, which has of course been called a separate species.

In their monumental work, *The Cactaceae,* Britton and Rose described a new cactus, *Opuntia macateei.* It was collected at Rockport, Texas, in 1910. It was described as a small, prostrate plant with orbicular to obovate, glabrous, dull green joints which were small and somewhat tuberculate, and as having 1 to 3 brownish spines up to 1 inch long. Nothing was said about the root form. The distinctive and really remarkable characteristic of this cactus was its production of flowers 3 to 4 inches long, including slender, subcylindric ovaries 2 to 2³⁄₈ inches long. These ovaries were said to bear leaves up to ¹⁄₂ inch long. We spent much time attempting to find and study this form.

It soon became evident that very little was known about the cactus. We studied the type specimen. It consists of one small pad with one flower, the flower being typical for the *O. compressa* complex, except that it possessed an extremely elongated, practically cylindric ovary slightly over 2 inches long but only about ¹⁄₂ inch in diameter, bearing several long leaves upon it. No evidence of any more recent collections of the plant was found. Later writers, even including Backeberg, have merely repeated the original description for the species, apparently without seeing further specimens. No one has even known enough about the cactus to propose relating it to any other form.

We then attempted to collect the living plant, making repeated trips to the type locality at Rockport, Texas, for this purpose. We found numerous specimens of variety *fusco-atra,* which is very common throughout that area, and of variety *macrorhiza,* which is less common there but occurs occasionally. We studied variety *fusco-atra* especially, as it was early noted that the descriptions of this plant and of *O. macateei* were identical as regards all features mentioned except the structure of the ovary, that of variety *fusco-atra* being described as leafless and only about 1 inch long, less than half as long as the minimum for the ovary of *O. macateei.* Britton and Rose used this difference as the sole means to distinguish these two forms.

For several years we found only the usual forms with typical short ovaries in the area. Then, in May, 1963, we discovered some plants producing elongated fruits. These made up a population of only a few dozen plants growing in almost pure sand inside a motte of live oak trees. The location was 4¹⁄₂ miles north of Rockport, Texas, and about ¹⁄₅ mile back from the waterfront known as Fulton Beach.

The fruits on these specimens were 1¹⁄₂ to 3 inches long, markedly clavate from very narrow bases, often widening near the ends to 1 inch in diameter. They were often curved, and the younger examples possessed several leaves up to ¹⁄₂ inch long. It was too late in the season to observe the flowers of these plants.

These specimens were identical to the numerous stands of variety *fusco-atra* common in the area, but the fruits certainly were different. No description has ever been given of the fruits of *O. macateei,* but we could easily visualize these greatly elongated fruits developing from the markedly elongated ovaries of that form, so we felt rather certain that we had found that cactus.

But almost immediately we noticed that the elongated fruits of our specimens remained green instead of coloring, and actually turned whitish with the passing of time. Soon one of them split open with one longitudinal furrow running the length of the upper, broadened part of the fruit. This furrow exposed a mass of black fungus growth resembling smut. Other fruits ruptured the same way. When we opened some of the fruits before they ruptured, we found them all to be sterile, the aborted ovules being much enlarged.

It was impossible to make further studies that season, but the area was watched closely at blooming time the next year. All cacti observed in the vicinity of Rockport bloomed and fruited normally with short, fertile ovaries, except those in the same motte of live oaks observed to have been atypical the previous year. Within this particular motte, which comprises probably two acres of dense tree growth, there are several dozen specimens of prostrate cacti. When they bloomed, many of their flowers produced the long ovaries described for *O. macateei;* these flowers were then followed by the large, clavate, sterile fruits observed the previous year. However, this year we noted that in some cases the same plant produced both elongated flowers and fruits and the normal flowers and fruits of variety *fusco-atra,* sometimes both on the same pad. There were also some specimens within the population which produced only entirely typical flowers and fruits.

It seems obvious that we have here an abnormal growth of ovary and fruit resulting in sterility, rather than a separate taxonomic form. Since some plants are found with both normal and abnormal ovaries, these sometimes side by side on the same joint, it does not seem that there could be a genetic basis for the difference. In vegetative characters and also in unaffected flowers and fruits the plants are clearly variety *fusco-atra,* and we feel that *O. macateei* must be regarded as merely a diseased form of that species.

The cause of the diseased condition has not proved easy to isolate. While the determination of the causative agent does not have to be made in order to understand the plants, we have been working with specialists in order to try to locate it. A fungus was at once suspected, but so far it has been possible to culture no organism from the abnormal fruit tissues except some common *Aspergillis* and *Penicillium* forms. It seems hard to imagine that such common fungi could have such drastic effects upon the most common cactus of the area in only one such localized habitat. Yet the fungi are in the abnormal fruits. But might they not be merely taking advantage of a breakdown of the tissues due to something else?

A new factor appeared in the affected plants the next year which we must have overlooked the previous year. Many of the plants with abnormal fruits were found to be the hosts of a species of Lepidoptera. At fruiting time larvae approximately $3/4$ of an inch long were found in the hollowed-out centers of some of the enlarged fruits, one per fruit. While these fruits were under observation the larvae became ready for the pupal stage and burrowed out through the sides of the fruits, left the cacti, and climbed nearby perennial stems, where they pupated. The insects entered the winter in the pupal stage, but we were unable to rear any adults from the pupae we had collected, as all of our specimens died during the winter. These larvae left round holes in the sides of the fruits as they burrowed out of them, and holes of this type were found in some of the pads as well. Dissection showed that each larva had entered its fruit by tunneling into it from the pad, through the narrow base of the fruit. Some of the tunnels were traced through two pads before entering the fruits.

This Lepidoptera has not been encountered by us in any other instance in the cacti of Texas, and we find no record of it. It is impossible to find it in the cacti on any side of this thicket.

It was thought that this Lepidoptera might be the cause of the abnormality in the cactus, since the larvae were observed only in the pads and the elongated fruits of these abnormal specimens, but exactly how this may be is not clear, since only a small per cent of the elongated fruits contained any larvae. Many of them showed no sign of the insect. Furthermore, the unusual growth originates at least as early as the flower stage, affecting the ovary when still in the bud stage, and the larvae were not observed to enter any fruit until much later than that. The presence of the larvae in the lower parts of the plant causing the abnormal growth of ovary is however a possibility, and the fungi may enter the plants with the insects.

Be that as it may, *O. macateei* seems clearly only a diseased form of variety *fusco-atra,* representing one of the few cases where such a diseased form in cacti has been called a species.

Opuntia compressa var. grandiflora (Eng.)
"Large-Flowered Opuntia"

DESCRIPTION   PLATE 55

ROOTS: Entirely fibrous in all specimens observed, with no tubers present, but in a few specimens the main roots were found to $3/8$ of an inch in diameter and somewhat fleshy before branching.

STEMS: The plant is speading and semiprostrate, but with new pads standing perfectly erect their first year or sometimes until there are two pads upright, before falling over, giving a maximum height of sometimes 12 inches. The pads are egg-shaped to rather spindle-shaped, narrowing at the base or both above and below, 4 to 6 inches long by $2^{1}/_{2}$ to 4 inches wide. They are medium in thickness, the surface conspicuously tubercled by elevated areoles, and except in very wet seasons usually markedly wrinkled. In color the surface is bright green.

AREOLES: Small and elongated, to only $1/8$ of an inch long on young pads, becoming round and to $1/4$ of an inch on old pads. In position they are $1/2$ to 1 inch apart.

SPINES: None.

GLOCHIDS: Straw-colored, many and conspicuous, although short and in a tight bunch at first, becoming to $1/4$ of an inch long in a spreading cluster on old pads.

FLOWERS: Normally very large and beautiful, 4 to 5 inches in diameter and 3 to $3^{1}/_{2}$ inches tall, but they can be stunted and reduced to 2 inches in diameter when denied good growing conditions. In color they are yellow streaked at random with reddish markings or yellow with reddish centers. The inner petals are about 8 in number and 2 inches long by $1^{1}/_{2}$ inches wide on normal sized flowers. The ovary is 2 inches or more long and slender clubshaped. The stigma has 5 white, thick, grooved lobes.

FRUITS: About $2^{1}/_{2}$ inches long, very elongated club-shaped, being only $1/2$ to $3/4$ of an inch wide at the thickest upper part, with a prolonged constriction below. The top is somewhat pitted.

RANGE. Given originally as "on the Brazos" in Texas. The only specific location known seems to be that of our collection in Bastrop State Park, Bastrop County. This is on the Colorado River about 30 miles southeast of Austin, Texas. This is about 60 miles southwest of the Brazos River where it passes near Bryan, Texas, and, although we have not been able to collect it on the Brazos River, the range could be assumed to be from the Colorado River at Bastrop to the Brazos near Bryan. If the debatable assumption is followed that Engelmann's *O. intermedia* from Industry, Texas, is the same plant, this would extend the range only slightly farther southwest between the two rivers.

REMARKS. This is a truly beautiful cactus when its huge blooms appear. It has the largest flowers of any Opuntia in the southwest except *O. compressa* var. *allairei,* which sometimes equals it in cultivation but seems always to have much smaller flowers in the wild. It would seem it would be better known than it is. However, except for that week or two when it flowers each spring, it is an uninteresting, sprawling prickly pear and so is usually overlooked or even avoided. It is also far from widespread, and no doubt few people have ever seen its flowers.

We have been able to discover it growing only in the Bastrop State Park, where there are, however, numerous specimens. Accepting all we can of the early, general statements about its locations, we come up with a total range for it consisting of a triangle about 60 miles or less on each side between the Colorado and Brazos Rivers just east of Austin, Texas.

This is, no doubt, a very local form of the *O. compressa* complex, more robust in size of pads and flowers, but totally without spines. It is interesting to note that no description has been given by anyone of the seeds of this plant, although several have described the fruits. In 5 years of cultivation in my garden, during which time it has bloomed repeatedly, no fruit has ripened and no seed has been set. We wonder if it may be some sort of sterile hybrid propagated entirely by separated pads.

Engelmann's *O. intermedia* was very incompletely described, but had similar flowers and fruits, and everyone since his time has assumed it to be the same plant as his *O. grandiflora.* However, he said that *O. intermedia* was erect and ascending to several feet high, which has always cast a doubt upon the combination. No erect plant with this flower and fruit is known in the area. However, noticing that Engelmann says he thinks he saw his *O. intermedia* also near Natchitoches, which is in western Louisiana, in the area of the larger and more ascending *O. compressa* var. *allairei,* and finding that that plant can produce flowers and fruits identical to those of variety *grandiflora,* I would advance the theory that Engelmann's *O. intermedia* from Industry, Texas, was variety *grandiflora,* but that he tempered the description of it from his memory of the similar but larger and more ascending plant which grows in western Louisiana and which was named much later by Griffiths as *O. allairei.*

Opuntia compressa var. allairei (Gr.)

DESCRIPTION   PLATE 55

ROOTS: Tuberous, with clusters of spindle-shaped enlargements on the fibrous roots of all specimens we have examined.

STEMS: A spreading plant, the joints of which only recline on one edge when very old and send up sprawling branches of 2 to 4 pads to a height of 12 or even 18 inches. Pads elongated egg-shaped or spindle-shaped, thick and firm, not becoming flabby or wrinkled even when desiccated, the surface often somewhat tuberculate when growing but when older always becoming smooth and flat. The color is blue-green to sometimes rather yellow-green. The size of the pads is 4 to sometimes 8 inches long by 2 to $3^3/4$ inches wide.

AREOLES: Small and oval to round on young pads, increasing to round and $1/4$ of an inch across on old pads. They are spaced $1/2$ to $1^1/4$ inches apart.

SPINES: Often spineless, but some specimens having 1 spine each on perhaps half a dozen of the uppermost edge areoles. This spine is straight, $1/2$ to $1^1/4$ inches long, medium in thickness, round or slightly flattened, gray or whitish, and sometimes slightly annulate above, with a brownish base.

GLOCHIDS: Yellow, many, and conspicuous, to $1/4$ of an inch long, in a compact tuft, as is typical in this complex.

FLOWERS: Entirely yellow, yellow irregularly streaked with red, or yellow with red centers. Plants blooming in the field presented flowers about 3 inches across by $2^1/2$ inches tall, but the same plants after 2 years of cultivation produced identical flowers except $4^1/2$ to 5 inches in diameter and 3 inches tall. There were always 9 inner petals up to $2^1/2$ inches long and $1^1/2$ inches wide. The ovary was slender and elongated to 2 inches on the larger flowers. Stigma lobes varied from 4 to 7 in number, and were white or cream in color.

FRUITS: $1^3/4$ to $2^1/2$ inches long by $3/4$ to $7/8$ of an inch thick, elongated club-shaped, constricted at both top and bottom. At first they have some glochids on them, but these soon drop off. When ripe they are bright rose-plum in color, the pulp light red. The seeds are about $3/16$ of an inch (4–5 millimeters) in diameter, thick, with narrow rims.

RANGE. The extreme southeast corner of Texas and southwest corner of Louisiana. Specifically, along the east side of the Trinity River from the mouth of that stream to near Livingston, Texas, and east into Louisiana, perhaps, if Engelmann's remark is taken to indicate this plant, as far north as Natchitoches, and known to grow as far east as Marksville, Louisiana.

REMARKS. It is obvious that this cactus is closely related to variety *grandiflora,* but I was greatly surprised to find the flowers, which have never been described before, becoming identical with those huge flowers of that form when the plant was grown in the most favorable conditions in my garden. It is different from variety *grandiflora* only in details of the pads and in sometimes having a few spines, and for the fact that it grows more robust and more upright and does not have the same difficulty with its fruits, these ripening and forming seeds in profusion. But the two forms respond differently to the same growing conditions in my garden in San Antonio. While variety *allairei* prospers and sprawls all over the place, variety *grandi-*

flora in the same bed does not grow well and only the most careful treatment will keep it alive here.

I consider variety *allairei* to be the largest, most robust form of the O. *compressa* complex, at least in our area. It is very much like a large edition of the small eastern form in nearly every character, although its pads are always elongated and never so broad as the eastern form shows.

Variety *allairei* grows in that unique and beautiful southeast corner of Texas called the Big Thicket. Most people are very surprised to find a cactus growing in this densely wooded and humid area, but this cactus thrives there. It accomplishes this by growing in alkali spots which occur naturally in that area, where the trees and brush are held back by the alkaline, almost sterile soil. Here, in these natural clearings, one will often find this cactus happily growing among the coarse grasses which share these special habitats. While these special natural situations are usually widely scattered, the oil fields of the area are among the oldest in existence and have for many years poured out salty water upon the ground. The cactus has quickly taken advantage of the alkali tracts so produced by man, and among the ancient oil tools and rusting pipes of these old fields, as for instance around Batson, Texas, in Hardin County, one can find variety *allairei* growing in some profusion.

Going east into Louisiana there are few records of the cactus, but it has been seen near Leesville. McAtee's collection of it near Marksville is by far the most easterly, and establishes the presently known eastern limit of its range. As has been mentioned in the remarks on variety *grandiflora,* if we explain Engelmann's statement about remembering having seen his O. *intermedia* at Natchitoches, Louisiana, by assuming that he saw this plant, that would push variety *allairei*'s known range some 60 miles or so north of any other record.

Rose and McAtee both collected plants on the lower Texas coast which they called O. *allairei,* Rose's from Brownsville and McAtee's from Matagorda Island, but having examined their herbarium specimens of these plants, I do not believe we can consider them this variety. They seem rather to be robust specimens of variety *fusco-atra* as are found all along the lower Texas coast. There is still no record of variety *allairei* west of the Trinity River.

Opuntia compressa var. stenochila (Eng.)

DESCRIPTION   PLATE 56

ROOTS: Usually entirely fibrous, but sometimes with some spindle-shaped to oval tuberous thickenings on them.

STEMS: Low and prostrate, with older pads usually resting on the ground, but young pads temporarily ascending. In the spring this often results in a small clump of the young, ascending pads standing to 8 or even 10 inches tall, but during the winter these pads become flaccid and the whole thing is

entirely prostrate. The pads are usually 2¹/₂ to 4 but sometimes to 6 inches long, nearly round with only a slight constriction below to elongated oval or egg-shaped with very pronounced constriction below. These pads are of medium thickness to very thick, often ⁵/₈ of an inch thick, tuberculate when growing but then nearly smooth, except often very shrunken and wrinkled from lack of water or from winter cold. The color is a light grayish-green or yellowish-green with a dull surface.

AREOLES: Small and inconspicuous on young pads, becoming to almost ¹/₄ of an inch in diameter on old pads. They are spaced ¹/₂ to 1 inch apart.

SPINES: 1 to 4 in number in the areoles on the upper edge to the upper one-half of the pad only. There is in these upper, armed areoles one main central spine which is porrect or deflexed a little, 1 to 2¹/₄ inches long, slender to medium thickness, and round to somewhat flattened. Besides this there are usually 1 or 2 upper spines porrect or spreading upward, ³/₄ to 2¹/₄ inches long, of medium thickness, and always round, plus rarely 1 lower spine ³/₈ to 1¹/₈ inches long, deflexed, slender, and flattened. All spines are entirely white or gray, or sometimes gray with bases light brown or yellowish. Rarely the upper spines have darker brown bases or brown mottling.

GLOCHIDS: Yellow, greenish-yellow, or straw-colored, few to medium in number and short at first, increasing somewhat in number and length until rather conspicuous and to ³/₈ of an inch long on old pads.

FLOWERS: Light sulphur or greenish-yellow in color, 2¹/₂ to 4 inches in diameter. The ovary is a slender club about 1¹/₄ to 2 inches long. There are 10 inner petals. The stigma has 6 small white lobes.

FRUITS: Club-shaped with constricted and more or less elongated bases. The umbilicus is deeply pitted. In size they measure 1¹/₂ to 2¹/₂ inches long. They seeds are approximately ³/₁₆ of an inch (4–5 millimeters) in diameter, thick to very thick, with narrow rims.

RANGE. Common only in northwestern New Mexico and adjacent Arizona, but found in very scattered locations over most of the northern two-thirds of New Mexico and also collected a few times in the upper Texas Panhandle.

REMARKS. I have found in all herbarium collections I have examined some small, prostrate New Mexico Opuntias which do not quite fit the descriptions of O. *cymochila* or O. *compressa* var. *macrorhiza,* but which are usually placed in the folder of one or the other of these species that everyone expects to find in New Mexico. Many of these specimens are so incomplete that there is little way to prove what they are, but taking those which present fruits and seeds as well as pads, and lumping them together, one gets a rather homogeneous group of specimens. In living collections I have found the same plants growing, and finally, we have collected specimens with the same characters in a number of places in New Mexico, Arizona, and Texas.

I soon noticed that when I compiled the description of this body of plants I had thus brought together, it paralleled remarkably well Engelmann's old description of *O. stenochila.* The only aspects in which it exceeds the limits of that description are in the maximum length of spines found on some of my specimens and in the slightly smaller seeds on some than he gave for the species. When it is noticed that the majority of these maverick plants are from northwestern New Mexico, including some from just east of Zuni, which must be from very near the type locality of *O. stenochila* (it having been given as "canyon of Zuni, western New Mexico"), it becomes very convincing that here we have a collection of that long-lost cactus.

But if so, then why has the cactus been so long overlooked, and why are there no specimens called by this name in any collection except the type specimens? I think this goes back to Wooton and Standley. These men were the acknowledged authorities on New Mexico plants in the next generation after Coulter, and somehow they misunderstood this plant so much that they dismissed it by saying, "Known only from the original collection by Bigelow. We have seen no material of this species." And almost everyone since has been all too quick to take them at their word; so, since we see what we expect to see, whatever specimens of this cactus have been found since that time have been quickly assigned to *O. cymochila* or *O. compressa* var. *macrorhiza,* where they almost, but not quite, fit. Being more careful, Peebles erected a new species, *O. loomisii,* to take care of the Arizona specimens of this same cactus, and so the more western examples of it were dispersed in other folders.

But perhaps this is one place where we should pay attention to Britton and Rose. After and in spite of Wooton and Standley's statement about *O. stenochila,* they said, "It is the common low, spreading Opuntia of northwestern New Mexico and Arizona." I agree with them, and think that many herbarium specimens would be shifted out of folders where they don't quite look comfortable into the folder of this form if we regarded it as a plant we might expect to find and if the specimens collected were complete enough and well-enough preserved to show its differences from the other forms.

The cactus is obviously one of the *O. compressa* complex. Engelmann himself reduced it in a later writing from a separate species to a variety, and Coulter followed him. Its fruits are almost exactly like those of variety *macrorhiza,* both in shape and in the limits of their sizes. The seeds of the two forms are very nearly alike, and both may have either fibrous or tuberous roots. But variety *stenochila* presents yellow glochids and longer spines than are typical of variety *macrorhiza,* and its pads are gray or yellowish-green and dull, while those of variety *macrorhiza* are deep and shining green. The flowers are also different.

When the fruits are considered, it is immediately obvious that variety *stenochila* is not just a poorly armed *O. cymochila,* as its pads have led many to believe. Its long fruits with constricted bases and its thick, narrow-margined seeds show that it belongs with the *O. compressa* group.

If this is truly variety *stenochila,* then it is, as originally stated, a plant of northwest New Mexico. One may actually find it fairly easily in that area. It is my opinion that it spreads into Arizona, where it was described as *O. loomisii* by Peebles. He states that that plant comes into New Mexico, and I know of nothing else in this state to equal his description. However, the eastern limit of its range is very hard to define. I have the cactus collected in the Mescalero Sands. This is east of Roswell, and getting near the southeastern corner of New Mexico. I have also collected what must be this plant in Gray County, east of Pampa in the Texas Panhandle, which marks by far the easternmost known record of it.

Opuntia pottsii SD

DESCRIPTION   PLATE 56

ROOTS: Always having a large central taproot $3/4$ to $1^{1/2}$ inches in diameter and 6 inches to more than a foot long. This may be smooth and carrot-like or, in rocky ground, is often contorted and constricted here and there by the edges of rocks. Sometimes it subdivides into 2 or 3 fleshy branches, but it is not ever a tuberous, spherical, or spindle-shaped, potato-like enlargement on otherwise fibrous roots. When damaged this root slowly exudes a milky sap.

STEMS: Although small, this is basically an ascending plant with pads only touching the ground when extremely dehydrated or in their winter-shrunken condition. It appears not to root from the pads, so it is not mat-forming, but stands as a small clump of upright pads 6 to 12 inches tall from a central base which is often a short, cylindrical trunklet. The pads are $1^{1/2}$ to 5 inches long by 1 to 4 inches wide, almost round to elongated egg-shaped, with some constriction at the bases. They are thin or medium thickness, the surface flat without raised areoles. In color it is glaucous blue-green, often purplish around the areoles when young and healthy, but fading to yellow-green when old or unhealthy. The leaves of this plant are extremely tiny, being around $1/8$ of an inch long.

AREOLES: To only $1/8$ of an inch long on young pads, but becoming to $1/4$ of an inch in diameter on old pads. They are spaced $3/8$ to 1 inch apart.

SPINES: Having spines on only the upper edge or at most the upper one-third of the pad. These upper areoles have 1 to 3 spines which are straight although usually twisted and rather slender. They may be round or flattened or sometimes ridged, and are whitish, gray, or sometimes gray mottled with tan, or brownish. There will be 1 or 2 upper spines 1 to $2^{1/2}$ inches long, deflexed or spreading, plus sometimes 1 lower, very deflexed spine ¹/₂ to 1 inch long. The plant has been said to be occasionally spineless, but I have not seen such a specimen.

GLOCHIDS: Greenish-yellow to dirty straw-colored, usually rather numerous in compact clusters, ¹/₈ to sometimes ¹/₄ of an inch long on old pads.

FLOWERS: Brilliant purplish or rose-red and very beautiful. 2 to 2³/₄ inches in diameter and 2¹/₂ to 3 inches tall. The ovary is very slender and 1 to 2 inches long, with some glochids on it. There are about 7 or 8 inner petals. The filaments are green below and yellowish above, the anthers bright yellow. The style is pinkish and the stigma lobes cream-colored, fat and velvety, and 5 to 7 in number.

FRUITS: 1¹/₂ to 2 inches long, slender club-shaped, being only ³/₄ of an inch in diameter at the upper, widest part above the slender, attenuated base. The apex is deeply pitted. When ripening, they become light red. The seeds are about ³/₁₆ of an inch or a little larger (4–5¹/₂ millimeters) in diameter in my observation, although Coulter says 3¹/₂ to 4 millimeters. These seeds are thick—Engelmann says they are the thickest of the Opuntias. The rims are of medium width, blunt instead of acute, and irregular.

RANGE. From Chihuahua, Mexico, north past El Paso and through the western part of the Big Bend into the Davis Mountains of Texas and on into southeastern New Mexico. Known to be found in the southern Guadalupe Mountains and to extend in New Mexico at least as far north as Caprock and Roswell.

REMARKS. This cactus is very close to the O. *compressa* group and more study may show that it should be included in it, but the step seems premature with no more than our present knowledge. At any rate, it has very distinct differences from any of the varieties of that group. It was first described from Chihuahua specimens by Prince Salm-Dyck. Engelmann redescribed it from Texas collections, calling it O. *filipendula*. Once it was determined by Britton and Rose that these two were the same, there has been little confusion over this species.

The cactus appears at a glance much like O. *compressa* var. *macrorhiza*, until one notices the more blue-green, glaucous coloring and the fact that, although it is no taller than the other plant, O. *pottsii* is not a fully prostrate, diffuse thing rooting and spreading from chains of pads on the ground, but a compact plant ascending from one center by many upright or sprawling pads. The spination is similar, each plant having either round or flattened spines on only the upper areoles, but O. *pottsii* has more slender and usually longer spines, although never reaching the maximum number found in some specimens of variety *macrorhiza* and always lacking the lower bristles often found on that other cactus. If one digs up the plants, he will find there an obvious difference between the two forms. The root of O. *pottsii* is always a central taproot extension of the thick, trunklike stem which often goes without interruption and

with very little taper up to a foot into the ground. It is basically different from the globular to spindle-shaped tubers often found on the fibrous roots of the O. *compressa* forms. There is also a striking difference in the leaves of this plant, those of O. *pottsii* being very tiny, while those of all forms of O. *compressa* examined in this study are 3 or 4 times as large. But when the beautiful purplish or rose-red flowers of O. *pottsii* appear one really appreciates the difference between the two plants. These are certainly some of the most beautiful flowers found among the Opuntias.

O. *pottsii* was reported by Anthony from western Brewster County in the Big Bend, although I have been unable to recollect it there. Dr. Rose collected it "in the valley of the Rio Grande below El Paso, Texas," and Engelmann's specimens were from near Dona Ana and San Elizario in the El Paso area, but I have seen no recent specimens from that locality. Engelmann said it was growing there on alluvial prairies, and in looking for likely spots, I found that almost everything there which might be described at all by the term of alluvial prairies is now a part of the city, in cultivation and irrigation, or otherwise developed, so I wonder if the cactus may not have been eliminated around El Paso by the developments.

The cactus does seem to be strictly a resident of alluvial flats. It still grows along stream beds in the Davis Mountains of Texas. Engelmann's statement that the eastern boundary of its range was the Limpia was correct. This is a creek in the eastern part of the Davis Mountains, and the plant has not been recorded from east of it in Texas. Nor does his additional statement of "El Paso and eastward on the Pecos," contradict this. It does not mean on the lower Pecos, as many have thought. Limpia Creek runs north out of the mountains into the Pecos River just below the town of Pecos, Texas, and the cactus occurs to the Pecos only above this point. Farther north it enters New Mexico, to be found in the creek valleys of the southeasternmost part of the Guadalupe Mountains and east across the Pecos to at least as far north and east as Caprock, New Mexico. If the New Mexico herbarium material usually labeled O. *ballii* were considered as this plant, as some think it should be, then the range would extend over all of the southeastern corner of New Mexico and along the eastern boundary of that state to Logan on the Canadian River.

Besides certain morphological differences, there is an ecological reason why I hesitate to lump these northern specimens with the Texas O. *pottsii*. There has been, in the past few years, a marked die-off of the O. *pottsii* population in the Davis Mountains, which has become so bad that in our old collecting spot north of Alpine, Texas (where a few years ago we could count dozens of healthy specimens), in 1966 I failed to find one remaining example. The preceding few winters had been very severe, setting new low temperature records for the area. Dr. Warnock, botanist at Sul Ross State College in Alpine, states that most specimens of this cactus in the area were killed by this unusual cold. Remembering that this is a Chihuahuan species restricted to alluvial bottoms in the south of its range and noting this evidence of tenderness in the plant, I wonder if it can be the same plant which grows rather profusely in the very severe conditions of the eastern New Mexico mountains and plains. Statements by those who have observed many of the plants growing far up in eastern New Mexico that they bloom yellow as well as red and often have tuberous roots instead of the typical taproot add to my doubts about them. Further study of these plants is needed to determine whether we have in them a transitional form bridging the gap between *O. pottsii* and the *O. compressa* complex or whether they are something entirely different.

The specimens definitely known to be *O. pottsii* show us a rather strange little Opuntia with beautiful flowers. While it grows over a rather good-sized area, it seems always to be far from common anywhere. It is an easy cactus to grow, in my experience, not being harmed by moisture as easily as are some others. Perhaps this is because it grows naturally in valleys instead of upon the more dry hills and ledges.

Opuntia ballii Rose

DESCRIPTION   PLATE 56

ROOTS: According to Rose, "somewhat tuberous." In our observation a large specimen had small, spindle-shaped tubers upon the fibrous roots, but plants started as cuttings from the original had not developed tubers upon their roots in several years' growth.

STEMS: Prostrate and spreading. The pads are 2³⁄₈ to 4 inches long, almost circular to broadly egg-shaped, very thick for their size, pale yellowish-green and glaucous, the surface entirely smooth without raised areoles.

AREOLES: Small, nearly round.

SPINES: 2 to 4 in number on most or all areoles. There are 1 to 3 main spines spreading upward or erect, 1¹⁄₂ to 2³⁄₄ inches long, plus 1 lower, deflexed, and much shorter spine. All spines are straw or pale brownish in color, heavy, very rigid, straight, and a little flattened.

GLOCHIDS: Very conspicuous, each areole having a great, compact mass of bright yellow glochids ¹⁄₄ to ¹⁄₂ inch long.

FLOWERS: Small, 1¹⁄₂ to about 2 inches across and about 2 inches tall, deep rose-red. The ovary is about 1¹⁄₄ inches long and very narrow club-shaped or almost linear, with very few yellow glochids in the areoles. The outer perianth segments have green midlines, the smaller ones shading to flesh-colored on the edges, the larger ones to burnt-orange pinkish on the edges. There are about 6 inner segments about 1 inch long and wide, with blunt ends notched at the apex. The base and most of each inner segment shade from old red through deep rose-red, the edges and tips cerise. The filaments are green at

the base, then cream-colored, the anthers cream. The style is short and whitish. The stigma has 5 cream-colored, fat, and thick lobes.

FRUITS: Small and very slender, ³⁄₄ to 1¹⁄₄ inches long, very narrow club-shaped, being only ¹⁄₄ of an inch thick at the center of the widest part, with greatly constricted bases and rather narrowed, pitted umbilici. They are spineless. The seeds are slightly over ¹⁄₈ of an inch (about 3¹⁄₂ millimeters) broad, and thick for their size.

RANGE. According to Dr. Rose, "the dry mesa beyond Pecos, Texas."

REMARKS. This remarkable little cactus was found and described by Dr. Rose in 1911. He gave for its type location Pecos, Reeves County, Texas.

Almost immediately after Rose described the species, Wooton said it was common in New Mexico, and later Wooton and Standley referred it to *O. filipendula* (*O. pottsii*) as a synonym. Dr. Rose had opportunity to publish a rebuttal and did so, stressing that *O. ballii* grows in a different habitat, has smaller fruits, stouter and more erect spines, and different areoles than that plant.

There thus arose a disagreement about this cactus which has continued until this day. Some students, influenced by Wooton, have expected to find it in New Mexico. We often convince ourselves that we have found what we expect to find, at least to our own satisfaction, and the New Mexico herbarium contains a whole series of plants labeled *O. ballii*, specifically from Eunice, Tatum, Caprock, Texico, near Tucumcari, and near Logan, New Mexico. If these are correctly assigned, the cactus extends its range all up along the eastern edge of the state.

I have studied the cacti growing in all of these areas as much as possible during a long search for the true *O. ballii*, collecting most of them in the field rather than relying on the herbarium specimens. The plants growing west of Tucumcari seem clearly to be *O. compressa* var. *macrorhiza*, which might be expected there, since I have collected it within less than one hundred miles both southeast and northwest of this location. The Logan specimens are too incomplete to identify certainly, and I was unable to find the plant growing in that area today. The Texico plants are quite certainly *O. cymochila*, which grows in profusion there. The Caprock specimens appear to be *O. pottsii*, which I have collected myself near Caprock. In short, I have found no New Mexican specimens under this name which seemed to me to be actually *O. ballii*, and most of them seemed clearly other forms.

But the plant was originally described from Texas, and Britton and Rose long ago denied New Mexico the plant in restating its range to be west Texas. What was the plant they actually collected near Pecos?

When I examined Rose's own specimens it immediately seemed clear to me that his was a different cactus, not only from *O. pottsii*, but from all those collected and labeled *O. ballii* in

New Mexico. His specimens are easy to recognize by their long, heavy spines, their yellow glochids mostly to ¹/₂ inch long, and very nearly the longest found on any Opuntia, as well as by their very small fruits. None of these characters are shared by *O. pottsii* or by any New Mexico plants I have seen, to say nothing of the difference in roots between *O. pottsii* and this plant. I became persuaded that we have here a unique small cactus perhaps not found outside of the Pecos area of west Texas. And there is only one sign of its ever having been seen again since Rose's original collection. There is in the Southern Methodist University herbarium a single unlabeled specimen which seems clearly to be this plant. It was collected by Warnock 22 miles northwest of Pecos, Texas. What was needed was the rediscovery of the thing itself so we could know more about it.

I made repeated trips to Reeves County and spent days scouring all of the region I could, but perhaps the most frustrating experience of this study has been the failure to relocate *O. ballii*. There is a large amount of dry mesa, and it must still be there, but also much of the area is now irrigated and farmed, and it may have been largely eradicated.

I had given up hope of ever seeing the cactus alive, when one day I was looking over the very interesting cactus gardens of Mr. Clark Champie, the widely known cactus student and dealer of Anthony, New Mexico-Texas. Mr. Champie began showing me some plants he could not identify, and there it was! Its small, thick, very light green pads with their very heavy spines often as long as the pads themselves and the brilliant yellow glochids so profuse and so long in each areole were unlike anything I had seen before. The tiny fruits less than an inch long in many cases and no thicker than a lead pencil were complete confirmation. Each fruit contained a dozen or so seeds hardly over ¹/₈ of an inch in diameter, but very thick.

So I have seen *O. ballii* alive, have my own cutting of it, and, thanks to Mr. Champie, am able to present a photograph of it, but still I can tell no more about where it grows than Rose's statement. Mr. Champie says that this plant was given to him some 8 or 10 years ago by a fellow cactophile who didn't remember where it was collected beyond the fact that it was in west Texas. This may very well be the only specimen of this interesting species living today. To those who might be intrigued and want to try to find it, I can say nothing more than for them to try the dry mesa beyond Pecos, Texas, and good luck! It must be there somewhere.

Opuntia plumbea Rose

DESCRIPTION   PLATE 56

ROOTS: Having a very unusual underground structure consisting of what appears to be a fleshy rhizome rather than a root. This structure is ¹/₂ inch or a little more in diameter, and runs horizontally just under the ground, giving off pads at intervals of 4 to 8 inches along its length. It has been observed with a total length of about 4 feet. Fibrous roots are produced from this apparent rhizome.

STEMS: Plants ascending at the point of each sprouting from the underground stem, but not standing over 1 or 2 pads high. These pads are almost circular to broadly egg-shaped and 1¹/₄ to 2¹/₂ inches long. They soon develop into a cluster of small pads standing to only 4 inches or so high but in time becoming to 8 or 12 inches across at each growing point. These separate clusters finally meet at their edges to form a more or less solid mat of pads up to several feet across. The pads are rather thin and the surface somewhat tuberculate by raised areoles. The color of the surface is very glaucous, dull blue-gray, sometimes described as lead-colored.

AREOLES: Large for the size of the pads, being oval and ³/₁₆ of an inch or so long, spaced ³/₈ to ¹/₂ inch apart.

SPINES: 1 to 4, but usually 2 in number, found in upper areoles of the pads only. They are gray in color, more or less mottled with pale brown. There is one main spine porrect or slightly deflexed, which is 1 to 1⁷/₈ inches long, slender, straight, and round, or nearly so, although sometimes slightly flattened at the base. Sometimes also present will be 1 or 2 upper spines standing porrect, or practically so, 1 to 2 inches long, slender, straight, and round. There may be also 1 lower deflexed spine ¹/₂ to 1¹/₄ inches long.

GLOCHIDS: There are conspicuous, bright, red-brown glochids in all areoles. They are in compact clusters and are ¹/₈ to ³/₁₆ of an inch long.

FLOWERS: Small, being 1¹/₂ inches or so long and wide, purplish in color. The ovary is less than 1 inch long, but fairly broad. The stigmas are white.

FRUITS: Small, being ⁵/₈ to ⁷/₈ of an inch long and broadly pear-shaped with pitted umbilici. The seeds are slightly over ¹/₈ of an inch (3¹/₂–4 millimeters) in diameter.

RANGE. The San Carlos Indian Reservation in Arizona and the edge of New Mexico west of Silver City.

REMARKS. Dr. Rose described this strange little cactus from a collection made on the San Carlos Indian Reservation of Arizona in 1904. The plant must be very rare, as there is no record of its ever having been seen again in Arizona. More recent works have generally ignored it or else submerged it as a synonym of *O. compressa* var. *macrorhiza*. It has never been considered a New Mexico plant.

Mr. Clark Champie of Anthony, New Mexico-Texas, who has a fine cactus collection, has a strange Opuntia which he has kept because of its uniqueness. He had had it for about 5 years when I first saw it, during which time it had spread in a most unusual, linear manner. When he transplanted it he was surprised to find that it had in this time developed a long, rhizome-like structure which, growing horizontally, was at that time nearly 3 feet long. It was observed that this structure had sprouted a series of pads at intervals of about 6 inches all along its length, each of these points in time forming a new growing center with numerous pads in a cluster. Since planted in the ground this cactus has continued the elongation of this underground structure, with new growth centers from it.

The manner of growth which results is rather well described by Rose's word, "creeping," in his description of O. *plumbea*. This is a term which Rose used concerning no other prostrate cactus and which I take to mean specifically the creeping, spreading growth outward which results in this cactus from these peculiar underground growths. I know of only one other cactus in the U. S. Southwest with a similar creeping and sprouting underground structure. This is O. *arenaria*, whose underground part has areoles with many glochids all over it. These are lacking on this plant, and the two cacti are different in almost all other respects.

Mr. Champie's strange cactus has small pads of a dull, bluish-gray color, long slender spines, and conspicuous, bright, red-brown glochids. It blooms with a small purplish flower and has small though broad fruits less than 1 inch long. It fits perfectly Rose's description of O. *plumbea,* and we are certain it is that long-lost plant. The specimen in Mr. Champie's garden was presented to him by a collector who gave little detail of the location of its collection, saying only that he found it in New Mexico somewhere west of Silver City. Although we have been unsuccessful in collecting it ourselves, I feel obliged to list it here as a species probably growing in New Mexico. Since I cannot give the exact location of it, I realize that this does not constitute an actual record in the strict scientific sense; however, I feel it is important to tell of this apparent instance of the plant in our area in the hope that it will stimulate someone to re-collect it and give us an exact location for it.

Opuntia drummondii Graham
   "Crow-Foot Prickly Pear," "Cock-Spur Cactus," "Cockle-Burr Cactus," "Sand-Burr Cactus"

DESCRIPTION   PLATE 57
   ROOTS: Either entirely fibrous or often having several oval tubers up to 2^1/$_2$ inches long and 1^1/$_2$ inches thick upon these roots.

   STEMS: A very prostrate and diffuse cactus, forming mats from 1 to sometimes at least 15 feet across, but hardly over 4 or 5 inches high, as all older pads lie on the ground. The pads are broadly oblong to elongated club-shaped, 1 to 4^1/$_2$ inches long by 1 to 2^1/$_4$ inches wide. They are often ^{3}/$_4$ of an inch and sometimes even 1 inch thick, young joints being almost globular. The surface is smooth, without raised areoles when well-watered. They shrink and wrinkle when dry, but can never be described as tuberculate. They are deep green with darker, bluish coloring around the areoles, becoming

lighter green when old. These pads are very loosely articulated, coming off the plant at a touch.

   AREOLES: Round or oval, ^{1}/$_8$ to ^{3}/$_{16}$ of an inch in diameter, ^{3}/$_8$ to ^{3}/$_4$ of an inch apart.

   SPINES: There are 1 to 4 straight spines on almost all areoles or often on upper edge areoles only. There is 1 porrect spine ^{1}/$_2$ to 1^1/$_2$ inches long, flattened, twisted, and of medium thickness. There may be 1 or 2 upper spines 1 to 1^5/$_8$ inches long and round in shape. Sometimes there is 1 lower spine ^{1}/$_4$ to ^{3}/$_4$ of an inch long, slender, round or flattened, deflexed or porrect. At first these spines are light brown, but they soon fade to gray with the tips remaining clear yellow or else becoming blackish.

   GLOCHIDS: Greenish-yellow or bright straw-colored, ^{1}/$_8$ to ^{1}/$_4$ of an inch long, average number to many, in compact clusters.

   FLOWERS: Clear lemon to greenish-yellow, sometimes with a slightly deeper yellow coloring in the center. They are 2^1/$_2$ to 3 inches in diameter. The ovary is ^{7}/$_8$ to 1 inch long, with a few short, red glochids on it. There are 8 inner petals. The filaments are orange, the anthers yellow. The stamens are very sensitive, moving at a touch. The stigma has 5 or 6 thick, yellow or slightly greenish-yellow lobes.

   FRUITS: Light red when ripe, club-shaped, with some constriction below and a shallow to rather deeply pitted umbilicus at the top. These fruits are 1 to 1^1/$_2$ inches long by ^{1}/$_2$ to ^{5}/$_8$ of an inch thick at the thickest point. The seeds are not quite ^{3}/$_{16}$ of an inch (about 4 millimeters) in diameter, regular, and rather thick, with rather narrow and blunt rims.

RANGE. Previously known from the beach areas of North Carolina through Florida to Alabama. It is known to grow in our area only in a strip a mile or so long near the tip of Bolivar Peninsula, in front of Galveston Bay. Perhaps it also grows in Louisiana.

REMARKS. I had been told by Mr. H. C. Lawson, the San Antonio cactus dealer so well known during more than 30 years of business, about the strange little prickly pear which grew on the Bolivar Peninsula directly across the pass from Galveston. I had repeatedly failed to locate it myself, and had about concluded that it had been eliminated by the developments which that area has undergone through the years. Then Mr. Glenn Spraker, a collector in Houston, told me of such a cactus which his father-in-law, Mr. Herman McGowan, had noticed during fishing trips on the peninsula. These men were so kind as to take me to the cactus, and it turned out to be O. *drummondii*, previously unknown in Texas.

The reason I had not found it earlier is that it grows only on the bay side of the peninsula from about Baffle Point toward the tip of the peninsula. This narrow strip is perhaps the highest part of the peninsula, but since the Intracoastal Canal was dredged down the length of the peninsula, it is entirely separated by this canal from the major part of the peninsula. It now forms a long, slender island not over ¹/₄ mile wide and totally uninhabited except by cattle, so anyone going to hunt this cactus has to have the interesting experience of hunting cactus by boat, since there is no other way to get to this island.

Once having gotten there, the collector will find the highest part of this strip to be almost covered by mats of *O. drummondii.* The small pads are flat on the very sandy ground or even partly covered by blowing sand. With the sparse grass growing up even higher through the cactus mats, they are almost impossible to see until one is within a few feet. And if a person fails entirely to notice them and makes the mistake of stepping into the mat of them, his foot comes up with sometimes half a dozen pads pulled loose and firmly stuck by their spines into his shoes, his trousers and, if he is little less fortunate, into his ankles. With its pads so loosely held, this cactus must be a constant hitchhiker on the legs of animals. It is well named the sand-burr cactus. Its adaptation for animal dispersal is probably even more cruel than that of the sand-burr or cockle-burr. However, no doubt the pads are broken off and distributed wholesale by storm tides as well, as there were unmistakable signs that the last hurricane had swept large logs across this ridge.

Although very common on and near beaches of the southeastern part of the U.S., *O. drummondii* has not been reported before in Texas. It is interesting, but probably fruitless to speculate upon how it happens to be growing here, so far west of Alabama, its previous definitely known western limit. This location in Texas is at the point where ships enter Galveston Bay and where more recently barges and boats come by constantly after having traveled west along the Intracoastal Waterway. It is not hard to imagine pads of this cactus moving west with them, but there is no evidence of this, and if it happened, it was long ago, as a large area is covered with this cactus now.

A specimen which appears to be *O. drummondii* is in the U.S. National Museum, collected, according to the almost illegible label, in 1910, by McAtee at Caudwerdee(?), Louisiana. I have not been able to find this location, but this raises the possibility that the plant grows somewhere along the coast of Louisiana.

This cactus was regarded by Coulter as very close to the eastern, typical form of *Opuntia compressa,* and it does have similarities, particularly of flower, fruit, and seed to that cactus. It is like the *O. compressa* group also in often having tuberous roots, but in thickness of pads it surpasses all of those forms.

Britton and Rose, on the other hand, in devising their series within the genus *Opuntia,* set up the series *Curassavicae,* made up of a number of small cacti from the West Indies characterized by fragile branches which separate at a touch, and naturally put this cactus into that series, thus separating it entirely from the *O. compressa* complex, whose pads have to be twisted off. However, this character seems a doubtful one upon which to erect a series. The looseness of joints is shared by a number of other cacti described for the U.S. One is *O. tracyi* Britt., which grows on the coast from Florida to Mississippi, and which seems very

close to *O. drummondii.* Another is *O. nemoralis* Gr., from northeast Texas, which would seem to be a typical *O. compressa* var. *humifusa* except for this feature. It has not been seen since its first description and nothing appears today in its area except variety *humifusa,* which makes it, in our estimation, of doubtful validity. A third is *O. fragilis* of northwest Texas and New Mexico and far into the north. However, even though this cactus has similar loose pads, it has dry fruits, and so Britton and Rose place it into another series entirely. *O. schottii,* a *Cornyopuntia* of south Texas has this character, and of course there are various of the large chollas, such as *O. tunicata* and *O. fulgida* featuring this. It seems to be a feature running through many major segments of the genus and not one upon which any major divisions of the group should be made.

Opuntia fragilis (Nutt.) Haw.
"Brittle Cactus," "Fragile Prickly Pear"

DESCRIPTION   PLATE 57

ROOTS: Fibrous.

STEMS: A low-growing cactus almost completely prostrate or with spreading branches rising to only 6 or 8 inches high, but forming very dense mats up to a foot or two in diameter. The joints begin as almost globular outgrowths up to ¹/₂ or even ⁵/₈ of an inch in diameter. In growing, they first elongate, reaching to 1 or 1¹/₂ inches long without broadening, so they are at this stage almost cylindrical. If the plant is not robust its whole growth may remain like this, but if it is situated so that it can proceed fully, these joints then begin broadening until they become small, very thick pads 1¹/₂ to 2 inches long by ³/₄ to 1¹/₄ inches wide by about ⁵/₈ of an inch thick. These joints are very loosely attached and separate at a touch. They are often very wrinkled and flaccid.

AREOLES: Small to medium size, with some white wool when young, situated about ³/₈ to ¹/₂ inch apart.

SPINES: 1 to sometimes at least 7, spreading, fairly stout, round or nearly so, and ¹/₄ to 1 inch long. They are whitish with darker tips or straw-colored when matured, but dark brown when growing.

GLOCHIDS: Very few and short, and yellowish in color.

FLOWERS: Clear yellow, sometimes with orange centers. They are up to about 2 inches in diameter. The stamens are yellowish. The stigma has 4 to 6 green stigma lobes. The ovary is small and almost spherical.

FRUITS: Oval or egg-shaped, ¹/₂ to 1 inch long, with pitted flower scars. They have some short spines on the upper areoles and become dry when ripe. The seeds are large, around ¹/₄ of an inch (5–7 millimeters) in diameter, flat, with broad, irregular rims.

RANGE. Extreme northern New Mexico into Colorado and Utah,

and extreme northwestern Texas across the Oklahoma Panhandle and on into Kansas. It is found at various scattered locations throughout the northwestern U.S. from Wisconsin to Washington and on far into Canada.

REMARKS. *O. fragilis* is the first of our dry-fruited Opuntias—that is, those in which the fruits become dry and their walls papery instead of juicy and pulpy when ripe—for us to study. These cacti have another character in common, the possession of green stigma lobes in the flowers. If one is fortunate enough to see both their flowers and fruits these two characters make them easy to know, but as some of them bloom and fruit very sparingly, most people see their vegetative parts only, and some of them are rather hard to recognize from just these parts.

O. fragilis grows in very sandy soil, and anyone who has tried to treat it to the same soil and extreme heat as he does most other cacti will find it is fragile indeed. It just will not grow in the typical hot desert situation or in heavy soil. But it is not fragile in regard to cold. It is one of our most northern cacti, said to grow in Canada almost to the arctic circle. Of course, its name comes from its loosely articulated joints, which are dislodged by a touch and which some say can even be loosened and distributed by the wind. A person or an animal, not seeing the low mat of these little pads, often steps away with pads securely stuck to clothing or fur—or flesh—to be shaken off later and to root wherever they fall.

One seeing the cactus only in the form it takes when less than robust might never think of it as a prickly pear, but as some sort of tiny cylindrical jointed cactus. However, when growing well, the joints broaden into thick, but definitely flattened little pads up to 2 inches long. The flowers and fruits are not well known because it does not flower at all unless very well situated, often relying upon the scattering of the little joints to propagate it for years at a time before every factor of season and soil pleases it and it blooms. For this reason it rarely blooms in cultivation.

This strange little northern cactus just enters the edge of our southwestern area, living only in extreme northern New Mexico and the panhandles of Oklahoma and Texas. Here its locations are not numerous and are very scattered. In Texas it can occasionally be found in the sandy breaks along the Canadian River north of Amarillo. There once was a good population of it along the railroad right-of-way northeast of Amarillo, but this is apparently all gone now, wiped out in the last few years, perhaps by the herbicides now used on such right-of-ways. Although I lived two years in the Oklahoma Panhandle and was in the field over much of that area, I know of no place where it grows there except on the Black Mesa, that remarkable formation in the extreme northwest corner of the state. It appears from old accounts that the cactus may have been more widespread in the past in the Oklahoma and Texas panhandles, but it is my theory that it has been practically eliminated by the farming which has been practiced on almost all of that area, or where there has not

been farming, by the drifting sand of the dust-bowl days. It would have been limited to the most sandy areas, the very areas where drifts sometimes covered automobiles and reached the eaves of buildings, and these would surely have covered and smothered this tiny cactus. Wherever we find this northern cactus in our area it is just the extreme southern extension of its range, and we get the feeling that it is not really one of ours, but merely one whose little pads have been carried in on who knows what animal's pelt and which is at best just hanging on with us. As treacherous as it is, we are not sure whether we wish it luck or not.

Engelmann received specimens from near Inscription Rock in northwestern New Mexico which he thought a different plant and named *O. brachyarthra*. Coulter made this a variety of the species, although saying that whether it should even stand as a distinct variety seemed doubtful to him. Britton and Rose considered it merely a synonym of the species. Boissevain, in his study of Colorado cacti, says that all of the specimens on the western slopes of the Continental Divide are more robust than those on the eastern side and that these western plants fit the description of Engelmann's plant, so he calls the whole western population *O. fragilis* var. *brachyarthra*. But upon examining specimens from Inscription Rock, we do not find constant enough differences from the more eastern specimens, in our opinion, to justify the variety.

Opuntia sphaerocarpa Eng.

DESCRIPTION   PLATE 57

ROOTS: Mostly tuberous, with small, oblong or spindle-shaped tubers on the fibrous roots, but sometimes lacking these and remaining entirely fibrous.

STEMS: A low, diffuse, and mostly prostrate plant with only the new pads temporarily upright. The pads are round or even wider than they are long to sometimes very broadly egg-shaped, $2^{1}/_{2}$ to 4 inches long and $2^{1}/_{2}$ to $3^{1}/_{2}$ inches wide. These pads are average thickness to thick, tuberculate by raised areoles, soft, shrinking to become very wrinkled when water is scarce or especially in the winter. They are bright green when young, fading to a somewhat lighter green when old, and often suffused with purplish coloring in the winter.

AREOLES: Elongated in shape, tiny or very small, $1/_8$ of an inch or less long on the sides of the pads, becoming oval, but hardly larger on the edges. They are $1/_4$ to $3/_4$ of an inch apart.

SPINES: Only upper edge areoles are armed. These have typically 1 to 3 spines consisting of 1 central which is deflexed, $1/_4$ to $1^{1}/_{2}$ inches long, slender to medium thickness, and flattened; sometimes 1 upper spine which is porrect, $1/_2$ to $1^{1}/_{2}$ inches long, slender to medium thickness, and round; plus occasionally 1 or 2 lower, much deflexed, slender spines, 3/16 to 1/2 inch long. The larger spines are brown or reddish-brown mottled above with tan or whitish. The lower, slender spines are gray with dark tips.

GLOCHIDS: Very few and short in a compact clump in each areole on the sides of the pads, becoming somewhat more numerous and longer to 3/16 of an inch on the edges. They are yellow to dirty straw-colored.

FLOWERS: Greenish-yellow, sometimes with some brownish coloring in their centers, 2 inches in diameter by 1 1/2 to 2 1/4 inches tall. The ovary is very broad club-shaped, 3/4 to 1 1/2 inches long, with some tan glochids on it. There are 7 or 8 inner petals. The stamens are cream or yellowish. The style is long and greenish, with 5 fat, bright green lobes making up the stigma.

FRUITS: Perfectly spherical to somewhat oval, 3/4 to 1 3/8 inches long and wide. The umbilicus is very broad and either flat or only very shallowly pitted. Having short white wool and many tan glochids up to 1/8 of an inch long in the areoles, but spineless. This fruit becomes dry, brown, and papery when ripe, but does this very slowly. It typically remains yellowish-green all summer and only dries the following winter. The seeds are just over 3/16 of an inch (5 millimeters) in diameter, irregular in shape, rather thick with narrow, acute rims.

RANGE. The Sandia Mountains east of Albuquerque, New Mexico, through the Jicarilla Mountains west of Capitan, New Mexico, to the Sierra Blanca Mountains north of Ruidosa, New Mexico.

REMARKS. This seems to have been one of the most sadly misunderstood of all cacti, and as a result it is almost unknown today. Being impressed by the fact that it is supposed to have dry, spherical fruits, many have seized upon any plant from the Sandia Mountains with such fruits as representing this species. But they forget that *O. polyacantha* is specifically stated by the original description to sometimes have spherical fruits, and that these can sometimes be almost spineless. As a result I have seen numerous herbarium specimens of *O. polyacantha* with round fruits called *O. sphaerocarpa*. Taking this one step farther, there have even been attempts to call this a variety of *O. polyacantha*. Such a mistake should not have been made, in view of Engelmann's very specific statement to forestall the confusion of these two. In his original description of *O. sphaerocarpa* he states that this form lacks the numerous small, bristle-like spines of *O. polyacantha,* which distinction will swiftly cull out the examples of *O. polyacantha* erroneously called this species. We have here a cactus with 1 to at most 4 spines, while *O. polyacantha* has always a total of 5 to 18 spines per fully armed areole.

The above error has so completely persuaded most students to regard *O. sphaerocarpa* as some sort of variation of *O. polyacantha* that Britton and Rose, for instance, describe it as light green in color like that other species. This has blinded most to the

idea that there might be another cactus in the Sandias and nearby mountains having round, dry fruits, but being by comparison almost spineless and bright green when in healthy color. Add to this the lamentable tendency to call any bright green, prostrate, sparsely spined, tuberous-rooted cactus found anywhere *O. compressa* var. *macrorhiza*, and the true *O. sphaerocarpa* has remained unknown for most of the time since its original description. Nor is it any wonder that it is often mistaken for *O. compressa* var. *macrorhiza*, which is also found within its range. Stumbling upon a cactus in central New Mexico having prostrate, bright green, fleshy, tuberculate, and often wrinkled pads, 1 to 4 spines more or less flattened on upper areoles only, and usually tuberous roots, almost anyone would call it that cactus. It keys out to that in any key I have seen that uses vegetative characters only. I called it that myself when I first collected it.

But then I saw it bloom, and I got a distinct surprise, for it had too short an ovary, and standing there in plain sight were bright green stigma lobes! No *O. compressa* var. *macrorhiza* of the hundreds I had seen flower ever had other than yellowish or whitish stigmas. So I watched this cactus closely, and when the fruits formed they were as round as marbles or at least very broadly oval with no constriction below and with the umbilici very broad and flat. I now knew that this could not be variety *macrorhiza*, which always has extremely elongated, club-shaped, constricted fruits, with deeply pitted umbilici.

What could this cactus be? All summer, as its fruits remained greenish way past the usual ripening time, I couldn't place it, but when, in the following winter, they dried to become brittle balls, I first thought of it as a dry-fruited species, and once I did that, it fell into place perfectly as *O. sphaerocarpa*.

Because this is apparently the first description of the flowers or the roots, and because I find no herbarium specimens since the type with the spineless, round fruits included, it is my opinion that any previously collected specimens, showing only vegetative parts, are buried in the *O. compressa* var. *macrorhiza* folders, from which they cannot be separated without reproductive parts. Nor do I think any collector will be able to tell when he has *O. sphaerocarpa* unless he is willing to wait in the New Mexico mountains until his specimens bloom and fruit, or unless he goes to the trouble to grow his specimens to these stages after he collects them.

As far as relationships are concerned, this plant is a remarkable intermediate between the dry-fruited species and the fleshy-fruited *O. compressa* group. It has the green stigmas of the dry-fruited, but its fruits dry tardily. By character of pads, spines, roots, and seeds it is much more closely related to the *O. compressa* group than to *O. polyacantha*.

I have collected this cactus from several locations in the Sandia Mountains, the type locality. I also have it from locations west of Capitan and from near Ruidosa, which enlarges its known range to include the mountains almost continuous with the Sandias on their southeast. It has been found only at comparatively high altitudes and usually in association with the forests of these mountains.

Opuntia rhodantha Schumann
"Wide Cactus," "Cliff Prickly Pear"

DESCRIPTION   PLATE 58

ROOTS: Fibrous in all specimens seen.

STEMS: Low-growing and spreading, only 6 inches to rarely 18 inches high, with the pads upright at first, later reclining and rooting. These pads are almost circular, egg-shaped, or oblong, 2 to 9 inches long by 2 to 6 inches wide, 1/2 to 1 inch thick, and often slightly tuberculate. In color they are deep green or glaucous and gray-green.

AREOLES: Oval and small to medium in size, being only about 1/8 to 3/16 of an inch long. They are spaced 1/2 to 7/8 of an inch apart.

SPINES: Usually 1 to 6 per areole in number, on only the upper one-half or less of the pad, except in one variety on which there may be up to 10 on most areoles. There are 1 to 4 main, spreading spines 3/4 to 2 inches long, medium to heavy, and somewhat to much flattened. These spines are whitish, yellowish, or variegated with brown. There are also 1 to 6 slender, round to slightly flattened, deflexed, whitish spines 1/4 to 3/4 of an inch long.

GLOCHIDS: Brown in color, very few in one variety, quite numerous in another.

FLOWERS: Yellow or pink or reddish in color, and 2 to 3 inches in diameter and 2 to 2¾ inches tall. The ovary is about 1½ inches long, tuberculate, with white wool and often some glochids, but with no spines on it. There are about 12 inner petals which are to 1 inch wide at the top. The filaments are greenish, yellowish, or reddish; the anthers cream. There are 8 to 12 long, slender, deep green stigma lobes.

FRUITS: Broadly club-shaped, tapering below, 1½ to 1¾ inches long. They usually have from a few areoles at the top to sometimes all areoles with clusters of short, whitish spines, but are occasionally spineless. They become dry and brittle when ripe. The seeds are between 3/16 and 1/4 of an inch (5–6 millimeters), flat, with wide rims.

RANGE. Southwestern Colorado and southern Utah into northern New Mexico and Arizona. In New Mexico found northwest of a line approximately from Taos to Albuquerque to Gallup.

REMARKS. This is perhaps the most beautiful of the small, dry-fruited Opuntias. Although not very big, it is the largest of them, with thick, fleshy, deep-colored pads having not too many spines but those it has being very rigid and heavy. Its beauty, however, lies in its flowers. Although many specimens have clear yellow blooms, others have the only definitely pink blossoms

I have seen in this genus. There are also specimens presenting shades intermediate between these colors, these often turning out to be salmon or reddish hues. The New Mexican plants tend to be mostly yellow, while in Colorado pink flowers are more commonly encountered.

O. rhodantha is a cactus of the higher elevations, usually found at 5,000 or more feet above sea level. Within our area it is limited to the mountains of northwestern New Mexico. While it is immune to cold, I find that it does not grow well or bloom very successfully in the extremes of heat that most of our southwestern cacti thrive in. In growing it, one should remember to provide all he can of the conditions of high altitudes.

Opuntia rhodantha var. **rhodantha** (Schumann)

DESCRIPTION

ROOTS: As the species.

STEMS: As the species, except pads to only 7 inches long by 4 inches wide.

AREOLES: As the species, except to only 7/8 of an inch apart.

SPINES: As the species, except to only 6 per areole, with the lower half or more of the areoles on each pad spineless, with the largest spines to only 1⅝ inches long, and with only 1 to 4 smaller, bristle-like spines per areole.

GLOCHIDS: Very few and inconspicuous.

FLOWERS: As the species.

FRUITS: As the species.

RANGE. As the species.

REMARKS. Originally, in describing this cactus, K. Schumann thought the red-flowered and the yellow-flowered specimens were different species, and he called them *O. rhodantha* and *O. xanthostemma* [sic] respectively. All students since then have realized that these two are one, and combined them under the name of *O. rhodantha*, with the exception of L. Benson, who has chosen to consider this a variety of the more westerly grizzly bear cactus, *O. erinacea* Eng., and so calls it *O. erinacea* var. *xanthostema*. This combination of our moderately spined cactus with the extremely spiny and hairy Mojave cactus does not seem too logical to us, and is not followed even by Earle in the most recent cactus book out of Arizona, so I continue with the original name for the plant.

There have been numerous names given to various garden varieties of this cactus by horticulturists, particularly in Europe. Examples of some of them are variety *pisciformis* and variety *schumanniana* Spath; variety *pallida*, variety *salmonea*, variety *rosea*, variety *ruba*, variety *gracilis*, variety *elegans*, variety *fulgens*, variety *orbicularis*, variety *brevispina*, variety *flavispina*, etc. Hort. These refer to the various flower colors and other characters which have appeared in cultivation, and have no significance except to show the extent to which this cactus has been grown and the degree of its popularity among collectors.

Opuntia rhodantha var. spinosior Boissevain

DESCRIPTION   PLATE 58

ROOTS: As the species.

STEMS: As the species, except pads averaging larger. When growing wild the pads are 4 to 8 inches long and typical in shape, but cultivated plants produced pads more spindle-shaped and to 9 inches long by 6 inches wide, the plants then standing to 18 inches tall in the most robust cases.

AREOLES: As the species, except a little larger and to 1 inch apart.

SPINES: 1 to 10 on almost all areoles of each pad. There are the same 3 or 4 main spines as on the species, except they are here up to 2 inches long. There are 1 to 6 smaller, bristle-like spines below these.

GLOCHIDS: As the species, except quite numerous and sometimes to $1/4$ of an inch long.

FLOWERS: As the species.

FRUITS: As the species, except not so spiny. About half of the specimens observed had spineless fruits and the rest had spines on only the upper edges of the fruits.

RANGE. From southwestern Colorado to near Albuquerque, New Mexico.

REMARKS. Boissevain and Davidson described this variety from the arid southwestern corner of Colorado. It has seldom been studied since, but in re-evaluating the species in 1944, Croizat concluded that this was a "geographic well established form peculiar of the species in the southwestern Colorado desert," and that it therefore deserves a position much higher than all of the garden varieties, which have been mentioned for the species. No one has reported it outside of Colorado until this time, however.

We were very surprised to find this plant growing in the yard of friends who live in one of the new subdivisions across the Rio Grande northwest of downtown Albuquerque, New Mexico. They had a whole row of the plants grown very large and beautiful with the care they had given them. There were both yellow and pink-flowering individuals in the row, and when they put on their fruits, the identification was unmistakable.

I visited the location where they had gathered their plants, only a few miles away on the flat, sandy mesa below the lava outcrops on the west and above the river valley a short distance to the east. The location is beside state road 448, in an area fast being developed, and the wild population is in real danger. I could not find the form growing anywhere else in the area. *O. polyacantha*, *O. hystricina*, and *O. phaeacantha* var. *camanchica* grew in profusion on the hills just to the west of this, but variety *spinosior* did not seem to be up there with them.

On the basis of this collection, and after observing the variety growing in Colorado, I feel it necessary to include this variety as another New Mexico cactus. One would assume that the form must exist in similar situations between this point and southwestern Colorado, and it will be interesting to see whether this supposition is borne out.

I have included in my description of the variety the larger measurements which the cactus has achieved in the above-mentioned garden. Although the specimens seen growing wild were somewhat smaller, they still averaged larger than the typical *O. rhodantha*, and since this garden was not over 4 miles or so from the collection point in the same soil and the larger growth could be the result only of some extra feeding and watering, I feel that the plant might attain the size in a favored natural situation also.

The cactus is clearly very close to *O. rhodantha*, and should probably be left as a variety of this species. Other relationships have not been worked out. I find that plants sent me from Arizona for *O. nicholii* are rather similar, and this similarity should be studied.

Opuntia polyacantha Haw.
"Hunger Cactus," "Starvation Cactus"

DESCRIPTION   PLATES 58, 59

ROOTS: Fibrous.

STEMS: A prostrate, spreading cactus rarely rising over 6 inches high, preferring to string out its joints along the ground, rooting on the edges of them, and thus often forming dense mats of growth. The pads are circular to oval, spindle-shaped, or broadly egg-shaped, but without any real constriction at the bases. They are average thickness to thick for their size, tuberculate by raised areoles, and also usually wrinkled. In color they are pale green or yellow-green, becoming reddish when suffering from extreme heat or cold. They vary from $1^1/2$ to 5 inches long and from $1^1/2$ to 4 inches wide.

AREOLES: Oval or elongated and small, $1/16$ to $1/8$ of an inch long on young pads, sometimes increasing in size on old pads and sometimes not. They contain much white wool when young. They are spaced $1/4$ to $5/8$ of an inch apart.

SPINES: Very variable. On typical specimens there are 1 to 15 spines present on all or almost all areoles. The main, interior spines may be missing or up to 5 in number. When present they consist of 1 main spine $1/4$ to 2 inches long, very slender to medium in thickness, round to somewhat flattened, porrect or deflexed; plus 0 to 2 upper spines $1/4$ to 3 inches long, upright or spreading, slender to medium thickness, and round; and 0 to 2 laterals $1/4$ to $1^1/4$ inches long, slender, and round or slightly flattened. These spines may be white, yellowish, brownish, red-brown, or variegated. Besides this there are from 1 to at least 10 outer, radiating spines $1/8$ to $3/4$ of an inch long, slender to very slender and bristle-like, white or gray, often with darker tips. On some forms of the species the larger, main spines may be missing on all but the upper edge areoles, the spination of the pad thus being made up almost entirely of just the lower, bristle-like spines radiating downward. On the other hand, specimens are occasionally seen on which only the upper areoles have spines and these only 1 to 3 of the main upper spines, with the lower bristles only 1 or 2 in number and very short. Quite often the radial spines of old pads increase greatly in number, especially toward the bases of the pads, and become flexible, hairlike, and elongated to 2 to 8 inches.

GLOCHIDS: Few and short on young pads, being a very compact cluster only $1/16$ of an inch or so long, but becoming sometimes to $3/16$ of an inch long and fairly numerous on old pads. In color, yellow to bright brown.

FLOWERS: 2 to $3^1/2$ inches in diameter, $1^1/2$ to $2^1/2$ inches tall. They are almost always—if not always—yellow in our area, but often pink, rose, or even reddish in color in Colorado and on north. The ovary is broad club-shaped to almost spherical, $3/4$ to $1^5/8$ inches long and $3/4$ of an inch or so wide. It is tuberculate by many elevated areoles containing much white wool and many yellow glochids plus some very slender spines sometimes up to $1/2$ inch long. There are 5 to 10 bright green stigma lobes.

FRUITS: Very variable. They are spherical to oval or egg-shaped, more or less tuberculate when growing, but without tubercles when ripe and dry. They measure $3/4$ to 2 inches long by $1/2$ to 2 inches thick. The top is usually somewhat pitted, but may be entirely flat. When completely ripe the fruit becomes dry with a thin, papery skin over the tightly packed mass of seeds. On typical specimens there are 2 to 12 slender spines $3/16$ to $5/8$ of an inch long on each areole of the upper third to three-fourths of the fruit, but fruits wholly spiny to wholly spineless may be found. The seeds are also extremely variable, ranging in size from $1/8$ to more than $1/4$ of an inch (3–7 millimeters), being however over $3/16$ of an inch (5–7 millimeters) in diameter on typical plants. The rim of the seed can be from narrow to very wide, this giving most of the variation in diameter which occurs.

RANGE. The northwestern United States far into Canada, and south through western Nebraska and Kansas across the western tip of the Oklahoma Panhandle into the upper part of the Texas Panhandle, as well as through Colorado, over all of New Mexico, south into the Hueco and Davis mountains of southwestern Texas, and west into Arizona.

REMARKS. This is one of the widest ranging of all cacti. It is probably the most northern cactus, growing practically up to the Arctic Circle, and followed north only by *Opuntia fragilis*.

It is, however, not a conspicuous plant, perhaps surviving so successfully because it lies half buried in the sand or lost in the grass. The mats it forms effectively hold the soil from erosion and even stabilize the sand which drifts into them on the wind. As a result there is usually grass growing up through these carpets of cacti, and the very pale coloring of the pads plus the many spines which blend with the dead grass and trash caught in them render the plant so nearly invisible that it is much easier to walk into a stand of it before seeing it than it is to get out again. It is an aid to soil conservation by this holding action against erosion, but it is an ally few people can appreciate properly.

The cactus was apparently first referred to by Nuttall as *Cactus ferox*, but his description was so inadequate that authorities take as the first valid name Haworth's *Opuntia polyacantha*. For a long period it was known by the name, *O. missouriensis* DC, but there is agreement now that this is merely a synonym.

Having such a huge range and living in such different climates, this cactus shows many variations—witness the spines numbering from only a few to 15 and the color from white to red-brown, the fruit from spherical to egg-shaped and its size from $3/4$ to 2 inches long, and most obvious of all, the seed size from about $1/8$ to more than $1/4$ of an inch in diameter. It has always been difficult to understand these differences. Engelmann found it necessary to list 5 varieties in the species, and Coulter increased that. More recently most of these have been ignored as mere growth forms, as for instance, variety *rufispina* Eng., and variety *albispina* Eng., based on spine color almost entirely, but some of them have, on the other hand, been elevated by various students to separate species, as *O. trichophora* (Eng.) B. & R. Then, some new species have been described, as for example *O. juniperina* Rose and *O. schweriniana* Schumann. Other students think these should hardly be carried even as separate varieties of the species.

Here is a place where classical taxonomy based on discernible structural characters has as bad a time and gives us as little hope of constructing a logical order of relationships as anywhere. Here is where we need help. And right here is about the first place in the study of cacti where the results of modern biosystematics comes forward with some very limited but suggestive data for us.

Chromosome counts have been made so far on only a few cacti, and most results published have been numbers from only single plants or plants from a single location. It happens, however, that chromosome counts of specimens of *O. polyacantha* from widely separate locations have been made and the results published by Stockwell. Here we find that there is variation in the chromosome number within the species. Where the typical 2N chromosome number for cacti is 22, specimens of this cactus checked by Stockwell had either 44 or 66 chromosomes, with the specimens having 44 chromosomes appearing typical and those with 66 chromosomes being Canadian specimens which were smaller plants with smoother pads, fewer spines, and the small-sized seeds.

What the modern technique seems to have given us thus far is a possible physical basis in the variation of chromosome numbers and a mechanism in the process of ploidy for some of the wide variation we have already seen in structural characters in the species. The only pattern we can see so far is that the chromosome number rises as we go north, which is as we would expect, ploidy often enhancing vigor and resistance to environmental extremes. All of the 66 chromosome counts reported were in the tiny-seeded Canadian form once described by Engelmann as *O. missouriensis* var. *microsperma,* which hardly enters the United States at all. This would seem to establish it as a definite variety based upon ploidy. But we are left with little aid in trying to logically separate the forms in our own area, since no variation in chromosome numbers among them has so far been shown. Therefore, we will leave the species as it stands, with our description wide enough to cover the usual forms, and deal individually with the most often separated of them.

A list of the named varieties which we do not see as distinct and consistent enough to be regarded separately is included here in order to try to eliminate as much confusion as possible. While we have seen specimens which fit the description of each one of these, we have not been able to find them making up any separate populations in any definite geographical range. Always we have found them existing as the extremes within a population of varying individuals on the same hillside with typical individuals, and more often than not 2 or 3 different ones of these variations have been found side by side with the typical. This is how they differ from what we consider the definite varieties of, for instance, *O. engelmannii.*

Variety *rufispina* Eng. is only the typical plant as it sometimes appears with its main spines brown instead of the more common white.

Variety *albispina* Eng. is the more common, pure white-spined form.

Variety *platycarpa* (Eng.) Coult. is the form as it often appears at high altitudes in the northern New Mexico mountains and on into Colorado. One will often find plants fitting this description growing under the rather dense shade of junipers, while typical specimens are usually only a few feet away in the open. Nor is this form distinct for having the fruits globose with broad, flat umbilici, as some have supposed. In Taos Canyon and in several other high mountain locations in northern New Mexico, I have seen *O. polyacantha* fruits from almost club-shaped to perfectly spherical and from 3/4 to 2 inches long, as well as from very spiny to spineless, all on the same mountainside. Many of them fitted Engelmann's description of this supposed variety, but they were only part of the one large, greatly varying population. It was noted that all of those fruits over

about 1¼ inches long were spherical or nearly so and spineless. Every one of these very large fruits which was opened was found to be sterile and apparently parasitized. We feel these exaggerated round fruits may be this species' reaction to fruit parasites just as the extreme enlargement by elongation is the response of *O. compressa* var. *fusco-atra* to something similar on the Texas coast. These abnormal fruits we have heard called both variety *platycarpa* and *O. sphaerocarpa,* as we have those more normal and smaller fruits which happen to be round and nearly spineless. Many otherwise typical *O. polyacantha* specimens have normally round fruits, and to separate those with fewer than typical spines on the pads from a mixed population and call them another species or even another variety does not seem proper.

Variety *subinermis* Eng. is yet another supposed variety. Plants fitting its description are occasionally found in the large, mixed populations of northern New Mexico. They have more elongated pads with areoles a little farther apart and only a very few short and slender spines on the upper edges. These plants often make up part of the same large population, with 2 or 3 others of these supposed varieties present as well as typical specimens. In each observed case, however, all of the specimens of this description were the result of environment, all of them growing far under junipers in deep accumulations of leaf mold. The elongated pads and poor armament are clear signs of etiolation. This form is very similar to *O. schweriniana* Schumann, which is not treated here because it is a Colorado form, but the relation between the two should be given careful study. I have seen a series of specimens from one location in Colorado which seemed to run all the way from fairly typical *O. polyacantha* through something like this form and on to something very close to *O. schweriniana.*

O. juniperina Rose has been considered a separate species. Early in this study, on a trip through the northern mountains of New Mexico during the dead of winter, I hurriedly dug out of the snow some specimens which exactly fitted Rose's description of this form. When I also saw similar specimens in the University of Colorado herbarium under this name, I was very sure of the species, and held out for it in some arguments with friends who said this was merely another form occurring in its type locality as part of the same sort of widely varying *O. polyacantha* population. More recently, when I studied the locality of my original collection of these specimens during the summer, I found the same thing there. There are typical *O. polyacantha* and all gradations between that and this supposed species wherever I have seen this form, including in its type locality at Cedar Hill, New Mexico. I therefore find it impossible to maintain it as even a consistent variety of the species.

Variety *trichophora* (Eng.) Coult. has been one of the most persistent varieties. This is the form of the species in which the radial spines of at least the lower areoles and sometimes of all areoles on older pads elongate greatly and become flexible and hairlike. They often grow to 4 inches long, and Boissevain says they sometimes reach 8 inches. At the same time they often increase in number to 25 or 30 per areole. Such a plant is surely a remarkable sight. This is naturally the most commonly noticed variant from the typical form of the species. Engelmann and Coulter called it a variety, Britton and Rose elevated it to a separate species, but most authors since have left it a variety.

We started out considering it as separate from the typical form, but we soon ran into the same trouble as with the rest of these forms. We found all degrees of this hairiness, sometimes in the same population. Where could we draw the line in separating them? We have wearied at trying to be consistent about this, and tired of reading the contradictory explanations of the variety by various authors. The condition intergrades all the way with the typical forms which fail to elongate and proliferate the spines. In our northern New Mexico locations mentioned above we have found this hairy form growing only yards away from very good variety *platycarpa*, variety *subinermis*, and *O. juniperina* specimens having their less than typical armaments. In Taos Canyon I once collected a specimen fitting the description of *O. juniperina* in all pads except one, this one aberrant pad having 20 to 30 hairlike, flexible spines to 3 inches long in each areole of its surface. It was literally a pad of variety *trichophora* growing from an *O. juniperina* specimen. I grew this specimen carefully for 4 years, and was very disappointed to find the two pads which sprouted from the hairy pad developing into typical *O. juniperina*, sparsely spined pads in the greenhouse. So we have begun disappointing all those who constantly ask, "Which do I have, *O. polyacantha* or *O. trichophora*?" by refusing to separate them. In this we claim the support of Wooton, who said long ago that variety *trichophora* may not be distinct from *O. polyacantha*.

The species, *O. polyacantha*, blankets all of the state of New Mexico. There are records from within 50 miles of each of the four corners of that state. However, it does not go far east or south beyond that. In Oklahoma it has been recorded only from Cimarron County, the end county of the Panhandle, and rarely seen east of the Black Mesa, which is the extreme corner of that county. It enters Texas in two separate areas, coming into the Texas Panhandle where it seems to grow only as far as the south breaks of the Canadian River. Not being seen in all of the Texas high plains south of that, it enters the state again from southeastern New Mexico along the Hueco and Guadalupe mountains, growing as far south as the Davis Mountains, but apparently no farther into the lower Big Bend. It is definitely a northern cactus.

Opuntia hystricina Eng.
"Porcupine Prickly Pear"

DESCRIPTION   PLATE 59
   ROOTS: Fibrous.

   STEMS: Low, diffuse, and spreading, but not prostrate. They form small clumps of upright pads standing 6 inches to sometimes 1 foot high. The pads are nearly circular to more often elongated obovate or even oblong, 3 to 5 inches long and 2½ to 3 inches wide, medium thickness, not tuberculate, and not becoming noticeably wrinkled from lack of water. They are medium or bright green in color.

AREOLES: Large and conspicuous, oval, and about ³/₁₆ of an inch long on young pads, becoming round and ¼ of an inch or more in diameter on old pads. They are situated ¼ to ½ inch apart.

SPINES: A total of 6 to 15 spines in each areole of the pad. There are in each areole 1 to 8, and in fully armed upper areoles always 5 to 8, main spines which are 1½ to 4 inches long. These spines are irregularly arranged and spread in all directions, including upward. They are brownish or gray or variegated in color. They are of slender to average thickness, somewhat flattened, often twisted or bent, and somewhat flexible. There are also up to 7 lower, very slender, white, radiating spines ³/₄ to 1 inch long in each areole. There is sometimes a tendency for a few very slender, white, hairlike spines 2 to 3 inches long to grow at the bases of the pads.

GLOCHIDS: Straw-colored or brown, often both in the same areole due to the existence of an outer ring of older, longer, darkened glochids and an inner cluster of younger, shorter, brighter, straw-colored ones.

FLOWERS: Ordinarily clear, pale yellow, but said to sometimes have various hues such as orange, rose, red, or even purplish. They are 2 to 3 inches in diameter. The ovary has white wool and bristle-like spines. The stigma lobes number 8 to 10 and are green in color.

FRUITS: Egg-shaped to broadly club-shaped and ⁷/₈ to 1¼ inches long by about ½ inch thick. The areoles of the upper half of the fruit possess 4 to 12 bristly spines ½ to ³/₄ of an inch long per areole. The umbilicus is flat, or nearly so. The seeds are very large, between ¼ and ⁵/₁₆ of an inch (7 millimeters or more) in diameter, with broad rims.

RANGE. From the Rio Grande in New Mexico west to Nevada and California.

REMARKS. Over 100 years ago Engelmann felt it necessary to distinguish a cactus closely allied to *O. polyacantha* from that species, calling it *O. hystricina*. He admitted that he himself had difficulty in keeping the two separate, and even conjectured that one might be only a form of the other. Everyone since then has had trouble with these two, but no one has actually combined them. When a combination involving this cactus did finally come, it was Benson's attempt to combine it instead with an entirely different California cactus, *O. erinacea* Eng., giving us *O. erinaceae* var. *hystricina* (Eng.) Benson.

Let us see first how we distinguish *O. hystricina* from *O. polyacantha* and what characters keep it from being united with that cactus. We find that it differs from *O. polyacantha* as follows:

it is diffuse and spreading with more upright growth than that cactus; its pads are darker green; it lacks distinct tubercles by raised areoles or marked wrinkling; it has more and longer and more erect main spines, which are also usually bent and somewhat flexible; and it has many more and longer glochids. I should state emphatically that it cannot be told from *O. polyacantha* by having flattened spines, as some have argued, since some specimens of that cactus have more definitely flattened spines than this does; nor by having more stout spines, since specimens could be matched with this character just reversed; nor larger pads; nor more widely spaced areoles. It is not just a robust version of the hunger cactus, as some articles about it would lead one to believe. Its whole manner of growth is different. But in many collections, both herbarium collections and fanciers' gardens, I see smaller specimens of *O. polyacantha* labeled correctly, but plants of that species merely more robust in size or spines wrongly called *O. hystricina*. This has made the tracing of this species very difficult.

Part of the trouble may be that although Engelmann says correctly that it grows all the way east to the Rio Grande, it is not at all common in New Mexico. It should be noticed that his descriptions were all compiled from specimens of Arizona and Nevada, and the only examples he actually mentions having seen from New Mexico were Fendler's specimens from near Santa Fe—these Engelmann says, "seem to be intermediate [between *O. hystricina* and *O. polyacantha*] and may make it necessary to combine them." These may have actually been only robust *O. polyacantha* specimens. If so, Engelmann himself would have been the first to make this often repeated mistake. It is interesting that Coulter found no New Mexico records of *O. hystricina* as late as 1896, and that in 1915, Wooton and Standley, those very complete students of New Mexico plants, said, "We have seen only one doubtful specimen [of *O. hystricina*]. It is reported here . . . on the authority of the first collector, Dr. Bigelow." So we should get over the idea which I find in some collectors that every New Mexico hill west of the Rio Grande can be expected to have this cactus on it, and stop calling all of our big specimens of *O. polyacantha* this.

This is not to say that it does not exist in New Mexico, but I believe it is rare anywhere in that state. I have seen only two definite specimens from New Mexico, and the one which I have growing before me is from only a short distance west of Las Cruces, so far southeast that it confirms nicely the fact that, although it is rare, it must range the whole state west of the Rio Grande.

These plants also show clearly why Benson combined this form with the more western form he calls *O. erinacea*. They are upright in growth, with ovate or oblong pads, having spreading, often erect spines up to 4 inches long and only moderately rigid, and with many conspicuous glochids. All of these are characters in common with the more western plant. In fact, it is easy to agree with Backeberg, who maintains that the two are actually the same. But Backeberg also points out that Engelmann himself

withdrew his name, *O. erinacea*, and so it would not be technically correct to combine anything under that name. We therefore follow him in leaving the name of our rare New Mexico plant *O. hystricina*. Whether it is the same as the California plant is outside the scope of our study. It is the same plant that grows at least to the Colorado River and Nevada, and it is more closely related to the equally upright *O. ursina* Weber, the extremely hairy grizzly bear cactus of the Mojave, than it is to *O. polyacantha*.

Opuntia arenaria Eng.

DESCRIPTION   PLATE 59

ROOTS: Unique among Opuntias in our area. The roots are not tuberous, but have large, rhizome-like structures up to ¹/₂ inch thick which sometimes run 3 to 6 feet horizontally just under the surface of the almost pure sand in which this plant grows. These underground structures are covered with many large areoles and long glochids like old stems, and they give off pads and fibrous roots all along them.

STEMS: If these underground structures are considered as rhizomes or stem structures, the main stems of the plant are prostrate strings up to 6 feet long of old pads which are buried in the drifting sand. However, if these underground structures are made up from old pads, the separate joints are not clearly observable; therefore some students have interpreted them as roots. But the presence of areoles and glochids upon them makes it difficult for us to consider them roots. From these structures there are ascending and spreading young pads which stand 6 inches or rarely a little higher. The pads are 1¹/₄ to 4 inches long by ³/₄ to 2 inches wide, and often are ³/₄ of an inch thick. When small these pads are almost cylindrical, but as they grow larger they widen and flatten to become elongated oval to very elongated egg-shaped or even clavate. Young pads are light, shiny green in color, tuberculate, but not becoming wrinkled when dehydrated. Old pads, on the prostrate, more or less covered stems become brown and woody.

AREOLES: Small, with a little white wool when young, enlarging somewhat on old stems. They are spaced ³/₁₆ to ³/₈ of an inch apart.

SPINES: Almost all areoles are armed with 3 to 10 spines white or brownish or white with brownish bases and tips. There are 1 to 4 main spines. The central one of these is ³/₄ to 2 inches long, rigid, of average thickness, flattened slightly, and standing porrect or turned upward. There are besides this 0 to 3 others ³/₈ to 1 inch long, round or slightly flattened, and spreading downward. Below these there are 2 to 6 bristle-like spines ¹/₈ to ¹/₂ inch long, radiating downward.

GLOCHIDS: Straw or brownish in color, few in number but

226

rather long on young pads, becoming very many and to ¼ of an inch long in large, spreading clusters which almost completely cover old pads.

FLOWERS: Yellow, 2 to 2¾ inches in diameter. The ovary is egg-shaped and ⅞ to 1¼ inches long. There are about 8 inner petals and 5 green stigma lobes.

FRUITS: Oblong or club-shaped, usually constricted at both the bottom and the top, and deeply pitted above. They are 1 to 1½ inches long by ¼ to ⅜ of an inch thick. They have 1 to 5 slender spines ¼ to ½ inch long on each areole of the broader central zone. The seeds are from nearly 3/16 to almost 5/16 of an inch (5–7 millimeters) in diameter, very thin, irregular, and rather elongated in shape, with broad margins.

RANGE. Known only from sandy areas along the Rio Grande just a few miles above El Paso, Texas. Those on the east side of the river would be in Texas and those on the west side in New Mexico.

REMARKS. This is a unique little cactus equipped with the extremely long, stolon-like root or stem structure of a plant adapted to survive in deep and shifting sand. And it is found only in such sand, where often three-fourths of the plant is entirely buried, with only the current year's new pads standing upright out of the ground.

This is an almost vanished species. Engelmann said it grew in the sandy bottoms of the Rio Grande near El Paso. Most of these have long since had buildings or irrigated farming upon them. Dr. Rose said he found the plant about 8 miles above El Paso on the New Mexico side of the river. I had spent some time slogging through the sand over there to no avail, and would no doubt never have seen the cactus but for Mr. Clark Champie, well-known cactus grower and dealer of the area. When I told him of my problem, I told the right person, for he has a definite corner on this cactus. He immediately took me to one of the two known living stands just a few hundred yards from his own cactus farm on the outskirts of Anthony, east of the river at the Texas-New Mexico border. The stand is only a few dozen yards in extent, and a road is now bull-dozed through the center of it, so let us hope Mr. Champie is a good custodian of the cactus, or it may be completely extinct very soon.

Coulter's opinion was that O. arenaria was allied to O. fragilis, because of the almost cylindrical form of its early joints, but O. arenaria's pads are tightly joined to each other instead of loose, and there are other differences.

Britton and Rose say that its flowers are red, which is definitely not true of the stand near Anthony. The blooms are very yellow there. However, Britton and Rose had plants from another location on the west side of the river, and knowing the tendency to variability of flower color in this whole group, we must admit that their plants might have bloomed with a different color.

In cultivation this cactus does not usually do well. It will not grow successfully in regular soil, and it is hard to provide a big enough and deep enough plot of sand containing the proper elements so that it can spread out and feel at home. While I have succeeded in keeping it alive for 4 years now, and in getting some growth, it has never flowered for me. So far as I know, to see it growing successfully one must make a pilgrimage to Mr. Champie's natural stand. We wish such a rare stand as this could have some sort of official protection.

Opuntia grahamii Eng.
"Mounded Dwarf Cholla"

DESCRIPTION   PLATE 59

STEMS: Joints elongated oblong, club-shaped, or sometimes spindle-shaped, 1½ to 2½ inches long, covered with low, oblong tubercles ½ inch or slightly more in length. Sometimes these tubercles are very indistinct. These joints form very dense mats up to about a foot across, those on the edges often lying prostrate, but those in the center ascending. The plant may round up into quite a mound, but this is due to sand blowing into it. The joints only branch once above the surface, and so stand to only 4 inches or so above the accumulated level of the sand. The joints are firmly attached.

AREOLES: Round, ⅛ to 3/16 of an inch across, with much white wool in them at first. They are located on the ends of the tubercles, and are about ½ inch apart.

SPINES: 8 to 14 per areole. There are 4 to 8 main inner spines spreading in all directions. They are 1¼ to 2½ inches long, straight, medium in thickness, round or nearly so, brown or red-brown and smooth at first, becoming grayish and rough when old. They are not cross-striated or edged. Besides these there are 4 to 6 outer spines spreading below, slender, round, whitish, ½ to 1 inch long.

GLOCHIDS: Few at first, becoming quite numerous and to ¼ of an inch long on old joints. They are brown in color.

FLOWERS: Yellow, 2 to 2½ inches across. The stigmas are whitish.

FRUITS: Elongated egg-shaped or oblong, 1¼ to 1¾ inches long, and yellow when ripe. They are tuberculate, with many areoles, each having white wool and several slender white spines, as well as 20 to 30 white glochids. The seeds are slightly over 3/16 of an inch (5–5½ millimeters) in diameter.

RANGE. As far as is definitely known, a rather small area of west Texas consisting of parts of El Paso and Hudspeth counties from the foothills of the Franklin Mountains through the Hueco Mountains and hills east and southeast of El Paso to near Sierra Blanca, Texas. It is known to grow in adjacent Chihuahua and is assumed to enter slightly into adjacent New Mexico, but I have not been able to confirm this. It is reported by Anthony from the Texas Big Bend, but this we also failed to confirm.

REMARKS. This species introduces us to the cylindrical-stemmed

Opuntias, sometimes called *Cylindropuntia* in technical language, and also almost universally known by the common name of chollas. It is also one of the low-growing chollas whose stems are more or less club-shaped, and so it is part of the group sometimes separated out of the *Cylindropuntia* as *Clavatopuntia* or *Cornyopuntia*.

O. *grahamii* is an interesting small cactus of the sand hills east of El Paso, Texas. It is very common on some of those hills, particularly near the Hueco Mountains. It grows more compactly and with its joints more ascending than those of any of its relatives except O. *clavata*. A typical specimen usually forms a little mound 3 to 6 inches high and up to about a foot or so in diameter. But the sand drifts with the wind into this compact mass, and soon covers the lower stems. As this happens, new ones grow above, and although no joint is over 4 inches or so above the surface, the accumulation often results in a mound a number of inches high. Covered as it is by its very many long, rather slender spines, the appearance from a distance is exactly that of a clump of short grass partly filled with sand, and the cactus is very hard to see.

O. *grahamii* can be told from all of its close relatives by the fact that its main spines are comparatively slender, smooth and round, or practically so, while all of the others have their main spines very heavy, very rough, cross-striated, and greatly flattened. Noticing this difference will enable anyone to distinguish it from O. *schottii,* with which it is most often confused.

Opuntia schottii Eng.
"Devil Cactus," "Dog Cholla," "Clavellina"

DESCRIPTION   PLATE 60

STEMS: Joints elongated, cylindrical, or more often club-shaped, lying prostrate or sometimes with the upper ends turned upward. The bases of these joints are constricted and around ¼ of an inch thick, from which they gradually broaden to almost 1 inch thick at the upper end. The over-all length of a joint is 1 to 3 inches. The joint is covered by broad, elongated tubercles about ½ to ¾ of an inch long. These joints are rather loosely attached, coming off the plant with only a small tug.

AREOLES: Round, or nearly so, located on the upper ends of the tubercles, small below to over ¼ of an inch in diameter toward the end of the joint.

SPINES: There are 8 to 14 spines per areole. Of these, 1 main central, which is very heavy and very flat, stands porrect or a little deflexed. It is 1 to 2½ inches long and 1/16 to 1/8 of an inch wide for most of its length. Its surface is very rough and usually distinctly cross-striated. In color it is at first straw to light brown with the tip translucent yellow and edged with light yellow or whitish the length of the spine. It

fades to rough gray when old. There are two lower centrals spreading downward, to 1½ inches long and as the main central in character. There are 1 to 4 centrals spreading upward, ¼ to 1½ inches long, heavy but triangular or completely round, darker brown or sometimes red-brown in color with the tips translucent yellow. Besides these there are 5 to 7 small, slender, round, whitish radial spines ¼ to ¾ of an inch long spreading below. There are no sheaths on matured spines of this plant.

GLOCHIDS: Few. In the upper areoles there will be up to a dozen straw-colored bristles to 3/16 of an inch long at the top of the areole.

FLOWERS: Yellow, about 2 to 2½ inches across and 2 inches tall. The stamens are whitish. The stigmas are whitish or very pale greenish.

FRUITS: 1 to 1½ inches long by 3/8 to ½ inch thick, elongated club-shaped, with perianth persistent upon it, and very light yellow when ripe. It is covered with narrow tubercles ¼ to 3/8 of an inch long, each ending in an areole above. These areoles are small, each containing white wool, 4 main central spines which are slender, round, 3/16 to 5/16 of an inch long, and arranged cross-wise, plus 25 to 35 radial spines which are very slender and bristle-like. The seeds are not quite 3/16 of an inch (about 4 millimeters) in diameter.

RANGE. Along the Rio Grande from near Brownsville, Texas, to Lajitas in the Big Bend. Becoming common from the area of Zapata, Texas, to the Big Bend, but never seen over 10 miles or so north of the river.

REMARKS. This is a very low, inconspicuous little cactus growing practically invisibly in the grass, but if stepped upon, it can become very painfully evident. The spines are strong enough to penetrate shoe leather sometimes, and being very barbed, they stick to shoes or clothing. The next step often pulls joints loose, and one has unwanted riders which it is a major chore to disengage without injury to oneself.

O. *schottii* grows on the gravelly hillsides overlooking the Rio Grande and the last few miles of its tributaries such as the Devil's River and the Pecos. Below the Pecos the plant usually grows as single chains of prostrate joints blooming and fruiting sparingly and apparently propagated mostly by separated pads. These can be pulled apart rather easily, but are not nearly so loosely attached as those of O. *fragilis* or O. *drummondii*. From the Pecos west the cactus grows more often in low, compact mats up to 2 feet or so across, and in season these are covered with very many flowers and fruits.

O. *schottii* is a Texas cactus, growing along an immense length of the Rio Grande, but never leaving the hills overlooking the river. Its westernmost range does not seem to quite reach the range of its nearest relatives, but it apparently has grown, at least in the past, almost to the mouth of the Rio Grande. Runyon's record of it, "near Brownsville," attests to that. We have not been able to find it below Zapata, and surmise that the great development of the area below there may have reduced its range considerably.

Opuntia stanlyi Eng.
"Stanley's Cholla," "Devil Cholla," "Creeping Cholla"

DESCRIPTION   PLATE 60

STEMS: Consisting of cylindrical, club-shaped joints, 3½ to 6 inches long, slender at the base, but enlarging to from 1 to 2 inches in diameter at the outer end. The plant consists of many of these joints lying prostrate or with the ends curving upward, or sometimes with the whole joint ascending, thus forming dense mats standing from 6 to sometimes 12 inches high and extending from several feet to sometimes 15 or 20 feet in diameter. The joints are covered with tubercles appearing as ridges 1 to 1¾ inches long by ¼ to ¾ of an inch tall by ¼ to ½ inch wide.

AREOLES: Round, or nearly so, located on the upper slopes of the tubercles, ¼ of an inch or slightly more in diameter, with some white wool at first.

SPINES: 10 to at least 20 in number. There are 5 to 9 large inner spines 1⅛ to 2⅜ inches long, spreading, with the largest one porrect or deflexed, very flat, and 1/16 to sometimes ⅛ of an inch wide, with the upper surface roughened by tiny pits and irregular cross-striation. The other main spines are not so heavy nor so flattened. All these are yellowish or reddish-brown at first, becoming ashy gray when old. There are also 7 to at least 15 outer spines ⅜ to ¾ of an inch long, whitish, round to flattened.

GLOCHIDS: Few in number, but to ¼ of an inch long and robust. They are yellow in color.

FLOWERS: Pale yellow, 1½ to 2¾ inches in diameter. The stigma lobes are white.

FRUITS: Broadly club-shaped or egg-shaped, 2 to 2¾ inches long, and very spiny. The seeds are about 3/16 of an inch (about 5 millimeters) in diameter.

RANGE. Entering our area from Arizona and Mexico, and ranging over southwestern New Mexico at least as far as the upper edge of Grant County, and east to Socorro and near El Paso. It is found in Texas along the Rio Grande from near El Paso to near Candelaria in Presidio County.

REMARKS. This is one of the worst cactus pests in existence, earning the common name, devil cholla. Fortunately it is not common in our area, but where it is met with it often renders whole hillsides impassible not only to men but even to goats, by covering many square feet with thickets only a foot or less high but so compact as to be impenetrable by all except small creeping things. Such stands are to be seen in western Grant County,

New Mexico, and along the Rio Grande in western Presidio County in Texas. Other than in these two locations in our area, we are not at all sorry to say, we encounter only isolated small stands of the cactus in widely scattered places. These locations are so scattered that it is hard to delimit the eastern edge of its range in New Mexico. The most northeastern record of it is an old one of Vasey's given as Socorro, New Mexico. There are old records from near El Paso as well, but the plant does not seem to have been collected nearly so far east in recent times.

O. stanlyi has had several other similar forms attached to it as varieties, but these occur only in Arizona, California, and Nevada. The cactus as we find it in our area is the typical form. It is most closely related to *O. schottii*. The main characters of the two are almost all the same, *O. schottii* presenting most of the features of the other in miniature. However, the joints of *O. stanlyi* are not easily separated, as are those of the smaller cactus. The ranges of the two are separated by only a short distance along the Rio Grande in Texas, and the Candelaria population of *O. stanlyi* has individuals averaging a little smaller than those farther west, but there is no actual intergrading in size between the two. Hester, who studied them both in the Big Bend, did not consider any combination of them, but a fair case could be made perhaps for considering one a variety of the other.

Engelmann apparently described this cactus under two names, first as *O. stanlyi*, and then later as *O. emoryi*. The two names are, therefore, considered synonyms.

Opuntia clavata Eng.
"Club Cholla," "Dagger Cholla"

DESCRIPTION   PLATE 60

STEMS: Each plant forming a low mat often 3 to at least 6 feet across but only 3 to 6 inches high. The joints are upright or nearly so, short club-shaped to egg-shaped, with some narrowing below but not markedly constricted below, 1 to 2½ inches long and to 1 inch thick above. These joints are covered with low, broad, rather indistinct tubercles about ¼ to ½ inch long.

AREOLES: Large, usually 3/16 to ¼ of an inch across, and round.

SPINES: There are 10 to 20 spines, all white and rough when mature, but bright pink when growing. 4 to 7 of these are main inner spines ½ to 1¼ inches long. The upper ones of these are more slender, shorter, only somewhat flattened, and stand erect. The lower 3 or 4 of them are spreading downward, larger, and flatter. The main central spine is deflexed and conspicuous for its flatness and thickness, to only 1¼ inches long, but about ⅛ of an inch thick at its base and tapering evenly to the point. The upper surface of this spine is conspicuously cross-striated and the lower surface is keeled.

There are also 6 to 13 outer spines radiating in every direction. They are only ³/₁₆ to ⁵/₈ of an inch long, slender, and round.

GLOCHIDS: Few to rather many, white or straw-colored, about ¹/₈ to ³/₁₆ of an inch long.

FLOWERS: Yellow and small, to only 2 inches in diameter and even less in length.

FRUITS: Elongated club-shaped or almost spindle-shaped, with a deep umbilicus. They are 1¹/₄ to 2 inches long and to 1 inch thick. The light yellow surface of the ripe fruit is almost completely covered with a large number of very slender, white or straw-colored bristles which grow from the many areoles. The seeds are slightly over ³/₁₆ to ¹/₄ of an inch (5–6 millimeters) in diameter.

RANGE. Central and a portion of northwestern New Mexico, sometimes said to extend into Arizona. From Tularosa and near Truth-or-Consequences, New Mexico, on the south to near Las Vegas on the northeast, to El Rito on the north, then back southwest to near Cubero. Said to enter Arizona north of the Zuni River, but I find no New Mexico record of it west of a line from El Rito to Cubero to Socorro to Truth-or-Consequences.

REMARKS. On all sides of Albuquerque, New Mexico, one can find large areas of almost barren flats and slopes where the short grass alternates with the often huge mats of O. *clavata*. At first glance the cactus appears much like grass, but one had better learn to distinguish the one from the other before he walks in the area. While some point out that it is a great pest to livestock, an unprejudiced observation reveals that it doesn't often compete with the grass, but usually occupies otherwise barren ground. The soil is usually bare and eroded away on all sides of these thick mats of cactus, leaving the stand elevated several inches on the soil it has held and showing clearly how valuable a soil holder it is where little else seems able to do the job. It is thus another "pest" which we should consider carefully before condemning entirely, and we should know very certainly what can be introduced to hold the soil in its place before the herbicide gunners are turned loose on it.

The cactus is well named the dagger cholla. The name comes from the shape and appearance of the largest spine, which is so short, but so broad and flattened that it does resemble a tiny dagger. The other common name sometimes applied to it, the club cholla, is probably not so apt, since the joints are at most only very broadly club-shaped without much constriction at the base and usually better described as egg-shaped. Although they stand upright, they rarely give off new joints except near their bases, and so the plant is seldom over 3 or 4 inches tall.

This is a cactus of central New Mexico. While it ranges most of the length of that state, it does not reach either the north or south border, and there are no known records of it near either the eastern or western boundaries. Records of it place it in a

strip only up to 100 or so miles wide. If it does in fact enter Arizona, as has been said, it must be very rare in the intervening western part of New Mexico.

This cactus is most closely related to O. *stanlyi* var. *parishii* Benson, which, however, does not seem to come east of western Arizona.

Opuntia imbricata var. arborescens (Eng.)
"Tree Cactus," "Cane Cactus," "Candelabrum Cactus," "Cholla," "Velas de Coyote (Coyote Candles)"

DESCRIPTION   PLATE 61
STEMS: Growing as an upright, bushy, or treelike plant, 3 to at least 8 feet tall. There is a round trunk quite often becoming up to 3 or 4 inches in diameter and said to have been seen 5 to 10 inches thick. This trunk is more or less covered with rough bark and enlarged areoles. The current year's joints are cylindrical, usually 2 to 6 inches, but occasionally to 8 inches long, and to about 1 inch in diameter. They are covered with elongated tubercles ³/₄ to 1¹/₄ inches long and to about ¹/₄ of an inch high, their upper and lower slopes about equal. The old stems have a woody skeleton.

AREOLES: Oval or oblong, about ¹/₄ of an inch long, enlarging somewhat with age. They possess some short, whitish, or yellowish wool.

SPINES: Very variable in number, from 2 to 10 on the current year's growth, increasing with age to 20 or 30. There are 1 to 8 central spines spreading in all directions. These are ¹/₂ to 1¹/₄ inches in length, slender to medium strength, round, yellow, brownish, or variegated in color. They are covered by loose sheaths. The remainder of the spines are radiating exterior spines, ¹/₄ to ⁵/₈ of an inch long, slender, white to brownish, at least partly covered with tight, whitish sheaths.

GLOCHIDS: Very few, sometimes apparently missing. Those present are found in the upper part of the areole and are so short as to be inconspicuous in the wool.

FLOWERS: To 3 inches in diameter, 1¹/₂ to 2 inches tall, purplish, lavender, or rose-pink in color. The ovary is 1 inch long or slightly more, and nearly as thick. It is very tuberculate and often has perianth segments and 2 or 3 long, white bristles ¹/₄ to ⁵/₈ of an inch long on its upper areoles. The filaments are reddish toward their bases, becoming greenish-pink above. The anthers are cream-colored. The style is reddish and slightly longer than the stamens. There are 6 to 8 long, fat, pinkish-white or tan stigma lobes.

FRUITS: Spherical or even hemispherical in shape, about 1 inch long, but often a little wider than they are long. They are unarmed, whatever bristles were upon the ovary being early deciduous, and have very deeply pitted umbilici, and the rest of the surface covered with pronounced tubercles around ¹/₂ inch long and $1/8$ to $3/16$ of an inch high. They become yellow when ripe, but not juicy. The fruits usually remain on the branches for at least a year, and sometimes even turn yellow and then turn brown and dry on the branches, but all this without ever losing their conspicuous tubercles. The seeds are regular, smooth, and $1/8$ of an inch or a little more (3–4 millimeters) in diameter.

RANGE. From southeastern Colorado into New Mexico east of a line approximately from the upper Rio Grande to the vicinity of Grants, New Mexico, to Silver City, and on into Chihuahua. The eastern boundary of its range runs from the extreme southwestern corner of Kansas across the western part of the Oklahoma and Texas panhandles, then southeast to near Abilene, Texas, then back southwest to near Fort Stockton, and into Mexico between Sanderson and the Big Bend. It is encountered in northwestern Coahuila.

REMARKS. This is the large cholla common over so much of the western part of our area, and seen almost anywhere else reduced to the canes, lamp bases, and other trinkets made of reticulated cactus wood and brought home from western trips. However, the larger and more firm cholla wood comes from other species growing even farther west than this one.

On the high plains of northwest Texas and at the tip of the Oklahoma Panhandle one may see proud old individuals of this cactus standing defiant of all the extreme elements, often miles apart, but clearly visible where no trees grow on the vacant prairies. Then again, some 20 miles northwest of Amarillo, the tree cactus somehow manages to take over whole stretches of the prairie and there are forests of individuals often 6 to 8 feet tall. And farther southeast toward Big Spring, Texas, this cactus alternates with the mesquite to make a spiny mixed forest. The cactus also grows on mountain slopes farther south and west, into Mexico and almost to the Arizona border. Sometimes in the mountains it becomes very numerous, but the individuals rarely seem to become as robust and proud as on the prairies, usually remaining low bushes 3 or 4 feet high and showing signs of dying back almost as fast as they grow. The best stands of robust, healthy individuals I have seen in a mountain habitat are in the southwestern parts of the Davis Mountains.

There is some variation in the color of the flowers of this cactus—the exact extent being hard to discover. Typically in Texas, the flowers are pale purple to lavender, with the outside of the segments often distinctly green and the center of the flower greenish. Almost everyone in the area of the Davis Mountains insists that occasional plants are seen there with white flowers, and that very rarely there have been seen flowers which were pale yellowish. These reports are so numerous as to be intriguing and, remembering the same sort of reports which, when finally investigated by an organized hunt during flowering season in the Arbuckle Mountains of Oklahoma, actually produced these flower colors in the also purple-flowered *Echinocereus caespitosus,* I have spent some time trying to substantiate them. So far,

however, I have not seen these flower colors myself. On the other hand, the flowers on the cactus as it grows in the mountains of northern New Mexico, as for instance in Taos Canyon, are a very bright rose-purple or almost red, with no green at all. This is unlike anything I have seen on this cactus elsewhere. Boissevain gives purple to rose-pink for the Colorado specimens.

The fruits of variety *arborescens* are entirely spherical or even broader than they are long, but always covered with large tubercles and having very large, very deep umbilici caving in the whole top of each. They ripen slowly, but by late summer are turning bright yellow. They remain on the plants most or all of the winter, usually falling in the spring. They do not change shape, however, remaining extremely tuberculate and pitted to the end. This shape distinguishes this plant most clearly from the following cactus which is probably another variety of the species.

I am using Engelmann's name, *arborescens,* for this cactus because we know this is exactly the form he was describing under that name. I have examined his types for his cactus, and this is his form.

An admittedly older name, *O. imbricata* (Haw.) DC, exists, but this was the name given for a cactus whose type specimens or even whose type locality are unknown (beyond that it was from Mexico) and whose original description is so vague that it would fit almost any large cholla we have. Many people have thought that our U.S. cholla is the same as the Mexican one, and so have used the name, *O. imbricata* for our cactus. Why, then, am I returning to the use of Engelmann's later name?

In studying this cactus, I have followed Engelmann's cactus which he called *O. arborescens* down from its southernmost U.S. range in the Big Bend of Texas into the mountains of northwestern Coahuila, Mexico. All along I saw the same plant with its greatly tuberculate, but small fruits, and no other, until it reached the end of its range and disappeared near Monclova, Coahuila.

Somewhat farther on, in the hills north of Saltillo, I came upon a similar but surely different cholla. This one grows with joints larger in both diameter and maximum length, and with its more or less ovate fruits becoming twice as big as those of the U.S. form, as well as becoming perfectly smooth as they ripen, all tubercles vanishing and the umbilici becoming flat. The resulting ripe fruit is quite like the shape of a fig. This cactus begins to appear near Saltillo, and is very common, becoming one of the dominants in much of the brush country all the way through San Luis Potosi, while our northern form does not appear anywhere at all in this whole area.

Both Coulter and Griffiths state clearly the differences between these two forms, as well as their proper ranges. Both use Engelmann's name *O. arborescens,* for the northern one, while assuming that the southern one is the original *O. imbricata* (as did Engelmann) and using that name for it.

Most later writers, following Schumann and Weber, ignored the differences between these two forms and united the two names as synonyms. While we feel that they may be too close to each other to be considered entirely separate species, we do not believe they are identical. They even show differing chromatograph maps, as we discovered in our own laboratory, which is added evidence for keeping them separate. While there is no certainty possible from only the very poor early descriptions of Haworth and De Candolle as to what the typical form of *O. imbricata* was, it is clear that it was a Mexican form, and that the much later discovered northern form Engelmann described was not for many years considered to be the same, although Engelmann himself speculated that his might not be a totally different species. We believe that, all evidence considered, our northern form can best be regarded as a variety of the larger species which all agree now must bear the original name, *O. imbricata*, and so we call it *O. imbricata* var. *arborescens*.

Opuntia imbricata var. viridiflora (B. & R.)

DESCRIPTION   PLATE 61

STEMS: Growing as an upright bush 1 to 3 feet tall. It is much branched and with no enlarging trunk, but the old stems are more or less bark-covered and with a woody support. The current year's joints are usually ¹/₂ to ³/₄ of an inch in diameter, but occasionally in cultivated examples reach 1 inch thick. The surface is covered with prominent tubercles ³/₄ of an inch or a little longer.

AREOLES: Circular or oval, with short gray or yellowish wool.

SPINES: 2 to 8 per areole on current year's growth, not increasing much with age. They are ³/₄ to 1 inch long, dark brown, with brownish sheaths.

GLOCHIDS: Fairly numerous, but short.

FLOWERS: 1 to 2 inches in diameter, not opening widely. They are coral-pink within, yellowish to pale green on the outside. The filaments are green, the anthers yellow. The pistil is long and reddish, and the stigma has 8 or 9 reddish lobes.

FRUITS: 1 inch or less in diameter, as those of variety *arborescens* in shape, with very prominent, persisting tubercles and deep umbilici. They have long, deciduous bristles at first, but are usually naked when ripe.

RANGE. Known only from the type locality, which is the hills just north of Santa Fe, New Mexico.

REMARKS. Although described by Britton and Rose as a separate species, I find it only possible to think of this form as at best a doubtful variety of the *O. imbricata* complex very close to the other northern form, variety *arborescens*. Growing wild, it appears in no essential character different from a small, stunted version of that cactus, all its elements present but reduced quantitatively. Many of the weaker specimens of variety *arborescens* found in the mountains of northern New Mexico which I have examined I could not distinguish from this form by their vege-

tative characters. Only when they bloomed with their bright purplish flowers could I be sure they weren't this form, and only when my specimens bloomed with their pale greenish flowers could I be sure that they were variety *viridiflora*.

It does not seem that flower color can be a basis in the cacti, at least, for separating species, and anyway, most of the very large, robust variety *arborescens* specimens in northwest Texas bloom with pale lavender flowers having traces of green in them. So if there were no other factors I would think the two should be combined. However, the cactus described as *O. viridiflora*, even in cultivation in New Mexico where it has the best situation, does not seem to grow large like the other forms of the species. The quantitative difference remains. Yet this is still little basis for separating the forms. Figuring even more importantly in our evaluation, the chromatograph map of the cactus is quite essentially different from that of variety *arborescens*.

For those reasons mentioned, I continue to keep this form separate, but I definitely do not feel that the differences are enough to warrant considering this more than a local variety within the *O. imbricata* complex.

Opuntia imbricata var. vexans (Gr.)

DESCRIPTION   PLATE 61

STEMS: A treelike cholla with cylindrical branches from an upright, bark-covered trunk. Old specimens stand 6 to 12 feet tall with a compact crown of many branches from a cylindrical trunk becoming at least 8 inches in diameter. The current years's branches are 4 to 16 inches long, the typical length being 6 to 12 inches. They are cylindrical, ³/₄ to 1³/₄ inches thick, usually narrowing gradually at their bases. They are tuberculate, the tubercles about 1¹/₄ inches long and ³/₁₆ to ³/₈ of an inch tall, with the upper slope abrupt and the lower slope much longer and more gradual.

AREOLES: Oval, ¹/₄ of an inch or slightly more in length, with gray wool at first, later enlarging and bulging outward.

SPINES: 1 to 10 in the areoles of current growth, increasing to 20 or 30 on old stems. Spreading in all directions, short, being only ¹/₄ to ⁵/₈ of an inch long, and very slender to medium in thickness. They are brown, more or less annulate, with lighter tips, and are covered with rather tight, yellowish, gray, or whitish sheaths.

GLOCHIDS: Yellowish in color. They grow from the upper part of the areole, and are always very few, and from ¹/₁₆ to ³/₈ of an inch long.

FLOWERS: 2 to 2³/₄ inches in diameter by 1¹/₂ to 2 inches tall. The ovary is 1 to 1¹/₈ inches long by about ³/₄ of an inch thick, very tuberculate, with a number of long perianth segments upon it. The outside of the flower is greenish, the inside light pinkish-purple. The filaments are pink suffused with green or brown. The anthers are yellow or cream; the style is short; and the stigma lobes number 6 to 9 and are brownish, tan, or whitish. This form tends to bloom repeatedly during the summer, whenever there is moisture.

FRUITS: When young, egg-shaped, about 1³/₄ inches long by 1 inch wide, very tuberculate with tubercles ⁵/₈ to ³/₄ of an inch long and about ¹/₈ of an inch tall, and with the umbilici deeply pitted. At this stage they have some short glochids and around the upper edge half a dozen or so very slender, white spines ³/₈ to 1³/₈ inches long. When ripening later in the summer, they become yellowish-green, egg-shaped to almost spherical or sometimes even wider than they are long, being then 1¹/₄ to 2 inches long and 1¹/₂ to 2 inches wide. These ripe fruits are spineless, wholly smooth, or with only the traces of a few tubercles at the base, and with the umbilici practically or completely flattened.

RANGE. Said in the original description to be Webb County, Texas. It has not been seen growing wild since, but is found as a cultivated plant in gardens in Laredo and Del Rio, Texas.

REMARKS. Dr. Griffiths described O. *vexans* as a new species in 1911. He said then: "The type specimen is . . . prepared . . . from plants cultivated from cuttings collected . . . in Webb County, Texas, March 13, 1908. Mature plants have not been seen elsewhere, but the species is frequently cultivated. The description is a compilation of several sets of notes taken from native and cultivated plants."

We carried on a long search for a cholla native to Webb County, covering as much of the area as possible ourselves, and asking everyone we could find who had reason to be abroad in the open, from ranch owners to cowboys, and particularly oldtimers, where the cholla grew wild in Webb County. Everywhere we met with complete surprise that anyone thought a cholla ever grew wild anywhere in that county. We were stymied entirely in trying to locate Griffiths' cholla this way.

But Laredo, in Webb County, is the site of one of the oldest and most famous cactus dealerships. In business continually for well over 30 years, first as the Shiner Cactus Nursery, and more recently as the Cactus Garden and Cafe, this establishment has sold literally millions of cacti from the local region, as well as imported cacti from all over Mexico. It still has a large garden with hundreds of huge old specimen plants which have stood there for decades. Mrs. Jones, the present proprietor, has been involved with the business almost since the beginning.

Naturally, since I believe that she knows the most about the cacti of Webb County of anyone living, I asked her about Griffiths' cholla. She says that she has never known of any such native plant. She has had crews of men in the field at various times during the years, digging cacti for her business, and says she was never shown a cholla from the region.

Although one hates to write off the statements of one so eminent as Dr. Griffiths, I was faced with having to do this, since I couldn't even find a clue to his plant. Then one day I walked out behind the Cactus Garden Cafe in Laredo, and there on the edge of Mrs. Jones's garden, fully 12 feet tall and vying successfully with the retama trees, stood a giant specimen of Griffiths' cholla. It had a trunk more than 6 inches in diameter, with its first branches 4 feet or more above the ground, and with a crown spreading 10 or 12 feet. On the branches were young, tubercled, spiny fruits, and also large, spherical, perfectly smooth and spineless, ripe fruits of the season's several blooming periods.

When I told Mrs. Jones that this was the cholla from Webb County, she disagreed, saying that it was instead an import from Mexico which had stood in that spot for very many years. There is a chance that this very specimen was growing there when Dr. Griffiths was collecting in Webb County, and it is entirely possible that he used it in writing his description. I have since seen several other specimens of this cactus in Laredo, but there are not many, and they are all in very old yards.

There was another old business dealing in rocks, cacti, and curios along the highway in Del Rio, Texas. This was run for many years by Mr. and Mrs. Basket. In the yard around this establishment was to be seen a whole grove of 20 or more specimens of this cholla 8 to 12 feet tall. I was privileged to know Mrs. Basket, and she said these cacti were not native to Texas, but had their source somewhere in Mexico. Mrs. Basket sold her property recently, and within the past year all of these giant specimens were grubbed out and destroyed. I do not know that the form exists any more in Del Rio.

There were also two fine specimens of this cholla beside a small roadside cafe and station some few miles west of Del Rio on U. S. 90, but this business has been razed and the plants went with it. So far as I know, the few Laredo specimens and some starts in my own collection are all that survive of the form.

It is impossible with only the present knowledge of this cholla group to know what to do with this cactus. It seems doubtful, from all accounts, that the plant ever grew wild in the U.S., and more likely that Dr. Griffiths saw examples escaped from very early cultivation, if he did see the cactus growing outside of yards. Neither is there any sign of the cactus growing wild anywhere near the Rio Grande in north Mexico. The nearest location to Webb County where I find chollas with fruits becoming smooth like this is in the hills around Saltillo, Coahuila, Mexico, and this might be a location from which it was introduced into Texas long ago; but the form with smooth fruits growing from Saltillo down through San Luis Potosi does not seem to be entirely identical with the form in Webb County. It does not grow so large anywhere that I have observed it, and there are differences of tubercle shape, spine development, and fruit details, which do not seem that they could be environmental.

What does seem very clear is that the cactus called O. *vexans* by Griffiths is different from the U.S. cholla which we are calling O. *imbricata* var. *arborescens*, having a different growth form when large, thicker joints, shorter spines, and different fruits. Since it is going to be noticed by some observant cactophiles in Laredo yards, if nowhere else, I feel we must list it here if we are to have a complete account. That it is definitely one of the *O. imbricata* group is also clear. But the problem of how it relates to the typical *O. imbricata* is a hard one, mainly because, the early descriptions of that cactus being in only the most general terms and no type or type locality being given, we do not really know the exact form of the typical species type. It is assumed by all that the original collection was in Mexico, and a logical choice for the typical species form would be the form which is so common as to be one of the dominant plants from southern Coahuila at least to San Luis Potosi. Griffiths himself flatly calls this form *O. imbricata*, and yet he never seems to have thought of the plant he saw in Webb County as this one. I have studied this cactus widely in Mexico, and Griffiths' *O. vexans* is very close to it, but I can see differences also. Yet even if I were to conclude that they are the same, I would still hesitate to state that the form was the typical *O. imbricata*, since Griffiths also describes an *O. spinotecta* from Durango, which I have seen, and which is still different from any of the above, with only 3 to 6 spines, even on old stems, but with these much longer than on the other Mexican forms. This form is the one which fits Coulter's description for *O. imbricata*, and could just as easily be the one which should bear the name.

With nothing more definitely known than all this, it seems most prudent to leave our cactus growing, probably as a visitor, in Webb County, Texas, as a variety of this complex under the name *O. imbricata* var. *vexans*. With all the lack of certainty about it, the name is certainly well enough chosen.

Opuntia spinosior (Eng.) Toumey
"Cane Cholla"

DESCRIPTION   PLATE 62

STEMS: A large, open-branching shrub or treelike plant 3 to 8 feet, and said to sometimes reach 12 feet tall. When large it produces a black, scaly trunk 2 to 4 inches in diameter, although smaller, shrubby examples will lack this. The young joints are 4 to 12 inches long, cylindrical, $5/8$ to $1^1/4$ inches in diameter, covered with conspicuous tubercles $1/4$ to $3/4$ of an inch long. The surface is grayish-green, often becoming purplish in the winter.

AREOLES: Oval or nearly so, $1/8$ of an inch in diameter when young, becoming larger and bulging outward with age.

SPINES: There are 6 to 12 spines per areole on the current year's growth, the number increasing to at least 20 or 30 when very old. They are short, mostly $1/4$ to $1/2$ inch long, but rarely to $3/4$ of an inch, and spread in all directions. They are white, gray, or brownish, all fading to gray. At first they are covered entirely, or the smaller ones on only the upper parts, with thin, comparatively inconspicuous sheaths which usually

fall off after a year. The sheaths are gray, sometimes with a pinkish tinge.

GLOCHIDS: There are a few short, inconspicuous, white or yellowish glochids at the top of the areole.

FLOWERS: $1^1/2$ to $2^1/4$ inches in diameter, very beautiful, but also variable in color. The most common color seems to be purplish, but it is not uncommon to find various shades of red, more or less yellowish, or even white blossoms. The ovary is tubercled and with very slender white spines on it. The stigma lobes are cream-colored or yellowish.

FRUITS: Yellow when ripe, 1 to $1^1/2$ inches long, almost spherical to oblong or rather egg-shaped. They are very tuberculate, with also deeply pitted apexes. At first the fruits have the very slender white spines of the ovary upon them, but these fall off long before they ripen. The seeds are a little over $1/8$ of an inch (about 4 millimeters) in diameter.

RANGE. Southwestern New Mexico from about Silver City to Hermanas and the Carrizalillo Hills, and on into adjacent Arizona and Mexico.

REMARKS. This is thought by many to be the most beautiful cholla of our area. Its treelike, open branching, and tidy manner of growth, its even covering of short, whitish spines, and its brilliant flowers make it a favorite. It is so often featured in the bright color photos of the southwestern desert which have become a fad these days that one might think he could find it anywhere he would look in that desert. The cactus really has a comparatively small range in the U.S., however, being found only in the southwest corner of New Mexico and over about the southeast quarter of Arizona. Other large chollas take its place farther west, and the casual traveler doesn't stop to notice the difference.

This cactus does have superficial similarities to the more northern and much smaller *O. whipplei*, and Engelmann confused them in all of his accounts, calling this cactus *O. whipplei* var. *spinosior*. There are various differences between the two, however, which will be noted in the following account of that other species.

O. spinosior is another of the large chollas having a woody skeleton of beautiful open pattern from which everything from canes to lamp bases has been made, hence the common name. It is a favorite especially for cane work, because of the straightness of its stems.

Opuntia whipplei Eng. & Big.
"Whipple's Cholla," "Rat-Tail Cactus," "Sticker Cactus"

DESCRIPTION   PLATE 62

STEMS: Ordinarily, and apparently always in our area, an erect but low-growing cholla 6 to about 24 inches tall. Plants may stand alone and be rather openly branched bushes, the joints 6 to 10 inches long, but more often they are very crowded with their branches extremely numerous and their joints only 2 or 3 inches long, these forming very compact, matlike thickets of sometimes up to 8 feet across while still only a foot or so high. In some locations in Arizona the plant is reported to grow much taller, but this has not been demonstrated elsewhere. The current year's joints are usually ³/₈ to ³/₄ of an inch in diameter, but occasionally to 1 inch. They are covered with conspicuous, broad, short tubercles ³/₈ to ⁵/₈ of an inch long. The surface is light or yellowish-green. The joints are rather easily detached.

AREOLES: Egg-shaped or elliptical, about ³/₁₆ of an inch long when young. They have some white wool at first, but very soon lose it.

SPINES: There are 3 to 12 spines per areole. 1 to 4 of these are main spines spreading from the center of the areole. The lower, rather deflexed one is usually the longer of these, and is often somewhat flattened. The uppermost one is flattened and the heaviest, but while all of these are rigid, none of them are very stout. They are from ¹/₄ to 1¹/₄ inches long. They are whitish to brown and covered with conspicuous, loose, straw-colored or whitish sheaths. There are 2 to 8 smaller, very slender, unsheathed spines ¹/₁₆ to ³/₈ of an inch long, radiating or often recurving against the surface of the plant around the areole.

GLOCHIDS: There are several white or pale yellowish glochids up to ¹/₈ of an inch long near the upper edge of the areole.

FLOWERS: Pale yellow, not opening widely. They usually stand ³/₄ to 1¹/₄ inches wide. The ovary tube is very tuberculate, with large white areoles and a few slender, white, soon-falling spines upon it. The filaments are greenish. The anthers are yellowish. The stigma lobes are about 5 or 6 in number and greenish or white in color.

FRUITS: Almost round to somewhat obovate, ³/₄ to 1¹/₄ inches long. They are very tuberculate, with deep umbilici, and without spines. They remain green a long time, and then become yellowish when ripe. The seeds are ¹/₈ of an inch or slightly more (3–4 millimeters) in diameter.

RANGE. Northwestern New Mexico from south of Ojo Caliente in Valencia County to western Socorro County around Puertecito, to near Farmington. Extending into southwestern Colorado and over almost the whole upper half of Arizona.

REMARKS. There has been much misinformation about this cactus because it has from the first been confused with two other chollas. Engelmann apparently never did distinguish clearly between this and *O. spinosior.* He began by having a species, *O. whipplei,* which encompassed both of these forms, and then describing under this species a variety *laevior,* which sounded much like this cactus, but for which he described the flowers as

being red, and a variety *spinosior,* which was the larger plant. Later, in his Whipple's Report, he stated his earlier described red flowers were actually those of variety *spinosior,* but he did not redescribe the flowers of the smaller plant.

Coulter restricted the name of the species to the small northern cholla, and it has been called *O. whipplei* constantly since that time, but he repeated the error of stating that it had red flowers, and still called the larger southern cactus *O. whipplei* var. *spinosior.*

The two cacti are so close to each other in many respects of stems and spines that it would be very easy to think of them as a large growth form in the south and a smaller one in the north due to more severe climate there, especially if one were thinking that the flowers were identical on both. Only later did Toumey separate the two as different species, and by Wooton's time it was clear that in New Mexico at least, which is the type locality of *O. whipplei,* the flowers of the smaller northern form are always yellow, and the ranges of the two are separated by a band of at least 100 miles where neither grows. Since then the two have always been considered separate species, although Arizona students have mentioned what they think may be intermediates in their state. These have not been demonstrated in New Mexico.

After all this had been pretty well settled, a new confusion arose between *O. whipplei* and another cholla of northeastern New Mexico, Oklahoma, and Texas, *O. davisii.* Here is another form surely very close to *O. whipplei.* It was only incompletely described by either Engelmann or Coulter, and Wooton seems the first one actually to try to distinguish between these two forms. Unfortunately, the only character he could find with which to try to tell them apart was the spine color. He said that *O. whipplei* has "spine sheaths pale yellowish to white," while *O. davisii* has "spine sheaths yellowish brown," or, as he put it again, "*O. whipplei* always looks whitish or very pale yellow, while *O. davisii* is a golden brown, the colors being due to the sheaths."

Now this distinction pointed out by Wooton is essentially accurate, but few things are more relative with us than color, both in the naming of the various shades and no doubt in the perception of them. The result was that other characteristics in which these two differed were not properly considered while people began to call their specimens whichever one of these they were more familiar with. Due to this confusion we have reports of *O. whipplei* in northeastern New Mexico and even in Oklahoma. All of these specimens collected outside of the above given range of *O. whipplei* which I have been able to investigate personally have proved to be *O. davisii.* A typical example is a collection made by Lahman in Greer County, Oklahoma, on the basis of which *O. whipplei* is often included in Oklahoma plant lists. I have examined Lahman's preserved specimen, and it is clearly *O. davisii.*

We need much more reliable characters with which to distinguish these two species, and I would mention that the length of spines of *O. whipplei* is usually no more than ³/₄ of an inch and never over 1¹/₄ inches, and the length of its tubercles is ³/₈ to ⁵/₈ of an inch, while the spines of *O. davisii* are to 2 inches long and its tubercles ⁵/₈ to 1 inch long. The flowers of the former are yellow and it produces seeds, while the latter has green flowers and is apparently sterile.

O. whipplei, when definitely recognized, is the small pest cholla of northwestern New Mexico and northern Arizona. It has little to commend it to us, and its impenetrable thickets, with its severe spines and joints which easily attach themselves to us and hate to let go again, make it less than appreciated by most who encounter it. Although it is one of the forms which give cacti little besides a bad name, we must acknowledge it as one of ours.

Opuntia davisii Eng.

DESCRIPTION   PLATE 63

STEMS: A low-growing, very much branched bush usually standing 12 to 18 inches tall, but occasionally reaching 30 inches. The main stem is very short because of the immediate branching and it hardly increases in diameter, but it does become more or less covered with gray, scaly bark. The current year's joints are cylindrical, often bordering upon being club-shaped because of the narrowing of their bases. They are 3 to 6 inches long, ¹/₄ to ³/₄ of an inch in diameter, very tuberculate, with the tubercles laterally compressed and ⁵/₈ to at least 1 inch long. The color of the surface is light green. The joints are easily detached.

AREOLES: Elliptical, about ³/₁₆ of an inch long, with some yellowish wool.

SPINES: Producing 6 to 13 spines per areole. 4 to 7 of these are main spines spreading in all directions from the center of the areole. They are from ³/₄ to 2 inches long, round, and heavy. They are bright brown or red-brown and somewhat annulate in color, but this coloring is not seen until their very large, very loose, bright, glistening, straw-colored, or light brown sheaths are removed. There are also 2 to 5 small radial spines which are ¹/₄ to ¹/₂ inch long, slender, brownish, and do not appear to be sheathed.

GLOCHIDS: There is a compact cluster of yellow glochids ¹/₁₆ to ¹/₈ of an inch long at the top of the areole.

FLOWERS: About 2 inches tall, but not opening widely, and so only about 1¹/₂ inches in diameter. They are deep green to pale green in color, the centers having yellowish coloring and the upper edges and outside surfaces of the petals tinted with brown or reddish. The filaments are greenish-red and very coarse, and the anthers yellow. The style is short, with 4 to 7

very large, cream-white to sometimes pale purplish lobes. The ovary is conic, about 1¹/₄ inches long by 1 inch wide, very tuberculate, with some yellow areoles and on the upper part some very slender, white, deciduous spines to 1 inch long.

FRUITS: Egg-shaped to clavate, 1 to 1¹/₂ inches long by ⁵/₈ to ³/₄ of an inch thick at the top. They are very tuberculate, with deeply pitted umbilici. There are short yellow glochids upon them, but they are otherwise naked. They become greenish-yellow and then dry up. All examples examined were sterile.

RANGE. From Greer and Harmon counties in extreme southwestern Oklahoma, west across the Texas Panhandle and eastern New Mexico to near the mountains, also south across Texas to Gillespie County in the south-central part of that state, and to the Rio Grande in the Big Bend.

REMARKS. *Opuntia davisii* is the eastern counterpart of the more western *O. whipplei*. The two have many characters in common, and since, in most keys, as for instance those of Wooton and of Britton and Rose, the only way mentioned to distinguish them is by spine-sheath color, they have often been confused. Frequently this has worked to the advantage of *O. davisii*, in terms of the range given to it. In Coulter's time, records were so confused between these two and even other small chollas that he gives the range of *O. davisii* as going all the way to California. Wooton seemed to be able to distinguish these plants well for himself, and put this cactus back in eastern New Mexico where it belonged, but his key led many others farther astray. There is just not enough difference between "sheaths pale yellowish to white—*O. whipplei*" and "sheaths yellowish brown—*O. davisii.*"

Perhaps the worst confusion was that of Boissevain and Davidson. Partly because of the above trouble with spine colors and partly because they repeat Engelmann's erroneous statement that *O. whipplei* has red flowers, they call their small, yellow-flowered, whitish-spined cholla of southwestern Colorado *O. davisii*, when it is in reality *O. whipplei*. To date there are no actual records of *O. davisii* in Colorado, much less in extreme southwestern Colorado as they would have it.

Conversely, Mrs. Lahman collected a cholla which she called *O. whipplei* in Green and Harmon counties, Oklahoma. Examination of her preserved specimens and re-collection of the living cacti show that they are clearly *O. davisii*.

How can this sort of confusion between these two interesting plants be avoided? Only by noting that beyond the glistening straw or golden-brown sheaths and the more or less red-brown color of the main spines, *O. davisii* has 4 to 7 of these main spines ³/₄ to 2 inches long, whereas *O. whipplei* shows no more than 1 to 4 main spines of which none are over 1¹/₄ inches long. Also, *O. davisii* has tubercles compressed and ⁵/₈ to 1 inch long instead of broader and shorter ones such as are found on the other cactus, and its flowers are at best yellowish-green while the flowers of the other are clear yellow. With this sort of careful observation the two can be distinguished with certainty unless, of course, one is looking at stunted, abnormal growths, and in this condition one can hardly separate any of the Opuntias. In extremely stunted conditions, purposely induced in my garden, *O. davisii* takes on much of the aspect of *O. kleiniae*, with long, very slender joints, very indistinct tubercles and down to 1 slender spine, while *O. whipplei* reacts in just the opposite manner, shortening its joints which remain very tuberculate and come to appear much like poorly armed, over-elongated examples of *O. grahamii*.

Hester reported *O. davisii* from the Big Bend of Texas, a very long way from any other report of it. Anthony later confirmed this, and I have re-collected it there myself. Some of Hester's plants had very long roots with tuberous thickenings strung along them. I have not been able to find this sort of root formation again.

Not only is the occurrence of the cactus in the Big Bend, so far from any other report of it, not surprising, but such isolated records seem to be the rule with this species. It occurs over a very large range, but is found in most of this huge area at only widely scattered locations. The center of its range is clearly a strip extending about 50 miles either side of the Texas, New Mexico boundary from about Nara Visa, New Mexico, on the north to about Tatum, New Mexico, on the south. In this strip of territory one can find a small stand every 30 to 50 miles wherever he goes, and there are some expanses of the prairie where the individuals are up to a dozen or so to the square mile. But when one goes any direction from this strip, the occurrences are very widely spaced. Going west we find records from the Tucumcari Hills, and then no sign of it again until between Chimayo and Espanola, New Mexico, we again find a real stand. Going southwest or south there has been no known sign of it past Tatum, New Mexico, except Hester's collections of it near Marfa, Texas, and at some unspecified place on the Rio Grande, and Anthony's and my own collections of it, both a few miles from Marathon. Going east from the New Mexico-Texas border one can quickly list the known locations. They are Abernathy in Hale County, Texas, north of Lubbock; in Kent County, southeast of Lubbock some 60 miles; and then not again until a location in the southwest corner of Beckman County, one in Harmon County, and one in Greer County, all in Oklahoma; and yet one more at Seymour in Baylor County, Texas. Going southeast from the original area one finds it again around Colorado City, Texas, once again 60 miles or so from any other record, and then not again until a small population is found in northern Gillespie County, Texas, fully 160 miles from the nearest location and well down into the Texas hill country.

This sort of widespread range with very scattered locations within it seems typical of many chollas. It may indicate, as some have conjectured, that these plants were previously much more common and that we have only islands of survival left, or it

may be the result of the highly developed ability in these plants to reproduce themselves from detached joints. These joints cling tightly to flesh, fur, or clothing, and perhaps these plants were spread to their widely separated locations by the migrating animals and wandering tribes of the prairies.

The flower of *O. davisii* is among the most unusual and remarkable I have seen in the cacti. Its petals are very firm and waxy, unlike those of any other Opuntias I know, and similar to the stiff, persistent flower petals of the *Echinocereus triglochidiatus* group. It is the largest green flower with which I am acquainted, except for some orchids.

Another peculiarity of this species is the fact that all fruits seem perfectly formed and developing normally, with many plants producing fruits in season, but seeds have never been described. While living in the Oklahoma Panhandle and traveling through the central range of this species in all seasons, I have opened many fruits, and all examples I have opened have been sterile. There did not seem to be any sign of parasites, and sterility appears to be a characteristic of the cactus, its reproduction apparently being solely by separated joints. What the significance of this is has not been determined.

The sight of a large, healthy specimen of this cactus standing as a glistening, golden bush on the prairie makes one look around for the Midas responsible. Its spine sheaths in shining gold are only equaled in brilliance by those of the next species which glisten as brightly in silver.

Opuntia tunicata (Lem.) Link & Otto in Pfeiffer, 1837
"Abrojo," "Clavelina"

DESCRIPTION   PLATE 63

STEMS: Erect, with a more or less definite woody stem, but with very many crowded, lateral branches, and, therefore, low and spreading in aspect. It grows from less than 1 to about 2 feet tall in our area, but is said to grow taller sometimes in Mexico. The current year's joints are 2 to 6 inches long, narrowly oblong or somewhat club-shaped when short, but almost cylindrical when longer. They are covered with prominent tubercles $3/4$ to $1^1/2$ inches long. The color is medium to light green. All joints are very easily detached.

AREOLES: Oblong in shape, $3/16$ of an inch long at first, enlarging considerably with age. They bulge outward with very white wool.

SPINES: There are 6 to 10 spines, all white, yellow, or rarely reddish, but all covered with very loose, very thin and papery, translucent, silvery white sheaths. There are 3 to 6 spreading central spines 1 to $2^1/2$ inches long. Underneath their sheaths these are more or less angular, and very heavy spines. There are also 2 to 4 radial spines from the lower part of the areole, these more slender and from bristle-like ones only ³/₈ of an inch long to sometimes fairly stout ones, to 1¹/₄ inches long.

GLOCHIDS: There is a small cluster of very short whitish or pale yellow glochids in the upper edge of the areole.

FLOWERS: Pale greenish-yellow. About 2 inches in diameter.

FRUITS: Spherical to broad club-shaped, tuberculate, yellowish-green. The seeds are apparently undescribed.

RANGE. Found in the U.S. only on the southeast slopes of the Glass Mountains just within the southwest edge of Pecos County, Texas. Ranging throughout central Mexico, and reported also in Ecuador, Peru, and northern Chile.

REMARKS. Miss Anthony reported this species not many years ago from the Big Bend of Texas, this being the first knowledge that it grew in the United States. Dr. Warnock, of Sul Ross College in Alpine, Texas, kindly sent me some specimens collected on the Glass Mountains, the same location where Miss Anthony found it. We seem to have in that small area a very isolated population of the species, as it has never been reported from any of the Big Bend south of there to the Mexican border. This population must be the northernmost point it attains, a remarkable outpost since, although I have watched for it on several trips through the mountains of northwest Coahuila, the first place I have seen it again was at the latitude of Saltillo, hundreds of miles into Mexico.

This gives the cactus ample reason to be considered for the title of the most widely ranging of all, since this means a range for it extending from the southern U.S. all the way into northern Chile. It is also said to have been found, probably as an escape, in Cuba.

This immense range is all the more remarkable since this is probably the most difficult cholla to grow in cultivation. Even here in Texas, when trying one after another of the treatments which enable me to grow and flower most of the other cacti successfully, I find my specimens of *O. tunicata,* both from Texas and from Mexico, which were large and beautiful when I got them, refusing to bloom at all and reverting to the curious dwarf form, 8 to 10 inches high, with very short branches and less than typical spination, which one sees here and there even among the robust examples in the mountains of Mexico. The lack of published details about the flowers and fruits of this cactus makes me think that others have had the same trouble with it, and that perhaps it blooms and fruits sparingly even in the wild. At any rate, it has managed to survive in many places. However, the dwarf form of it is widespread even in the best locations, as Britton and Rose mention.

When growing robustly, *O. tunicata* is an amazingly beautiful plant. A good specimen is a small bush so compact in its branching and so covered with its shining silver-sheathed spines that it glistens, even from across a canyon, like an ice-covered bush in the sunlight of a northern winter, or like a globe of the finest Spanish silver filigree. But for all the magic of its appearance, it is a cactus which must be skirted by man or beast with the proper respect.

Opuntia kleiniae DC
"Klein Cholla," "Candle Cholla"

DESCRIPTION   PLATE 64

STEMS: Erect, shrubby stems 3 to 6 feet tall, openly but rather sparingly branching from woody trunks 1 to 1¹/₂ inches in diameter and covered with brown, scaly bark. The current year's joints are 4 to at least 12 inches long, cylindrical, ⁵/₁₆ to ¹/₂ inch in diameter. They have low, broad, more or less indistinct tubercles ¹/₂ to as much as 1³/₈ inches long. The lateral branches are fairly easily detached, but are not as loosely held as on some chollas.

AREOLES: Round to egg-shaped or even practically triangular, and about ³/₁₆ of an inch long. They have white wool in them.

SPINES: 1 to 4 per areole, with most often only 1 present. This main spine is ¹/₂ to at least 1¹/₂ inches long, and said to reach 2 inches; reddish to gray, with a loose yellowish sheath which usually falls off soon after the spine matures. There may be 1 to 3 additional shorter spines.

GLOCHIDS: A small, compact cluster of yellowish or brown glochids about ¹/₁₆ of an inch long is found at the upper edge of the areole.

FLOWERS: 1 to 1¹/₄ inches in diameter, pale greenish-purple, lavender, or pinkish in color. The ovary is egg-shaped, ¹/₂ to ³/₄ of an inch long, with woolly areoles on indistinct tubercles. The filaments are pinkish, the stigma with 6 or 7 small, whitish lobes.

FRUITS: Egg-shaped or sometimes almost club-shaped, ³/₄ to 1¹/₂ inches long, red or bright orange, naked or with clusters of brown glochids ¹/₈ of an inch long in the areoles when ripe. They are more or less tuberculate when growing, and sometimes remain strongly tuberculate but more often become almost completely smooth when ripe. The amount of growth influences the degree of smoothness attained, since smaller fruits are consistently more tuberculate. The seeds are between ¹/₈ and ³/₁₆ of an inch (about 4 millimeters) in diameter.

RANGE. From deep in central Mexico far north into the United States, having been reported from Texas, New Mexico, Oklahoma, and Arizona. The most northerly records from within our area, going from west to east, are as follows: Columbus, in southwest New Mexico; the hills west of San Antonio, New Mexico; Santa Rosa, New Mexico; Clayton, in the extreme northeast corner of New Mexico; then back to the Davis Mountains of Texas and the lower Big Bend, except for one remarkable report of its having been found growing wild near Kingfisher in north-central Oklahoma.

REMARKS. *O. kleiniae*, while a tall-growing cholla, is an inconspicuous one. Its branches and stems are so long and slender and so weakly spined that from a distance it looks more like some leafless bush than a cactus. Many collectors no doubt pass right by it, thinking it is just another of the assorted desert shrubs with which it usually mingles in thickets. Few of them would care to take this cactus home with them anyway, since by either form or flower it has little to offer to a garden.

If it grew over large areas of our country, this would certainly be one of the worst of the pest cacti, as it is in parts of Mexico, since, where it is found, it often makes large thickets of tall bushes which man or beast must avoid. Some of the creek flats in the Davis Mountains of west Texas are fairly choked with the cactus, and a large thicket grew, when I was last there, in a ditch in almost the center of Fort Davis, Texas. Here it was obvious that it was scraped away with each cleaning of the ditch, but it returned immediately from the roots with stems reaching 4 or 5 feet tall in one season.

It is fortunate that in the U.S. this potentially dangerous cactus is like so many of the chollas in occurring only here and there within its wide range. Although its range includes about half of New Mexico, in this huge area it has been found at only a dozen or so places, all of these more or less localized populations covering small areas. In Texas the same is true, the population in the Davis Mountains being the largest, with occasional thickets being found down around Presidio and up in the foothills of the Guadalupe Mountains.

It is hundreds of miles from any of these locations to the location mentioned for the plant near Kingfisher, Oklahoma. There have never been any other reports of this species from Oklahoma. Were it not that this collection was made by Mr. Charles Polaski, the well-known cactus collector of Oklahoma City, who is a very careful observer and who has provided most of the recent specimens for European studies of Oklahoma forms, and that I have seen specimens collected at that site growing 6 feet and more tall in Mr. Polaski's garden, I would be skeptical, but apparently there is this isolated colony of the cactus far in north-central Oklahoma.

There has not been much confusion over this cactus. Engelmann, overlooking De Candolle's earlier description of it, renamed the species *O. wrightii*—this not to be confused with *O. wrightiana* (Baxter) Peebles, which is a low-growing, club cholla closely related to or a variety of *O. stanlyi*. Almost immediately the earlier name was recognized as the correct one, and I believe no one else has used Engelmann's unfortunate name for the plant since.

O. kleiniae is probably most closely related to *O. arbuscula* Eng., a cholla with similar slender, though much shorter branches from a much thicker trunk, which is therefore a much more compact, bushy shape when grown. The two have similar spines, but, so far as I know, *O. arbuscula*, which has yellowish flowers and green fruits, is an Arizona plant which has never been found in New Mexico, so we should have no problem with the two in our area.

It may be noticed that this description gives a longer maximum spine length and larger maximum fruit size than is stated for *O. kleiniae* in most of the major works on cacti. The first few descriptions of the cactus do not give us either the length of the spines or the size of the fruits. Coulter seems to have been the first to state sizes for these, and his maximums are the smallest given by anyone—³/₄ inch for the spines and about ⁵/₈ inch for the fruits. Most others have increased his figures only slightly. Most of them give the maximum spine length as between ³/₄ and 1 inch, and the largest fruit size is stated variously as from ⁵/₈ to 1 inch long. Only Borg differs from the rest in this, and he gives the spine length as to 2 inches—a startling maximum, double that of any other authority, which at first looks doubtful.

It is our conviction that stopping the study of cacti which enter the U.S. from Mexico at the north bank of the Rio Grande and drawing up our descriptions of such species from only the U.S. segment of the population, which may be only a northern clone, as is so often done, is not good practice and may be the cause for some of our confusing problems in cactus study. Here, in this cactus which ranges hundreds of miles into Mexico and occurs widely there as huge, dominant populations rather than in scattered small numbers as in the U.S. seems to be one place where more attention should have been paid to the Mexican specimens. It is significant that Borg, who was much more a student of Central and South American cacti than of the U.S. forms, gives a spine length for the species double that given by our students.

With this in mind, I have observed this cactus carefully on numerous trips throughout Coahuila and as far south as San Luis Potosi, where it grows in great profusion. In Mexico I find it identical to our northern specimens in all respects except that the spine length is quite commonly to 1¹/₂ inches and the fruit size often to 1¹/₂ inches also. I have never been able to measure a spine on it 2 inches long, as Borg must have done, but must presume that since he is right in that the usually stated limits are too short, he may well be right in his new maximum also. The value of considering the Mexican population is shown in that it made me return to the U.S. situation with new questions about our long-accepted limits. I measured plants wholesale, and in the Davis Mountains, where the cactus grows most profusely in the U.S., I finally found a few examples equaling the best Mexican specimens I had seen in both spine and fruit size. I have not been able to find equally developed plants in New Mexico, where it seems the cactus is less successful and, therefore, less robust.

While these are small and technical points, their importance may be greater than at first appears. Engelmann described another slender-stemmed cholla from "in mountains near El Paso." He said it had a main spine 1 to 2¹/₂ inches long. He at first thought it another new species and called it O. *vaginata*. In his earliest report of it he said it had pale yellowish flowers with a green tinge, which were ¹/₂ to ³/₄ of an inch in diameter. Now these flowers would be exactly like those of O. *leptocaulis,* and perhaps because of this he said later that it might be a stout form of O. *frutescens* (his name for O. *leptocaulis*). Watson took him seriously on this and made the combination, O. *leptocaulis* var. *vaginata.*

Whether or not Engelmann ever actually meant to submerge the form into the species O. *leptocaulis* is not clear, but seems unimportant in the light of later developments. What is important is that in later reports he retracts his description of the flower and says that the flower of O. *vaginata* is unknown. It is impossible to tell whether, without the earlier, erroneous concept of the yellow flower it would ever have occurred to him that there could be a stout form of O. *leptocaulis,* but what has happened is that all students since have either made this a variety of that species or considered it a synonym and ignored it.

But what if the flower, which is unknown still, were purplish? Wouldn't we then think of the cactus as a long-spined form of O. *kleiniae* instead? It is clear that while in several characters this cactus exceeds the usual limits of O. *leptocaulis* so that to include it in that species would require a redrawing of the species description, vegetatively, except for the spine length, the description of O. *vaginata* falls entirely within the limits of O. *kleiniae*. Even the longer spines, with our new knowledge of the length of spine sometimes attained in O. *kleiniae,* is no more of a problem here than it would be in combining this form with O. *leptocaulis*. The fruits were said to be small, yellowish, and strongly tuberculate, but they were within the range of size found easily on plants of both the other species. Both species sometimes have orange or yellow-orange fruits, but the smaller, less well developed fruits of O. *kleiniae* sometimes remain tuberculate, as was its ovary, while neither the fruits nor the ovaries of O. *leptocaulis* are ever seen distinctly tuberculate.

This gives the idea of O. *vaginata* being an extra long-spined form of O. *kleiniae* somewhat the advantage, it seems to me. And here the fact that we now know O. *kleiniae* grows longer spines than before supposed becomes important. Now who can tell—may it not be that Engelmann merely had before him, from near El Paso, an O. *kleiniae* with spines yet a little longer than Borg's?

Attractive as this possibility is, it is impossible to know. It would seem to be essential to have living specimens to which to refer and from which especially to learn the characteristics of the flower, yet I know of no specimens which fit the description of this form collected since the type, and admit that it has eluded me. All of the herbarium specimens so labeled which I have examined, other than the type, have proved to be, like Lindheimer's O. *vaginata* from New Braunfels, Texas, ordinary O. *leptocaulis* and have lacked the dimensions given for the species by Engelmann. In this situation it would be almost as great an assumption to call it a synonym or a variety of O. *kleiniae* as it has

been on the part of Watson and others to place it in O. *leptocaulis*. Here is a place where there is real need of further work, and we hope by this discussion to clarify the problem which has been glossed over for too long and to stimulate someone to find the plant and place it properly.

Opuntia leptocaulis DC

"Desert Christmas Cactus," "Slender Stem Cactus," "Tasajillo," "Aguijilla," "Garrambullo"

DESCRIPTION   PLATE 64

STEMS: A small, upright bush 2 to sometimes 5 feet tall. It is usually compactly and extensively branched from a main trunk which, on old plants, becomes covered with scaly bark and grows to 1 to 1¹/₄ inches in diameter. The current year's joints are cylindrical and 1 to 12 inches long, but only ¹/₈ to ¹/₄ of an inch thick. The surface of these joints may have indistinct tubercles ¹/₄ to ¹/₂ inch long, but are more often completely smooth. The color is deep green, often with purplish spots around the areoles. The lateral joints detach very easily.

AREOLES: Ovate or often almost diamond-shaped. They are about ¹/₈ of an inch long, with short, white wool.

SPINES: 0 to 3 per areole, but most commonly 1. The main spine is porrect, gray, and very variable. It may be ¹/₈ to 2 inches long. When short, it is usually very slender with a close-fitting sheath. When long and well-developed, it is stout, more or less flattened, and covered with a loose, papery, white, yellow, or tan sheath. There may be 1 or 2 additional short, slender, bristle-like spines.

GLOCHIDS: Few and very short in 1 to 3 small bunches in the upper part of the areole. They are yellowish to brown in color.

FLOWERS: ¹/₂ to ⁷/₈ of an inch wide by ³/₄ to 1 inch tall, opening very wide. They are greenish-yellow in color. The ovary is about ⁵/₈ of an inch long, egg-shaped to conical, slightly if at all tuberculate, with brown glochids and elongated perianth segments upon it. The outer segments are greenish-yellow with soft green spines at their summits. The inner segments are oblong and pointed. The stamens are greenish-yellow. The style is long, with 3 to 6 short, thick, greenish-yellow stigma lobes.

FRUITS: Bright scarlet, orange-red, or yellowish when ripe. Almost globular, pear-shaped, or club-shaped, and ³/₈ to 1 inch long. The surface is smooth, often with brown glochids in the areoles and with a deeply pitted umbilicus. These fruits are persistent on the plant and often proliferous, sometimes having shoots 2 or 3 inches long from them while still in place on the branch. There are usually a dozen or less seeds per fruit, these ¹/₈ of an inch or a little more (3–4 millimeters) in diameter.

RANGE. From south-central Mexico north into Arizona, over all but approximately the northwestern quarter of New Mexico, over all of Texas south of the Canadian River east to the Dallas area and the lower Brazos River, and entering Oklahoma as far as Harmon and Greer counties in the extreme southwestern corner and the Arbuckle Mountains in the south-central part of the state.

REMARKS. This, probably the most hated cactus of all in our area, and surely the one with the least to endear it to us, is a very wide-ranging species and one which unfortunately grows in great numbers in much of its territory. No one who has ever carelessly brushed up against what he ignored as just another scrubby little bush, but which was really this cactus, will ever forget it. Its nefariousness lies not in its being so spiny—many other cacti far surpass it in that—but in that it is so uncactus-like that we often fail to give it the proper respect and so it pricks us worst of all. It likes to grow within other bushes, and reaches out stray branches to snare us as we pass. The Spanish names for it, which anyone who understands them will realize are not exactly terms of endearment, are most appropriate. The person who had charity enough to coin the name, desert christmas cactus, for it, after the brilliant fruits which do remain on the bushes and beautify the otherwise dull brush all winter, was a rare soul or else only saw it from the highway and never tried to walk between plants of the garrambullo.

The cactus varies greatly in size in different situations, being often only 2 feet high, but in the southern part of our area, in good alluvial soil it sometimes becomes 5 feet tall. However, robust as it may grow, it does not increase the diameter of its terminal branches over about 1/4 of an inch nor of its trunk over about 1 1/2 inches. I believe this distinguishes it from O. arbuscula, a close relative found in Arizona, upon which I have seen old trunks over 4 inches in diameter. Fruit color also distinguishes these two. Another close relative sometimes found in the same thicket with this species is O. kleiniae. Although the trunks of that species do not get much larger, its current year's stems do, and it also has larger, purplish flowers.

The garrambullo was noticed early and has had its share of names assigned to it. The first and valid one is O. leptocaulis, given it by De Candolle in 1828. Afterward there followed various others, among them O. ramulifera SD and O. virgata Link, but the ones causing the most confusion were the array of different names used for it by Engelmann. At first he thought it was a variety of another cactus we have recently looked at, and so

called it O. fragilis var. frutescens. He himself later realized the error in this, and so raised it to a separate species, but at the time he apparently did not know of De Candolle's previous name, and so he burdened us with O. frutescens as a species name, which is of course superseded by the earlier one.

But then Engelmann thought he saw consistent varieties in the species. He therefore described variety longispina and variety brevispina, the former with its spines 1 to 2 inches long and with a loose sheath, and the latter with its spines short, slender, and tightly sheathed. Coulter, later, when trying to get the names correct, only compounded the confusion by rechristening the long-spined variety O. leptocaulis var. stipata because of a supposedly consistent difference from the other in joint shape. Still later, Britton and Rose described what seems to be nothing but this same long-spined form as a new species, Opuntia mortolensis. There was also commonly listed an O. leptocaulis var. vaginata. This supposed taxon and the almost complete uncertainty concerning it is discussed in the remarks upon O. kleiniae, to which it seems to us much more closely linked. There followed variety badia, variety robustior, and variety pluriseta, all by Berger, and all for minor differences of spines, joints, or areoles.

Most authors have long since dropped any attempt to maintain these varieties, and I agree that they seem only minor growth forms, probably environmental or else mere phenotypes. They are often found growing together, although in some areas one form does predominate and often only the weak-spined type is present at all. In numerous cases where I have watched over a period of several years, long-spined specimens have reverted to the short-spined, making it appear that we have here again the robust versus the stunted forms of the same plant, as we have seen so commonly in the Opuntias. At least there seem no separate ranges for these forms.

O. leptocaulis is placed last in our account of the cacti. This has no significance except to indicate that it is probably last in the interest of cactophiles. Many would say it should have been first in our account, since it seems probably the most primitive of the cacti in our area. Be that as it may, the cactus is a major pest cholla, and hardly the form to use in introducing the cacti to anyone. So we place it here at the end of our account. Whether it is thought of as the unpleasant thing from which others so beautiful and fascinating arose or as an example of how degenerate a cactus can become, it is the poor relation of all the beautiful ones, and it cannot be left out.

GLOSSARY

The terms below are defined as they are used in this work to refer to the cacti described, and the definitions are not intended to be so broad as to cover their usage for all other plant groups.

Anther. The enlarged, pollen-bearing sac at the tip of a stamen.

Apex. The tip or summit of any structure.

Apical. Referring to the apex.

Areole. A spot in the form of a pit or a raised area marking an opening through the epidermis from which leaves, spines, or other structures grow.

Ascending. Not standing perfectly upright, but growing upward.

Axil. The angle between a leaf, branch, tubercle, or other outgrowth and the stem.

Basal. At or referring to the base or lower part of any structure.

Berry. A pulpy or fleshy fruit with numerous seeds embedded in the flesh.

Bud. An unopened flower; a growing tip surrounded by its immature perianth segments or leaves.

Caespitose. Forming a cluster or clump of stems by repeated branching of the stem at or near the base.

Calyx. The outer series of perianth segments, whenever these are distinct from the inner series.

Central. Positioned at or near the center of an area, as opposed to being peripheral in position. A spine originating in the center of the areole as opposed to those growing around the edge of the areole.

Character. A characteristic or feature unique enough to have value in distinguishing forms and setting up relationships.

Cholla. Any cylindrical-stemmed member of the genus *Opuntia*.

Cilium (pl.: *cilia*). Very fine, hairlike filaments sometimes forming fringes on the margins of perianth segments.

Clone. A local population usually propagated from one individual by vegetative means and therefore uniform genetically and in appearance.

Confluent. Running together or more or less coalescing.

Corolla. The inner series of perianth segments, when these are distinct from the outer ones; the petals collectively.

Decumbent. Lying prostrate on the ground with the tip turning upward.

Deflexed. Curved or bent back, down upon itself, or toward the surface of the plant. Recurved.

Dehiscent. Splitting open at maturity.

Dimorphic. Having two forms.

Distal. Situated opposite the point of attachment or origin.

Divergent. Spreading apart so as to form opposites.

Ecotype. A population which is recognizable by distinct morphological and physiological features and which is the result of, but kept separate from its near relatives by environmental barriers; an ecological "race."

Entire. Having the margin continuous and not toothed, lobed, indented or interrupted.

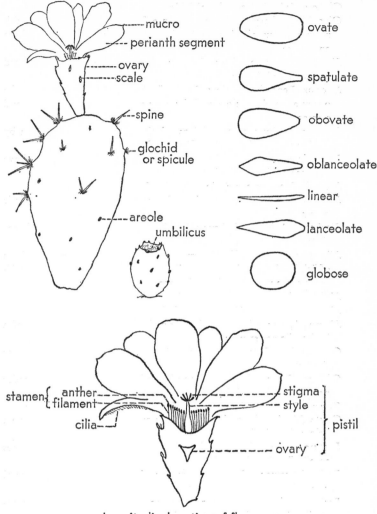

Longitudinal section of flower

Epidermis. The outer layer of cells on a plant, forming a protective covering. In ordinary usage thought of as including the waxy non-living layer that overlies the living cells.

Erose. Ragged, with irregular indentations, as though bits were randomly chewed away.

Felt. A very thick covering of hairs, filaments, or fibers.

Fibrous roots. Finely subdivided roots with no obvious thickening or enlarged central root beyond the base of the plant.

Filament. The stalk of a stamen; the threadlike part of the stamen that supports the anther.

Genotype. A group of organisms having a common genetic makeup.

Genus. A grouping of species possessing common characters unique enough to be treated as a unit distinct from others.

Glabrous. Smooth and shiny; not pubescent, rough, or hairy.

Gland. A secreting structure, usually in the form of a protuberance or appendage, but sometimes a surface.

Glaucescence. A thin layer of whitish substance, often called the "bloom" and usually made up of tiny particles of wax, which rub off.

Globose. Spherical or spheroidal in shape.

Glochid. A sharp, hairlike or bristlelike outgrowth equipped with minute and usually invisible barbs so that it resists withdrawal from any tissue.

Hilum. The scar on the seed that marks the point at which the seed was attached during growth.

Inferior. Beneath or below; in the flower, descriptive of having the ovary appearing below such flower appendages as the perianth and stamens.

Intergrade. Not separated by any division into sets, but merging by having an unbroken series of intermediate forms.

Lanceolate. Lance-shaped; much longer than broad, widest just above the base, with a gradual taper from there to the tip.

Lateral. Growing or positioned at the sides.

Linear. Long and narrow, with sides parallel or nearly so, as a blade of grass.

Meristem. A body of tissue with the power to divide and differentiate.

Microgenus. A nonofficial term used here for genera that have been officially described, but seem distinguished by less obvious or significant characters than the major genera.

Midrib. The main or center rib of a leaf or perianth segment.

Monomorphic. Having but a single form and not subdividing.

Mucro. A short, abrupt, and more or less sharp point on the tip of a leaf or flower structure.

Oblanceolate. Reversed lanceolate in shape, with the widest part near the tip.

Obovate. Reversed ovate; the outline of a hen's egg with the broader part above the middle.

Ovary. The enlarged lower part of the pistil containing the ovules.

Ovate. Having the outline of a hen's egg, and with the broader part below the middle.

Pectinate. Comblike; used in referring to spines or other structures spread flat like the teeth of a comb.

Perianth segment. One of the parts making up the perianth; a petal or sepal.

Perianth tube. A tubelike arrangement of the perianth segments extending in some forms to some distance above the ovary.

Petal. One of the inner set of perianth segments or corolla.

Phenotype. A group of organisms recognized by their common visible characters irrespective of their genetic composition.

Pistil. The central, female part of the flower, made up of the ovary, style, and stigma.

Porrect. Positioned outward; standing perpendicular to the surface of the plant.

Prostrate. Lying completely flat upon the ground.

Pubescent. Covered with short, soft, fine, hairlike outgrowths; downy.

Ramose. Branching or having branches.

Radial. Positioned around the edges of an area; peripheral, as opposed to central. A spine positioned somewhere upon the periphery of an areole.

Radiating. Positioned outward like radii.

Reclining. Sprawling or leaning against something.

Recurved. Curving back upon itself; deflexed.

Rib. A ridge; a raised surface running vertically or sometimes spiraling, and bearing areoles in a row along its summit. Often thought of as being composed of more or less coalescent tubercles which may be evident as bulging masses along it.

Rotate flower. Spreading widely rather than remaining bell-shaped or funnel-shaped; wheel-shaped.

Scale. A small, scarcely expanded leaflike structure; also a narrow, triangular, or sometimes spinelike lower perianth segment often found on the ovary or flower-tube surface.

Sepal. One of the outer perianth segments of the calyx.

Spatulate. Spoon-shaped; oblong or rounded above, the base long and narrow.

Species. A population recognizable by characteristics of form and genetic relationship as a unit, often capable of subdivision into varieties all genetically close enough for interbreeding.

Spicule. A very small, fine spine. A glochid.

Spine. A sharp outgrowth, either rigid and woody or sometimes flexible and hairlike. In cacti always arising from an areole and thought of as a modified leaf.

Spreading. Growing outwardly. Used in referring to a series of radial spines projecting obliquely outward around the areole, as opposed to lying flat against the surface of the plant. Used also for plant growth advancing outward by new shoots or by rooting from old, reclining stems.

Stamen. The male part of the flower consisting of the filament and the anther bearing the pollen.

Stem. The main upward axis of a plant.

Stigma. The uppermost part of the pistil, at the tip of the style; the part that receives the pollen; in cacti usually divided into lobes.

Stigma lobe. One of the expanded sections of the stigma.

Stoma (pl.: *stomata*). A microscopic opening through the epidermis of the plant allowing for respiration and transpiration.

Style. The central portion of the pistil, connecting ovary and stigma.

Subgenus. A taxonomic rank sometimes used to divide a large genus into subdivisions above the species level.

Subspecies. A subdivision of the species unit recognizable by certain morphological characters, but not isolated by genetic barriers from others within the species. (No attempt is made in this work to distinguish between the subspecies and the variety.)

Taproot. The primary root axis, when larger and longer than the branch roots, and often thick and used for storage, as a carrot.

Taxon. A formally described category in classification; a series of individuals distinct by some visible characteristics.

Terminal. At the tip or end.

Transpiration. The giving off of water vapor through the stomata by a plant.

Trichome. A hairlike structure found on plants; a slender filament growing from the plant's epidermis by one end.

Tuber. A short, thick, fleshy underground stem or stem branch for storage and having buds. The potato is an example.

Tubercle. A knoblike protrusion from the surface of any structure; a more or less pyramidal knob rising from the stem surface of a cactus and having an areole on or near its summit.

Tuberous root. A root of undistended size overall, a generally fibrous root, but having thick, fleshy sections like tubers scattered upon it. Not a taproot.

Tuberculate. Having tubercles.

Umbilicus. On those species which drop the perianth and upper parts of the flower, the scar left at the summit of the fruit after the floral parts are shed.

Variety. *See* Subspecies.

Woolly. Covered with long and very thick hairs.

INDEX OF SCIENTIFIC NAMES

The number of the page on which the principal description of a form begins is in italics. The number of the plate where the illustration of the plant appears is in parentheses. All other numbers refer to pages on which there is incidental reference to the plant.

INDEX OF COMMON NAMES

The spelling of the Spanish names is that of local usage where the plants grow, without correction or standardization.